The Religious Orders in England

❋ ❋

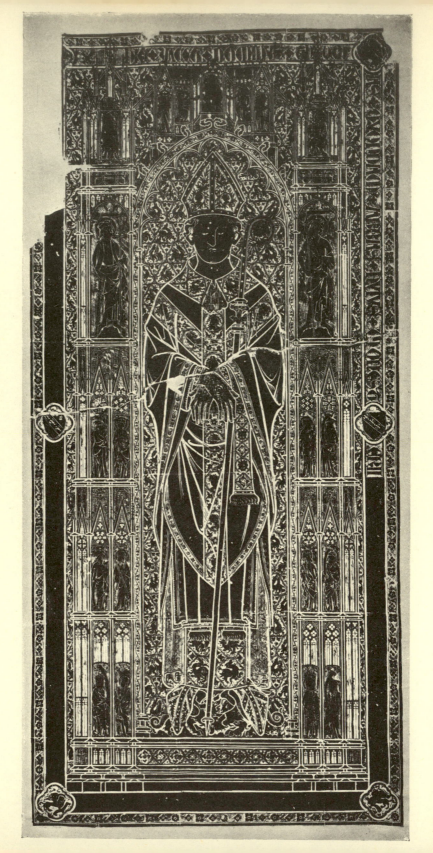

The Religious Orders in England

VOLUME II
The End of the Middle Ages

BY

DOM DAVID KNOWLES

formerly Regius Professor of Modern History in the
University of Cambridge

CAMBRIDGE UNIVERSITY PRESS

CAMBRIDGE

LONDON · NEW YORK · MELBOURNE

Published by the Syndics of the Cambridge University Press
The Pitt Building, Trumpington Street, Cambridge CB2 1RP
Bentley House, 200 Euston Road, London NW1 2DB
32 East 57th Street, New York, NY 10022, USA
296 Beaconsfield Parade, Middle Park, Melbourne 3206, Australia

ISBN 0 521 05481 8 hard covers
ISBN 0 521 29567 X paperback

First published 1955
Reprinted 1957, 1961
First paperback edition 1979

First printed in Great Britain at the University Press, Cambridge
Reprinted in Great Britain by
REDWOOD BURN LIMITED
Trowbridge & Esher

CONTENTS

Part One

The Historical Framework

Part Two

The Institutional Background

PREFACE

The present volume treats of the history of the religious orders in England from the pontificate of Benedict XII (1334–42) to the end of the period of strife between the houses of York and Lancaster, though no attempt has been made to keep rigidly within either of these limits. This epoch has been neglected by monastic historians in general, or dismissed in a few words, and the present writer had every expectation that a single volume would suffice to carry the story from the Benedictine Constitutions to the Dissolution. When, however, the sources were regarded more closely, they revealed a number of important developments and activities which hitherto had been either ignored or treated in isolation; the diffusion of Ockhamism in the English universities, the various controversies between the monks and the friars, and the literary work and controversial interests of the university monks, have never been considered in detail with all their mutual relationships. Similarly, no historian has taken account of the varied activities of the most notable group of monks to appear since the twelfth century, men so diverse in gifts and achievements as Alan of Walsingham, Thomas de la Mare, Simon Langham, Uthred of Boldon, Adam Easton and Thomas Brunton. A little later, at the end of the century and during the reigns of Henry IV and his son, the crisis of an attack launched upon the religious from several angles was followed by a conservative reaction which was in fact something of a spiritual revival, not only by reason of the new contemplative foundations of the Carthusians and Bridgettines, but also owing to the energy of the friars, and in particular of the Carmelites, who by their theological writings, their preaching and their spiritual direction gave distinction to the religious life of the towns. These and other topics of the same kind seemed to deserve, if not to demand, a fuller treatment than they had received in the past.

Already in the preceding volume it was found hardly possible to weave the external history of the monks and friars into a continuous narrative such as had served for the earlier years of the monastic order. In the fourteenth and fifteenth centuries the impossibility was found to be absolute, not only through a dearth of narrative and biographical sources, but also from the very nature of the growth of great institutions. It is with religious orders as it is with medieval universities or with modern public schools. The beginnings, when the shape of the organism is moulded by distinguished pioneers and through acute controversies, and when numbers are small and diversities great, can readily be treated as parts of a connected story, in which individuals play their part in perfecting the type. But when the members of the class have become numerous, and interaction between them frequent, and an age of maturity and stability has developed in which no individual, however eminent, can change the character of the institution, the historian has no longer a thread or pattern that he may take as his guide. He must abandon the hope of presenting an ordered or chronological account of the events and changes of the period, and be content to consider particular topics or take cross-sections and soundings.

The plan has therefore been adopted of treating chapter by chapter a series of varied aspects or activities of the religious, thus building up, stroke by stroke, a picture of the life of the period. *Quidquid agunt monachi....* In so doing, an endeavour has been made to make each section self-contained, and, as in previous volumes, some repetition of detail has been retained of set purpose. A book of this kind may well be treated by some as a work of reference, and the reader who consults it for a single broad topic may find it convenient to meet with all the relevant facts, even if a few of them have been noted in another connexion elsewhere.

A reviewer of the preceding volume regretted the absence of a detailed treatment of the nuns: I fear he will still be able to charge me with neglect. In truth, intimate or detailed records of the nunneries are almost entirely wanting over the whole period between *c.* 1200 and the Dissolution. Doubtless it would be possible, after a long course of research, to describe the social and economic relationships of the nunneries in some detail, but the absence of information on the spiritual life of the nuns is all but complete. The religious historian of medieval England cannot help remarking, in every century after the eleventh, upon the absence from the scene of any saintly or commanding figure of a woman. While all the other regions of Europe, not excluding Scandinavia, witnessed the appearance of women saints of great distinction and individuality, whose lives and writings gave lustre to their age, it is not too much to say that the only two names known even to the specialist in England between St Margaret in the eleventh and Mary Ward in the seventeenth century are those of Dame Juliana and Margery Kempe, neither of them either a leader by nature or indeed, technically speaking, a 'religious' at all. Of the nunneries of England the only one of which we can have something like a clear picture is Syon, and even there it is the formal details of the life, and the composition of the library, not the acts and thoughts of the inmates, that we know.

As might be expected from what has been said above, the monastic historian of the later Middle Ages cannot expect to enter in upon a harvest which others have prepared. There is no Wilmart, no Stenton of the fifteenth century. The one indispensable work, without which the history of the black monks would have been far more difficult to elucidate, is the collection of official documents published by Mr W. A. Pantin, and the same writer, in a series of carefully documented studies, has made it possible to gain a general view of the literary activities of the monks. On particular aspects Miss R. Graham, by a series of papers on the Cluniac houses and on the Great Schism, and the late A. H. Thompson, by his publication of visitation records, have laid all subsequent writers in debt, while Mr H. M. Colvin and Miss E. M. Thompson have firmly based the story of the Premonstratensians and the Carthusians. The works of these scholars are well known to all medievalists, but in this volume I am particularly indebted to a number of less familiar works, the dissertations of research students in various universities during the past thirty years. One of the problems yet to be solved by those concerned is how to avoid the waste of so much meritorious investigation, which is at present buried in theses that have never been printed or otherwise made public by their authors, and whose very existence can so easily be forgotten. I have tried to acknowledge my debts in this respect both in the footnotes and by giving a separate list of such theses in the bibliography, but I should wish to record a particular obligation to Miss E. M. Halcrow who, besides lending me her thesis, allowed me to read and make use of many additional papers and transcripts.

Finally, I must thank those friends who have read and criticized the parts of this book in which they had particular competence: Dr H. M. Chew, Fr. Daniel Callus, O.P., Mr W. A. Pantin, Professor M. M. Postan, and Professor R. A. B. Mynors. I have also to thank the Dean of St Albans (the Very Rev. C. C. Thicknesse) for permission to illustrate the brass of Abbot de la Mare, and Dr G. H. S. Bushnell, for providing the rubbing from which the photograph was taken.

DAVID KNOWLES

PETERHOUSE, CAMBRIDGE

8 December 1954

A second printing has made it possible to make a number of small corrections and a few additions suggested by readers and reviewers. These appear in their relevant places throughout the book. In addition, the following more important notes are added here. I owe them to the kindness of Professor V. H. Galbraith.

Henry Knighton. It has hitherto been generally assumed that Knighton died in 1366 and that the rest of his chronicle was the work of a continuator (*v. infra*, 185–6, 263). Professor Galbraith, in an article not yet (June, 1956) published, has shown that Knighton in fact lived till the very last years of the century, and that the whole chronicle is therefore his work.

Thomas Netter. Netter has usually been credited with the compilation of *Fasciculi Zizaniorum* (*v. infra*, 147) owing to the assumption of his editor, W. W. Shirley, that the last document in the collection dated from 1428, two years before Netter's death. It has now been shown that the manuscript was not written before 1436–9; this leaves the identity of the author or editor uncertain for the present.

DAVID KNOWLES

PETERHOUSE, CAMBRIDGE

15 June 1956

LIST OF ABBREVIATIONS

AC	H. E. Salter, *Chapters of the Augustinian Canons*
ACant.	*Archaeologia Cantiana*
AJ	*Antiquaries Journal*
ALKG	*Archiv für Litteratur- und Kirchengeschichte*
Amundesham	*Annales Joannis de Amundesham*
[T]BGAS	*[Transactions of the] Bristol and Gloucestershire Archaeological Society*
BJRL	*Bulletin of the John Rylands Library*
CBEL	*Cambridge Bibliography of English Literature*
CClR	*Calendar of Close Rolls*
CEH	*Cambridge Economic History*
CHEL	*Cambridge History of English Literature*
Chron. Mels.	*Chronicon monasterii de Melsa* (Meaux)
CMH	*Cambridge Medieval History*
CPL	*Calendar of Papal Letters*
CPR	*Calendar of Patent Rolls*
CS	Camden Series
C & YS	Canterbury and York Society
DAR	J. T. Fowler, *Extracts from the Account Rolls of the Abbey of Durham*
DHG	*Dictionnaire d'Histoire et de Géographie ecclésiastiques*
DNB	*Dictionary of National Biography*
DR	*Downside Review*
DV	A. H. Thompson, *Visitations of the diocese of Lincoln*
DTC	*Dictionnaire de Théologie catholique*
EcHR	*Economic History Review*
EETS	Early English Text Society
EHR	*English Historical Review*
GASA	*Gesta Abbatum Sancti Albani*
HBS	Henry Bradshaw Society
Henry IV	J. H. Wylie, *History of England under Henry IV*
Henry V	J. H. Wylie, *The Reign of Henry the Fifth*
HMC	Historical Manuscripts Commission
JBAA	*Journal of the British Archaeological Association*
JTS	*Journal of Theological Studies*
L & P	J. Brewer, J. Gairdner and others, *Letters and Papers of the reign of Henry VIII*
Lit. Cant.	J. B. Sheppard, *Literae Cantuarienses*
LV	A. H. Thompson, *Visitations of religious houses of the diocese of Lincoln*
MC	W. A. Pantin, *Chapters of the Black Monks*

MO	D. Knowles, *The Monastic Order in England*
Monasticon	*Monasticon Anglicanum* (Dugdale)
MSAC	*Monasterii S. Albani Chronica* (Rolls Series 28)
n.s.	new series
OHS	Oxford Historical Society
o.s.	original series (EETS); old series (CS)
PL	*Patrologia Latina*, ed. J. P. Migne
PMLA	*Publications of the Modern Languages Association*
RB	*Revue Bénédictine*
RO	D. Knowles, *The Religious Orders in England*, vol. 1
Rot. Parl.	*Rotuli Parliamentorum*
RP	Record Publication
RS	Rolls Series
RU	H. Rashdall, *Medieval Universities* (ed. Powicke and Emden)
Scriptores tres	*Historiae Dunelmensis Scriptores Tres*
SRS	Somerset Record Society
SS	Surtees Society
TRHS	*Transactions of the Royal Historical Society*
VCH	*Victoria County History*
WHS	Worcestershire Historical Society
WS	Wyclif Society
YAJ	*Yorkshire Archaeological Journal*

NOTE

For all details of date, place of publication, and (in the case of articles and papers) title of periodical or series, etc., the reader is referred to the full Bibliography at the end of the volume. The works cited in the footnotes to the text are there listed under the author's name or (where only the title is given in the notes) under the title of the work.

Part One

The Historical Framework

CHAPTER I

THE OPENING OF THE PERIOD

I. THE BENEDICTINE CONSTITUTIONS

The constitutional and capitular history of the black monks between the Fourth Lateran Council and the Dissolution is divided conveniently, if somewhat accidentally, by the constitutions issued in 1336 by Benedict XII.[1] That pontiff, who reigned from the last days of 1334 to the spring of 1342, was in many ways the most distinguished of the popes of the fourteenth century after the death of Boniface VIII, and his comparatively short reign left a permanent mark both on church discipline and the history of dogma, while a more tangible monument of his energies remains in the massive ochre walls of the Palace of the Popes at Avignon. Himself a French Cistercian who had ruled as abbot before his elevation to the episcopate, he earnestly worked as pope for such a reform or reorganization of the monastic and religious orders as should be in harmony with the ideas of the time. He was a practical and energetic ruler, and within five years of his accession had accomplished a large part of his task, as he saw it, by preparing and promulgating comprehensive statutes for the three great orders of monks and canons. His first care was to issue a bull (*Pastor bonus* of 17 June 1335) against apostate religious; this was followed by constitutions for his own order in *Fulgens sicut stella* of 12 July; then came the decrees for the black monks in *Summi magistri* of 20 June 1336; and finally the Augustinian canons received the *Ad decorem* of 15 May 1339. In each case a small but strong papal committee of zealous superiors of the order concerned had framed decrees which were submitted to the pope and approved. There was to be no question of a return to primitive observance or the letter of the Rule, or even to the strictest practice of two centuries before; Benedict aimed at securing the financial and numerical prosperity of the monastic body and at maintaining a good level of intellectual training, while he frankly accepted the common mitigations of the Rule; he attempted to check the abuse of power and dilapidation by superiors by legislation not always in harmony with monastic tradition, and to abolish some of the most inexcusable deviations from the common life. It was, in fact, a sincere attempt, similar to but less energetic than that of Innocent III, to make of the uncentralized monks a prosperous, efficient and well disciplined body; the scheme had in it no pregnant, germinal force, no dynamic ideas. It did, however, pass immediately into current canon law and remained the norm till the Dissolu-

---

1 These are in Wilkins, *Concilia*, II, 588 *seqq.* There is a summary in *MC*, II, 230–2. Cf. also J.-B. Mahn, *Le Pape Benoît XII et les Cisterciens.* For a further account of the Benedictine legislation as affecting studies and the Cistercians, *v. infra*, pp. 15, 24–5.

tion; some of its enactments, indeed, remain almost unchanged in the monastic constitutions of the present day.

To achieve his purpose for the black monks Benedict XII set up a commission in the first months of his reign, and the outcome of their deliberations was the bull *Summi magistri*. While this was in large part a re-enactment of old legislation it contained some novel features and laid a new emphasis on old things. In England, henceforth, a single triennial provincial chapter was to replace the two of North and South; in each monastery a yearly chapter was to be held, at which the superior was to render a full financial account; a list was given of measures for which the consent of this chapter was needed. Certain current practices leading to abuse were directly envisaged: thus the holding of private property was banned and the common practice of giving the monks a money allowance for food and clothing was reprobated; all were to receive from the common store; on four days of the week (Sunday, Monday, Tuesday and Thursday) meat-eating on the part of half of the community was accepted, but this was to be outside the refectory and was forbidden in Advent and from Septuagesima to Easter; it was forbidden for monks to have rights of maintenance at any house save their own, and the presidents were given power to deal with unfortunate or decaying houses. Finally, the study movement received an important recognition: in each house a master was to teach the young monks grammar, logic and philosophy, and one out of every twenty subjects at least was to be sent with an adequate pension to the university.

Though lacking the fire of intense spiritual endeavour, Benedict was an efficient administrator. Within six months of the issue of *Summi magistri* the abbots of St Mary's, York, and St Albans—the latter the distinguished Michael de Mentmore—were appointed executors of the bull and were charged not only with convening and setting in motion the first of the new series of chapters, but also with visiting every monastic house with a view to reporting upon its financial resources, in order that the pope might settle the number of monks to be maintained at each for the future.[1] The latter charge raised protests both from individual houses and from the king, who scented a new papal tax in the inquisition, and there is no evidence that it was ever carried out in entirety.[2] The new constitutions, however, were duly sent to England with a covering bull early in 1337,[3] and in spite of royal prohibition the first joint chapter was held in June 1338 at the Cluniac house of Northampton, the central point of medieval England.[4]

At this meeting diffinitors were chosen to draw up a new set of statutes consisting of the old ones modified and augmented by the recent papal pronouncements. In addition, every monastery was to examine its own code of customs to ascertain if they conflicted with the Benedictine con-

1 *MC*, III, 7–11.
3 *Ibid.* 3–4.
2 *Ibid.* 13–15.
4 *MC* II, 5–12.

stitutions, while the diffinitors were to explain themselves, or refer to the pope, any points on which the new legislation might appear alarmingly strict. At the next meeting in 1340 it was found that the diffinitors had not yet achieved their task, owing to lack of information from certain houses; they were therefore instructed to meet again shortly at Oxford, while at the same time three emissaries were chosen to obtain from the Curia the mitigation or interpretation of certain decrees.[1] The latter object was attained by the receipt of a bull from Clement VI; the former by the production in 1343 of a comprehensive code of statutes which was on the whole little more than a revised version of the code of 1273, with some added details and the assumption of the Benedictine constitutions.[2]

For twenty years after this the records of the chapters are wanting, but in 1363 the sole president, the great Abbot Thomas de la Mare of St Albans, published yet another code. Whether this, too, was the work of diffinitors is not clear.[3] De la Mare, as will be recounted elsewhere, was an energetic reformer and legislator whose activities had ranged from his own abbey and her satellite priories to a number of houses which he had been appointed to visit, and it may be that the statutes were his own work, based in part on the representations of a few contemporary abbots. Certainly, where they differ from the older code they bear a strong personal impress, particularly in the long disquisition on extravagances of dress and in the detailed enactments for the financial support and discipline of the students at Oxford.

Henceforward, for almost eighty years, very little material has survived regarding the business of chapter, but as there is no reference in subsequent documents to any further legislation, and as it was even found necessary to obtain from Innocent VII in 1405 a bull enforcing the constitutions of Benedict XII,[4] it may be assumed that none was enacted.

At last, twenty years after the death of Henry V, an attempt at codification was once more made. This time, so we are told, it was brought about by the accumulation of decrees and by the uneasiness of those who saw statutes conflicting with each other and with common usage. The reference, no doubt, is to the customs connected with meat-eating and with the *peculium*, which many wished to see fully legalized by papal indult. The resulting code of 1444 is the least original and important of all in the history of the chapters.[5] Though lengthy, it contains scarcely any new matter save for a number of regulations for studies at the universities. While there is no notable relaxation, there is likewise no tendency to reform; the statutes are in fact a faithful echo, pitched in a slightly lower key, of the legislation of the two previous centuries. The statutes of 1444 were, so far as surviving evidence shows, the last comprehensive code to be drawn up. Henceforward, the only new legislation consists of a number

---

1 *Ibid.* 13–18.
3 *Ibid.* 64–82; *v. infra*, pp. 42–3.
5 *MC*, II, 187–220.

2 *Ibid.* 28–62.
4 *MC*, III, 88–92.

of scattered diffinitions concerned with the universities. No references to later statutes exist, and it may therefore be assumed that the black monks of England had as their norm of life until the Dissolution the statutes of 1444.

Thus for more than three centuries the autonomous English monasteries were governed by a body of decrees, modified and added to from time to time, but retaining in all essentials the form first taken immediately after the Fourth Lateran Council of 1215. Since that date there had been three or four occasions on which a comprehensive reform had been envisaged—in 1273, in 1336 and the following years, and in 1421. None of these had fully succeeded, and each had been less drastic than its predecessors. In 1273 there had been a real endeavour to restore to the monasteries the fully regular life of the early twelfth century; in 1336 a regular and respectable, if somewhat mitigated, observance had been the goal; in 1421 the aim had been to remove a number of abuses which had seriously modified the common life. As has been said, all these efforts were in the long run failures, and the rhythm of the monastic life shows, during the three centuries concerned, a slow but continuous tendency to slacken, save in two or three periods of twenty years.

Yet so far as legislation goes, the life lived in 1500 was essentially that of 1200 and 1300. The horarium, the practices, the dietary regulations, were in essentials the same. So far as essentials went, in the forensic order at least, the critical century had been the twelfth. What changes had followed for the worse are scarcely reflected in the legislation, but must be sought in the indications given elsewhere. During these three centuries, the positive legislation chiefly concerned two matters: the accountability of superiors and officials to the community in general, and the rights of the latter to veto certain undertakings; and the regularization and development of higher studies. The progressive mitigations gave step by step the sanction of law to existing customs as regards meat-eating, periodical periods of recreation, and certain less important deviations from the strict following of the Rule; they also came to tolerate some important relaxations from the strictness of the common life, notably as regards the *peculium* for clothes and the provision of private apartments for a growing number of the senior monks. As for the life of the choir, this remained substantially unaltered to the end, save that the additional psalmody was curtailed in many houses in accordance with the decrees of chapter at the end of the thirteenth century.

During the period following the union of the two provinces in a single chapter the functions of the body and its presidents differed little from those exercised previously. From 1336 to 1498, without a single known exception save the 'irregular' meeting at Westminster in 1421, the chapters were held at Northampton. The central position was of obvious convenience, but it is curious that the regular meetings of some seventy English heads of houses should have taken place in a monastery which until 1405 was a member of the Cluniac congregation. Perhaps, however, there were advantages in a neutral venue. From 1498 onwards Coventry and Westminster were the places of meeting.

The list of presidents is unfortunately very incomplete.[1] After 1336 they were three in number, doubtless in order that a northerner might be added to the existing two from the south. In practice, however, this rule was not rigidly kept, though in the majority of cases where three names have been preserved one is that of a northerner, almost invariably the abbot of York or the prior of Durham. In 1426 a decree was passed that one president should come from the south or east, one from the west, and one from the north, but there is not sufficient evidence to show how far, if at all, this rule was observed. The presidency, as might have been expected, was usually held by superiors of ten or a dozen of the larger houses, including the cathedral priories, but it remained strictly elective and never became the monopoly of a ring. So far as can be judged, the chapters elected the men deemed ablest, not merely amiable nonentities, and some of the most distinguished prelates of the period were re-elected for a number of terms. Thus the two great abbots of St Albans, Michael de Mentmore (1335–49) and Thomas de la Mare (1349–96) were presidents in succession for all the years of which there is record between 1340 and 1369, and John Chinnock of Glastonbury held office from 1387 to 1399.

On the whole, the presidents would appear to have exerted a greater influence than might have been expected. The fact that they were two (later three) in number was possibly a source of strength rather than weakness; the black monks would not have brooked a general, and a weak man would have felt the isolation of his position. As it was, they could advise and support each other, and the large number of monasteries concerned militated against jealousies. Elected as they were three years before the chapter at which they were to preside, they could when necessary prepare the main lines of future legislation, and on more than one occasion a really eminent president left a permanent mark on the body. Their greatest permanent task was, however, the supervision of the common houses of study at Oxford and (later) Cambridge; they also supervised the visitors of the various circuits appointed by chapter.

This would seem a fitting place to record the slight constitutional changes of the Austin canons. The decrees of Pope Benedict XII in their regard were in their main lines and general temper similar to those for the black monks, though special attention was given to practices peculiar to the order such as the serving of churches, and a somewhat less austere regime of fasting and abstinence was accepted: Saturdays were not days of abstinence, and the ancient custom of each house was to be followed as regards the keeping of abstinence on Wednesdays and the season between Septuagesima and Lent. Other decrees prohibited the carrying of arms

1 *MC*, III, 259–62.

and countenanced hunting and hawking on the canons' properties, though they themselves were to take no part.[1]

The united chapter of the two English provinces duly met for the first time at Newstead in 1341 and accepted the Benedictine constitutions;[2] there is no record of protests or of application for dispensations as there is among the black monks, though in the event the canons showed even less disposition to honour such of the decrees as sharpened their traditional observance. In any case, no drastic revision of legislation was undertaken; indeed, it was decreed at Oseney in 1353 that all houses, northern and southern, were to adopt the Northampton statutes of 1325,[3] and this decree, presumably ineffective, was reaffirmed as binding on the northern houses in 1380.[4] This attempted unity, however, did not long endure; after three years the north reverted to the statutes of Healaugh Park, dating from c. 1265 to 1285, with which they were familiar.[5] The only considerable change was that from 1353 onwards three presidents, of whom two were of the south, and one of the north, replaced the two hitherto elected. They were to hold office for three chapters (i.e. nine years), and the chapters were to be held alternately at Northampton and Newstead (Notts), each near the confines of its province.[6] This last regulation lapsed after a time, and Northampton became the normal venue for all chapters. Presidents were elected from a wide selection of houses, but Leicester, Northampton, Oseney and Waltham in the southern province, and Gisburn, Nostell and Thurgarton in the northern maintained their pre-eminence. Unfortunately, detailed records of the chapters cease after the first decade of the fifteenth century.

II. THE BLACK DEATH

Towards the end of the nineteenth century there was a tendency among English historians to regard every symptom of languor and decadence in the religious life of the country after 1350 as a direct consequence of the great plague of 1348-9.[7] In particular, this visitation, by permanently reducing the numbers and stamina of the religious, was taken as marking the moment when a material, soon to be followed by a spiritual, decline

---

1 The constitutions are printed in Wilkins, *Concilia*, II, 629 *seqq.*, but the best text is that of H. E. Salter, *Chapters of the Augustinian Canons*, Appendix II, pp. 214–67.

2 *AC*, 49–52.   3 *Ibid.* 59–61.   4 *Ibid.* 73–5.
5 *Ibid.* 76. Cf. *RO*, I, 30.   6 *Ibid.* 59, 61.

7 For a short account of the Great Pestilence in England and the losses in the religious world Abbot Gasquet's *The Black Death* is still useful, though it has been corrected and supplemented by subsequent research. G. G. Coulton, *The Black Death* has a good bibliography to date of writing. The work of P. G. Mode, *The Influence of the Black Death on the English Monasteries* contains valuable information but, as often happens with doctoral dissertations, shows a lack of historical perspective and traces in every subsequent monastic vicissitude the influence of the Black Death. The author also makes the mistake of supposing that the monks served in person many of the churches they owned. A. M. Campbell, *The Black Death and Men of Learning*, is concerned with the whole of Europe, but has interesting references to England.

set irrevocably in. It was the great divide, one of the few decisive fractures in the continuity of European history.[1] This hypothesis, as regards its moral and spiritual implications, can be neither established nor demolished by direct evidence. The precise influence of a great catastrophe—war, famine or pestilence—on the moral and spiritual resources of a country must always elude the historian. It should, however, be possible to establish a few facts to show in particular cases how severe were the losses in personnel, and to pronounce in general on the relative excellence of discipline and observance in the generations before and after the series of plagues that devastated the country between 1348 and 1370. On the latter point, indeed, judgement is given by implication in many chapters of this work; here, it will be needful only to give a summary decision after the direct and tangible results of the plague have been passed in review.

The Black Death, a variety of the contagious bubonic plague of the East, of which rats through their parasites were the chief carriers, reached England from the Continent in the late summer of 1348. It entered the country on the Dorset coast, probably at Weymouth, and spread rapidly up and across the land, raging in London all through the winter and until the following May. By the midsummer of 1349 it had all but exhausted itself, though a parting shaft carried off the great Bradwardine in August. It returned in 1361-2 and again in 1368-9, and these later visitations, though less catastrophic in character, were very severe, and attracted more attention from contemporaries than the references in text-books might suggest. The disease appears to have taken two forms, the one implying a longer period of sickness and danger than the other; in the more common form, death was the probable, though not the inevitable, outcome, and took place within three days or less.

A consensus of opinion, after the discussions of the past half-century, acknowledges that, when all allowance has been made for contemporary exaggeration, the population of the country during the fatal twelvemonth was reduced by more than a quarter and perhaps by as much as a third.[2] Individual districts suffered still more heavily, while individual groups, such as villages or religious communities, might escape altogether or be annihilated. The disease left behind it a train of *sequelae* in those who had

1 Mode, *op. cit.*, in his early pages cites several of the emphatic pronouncements of historians of fifty years since, and echoes of their opinion may still be heard even in the works of careful scholars such as Fr P. Hughes, who remarks (*The Reformation in England*, I, 40): 'In many respects the monasteries in England never regained what they now lost [i.e. by the Black Death]. Very few indeed of them—comparatively speaking—were henceforward sufficiently staffed to carry out their primary function of choral prayer in the way this needs to be done.' The wording is cautious, but the reader would scarcely be led to expect such post-plague numbers as the following: Bury St Edmunds, 62; Canterbury, Christ Church, 70; Canterbury, St Augustine's, 54; Durham, 74; Gloucester, 54; St Albans, 54; Worcester, 45. Downside Abbey, with a large public school and other commitments besides choral duties, has (1953) some 50 permanently resident monks.

2 So, for example, M. M. Postan in his important article, 'Some economic evidence of falling population in the later Middle Ages', 221–46. This estimate is adopted *passim* by writers in vols. I and II of the *CEH*.

survived its attack, and this lack of physical resistance, added to the recent memories of terror, no doubt added to the apprehension when later visitations struck a reduced population.

When the fearful severity of the scourge is borne in mind it may appear strange that it has left such scanty traces in the monastic records. There was no English rival to Thucydides or even to Boccaccio, and the rare mention is often a passing allusion only. Even the chronicler of St Albans, who devotes so much space to the doings of contemporary abbots, has no graphic phrases to describe the disaster that affected the domestic history of his house so deeply[1]. Such notices as survive make it clear that the incidence of mortality was very uneven in the different houses, but there is no way of ascertaining, as has been done with some certainty in the case of the parochial clergy by use of the records of institutions to benefices, whether the total losses were lower or higher than the average losses of the whole population. On the one hand, a large household in close contact by day and night would be a natural field for rapid infection; even at the present day, with scientific techniques of isolation and disinfectants, groups and institutions such as a ship's company or a school are peculiarly liable to suffer when once hit by an epidemic. On the other hand, the religious, as living regular, well-nourished lives, might be expected to have had greater resistance, while the level of cleanliness, sanitation, medical service and nursing, though low by modern standards, must have been high indeed in the great monasteries when compared with the conditions prevailing in villages and towns. Detailed notices are relatively scanty. The most familiar, perhaps, is that in the ample chronicle of St Albans, a house which lost its abbot, prior, subprior and forty-six monks, in addition to others in the dependent cells, in the course of a few days when the pestilence struck the abbey at Eastertide, 1349.[2] At Westminster in May, a month later, the abbot and twenty-six monks were carried off,[3] but the still larger community of Christ Church, Canterbury, escaped with only four deaths[4]—an escape that can scarcely have been wholly due to its copious supply of pure and running water. Other figures are known from scattered sources: thus Lewes[5] and Reading[6] lost large numbers; Louth Park the abbot and many monks.[7] A few houses were even harder hit, and the record perhaps owes its existence to that circumstance. Thus among the Cistercians at the Devonshire house of Newenham twenty monks and three converses died, leaving the abbot with only two monks behind;[8] at Meaux in Yorkshire only ten monks

1 *GASA*, ii, 369–70.   2 *Ibid.*
3 Flete, *History of Westminster*, ed. J. A. Robinson, 128.
4 *Lit. Cant.* ii, xxii–xxiii.
5 B.M. MS. Cole 5824 fo. 78 (cited by Gasquet, *Black Death*, 134).
6 *VCH*, Berks., ii, 66.
7 *Chronicon abbatie de Parco Lude*, ed. E. Venables, p. 38. The writer, though diffuse in his expressions of emotion says merely: *obierunt multi.*
8 Gasquet, *op. cit.* 103, with references.

survived from a community of forty-two monks and seven converses.[1] Among the canons Croxton in Leicestershire was all but exterminated,[2] Lanthony lost nineteen out of thirty,[3] and at Bodmin the prior and all but two of the canons went, leaving only an invalid and a simpleton to look after each other,[4] while at some of the smaller houses, such as Hickling, Ivychurch, Mountjoy and Sandford[5] such a clean sweep was made that regular observance was at an end and an appeal was made at the general chapter for drafts from elsewhere. For the friars figures are extremely rare, but we are told that the Norwich house of Preachers was emptied to the last friar.[6]

In addition to these direct and precise references to losses, it has been noted that the recorded deaths of heads of houses in the fatal twelvemonth are strikingly more numerous than in normal times. Gasquet collected some forty references to the death of an abbot or prior, and a more recent investigator has reckoned that whereas the average annual number of voidances for the previous nine years was twenty-one, in the year 1348–9 this number rose to 144; it may be noted that the same authority found the average for the years 1350–60 to be twenty, while in the year (1361–2) of the second visitation of the plague it rose to fifty-six.[7] A further means of calculation has been found in a comparison of the numbers of religious shortly before 1349 and those at a later date in the century. In almost every case a very sharp fall is seen, at once most noticeable and most significant at some of the largest houses. Thus Bath, Glastonbury and St Swithun's, Winchester, all show a reduction by nearly a half between the first and last quarters of the century.[8] It is natural, and perhaps allowable, to connect this steep fall with the plague in its three visitations, but it is impossible to be certain whether the drop was primarily due to the mortality within the house or to the falling-off of recruits from a diminished population now in what we may anachronistically call 'full employment'. It may be significant that at Christ Church, which all but escaped the plague of 1349, and Durham, from which no record of any kind survives, the numbers fell by only a third or less.[9]

Yet another argument has been found in the appearance of a series of petitions to Rome from monasteries all over England asking for faculties to ordain a specified number of monks to the priesthood below the

1 *Chronicon monasterii de Melsa*, ed. E. A. Bond, III, 37.
2 *V. infra*, p. 12, n. 1.   3 *VCH, Glos.*, II, 90, with reference.
4 *Reg. J. Grandisson*, ed. F. C. Hingeston-Randolph, II, 1076–8.
5 *VCH, Norfolk*, II, 241; *AC*, no. 34, p. 58: 'Ivychirche et Sandford per mortalitates fratrum adeo sunt collapse quod nulla ad presens in eisdem viget religio.'
6 *VCH, Norfolk*, II, 241.
7 Mode, *The Influence of the Black Death on the English Monasteries*, 18. The writer apparently includes some heads of hospitals and colleges in his calculations, but this does not affect the ratio of the totals.
8 A glance through Gasquet's *Black Death* or Knowles and Hadcock, *Medieval Religious Houses* will provide numerous additional examples.
9 For Canterbury (65 falls to 46) *v*. R. A. L. Smith, *Canterbury Cathedral Priory*, 3; for Durham (70 falls to 56) *v*. Knowles and Hadcock, *op. cit.* 69.

canonical age (the petition usually specifies the very early age of twenty years) in order to remedy the dearth of priests caused by pestilence. All orders are concerned, and the stream of petitions continues for some twenty years. St Albans, Bury, Coventry, Durham, Norwich, Reading, Shrewsbury, Spalding and Worcester are among the black monks, Croxden, Kingswood and Newenham among the Cistercians, Cockersand, Hickling, Leicester, Nostell and Walsingham among the canons.[1] It is perhaps noteworthy that several of the houses known to have been hardest hit are on the list, but it is even more remarkable that the spate of petitions does not begin till 1363, and is at its highest flow in that and the two following years. It is not clear why some of these houses did not express their needs earlier; possibly it was only under Urban V, who succeeded in 1362, that there was assurance of a favourable reception; possibly the visitation of 1361–2 had made a difficult situation more urgent. It is at any rate the indication of a *bona fide* state of emergency, for the monasteries were not naturally eager to advance to fully privileged status recruits of only a few years' standing.

If it is difficult to assess the numerical losses, it is almost impossible to assert that the quality of the next generation had deteriorated. It has been suggested that the smaller communities which henceforth were to gaze daily at tiers of unoccupied stalls, and hear the echoes in a refectory and chapterhouse vaster than their needs, must have felt that they were living in an age when fervour had cooled and less could be demanded of the puny race that remained. It is true that at a number of houses the refectory and even the dormitory were either abandoned or curtailed; Durham, Furness and Cleeve provide well-known examples. On the other hand, a very large community is not always the best nursery for individual fervour or contentment; useful employment and individual relationships are easier to come by in one of moderate size. And, if we abandon the realm of fancy for such facts as are available, we do not receive the impression that the monks acted as if an epoch had ended. One of the accidental results of the plague was to open the way to high office for Thomas de la Mare at St Albans and Simon Langham at Westminster, each of whom in his own way inaugurated a period of development for his house. At Gloucester and Ely the great building schemes may have halted for a moment, but continued almost at once on their course. It was within the decades immediately after the pestilences that both Canterbury and Durham established themselves more firmly at Oxford, while in general such statistics as are available show that there was a general, if not spectacular rise in numbers towards the end of the century.

In the economic field also the Black Death has been invoked as the great dissolvent agency, and as the cause of permanent manorial disruption

---

1 Mode, *op. cit.* 62–3, gives a list, by no means complete, of those houses, which may be supplemented by reference to the volume of *CPL* in question.

and financial deterioration within the monastic boʊy. Opinions are still divided as to the extent of the change wrought by the plague in society. The view of early economic historians that a dearth of tenants in villeinage and the demand for well-paid labour caused a whole series of revolutionary changes, such as the disappearance of labour service, the decay of the manorial economy and the introduction of a regime of rents, has been successfully challenged. It has been shown that all these processes, including the fall in population itself, were well under way before 1348, either generally or in certain districts, and that on the other hand some of them did not develop everywhere till late in the century. On the other hand, some findings that suggested little or no economic or social change immediately after the pestilence have not been endorsed by more recent scholarship,[1] which is almost unanimous in attributing to the Black Death, if not an originating, at least a marked accelerating, influence upon all these developments. There is certainly no reason to think that the financial situation of the monasteries as a whole was changed finally for the worse. The numerous instances that have been alleged from the later fourteenth century can easily be paralleled from almost any other period of the Middle Ages. The case of Canterbury, whence an impressive tale of woe was dispatched to Avignon in 1350, is perhaps representative. Finances soon recovered, and by the end of the century the cathedral priory, with almost all its lands at rent, was drawing a revenue considerably higher than that produced by Henry of Eastry in his best years. Canterbury is also a warning against other generalizations, for in the latter decades of the fourteenth century she was demanding more labour services than in Eastry's later years. In other words, though the economic shock was great, and its consequences permanent at least in part, the view cannot be accepted that sees in the Black Death and its satellities the chief cause of the alleged economic distress of the monasteries in the later Middle Ages.

1 In particular, the important study by Miss A. E. Levett, 'The Black Death on the estates of the see of Winchester', showing that vacant holdings were soon taken up after the plague, has been examined by Professor Postan in his article noted above (p. 9, n. 2), where he suggests that the author selected a peculiarly profitable group of manors and failed to make allowance for the possible existence of a 'queue' of unsatisfied would-be landowners even after the Black Death.

CHAPTER II

MONKS AND CANONS AT THE UNIVERSITY,
1300–1450

An account has already been given of the establishment of a house of studies at Oxford by the authorities of the chapter of the black monks of the province of Canterbury.[1] The first tentative moves had issued, shortly before the end of the thirteenth century, in the occupation of an adequate area in Stockwell Street, on the site occupied by the original buildings of the present Worcester College. Owing directly to the circumstances of its origin Gloucester College, as it came to be called, was both in ownership and organization something of a patchwork. The abbot and community of Malmesbury were the ground landlords, and they also owned and occupied part of the building; the parts of the fabric common to all— chapel, hall and perhaps in time lecture rooms and library—had been erected and were maintained at the cost of the authorities of the provincial chapter, who had also secured an additional parcel of land; the apartments occupied by monks from the various houses were erected and maintained by the communities concerned. The head of the establishment was a prior, originally appointed by the abbot of Malmesbury; but the presidents appointed the regent master.

Gloucester College was not the only foothold of the black monks at Oxford. The northern province, which contained only four houses of any size, had made no attempt to set up a common house, but the great cathedral priory of Durham, which throughout the Middle Ages dominated the northern monastic scene, had begun to send monks to study at Oxford during the second priorate of Hugh of Darlington (1286/7–1289/90), the first purchase of land having been made in 1286.[2] The first steps towards the building of a college were taken by his successor, Richard of Hoton, but without much success, and the project languished, though Durham monks continued to frequent the university.

The third establishment of the black monks was that set up by Christ Church, Canterbury.[3] The cathedral monastery, which had been always in the past, and still remained, the largest house of black monks in the country, and which was also one of the two or three wealthiest and most distinguished, had consistently held aloof from the provincial chapter and all its works. In the mid-fourteenth century, as we shall see, a final trial of strength took place between this community and the greatest of the

1 *RO*, I, 25–7.
2 The best account of this is still that of H. E. D. Blakiston, 'Durham Account Rolls'. For shorter accounts *v. RU*, III, 186–7, and H. E. Salter in *VCH, Oxon.*, II, 68–9.
3 The voluminous and interesting records of the college have been printed by W. A. Pantin in *Canterbury College*.

abbots-president, and Christ Church emerged finally unconquered. It is not surprising, therefore, that the cathedral priory had taken no part in the foundation of Gloucester College, and had refused contributions to the common fund. At the same time, such a great monastery could not neglect the advantages of a university training in theology and canon law. Although Christ Church had long ago made use of the services of Franciscan lecturers, and in the early decades of the fourteenth century maintained a teacher in theology, presumably a monk,[1] the attraction of Oxford persisted, and at about the same time the priory owned a hall at Oxford, where three monk students resided.[2]

Such was the state of the black monks·in academic life on the eve of the publication of the constitutions of Benedict XII.[3] These affected the situation in two ways. By uniting the provinces of Canterbury and York in a single capitular body the papal measure made Gloucester College the concern and the resort, at least in legal theory, of all the English black monk houses. At the same time the relevant chapters of the bull *Pastor bonus* laid down regulations for the common house of studies, and imposed on all the obligation of supporting it by contributions and of despatching thither a fixed quota of their subjects. One monk from a community of twenty and so upwards *pro rata* must be sent to one of the approved universities to take a degree in theology or canon law.[4] The pension to be paid for each monk by his superior, and the salary to be found out of the common fund for the regent in theology, were fixed. Nothing was laid down as to the financial responsibility for the first capital outlay: at Oxford, as has been seen, an establishment was already in existence, with the individual houses as part-owners of the buildings, and no change took place in this respect.

The Benedictine constitutions had been drawn up with the advice of a committee of French abbots, and they reflected in their details the distaste for strong central control always shown by the black monks. Thus it was decreed that the house of studies, which in the case of the Cistercians at Paris had been put under the control of the general chapter, should be under the general supervision of an abbot of the vicinity; it was his duty to choose from among the students one to be their prior, with all rights of maintaining discipline. This arrangement, which did not conform to any traditional black monk method of relating a dependency to its mother-house, may have aimed, in the earlier Cistercian bull, at giving canonical sanction to conditions already obtaining at Paris; certainly it

---

1 *V.* letter of Archbishop Reynolds to Prior Eastry, 27 April 1321, in *Literae Cantuarienses*, ed. J. B. Sheppard, I, 46.

2 *Lit. Cant.* I, 392 (September 1331), 417 (27 December 1331).

3 These have been printed in Wilkins, *Concilia*, II, 588 *seqq.*, and in the various editions of the *Bullarium Romanum*. The relevant passages on the studies have been extracted by Denifle and Chatelain, *Cartularium Universitatis Parisiensis*, II, 448–50 (Cistercians), 463 (black monks) and 480–1 (Austin canons).

4 *Cart. Paris.*, II, 463: 'De quolibet vicenario numero monachorum unum.'

coincided with contemporary practice at Oxford, and could thus be implemented without difficulty. The simplest course might have been to depute the abbot of Malmesbury, who up to the present had exercised an ill-defined control, as abbot-protector. The presidents, however, either from a desire to carry out the papal instructions as literally as possible, or from a fear that Malmesbury might acquire a quasi-proprietary control, deputed the abbot of Abingdon, who was in fact the nearest prelate, to oversee the house and appoint the prior.[1] This he duly did, but it would seem that Malmesbury, still the ground landlords of most of the property, and with a contingent of their students in residence, continued to treat their own part of the fabric as a dependency, and to appoint a *prior loci*, who exercised authority alongside of, and occasionally in conflict with, the *prior studentium*, who was always regarded as having personal, rather than local jurisdiction.[2]

Meanwhile the chapter, and its representatives the abbots-president, continued to implement still further the Benedictine constitutions. It was decided in 1343 that a doctor of divinity should be maintained at the common cost to act as domestic regent to the college, and that the houses of the united provinces should contribute to his salary and to the expenses of monks incepting in theology and canon law. They further drew up regulations for the life of the college, establishing Office and Mass in common on festal days.[3] Gloucester College, nevertheless, remained something of a composite body. It never became a family with a fully common life, but remained a collection of 'staircases' owned or leased by particular monasteries, over which the prior of the Malmesbury monks continued to exercise, or at least to claim, some of the powers of a superior.[4] The *prior studentium*, for his part, and with some show of legal justification, claimed jurisdiction over the monks who resided in Oxford outside the walls of Gloucester College, either in the rival colleges of Durham and Canterbury or in halls.[5] His chief function was to keep the presidents informed on matters concerning the common house as such: he it was who applied to the individual houses for their money contributions, and who reported to the presidents the monasteries that defaulted in maintaining their canonical quota of monks at Oxford. He also reported notable breaches of discipline or morals which demanded some sort of judicial process.[6] The internal organization of Gloucester College developed gradually, and owed much to the impulse of energetic abbots

1 *MC*, III, 23–4.

2 *Ibid.* 25, 104; cf. *Snappe's Formulary*, ed. H. E. Salter, 347 n. For an excellent account of the college *v.* W. A. Pantin, *Gloucester College. V.* also *infra*, p. 28.

3 *MC*, II, 55–8, especially 57: 'Statuimus ut studentes nostri ordinis qui in loco nostro communi Oxon' moram trahunt, conveniant in capella communi diebus solemnibus et festivis ad diurnum servicium decantandum.'

4 *MC*, III, 104.

5 'Durham Account Rolls', 27 *seqq.*

6 *MC*, II, 80; cf. the action of Adam Easton in 1366 (*MC*, III, 60) and the instructions of the chapter of 1363 (*MC*, II, 74–5).

who might or might not be presidents at the time, such as Walter de Monington of Glastonbury (1341–75) and Whethamstede of St Albans half a century later. Thus the former, unable to be present at the chapter of 1360, made a number of suggestions tending to increase the monastic observance of the college: he wished for a monthly chapter of faults and less freedom for the monk-students in social contacts in the town.[1] Three years later, c. 1363, the chapter did in fact issue a number of decrees, though of different and somewhat wider scope: while the *prior studentium* is called upon to maintain discipline more strictly, the domestic autonomy, so characteristic of the black monks, is shown in the designation of the senior monk in each group to act as superior *in spiritualibus*, that is, ʋ administer the sacraments of Penance and the Eucharist to his confrères, and to dispense them when necessary from regular observance.[2] A number of further decrees concerned the studies and degrees. Half a century later John of Whethamstede is said to have drawn up a body of statutes when *prior studentium*, c. 1414–17, and in 1444 the earlier decrees of chapter were republished with additions.[3]

Gloucester College, reflecting so well the distaste of the black monks for any submission to central control, continued till the Dissolution as a loose federation of small groups rather than a college. It had no fellows, no property of its own, no seal; it is not certain that even the modest measure of liturgical service in common aimed at by the chapter was ever, or constantly, achieved. Moreover, and for similar reasons, it never fully realized the aim of Benedict XII and its still earlier first founders, who had intended it to be at once the only and the fully representative focus of academic life for the black monks. Two of the very largest and intellectually most distinguished houses not only stood aloof but maintained rival establishments which from time to time gave lodging to monks from various other houses. In addition, some abbeys, at least occasionally, either from set purpose or because Gloucester College was at the moment full, allowed their subjects to lodge in halls about the town, while others sent their monks to Cambridge where, from the middle of the fourteenth century, a rival with a more legitimate title recognized by the chapter came into being.[4]

Quite apart from rivalries and neglect of these kinds, there was always a fairly numerous minority among the houses who defaulted in their duty of sending monks to study—a minority partly, though not entirely, coincident with a large group that defaulted in their payment of the monetary contribution. Leaving out of the reckoning the small independent priories (and indeed the capitular authorities seem never to

---

1 *MC*, III, 29–30.   2 *MC*, II, 80.
3 *MC*, II, 211–16; for Whethamstede *v. MC*, II, 214.
4 *MC*, II, 76 (chapter of 1363): 'Volumus ut in universitate Cantibrigg prior studentium juxta modum et formam in ipsis Benedictinis [*sc.* constitutionibus] traditum amodo deputetur, qui monachorum ibidem studentium sollicite curam gerat.' In subsequent chapters the *priores studentium* of Oxford and Cambridge are named together.

have reckoned with these at all consistently), the most constant culprits were, as was to be expected, the small and relatively poor upland abbeys, mostly Saxon foundations, in Somerset, Dorset, Devon and the midlands. Lists have survived of the defaulters reported to the chapters of 1343, 1393, 1423 and 1426. Burton-on-Trent appears in all four; Tavistock and (somewhat surprisingly) Evesham in three; Abbotsbury, Battle, Eynsham, Muchelney and Whitby in two, and among the numerous single culprits are Cernel, Milton and Athelney.[1] It may be suspected that several of these houses were in fact chronic defaulters. Indeed, it is perhaps scarcely fair to use the term defaulter of many of these monasteries. The Benedictine constitutions, like all similar legal enunciations of a 'flat rate', could not with equity be rigidly or universally applied. In almost every case noted above, the defaulting house can be shown to have contained at most twenty, and often considerably less than twenty, monks in the century between 1350 and 1450. Not all these would be able-bodied; they might all be over the age of thirty, and if by any chance a remote community of that size contained a young monk capable of doing himself credit in the long and arduous course of philosophy and theology at Oxford, it is obvious that he could ill have been spared for eight years' absence.[2] Unfortunately, no figures for the strength of the college exist save for the year immediately before the Dissolution, when there were thirty in residence.[3] From the analogy of all other similar figures, this cannot have been a maximum, and perhaps the college at peak periods may have held fifty or more. This, of course, fell far short of the full statutory number to be housed, if the Benedictine constitutions had been exactly honoured. This figure has been set as high as 125, but this would seem an overestimate.[4] In the second half of the fourteenth century, the number of houses with more than twenty monks stood at little more than thirty, while many had fallen to a population of sixteen or less, and it is clear that no attempt was ever made, or could reasonably have been demanded, to extract the best young men from all these struggling or decayed communities. As might be expected, it was the greater monasteries that resorted most regularly to Oxford. There is certain evidence of half a dozen, and almost certain indications of seven or eight others having owned or leased groups of rooms for at least considerable periods.[5] Eminent among all was a small group—St Albans, Norwich, Worcester,

---

1 Cf. *MC*, II, 21–2, 90, 150–1, 172.

2 The view had been put forward, apparently, that no house with less than twenty monks lay under any obligation, but the chapter of 1363 drew attention to a declaration of Benedict XII which laid upon the regular visitors the task of inquiring, at any house with more than six monks, whether there were funds sufficient to send one or more to study. Such a regulation could have little effect in practice.

3 University Archives Reg. B (reversed) fo. 194v. This reference is taken from Pantin, *Gloucester College*, 71.

4 Pantin, *Gloucester College*, 70. C. H. Daniel, *Worcester College* (1900), 27, argues from architectural and other evidence for a monastic population of 100.

5 *VCH*, *Oxon*, II, 71.

Westminster and Bury St Edmunds—which consistently maintained students, provided *priores studentium* or, as they came to be called, wardens, and from time to time made free-will additions to the fabric of the college, such as the block of rooms and hall built by Abbot Curteys of Bury (1429–46) and the private chapel and common library provided by Whethamstede of St Albans (1420–65).[1] It has been calculated that from Westminster, where the evidence is very full, no less than sixty-five, or more than one in ten of the total number of monks between 1300 and the Dissolution, went up to Oxford, and it is possible that one or two of the other houses could have shown comparable figures. On the other hand, two or three notable houses are conspicuous by their absence from most of the lists of those supporting students that have survived; Winchester Cathedral Priory is one (it is even found defaulting in 1343 and 1408), St Augustine's, Canterbury, is another, Coventry is a third.[2] Material probably exists, in printed and unprinted form, for a fairly full survey; till this is accomplished further precision is useless.

Meanwhile, the two other establishments of the black monks at Oxford had grown to full stature. The northern province, as has been noted already, had hitherto made no attempt to inaugurate a common house of studies at Oxford, though Durham had made a tentative beginning on its own. Further progress may have been delayed by hopes, raised first in 1260 and renewed in 1333–4, of establishing a northern university at Stamford,[3] where Durham had long possessed a house to which students in arts appear to have been sent; among them, at a later date, was Uthred of Boldon. Shortly after the Stamford secession of 1333, Richard de Bury contemplated a re-foundation on a larger scale at Oxford, where individual monks of Durham had continued to study, and intended to bequeath to it his great collection of books. In the event, however, he achieved nothing, and his books were dispersed in settlement of his debts. Meanwhile the cell of Durham near the Canditch, supported by contributions from the obedientiaries at the mother-house and by the more irregular payments from the dependent cells of the north, had continued its modest career for almost a century when Thomas Hatfield, one of the most munificent of all the wealthy occupants of the see of Durham, decided to erect the house into a college, acting in close concert with the then prior, Robert Walworth.[4] Walworth would seem to have been a relative of the distinguished mayor of London, William de Walworth, and Hatfield, who for some time before his death had been living in his London house, had been associated with Walworth in the establishment of the London Charterhouse, then just beginning its existence. Hatfield left for his college a legacy of £3000; land was acquired to the extent of several acres in the suburbs of Oxford north

1 *V. Snappe's Formulary*, 352–3; *Amundesham*, II, 200, 264.
2 *MC*, II, 22; cf. *MC*, III, 149.
3 For Stamford, *v.* A. F. Leach in *VCH Lincs*, II, 469 *seqq.*
4 For this see H. E. D. Blakiston, 'Durham Account Rolls', 27 *seqq.*

of the walls and the present Broad Street, probably consisting of the whole area which ultimately passed to Trinity College. Buildings on a small scale were erected, without a large chapel or hall, and henceforward a small group of Durham monks under a prior were in residence. Hatfield's legacy was under the charge of Walworth and a colleague, and was expended somewhat wastefully by a monk of Durham, John de Berington, probably the prior's brother, in buying and stocking estates, in purchasing advowsons to build up an income for the college, and in certain capital expenses on the Oxford property.

The college, as established by Hatfield, was for eight student monks (of whom one was to be appointed warden by the prior of Durham) and eight secular students in grammar and philosophy, two from the diocese or city of Durham, two from Allertonshire, and two from Howdenshire, who were to act as general servants to the monks. From its inception onwards it was carefully maintained, and a regular succession of students passed through it. Perhaps more than any other monastery Durham came to be governed and administered by 'university monks'. Six wardens of the college became priors of Durham, and between them ruled the cathedral monastery for nearly eighty out of its last hundred years of existence.[1] Almost all the wardens, and many other *alumni*, filled other important posts as priors of Coldingham or Finchale, or as greater obedientiaries at Durham itself. Durham College also gave occasional lodging to monks of other northern houses, such as York and Whitby.[2]

Shortly before Durham College attained full development, the position of Christ Church, Canterbury, at Oxford had changed.[3] The hall which the house owned in the early decades of the century would seem to have been disused shortly afterwards, for in 1355 Archbishop Islep is found exhorting the prior to send young monks to the university,[4] and it is clear that at some time after this date they actually leased rooms in Gloucester College.[5] Six years after his letter, however, Islep took decisive action by founding Canterbury Hall at Oxford. That the initiative should have come from the archbishop is noteworthy, and it is possible that the move may have been occasioned by the serious attempt that was being made at the time by the black monk chapter under the direction of Abbot de la Mare to bring Christ Church fully under its jurisdiction.[6] The archbishop's

1 See list of wardens given by Blakiston, *op. cit.* 23–5.   2 *Ibid.* 19.

3 The tangled story of the beginnings of Canterbury College has been outlined, with growing precision, by J. B. Sheppard (introd. to *Lit. Cant.* II, xxv *seqq.*), H. B. Workman, *John Wyclif*, I, 171–84, and W. A. Pantin (cf. in particular the long note to Rashdall, *Medieval Universities*, ed. Powicke and Emden, III, 212, n. 1). Pantin also, in the third volume of *Canterbury College*, prints many of the vital documents.

4 *Lit. Cant.* II, 332–3 (25 Feb.): 'Cum...improperaverint nobis multi quod juniores monachos in Universitatibus studentes non habemus.'

5 Pantin, *Canterbury College*, III, no. 26, p. 21. Shortly after 1363 the monks of Christ Church granted their old chambers at Gloucester College to Westminster with right of re-entry. The grant was later made absolute.

6 *V. infra*, pp. 43–4.

reputed rights, no less than the monks', were at stake in the quarrel, and the presence of monks from Canterbury either in Gloucester College or in unauthorized lodgings would have put all parties at Canterbury at a disadvantage.

Islep's original intention seems to have been to found a college for twelve students, partly monastic, partly secular, and after due preliminaries it was opened under a monk-warden, Henry Woodhull, in March 1363.[1] Islep, however, for some reason thought better of his scheme and ejected the monks and their warden, filling the house with secular students under the wardenship of the celebrated John Wyclif.[2] The archbishop died in the spring of 1366 and was succeeded by Simon Langham, sometime abbot of Westminster, who naturally favoured the monks and dismissed the secular warden. As a practical measure to force the secular students to capitulate he endeavoured to revoke the valuable gift of the living of Pagham, which the monks of Christ Church, whose property it had been, had made over to the support of the college. In consequence, two suits developed in Rome: that of the dispossessed master and fellows of the secular college against the archbishop, and that of the archbishop and community of Canterbury asserting their claim to Pagham. Before any decision had been reached Langham, created cardinal, was compelled to resign his see, whereupon his successor, William Wittelsey, gave his support to the seculars. The monks appealed for help to Langham at the Curia and after litigation the decision was given in their favour. The college, thus restored and now also restricted to the monks, was constituted in its final form by Archbishop Courtenay and furnished in 1384 with statutes which remained in force till the Dissolution.[3] These statutes established the house as a college in the full meaning of the term: it consisted, that is, of a warden and fellows who possessed a common seal, and acted as a corporate body in financial and legal transactions. In this it differed from the federal association of groups and individuals at Gloucester College, and from the quasi-collegiate status of Durham College. The warden and fellows, however, of Canterbury College, though they appeared before the world in all transactions as a governing body, were in fact still under the jurisdiction of the prior of Christ Church and bound by the decisions of the Canterbury chapter; they were also, in certain specified ways, under the jurisdiction of the archbishop, and could not move in any important transaction without obtaining the consent of these two authorities.

Residence at the university in the Middle Ages affected the whole pattern of a monk's life far more than it does in the modern world. Whereas nowadays it makes a break of less than three (or at most of less than four) years, punctuated by long periods of 'vacation' spent in the monastery, in the Middle Ages it implied an almost complete absence

1 Pantin, *op. cit.* III, 3–4.   2 *Ibid.* III, 11.
3 They are printed in Pantin, *op. cit.* III, 172 *seqq.*

from the monastery for a long space of time in early and vigorous man-hood. There is indeed some evidence that at a few great houses the students returned for the three months of the summer vacation, but the normal 'vacation' from the Oxford monastic colleges seems to have been only one of a few weeks, granted to individuals for recreative or domestic reasons, and spent at home or on a visit of travel.

For the degree of Master of Arts eight years' study was required, and nine for that of the doctorate in theology, and though perhaps a majority of the monk-theologians had been through their arts course in their monastery, there must have been some who spent seventeen years or more at Oxford, and the theologians would all spend the needful nine years, even if they did not remain for a time as regents after inception. They were therefore all but strangers to their monastery from their mid-twenties to their mid-thirties, and though monks from houses in southern and south-eastern England often returned for a month or two in the summer, or for an abbatial election or important visitation, others must have resided almost without a break at Oxford, outside the conditions of monastic life, and ineligible for the minor administrative offices that would have come the way of a capable young man. This latter disability was no doubt offset by the eligibility for high office conferred by the doctorate in theology or law, but the long usage of private rooms, and the disposal of one's daily work and movements, must have made it inevitable for univer-sity monks to expect similar indulgences on their return home. In the case of weaker characters, or those without a strong bent for study or for devotion, the long residence at Oxford must not only have given occasion for disciplinary lapses, but also have implanted a permanent taste for liberty and social intercourse. Besides the inevitable scandals, there is evidence of a certain amount of dissipation and waste of time in social visits. The less distinguished students, who had taken an arts course only, or who had spent a year or two learning to preach, may well have found claustral life irksome on their return.

The little evidence that has survived confirms these suggestions, though it must be remembered that here, as with visitation records, and with the modern press, it is the troublesome type that receives publicity, while the clerk of Chaucer's *Prologue* is preserved only by the accidental touch of poetry. A welcome glimpse of real life is given us in a short sequence of letters written in 1360-1 by the capable abbot of Glastonbury, Walter de Monington, who appears throughout in a very attractive light. The first letter[1] is written to one of his monks, William Nye, a student at Oxford, and contains the proposals for new chapter decrees already mentioned. The abbot is sending two young monks to Oxford whom he places under Nye's tutelage. A month or so later he writes again to Nye,[2] giving him full jurisdiction over one of these young monks, and a third: they are not to leave the house without his permission, nor to entertain in their rooms;

1 *MC*, III, 29–30.　　　2 *Ibid*. 30–1.

they are to keep the regular fasts unless dispensed. Some months later Monington is found writing direct to the young monks, as Nye has failed both to act and to report, though they have been hunting and fishing and trespassing.[1] The abbot summons them back to Glastonbury to give an account of themselves, though they are to leave their possessions at Oxford. One of them, at least, was allowed to remain at the university, but four years later he has run out of cash and Monington has to reprove him for extravagance; advising him to take pupils in philosophy as a means of raising funds, he sends him eleven shillings and eightpence with no hope of more to follow.[2] Sambourne, the monk in question, apparently mended his ways, for a year later the abbot entrusts him with the care of his cousin, 'little Bodenham', with some observations as to the known dangers of university life for the young.[3] The other monk of the original pair, John Lucombe, was not so satisfactory. In the autumn of 1366 the abbot-president, Thomas de la Mare, acting on the information of Adam Easton, the future cardinal, then *prior studentium*, is found delegating to the abbot of Glastonbury the examination of Lucombe on a charge of incontinence.[4] The issue is not known, but the series of letters gives a vivid picture of the anxieties that could be caused to an abbot who was doing all in his power to implement the Benedictine constitutions.

The prime purpose of sending monks to the university was declared to be the encouragement of the study of theology and canon law. Allotment of students to these two subjects was to depend upon abilities and personal choice, but legists were never to outnumber the theologians.[5] Both courses were, both by statutory requirement and normal practice, preceded by a course in arts and philosophy. This requirement, as is well known, gave rise from the mid-thirteenth century onwards to a quarrel of long standing between the universities and the friars, who claimed that they had themselves given their subjects a grounding in letters and philosophy, and who always sat loose to university regulations. A practical outcome to the struggle at Oxford and Cambridge had been to give the friars exemption from the arts and bachelors courses by means of a grace in each case, which was never refused. When the monks arrived, they seem from the first to have been the beneficiaries of this system. Benedict XII, when legislating for studies, had laid it down that all monasteries were to have a master in grammar, logic and philosophy. No doubt this was honoured in the greater monasteries; evidence of such teaching does indeed exist at Canterbury, Durham[6] and elsewhere, but it was clearly an ideal unattainable in the smaller houses, and it was presumably for

---

1 *Ibid.* 31–2: 'In garennis prohibitis discurrere, venari et piscari minime pepercistis.'
2 *Ibid.* 53–4: 'Mittimus tibi undecim solidos et octo denarios et non plus.'
3 *Ibid.* 54: 'Parvulum Bodenham inscium et indisciplinatum tuo regimini destinamus.'
4 *Ibid.* 60.   5 Wilkins, *Concilia*, II, 595 (cap. viii).
6 For Canterbury *v. Lit. Cant.* I, 46. For Durham *v. Rites of Durham*, ed. (1) J. Raine, 81; ed. (2) J. T. Fowler, 97, where some sort of instruction is presumed for those who do not go to Oxford.

students from these that lectures in philosophy, usually by one of the students of theology, were decreed as necessary in Gloucester College, with weekly disputations in the subject.[1]

Besides artists, canonists and theologians, a certain number of monks, at least in the thirteenth century, went to Oxford to learn preaching, partly with the aim of dispensing with the services of friars in the cathedral priories, where friction had developed between the mendicants and the possessioners. Preaching both in Latin and in English was contemplated: occasions for Latin sermons were provided by the solemn inaugurations of chapters and visitations, and the rarer synods where the preacher was sometimes a monk.[2]

Each monastery was responsible for some, at least, of the running expenses of Gloucester College, and for the current expenditure of its students. These, it would seem, settled accounts individually with the manciple of the college.[3] The rooms were rented, if they had not been built by the house concerned, and the monasteries paid the salary of the manciple and servants. On the other hand, the salary of the regent in theology was paid by the chapter out of the contributions levied from all, and in early days, to forestall the excuses of impecunious abbots who refused to send their monks or withdrew them before taking their degrees on account of expenses incurred, the chapter, as early as 1343, agreed to subscribe £20 for an incepting master of theology (the sum to be shared if two or more incepted simultaneously) and twenty marks for an incepting canonist.[4] Large as these sums were, they were probably far from covering even the normal expenses, especially if, as seems to have been the case, they remained fixed while prices in general rose. Thus at Canterbury College in 1395 a degree feast of two monks cost almost £47, and this relatively moderate outlay was far exceeded by a similar entertainment in 1410 which cost £108 and another in 1428 costing £92. In 1498 a single degree cost £43.[5]

Before legislating for the black monks, Benedict XII had, in the bull *Fulgens sicut stella* of 12 July 1335, promulgated his most carefully prepared scheme of reform, that addressed to his own order, the Cistercians. In this document the organization, or to speak more accurately, the normalization of university studies for the white monks was taken in hand. The pope had consulted a number of leading abbots, and current practice was taken up into the legislation, but a new breadth and precision was given, and a detailed tariff of sanctions imposed. Each region of western Europe was assigned as the recruiting ground for a university, while Paris was given a place apart: thither were to go select students from every country to which the order had spread. The ratio of students

---

1 *MC*, II, 75.   2 *Ibid.* 11–12; *MC*, III, 28–9.
3 Cf. *MC*, III, 54.   4 *MC*, II, 23, 56–7, and elsewhere.
5 Pantin, *Canterbury College*, III, 54–6, 63–7, 84–7, 132–4.

to the total number of monks was fixed exactly: every monastery with forty or more was to send two to Paris; those with thirty to forty monks were to send one. Monasteries having more than eighteen and less than thirty were to send a monk to the regional house of studies. Similar precision was observed in the salaries payable. Teachers at Paris were to be supported partly by the order, partly by the convent concerned; those elsewhere by the abbot-rector, drawing on contributions from the individual abbeys. The regional houses of studies were administered by provisors under the general oversight of an abbot-rector who might be either, as in the case of Paris, a prelate of exceptional dignity (the abbot of Clairvaux) or simply the abbot of a neighbouring house (as of Thame at Oxford). A general supervision of the *studia* was shared, on different levels, by general chapter and the abbots-rectors. Individual students, however, were to remain subject to the overruling jurisdiction of their own abbots. There was one notable difference between Cistercian and Benedictine practice: in the regulations for Cistercian studies canon law was severely banned.[1]

The Cistercians of England, following the example of their French brethren, had moved towards the university even earlier than the black monks, to whom, indeed, they served as a reproach and a stimulant. Rewley Abbey had been founded on the outskirts of Oxford in the last weeks of 1281. The original intention had been to found a college, similar to the college of St Bernard at Paris, which should be under the jurisdiction of the neighbouring abbot of Thame, but the house was in the event given abbatial rank from the first in honour of its founder. The community consisted in the early days of fifteen monks, but it was understood, and approved by the assembly of English abbots, that it was to be a place of residence for students, and as such it was probably inaugurated at the beginning of the academic year in the autumn of 1282.[2] Accommodation was erected by various houses for their students within the precinct, and a reference in 1315 would seem to suggest that it was then largely, if not wholly, made up of student monks. So matters stood at the time of the legislation of Benedict XII, in which the pope decreed that the abbeys of England, Scotland, Ireland and Wales were to send their quota to Oxford for primary education and theological studies. No change was made in consequence of this; it was no doubt considered that Rewley satisfied the spirit, if not the letter, of the new law, and it may be that additional camerae were constructed to hold more students, though there is no evidence whatever of a sudden increase.

The decades immediately following the Great Pestilence saw the fortunes of a number of Cistercian abbeys reach a very low ebb, with greatly reduced numbers. Those with a population of choir monks notably

---

1 For Benedict XII, *v.* J.-B. Mahn, *Le Pape Benoît XII et les Cisterciens.* For *Fulgens sicut stella, v.* Coquelinus, *Bullarium Romanum*, III, ii, 203 *seqq.*

2 *RO*, I, 26. Cf. also W. H. Stevenson and H. E. Salter, *The Early History of St John's College, Oxford*, 6 *seqq.*

exceeding the lowest mark (18) of the Benedictine constitutions were not numerous. Whether for this or other reasons, Rewley seems gradually to have ceased to harbour a student community of any size, and when the buildings erected by other abbeys had, with Rewley itself, fallen forfeit to the king in 1381 they were, when released, restored directly to that abbey.[1] The number of monks there fell at one time to five only.[2] At last, in 1398, the Cistercian scholars then at Oxford petitioned the chapter of England and Wales, which during the Great Schism met annually with authority, for suitable accommodation. The Cistercian students, they said, were living at Oxford in various colleges and halls, including Trillock's Inn, and it often happened that monk-students, realizing that this did not accord with the principles of the monastic life, returned home without finishing their course, while others refused for similar reasons to come to Oxford at all. The abbots agreed, in 1400, to make an assessment of the order for new buildings, but the contributions were not paid and no further steps were taken.[3]

The decisive move was probably occasioned by the action of the university in proceeding against 'chamberdekyns' living in separate lodgings c. 1421, and the initiative came from an unexpected quarter. Petition was made to the king by Archbishop Chichele for permission to purchase land; the Cistercian monks, he said, were scattered in private lodgings which gave uneasiness to the more conscientious among them. Chichele not only gave land on part of the site of the present St John's College, but also proposed to compile statutes for the college and to have the right of appointing the prior.[4] This seems clearly to indicate that the archbishop's interest was more than merely formal, though he subsequently withdrew his claim as contrary to the statutes of the order. In the sequel, St Bernard's College was governed by statutes drawn up in 1446 by Abbot John of Morimond, visitor in that year.[5]

The original building seems to have been on a modest scale, for from 1480 onwards there are repeated references to further undertakings. Not only did the general chapter in that year extend the obligation to send students to the university, but Richard III, both before and after his accession to the throne, is found circularizing the Cistercian abbeys with an exhortation to contribute more liberally.[6] The general chapter maintained its interest in English affairs, and, though no figures exist, the references to building, even on a fairly extensive scale, which continue into the first decade of the sixteenth century, seem to show that both funds and students were forthcoming.

Though all attempts to trace the origin of the schools of Oxford to a religious house have so far failed from a complete lack of evidence, the

[1] Stevenson and Salter, *op. cit.* 10–11.   [2] *Ibid.* 12.
[3] *Ibid.* 11 *seqq.*   [4] *Ibid.* 14.
[5] They are printed in *Early History of St John's College*, Appendix VI, 75–81.
[6] Printed in *Early History of St John's College*, Appendix VII, 81–2.

black canons, with their houses of Oseney (1129) and St Frideswide's (1122) had had from the earliest times a close local connection with the nascent university, and continued to be landlords of many of the halls and lodgings of the town. The canons, like the monks, doubtless felt the pull of the stream towards the universities, but there is apparently no clear evidence that either of the two Oxford houses made a practice of harbouring students from elsewhere. The black canons had even less solidarity as a body than the black monks, and a less widely diffused tradition of letters, and their chapters in the thirteenth century never achieved even the modest degree of directive and initiative energy which had as its most notable fruit the foundation of the Benedictine Gloucester College. The greater houses must indeed have sent students to the schools; some no doubt went to Paris, but others went to Oxford, and there is evidence that individual houses had tenements in the town.

This irregular system continued throughout the fourteenth century, and the legislation of Benedict XII had little effect. It was not till the early years of the fifteenth century that a change was made that was almost simultaneous with the Cistercian development and was probably due to the same cause.[1] At that time, from a variety of reasons among which may be reckoned the fall in the total number of students and the foundation of several new colleges and halls, the practice of individuals lodging by themselves fell into disrepute and was forbidden by the statutes of 1421. The intentions of the university had no doubt been previously known, for in 1419 the annual chapter of the canons had discussed the possibility of founding a college. The debate issued in a petition to the Parliament of 1421 asking the King to buy some land on the site of the present Trinity College for a house of studies. Henry V received the petition with favour, but died shortly after, and in 1422 the *prior studentium* of the scattered canons hired Deep Hall as a focus. Chapter records are defective at the time, but discussions proceeded, and in 1434 it was still a question of finding ways and means to finance the construction.[2] At this stage the canons were fortunate in finding a benefactor in a certain Thomas Holden, a member of a landed family of Lancashire who had served John of Gaunt and Henry IV and became under Henry V Surveyor of the King's Works at Chester and the castles of North Wales. He had also worked for Thomas Langley, bishop of Durham (1406–38), whose executor he became, serving in that capacity with William Alnwick, the energetic bishop of Lincoln. Both Langley and Alnwick were educational reformers, and each had already assisted academic enterprises, Langley Durham College and Alnwick King's College, Cambridge. In addition, the two bishops had worked together in helping to found the Benedictine house of studies at Cambridge, later known as Buckingham College. This last

---

1 The fullest account is in an article by Miss E. Evans, 'St Mary's College in Oxford for Austin Canons'.

2 *AC*, 83.

enterprise may well have served to suggest to Thomas Holden a worthy destination for his property, much of which was given during his lifetime to provide a house for the black canons at Oxford. The site chosen was in part coincident with the present Frewin Hall, and its garden; the chapel and possibly the library were built immediately, and other buildings were added by the order itself. The revenues of the house were never satisfactorily established; the chapter decided that the fines accruing from houses failing to send their quota of students should be used for this purpose—an unsatisfactory arrangement from more than one point of view. Nevertheless, the chapel was in use by 1443 and statutes were compiled in 1445.[1] By these the college was ruled by a prior, one of the senior students, who had full jurisdiction subject to oversight by the abbot of Oseney, who was also allowed to authorize canons to live in halls under the general control of the prior. There were no fellows. The inmates were canons studying theology and canon law, together with younger brethren studying logic and grammar, and some secular pensionary students. The first prior, William Westkarr, helped to establish the good name of the college. Originally a canon of the small Lancashire priory of Burscough, he was a doctor of distinction who often acted as commissary for the chancellor and was recommended by the university to the pope for promotion; he became in due course prior of Mottisfont, and as bishop of Sindon *in partibus* he acted as suffragan to the archbishop of Canterbury and several other bishops.

St Mary's College, like the monastic colleges, served to provide a leaven—though in this case one of no great strength—for the whole body of the order. Several of the greater houses such as Dunstable, Cirencester, Leicester and Merton were consistent patrons, and priors and abbots of a number of houses were drawn from its alumni, while priors of St Mary's College almost without exception passed to high office in their own or other monasteries. But the numbers, always small, bore no proportion to the large body of Austin canons scattered over the land in so many priories of modest or minute size.

1 Bodl. MS. Rawlinson Statutes 34, summarized by Miss Evans, *art. cit.* 376–9.

Note added in proof

When the above pages were in type, the article on the buildings of Worcester College in *VCH Oxon.* III, 301–9, by Professor A. H. M. Jones, appeared. From this it seems clear that the following houses had rooms: Abingdon, Bury (4), Eynsham ($\frac{1}{2}$), Glastonbury, Gloucester, Hyde, Malmesbury, Norwich, Pershore ($\frac{1}{2}$), Ramsey, St Albans, St Augustine's, Canterbury (2), Tewkesbury, Westminster, Winchcombe, Worcester (3). Three unidentified rooms remain.

CHAPTER III

PATRONS AND ARCHITECTS:
ELY AND GLOUCESTER

Monastic architecture as such, the conception, that is, and the detailed designing and building of the fabric of monastery and church, lies outside the scope of these chapters. No department of monastic antiquities has been more fully and, in general, more adequately treated. Moreover, the period in which monastic architecture influenced all ecclesiastical building, and the somewhat later epoch in which the plan of the great black and white monk abbey was finally evolved and standardized, were alike over before 1216. Indeed, by that time, or at least by c. 1260, the vernal burst of bloom was over. The cathedrals and abbeys of England and Wales were in existence with all their main dimensions as we know them now, and save in a very few cases the additions made between 1250 and 1540, great as was their effect upon the external appearance, consisted almost entirely in reclothing the existing fabric, in adding screens, stalls and chapels, and in augmenting the number of towers or repairing those already in existence. Yet though it is not easy to recall a single occasion, after the building of Salisbury, on which a medieval architect had such a clear field and great commission as have since been given to a Wren, a Pugin, a Scott or a Lutyens, yet the sum total of building, even in the monastic churches alone, was very large, and in some cases the work was all but continuous.

With the actual mason's work, and with the small-scale architectural designing the monks, save in the rarest cases, had nothing whatever to do.[1] They might, however, influence or guide the construction in three ways: by deciding to undertake such and such a work on such and such a scale; by actually planning the main features of a building; and by directing the *main d'œuvre* in the capacity of clerk of the works. In the first of these departments the abbot and monks were in the position shared by all collegiate and corporate bodies of the modern world, with the important difference, however, that a great church can be enlarged, rebuilt and decorated to an indefinite extent, whereas colleges and public buildings in general soon reach the limit beyond which additions are undesirable. In the second department, again, the monks held a unique position: a

---

1 The vaulting of Gloucester nave in 1242 is perhaps an exception. This, according to the chronicler, 'completa est...non auxilio fabrorum, ut primo, sed animosa virtute monachorum item in ipso loco existentium'. (*Historia et Cartularium monasterii S. Petri Gloucestriae*, ed. W. H. Hart I, 29). This sentence, whatever its precise meaning may be, occurs in a compilation of the late fourteenth century. Doubtless it embodies an earlier record, but the business of vaulting a great nave such as Gloucester would have been a peculiarly difficult task for amateurs; the vaulting, however, does in fact exhibit faults of construction (F. Bond, *The Cathedrals of England and Wales*, 143).

bishop had many other and distant occupations, whereas the officials of a monastery, whose daily work and life's interest had been built up with every stone and doorway, would inevitably have a very clear notion of the needs and amenities of their church. In early times, indeed, and in individual cases as late as the fifteenth century, the monastic official, the prior, sacrist or chamberer,[1] acted for all practical purposes as clerk of the works; later, this function was normally discharged by the master mason or carpenter, but until the end of the fourteenth century a monastic superior or official with a flair for building took a more direct and ceaseless part in the work of overseeing and daily decision than does a dean or a college bursar or a monastic procurator at the present day. Although it was an age when every kind of pecuniary transaction was farmed out and sub-contracted there was by no means always a financial contract in monastic building operations. Payments, therefore, not only for wages and material, but for the smallest additional expense of carriage or firing, often passed through the books of the sacrist. He could not therefore avoid, even had he wished, the assumption of a responsibility which to-day is shared between architect and building contractor.

It is, indeed, not easy for us to reconstruct the medieval process of building, which with an apparently elastic organization and primitive technical apparatus was able to achieve such stupendous monuments of beauty and engineering skill. In the modern world the patron, often without either knowledge or taste, the architect and his draughtsmen in a city office, the quantity surveyor in another street of the city, and the contractor from another part of the country, with his clerk of the works and his casual labour, building mechanically from large-scale drawings and stencilled instructions[2]—all these work independently, each within a well-defined province. In medieval England the architect as distinct from the builder did not exist, and the province of the modern architect was a no man's land with a shifting boundary which a skilled and interested patron might usurp to a greater or less extent. Modern writers, while avoiding the mistake of making the sacrist or *magister operis* or *magister caementarius* the exact equivalent of the architect of to-day,[3] not infrequently give the impression that an immense structure such as Salisbury, demanding exact dynamic calculations and the artistic harmony of detail and part, part and whole, grew by some inner process of life under the hands of a group of talented masons working by genius and rule-of-

1 An example of the chamberer thus acting may be found in *GASA*, 1, 280. A thesis for the M.A. Degree at London University by Mr R. A. Smith with the title 'The Organization and Financing of Monastic Building', gives a survey of parts played by the various monastic officials in constructing and repairing the fabric of church and monastery. For the material side of the building operations, with detailed descriptions of construction, the classic work is now that of Mr L. F. Salzman, *Building in England* (1952).

2 In elaborate modern ashlar work the whole wall-face is designed in the drawing office, and the blocks of stone cut with precision at the quarry, where they are marked or numbered. The mason has nothing to do but to fit the blocks together.

3 The article on Alan of Walsingham in *DNB* commits this error.

thumb. Avoiding both extremes of error, and realizing that many of the processes of medieval planning cannot be traced in the documents, we shall probably be correct in supposing that in monastic building, at least, the superior or obedientiary concerned had often a very real, if indeterminate, share in the creation of the masterpiece, a share more intimate and direct than that of the most enlightened patron of later centuries—a Wolsey or a Louis XIV—though one less exclusive and creative that that of a Bramante or a Wren. Such a consideration may assist in the examination of two or three celebrated undertakings of monastic building. It will be found there, and almost invariably, that an epoch of extensive construction is due to the personal initiative and direction of a monastic official.

The cathedral monastery of Ely, whose history had been undistinguished during the thirteenth century, housed in the early years of the fourteenth several men of unusual ability. Fortunately, the chronicler who records the careers of the bishops of the see digresses during these years into what is in effect an account of three of these monks, and thus gives us a most welcome picture of administrative skill and monastic enthusiasm.[1]

The first in origin of the notable series of operations at Ely was the Lady Chapel. So far as can be ascertained, its erection was due to the efforts of the monk John of Wisbech. At that time many, if not most, of the greater churches of England had substituted for the original altar of the Blessed Virgin a Lady Chapel of architectural significance, and considerations both practical and aesthetical had led to the addition being made as a rule to the east of the presbytery. At Ely there had been no major building since Bishop Hugh's presbytery was finished c. 1250; there was no Lady Chapel, and it was impossible to prolong the church in an easterly direction without destroying existing monastic buildings. It was therefore decided to build on a most unusual site, all but detached from the church, to the north-east of the north transept, the position usually devoted to the chapter-house in secular foundations. This gave the fabric the character of an aisleless church, with scope for elaborate carving and glazing. It is not known who inspired the choice of site, or whether the edifice as completed almost thirty years later was designed from the start in its final form; it is, however, remarkable that the first stone was laid in March 1321, by the young and recently appointed subprior, Alan of Walsingham.[2]

The name of this distinguished monk will always be associated with those features of his monastic church which, supremely beautiful in

---

1 This is the *Chronica abbatum et episcoporum Eliensium*, printed as *Historia Eliensis* by H. Wharton in *Anglia sacra*, II. The digression referred to is on pp. 643–9. Wharton's is the only printed text, and as Canon Chapman noted (*Sacrist Rolls*, I, xi *et al.*), it contains some unwarranted interpolations. The Dean and Chapter of Ely possess also numerous compotus rolls of obedientiaries covering the period. Those of the sacrist which survive from 1292 to 1360, a rich but incomplete series, have been published with valuable introductory and other notes as *Sacrist Rolls of Ely* by the late Canon F. R. Chapman.

2 *Hist. Elien.* 651: 'Vir venerabilis et artificiosus frater Alanus de Walsyngham.'

themselves, are also those which give it unique distinction among the cathedrals of England.[1] Sprung, as it would seem, from a family of hereditary craftsmen long settled in Ely,[2] one of whom had recently been chosen successively prior of the monastery, bishop of the see and bishop of Norwich,[3] Alan had himself learnt the goldsmith's art before becoming a monk.[4] He was already a marked man in 1314, and in 1321, when Prior Fressingfield resigned, the office of subprior also fell vacant and he was appointed to it. He was thus acting superior during the interregnum, and as such performed the ceremony of laying the foundation stone of the Lady Chapel. A few weeks later the community elected as superior John of Crauden.

The new prior, a man of distinguished presence and handsome features, had also a compelling charm of character which won him the affection alike of his monks and of many outside the monastery, from Queen Philippa to less exalted friends.[5] The chronicler dwells on his love of peace and his warmth of feeling, as also his religious fervour.[6] His monument for later generations is the chapel which he added to the prior's lodging,

---

1 Alan of Walsingham has in modern times gradually acquired credit in successive popular accounts, lectures and handbooks for complete architectural responsibility for all buildings erected at Ely between 1320 and 1360, and has been ranked among the greatest architects of western Europe. Such a view, as has been noted, rests upon a complete misconception of medieval conditions, as also upon a strange disregard both of documentary evidence and the most cogent arguments from style. The Lady Chapel, octagon and western bays of the choir are so different in every respect that it would be inconceivable that a single medieval architect should have 'designed' all three. A fourteenth-century architect was not expected to produce on demand designs for an Anglican cathedral, a Catholic abbey, a Cambridge college, a London power-station and a telephone kiosk. The choir, in particular, was outside Alan's province, being the bishop's responsibility, and the same may be said of Prior Crauden's chapel, which has been attributed to him by admirers.

The opposite extreme must, however, be avoided, of regarding him as a mere patron or paymaster. He was a trained craftsman (though neither a master mason, sculptor nor carver) with a genius for conducting building operations. Moreover, in the case of the octagon and lantern, there is a stream of tradition associating his name with their conception.

2 Cf. *Sacrist Rolls*, I, Appendix C, 'The Hereditary Goldsmiths of Ely'. In this interesting excursus Canon Chapman makes the descent of Alan from the goldsmiths of Ely all but certain. The first member of the clan to attain celebrity was Salamon of Ely who worked at St Albans *c.* 1130 (*GASA*, I, 83–6). Chapman (*loc. cit.*) suggests very reasonably that a daughter of Alan of Ely married Adam (of Walsingham) and became mother of the future prior.

3 This was Salomon or Salmon, prior of Ely 1291–9, bishop of Norwich 1299–1325, and Chancellor of England 1320–3.

4 Cf. Thomas of Walsingham, *Hist. Anglicana*, ed. H. T. Riley, I, 138–9, where the opening of the (alleged) shrine of St Alban at Ely in 1314 is described: 'Feretrum solutum est apertum est per quendam monachum Alanum de Walsingham dictum...qui et ipse peritus erat in opere aurifabrili et ideo ad solvendum feretrum tunc vocatus.'

5 *Hist. Elien.* 649–50: 'Pulcher erat aspectu et corpore formosus ac in oculo omni apparuit gratiosus. Ita quod...Philippa...Anglorum Regina ipsum in amicitiam praeclaram collegit et familiaritatem, tum propter amabilem et graciosam ipsius affabilitatem et eloquentiam, &c.' Chapman, nevertheless, notes that Crauden was the object of attack, both personal and forensic, from enemies of the priory.

6 *Ibid.*: 'Dilectus Deo et hominibus, cujus memoria in benedictione sit sempiterna. Diebus enim suis cum omni pace et tranquillitate ac sacrae religionis dulcedine, sicut pastor pacificus, toto cordis conamine conventum suum tractavit caritative.'

and in which he spent long hours each night, a work which contemporaries praised and which survives in a mutilated state to perpetuate his name.[1] He must not, however, be denied the ultimate credit for greater works, for he accepted the advice and countenanced the expenses of his sacrist at a crisis of the priory's fortunes.

Alan, doubtless at Prior Crauden's wish, exchanged the office of sub-prior for that of sacrist on 21 December 1321, and in less than eight weeks was called upon to remedy a catastrophe of the first order. In the early morning of 13 February, when the monks had retired to the dormitory after mattins, the great Norman tower over the crossing, which had long shown alarming signs of weakness, collapsed, forming an immense pile of rubble and filling the whole edifice with dust. The normal course would have been to rebuild the tower in the style of the day. This, the new sacrist may have felt, would have been to put an unbearable weight on the insecure subsoil.[2] In any case, he took the momentous decision not to build a new tower or to re-lay the four piers of the crossing, but to work upon the eight piers of the first bay of nave, choir and transepts, and to superimpose upon an open octagon of masonry a wooden campanile or lantern. This conception, unique on such a scale in English architecture,[3] and producing an effect of marvellous light and grace, has always been attributed to Alan of Walsingham, and one who examines the evidence of chronicle and account rolls will probably acquiesce in the verdict which gives him the credit for the main lines of the scheme, though the actual designs of the vaulting and the ingenious framework of the lantern were doubtless drawn out by the master mason and master carpenter he employed.[4]

1 *Ibid.*: 'Fecit novam capellam mirandi decoris.' The attribution (common in guide-books of the past) to Alan of Walsingham as architect is without evidence and probability.

2 F. Bond (*Gothic Architecture in England*, 25) notes that whereas the foundations of Hugh of Northwold's presbytery go down to the rock, those of the Norman choir fail to do so. The words of *Hist. Elien.* 644, are not conclusive: 'fodere fecit...donec invenit locum solidum'.

3 While it is true that 'towers with eight sides are not uncommon' in England (Bond, *Gothic Architecture*, 600) and that 'the octagon in plan...was to become popular in this part of England' (T. D. Atkinson in *VCH, Cambs*, IV, 62) and true also that 'Walsingham's dome is really a development of the wood vaulting of York Chapter House, combined with the common construction of the Monastery kitchens and their central ventilators' (E. S. Prior, *The Cathedral Builders in England*, 75), it must nevertheless be repeated that the Ely octagon and lantern are, alike in conception, design and aesthetic effect, unique in England. They have not, however, satisfied all tastes. The distinguished French medievalist, M. É. Perroy, has had the courage to refer to 'la hideuse tour-lanterne qui défigure Ely' (*Revue Historique*, CCVIII (1953), 84).

4 The chronicler (*Hist. Elien.* 644) seems to imply that Alan himself directed the clearing and surveying of the crossing, and the erection of the eight piers. The compotus rolls note a visit from Peter Quadratarius in 1323 (*Sacrist Rolls*, II, 33) and the presence of a salaried John, the master mason, in that and subsequent years (*ibid.* 34, 48, 61). They do not, how-ever, indicate that Master John held a position equal to that of Master William of Hurley the carpenter, who was clearly the designer of the lantern and the stalls. Canon Chapman notes the presence in later years of several craftsmen known to have been occupied at this time on the king's works. Queen Philippa, Bishop Hotham and Alan's relative Salmon of Norwich the Chancellor would all have been means of contact between the royal works and Ely.

The work went forward slowly: the masonry was complete in about six years,[1] but twenty had passed since the disaster before the monks resumed the choir office on the old site, now illuminated by the shafts of light that poured down from the lantern, and soon to be beautified yet more by the magnificent stalls which still remain. During these long years, when the western bays of the choir were also being rebuilt at the direction of the bishop, the great church, full of dust and noise and currents of fenland mist, was an abode of discomfort,[2] and the cost of the sacrist's works mounted steadily to £2400, which donations did little to meet.[3] It is not surprising that during the first years of construction the source of funds for the Lady Chapel dried up. John of Wisbech, however, did not lose heart, and he succeeded in inspiring with his enthusiasm some of his brethren. Together with some lay helpers, they worked as a team upon the foundations, and year by year the walls rose. When John of Wisbech was carried off by the Black Death in 1349 the work was almost complete; the chapel was consecrated in 1352.

Meanwhile, Alan of Walsingham, not content with the amount of work already on his hands, put a wall round the property of the sacrist, built offices, and constructed a new wing for the infirmary, while his carpenters, as the lantern advanced, began to carve the stalls for the new choir.[4] Prior Crauden, for his part, added to his quarters by building the chapel and the range facing it where he had his working room and private study. Ely was a rich house, but the prior had inherited debts from an improvident predecessor, and it says much both for the resources of the place and the general efficiency of the administration that all these undertakings were carried forward without complete financial ruin.

Early in 1337 the monastic chapter elected John of Crauden to the see of Ely. The king, however, wished to translate Simon of Worcester thither, and papal permission was obtained. Four years later the prior died, and Alan of Walsingham was elected in his stead. By this time the great buildings were approaching completion; Hotham's choir was finished, and within a year of Alan's election the monks were singing office under the lantern.[5] In 1345 the bishopric again fell vacant, and the

1 *Hist. Elien.* 644: 'Usque ad superiorem tabulatum per vi annos consummatum anno Domini MCCCXXVIII.'

2 The sacrist roll of 1341–2 (*Sacrist Rolls*, II, 116), contains many items relating to the furnishing of the choir, including a large net and ropes to keep the pigeons out (*pro excludendis columbellis*).

3 The chronicler (*Hist. Elien.* 644) gives the total cost of the new tower (presumably the octagon and lantern together) as £2408. 19s. 3½d., but this figure, he expressly states, does not include the food and drink of the workmen, nor the horses, carts *et omnia alia* (an exasperating phrase). Gifts amounted to a mere £102. 1s., a sum which, when compared with the riches pouring in upon Gloucester at this very time, is an interesting evidence of the currents of medieval sentiment.

4 For Alan's works outside the church *v.* Chapman, *Sacrist Rolls*, I, Appendix B: Buildings...erected or restored in the time of Alan of Walsingham' and the still more elaborate and sumptuous work of T. D. Atkinson, *An Architectural History of the Benedictine Monastery of St Etheldreda at Ely.*   5 *Hist. Elien.* 649.

monks, with royal permission, chose their prior. This time they were frustrated by the pope, who on the news of a vacancy had provided the Preacher, Thomas de Lisle, then at Avignon. Alan lived almost twenty years longer, till 1363 or 1364, but the chronicler tells nothing of his latest years.[1] They certainly saw no external works comparable to those he had undertaken forty years before, but he had done enough for fame, and if others may have surpassed him in the magnitude of their works, the grace and freshness of all the building that he had watched over gave full justification for the title—*Flos operatorum*—which his brethren inscribed upon the stone beneath which he was laid.

While the lantern of Alan of Walsingham and the carvings of the Ely Lady Chapel were approaching completion, an architectural scheme of a very different kind but of even greater significance was being developed in the west.

The abbey of St Peter at Gloucester, though not of the very first rank in point of wealth or numbers, held a place among the greatest on account of its position in a city so often visited by the court, and of a distinguished series of abbots which had opened with Serlo, the friend of the Conqueror, and had included the great Foliot. At the end of the thirteenth century the beneficent rule of Abbot John de Gamages had left it free of debt and rich in flocks,[2] while it had won distinction of another kind by being the first black monk house to have a priory for students at Oxford whence, after Gloucester College had become a common house of studies, a monk of St Peter's had been the first to incept in divinity.[3]

Gamages was succeeded by Abbot Thokey, and under his rule the abbey had a windfall that was to make its fortune. Thokey had a personal affection for Edward II, whom he had entertained at Gloucester, and when other religious houses of the neighbourhood fought shy of incurring the enmity of Mortimer he had the courage, and perhaps also the foresight, to despatch a carriage to Berkeley for the body, which he buried with great pomp on the north side of the presbytery.[4] The tomb immediately became a shrine, and in the decades before the Great Plague, when the country was wealthy and populous, a stream of pilgrims and a shower of oblations and gifts poured in upon the abbey. Thokey died before the consequences of his action were fully visible; he was succeeded by the prior, John of Wigmore, who was himself a skilled sculptor and embroiderer,[5] and had

1 In his last years of office as sacrist Alan was putting the octagon and bells on the western tower. As prior, he paid for the fourth bell of the series *IHS, John, Mary* and *Walsingham*.

2 *Hist. Gloucestr.* I, 39. This brief chronicle was compiled from existing materials in the time of Abbot Walter Frocester (1382–), but there is no evidence that he was the author; all indications are to the contrary.

3 *Ibid.* 34. The event occurred in June 1298.   4 *Ibid.* 44–5.

5 *Ibid.* 45: '[Secta vestimentorum] de viridi samyt cum volucribus deauratis quam propriis manibus texuit et fecit.' 46: 'Qui in diversis artibus multum delectabatur, ut ipse saepissime operaretur, et multos diversos operarios in diversis artibus praeexcelleret tam in opere mechanico [? metalwork and carving] quam in textura.'

already shown ability as a director of building and decoration. Thokey had made a beginning on the south aisle in the style of the day, employing, it would seem, masons from the Herefordshire border who powdered the windows with the ball-flower characteristic of the district between the Malverns and the Marches, but now funds were ample enough to rebuild the whole church, and Wigmore decided upon a more drastic treatment of the problem.[1] The choir and east end of Gloucester had always been peculiarly gloomy, even for a Norman church, owing to an absence of light from the aisle windows and the presence of a floor carried along the aisles at triforium level and holding chapels. The concourse of visitors to the shrine accentuated the disabilities of the building. Under other circumstances, the monks would probably have rebuilt the whole choir in the contemporary manner, but they were unwilling to dislocate the pilgrimages and so decided to raise and recase the choir, thus obtaining clerestory windows. The Norman work, unlike similar building at Hereford and elsewhere, had been well done and was capable of standing the weight. The scheme therefore went forward. In the event, however, the end, which was by no means abnormal, was achieved by the most revolutionary of means.

In default of a detailed narrative and account rolls, the genesis of the new choir must be largely a matter of conjecture, but it seems probable that Wigmore, himself a craftsman, engaged the services of a group of masons from the Severn valley whose resource in dealing with structural problems had already been shown in the inverted arches recently devised to shore up the central tower at Wells and in the high aisles and transoms of St Augustine's abbey at Bristol. The work at Gloucester was on a far larger scale and wholly original in design. A lofty clerestory, full of glass, was set on the Norman triforium, and the whole panel from vault to floor cased in rectilinear tracery covering the circular arches.[2] The long vaulting shafts rose from the pavement to the springing of the ribs unbroken by capital or band, and to crown all the choir was spanned by an elaborated lierne vault. With such a choir it would have been impossible to deal with the Norman apse by the method so successfully adopted later at Norwich; moreover, after centuries of gloom, they could not have too much light at Gloucester. The east end was therefore knocked out and the space filled

1 For an exposition of the problem at Gloucester and its solution *v*. Bond, *Cathedrals of England and Wales*, 140 *seqq*. The hypothesis (for it does not seem to be a statement resting on any written evidence) of the existence of a revolutionary school of Severn masons, responsible for work at Bristol, Wells and Gloucester, apparently originated with the late Professor E. S. Prior, *The Cathedral Builders in England*, 78–85, where the 'clever Bristol constructionists' (p. 79) become insensibly 'Gloucester masons' (p. 81). It has often been adopted subsequently, with assurance and without acknowledgement. More recently, an endeavour has been made to trace the genesis of the so-called Perpendicular style to the cloisters and other parts of Old St Paul's, or to St Stephen's Chapel, Westminster.

2 By a curious vagary, typical of the school of masons concerned, the designer of the new choir outlined the Norman arches of the main arcade and triforium with semicircular hood-moulds instead of masking them.

with an enormous window of small panels of glass held together by horizontal transoms and vertical mullions. In the glass itself white predominated, with tiers of figures surmounting a band of heraldry which perpetuates the memory of knights from the Severn and Wye who fought at Crécy.[1]

The masons at Gloucester had thus created, earlier than 1350 and almost at a stroke, the elements of a new style in which vertical lines predominated and in which the whole elevation of the church became in effect a single storey, while the utmost economy of material left the greatest possible space for light and glass. How much of this conception was due to Wigmore will never be known, but he and his successor must at least have assumed full responsibility for such thorough remodelling, which both in its use of existing masonry and in its main features of design was to become the archetype of so much building during the next hundred years. As to the intrinsic value of the experiment the most divergent judgements have been expressed on almost every detail in a design which has many elements of supreme beauty, not a few brilliant feats of engineering and some features that are toneless or even displeasing.[2] Those, however, who deplore the light that pours in floods from east window and clerestory may not have made a sufficient effort to reconstruct in imagination the sanctuary of Gloucester as it was in the days of Abbot Frocester. It would indeed be difficult to find a more admirable setting for a pontifical Mass[3] than that spacious pavement bathed in light that would have fallen upon the cloth of gold, the lawns and linens and damasks, the silver candelabra and the rising clouds of incense. And perhaps only those who have known by long experience year in, year out, what rest is given by natural light to eyes tired by glare and shadow will feel the full refreshment of Gloucester choir, and only those who have watched the dawn stealing upon the end of a long Office—*lux intrat, albescit polus, Christus venit*—will know how the shafts of June sunlight over Cleeve brought hope and faith to many who saw that great window gleam in the level rays.

Abbot Wigmore died in 1337, but his prior, Adam of Stanton, who

1 For the date of the window and its subjects *v.* C. Winston, 'The East Window of Gloucester Cathedral', in *Archaeological Journal*, xx (1863), 239–53; 319–30; T. D. Grimké-Drayton (same title) in *BGAS.* xxxviii (1915), 69–97; and G. McN. Rushforth (same title) *ibid.* xliv (1922), 293–304.

2 The rich vault and slender vaulting shafts, and the effect of space and light given by the shallow mouldings and expanses of glass certainly combine to produce a 'view...of an unforgettable beauty' (H. Batsford and C. Fry, *The Cathedrals of England*, p. 47). On the other hand, the web of transoms, buttresses and skeleton arches about the transepts, found only here and at Bristol, gives an impression of *bravura* rather than of firm repose, while the east window has been characterized by no mean judge as 'one of the ugliest in the world' (Bond, *Cathedrals of England and Wales*, p. 150), the sole function of which, as another critic sees it, is to let in floods of grey English daylight which would be better kept out (E. Hutton, *Highways and Byways in Gloucestershire*, 360).

3 Abbot Frocester was the first to obtain the use of *pontificalia* (*Hist. Gloucestr.* i, 56–7). For vestments and silver plate given to the abbey about this time *v. Hist. Gloucestr.* 45, 49, 51, 55, 57.

4

succeeded him, was a pupil or at least a follower,[1] and the work was continued without a break through the vaulting of the choir and the first range of stalls. Adam of Stanton was followed by Thomas of Horton, the sacrist. He completed the high altar and the stalls, and began on the cloisters, where once again the versatile Gloucester masons originated—or at least brought for the first time into large-scale work[2]—a new and unusually beautiful type of vaulting which, more than a century later, was to be a principal feature in the latest and richest examples of medieval architecture. The cloisters were the last flower of the long and prolific second spring at Gloucester:[3] in fifty years Wigmore, his followers and their masons had originated and displayed on the grand scale in a great pilgrimage church almost all the methods and *motifs* which architects all over England were to exploit for the next century and a half. They had also shown what could be done by the skilful masking of old work without complete rebuilding, and this lesson too was duly learnt and repeated at Winchester, Norwich and elsewhere. At Gloucester itself important building was carried out at intervals until the end, in a style which shows scarcely anything to distinguish it from the work of the mid-fourteenth century, and which bears in its latest example, the Lady Chapel of *c.* 1500, the same marks of resourceful ingenuity in meeting structural problems.

1 The phrase of the chronicler—'successit venerabili magistro suo'—is unusual and seems to imply a relationship of more than common dependence.

2 It has been suggested (Bond, *Gothic Architecture*, 342) that a model was found in tomb-canopies such as that of Despenser at Tewkesbury.

3 The chronology of building at Gloucester would seem to have been:

South aisle of nave (Abbot Thokey) . . .	1318–29
Shrine of Edward II (? Thokey and Wigmore) .	1329–34
South transept (Wigmore)	1331–7
Choir and north transept (Stanton) . . .	1337–
Choir vault and north stalls (Stanton and Horton)	1337–57
Glass in east window (Stanton)	1347–50
East walk of cloister (Horton)	1351–77
Remainder of cloisters (Frocester) . . .	1381–

The length of time that elapsed before the Gloucester innovations influenced other work (Edington *c.* 1352–61; Winchester nave (1360–) is fully explicable on the hypothesis that an original, even 'eccentric', school of local or regional masons was on the work at Gloucester. They were busy enough for thirty years, and other masons would have had to adopt not only designs and ideas, but what is almost an idiosyncrasy of mind. In the event, the peculiar methods and mannerisms of Gloucester were never imitated, though the basic principles were soon found in countless designs.

CHAPTER IV

PORTRAITS OF MONKS

I. THOMAS DE LA MARE

The first monk to be taken as a representative of his age is the long-lived abbot of St Albans, Thomas de la Mare, who held office for almost half a century and whom a distinguished modern historian has named the greatest in the long line of abbots of the premier house of England.[1] Certainly, whether we assent to this judgement or not, it will not be disputed that Abbot de la Mare displays, magnified as it were to several dimensions, the qualities to be found in numerous prelates of his age; he occupies, in fact, very much the same place in monastic history as does Samson of Bury two centuries earlier, and had he found, like Samson, a *vates sacer* with a memory and a *naïveté* rivalling those of Jocelin of Brakelond, his name would doubtless be as familiar to his countrymen to-day.

His two predecessors had been men of marked individuality, if no more, and had shown, each in his own way, how such a house as St Albans could foster and give expansion to talents of all kinds that might otherwise have failed to blossom.[2] Richard of Wallingford (b. 1291), the son of a blacksmith, was adopted, no doubt on account of his manifest promise, by the then prior of Wallingford, who sent him to Oxford—the Oxford of Duns Scotus—where he passed successfully through the arts course (1308–14), and at the age of twenty-three asked for the monastic habit at St Albans. This no doubt fulfilled the hopes, amounting almost to a tacit bargain, which had inspired Prior William Kirkby's original patronage. After only three years of monastic life he was back at Oxford, this time at Gloucester College, to study theology. In after years he lamented his short abode in the cloister, as also an excessive addiction, while at Oxford, to the mathematical studies for which the university of Grosseteste and Roger Bacon was famous, and which included both astronomy and astrology. Becoming a Bachelor in 1326, he returned to St Albans, to ask for the festive expenses of his inauguration, just in time to be present at the death of Abbot Hugh of Eversdene. Richard was clearly the most brilliant of the coming generation at St Albans, for he was chosen as preacher on

1 So C. L. Kingsford in *DNB*; cf. L. F. R. Williams, *History of St Albans*, 166.

2 The principal authority for all personal details of these three abbots is *GASA*, II, 181–III, 372, which is here the work of Thomas of Walsingham using earlier material. The main narrative breaks off c. 1381–2, but another parallel account, mutilated at the opening, covers the whole period of rule of Abbot de la Mare, and is in *GASA*, III, 375–423. At the time of de la Mare's death Walsingham was prior of Wymondham (*ibid.* III, 425). Unless otherwise noted, these accounts are the authority for what follows; for Abbot Richard, Walsingham is clearly following an earlier 'Life', which he occasionally fails to adapt, as for example on p. 182 he writes: 'eum [*sc.* Ricardum] conqueri frequenter audivimus'.

election day and as one of the nine to whom the election was compromised. We are told that at Mass that morning he had resolved to accept as from God the result of the day's debate and when, after long discussion, the choice of his fellow-electors fell on him, he accepted the omen. Unlike his immediate predecessors he lived simply as abbot, dispensing with servants and companions and customary presents, and having with him only a single chaplain, while at the solemn feast on his reception at the abbey on returning from Rome he dined with the brethren, leaving the magnates to dine by themselves in the abbatial hall.

Like other abbots of St Albans, he revised the constitutions of the house, and made decrees for Redburn, the holiday resort of the monks. He also drew up a list of the decrees of the provincial chapter, while continuing his own astronomical and geometrical studies. Among his additions to the abbey were the new mechanical clock and the almonry school with its offices, and the private chapel in his lodging, with its adornments. His biographer notes, in the fashion that Matthew Paris had set in the *Gesta Abbatum*, that many thought he would have been better advised to pay off some of the debts of his predecessor before making any of his own. What might have been a distinguished reign was, however, shadowed from the first and prematurely ended by a long illness, diagnosed as leprosy, which attacked his sight and later his voice and rendered him all but impotent in the last few years of his life; from 1333 he had his prior as coadjutor. He died in May 1335.

His successor was, like himself, a scholar, and the type throughout the ages made a peculiar appeal to the electors of St Albans. Born of parents of easy circumstances, he was sent by them to Oxford, and took his mastership in arts. Then Michael of Mentmore, like Richard of Wallingford before him, took the habit and in due course returned to Oxford, where he proceeded bachelor in divinity. He was apparently still at Oxford when Abbot Richard died, and was chosen to succeed him ten days later. His visit to Rome coincided with the preparation of the constitutions for the black monks by Benedict XII, and when these were promulgated a year later they were sent for publication to Abbot Michael, either (as his biographer implies) because his good qualities were familiar to the pontiff, or (as seems more probable) because he was one of the presidents at the time, perhaps as having earlier deputized for Abbot Richard. In any case, he published the Benedictine constitutions at the Northampton chapter of 1336, and eighteen months later held a general chapter of St Albans and its dependencies (as ordered by the pope) at which he published the constitutions once more and implemented for his house the new regulations for the eating of meat.

Abbot Michael was an indulgent patron of scholars, rearranging the time-table in their favour and building out of his own revenues a group of studies between the dorter and the chapel of the guesthouse, so that they might not suffer the disturbances of the cloister. He continued to take part in the monastic affairs of the province, and was elected president for the whole of his reign save for an interval of three years; he was also sufficiently in favour with the young Edward III to be asked to stand god-father to his youngest son, Edmund of Langley, the future Duke of York. Premature death, however, took him away; he was one of the first to die when the Black Death struck St Albans; taken ill on Maundy Thursday, he died on Easter Day.

Thomas de la Mare, in contrast to his predecessors, was of distinguished family, with forebears who had taken their part in public life, and with connexions among the baronial houses such as the Montagus, the de la Zouches and the Grandissons. Sir Peter de la Mare, Speaker of the Parliament of 1376, was probably a relative.[1] Strikingly handsome both as boy and as man, he had the refined features, the long, thin hands and the pure complexion that observers noted in more than one of the out-standing men of that age, and which have been perpetuated in the effigies of Gloucester and Westminster, and in the Wilton diptych. Educated in letters by his parents, he never passed through the schools of Oxford; though highly intelligent, he had not a scholar's or a theologian's mind, but as a young monk he studied composition, and later, when prior of Tynemouth, he became expert in the current fashion of preaching both in English and Latin with the help of some Austin friars, and in particular of John Waldeby, later provincial, who dedicated to him a series of homilies which he had written at the prior's request.[2] He also studied the *dictamen*, and in later life Abbot Thomas was able to compose his own official letters, even those to the papal Curia.[3]

Attracted from youth to things religious and to the liturgy of the Church, he resolved to become a monk, apparently at the early age of seventeen. He was one of a large family, and three brothers and a sister followed his example; of his brothers one came to St Albans, one went to the Cluniac house of Thetford, and a third became a canon, and ultimately abbot, of Missenden; the sister took the veil at the nunnery of Delapré, near her brother's abbey. The vocations of the family are an interesting indication that aristocratic recruits still found their way to the most varied homes. It is equally interesting to learn that an aspirant of such high rank and promise should have been sent to pass his noviciate at a distance from St Albans at the dependency of Wymondham. There he remained till the death of Abbot Richard in 1335, when Abbot Michael

---

1 The suggestion is made by C. L. Kingsford, in *DNB*.

2 *GASA*, II, 380: 'Tres...[annos peregit] in studio predicandi verbum Dei, tam in lingua Anglica quam Latina, ac propter hoc secum detinuit semper clericos et magistros... Ordinis Mendicantium.' There is a previous reference (*GASA*, II, 376) to *fratres Augus-tinenses*, and the chronicler attributes to this training the abbot's subsequent success in preaching and publishing monastic doctrine as president. Fr A. Gwynn, S. J. (*The English Austin Friars*, 119–21) drew attention to the friendship between de la Mare and Waldeby. The homilies written at his request are in Bodl. Laud Misc. MS. 296, fo. 57.

3 *GASA*, II, 374: '[Habebat] peritiam dictandi sive scribendi irreprehensibiliter ipsi Papae.'

recalled him to fill in rapid succession the posts of abbot's chaplain, kitchener, cellarer and lastly prior of Tynemouth. There his prudent administration, his social gifts and his zeal for observance gained him a name in the north among nobility and common people; he also gave evidence of his readiness—never wanting throughout his long life—to vindicate in the courts on behalf of his house any claim that he regarded as just.

He had been nine years at Tynemouth when the first visitation of the Black Death carried off Abbot Michael on Easter Sunday, 1349. More than fifty of the monks died with him, including prior and subprior,[1] and this may have smoothed the way for de la Mare's candidature. Even so, he was apparently not the first choice of the electors to whom the convent had delegated powers, but when the prior of Wymondham refused to take office Thomas was chosen. He was about forty years old.

As abbot, he speedily made a name for himself. Edward III made him a Privy Councillor and remained on friendly terms, though with intervals of misunderstanding. The Black Prince was a closer friend, to whom the older man acted as counsellor and confidant; the Prince became a confrater of the abbey, and on at least one occasion defended the abbot with filial piety. A third distinguished friend was the captured King John of France, who spent some time at St Albans. The close friendship with the Black Prince, and the sympathies of a St Albans chronicler with the abbot's namesake (or relation), the Speaker of the Good Parliament of 1376, suggests that de la Mare's interest lay with the opposition in the later decades of the old king's reign, but of this the abbey chronicler says nothing.[2]

In monastic affairs, Abbot Thomas succeeded on election to the office of first president of the black monks, held by the late Abbot de Mentmore, and three years later he was elected to the post in his own right. He remained president, with or without a coadjutor, for twenty years, and fulfilled his duties with energy. In addition to framing two sets of statutes for the province,[3] he drew up minute constitutions for his own house and its dependencies, giving especial attention to the devout performance of the liturgy, prescribing a slower recitation and some added chant, while at the same time pruning off excrescences of vocal prayer.[4] His position and reputation combined to make him the outstanding abbot of his day, and the king employed him to visit the monasteries of Eynsham, Abing-

---

1 *GASA*, II, 370: 'Decesserunt eo tempore, praeter illos qui copiose defungebantur in Cellis, quadraginta septem monachi.' In 1396 there were some sixty monks in residence at St Albans itself (*GASA*, III, 425–6); no doubt the number was greater fifty years before.

2 The point is discussed by Sir E. M. Thompson in *DNB*, article 'Peter de la Mare'.

3 These are in *GASA*, II, 449–66 and in *MC*, II, 65–81.

4 These were published in 1351, 1352 and 1355 (*GASA*, II, 418–49). In the rubrics of the chronicle they are described as promulgated *in capitulo generali* (*sc.* S. Albani), which the editor wrongly renders as the 'general chapter of the Benedictines' (p. 419). It was the yearly assembly at the mother-house.

don, Battle and Reading, where various degrees of royal patronage existed, and he performed the same duties elsewhere, as at Chester and Bury.[1] It may be remarked that the only charges of extravagance made against him were in connexion with his expenses as president;[2] it is also perhaps characteristic that he was the most energetic collector of funds on behalf of Richard Fitzralph during his controversy with the friars.[3]

Extravagant or not, de la Mare was certainly in his years of health an abbot in the grand style. In parliament he asserted his right of precedence before all other abbots. He was a tireless litigant against great and small, ecclesiastical and lay, local and remote adversaries, and was almost as often a defendant; besides the innumerable miscellaneous suits on which he embarked or into which he was drawn, he contributed his page to the time-honoured controversies with the bishops of Lincoln and Norwich concerning exemption, and with the townspeople of St Albans regarding their liberties. Though often victorious, he had his reverses, and shared in the calamities of the times. If the first visitation of the plague had put him into power the second, which struck him down, left him with a painful legacy of disease and in his old age he was disturbed, and forced for a time to capitulate, by the rising of 1381 in which the inhabitants of St Albans exploited their private grievances.[4] A man of practical rather than speculative intelligence, he took no direct interest, so far as can be seen, in the new and vital controversies that were sapping the foundations of his world; his support of Fitzralph was probably an act of the president's *esprit de corps*, and in the polemics between Wyclif and the possessioners, and in the later Lollard controversies he appears only as a cautious counsellor.[5]

De la Mare was indeed the most active and influential president the black monks were to know. Perhaps his only considerable failure was when he attempted to bring Christ Church, Canterbury, within the ambit of his jurisdiction; before those redoubtable opponents, whose predecessors had humbled archbishops and defied kings, even the abbot of St Albans had to hold his fire, though he did not admit defeat.

The cathedral priory of Christ Church had from the first refused to attend the provincial chapter and to submit to visitation.[6] Their case rested on the metropolitical and legatine status of the archbishop, their immediate superior; any attempt to assert authority over his church and its community was of necessity the attempt of an inferior, and therefore of no validity or standing.[7] The Lateran decrees of 1215 had in fact come

1 For references *v. MC*, iii, 34–5. 2 *GASA*, iii, 418.

3 *GASA*, ii, 404–5: 'Ipse etiam dum Praesidens existebat Magistrum Ricardum Fitzrauf ..in causa Dei, ut credimus, contra Fratres dimicantem, collecta juvit pecunia plus de suo conferens quam omnes alii conferebant.'

4 *V. RO*, i, 268, and references there given.

5 Cf. K. B. McFarlane, *John Wycliffe*, 66, 113. 6 *RO*, i, 17.

7 Cf. the words of Archbishop Sudbury (letter of 7 June 1375, in *MC*, iii, 74–5): 'Cum vos prior et capitulum predictum nobis tam metropolitico quam legacionis jure sedis apostolice speciali et nulli alii nobis inferiori. . .subjecti sitis, nullusque nobis inferior mandando, visitando aut inquirendo de vobis. . .intromittere debeat aut possit quovismodo', etc.

too early, by a narrow margin of years, to be familiar with the canonical concept, owing its origin to the friars, of a body of religious persons forming a single articulated whole and pivoting upon Rome, and the monks of Christ Church succeeded in retaining, under canonical terminology, what was in all essentials the position of an episcopal *Eigenkirche*, able to keep off all external interference by reference to their metropolitan legate, while they warded off his undesirable attentions by appeal to the Rule and to ancient custom.

Pursuant to their policy of non-cooperation, the monks of Christ Church had stood aloof from the establishment of Gloucester College, and had successfully and repeatedly withstood all attempts to extract contributions for its upkeep. As a corollary, they were debarred from enjoying its advantages, and, as has been seen elsewhere, after some unsatisfactory compromises they accepted the position and established a college of their own.[1] It may well have been this last move that precipitated the crisis with de la Mare, and he may have seized his opportunity in the momentary discomfiture of the monks under Islep. In any case, some time during the pontificate of Innocent VI (1352–62) he obtained a declaration that the constitutions of Benedict XII applied to metropolitan cathedral monasteries, and in 1360 he proceeded to bring the prior to heel in virtue of this document.[2] The prior, the long-lived Robert Horthbrand, appealed to the king, doubtless alleging the slight implied by the papal bull (for the first Statute of Praemunire was only seven years old) as well as old friendship.[3] The king, however, was also the friend of de la Mare and reserved the matter for discussion in council, meanwhile bidding the president call off his proctor in Rome and himself writing to the pope in support of Christ Church.[4]

There is no record of what happened, but no decision can have been given in Rome, for the case was pending in 1363, and in 1366 de la Mare cited the prior to the impending general chapter. Clearly there was soreness at Canterbury, for the prior's servants set upon the messenger and having beaten him put him in prison.[5] De la Mare protested to his friend the Black Prince, who took the prior so effectively to task that he sent two of his monks as proxies with full powers to the chapter, and even went so far as to admit that appearances in the suit still pending were against him.[6] He himself could not come, partly because the manifold cares of the harvest were upon him—as a worthy successor of Henry of Eastry, he thrice repeated the point—and moreover he was in charge of Canterbury during the vacancy. This last circumstance was significant; with no

---

[1] *V. supra*, pp. 20–1.

[2] *GASA*, II, 403; *Lit. Cant.* II, 449. For the whole episode *v.* the summary of events and references in *MC*, III, 56–7.

[3] *Lit. Cant.* II, 398–405.   [4] *Lit. Cant.* II, 448–9.

[5] *GASA*, II, 403–4.

[6] Cf. his letter in *MC*, III, 58: 'qui processus ad comparendum et interessendum in dicto capitulo communi...videatur saltim prima facie nos artare'.

powerful patron and with unpleasant memories of Islep the prior was in a weak position. Nevertheless, he obtained the advocacy of John of Gaunt, who presented himself at the chapter, and having solicited and received some kind of confraternity urged the Canterbury case.[1] The litigants then disappear from sight, and it is possible that the new archbishop, Simon Langham, effected some sort of compromise. When he, too, had gone pressure was once more put upon the prior, and at least two attempts were made by capitular visitors to exercise their functions in the priory; each time, however, they were kept at bay by Archbishop Sudbury.[2] Finally, after the abbot of St Albans had relinquished office, Christ Church obtained a papal bull formally exempting them from any connexion with the chapter.[3] This was the end of the affair.

De la Mare was a munificent superior and a magnificent builder. The great gateway, the washing-place in the cloister, the King's Hall and the New Chamber for distinguished guests were probably his most memorable undertakings, but his hand was present everywhere repairing, furnishing, rebuilding and enlarging in the airy, more comfortable manner of domestic planning that was becoming the fashion. The cloister was glazed and furnished with seats, a room was fitted up for his chaplains and studies for the Oxford scholars, a set of apartments was constructed with ornamental ceilings and a decoration of shields and stars in gold and green; furniture of all kinds, silver-plate, chests and books added wealth and beauty to the cluster of buildings where the new cream ashlar met the warm red of the Roman tiles. Nor were sacristy and church forgotten; vestments, vessels, service-books, lamps, hangings and pictures poured in, and among the last was one brought at great expense from north Italy; not the least costly item (which formed a less justifiable article in the charge of extravagance) was a great clock of the kind now coming into fashion. De la Mare's personal taste in things rich and beautiful appears in the gift of a silver-gilt eagle with wings outspread to stand on the crest of the shrine of St Alban, and in the provision, during his lifetime, of a marble tomb and elaborate brasses for his predecessor, Abbot Michael, and himself.[4] When the reader of the long catalogue pauses to form a picture of the roofs and pillars and windows and panelling of the vast group of buildings, of the shimmer of silks and velvet, the lustre of precious metal, and the glow of lamps on candelabra and jewels, he can well understand that Thomas de la Mare was prepared to contribute generously to any collection taken up on behalf of the protagonist of the *possessionati*; he can understand also something of the grievances of the townsfolk in 1381 and of the members of the parliament of 1410 who suggested that the religious houses should be nationalized to provide funds for foreign wars and social services at home.

1 *GASA*, II, 403–4. The curious phrase *fraternitas capituli generalis* presumably implies a confraternity given *honoris causa* in the name of the whole body of black monks in England.
2 *MC*, III, nos. 227, 230A, B, C.   3 Wilkins, *Concilia*, III, 126.
4 For an account of Abbot Thomas's benefactions, *v. VCH, Herts.*, IV, 395–6.

Whatever value we may set upon the objects of the abbot's benefactions, and however great their intrinsic beauty, the funds came for the most part neither from spontaneous offerings nor from payment for work done or services rendered by his monks, but from the labour of peasants on the abbey estates and from those burdened in various shapes and forms with the charges of the abbey's churches.

Yet if we compare de la Mare with the great ecclesiastical patrons of a century and a half later—with Cardinal Wolsey and Cardinal d'Amboise, to say nothing of the Medici and Colonna and d'Este—the man and his works stand in strong contrast. In the abbot's expenses there was no directly personal luxury and little personal display; his gifts adorned the abbey church or added to the amenities of the monastery; they did not primarily cater for the pride of life; they were for the enjoyment of many and would, had the fates been more kind, have remained for the eyes of posterity till they crumbled. The man himself stands in still stronger contrast. It comes, perhaps, as a surprise to those who have read widely in the sources of monastic history of the fourteenth century to find how practical was the devotion and how ascetic the life of Thomas de la Mare. Here he could have learnt little from Samson or the most observant of the Anglo-Norman monks. He rose before midnight, from a bed penitential in its roughness,[1] while the community still slept, and recited his private Office or lengthy prayers;[2] after celebrating Mass he heard three or four more. He let no occupation, however absorbing, no visitor, however distinguished, stand in the way of his punctual observance of the Hours, and when he had a spare half-hour in his room or on a journey, he recited the Penitential Psalms or the Office of the Dead, as had Wulfstan of Worcester almost three centuries before. He seldom ate or drank more than once in the day,[3] and practised fixed fasts and abstinences in addition to those of the Church and monastic custom; he wore a hair-shirt and received the discipline at the hands of another every week; he observed strictly the times and places of monastic silence. Though as a boy he had known and enjoyed as an expert the field sports of his class, he refused as a monk to take part even as a spectator in hunting or hawking, nor would he allow those under his rule to do so. Yet if rigid himself, he was an excellent host, studious of the comfort of others and with the easy urbanity of a man of breeding.

Though we possess a long and detailed account of his administration and his lawsuits there are few of the intimate details, domestic incidents and revealing snatches of conversation that enable us to catch glimpses of

---

1 *GASA*, III, 403: 'Super mollia pulvinaria et chlamyde et furruris calidis sedere videbatur, quando lapilli duri et urticae...erant intermedia'.

2 *Ibid.* 'Nunquam, ut putabatur, ad medietatem noctis dormiebat, sed pluries ante Vigilias Conventuales Psalterium integrum dicere solebat [!], ultra alias suas orationes solitas.'

3 *GASA*, III, 402: 'Raro, et hoc modicum, coena[vi]t; a prandio etiam unius diei usque ad prandium alterius a potu pluries abstin[ui]t.'

the living Samson or Ailred, nor do any personal letters remain. It is therefore not possible to judge how far de la Mare's austere rule of life was the reflection of a character that was by nature serious, determined and energetic, or whether he gave also an impression of a deeper spirituality drawing its strength from a hidden source. We may perhaps be allowed to feel that the ultimate touch of holiness is wanting, and that de la Mare was neither a Wulfstan nor an Anselm. He ruled, however, with love, never happier than when among his monks, whose voices in the liturgy delighted him above all other melody.[1] He often stayed at Redburn with the monks in *villeggiatura*, ringing the bells for office when others failed to do so,[2] and smilingly putting a forfeit of wine on latecomers to dinner. On a deeper level, the chronicler tells us of a service of the sick which is in the true line of Christian and monastic charity; he visited and consoled them, and did not hesitate to perform the most menial services or to give the most delicate marks of affection.[3] It is pleasant to learn that in his own long-drawn decay he received a willing return. His wishes were gladly met when he desired, between Compline at night and Mass of the next day—the monastic greater silence—to be served by none save his own monks; he preferred their services freely given, he said, to those of any others, however skilled.

Attacked by the plague at its second visitation (no doubt that of 1361–2) he never shook off its legacy of infection and disease, but he long continued the ascetic practices of his vigorous manhood; he bore his growing infirmities with dignity and refused to interrupt the tenor of his life and its occupations until extreme old age sapped his physical and mental powers. It should, however, be remembered that he made a genuine attempt to resign his office, but was prevented by the instance of the Black Prince and the remonstrances of his monks.[4] He remained abbot, therefore, until his death, but for the last nine years he was a complete invalid, suffering from a complication of painful maladies which ultimately rendered him helpless in body and weakened in mind, though he retained full consciousness. Throughout these trying years he was nursed assiduously

1 *GASA*, ii, 399: 'Prout saepius asseruit, videbatur sibimet desolatus...quotiens monachorum multitudine caruisset'. *Ibid.* 401: 'multum gaudens modulatione suorum monachorum, quibus aestimabat optimos cantores comparari non posse'.

2 It may be perhaps permissible, as showing how human nature remains the same now as in the fourteenth century, to quote some words written of a modern abbot, Dom Cuthbert Butler of Downside (1859–1934): 'Many years ago a certain junior monk, when "antiphoner", omitted to ring the prescribed bells. Abbot Butler often supplied the defect. One day he left in the junior's room a note to this effect: "Shall be away to-day. Please get another to ring Angelus. E.C.B."' (*Memoir* in *DR*, xxxiii (1934), 430.)

3 *GASA*, iii, 406: 'Si opus esset, ipse primus et prae familiaribus [i.e. servants], si eos vomitus aut fluxum pati contingeret, vasa supponeret et capita manu firmaret, et infici turpi et viscosa materia non refugeret.'

4 *GASA*, ii, 407–9. The episode can be dated to 1360 by the reference to the final agreement at Calais after the return to France of the captured King John. The abbot of St Albans, an exempt abbey depending directly upon the Holy See, needed the papal permission to resign. Hence the search for influential advocates.

by his monks—'in motherly wise', the chronicler records, adding that no son could have watched over his father, no wife over her husband, with more patience. Failing slowly, he died on the octave of the Nativity of Our Lady, 15 September 1396, aged eighty-seven; seventy-one years had been spent in the habit and forty-seven as abbot. He had led, in a certain sense, a double life. That of the great prelate was open for all to see; of the other how much, we may wonder, did the eyes of a Wyclif, a Langland or a Chaucer perceive, when they fell upon the abbot of St Albans riding from London to Westminster to take precedence of all the abbots of England? Did they know of the hair-shirt, the vigils and the fasting? We cannot say, nor do we ourselves know how many of the abbots of England, in an age when the medieval world and its faiths were crumbling, lived as devoutly and as austerely. We can, however, well say that had many thus lived in the days of Henry VIII their order would not have passed, and would not have deserved to pass, so easily from the English scene.

II. UTHRED OF BOLDON

The next monk to be portrayed as an outstanding member of his order in the fourteenth century never held office as superior of a great monastery; he may nevertheless not inaptly be regarded as the most eminent English monk of his time after the abbot of St Albans, while he is certainly the only monk from north of the Humber to win a high reputation in the south during the century. He is, besides, the most distinguished of all the 'university monks', and a principal ornament of a house that inherited a long tradition of fine culture. John Uthred, called of Boldon,[1] may indeed stand as the representative monk-scholar of his age, the century's typical figure in the long series that stretches in England from Bede to Aelfric,

[1] The fullest account of Uthred in print is in *Uhtred de Boldon, Friar William Jordan, and Piers Plowman*, a thesis by Miss M. E. Marcett, privately printed in New York, 1938. This contains an edition of Uthred's *Contra injustas fratrum querelas*. A more complete and in some ways more accurate account is contained in an unpublished Manchester University Ph.D. thesis by C. H. Thompson, entitled *Uthred of Boldon, a study in fourteenth-century political theory*, which contains the text of Uthred's treatises *De dotacione ecclesie sponse Christi* and *Contra garrulos fratrum dotacionem ecclesie impugnantes* (1936). *V.* also R. B. Hepple, 'Uthred of Boldon'.

A chronological skeleton of Uthred's career exists in B.M. Add. MS. 6162, fo. 31ᵛ, entitled *Vita compendiosa Uthredi monachi Dunelmensis* and probably compiled by Prior Wessyngton of Durham; it has been printed in the *Bulletin of the Institute of Historical Research*, III, 46, and in default of any contrary evidence may be accepted as correct, though the information it gives is meagre, and sometimes appears to conflict with other sources (*v. infra*, p. 49, n. 3). W. A. Pantin has a short biographical note and many references to Uthred in *MC*, III (*v.* index), and has in various articles dealt with aspects of his work. The article written *c.* 1898 by A. F. Pollard for the *DNB*, though using the accepted sources, is surprisingly inaccurate in detail.

Uthred—the name is spelt by medieval and modern writers in at least half a dozen different ways—was a common family and Christian name in the north; it occurs often in the *Liber Vitae* of Durham (for the entry of John Utred *v.* facsimile in *SS*, 136, 69ᵛ) and was borne in the fourteenth century by a distinguished family of the East Riding. It was also common in Wales.

William of Malmesbury and Matthew Paris, and is taken up later in France by Luc D'Achéry and Jean Mabillon, to be continued in our own day by Dom Ursmer Berlière, Dom André Wilmart, Dom Germain Morin and Dom Jean Leclercq.

John Uthred, a northerner, if not a Scot, by birth,[1] probably spent much of his childhood on the coastal flats between the estuaries of Wear and Tyne; his home, with its distinctive, far-seen church, lay almost exactly midway between the two monastic settlements of Jarrow and Wearmouth hallowed by memories of Bede and Benet Biscop. The manor from which he took his name belonged to Durham, and it may have been there that the bursar or some other official on his rounds heard of the promising boy. He did not, however, go to Durham for his schooling, and when, at the age of thirteen or so, he began his arts course at Oxford it was as a secular student.[2] The course was interrupted by his decision to become a monk; he was professed at Durham in 1342 and five years later returned to Oxford after three years at the Durham cell of Stamford. Oxford was his home for twenty years; he took his doctorate in 1357,[3] a little before Fitzralph's final onslaught on the friars, and almost fifteen years before Wyclif left philosophy for divinity.

Uthred's working life, so far as it is visible, falls into two periods, though some of his interests and activities were common to both. There is the continuous residence of twenty years at Oxford (1347–67) during part of which he was regent master, and during the whole of which he was occupied with academic questions, and became involved in a series of academic controversies; and there is the later period of thirty years (1367–96) during the whole of which, save for a short interlude at Oxford (1383–6), he was in office either at Durham or the neighbouring Finchale, and was occupied principally in monastic and other ecclesiastical business.

Uthred soon became one of the most distinguished teachers at Oxford. Had we only his historical and monastic treatises by which to judge him,

1 Tryvytlam, *De laude Universitatis Oxoniae*, ed. Furneaux (the lines devoted to Uthred are 449–92), calls him a Scot—'Hic Scottus genere perturbat Anglicos'—while Leland assigns a Welsh origin. The former is probably only using a general term of abuse for a northerner; the latter is merely employing conjecture. There can be no doubt of his northern and English provenance, and in all probability the Boldon or Bolton is not Bolton in Northumberland, where Durham had a property, but Boldon of the *Boldon Buke*, a manor owned by the priory near the coast south of Gateshead. This we should naturally take to be his birthplace, or at least his boyhood's home, were it not that the first entry of the *Vita compendiosa* runs 'a.d. mcccxxxiii primo ad Bolton ad festum Michaelis'. In 1333 he would, according to other data, have been about eight years old, and according to the same source, he was at Newark a year later. Possibly, however, *primo* indicates simply the 'discovery' of the boy by the bursar on his Michaelmas rounds.

2 This seems to follow from the entries in the *Vita* which send him to Oxford in March 1337, and give the date of his clothing as a novice as 26 August 1341. He would then have been sixteen or seventeen years of age. His jubilee in the order is recorded under the year 1392 (i.e. fifty years from his profession at the end of the year's noviciate).

3 So the *Vita*. But the Jarrow accounts (*Inventories of . . . Jarrow and Monk-Wearmouth*, ed. J. Raine) for the half-year December 1358 to June 1359 contain (p. 42) an entry recording a sum paid to Uthred *ad incepcionem suam*.

we might picture him as a venerable and peace-loving student. In fact, he took a leading part in the controversies of his day, showing something of the pugnacity and partisan zeal that was to become so familiar under Wyclif, and as regent proposed a number of theological opinions (which he defended with acerbity) that were both novel and rash.

His first excursion into polemics seems to have been during the last phase of the great controversy on evangelical poverty and the mendicant ideal which had recently been given a practical turn by Archbishop Fitzralph.[1] Uthred was the author of at least two tracts against mendicancy, and it was this, no doubt, that ranged the friars against him and ultimately led to his academic undoing. When (c. 1365) the friars turned their apologetics into a frontal attack upon the property-owning clerks and religious, and even gave support to the demand for some sort of confiscation, Uthred came forward as the protagonist of his order as the author of two treatises on the superiority of the spiritual over the temporal power and on the lawfulness of church endowment, and determined against Wyclif on these matters. In this he once more attacked the Minors' interpretation of evangelical poverty, and added for full measure a sharp rebuke to the false brethren attacking their Mother's dower. However well deserved his attack may have been—and his arguments in general are sane and persuasive—he could not have expected it to act as an emollient.

Meanwhile Uthred had, with the majority of his contemporaries, chosen his theological opinions from many schools, including that of the Ockhamists, while his views on grace resembled those of the doctors stigmatized by Bradwardine a few years previously as 'Pelagian'. This by itself, however, would probably not have brought him to grief. He had, however, excogitated a particular opinion to which he was firmly wedded, and which he applied to a whole series of problems; this was the thesis of the *clara visio*, the vision of some aspect of divine truth granted to all between apparent and real death, carrying with it the fateful choice or rejection of God upon which depended the eternal salvation or shipwreck of the soul.[2] This in the fullness of time was attacked by the Friars Preachers and delated to the archbishop of Canterbury; Uthred fought back with spirit, and his vituperation must have supplied any stimulus that was still wanting to his opponents; after a solemn examination by a panel of theologians the majority of the propositions were censured by Archbishop Langham and declared inadmissible in public teaching at Oxford.

No contemporary account of the affair exists, but it is at least remarkable that at the very crisis of the episode Uthred was recalled to be prior of Finchale,[3] a small dependency of Durham within easy reach of the

1 For a fuller account of this, *v. infra*, pp. 66–7.
2 Uthred's opinions are discussed more fully *infra*, pp. 85–8.
3 There is some doubt as to the exact date of Uthred's recall, or at least of his return. The dated letters in Langham's register make it certain that the examination of Uthred's

priory, which was used as a rest-house by monks in *villeggiatura*. His confreres clearly did not regard the episode as a disgrace; they may even have regarded Uthred as something of a martyr at the hands of the mendicants, but his prestige and self-confidence as a speculative theologian must have been shaken, and while it would be false to regard Uthred as a fourteenth-century Loisy or Fénelon, or to think of the censure as comparable with the condemnation of Wyclif a few years later, yet the blow must have been a sensible one, and may well have played its part in bringing to an end the era of free academic speculation at Oxford.

For the next fifteen years Uthred passed in rotation from the post of prior at Finchale (1367–8, 1375–81) to that of subprior at Durham (1368–75, 1381–3) and we can trace his activities in the former office both in the accounts which he presented to the mother house, and in the record of expenses incurred by him on various journeys.[1] Already from early days at Oxford he was a well-known figure among the black monks, and from 1360 onwards for a series of years he represented his house at chapter; in 1363 he was one of the committee of diffinitors who considered the new statutes of de la Mare,[2] and in 1366 he was delegated to visit the troublesome abbey of Whitby, the scene of recent scandals, and together with the abbot of St Mary's, York, to report on the success of the recent disciplinary measures.[3] Such commissions, given to a man of forty who had held no high office, are evidence of the reputation for sound judgement and tactful dealing acquired by Uthred among his brethren. His fame, indeed, had spread outside his order in circles which would have taken little heed of Langham's censure, and he was generally regarded as the representative spokesman of the monastic body in the country. This is shown in a striking manner in a chronicle which under the year 1371 introduces four regular theologians to be questioned by the Black Prince at a royal council as to the degree of jurisdiction enjoyed by the pope in temporal matters; side by side with Uthred on the bench were the

opinions took place between the archbishop's letter to the chancellor of Oxford (18 February 1367/8) and the promulgation of the censure on 11 November 1368. On the other hand the *Vita* gives the date of his appointment to Finchale as 10 August 1367 and his appointment as subprior of Durham as 2 February 1368. Some assistance in reconciling the various data is given by the Finchale accounts (*v.* next note) where under the period St Lawrence (10 August) 1367 to Ascension (18 May) 1368 the *Compotus D. Uthredi* has (p. lxxxi): 'In expensis Prioris cum hominibus et equis suis, scilicet ad Witeby, eundo et redeundo, et alias ad Oxoniam et London. et ibidem per medium anni morando £xxi–xvi–viii. Et in expensis clericorum diversis vicibus missorum ad Archiepiscopum et alibi pro eadem causa [none has been specified] £viii–vii–xi.' Langham's letter of February, however, alludes to Uthred as still publicly disputing and determining *in scolis et alibi*, and imposes silence on him *pendente lite*. Similarly in the list of Uthred's alleged errors, drawn up by his opponents and certainly used by Langham, he is spoken of as *sacrae theologiae professor in Universitate Oxoniensi*. But *v. infra*, p. 84, n. 2.

1 Cf. *The Priory of Finchale*, ed. J. Raine, for several of Uthred's account rolls, and *Extracts from the Account Rolls of the Abbey of Durham*, ed. J. T. Fowler, where more than twenty entries (*v.* index) refer to grants made to him.

2 *V.* Uthred's biographical entry in *MC*, III. For de la Mare's statutes *v. MC*, II, 66–83.

3 *MC*, III, nos. 350–4.

provincials of the Minors and the Preachers.[1] The probability that the passage is a tendentious exaggeration or even an entirely fictitious squib does not diminish its significance for Uthred's reputation, and it is not surprising to find that in 1373 he should in actual fact have been chosen one of the small embassy sent by the king to Avignon to negotiate on a question of papal subsidy. Here again the appointment of a monk who was not a prelate is probably without parallel in the century.[2] His engagement in ecclesiastical affairs continued, and casual notes in account books show him to have been at York for convocation in 1370–1; as visitor of the churches of Howdenshire in 1379–80, and again in 1383–4; and as visitor of the northern monasteries as delegate of the chapter in 1380–1.[3] He was one of the trustees of the fund left by Bishop Hatfield for the endowment of Durham College, and travelled to London and Oxford on business connected with this.[4] He took no direct part in the various moves and councils issuing in the condemnation of Wyclif, but it is probably to the later part of his career that belong two treatises in which he defended traditional doctine on two burning questions of the day, the Eucharist and Predestination. To this period, perhaps, belong also his apologetics of the monastic way of life as against the friars, who were urging their claims to superiority on the score both of their poverty and of their greater antiquity. On the last point something of a *mêlée* was in progress in which all the orders were engaged; the Augustinians of every description claiming unbroken descent from their patron, while the Carmelites, by tracing their pedigree back to the prophet Elias, successfully outbid all the regulars save for a small group of Preachers who had the enterprising courage to rely on their popular title in staking out a claim upon the patriarch Jacob as their founder.[5] To the literature of this controversy Uthred contributed several writings of greater solidity and worth than the topic might have seemed to promise.[6] One of these, a revised version of a treatise on monastic origins, became an extremely reasonable, persuasive and historically accurate account of the development of the monastic ideal, as seen first in kindred endeavours in the Old Testament and by St John the Baptist, and traced from apostolic times through

1 *Eulogium Historiarum*, ed. F. S. Haydon, III, 337–9. Despite the absence of any corroborative evidence and the argument of Tait (article 'Whittlesey' in *DNB*) as well as the tone of the whole narrative, the passage has been accepted as sober history by Workman, *John Wyclif*, I, 228–30, Marcett and others.

2 The article in *DNB* makes Wyclif one of the party, apparently through confusion with the embassy to Bruges in the following year.

3 *Account Rolls of Durham*, ed. Fowler, 576, 579, 589, 593.

4 *Ibid.* 591. Uthred goes to London 'ad tractandum cum Episcopo et consilio suo pro Collegio Oxon'.

5 The Preachers were known in France and England as *Jacobitae* from their Paris convent of St James; hence their adaptability to the 'I' of Caim (for Cain). Uthred or the writer he is copying gives the facts about this name. Cf. *Monasticon*, I, xxii–xxiv.

6 A list of Uthred's writings is given by W. A. Pantin in *Studies in Medieval History presented to F. M. Powicke*, 364–6. The Durham MSS. there listed no doubt contain the changes and additions made by Uthred to the monastic treatises as he found them.

Cassian and the monks of Palestine to the Italian monks of the age of St Benedict. This treatise had as complement one on the essence of the monastic life, perhaps composed as a manual for novice-masters, which again with extreme reasonableness, if also with some quaint touches and topical references, showed that the monastic life was in effect the perfect Christian life; that it was, in fact, that lived by our first parents in Paradise.[1]

Uthred was again in Oxford for three years from 1383. It was the year after the solemn condemnation of Wyclif, and the academic climate had changed greatly since the days of Uthred's inception. Wyclif had gone, and was pouring forth a molten flood of pamphlets from Lutterworth; the university had been roughly handled by Courtenay, and the friars and monks of all orders had drawn together to defend the Eucharist and resist the attacks of the followers of Wyclif, the first generation of Lollards, on the religious life and on the whole framework of the Church as they knew it. What Uthred thought or did in this new world we do not know; he may have returned merely in order to set the newly organized college on its feet. He returned to be prior of Finchale for the third time in 1386, and there, ten years later, he died. To his last years belongs, perhaps, the group of devotional writings and notices of monastic saints and writers that are still extant.

Uthred is in large part hidden from us by that veil which covers so many of the distinguished thinkers of his century, from Marsilius to Wyclif, and which baffles all search for personality and intimacy. His writings hold no allusions to his own life; they are formal in construction and often depend so largely on previous work that it is impossible to separate his own contribution. His theological opinions, as known to us from his tract, are of interest chiefly as showing the lack of any fixed tradition in the Oxford of his day, but they show also an independent mind, at grips with real problems, not merely a technician in theological gymnastic. His reputation was very high; it is not possible to recall another black monk beneath the rank of abbot who held a position in the age at all comparable to his; that his memory was held in honour at Durham is shown by the care taken, forty years after his death and possibly by Prior Wessington, to assemble a series of dates covering the changes of residence and office in his life. Yet only one saying, 'that the accidents should never be preferred to the substance' by the student, remains to reveal his character. He wrote and thought in the academic idiom of his day, and this, though it may have advanced his fame among his contemporaries, rendered his work sterile; the future, the distant future, lay with the hidden, spontaneous writers of English, with Rolle, with Langland, with the unknown authors of *The Cloud of Unknowing* and *The Pearl*. Uthred lived to see the age of Chaucer and Piers Plowman, but there is nothing in his work that speaks of it. Laborious, sane and often convincing in his argument, he had neither the fresh outlook on his own world nor the

1 For a fuller notice of these tracts, *v. infra*, pp. 270–2.

resources for a critical survey of the past which both before his time and after have given to the work of monastic scholars a permanent value for the ages. His adult life was divided almost equally between the routine of a teacher at Oxford, the liturgical and social round of community life in its most dignified form at Durham, and the quieter, simpler days in the shady valley by the Wear with its old memories of Godric and its present succession of brethren taking their rest and refreshment by the pleasant waters. Through all this he passes, a figure to us dignified and not un-sympathetic, whom few of to-day's visitors recall as they walk over the fields from Durham along the path that must have been so familiar to his eyes, and stand on the grass *ante introitum chori* beneath which his bones are lying.

III. SIMON LANGHAM

Thomas de la Mare was probably, both in character and influence, the most notable English monk in the public life of the fourteenth century, but he was not the most eminent member of his order nor the one whose name is most commonly found in books of to-day. That place is occupied by Simon Langham, abbot and, as he was sometimes called, second founder of Westminster, the only black monk to sit in the chair of St Augustine since Richard, the successor of St Thomas; he spent his last years as cardinal at the papal court and his benefactions and legacies made possible the building of part of the cloisters and much of the nave of the Abbey as we know it to-day.[1]

Langham was born in the village of that name a few miles north of Oakham in Rutland; nothing is known of his father or of the reasons that prompted the boy to seek admission at Westminster. His name occurs first in the abbey documents in 1339–40, when he was not yet a priest and may have been some twenty-three years old. He did not go up to Oxford, and nothing in his later activity suggests that he had literary or speculative talents beyond the ordinary, but as early as 1346 he is found representing his abbot at the general chapter of the black monks.[2] Three years later the path to a career was opened for him in a remarkable manner. The spring of 1349 was that in which the Black Death raged in London and its neighbourhood. At Westminster, between January and the late summer, twenty-seven of the inmates—almost exactly half the community—were carried off.[3] Among the early losses was the prior, and Langham, who had probably been the close assistant of the abbot, was chosen in his stead on 10 April. A month later the abbot himself died, and on 27 May Langham was elected abbot by a stricken and still dwindling community. It was a strange coincidence that the other eminent monk whose career we have

---

1 For Langham, *v. DNB*; E. H. Pearce, *Monks of Westminster*; H. F. Westlake, *History of Westminster Abbey*; and J. A. Robinson, 'Simon Langham, Abbot of Westminster'.
2 *MC*, II, 62.
3 Flete, *History of Westminster*, ed. J. A. Robinson, 128.

already glanced at should have come young to office by the same chance of death in the same year—the year in which the great Bradwardine, twice within six months elected to Canterbury, was taken so swiftly from the high station that he might well have filled so ably.

The new abbot took over an administration in debt and a community shaken and dislocated rather than renewed in spirit by the pestilence. He showed himself from the first a capable man of business and a strong, perhaps even a severe, ruler. His judgement and his strength alike appear in his immediate appointment of Nicholas Litlington as prior. No doubt his later eminence and still more his later benefactions caused his period of rule to be seen in something of a golden mist, but his tightening of discipline and observance is specifically recorded,[1] even if there is a suggestion that personal ambition was a motive in much of his external activity.[2] Whether this was so or not his ability had made its mark; he was elected one of the abbots president of the black monks[3] and at the end of November 1360, the abbot was appointed Treasurer of England, an office that one of his predecessors, Abbot Ware, had held eighty years before. A year later he was elected to the see of London and almost simultaneously provided to that of Ely, whose bishop, Thomas de Lisle, had died at the papal court. He had already left his mark on the buildings of Westminster by rebuilding a part of the cloister. A year after his consecration he was appointed Chancellor, but did not neglect his see, where he left a reputation for severity behind him. On 24 July 1366 he was provided to Canterbury with the king's approval.

He held that great office for little more than two years, but even in that short time showed once again his desire to enforce discipline, this time against the pluralists and their protagonist, William of Wykeham. He also had the fortune to receive appeals in two cases of some historical interest. The one came from his own monks of Canterbury, who resented the ejection of their brethren from the new Oxford foundation by Archbishop Islep; here Langham's decision in favour of the monks, which was in fact a reasonable one, had the accidental effect of turning Wyclif out of office and may thus have contributed to the feeling of resentment against the organization of the Church that was to have such important results a decade later.[4] The other, from the Dominicans, lay against his confrère,

---

1 *Ibid.* 130: 'Quantaque industria quorundam insolentias, abusiones, singularitates, superfluitates et malitias exstirpaverit, qualem ordinis disciplinam jam per aliquorum voluntarios usus vitiatam sagaciter introduxerit, calens adhuc [? *c.* 1430] recolit memoria.' *Ibid.* 131: 'Monasterium praedictum in tam debita regula et sub tam bono gubernaculo stabilivit quod etsi nihil aliud boni fecisset [Flete clearly has his legacy in mind] secundum dicta seniorum loci praedicti ecclesiae fundatoris merito poterit comparari.'

2 The suggestion is made by the chronicler John Redyng in B.M. MS. Cleopatra A 16, cited by Robinson, *art. cit.* 352: 'in the aforesaid matters [i.e. papal negotiations for the peace between England and France] and in others, Simon de Langham, then abbot of Westminster—perhaps to get a name for himself and fatter promotions—laboured more abundantly than all'.

3 *MC*, II, 4.   4 *V. supra*, p. 21.

Uthred of Boldon, and here, as we have seen, the archbishop's decision, based on the findings of a panel of theologians, was against Uthred.[1]

In September 1368, what might have been a notable episcopate was cut short by Langham's appointment as Cardinal of St Sixtus by Pope Urban V. He resigned his see and went to Italy and later to Avignon. He returned to England, however, as one of the two ambassadors sent by the pope to mediate between the kings of England and France. He stayed for a considerable time in England, visited Westminster and made dispositions of his many benefices, but his mission was foredoomed to failure and he returned to Avignon in 1373. When Whittlesey, his successor at Canterbury, died in 1374 he was again, it would seem, desired by the monks, but the pope refused to let him go. In the sequel, he died two years later, leaving his fortune, equal to some £300,000 in present-day value, his books, his plate and his ornaments to the house of his profession. He was buried in Westminster Abbey, in a tomb designed by Henry Yevele, and his princely legacy helped to build his other monument, the present nave of the Abbey.

Langham has naturally fared well at the hands of Westminster writers, both medieval and modern, to whom we owe most of our knowledge of him. Criticism, indeed, or even candour, could scarcely be expected from those who had accepted and were spending more than a quarter of a million, and the Westminster scholars of our own day have yielded nothing in piety to their predecessors.[2] Langham, indeed, was certainly morally blameless and an upright abbot and bishop. In four entirely different worlds he attracted men's notice and won the tribute of their satisfaction.[3] Whether, as some contemporaries hinted, he played his cards well with a clear view of the material prizes at stake can scarcely be decided from the evidence that survives, but it is not easy to justify his willingness to amass a very great fortune in a very short time largely by means of the very pluralism which he had so rightly attacked,[4] even if his wealth went in great part to the Carthusians of Bonpas and the monks of Westminster.

IV. ADAM EASTON

Only a little less eminent, and perhaps more mentally distinguished and personally attractive than Simon Langham was Adam Easton, his younger contemporary.[5] Born of humble parents, probably at the Easton that lies

1 *V. supra*, p. 50.

2 Even Robinson (*art. cit.* 366) is conscious that he might be accused of partiality.

3 Flete, *History of Westminster*, 132, gives a general judgement: 'Fuerat enim vir magni consilii et sapientiae excellentis, tenacis memoriae et eloquentis facundiae'.

4 Robinson, *art. cit.* 356, gives a list; besides English benefices which Langham in 1372 leased for 1360 marks, he held the deanery of Lincoln with the Lincoln prebend of Brampton; the treasurership of Wells and archdeaconries of Wells and Taunton; the archdeaconry of the West Riding and the York prebend of Winstow. The bill *Execrabilis* and other papal decrees did not apply to the Sacred College.

5 There is no study of Adam of Easton. For events of his life *v. DNB*; *MC* (index); and Workman, *John Wyclif* (index).

some six miles north-west of Norwich, Adam was a student at Gloucester College at least as early as *c.* 1365–6, and in 1366 he was prior of the monk-students of Oxford; he had then recently incepted in theology. It is possible that he accompanied Langham to Rome when the latter became cardinal in 1368; certainly in that year he was sent by the pope on a mission to the English king. He was back again in Rome in 1370, and may have succeeded his friend and confrère of Norwich, Thomas de Brunton, as procurator in Curia of the black monks *c.* 1373. He was closely associated with Cardinal Langham in his last months, and as one of his executors was concerned to transmit the legacies safely to Westminster. In the same year, 1376, he had been informed of Wyclif's attacks on the monks, and asked Abbot Litlington for a copy of his writings.[1] A year later it was he almost certainly who was primarily responsible, like Langham eleven years earlier, for precipitating a crisis in Wyclif's life by urging Gregory XI to issue his bulls against him. Meanwhile his work of twenty years on the seat of authority in the Church was brought to a point by the appearance of this new opponent, and issued in the completion of his *Defensorium ecclesiasticae potestatis*, 'a strong defence of the highest papal and ecclesiastical claims', directed chiefly to the addresses of Marsilius of Padua and William of Ockham, and only mentioning Wyclif in passing.[2] Adam's services at the Curia were rewarded in 1381 with the cardinalate, with the title of St Cecilia, but he was not destined to end his days in dignified leisure. Though originally one of the supporters of Urban VI, he was one of the most determined in his rebukes to the pope, and he was imprisoned by the now frenzied pontiff as the alleged ring-leader of a revolt in 1385. Two years later we find the three black monk presidents petitioning Urban for his release. In the event, Easton did in fact escape the fate of some of his colleagues and regained his liberty, dying at length in the Curia in 1397.

Adam Easton was a man of great learning and industry, and prepared for his task of defending the papacy by learning Hebrew and translating the Old Testament from that language to avoid any charge of error should he use the Scriptures in his arguments. In his last years he interested himself in the cause of St Bridget of Sweden, whom he may have known and to whose intercession he attributed his escape from the worst rigours of persecution under Urban VI; in gratitude he defended her memory and urged her canonization, which took place in 1391.[3] It is to be hoped that he will within a short time find a chronicler. Though still very imperfectly known he is in many ways a more attractive figure than Langham. His ability is unquestionable, and he did nothing, so far as is known, to further his advancement, from which in fact he reaped more sorrow than

1 *MC*, III, 76–7. Also *v. infra*, p. 69.
2 Cf. 'The *Defensorium* of Adam Easton', by W. A. Pantin, in *EHR*, LI (1936), 675–80. Research under Mr Pantin's direction has since made the ascription of this to Easton certain, and has added considerably to the material for a biographer.
3 *V. infra*, p. 277.

honour, and both in his opposition to the outrageous behaviour of Urban VI and in his advocacy of the Swedish saint he shows a sense of spiritual principles and obligations. At the least he is, as he has been justly called, 'one of the worthiest products of the English Benedictines' contact with Oxford'.

V. THOMAS BRUNTON

After the greatest abbot of the age and the two monk-cardinals, a place may be found for a monk who had a well deserved celebrity in the pulpit and in public life while occupying the humblest episcopal see in the land.

Thomas of Brunton[1] hailed from the hamlet of Brinton, which lies between Melton Constable and Holt, twenty-five miles north-west of Norwich and not far from Blakeney and the coast. He was born c. 1320 and entered as a boy the cathedral priory of Norwich, being perhaps eight or ten years senior to Adam Easton. The house was then entering upon the most distinguished phase of its history, and between 1350 and 1420 gave to Gloucester College and the English monastic body a series of able theologians and administrators; the excellence of its library can still be measured by the books that remain in Cambridge and elsewhere.[2] After studying canon law for a short period (1352–3) at Cambridge, probably at Trinity Hall, the recent (1350) foundation of Bishop Bateman of Norwich, Brunton passed to Oxford, where he was a student with Adam Easton at Gloucester College (1355–63), and was recalled along with Adam for a time to preach the customary sermons in the cathedral.[3] In 1362 he was appointed papal penitentiary, no doubt to meet the needs of English pilgrims and travellers, and in the following year incepted as *doctor decretorum* at Oxford; Adam Easton probably incepted in divinity at the same time. Henceforward for some ten years he was at the papal court, first at Avignon and then at Rome, and he is found acting as proctor for the English monks. While in Rome he was associated with a redoubtable compatriot, Sir John Hawkwood, in establishing a hospice for English pilgrims which ultimately developed into the Venerable English College,[4] and early in 1369 he was joined in Rome by his confrères in the habit, Simon Langham, newly created cardinal, and Adam Easton, who may have accompanied Langham in some kind of secretarial position. It may well have been the recommendation of the late archbishop of Canterbury

---

1 The first modern writer to 'discover' Brunton was F. A. (later Cardinal) Gasquet, in his essay 'A forgotten English preacher' (1897). Since then, the bishop and his sermons have been discussed by G. R. Owst in *Preaching in Medieval England, passim*, especially 15 *seqq.*, and a full and scholarly study of his career, with references to printed and manuscript sources, has been given by Sister M. A. Devlin in 'Bishop Thomas Brunton and his sermons'; her edition of his sermons has recently (1954) appeared (*v.* Bibliography). Cf. also W. A. Pantin, *The English Church in the Fourteenth Century*, 182–5.

2 H. C. Beeching, 'The library of the cathedral church of Norwich', and N. R. Ker, *Medieval Libraries of Great Britain*, 75–7.

3 *MC*, III, 28–9.

4 F. A. Gasquet, *A history of the Venerable English College in Rome*, 30.

that led Gregory XI, early in 1373 and acting apparently on his own initiative, to provide Brunton to the recently vacated see of Rochester.[1]

Though the smallest and poorest of the bishoprics of England, Rochester had given a home to more than one saint, and the tale was not yet complete. In a period of social and religious turmoil Thomas Brunton, untainted by wealth or worldliness, came to hold a position of considerable weight as a conscientious bishop who was also one of the most learned and fearless preachers of his age. He was indeed, far more than his contemporaries Simon Langham and Thomas Merk, of the type of monk-bishop that recurs throughout the ages and has been seen in recent times in an Ullathorne and a Hedley, combining a sound, though not brilliant, theological talent, and an outlook neither conservative nor revolutionary, with a solid piety that never blossoms fully into sanctity. In the ten years of active life that remained before infirmities came upon him, Brunton made his mark upon his generation not only as a bulwark of stability when the peasants and Wyclif attacked in their different ways the old order of things, but also as a resolute critic of moral and social evils in high places and in low alike, fighting both the corruption of the court and city, and social injustice in landowners and government officials. Already in the Curia he had been noted as a preacher, and now for a decade he was the public orator among the bishops. He preached on public affairs at a provincial synod in 1373, at a meeting of convocation in 1376, and on the morrow of the coronation of Richard II.[2] He was active in parliaments between 1376 and 1380, and in the last named year was one of the ambassadors to France; he was one of the commission that tried the rebels of Kent in 1381, and in 1382 was present at the council of Blackfriars when Wyclif was condemned. In all these circumstances he is consistent and firm, the advocate of justice as well as moderation, loyal, without hypocrisy if also without an apostle's fire, to his motto: 'the truth shall make you free'.[3]

Recent scholarship has taken an interest in Brunton's relations with more than one of his celebrated contemporaries. A resemblance has been noted between his social programme and that of John Ball, the leader of the Kentish rebels,[4] as also between his motto and some lines of Chaucer.[5] Certainly both the rebel and the poet must have been aware of Brunton. Still more interesting, though more elusive, is his relationship to the poet

1 Devlin, *art. cit.* 328, n. 5, cites from the Vatican Library *Reg. Aven.* 190 fo. 21ʳ the papal act of provision.

2 Devlin, *art. cit.* 335, 336, 338.

3 Devlin, *art. cit.* 324, n 3, cites B.M. Harley 3760, fo. 309ᵛ: 'Et ego a primo die consecracionis mee pro vulgari meo recepi et postea continuavi verbum pro themate prius sumptum *veritas liberabit.*' [Cf. St John, viii. 32 (Vulgate): 'cognoscetis veritatem, et veritas liberabit vos'.]

4 B.M. MS. Harley 3760, fo. 112ᵛ has been discussed by Gasquet, 'A forgotten English preacher', 87, and G. R. Owst, *Literature and Pulpit in Medieval England*', 291–2.]

5 Cf. the refrain to the *Balade of Bon Conseyl*, 'And trouthe shall thee delivere, it is no drede'.

of *Piers Plowman*. A scholar has seen in Brunton the Angel of the Prologue of the B-text; another has found in him the source of the poet's fable of the rats;[1] others have noted further resemblances between his sermons and the poem,[2] while the identification of John Butt who wrote part of passus xii of the A-text with the John Butt who carried a message to Brunton at Calais in 1380, and the further connexion of Butt with William de Rockayle of Norwich, takes us deep into the thicket that has hitherto protected the author of the poem from the advancing army of learned beaters.[3]

Brunton died in 1389 after a long period of inactivity, a relatively poor man who did not forget his relatives and friends in Norfolk.[4] His voluminous sermons, explored by more than one student, still remain to be fully exploited as a mine of information on the social and political ideas of the time. To the monastic historian, however, Brunton's chief title to a restricted fame must be the picture he leaves of a devout, sober and sturdy monk-bishop of a type that does not recur in the English medieval church.

1 G. R. Owst, 'The *Angel* and the *Goliardeys* of Langland's Prologue'; Eleanor Kellogg, 'Bishop Brunton and the Rat Parliament'.

2 Gasquet, *art. cit.* 71–83.

3 Edith Rickert, 'John But, Messenger and Maker'; O. Cargill, 'The Langland myth', and, for the thicket itself, still budding strongly, M. W. Bloomfield, 'Present state of *Piers Plowman* studies'.

4 Among the legatees was one Matilda Pynsware, who owed suit to the manorial court of Thornage, the manor which included the hamlet of Brinton, and who had lately been fined there for brewing beer of inferior quality (Devlin, *art. cit.* 325).

CHAPTER V

MONKS AND FRIARS IN CONTROVERSY

I. DOMINION AND GRACE

It is a characteristic of the century that elapsed between the death of Aquinas and the outbreak of the Great Schism that both thinkers and leaders of parties followed out their ideas or their principles of action to what seemed their logical issue but what was in fact a point outside the sphere—beyond the horizon, so to say—of a world of human beings and practical relationships: to a point, that is to say, where logic becomes fallacious and harmful. The extreme papalist writers, the no less extreme secularists, the Franciscan advocates of the Poverty of Christ, though especially notable, are but examples of this general tendency. No less striking in their intransigence are the various leaders on either side of the controversy on Lordship and Grace.

The theory of Lordship or Dominion and Grace first became a living issue in the worlds of thought and politics with the appearance in 1302 of the work *De ecclesiastica potestate* of the Austin friar Giles of Rome.[1] In this treatise, which is throughout an assertion of papal claims in their most extreme form, Giles maintained that dominion can only exist within the Church or with the permission of the Church, and that in fact only faithful Christians can have just dominion since they alone can derive their right through the Church from Christ the supreme Lord of all things.[2] The basis of this position consists of the two propositions that only the just are susceptible of God's gift of dominion, and that only those in a state of grace within the Church are truly just. Giles thus demanded a twofold condition for dominion, part internal, part external; in other words, he demanded in the owner a state of grace and communion with the Church. Nevertheless, he appears to have avoided the immediate and obvious difficulties of his position by omitting to consider any kind of fall from grace save that by the sin of infidelity, which would inevitably carry with it defection from the Church. This, however, was clearly not a satisfactory permanent solution of the difficulty, and those who followed his lead split ultimately into two widely opposed groups: those who held that the

1 The best account of this subject up to and including the contribution made by Fitz-ralph is that of Fr A. Gwynn, S.J., *The English Austin Friars*, 59–73. Wyclif's teaching is mentioned in other parts of this book, which is a mine of precise information, not easily come by elsewhere and informed by clear and cool judgements, though the arrangement of topics does not make for ready reference. An excellent short account of Wyclif, by B. L. Manning, is in *CMH*, VII, ch. 16, and longer discussions in H. B. Workman, *John Wyclif*; v. also articles on Wyclif and others in *DTC*.

2 Throughout this controversy the term *dominium* carried much of its feudal connotation: the supreme feudal lord (as the king) had *dominium eminens*, the actual holder of the fee had *dominium utile*.

visible Church alone had a right to dominion, and those who gave this right to the invisible body of the just.

Across this controversy of publicists there cut another which had an equal fascination. This was the question of the transcendent worth of Poverty, conceived as the absolute renunciation and lack of material possessions which the mendicant friars, and particularly the Friars Minor, had made a living and all but œcumenical issue.

The early decades of the fourteenth century might have seemed to witness the termination of this long quarrel, at least so far as the pronouncements of authority were concerned. Pope Clement V, who had hoped to reconcile the warring Spirituals and Conventual Minors by something of a compromise did in fact by the bull *Exivi de paradiso*[1] (5 May 1312) destroy for ever the hopes of the stricter party by declaring that the religious vows of the Minors did not bind them to the observance of all the gospel counsels and that absolute personal poverty of life (the so-called *usus pauper*) was not essential to their profession. A decade later (8 December 1322) John XXII, by his bull *Ad conditorem canonum*,[2] revoked the act by which his predecessor Nicholas III in the bull *Exiit qui seminat* (14 August 1279) had taken into the ownership of the Holy See all the material possessions of the Minors, thus restoring full ownership to the friars. A year later, in the constitution *Cum inter nonnullos*[3] (13 November 1323) he condemned as heretical the opinion of the strict party of the Minors that Christ and His apostles owned no property either in private or in common. At almost the same time the external relationship of the mendicants with the bishops and secular clergy was settled for the remaining two centuries of the medieval period by the reissue by Clement V (1312) of the celebrated bull of Boniface VIII *Super cathedram*.[4] From this time forward, therefore, the great issues of Franciscan theory and practice were no longer debatable by orthodox controversialists, and though a large section of the order went into schism and maintained a long rearguard action against both papal pronouncements and the authorities of the order, this very fact increased the unity and respectability of the moderate or Conventual party, and the English friars at least had no further share either in the forlorn hope of the Spirituals or in the orthodox reform of the Observants early in the next century.

But if internecine strife and forensic controversies no longer tore at the vitals of the Minors, they and the other mendicants, by reason alike of their ideals and of their failure to realize those ideals remained a focus of friction in the English Church. Something will be said later of the attacks made upon them by their contemporaries for their failures, real or alleged; here we have only to consider the academic and public controversies to

---

1 *Bullarium franciscanum*, ed. J. H. Sbaralea (1759–68), v, no. 196.
2 *Bullarium franciscanum*, v, 235.
3 Denzinger-Bannwart, *Enchiridion symbolorum*. no. 494.
4 *Bullarium franciscanum*, IV, 498–500.

which they were a party. Among these an important place was taken by the question of Dominion and Grace.

The opinion that the just or the elect alone had a true title to possession and rule in this world, and the almost opposite opinion that all possession was evil, had been held by various heretical sects during the Christian centuries, but the new form taken by these theories in the fourteenth century cannot be traced directly to any ancient source; it was rather the outcome of the two great controversies mentioned above between papalists and secularists, Spirituals and Conventuals. Even after the papal condemnation of the theological issue of the Poverty of Christ the Minors continued to preach the sinfulness of possession. This had a great, if indirect, influence on the dispute as to Dominion and Grace on account of the practical consequences of the Franciscan view. If possession of material wealth was sinful, churchmen and the papacy above all were among the greatest sinners, and therefore incapable of lordship. Eventually, therefore, the same arguments were used by the bitterest opponents, though with different applications. While one party held that the Church, the only spiritual and holy society, had the sole and complete title to all things, the other maintained that the existing, official Church had sinned grievously through avarice and luxury and therefore deserved and indeed required to be despoiled of all things, while the poor just man alone was lord of all.

The views of Giles of Rome, already noted, reappeared, though modified and even criticized, in the writings of his two confrères James of Viterbo and Agostino Trionfo, and are found almost in entirety in a treatise which another Austin friar, later prior-general of his order, William of Cremona, wrote, c. 1328, against the *Defensor pacis* of Marsilius of Padua.[1] William of Cremona was in touch for the next sixteen years (1326–42) with the papal court at Avignon, and for the last five of these years Richard Fitzralph, dean of Lichfield, was in residence at Avignon and, like William of Cremona, a frequent preacher before the pope. This near neighbourhood no doubt accounts for the clear traces of the Aegidian doctrine of Lordship and Grace in Fitzralph's writings even as early as 1340–4. In 1346 he was elected archbishop of Armagh, of which diocese he was probably a native, and he spent an active year in Ireland in 1348–9, but he returned in the latter year to Avignon as ambassador from Edward III, and remained to negotiate a settlement in a controversy between his see and that of Dublin. Fitzralph had probably by this time had unpleasant experience himself of the mendicants in his diocese, and in the first year of his second visit to Avignon the fires of the old strife had been stirred by an attempt on the part of the friars to obtain a more favourable interpretation than was customary of the *Super cathedram*. This move was countered by a group of bishops who proposed to appeal for a more rigorous interpretation of the bull; Fitzralph became their leader and spokesman and

---

1 Gwynn, *op. cit.* 64 ff.

was drawn gradually forward to make a frontal attack not only on the privileges of the mendicants, but upon their whole conception of poverty. Before he had finished his treatise, which had developed into a very long work, he was recalled to his diocese where he soon ran foul of the friars, who were naturally disposed to see in him an enemy. Thus action and reaction succeeded one another, and the matter came to a crisis when Fitzralph, visiting London on some business in 1356, was invited by his old friend the dean of St Paul's to give his views in a course of public sermons at Paul's Cross. This he duly did in the winter and spring of 1356–7, and his sermons, in which he attacked the practice as well as the theory of the mendicants, caused the four orders to form a solid front against the archbishop and to carry their cause to Avignon, where Fitzralph died in 1360.

While at Avignon and in Ireland, between 1350 and 1356, Fitzralph, as has been mentioned, had composed his chief work *De pauperie salvatoris*.[1] This consists of seven books, in the first five of which the writer elaborated his theories of property and its rights—that is, of Lordship and Grace— while in the two last he turned to an attack on the papal privileges enjoyed by the friars; these, he maintained, were so seriously abused by their holders that they no longer had any right to them (here the doctrine of Lordship and Grace was used) and he trusted that the pope would take them away.

By this treatise and still more by his sermons at Paul's Cross Fitzralph scattered fire among very inflammable material, and a general conflagration ensued. He was answered immediately by Geoffrey Hardeby, an Austin friar who was in 1356 regent master at Oxford and who soon became prior provincial. In his long treatise *De vita evangelica* Hardeby travelled over the whole area of the controversy.[2] As an Austin friar he was chary of attacking directly the doctrine of Dominion and Grace, but he defended the friars in their use of privilege and their conception of poverty. In his final chapters he travelled outside his brief into another field of strife, the respective claims of the various orders to founders in the remote past, and endeavoured to vindicate for the Austin friars, as against the Austin canons, the bishop of Hippo as their founder. Of this controversy, which gave birth to a small literature of its own, mention has been made in another place.[3]

Meanwhile in the years after 1360—the decade in which Wyclif began his career as teacher and writer, and in which his elder contemporary Uthred of Boldon was at Oxford for his second long period of residence— the area of controversy among the religious was still further extended. Either in answer to further provocation of which nothing is known, or acting on the maxim that attack is the best method of defence, the friars

---

1 Books 1–4 were published by R. L. Poole in his edition of Wyclif's *De Dominio Divino*.
2 Gwynn, *op. cit.* 71. 3 *Supra*, p. 52.

began to take the offensive in academic circles with attacks upon the endowed religious bodies, known in the phrase of the day as 'possessioners'; these were the older orders of monks and canons, among whom, in a dispute of this kind, the greatest and richest houses, such as Durham, Canterbury and Glastonbury, were obviously the most vulnerable. Among the leaders of this attack was the Franciscan John Hilton, who 'determined' on the question of apostolic poverty and was 'opposed' by Uthred. Whether the Durham theologian was first in the field on parchment, or whether he did no more than riposte to an attack is not certain, but in the years around 1365 he composed two or possibly three treatises against the 'mendicancy' (i.e. the dependence upon alms) of the friars, and against their views on ecclesiastical endowments, for it would seem that the Minors at least had gone beyond a criticism of monastic property-holders to an attack, almost in the spirit of the *fraticelli*, on church possessions in general.

This attack had indeed far wider implications than were originally foreseen by the Minors, for in addition to the disquisitions of the theologians on Lordship and Grace, and the theories of the friars on the value of absolute poverty, the title of the clergy and the older orders of religious to their great possessions had been shaken by another class of critics, the secularist and anti-papal controversialists. Chief among these in logical ruthlessness, though perhaps not the most widely influential, was Marsilius of Padua, who in his *Defensor pacis* (1324) had drawn in firm outline what would now be called the autonomous secular state, in which organized religion was a subordinate function or department of government, while the traditional Church and its activities, professedly relegated to the purely spiritual, super-social sphere, was in fact urbanely reduced to nonentity. In this view it was illogical and harmful for the Church to own independent property: the rulers had complete ownership, with the task of giving sustenance and no more to the clergy and religious. In phrases which echo the doctrines of the austere party of the Minors on the subject of papal ownership of their goods and the *usus pauper*, Marsilius explains the benefits that will come from the entire abandonment of the right to property into the hands of the lay power.

From a somewhat different angle the contemporary and sometime ally of Marsilius, William of Ockham, arrived at conclusions less explicitly subversive of the existing state of society but perhaps of almost equal dissolvent power on a long view. Penetrated as he was by a hatred of the wealth and luxury of the papal court and holding as he did the strict theories of his party, he was the enemy of all wealthy religious corporations. Just as he seems to have felt that all authority within the Church existed solely for the common good and could be judged by its degree of care for this, so the common good or common danger of a people might demand the partial or total confiscation of the goods of wealthy churchmen. Ockham, indeed, went out of his way in 1338–40 to write a small tract maintaining that the king of England could rightly, even without papal authority, confiscate some of the possessions of the Church to implement the war against France.[1] How far his views passed beyond academic circles cannot be accurately decided; within those circles they were most influential.

The champion of the 'possessioners' in the controversy with the mendicants was Uthred of Boldon. His determination against Hilton would seem to have been preserved, at least in general, in his treatise *De dotacione ecclesie sponse Christi*.[2] This is an elaborate defence of church endowment by means of arguments drawn from history and Scripture, and the writer is at pains to combat the mendicant teaching on the poverty of Christ and His apostles. Concurrently with his direct attack upon the friars Uthred was acting as apologist for the clergy on a more theoretical and academic level. Considerable uncertainty still exists as to the dating of his treatise, *De naturali et necessaria connexione ac ordine sacerdotalis officii et regalis*,[3] but it seems probable that it was composed before his departure from Oxford in 1367. The principal concern of the writer is to establish the priority and superiority of the priesthood as against the kingly office, both being of divine institution. The priesthood, Uthred concludes, has authority over all, but it is noteworthy that he never refers to the papacy by name, although in the passage from the *Eulogium Historiarum* mentioned on an earlier page he answers the chancellor's question on the papal claims with a sermon on the text: 'Lo, here are two swords,' proving that Peter had both spiritual and temporal power. This in turn was followed by a shorter tract, *Contra garrulos fratrum dotacionem ecclesie impugnantes*.[4] This is a shorter and more practical answer to the false brethren who are stirring up lay lords to take away the temporal possessions of the Church, and who suggested that religious houses can rightly be deprived of goods given them. Uthred in reply maintains that gifts of this kind are made to God and not to man, and that God can never forfeit His rights to the gift; that the donor had received a *quid pro quo* in the form of spiritual benefits, and that therefore the transaction is complete and irrevocable. Neither can it be annulled by any earthly court, for God is a party concerned, and no earthly power can have jurisdiction over Him. Moreover, gifts given in pure alms imply a renunciation of all rights in their regard, and gifts which have become sanctified cannot be claimed back by secular owners. This short treatise, though scholastic in form and clearly intended for an academic reader, is a workmanlike and sensible contribution to a living issue. The gist of the argument, that a gift given to an ecclesiastical cause

---

1 The treatise *An rex Angliae pro succursu guerrae possit recipere bona ecclesiarum* was published by R. Scholz, *Unbekannte kirchenpolitische Streitschriften*, II, 432.

2 This has not been printed but exists in typescript, in a Manchester M.A. thesis by C. H. Thompson, taken from Durham, Dean and Chapter Library, MS. A III, 57, 69^r–99^v.

3 The same MS., 24^r–64^v.

4 The same MS., 99^v–110^r. For a description of these MSS. and other fragments *v.* M. E. Marcett, *Uthred de Boldon*, 70–1; the tract is printed there, 25–37.

is given to God, not man, and is therefore irrevocable, and that the donor has received a recompense in the spiritual sphere, is a sane and valid one. It is worth noting that Uthred in these treatises accepts the Aegidian doctrine of Dominion and Grace, though he does not regard it as of importance.

Uthred's activity on behalf of the possessioners drew no less a person than John Wyclif into the lists, with a determination against his treatise on the relationship of the priestly and royal offices. This document, which opens with a respectful address to his opponent, is equally academic and formal, but Wyclif followed it up with a second part addressed to William Binham, a monk of St Albans, who had attacked him with less restraint than Uthred. In this, after a long formal argument, he interrupts his exposition of the thesis with the well-known report of the opinions of seven lay lords, alleged to have been given in a royal council on the subject of the papal claims to lordship in England.[1]

Though academic in origin and form the treatises of Uthred and Wyclif make it clear that the attacks on the possessioners were passing from the theoretical to the practical plane, and that Wyclif, who had taken over from Fitzralph the doctrine of Dominion and Grace, was making a common front with the friars against the monks.

II. MENDICANTS AND POSSESSIONERS

The controversy between the mendicants and the possessioners, which, like the concurrent theological issue between Uthred and the friars, had been for several years an academic and almost a domestic question that affected only the parties concerned, had become, shortly before 1370, a living, practical issue. The change in its nature, which was not without effect upon the subsequent course of ecclesiastical policy in England, was due in the main to two causes: the emergence of the controversy over the right to endowment of the Church as a matter of practical politics; and the entrance of Wyclif into the lists as the opponent of the possessioners.

English kings ever since the Conquest had always in practice maintained their right of mulcting the Church in a national emergency, and despite the stand made by the papacy and the episcopate during the pontificate of Boniface VIII the kings had usually had their way. From that time, also, there had been attempts even in England to justify the practice as flowing from an indefeasible right. There had, however, never been a widespread and influential anti-clerical movement such as began to appear shortly before 1370. Discontent with the sordid, unsuccessful and costly war with France, and dissatisfaction on the part of lay magnates with the freedom from taxation enjoyed by the clergy and the freedom from control of great clerical ministers such as William of Wykeham the

1 These two tracts are printed from Paris B.N. Cod. Lat. 3184 by J. Loserth, in his edition of Wyclif's *Opera Minora*, 405–14; 415–30.

Chancellor and Thomas Brantyngham the Treasurer were now added to the secularist and anti-clerical doctrines of Marsilius and Ockham, which had penetrated, or at least reached, educated and political circles some years earlier; this reinforced the propaganda of the friars against such religious as professed poverty, being themselves rich. The support of lay magnates, anxious to ease their own burdens, for what had hitherto been simply a plea of government eager for funds, resulted in the rise of a party which demanded not only heavy taxation of the clergy, but a measure at least of confiscation as well. This party, which owed its programme remotely to the secularist writings of Marsilius and Ockham, drew much of its direct inspiration from the friars and from Wyclif. Here, as in more than one phase of his activity, Wyclif gave a decisive turn to affairs both by leaping, so to say, the academic fence, and by continuing in his course even though ecclesiastical censure on the one hand, and social dislocation on the other, might result from his action.

When Wyclif wrote his rejoinders to Uthred and Binham in 1366 or 1367 the controversy was still being conducted on the purely academic plane. In the years that followed, however, Wyclif continued to develop and publish his views on the polity of the Church and its right to endowment in his treatises *De dominio divino* and *De civili dominio*. In both of these his theory of Lordship and Grace appeared, and in the latter it was maintained in all its logical austerity: those in mortal sin are incapable of lordship; those in grace have dominion over all creation.[1] When the institutional Church in the person of its representatives falls from grace, the secular power has the right and duty of disendowing it.[2] Some of the friars, also, and in particular the Austin Friars, were in the forefront of those who were making the issue a practical one. This is strikingly corroborated from what we know of the proceedings of the Parliament of 1371. At that meeting a warm debate took place on the liability of the clergy to pay their fair share in easing the national stringency. In support of the move to mulct the possessioners and the clergy a number of articles[3] were submitted to parliament, the work of two Austin friars, one of them John Bankyn, and it was probably on this occasion that one of the lords of parliament retailed the old fable of the owl who, when featherless, had been charitably provided with feathers by the other birds; these, when the approach of the hawk stimulated flight, demanded their feathers back again, leaving the owl once more wretched.[4]

We are not concerned with the further political moves, which were less the result of a general movement, and derived chiefly from the more violent party of the Lollards. The controversy had, however, important consequences in other quarters, and in particular in the career of Wyclif. Until 1367 the conservative view had been defended by Uthred of

---

1 Wyclif, *De civili dominio*, ed. R. L. Poole, I, cc. 1–14.   2 *Ibid.* I, c. 37.
3 Printed with introduction by V. H. Galbraith in *EHR*, xxxiv (1919), 579–82.
4 Wyclif, *De civili dominio*, II, c. 7; Workman, *John Wyclif*, I, 210.

Boldon, but he was now at Durham concerned with other things and perhaps even under a cloud in academic circles. His mantle had, however, fallen upon another black monk. Adam Easton, of the cathedral priory of Norwich, was at Oxford at least as early as 1356–7 and in 1366 was *prior studentium* at Gloucester College.[1] He must therefore have known well both Uthred and his activities, as well as Wyclif. He tells us himself that from the beginning of his academic career he had realized the importance of the secularist attack upon the Church, and had embarked upon a long and exacting course of studies, which included the acquisition of Hebrew and which was prolonged for twenty years, in order to be able to compose a solid work of apologetics. From 1370 onwards he was at Avignon, perhaps as proctor of the English presidents, and certainly taking part in curial activities while he continued to compose his treatise. To him, in 1376, came alarming reports of the writings of Wyclif directed against the black monks and their interests; the source of these reports is not known, but possibly is to be found in the Westminster monks who came to the Curia in connexion with the estate of Simon Langham, of whom Easton was one of the executors. In any case, it was to the abbot of Westminster, at that time one of the presidents, that he wrote, asking for a copy of Wyclif's writings.[2] As he requested the abbot to use his influence in the order for this purpose, as a chronicler points to Oxford as the source, and as Wyclif refers to the youth of those who secretly delated his writings, it seems clear that the students of Gloucester College were responsible for giving Adam Easton the copy of Wyclif's writings for which he asked, and it seems fairly clear that they sent him more than he asked, and included Wyclif's determinations on the Church and the Eucharist.

Meanwhile the young and energetic bishop of London, William Courtenay, who had witnessed Wyclif's incursions into political life and activities in London, had summoned him to appear in St Paul's Cathedral on 19 February 1377, before himself and Sudbury, the archbishop of Canterbury, to answer for his views. Wyclif was able, under the patronage of John of Gaunt, to produce four friars, one from each of the great orders, to support his opinions, thus providing us with evidence that his teaching was still regarded as tenable by the orthodox, and that the division in academic circles was still between Wyclif and the friars on the one hand, and the possessioners on the other.[3] As is well known, the

1 For Easton, *v.* W. A. Pantin, 'The *Defensorium* of Adam Easton' and *supra*, pp. 56–8.

2 *MC*, III, 76–7: 'Suppliciter vestram paternitatem et cordialiter interpello quatenus per studentes vestros possim habere copiam dictorum cuiusdam magistri Johannis Wyclyf, que contra ordinem nostrum sicut dicitur in Oxonia seminavit.' This is a curiously hesitant reference to Wyclif on the part of one who had been *prior studentium* in 1366, if not later; it may indicate that Wyclif did not take part with the monks against the friars much before that date. Wyclif's reference (*De ecclesia*, 354) to a 'canis niger' and his whelps suits well enough with Adam Easton's request for help from monks at Gloucester College.

3 For these events *v.* Workman, *John Wyclif*, I, 286 *seqq.* The names of the friars are not known.

judicial process turned into a brawl, which merged into a political riot which had had other origins, and judgement was never passed. Within three months, however, Gregory XI, doubtless incited by Adam Easton, submitted Wyclif's teaching to a commission of cardinals and on 22 May issued bulls to king, archbishop, and the university of Oxford in which he condemned eighteen propositions taken from the fifty delated to the Curia and called on the prelates and the university to take firm action. Edward III died within a month, and though the relevant bull was re-directed to the new king no promulgation took place till 18 December. The university of Oxford acted half-heartedly and the bishops were prevented by the king's mother from giving a final judgement. Wyclif's opinions were officially suppressed without formal condemnation; and their author still protested his submission to the pope, even after the disputed election which opened the Great Schism.

Yet although Wyclif may have announced his readiness to submit, 1378 and the following year were in fact the season of the parting of the ways. In his Oxford lectures on the Church and the Eucharist in those years he clearly crossed the boundaries of orthodoxy, wide as was the freedom accorded to academic disputants, and severe as had been the criticism of the papacy by the majority of English spokesmen in recent years. Before the divide had been reached more than one friar had been a friend as well as a colleague of Wyclif at Oxford. Thomas Winterton, regent master at Oxford *c.* 1372, and later (1387–93) prior provincial of the Austin friars, was one such. Another was William Wodeford the Franciscan, a distinguished doctor and controversialist, and the master of Thomas Netter. Others, possibly without relations of personal friendship, were respectful hearers of his teaching: such were Adam Stocton, *lector* of the Austin friars at Cambridge in the seventies, and John Kenningham (*not* Cunningham), confessor of John of Gaunt and provincial of the Carmelites from 1393. The friendship and respect of these men did not prevent them from joining issue with Wyclif, either early or late. Wodeford, who had lectured on the Sentences simultaneously with him when both were bachelors, relates how the two had interchanged lecture-notes and how, even thus early, he had challenged Wyclif's Eucharistic doctrine, while Wyclif tells us of their disagreement on the scope of authority in Church and State. Kenningham, as early as 1373, had attacked Wyclif's extreme realism, but all his references are courteously addressed to 'my reverend master'. Equally deferential was the early language of Adam Stocton when he spoke of the 'venerable doctor master John'. Of all the friars the Carmelites seem to have been the most determined opponents when Wyclif's teaching on the Eucharist became clear, and Adam Stocton altered the *venerabilis doctor* of his comment on Wyclif's anti-papal argument to *execrabilis seductor*.

Wyclif's teaching, as has been said, was delated to Pope Gregory XI in 1376–7 by the monk of Norwich, Adam Easton, and was condemned forthwith. In the years immediately following the characteristic Wyclifite doctrines appeared in full strength in the treatises *De ecclesia* (1378), *De potestate papae* (1378) and *De eucharistia* (1380). It was the last of these that drew from William Wodeford his lengthy reply *De sacramento altaris*. It was also probably the occasion of the condemnation of Wyclif's teaching by the council at Oxford summoned by the Mertonian chancellor, William Berton, in 1380/1. Here, as in the more solemn condemnations that followed, we have the names of those present, and can trace the influence of the friars. Berton's council was made up of four seculars and eight regulars; the latter were Henry Crump, the restless Irish Cistercian, John Wellys, monk of Ramsey, three Preachers, and one from each of the other three orders.[1] Although, if Wyclif's account is to be trusted, he was condemned only by seven votes to five, it is very probable that at least five of the friars were against him, as the seculars may presumably be counted his friends. It would be interesting to know if the friars from the order of Austin Hermits, hitherto friendly to him, voted in his favour. We know only that he was lecturing in the school of the Austin friars, and precisely on the Eucharist in the sense of his propositions, when the news of his condemnation reached him.

Wyclif replied to the condemnation with his *Confessio*, and this in turn drew from the Franciscan, John Tyssington, one of his judges, and from the Austin friar, Thomas Winterton, instant rejoinders. The rubicon had now been crossed, and though Wyclif, in his *De apostasia* of 1381, made a last earnest appeal to the friars to join with him in the fight for truth, begging his 'dear sons' not to turn back through cowardice or worldly wisdom, the tone of the whole treatise is hostile to the four orders in their existing state.[2]

Within a few months the Peasants' Revolt broke out. Though not in fact desired or supported by Wyclif, he was accused by the friars and others of having supported it through the agency of his disciples, and on 17 May 1382, William Courtenay, now archbishop of Canterbury, held his celebrated 'Earthquake' synod at the Blackfriars. Among the ordinaries present were two regulars, both old opponents of the accused: John Gilbert of Hereford, a Dominican, and Thomas Brunton of Rochester, a Norwich confrère of Adam Easton; another Dominican, William Bottisham, was present as suffragan of William of Wykeham. Of the seventeen doctors of theology present besides the bishops all were regulars and all, save for the monk John Wellys, were mendicants.[3] Their distribution was symmetrical: four from each order, and of the four two from Oxford and two from Cambridge save in the case of the Austin friars, where only one was a Cambridge man. It was a strong panel:

1 Workman, *John Wyclif*, II, 142 *seqq.* Very useful notes and references are given for the friars and others concerned in the trial.
2 Cf. *De apostasia*, ed. Dziewicki.
3 Workman, *John Wyclif*, II, 246 *seqq.*, for notes on individuals.

alongside of Robert Waldeby, the tutor of Richard II and later (after no less than three translations) archbishop of York, were Walter Diss the Carmelite, a well-known preacher and confessor of John of Gaunt, John Bankyn the Austin friar, who had as his colleague from Oxford Thomas Ashbourne, who with him had presented the petition for disendowment to parliament in 1371. Among the Preachers was William Siward, confessor to Edward III; of the Minors the most eminent was John Kenningham, the preacher and controversialist. Besides the doctors there were seven bachelors, of whom all save John Bloxham, the Warden of Merton, were friars; three were Dominicans, among them William Pickworth the prior provincial. It was indeed a notable gathering, of which almost every member, if not yet distinguished, attained sooner or later to some kind of name in the ecclesiastical life of the day. Wyclif might call it in reproach a 'council of friars'; the historian is more interested in the evidence it supplies that, whatever might be the general abuse of the friars, when an archbishop of Canterbury needed expert theological advice in the cause of orthodoxy, it was to the friars he turned.

Condemned by such a galaxy of talent Wyclif broke into his bitterest vein. Henceforward friars appear in the story at every turn, just as two centuries before, Cistercians had risen from every bush to plague Gerald of Wales. One such was Peter Stokes the Carmelite, red-faced and white-cloaked, who had earned the name of 'white dog' from Wyclif, and who had been fighting Nicholas Hereford for a whole year at Oxford.[1] Now he was detailed by Courtenay to prevent the heretical sermon of the young Austin canon, Philip Repyndon, at Oxford on Corpus Christi Day, 1382. He was opposed by an obstructive chancellor, Rigg, and by young artists who threatened violence, and according to his own story was lucky to escape with his life. In consequence, Courtenay held a second synod at Blackfriars on 12 June, for the benefit of the Oxford chancellor, and a second condemnation of Wyclif's doctrines followed. The composition of the panel of theologians was largely the same as before, but there were notable additions: two monks of St Albans, Simon Sutherey and Nicholas Radcliffe, both doctors; the celebrated Dominican preacher, John Bromyard, and the young Carmelite bachelor, Stephen Patrington, who was to have a distinguished career. Twenty-four conclusions were condemned, and Courtenay and the friars combined to impose silence on the secular masters of Oxford, who were still restive.

With these events the story of the Lollards, the development of the school of divinity at Oxford, and the activities of the friars and monastic doctors all entered upon a new phase. The days of care-free academic discussion and debate were over; what might have remained opinions of the lecture-room had been preached to all and sundry and had been

---

1 So Bale, *Illustrium maioris Britanniae Scriptorum Catalogus*, I, 496; cf. *Political Poems and Songs*, ed. T. Wright, I, 261: 'Rufus naturaliter et veste dealbatus.' Wyclif's 'canis niger', with face 'yellow as gall', was Dom John Wellys of Ramsey (*Sermons*, III, 246).

translated into what seemed to the orthodox teachers to be explosive and subversive tenets; the friars had joined together in defence of threatened tradition, and the possessioners, threatened by social as well as by dogmatic revolution, had made common cause with them. For more than thirty years all the academic talent of the religious orders was engaged in the attack on Lollardy, and the distinguished friars were no longer speculative disputants, but controversialists and writers of topical treatises.

CHAPTER VI

TRENDS IN THEOLOGY: OCKHAMISM, JUSTIFICATION AND GRACE

About the middle of the fourteenth century a very real change took place in the interests and outlook of philosophers and theologians at the English universities. The early decades of the century had been for Oxford as for Paris a time of criticism and eclectic thought. The age of the absorption and interpretation of Aristotle had come to an end with the Paris condemnations of 1277, which followed hard upon the deaths of Bonaventure and Aquinas, and the early death of Duns Scotus in 1308 had taken from the scene the last great builder of a system embracing the whole of philosophy and theology. The acutest minds of the years immediately following were mainly engaged in criticizing, blending or prolonging certain important features of one or other of the great thinkers of the preceding generations, or in elaborating particular aspects of philosophy and theology. There was a noticeable drift away from metaphysics and natural theology, and a tendency to separate the realms of faith and reason. The change, however, was slow and not abnormal, and took place at a similar rate both at Paris and Oxford, which continued as the two great international centres to attract and interchange students and masters. Shortly before the middle of the century, however, two changes occurred, the one in the realm of ideas, the other in that of events, which profoundly modified this state of things. In the realm of ideas there was produced the original thought of William of Ockham; in the realm of events the Hundred Years War with France, which began in the last months of 1337, began that process of isolation that was to make England once again a self-contained and insular intellectual region. The process was slow and the isolation was never complete, but it is true to say that from 1350 onwards the masters of Oxford and Cambridge pursued their own interests and engaged in purely provincial controversies with little relation to anything that was happening in Paris.

The phases and movements of thought in the schools of Oxford and Cambridge during the fourteenth century are discernible only in part and can as yet be described only with the greatest hesitation. One reason for this is that the works of the theologians of that period have not yet been published and studied as fully as have those of the so-called 'golden age' of scholasticism. A second reason is the form of expression adopted by these thinkers. In the thirteenth century the leading masters either wrote in the clear rhetorical style and used the traditional vocabulary that had descended from Augustine through the Victorines and others (of which style Bonaventure is a notable exponent), or else made use of a drier and more technical treatment (as did Aquinas) which nevertheless followed very closely the scheme and terminology of Aristotle's writings. In the fourteenth century, on the other hand, a series of thinkers, beginning with the great Duns Scotus, made use of ideas and methods for which a new vocabulary of technical terms was necessary, while they redefined old concepts in a new way. Finally, Ockham, when his day came, employed methods of thought and expression which, however traditional he may have considered and intended them to be, did in fact effect a revolution in logic comparable to that brought about by Einstein in the realm of Newtonian physics.

More fundamental, however, than either of these two reasons for the difficulty experienced in interpreting these writings is the direction taken by their speculation. All the great scholastics up to and including Duns Scotus had worked in their different ways at the task of elucidating and formulating with greater precision the vast corpus of theology, the deposit of the faith, handed down in the Scriptures and the writings of the Fathers, the pronouncements of popes and councils, and the decisions of 'authorities' such as the Victorines and Peter Lombard. Whatever their disagreements, they are at one in the acceptance of the wisdom of the past. Archbishop Pecham, indeed, could write in 1285 in a moment of irritation, that the concert had been broken, and that Preachers and Minors were at odds all along the line, but he hastened to add 'save in matters of faith', and indeed in the light of subsequent events the points at issue between Thomists and 'Augustinians' seem indeed peripheral. But from the early years of the fourteenth century the speculative theologians abandoned the task of expression and elucidation for that of subjecting many of the basic ideas and propositions to a philosophical criticism and restatement. God, His attributes and His dealings with creatures; grace, predestination and free will, were no longer examined in an endeavour to understand and explain the Scriptures and tradition, but were treated as topics to be freely discussed in an exacting dialectical process, often with the help of novel concepts and of new meanings attached to old terms. The theological writings of the fourteenth century therefore no longer pass over familiar ground where the feet can rest firmly on the authorities of old, but move in a rarer atmosphere, half theological, half logical, from which the lights of Christian theology—God the Father of all and Christ, the Brother, the Master, the Redeemer—have disappeared, and in their place is a God of illimitable, indefinable power, whose action is so unpredictable as to fall outside the sphere of attention.

The departure from the traditional topics and methods was emphasized by the frequent employment, with a new extension, of a time-honoured traditional distinction: that between the 'absolute' power of God, and his normal use of that power in His 'ordained' or established economy. In the past theologians had considered the normal action of God in human affairs, as known from reason and revelation, to be the subject of their study and argument, while the 'absolute' power was indeed to be safeguarded with reverence, but could be left out of the reckoning. Gradually this position was reversed. Theologians from Scotus onwards, largely through their emphasis on what has been called the 'primacy of the will' in theodicy, gave more and more attention to the possible use by God of His absolute power, until the realm of the absolute becomes their only interest. All the elaborate hierarchy of means and laws—the clumsy but indispensable method by which the human mind can express the fragmentation of eternal Truth—disappears from sight, and the incomprehensible, illimitable power of God alone remains. The results of this were felt in particular in the theology of grace, of the theological virtues, and of merit. The elaborate scheme of supernatural virtues and gifts, together with grace itself, fades from view, and only the free and absolute will of God remains. A corollary of this outlook, in a slightly different sphere, was a new use of the distinction between man as a member of the visible Church, and man as the immediate dependant of God. The distinction between the laws and judgements of human agents and those of God had always been fruitfully made: it had always been admitted, for example, that a sentence of excommunication, or the refusal of absolution, might be based on false information or unjust motives, and might therefore remain unratified by God, but hitherto He had been regarded, so to say, as a judge in equity and of second instance, readjusting errors due to the frailty of accredited agents or to the hardship of laws normally just. Now, if the comparison may be allowed, God was becoming the Immediate Universal Ordinary, overriding at His own will and pleasure the normal working of His laws for creatures and for His Church. Thus, as will be seen, an orthodox theologian, while admitting the necessity of baptism from the point of view of the visible Church, could maintain that God, of His absolute power, gave to all and sundry an alternative, unseen means of salvation. When all was thus, in a sense, uncertain, it was only a stage to pass by the whole economy of salvation and grace as something that could not be grasped or formulated, and to concentrate on what could be seen and known by man's unaided powers: to adopt a kind of theological positivism: and this step was in fact taken very generally.

This attitude of mind was encouraged by the tendency of all contemporary theologians to move away from a universe governed by the Divine Reason to one resulting from the Divine Will. Ever since Christian thinkers had turned to Greek philosophy for a rational statement of the world of being, the material universe and the universe of spirit had alike been regarded as reflecting in their ordered harmony the eternal Truth of God, seen in a manifestation of reason and law. This attitude had in the thirteenth century received full and precise expression in the theologians who took Aristotle, the philosopher of reason and order, as their master, and above all in Aquinas, whose celebrated treatment of Law is perhaps the clearest expression of the idea: created being, the work and the reflexion of Uncreated Being, follows the immutable law of God in its varying modes and degrees; all creatures are as they are because God has seen them in Himself and willed them to exist outside Himself.

This doctrine in St Thomas was a wholly spiritual conception, but in its application to the universe it rested upon an Aristotelian basis, and to those who looked only to its foundations it appeared an almost mechanistic, predetermined, self-contained structure to which God was no more than a First Cause, an unmoved Mover. Aristotelian determinism had indeed been taught in the lifetime of Aquinas by the radical Aristotelians of Paris; it had been condemned by Bishop Tempier in 1277 and had gone near to taking Thomism with it in its fall. Thenceforward, there had been a rejection of anything savouring of determinism, or of an attitude which regarded God as the servant, so to say, of His own laws; especially was this so among the Franciscans, and Duns Scotus in particular had stressed the divine liberty. God's beneficent Will, rather than His directive Reason, was regarded as the cause of all things and their guiding norm. Scotus, however, was a great traditional theologian, to whom God's will was primarily His all-embracing, creative, outgoing Love. For many of those who came after, this rich and genial teaching gave place to a purely schematic conception of the divine Will as pure Liberty. This almost inevitably had a twofold result, especially when it was combined with the Ockhamist teaching on knowledge: on the one hand God's liberty, being bound by no law, not even by His own (for His knowledge was regarded as a function of His will), could everywhere dispense with any of His ordinary means of enriching or rewarding his creatures, thereby rendering superfluous the traditional structure of supernatural habits and virtues, and even grace and merit themselves: secondly, given this divine liberty, theodicy, the study of God and His ways with man, was something so flexible and undetermined that it was useless to devote energy to its consideration; the theologian's task was with what could be seen of men's actions. Thus, under the plea of honouring God's liberty, He was for all practical purposes left out of sight.

Side by side with this causal indeterminism, and undoubtedly influencing its development, was the theory of knowledge which it is perhaps best to call Ockhamism,[1] since the name of Nominalism or

1 As all recent studies of Ockham have criticized or qualified the notions previously current of his Nominalist teaching, it is perhaps in the interests of clarity to refer to the complex of tendencies deriving from him as 'Ockhamism' rather than to use a more question-begging name. Here, moreover, we are concerned with theology rather than epistemology or logic, and in this field the critical and dissolvent tendency of his thought remains, whether he was in fact a 'Nominalist' or not. The only general sketch of fourteenth-century philosophy which takes account of recent work is that of M. de Wulf, *Histoire de Philosophie Médiévale*, III, but there are many assertions and judgements in this work which must be received with caution, as they are based on insufficient evidence. The picture of this period has been radically transformed within the past few years, and the process is continuing. This circumstance has unfortunately antiquated the relevant sections in Ueberweg-Geyer, *Grundrisse*, II, which, excellent as they are, are now more than twenty-five years out of date. Ockham has received much attention in the past few years, but it will be many more before

Terminism predetermines its character. Ockham has often been considered a philosophical sceptic, or at least as denying any connexion between the mind and extra-mental reality. His recent expositors deny this, and it would seem with reason. Yet the only knowledge of extra-mental reality, in Ockham's view, was the intuition of the individual; the function of the intellect was not, as with Thomist Aristotelianism, to abstract the essence from being outside itself, but to work with the term or sign which the mind attached to the objects of which it had intuition. This, however, eliminated the conception of the universe of being as an ordered whole, sharing in its different degrees the contingent being given to it by the Subsistent Being, as it also eliminated the Thomist analogical knowledge of God's perfections. The human mind could not rise to a valid knowledge of God as First Cause or Final End or Supreme Exemplar; God, therefore, was attained by faith alone; knowledge was limited to the individual objects of which the mind had experience. Consequently, for Ockham the philosopher and speculative theologian, God remained, as has been aptly said, 'outside his terms of reference'; although admitted as ever-present, His influence is indeterminate, and cannot enter into the argument.

Ockham's theory of knowledge thus chimed in with the doctrine of divine liberty which he took from his predecessors. Already from the time of Duns Scotus theologians had been giving greater attention than before to the problems connected with justification and grace.[1] Whereas the great doctors of the thirteenth century, such as Aquinas and Bonaventure, had been principally concerned to define and analyse the gifts and graces and virtues with which the Christian's soul was adorned, and to consider grace as a quality of the soul, the principle of the new life with Christ in God, there had been a tendency from Scotus onwards to identify it with 'charity', the supernatural love of God, and then to regard it either as merely another name for the Holy Spirit, the Spirit of Love, or proceeding still further, to consider grace as a mere relationship to God or even simply as the state of one whom God had chosen to love. At the same time the 'voluntarist' theologians of the school of Scotus, who was followed here by Ockham, laid stress both on the absolute freedom and liberality of God, and on the freedom of the human will; by so doing they came on the one hand to admit the possibility of God's accepting and saving one still actually sinful, while on the other hand their optimistic view of human nature—or, to speak more precisely, of human beings and their powers of love and choice—led them to minimize the part played by

a definitive judgement can be passed. In the meanwhile articles 'Nominalisme' and 'Occam' by J. Vignaux in *DTC* should be consulted, and, for the spread of Ockhamism, F. Ehrle, *Der Sentenzenkommentar Peters von Candia*.

1 For this, *v.* the excellent study of J. Vignaux, *Justification et Prédestination au xive siècle*. Cf. also the various writings of K. Michalski, especially *Le problème de la volonté à Oxford et à Paris au xive siècle*; but the reader of these may be reminded that subsequent research has revised a number of Michalski's findings.

God in the work of salvation. Ockham himself, indeed, went very far in denying the absolute necessity of forgiveness of sin as part of the process of justification, and in considering habitual grace little more than a right relationship of a man to God, while in emphasizing the part played by free will he came very near to (if indeed he did not completely reach) what theologians were agreed to call semi-Pelagianism.[1] He was led to this by his preoccupation with the absolute liberty of God and his unwillingness to admit the existence of any power or quality of which the mind had no immediate experience. God can do anything, as He wills and without means. Grace as a created entity and quality of the soul, the supernatural virtues as habits, cannot be established by any proof as existing or necessary, and God can in fact dispense with them.[2] Therefore, on the principle of economy, they may be neglected in the theologian's calculations. With grace and the virtues gone, and God's power illimitable and unconditioned, Ockham was in this realm also interested only in what could be known as matter of experience, the human volition. The human act alone interests him; it is the pre-condition of all merit and reprobation; it must be performed before God can accept it and thereby render it meritorious; God's will alone makes one deed good and another bad; of themselves they are merely acts.[3] Regarded merely as agents, it is clear that men can do anything; they can even love God above all else and keep all His commandments.

This relegation of God to a place of honour outside the sphere of thought has an important consequence—if indeed it is not itself the consequence of an existing disposition in the mind of the thinker. God is no longer the only Reality, the source and giver of all life and light, who raises His creatures by a new birth of grace to a share in His own divine life by fellowship with Christ. This is, indeed, for a theologian the head and front of Ockham's offending; it would remain even if the charges of philosophical scepticism were shown to be groundless.

In his earliest work at Oxford, composed between 1318 and 1325, Ockham had clearly outlined his theological position,[4] and had given to grace a definition which drained out all the rich content of traditional teaching and gave to the human free will an independence that struck at

---

1 For Ockham on grace v. also article 'Occam', by J. Vignaux in *DTC*, and G. de Lagarde, *La Naissance de l'Esprit laïque*, VI, 77–88.

2 So many reserves and technicalities lie behind Ockham's statements that little is conveyed by isolated quotations, but two may perhaps be given. 'Ideo dico... quod aliquis potest esse deo acceptus et charus sine omni forma supernaturali in anima' (*In Sent.* I, dist. XVII, q. I). 'Deus potest aliquem acceptare in puris naturalibus, tanquam dignum vita eterna, sine omni habitu charitatis' (*ibid.* III, dist. XIII c).

3 'Deus potest acceptare actum naturalis dilectionis sicut quemcumque alium actum elicitum mediante charitate' (*In Sent.* III, q. 5). 'Nihil est meritorium nisi quod est in nostra potestate, ergo actus non est meritorius principaliter propter illam gratiam, sed propter voluntatem libere causantem, ergo posset Deus talem actum elicitum a voluntate acceptare sine gratia' (*Quodlibetum*, VI, q. I).

4 L. Baudry, *Guillaume d'Occam; sa vie, etc.* By 1323 Ockham had composed his Commentary on the Sentences, his Quodlibets, and almost all his theological work.

the roots of the theology of grace. The contemporary authorities at
Oxford, and the masters who examined his works with vexatious slowness
at Avignon, considered that he gave to free will and not to grace the role
of chief agent in human good actions, and that by so doing he incurred the
charge of falling into the heresy with which medieval theologians who
knew their Augustine were most familiar, that of Pelagius.[1] It was realized
at Oxford that he was not alone, nor the first to lean towards this dangerous
doctrine, and there was a widespread desire that the movement should be
stemmed. The great Mertonian, Thomas Bradwardine, who had been
proctor of the University of Oxford when John Luttrell, Ockham's first
adversary, was chancellor, was approached with a request for aid.[2]
Bradwardine was a deeply religious man, who at a crisis of his own
inner life had been penetrated by a sense of the all-embracing, ever-
present power of God. He had found in Augustine the fullest answer
to the problems of grace and predestination, and like others before and
since he had interpreted the Doctor of Grace according to his own prepossessions.

The whole cast of Bradwardine's mind and personality fitted him to be
the antithesis of Ockham. Each abandoned the lucid balance of natural
and supernatural that had been established by Aquinas. To Ockham as a
thinker human action, and human action in all its freedom, was the concrete reality; God was in the background and supernatural qualities had
only a questionable existence. To Bradwardine God was all. His knowledge embraced all things past, present and future, and by embracing them
determined them. His power as author of grace controlled all men at
every moment, absorbing and all but obliterating their human powers.
To Bradwardine, as to Augustine, man was the individual predestined to
an eternity of glory or foreknown as lost; he was never considered as a
being with a nature and faculties of his own to whom God had given
a supernatural life. To Bradwardine, therefore, Ockham, his forerunners
and his disciples were anathema; they were 'Pelagians', and the term in
Bradwardine's lexicon is little more than one of abuse, and covers all who
in any way limit the supreme dominion of God over His creatures or who
deny reality to the supernatural order. Against them he composed his
great work *De causa Dei adversus Pelagianos*.[3]

Bradwardine nowhere names his opponents, but it has been shown
convincingly that Durand de S. Pourçain, Pierre Auriole, William of
Ockham and Robert Holcot were the principal adversaries engaged, and
that Ockham comprehended in himself all that Bradwardine fought against

1 Cf. A. Pelzer, 'Les 51 articles de Guillaume Occam censurés en Avignon en 1326'.
2 Bradwardine has not yet formed the subject of a full-length study; the articles in *DTC*
(*s.v.* 'Thomas') and *DHG* (*s.v.* 'Bradwardine') are the most recent outlines; the latter is
entirely biographical. Mr G. Leff, of King's College, Cambridge, is at present engaged in
research on Bradwardine and the Pelagians, and I owe to him the quotations from Bradwardine and Holcot, and much else in the above exposition.
3 Bradwardine's *De causa Dei* was first printed by Sir Henry Savile at London in 1618.

most sternly.[1] If, as seems probable, he began writing the *De causa Dei* between 1325 and 1328, that treatise must have been designed as a direct counterblast to Ockham, whose condemnation at Avignon, after three years of delay, took place in 1326, and had been preceded by one at Oxford. Yet despite the great reputation and influential position enjoyed by Bradwardine during the last fourteen years of his life (1335–49), when he was constantly at court or near the king, despite also the compelling power and eloquence of the work itself, no evidence of its immediate influence in England has as yet come to light. This is the more surprising if, as has been said, the traditional date of the completion of the work (1344) is possibly only the date of its final form.[2] For whatever reason, Bradwardine's tremendous artillery made no impression on its target. Not only did 'Pelagianism' and Ockhamism continue to spread, but there is no evidence that any reply was made to Bradwardine or that debates on grace and free will formed any part of the next decade's controversies at Oxford. When Uthred of Boldon's opinions were under examination in 1367, those in which he denied the existence of grace as a quality of the soul were among those left uncensured. In the long run, however, the great Mertonian's influence was so important as to be epoch-making, although, by another of the ironies of history, it was the heresiarchs who borrowed his teaching. Fitzralph knew and admired his work and, through Fitzralph, Wyclif, who drew from *De causa Dei* his determinist principles which were to exercise such a profound influence in after times.

There were thus two main streams of thought in the schools of Oxford between 1330 and 1370: the triumphant invasion of Ockhamism in all its forms and the concentration on the problems of grace and justification.

Ockhamism or, as it is so often called, Nominalism, unlike the teaching of Aquinas or Scotus, was at once a body of doctrine, an attitude of mind, and a new technique of thought. Coming as it did into a mental climate that was already critical and eclectic, it attracted minds of every shade of opinion. Even the Dominicans felt the pull, as may be seen when the essentially Thomist Nicholas Trivet (*ob.* 1320)[3] was followed by the Oxford master Robert Holcot (*ob.* 1349). Holcot was an exact contemporary of Bradwardine, and can be shown to have been ranked by him among the 'Pelagians'.[4] In the realm of epistemology he would seem to have gone beyond Ockham in asserting that the object of knowledge is

1 This has been clearly shown by Leff, in a thesis as yet unpublished.
2 Savile dated the work 1344, following the indication of the *explicit* of his MS. Michalski, *La problème de la volonté*, 236–7, shows that the words 'explicit istud opus...perscriptum Parisius' on such-and-such a date, occur in different codices with different dates. He therefore took *perscriptum* to mean 'copied'. Michalski, however, had failed to take account of three MSS. (Lambeth 32; New College, Oxford, 134; Merton College, Oxford, LXXI) in which the date of writing or publication, as opposed to that of transcription, is given as 1344. This evidence, to which my attention was drawn by Professor E. F. Jacob, seems compelling.   3 *RO*, I, 234.
4 J. Wey, *Medieval Studies*, XI (1949), 219, vindicates Holcot for Oxford.

the proposition in the mind, and not the individual which this proposition represents. In regard to grace and the supernatural he adopts all Ockham's opinions, and draws them out still further. With Holcot, as with Ockham, the absolute power of God is not a speculative hypothesis, contrasted with His known way of acting, but an ever-present possibility more real than the artificial 'ordained' power which can always be superseded—and by this absolute power God can reward where there is no grace or supernatural habit or even love; he can accept purely natural human actions in lieu of merit. Thus man's natural powers are sufficient for loving God, and are worthy of reward. Holcot goes a stage further than Ockham in another way: since God can reward without precedent merit or grace, He can also reward without human action at all: he could even allow men to act without any sense of right or wrong and reward them for it.[1] Here, as in Durand and Ockham, the wheel has come full circle; God's way of acting is so indeterminate, so untrammelled by law, that it cannot come into the reckoning, and we are thrown back on what we see and experience. It is indeed true that Holcot (like Durand and Ockham before him) safeguards all his most alarming assertions by his appeal to God's 'absolute' power, but it is clear that this distinction, like that between the teaching of Aristotle and Christian revelation, or that between 'historical' and 'religious' truth, is a safeguarding formula only. The Ockhamist, like the radical Aristotelian or the extreme Modernist, lives in a mental climate which is not that of traditional Christian theology.

Holcot's contemporary at Oxford, his confrère Crathorn, was equally, though differently, susceptible to the attraction of Ockhamism.[2] Among the Minors a similar tendency can be seen. The relatively strict Scotism of Richard of Conington (*ob.* 1310), John of Reading, William of Nottingham, Robert Cowton and others was replaced by the new thought. One of the first of the school was Ockham's pupil Adam of Woodham (*ob.* 1358), who followed his master in his contempt of natural theology, and went beyond him in the identification of the intellect and the will in God. A pupil of his, John of Rodington (*ob.* 1348), continued the Nominalist tradition.[3]

The Carmelites, who entered the schools some fifty years later than the Minors and Preachers, and who took some time to establish a tradition of learning, did not in the medieval period produce a master of the first eminence, and in consequence were always eclectic in their thought. Their

---

1 To the question: 'an homo ex suis naturalibus sine habitu supernaturali possit diligere Deum super omnia', Holcot answers that there are two conclusions: 'Prima est affirmativa talis. Homo potest ex suis solis naturalibus diligere Deum super omnia.' This he proves by five arguments, and continues: 'Secunda conclusio est ista. Nullus homo potest libere implere preceptum de dilectione Dei super omnia per sola naturalia stante lege quae nunc est.' We may note that the second conclusion, whether operative or not, implies that the ability to love God above all things is merely a question of God's decision; it does not depend upon the intrinsic nature (i.e. supernatural or natural) of the act in itself.

2 M. de Wulf, *Histoire de Philosophie Médiévale*, III, 55–7.

3 *Ibid.* 72–5.

greatest doctor, the English John Baconthorp (*ob.* 1348), was a critical, rather than a constructive theologian. Though the charges of Averroism which have freely been made against him are unjustified, it is equally impossible to see in him a follower of Aquinas. Fifty years after his death, the English Carmelites were to be among the leaders of the orthodox party, but in the interval all that can be seen is a tendency to adopt some of the principal Ockhamist views.[1]

The fourth order, that of the Austin Hermits, had remained longer than the rest uncontaminated by Nominalism. Its first distinguished master, Giles of Rome, who had been a pupil and remained in essentials a disciple, of Aquinas, was accepted as the authority for the schools of the order, and in the middle of the fourteenth century Thomas of Strassburg, a great theologian who ultimately became prior general, was responsible for decrees forbidding Ockhamism to the Austin friars. It is true that Thomas's successor, Gregory of Rimini, adopted several of the Nominalist positions, but he was at the same time an ardent anti-Pelagian and supporter of the strictest Augustinian teaching on grace and free will.[2]

Finally, the secular masters of Oxford, of whom the most notable were the group of Mertonians, while devoting much of their attention to logic and mathematics were, like their other contemporaries, eclectic and in some respects influenced by Nominalism.[3]

All this evidence, scanty though it is and must remain till much further research has been accomplished, shows that Ockhamism had penetrated into all the schools of Oxford and Cambridge, though many of the elements of Scotism existed in combination or competition with it. Above all, the general impression remains of an academic society which lacked both the impulse of creative thought and the ability to judge all things by the acquired wisdom of the past. In the only two Oxford theologians whom we can see at all clearly between Bradwardine and Thomas Netter— that is, John Wyclif and Uthred of Boldon—there is the same *naïveté* in putting forward new views on matters that had long ago been debated by some of the greatest minds of the past: these views are put forward without any of the acumen or dialectical technique of a Scotus or an Ockham, and even (as it would seem) without any clear realization that they ran counter not only to the tradition of the schools but to the mind of the Church. With Wyclif we are not directly concerned, but a few words may be said of an interesting and little-known episode in the career of Uthred of Boldon.

Uthred of Boldon had been at Oxford for some twenty years as student and teacher when the controversy occurred. As we have seen, he had often

---

1 *Ibid.* 108–12.
2 The best account of this school is in Gwynn, *Austin Friars*, 35–53, with articles in *DTC* on the theologians concerned.
3 M. de Wulf, *Histoire de Philosophie Médiévale*, III, 160–74.

found himself ranged against the friars, especially in the years after 1360, but it is not clear whether the attack made on him by the Dominican, William Jordan, was made with the intention of discrediting an old enemy, or whether it was a purely theological dispute in which a somewhat combative man felt it his duty to defend the traditional teaching. Such facts as can be discovered seem to suggest that the two theologians had long been opponents and that the appeal to authority was the climax of a long academic strife.[1]

William Jordan, a northerner by birth, had been at the papal court in 1355, and was prior of the Preachers' house at York in 1358, in which year he was again in Avignon, where he was one of the friars who argued against Fitzralph. At about the same time he was engaged in controversy at York with Mardisley, the provincial minister of the Minors, on the subject of the Immaculate Conception of the Blessed Virgin; in this the two friars took up each the position traditional in his order. It is not known when his opposition to Uthred began; a letter written to the latter by a confrère shows that the two were at odds at the end of 1366,[2] and the titles of three works attributed to Jordan suggest that he had attacked Uthred both on the question of the mendicants' poverty and on his theory of the vision of God at the moment before death.[3] Soon after this, perhaps in 1367, the friars, no doubt led by William Jordan, drew up a list of propositions from various academic pronouncements of Uthred which they held to be contrary to sound doctrine.[4] This list, according to Uthred, they published in many places, and spoke against its alleged errors before general audiences, without coming forward in due form at Oxford. To defend his reputation, therefore, Uthred himself published the list, together with his own corrections and replies. On the whole, he stood firmly to his guns, and his corrections and explanations do not bear out his complaint that he had been seriously and maliciously misrepresented.

1 For a more detailed account of this affair, v. M. D. Knowles, 'The Censured Opinions of Uthred of Boldon'. The work of Miss M. E. Marcett, *Uthred de Boldon* (*v. supra* p. 48, n. 1), while creditable as a piece of pioneer research by one who was primarily a philologist, fails to express the theological significance of the dispute; through sympathy with Uthred, the author dismisses Jordan as a quarrelsome heresy-hunter. This he may have been, but he was nevertheless theologically justified in his attack on Uthred.

2 The letter (*MC*, III, 309) is written by a monk of St Mary's, York, most probably to Uthred, and can be dated *c.* 8 December 1366. In a sentence decipherable only in part the writer asks for information 'de modo accessus et recessus fratris Willelmi Iordan de Oxonia'. The date would accord with all the other indications. Uthred was apparently still at Oxford (i.e. it was before his departure for Finchale in the late summer of 1367) as he complains that he had been 'per ipsos [*sc.* fratres] in diversis provinciis nequiter diffamatus', and that these attacks had been launched 'non in scolis nec in locis aliis aptis pro veritate discucienda set a tergo resistunt veritati scolastice, ubi eorum mendacia per audientes non poterunt reprehendi' (Knowles, art. cit. 332).

3 Antonio Senensi Lusitano, *Biblioteca ordinis fratrum praedicatorum* (Paris, 1585), p. 99 (cited by Marcett, *Uthred de Boldon*, 50) gives *Pro mendicitate contra Utredum* and *Tractatus de libera electione ante mortem* (al. *De clara Dei visione*).

4 The list is cited and discussed by Uthred in his short treatise *Contra querelas fratrum*, of which the relevant part is printed by Knowles, *art. cit.* 332–40.

The friars, therefore, seem to have been justified in pressing their attack, and early in 1367/8 the list of Uthred's propositions was delated to the archbishop of Canterbury, Simon Langham, who as a monk would naturally have been unwilling to take strong measures against one of his habit, though he himself had never been a master at Oxford. Langham wrote on 18 February to the chancellor of Oxford, ordering him to silence both parties and their adherents, who were continuing to dispute upon the articles delated. The matter, the archbishop wrote, was about to be judicially decided.[1] The examination duly took place the same year, and on 9 November, less than three weeks before his resignation of the see, Langham condemned thirty propositions, which he forbade to be defended in the schools. The names of Uthred and Jordan do not appear in the decree, but twenty-two of the articles repeat with a few small verbal changes propositions on the list quoted and defended by Uthred. The remaining eight are entirely different from Uthred's list, and may represent propositions delated by Uthred from Jordan's writings.[2] This supposition seems to be confirmed by the last item in the process, a testimonial from Langham on 17 November in favour of William Jordan, bearing the archbishop's witness to the fact that Jordan had denied ever having taught or held certain articles which Langham had recently condemned as having been held by him.[3]

The articles thus acknowledged and defended by Uthred and condemned by Langham and his theologians are of considerable interest, and deserve detailed study. Here only a summary account of them can be given. In the list as drawn up by the friars the order is arbitrary and confused, but in Langham's condemnation they are rearranged in a more logical order. The first and longest group is concerned with an extraordinary opinion which would appear to have been of Uthred's own invention, though it has been revived in the early nineteenth century by a Catholic theologian and has since been favoured by a number of writers, Catholics and others.[4] This is the opinion that in the moment between apparent and real death the soul is given a clear sight (that is, an intellectual vision of God, no longer hidden by faith) and that its fate for all eternity is decided by the choice or rejection that it then makes. This vision, in Uthred's view, is given to all, whether Christians or pagans,

---

1 Lambeth Reg. Langham, fo. 60ᵛ, printed by Knowles, *art. cit.* 340–1. The letter is dated 18 February, and refers to a *cedula* of delated propositions; careful examination shows that the archbishop had read Uthred's rejoinder.

2 Wilkins, *Concilia*, III, 75–6.

3 Lambeth Reg. Langham, fo. 72, printed by Knowles, *art. cit.* 341. This is dated 17 November, and speaks of 'diversis conclusionibus... dampnatis per nos pridie', but as a reference to the register is given for these articles, they are clearly those censured on 9 November. The letter may have been written on the 10th, but not dated and dispatched till the 17th. *Pridie*, however, in post-classical usage, can mean 'recently'.

4 For the modern opinions *v. DTC*, article 'Persévérance' (at end); also *Nouvelle Revue Théologique* (1932), 865–92, where P. Glorieux puts forward an opinion similar to that of Uthred. He is answered by E. Hugueny in *Revue Thomiste* (1933), 217–42, 533–67.

infants or adults; even the unborn child dying before birth has it.[1] The primary motive for Uthred in devising this theory would seem to have been dissatisfaction with the common medieval opinion that all those dying without being baptized or having made an explicit act of faith were lost. So far forth Uthred shows a sensitive humanity and charity of a kind which we are often disposed to consider modern rather than medieval. He appears, however, to have been strangely unperceptive of the difficulties into which such an opinion would lead him. To begin with, the universality of such a final moment of vision and choice threatened to dislocate the whole Christian economy. If a pagan could be saved without any precedent act of faith, such an act could not be necessary as a means to salvation; the same might be said of baptism, whether for the ordinary Christian or for the unborn infant. Moreover, if all were to see God with the possibility of choosing or rejecting Him, no one could be lost owing to original sin, while those who were in fact lost would have the guilt of actual sin. Also, while it would no longer be possible to assert that a stillborn (and thus unbaptized) infant was lost, it would be equally impossible to assert that a child dying baptized was certainly saved, for it might have rejected God in the clear vision. Finally, since *ex hypothesi* the choice was final, those who rejected God committed a sin for which the Passion of Christ could not satisfy, even though (again *ex hypothesi*) it was committed by one who was still a *viator*, on this side of death.

It is indeed remarkable that so experienced a theologian as Uthred, who was clearly a man of moderate and judicious views in all affairs of common life, should have been attracted into such slippery paths. It is perhaps an indication that speculation in academic circles had lost touch both with tradition and with the conclusions of the great schoolmen of the previous century. It may be remarked that the strange episode of Pope John XXII

---

1 The essential proposition is the third in the *cedula* and runs as follows (Knowles, *art. cit.* 334): 'Quod viator quilibet, de lege communi in via, tam adultus quam non adultus, habebit claram visionem ipsius dei.' And Uthred comments: 'Hunc eciam tenui et persuasi et reputo verum esse.' He goes on to insist that by 'lex communis' he intends to include all men, not Christians only. It is difficult to think that Uthred devised this opinion with no previous authority to support him, but such an authority has not yet been found either by the present writer or by the theologians and historians of medieval thought he has consulted. Uthred's contemporary opponent, indeed, in Worc. Cath. MS. F65, fo. 7, says, 'solet...dici et specialiter per Utredum', but this by itself cannot be taken as proof that others had held this opinion before Uthred. Though this same opponent understands Uthred to have understood by his *clara visio* a clear sight of the Divine Essence, it is hardly possible that Uthred can have been so inept. Christian tradition has always held that the Beatific Vision, save in the altogether unique case of the human intelligence of Christ, is incompatible with mortal life, and the rare and momentary exceptions allowed (e.g. St Paul and Moses) by some schoolmen, largely in deference to St Augustine, formed no real exception. More recently the tendency among both dogmatic and mystical theologians has been to reduce even the experiences of St Paul and Moses to the class of sublime 'intellectual visions', and it would seem that Uthred's *clara visio* was of this kind (cf. St John of the Cross, *Ascent of Mount Carmel*, II, xxiv, xxvi). Moreover, all theologians agree that when the human intelligence sees the Divine Essence it is not free to choose anything but God; the *clara visio*, if of this kind, would have given no alternative choice to the soul.

and the Beatific Vision, forty years before, shows very similar preoccupations and an even greater want of theological tact.

Uthred, it may be added, fell easily into unfamiliar opinions by reason of his views on grace. Here it is clear that he followed the line of thought started by Pierre Auriole and Jean de Mirecourt and followed by William of Ockham. Sanctifying grace, in his view, was not a quality of the soul infused by God, but a relationship to God, the heavenly Father, by which a man could merit eternal life.[1] This relationship was due to the mere liberality of God, and could not therefore be attained by any natural powers, but Uthred seems to have held that a man's actions, both before and after this relationship had been bestowed, were essentially and solely his own, though God might in various ways give his assistance. Thus he held firmly that a man could of his own natural powers attain to his natural end;[2] that he could equally turn from sin and regain his previous state before God.[3] He was further accused of holding that a man could by his purely natural powers merit everlasting life.[4] This, of course, would have been sheer Pelagianism, and to admit it would have been to incur numberless anathemas. Uthred therefore had recourse to his God-given 're-lationship', adding that he did not exclude the general providence of God in protecting and helping man. He stood firmly, however, to his forthright statement that grace as generally understood was moonshine.[5] This statement, alone of the censured propositions, was not condemned simply as erroneous, but as erroneous because ill-sounding. It is noteworthy, also, that Langham and his theologians passed over without condemnation three propositions concerning the nature of grace which certainly would not have escaped stigma in a post-Tridentine world; these show that Uthred held the Ockhamist view that grace as an infused quality, together with the *lumen fidei* and *lumen gloriae*, was a figment of the imagination, and that theories of merit based upon it were open to serious criticism. In this field, then still open to speculation, Langham was

---

1 The fourteenth article reads (Knowles, *art. cit.* 337): 'Quod nulla gratia in viatore ad vitam eternam promerendam est ponenda que sit aliud infusum distinctum a creatura merente.' Uthred's comment is: 'Hunc dixi et reputo quod sit verus, eo quod hec vocabula "gratus" et "gratia" et huiusmodi sint relativa seu respectiva. Nec notant principaliter aliquid, sed ad aliquid, non absolutum sed respectivum.' He therefore accepts without essential change responsibility for the fifteenth article: 'Quod nulla potest esse gratia creata que sit aliquid positivum creatum vel infusum gratificans viatorem.'

2 Article xix (Knowles, *art. cit.* 338): 'Quod est medium sufficiens in natura ad attingendum finem hominis naturalem.' Uthred comments: 'Hunc tenui et persuasi et reputo esse verum.'

3 Article xx (*ibid.*): 'Quod pro quolibet peccato...est remedium sufficiens in natura per quod redire potest viator ad gradum deperditum per peccatum.' Uthred accepts this, but adds that he does not wish to exclude divine supernatural assistance in the concrete case.

4 Article xvii (*ibid.*): 'Quod quis potest mereri ex puris naturalibus.' Here Uthred draws the line: 'Hunc non tenui nec intendo tenere.'

5 Article xviii (*ibid.*): 'Quod gratia juxta communiter ponentes est truffa.' Uthred comments: 'Hunc dixi eo quod juxta communiter ponentes gratia ponitur aliquid absolutum, creature superinfusum, et ab ipsa creatura distinctum.' *Truffa*, from the Old French *trufle*, *truffe* (whence English *trifle*) = 'trick', 'mockery', 'worthless thing'.

unwilling to trespass. Of another neighbouring field, however, he was not so respectful. Since the days of Scotus there had been a continuous dispute between 'intellectualists' and 'voluntarists' as to the essence of moral evil. The former held that actions were of themselves either good or bad, and that God's commands did no more than declare and sanction this fact. The latter held that acts in appearance essentially evil (e.g. hatred of God or adultery) could very well have been the object of God's command and therefore morally good. In this respect Uthred held the opposite view to Ockham; his error lay in making a universal and exclusive statement, thus depriving God, so to say, of the right of forbidding acts in themselves of no moral turpitude.[1] Uthred, as another condemned article shows, was prepared to apply his theory to the well-known test case of the prohibition of the fruit of the Tree of Knowledge in Paradise. This fruit, he maintained, though excellent in other respects, was not suitable for eating, and therefore forbidden to Adam.[2] Finally, Uthred's eclecticism is shown by his firm adherence to the ultra-Realist opinion, almost certainly derived from Wyclif, that not even God could annihilate anything.[3] This, it may be supposed, was condemned as unduly limiting the omnipotence of the Creator; as will be remembered, it was soon to be the basis of Wyclif's denial of transubstantiation, and it is worth noting that he must have been aware of this previous decision.

After condemning twenty-two propositions clearly taken from the schedule criticized by Uthred, Langham continued without any indication to stigmatize a further eight which, as we have seen, had apparently been attributed to Jordan by his adversary. As Jordan (unlike Uthred) stated solemnly that he had never held these opinions, and as these may therefore represent erroneous or exaggerated interpretations of his words, there is little to be gained by examining them in detail. The occasion of some, at least, was probably the controversy with Mardisley on the Immaculate Conception, since in one of the articles the 'peccability' of Mary is asserted. Most of the articles turn on the then familiar distinction between the *potentia absoluta* and the *potentia ordinata* of God, and they may represent a paradoxical controversial use of this which has been confused and deformed by Jordan's adversaries.[4]

Uthred's condemnation is of interest in many ways. In the first place, the troubles into which he had run, and the impending delation, may well have been the reason why, in 1367, he was recalled from Oxford to be prior of Finchale. It is true that he succeeded a prior who had died, and

1 Article xxi (Knowles, *art. cit.* 338): 'Quod nichil est nec esse potest malum solum quia prohibitum.' Uthred comments: 'Hunc tenui et persuasi, et adhuc reputo verum esse.'
2 Article xxiii (*ibid.*).
3 Article ii (Knowles, *art. cit.* 334): 'Quod deus non potest aliquod adnichilare.' Uthred remarks: 'Hunc articulum sepius tenui et persuasi, et adhuc dictat mihi ratio quod sit verus.'
4 Cf. the proposition of Autrecourt condemned by Clement VI in 1348 (Denzinger-Bannwart, *Enchiridion symbolorum*, no. 565): 'Quod propositiones Deus est, Deus non est, penitus idem significat, licet alio modo.'

that therefore there is no clear evidence that the appointment did not take place as a matter of domestic routine, but the post was not a distinguished one for a man in the prime of life (in fact, Uthred soon became subprior of Durham) and had there not been good reason for an honourable retreat from Oxford such a transference would have seemed remarkable.

Next, there is some additional evidence both of the novelty of Uthred's views on the vision of God before death and on the notice taken of him in academic circles. There are in the library of the Dean and Chapter at Worcester several determinations and other notes attributed to one Hatton or Acton in which the *clara visio* and several other of the articles censured are attacked in academic form.[1]

Finally, the form and consequences of Langham's censure should be noted. No name is given and no kind of abjuration is imposed. The propositions are simply branded as erroneous and not to be taught or disputed upon in the schools. The contrast between this and the more severe and personal proceedings taken against Wyclif only a few years later is noteworthy, but readily explicable. Uthred, however erroneous or fanciful his opinions may have been, was clearly speaking as a theologian among theologians, and took his quietus in good part. Wyclif's attack on transubstantiation implied a novel attitude towards the Eucharist in public and in practice, and he was not prepared either to retract or to keep silence[2].

---

1 Worcester Cathedral MS. F 65, fo. 1v ('Determinacio Hatton contra Utredum'); fo. 7; fo. 11ᵛ; and fo. 19ᵛ. Fr S. L. Forte, O.P., has worked upon this manuscript, and it is hoped that his conclusions will be published.

2 When the above pages were already in type, the second part of Langham's register was published (*v.* Bibliography), containing (pp. 184, 219–22, 226–7) the documents referring to this case.

CHAPTER VII

CRITICISM OF THE RELIGIOUS IN THE FOURTEENTH CENTURY

I. FITZRALPH AND WYCLIF

During the latter half of the fourteenth century the religious orders, and in particular the friars, were subjected to attacks both public and literary, to which an earlier parallel can only be found in the simultaneous assaults by a group of bishops and by the court circle of writers upon the monks in the last years of Henry II. In the previous onslaught, a number of prelates had sought to eject the monks from their cathedrals or to render them innocuous by the foundation of colleges of secular canons, while at the same time Gerald of Wales and Walter Map were accusing the whole monastic body of luxurious and immoral lives, and of avaricious and dishonest behaviour.[1] Both these attacks had died away with the reign of John: the relations between monks and bishops had been firmly determined by Innocent III, while the extinction of literary humanism and the court culture had put an end to literary polemics. Henceforward for almost a century and a half criticism of the religious in this country had been personal and private only, save for faint echoes at Oxford of the quarrels between the secular masters of Paris and the mendicants. Of literary criticism during this period scarcely anything of weight has survived; the thirteenth century, as is well known, is a barren one in the annals of national literature when compared to the age of Latin culture which preceded it, and the epoch of English renaissance that followed.

When, half way through the fourteenth century, attacks were once more directed against the religious orders in England, external circumstances and the intellectual climate of the times had alike changed. The monks, indeed, still stood in very much the same position towards society as in the reign of Henry III, and the criticisms passed upon them followed the old pattern. The arrival of the friars, however, their wide diffusion and their stormy history had opened the way to attacks of an entirely new kind, and it was in fact the friars who drew most of the fire of the new generation of critics.

The four orders of friars, and above all the Friars Minor, had been from the first in a peculiarly delicate position, both by reason of their habitual mingling with the people and by reason of their intrusion into the organization of the diocese and parish. Both of these circumstances made demands upon their virtue and tact which could not normally be met by the rank and file, and the difficulties of their position were aggravated by their dependence for material support upon the daily alms of those with

1 For this *v. MO*, ch. xxxix.

whom they came into contact. All controversies apart, therefore, it is not surprising to be told, when the first enthusiasm had passed, that they are gossips and meddlers, that they live like lords at the charges of others, that by wheedling and *bonhomie* they filch penitents from the local clergy and pocket dainties and comforts from the housewives of the parish, to say nothing of the inevitable charges of a more serious nature. Such grievances form the basic theme upon which endless variations were played.

Criticism of the friars, however, had from early times been rendered at once more bitter and more dignified by the ramifications of two great controversies which agitated the higher circles of the Church from 1250 onwards for almost a century: the exact canonical position of the friars *vis-à-vis* the bishop and parish priest, a question which led on to the more radical controversy as to the right of the friars to preach and administer the sacraments under any circumstances; and the still more warmly debated topic of the nature of religious poverty and the ethics of mendicancy. Both these controversies broadened gradually into a doctrinal issue and ultimately demanded the attention and judgement of the pope. Some mention has already been made of them, but a recapitulation will be necessary as a prelude to an understanding of the accusations of Fitzralph and Wyclif.

Although all the four great orders of friars that survived the council of Lyons in 1274 were objects of criticism, the Minors were always the mass of ferment at the heart of all controversies, partly on account of the internecine strife which distracted their body, and in part because truancies and heterodox enthusiasm of individuals and groups gave a handle to their opponents, but principally because the original legislation of St Francis on poverty and the apostolic work of the friars, resting as it did on purely spiritual principles, remained a perennial source of doubt and discussion, from which zealous friars and bitter opponents alike drew conclusions against existing compromises or abuses.

As it happened, even before the regular attacks on the mendicants had begun, their opponents had been presented with a wide target by one of the many Minors with Joachimist sympathies, Gerard of Borgo San Donnino, who had represented the friars as the sole spiritual leaders of the new dispensation in which the hierarchy and all ecclesiastical organization would disappear. His celebrated opponent, the Paris master William of St Amour, besides attacking mendicancy, naturally took up a diametrically opposite position to Gerard, urging that the secular clergy alone were divinely commissioned to teach and to preach. Henceforth the theological controversy was carried on alongside of the forensic struggle between the bishops and the friars. The stages of the latter have already been noted down to the issue of the bull *Super cathedram* by Boniface VIII. This was revoked by the constitution *Inter cunctos* of Benedict XI in 1304, but this in its turn was superseded by the decretal *Dudum* issued by Clement V in

1312 shortly after the Council of Vienne, in which the *Super cathedram* was reaffirmed. This, while giving full rights of selection and control to the bishops, ensured to the friars a foothold in each diocese as preachers and confessors.[1]

At almost the same time the extreme opponents of the friars in the theological sphere had fallen under a papal condemnation. The contention that the friars were unlawfully usurping the rights of the secular clergy had been unanswerably met, when raised from a practical to a theoretical level, by references to papal declarations and privileges. The spokesmen of the seculars, therefore, were driven back to the question of jurisdiction, and maintained that bishops and parish priests had *jure divino* the exclusive right of government over their own flock, that the pope's claims as universal ordinary could not be upheld, and that therefore he had no power to authorize external persons such as the friars to exercise any sacerdotal functions in the diocese or parish. These views, as enunciated by the Paris master Jean de Pouilly, were condemned by John XXII in his bull *Vas electionis* of 1321.[2]

Despite these papal interventions, both controversies dragged on, as on the one hand the clash between friars and secular clergy continued in practice, while it was still possible for a hardy controversialist like Fitzralph to restate the arguments against apostolic work by the friars and suggest that another pope might undo the work of John XXII.

The controversy on mendicant poverty had meanwhile continued with still more intense bitterness, and had in time resolved itself into at least three great theological disputes: that on the essence of the virtue of poverty, in which the Minors were opposed by the Preachers and other friars;[3] that on the lawfulness of mendicancy and the excellence of the evangelical counsels, in which all the friars formed front against the seculars; and that on the absolute value of material poverty, which ultimately became a dispute as to the absolute poverty of Christ, in which a section of the Minors, known as the Spirituals, stood against all others.

In the early years after the death of St Francis, the followers of the Rule according to the letter, who came to be known as the *zelanti*, had been content to live a life of absolute poverty with the sincere conviction that they were thus imitating the nakedness of Christ, who lived without a home

---

1 For this *v. RO*, I, ch. xxi and, for England, the thesis of Jean Copeland there cited, p. 184.

2 The best account of this episode is that by J. G. Sikes, 'John de Pouilli and Peter de la Palu'.

3 The Minors, when driven to set forth in apologetic form the Lady Poverty of St Francis' spiritual vision, found it hard to avoid laying stress on the absolute value of material poverty in its two aspects: the absence of ownership and control and the pressure of real want. The Preachers, of whom the most illustrious spokesman was St Thomas, laid emphasis rather on the purely moral and spiritual aspects: that the virtue was not material want, but poverty of spirit, the lack of all attachment. As in fact real spiritual detachment can only be achieved by those whose love of God is perfect, both parties often laid themselves open to the charges of hypocrisy and laxism.

and died on the Cross stripped of all. Such, no doubt, continued to be the frame of mind of the simplest and most zealous Minors throughout the century. As time went on, however, the successive mitigations of the Rule by the papacy, accompanied as they were by what seemed to many to be disingenuous evasions, added to the need for a spiritual doctrine to set against the opinion that the essence of personal poverty was not diminished by corporate ownership, as also against the teaching of the Preachers who stressed the value of renunciation of ownership by the will, even if material possession remained[1]—all this, combined with an exaggerated estimation of poverty as a condition of all good living, drove the Spirituals gradually into an untenable position.[2] From asserting the essential value of material poverty among the virtues it was an easy step to assert that the perfection of St Francis's Rule in this respect made it an instrument of the highest possible religious perfection. A further step was taken by asserting that Christ, the exemplar of all religious, must have been, throughout His public life, free of private ownership, and a further corollary set this absolute poverty as a goal for all those, such as the pope, bishops and priests, who stood in the place of Christ in His Church. Viewed thus, with all its consequences for the fabric of ecclesiastical society and for the spiritual life of the individual, the question of the absolute poverty of Christ, however academic it may at first sight appear, is clearly seen to be a practical one and no mere debate of the schools. In the spiritual sphere it has many characteristics in common with the later controversy on the contemplative life which issued in the condemnation of Quietism. In each, an important element of Christian perfection was materialized and deformed, and then advocated with an unbending logic and an intemperate zeal which, had the premises been correct, would have utterly revolutionized Christian ethics. In both cases, also, the party which held to the false opinion counted among its number estimable and disinterested men who appear to posterity more admirable, or at least more amiable, than their orthodox opponents.

The papal decision on the poverty of Christ was pronounced in 1323 by the decretal *Cum inter nonnullos* of John XXII, but though the doctrinal question was thus settled in a way that clearly combined theological precision with sound sense, and although the considerable schism which took place among the Spirituals was healed after twenty years, the Minors, as was their right, continued to profess, and in many circles in Italy and Provence to practise, an absolute poverty superior to that of other religious. In addition, the system of mendicancy, with all its disabilities, continued as before. There was, therefore, still room for controversy, especially of the abusive, *ad hominem* kind.

1 As St John of the Cross, who will not be accused of laxism, wrote (*The Ascent of Mount Carmel*, I, iii § 4 (trans. Peers)): 'It is not the things of this world that either occupy the soul, or cause it harm, since they enter not within it, but rather the will and desire for them, for it is these that dwell within it.'
2 This is well analysed by Ehrle, *ALKG*, IV, 45–50.

This large store of material for dispute and recrimination between the friars and their opponents was rendered more corrosive by the spirit of the age, in which radical views on the whole constitution of the Church and society were being bandied about with a hardihood never before experienced in Western Christendom. The attacks of Wyclif on the orders have been compared to those of Gerald of Wales upon the monks, but in spite of a superficial resemblance the differences are profound. In the earlier age all, if we except shallow atheists of the type of Walter Map, took for granted the traditional balanced constitution of the Church and the ideals of the monastic life. The only question was of the worthiness of the practitioners. Even in the thirteenth century, when a group of Averroist philosophers and more than one powerful heretical sect were sapping the foundations of medieval religion, the vast mass of theological speculation was in essence traditional and sound. In the fourteenth century, however, this had to a large extent changed, and in every direction publicists, philosophers and theologians were advocating with the utmost hardihood radical opinions of every kind. Thus the extravagant claims to total and immediate dominion in the spiritual and temporal spheres put forward on behalf of the papacy by Giles of Rome and others were echoed not only in such pronouncements as the bull *Unam sanctam* of Boniface VIII, but also in the papal claims for taxation and the provision to all kinds of benefice, supported often by alleged historical surrenders such as those of Constantine or King John. They were countered by a no less thoroughgoing advocacy of the absolute rights of the secular state in the writings of Marsilius of Padua, William of Ockham and others, which in their turn found echoes in the various proposals to secularize Church property, or to suppress religious institutes such as the Templars or the friars. In another sphere, where on the one hand absolute poverty was being held up as the Christian ideal derived from the practice of Christ, on the other religious mendicancy was being no less warmly attacked as the bane of civil society. In theology, both the reasoned synthesis of St Thomas with its clear division between natural and supernatural, and its wise use of analogy, and the moderate Augustinianism of St Bonaventure had given place, in the majority of schools, to a theology divorced from rational exposition and resting on a basis of authority (or, alternatively of Scripture) alone, while in philosophy the Nominalism of Ockham, which gradually won for itself an almost universal supremacy, provided masters and students in arts with an instrument of great delicacy and cutting power and a technique which could deal with the deepest truths of theology on its own terms and from a purely intellectual standpoint. When to all these tendencies which gave a peculiar character to the mental climate of the times there are added the deplorable results of the residence of the papacy at Avignon and the scandal of the Great Schism, it will readily be understood that criticism of all kinds was likely to be radical and daring. In addition, the conflict between parties had become still further confused by strange alliances, such as that between the Spiritual William of Ockham and the frankly secularist Marsilius of Padua, who were both opposed to the papacy and to the ownership of property by ecclesiastics, while the legislation of the popes in favour of the apostolic work of the friars was opposed both by the secular clergy and those among the Minors themselves who wished for a return to the simple 'unprivileged' conditions of the original Rule. Sometimes, indeed, in the course of the long scuffle, the opponents, like the duellists in the play, had exchanged weapons; thus Gerard of Borgo San Donnino had maintained that the Church of Rome was the whore of Babylon and the pope antichrist, and was for supplanting the whole sacerdotal system by the friars; Wyclif, a century later, found himself in agreement with the exegesis and general aim of Gerard, but put the friars among the most trusted followers of antichrist. Similarly, the doctrine of Dominion and Grace, which had at first been exploited in favour of the papacy, was later used to prove that all property should be in lay hands, since the clergy had fallen from grace, and was finally turned by the opponents of the friars to exclude them from all ecclesiastical jurisdiction, however fully authorized by Rome.

Some account has been given in a previous volume of the controversies between bishops and friars to which the bull *Super cathedram* of Boniface VIII was intended to put an end. As has been noted, the bishops of England observed the letter and spirit of this decree with considerable fairness, and though it was for a time revoked by the constitution *Inter cunctos* of Benedict XI in 1304, there is little evidence that the friars of this country took advantage of the more favourable position then accorded to them. Shortly afterwards, the decision of John XXII on the question of the poverty of Christ brought about the schism among the Minors with its important political consequences; this was finally healed in 1349, and in the same year representatives of the four mendicant orders approached Clement VI with a formal request (*propositio*) that he should issue a fresh bull interpreting and mitigating in their favour some points of the *Super cathedram*. This *démarche* was immediately countered by a group of secular prelates at Avignon, who chose for their spokesman the able Anglo-Irish doctor Richard Fitzralph, sometime chancellor of Oxford and now for three years archbishop of Armagh, who had already come into collision with the Friars Minor in the course of diocesan administration when he had been conservator of their privileges. He was at the time on a long visit to the Curia on a commission from Edward III and on his own affairs; in an earlier period of his life he had spent some ten years at Avignon; he was therefore *persona grata* in the Curia, while his great theological reputation and natural talent for controversy made him a formidable opponent.[1]

1 Fr A. Gwynn, S.J., has made of Fitzralph a subject peculiarly his own. Cf. his articles, 'Archbishop Fitzralph and the Friars' and 'The Sermon-Diary of Richard Fitzralph,

Fitzralph countered the friars by putting up an alternative *propositio*, known from its initial word as *Unusquisque*,[1] in which he demanded a complete repeal of *Super cathedram* and the restitution to the secular clergy of their primitive monopoly of the care of souls. He based his demand on the Pauline precept that each should abide in the vocation to which God had called him: the reader of his oration must judge for himself the precise degree of candour exhibited by the archbishop in his plea that he is defending the truest interests of the friars themselves, and that he feels deeply for the souls of those who, buried in the friars' churches, are deprived of the fruits of pious suffrages, since such places are less acceptable to God than are the parish churches.[2] He is perhaps more unquestionably sincere when he asserts that hope of financial gain is the sole motive behind the desire of the friars to hear confessions. The speech, however, is on the whole temperate, though the basic argument that confessing (and to a lesser degree, preaching) are inconsistent with the vocation of a friar would only have been admitted with reserves by the most zealous Spiritual and was in no sense true of the Friars Preachers.

As a result of the move, the pope set up a commission of three doctors, of whom Fitzralph was one, to go into the whole question of the Mendicants' privileges.[3] The nature of their decisions is not known, and certainly had no immediate result at Avignon. Fitzralph, however, once his interest had become engaged, resolved to go to the bottom of the matter, and began to investigate the whole economy of the friars, their ideals and their rights, in a long treatise *De pauperie Salvatoris*,[4] which is not, as its title might suggest, an addition to the literature of the controversy regarding the poverty of Christ, but is an elaborate statement of the Augustinian theory of lordship and grace, constructed to prove that the friars, by sinfully soliciting and discharging tasks foreign to their vocation, have forfeited any title they might be supposed to have possessed to the privileges given by popes. The treatise was circulated among friends at Oxford in the winter of 1356–7,[5] and was answered point by point by Geoffrey Hardeby, later prior provincial of the Austin friars.

Meanwhile Fitzralph, who had been having harassing times with the Minors in Ireland, had come to England to solicit help from the king against their privileges, and while in London accepted an invitation to

Archbishop of Armagh'. The conclusions reached in these articles are summarized and developed in *The English Austin Friars*. Prof. L. L. Hammerich of Copenhagen has also studied Fitzralph in a paper *Richard Fitzralph and the Mendicants* (*v.* Bibliography).

1 This is printed with notes by Hammerich, *op. cit.* 53 *seqq.*

2 *Proposicio*, ed. Hammerich, 68.

3 Cf. his account in the preface to *De pauperie Salvatoris*, p. 273 (*v.* following note).

4 The first four books were edited by R. L. Poole as an appendix to his edition of Wyclif's *De dominio divino.*

5 So Fitzralph himself, in a sermon, not yet printed, in Bodl. MS. 119, quoted by Gwynn, *The English Austin Friars*, 92, n. 2. For the date (1385) of Hardeby's *De vita evangelica*, *v.* B. Hackett, 'The Spiritual Life of the English Austin Friars', in *Sanctus Augustinus*, 1959, 448, n. 81.

preach on the topic at Paul's Cross. In a series of sermons from December to March, which became more and more personal in tone, he finally attacked the motives and methods of the friars as confessors, together with their avarice, their luxurious lives, and their sumptuous buildings.[1] Roused and united, the friars appealed to Rome, and at the same time obtained a royal injunction against the archbishop. The latter, after a parting assault, repaired to Avignon, where in November 1357 he wound up his course with the well-known *Defensorium curatorum.* The friars, however, were also at the papal court, the prior general of the Austins and the English prior provincial of the Minors being especially active in their attempts to safeguard their privileges and to secure the condemnation of Fitzralph's doctrine of dominion. In the latter endeavour they were formally unsuccessful, but the English provincial of the Minors, Roger Conway, was able to obtain a bull confirming the *Vas electionis,* the document which had condemned the errors of Jean de Pouilly. This was in 1359, and a year later the archbishop of Armagh died in the Curia. He may or may not have lived to read the treatises in which Roger Conway traversed his arguments and restated the position of the Minors with regard to poverty and mendicancy.[2]

The London sermons of Fitzralph had given authority and a maximum of publicity to the current charges against the friars. Within a few years it was the turn of the older orders to come under fire.

Attacks on the wealth of the Church, and in particular on that of the monasteries, were no new thing, but before the fourteenth century they had come from critics who were primarily satirists or moralists. Early in the fourteenth century, however, a radical attack on ecclesiastical and monastic endowments *in toto* had been developed by social reformers of widely divergent ideals: by Marsilius of Padua and his associates, who upheld the claim of the secular state to all ownership, giving to the Church only a pension, and by the extreme Spirituals among the Friars Minor, who held that ownership of property was contrary to the Christian ideal. A modified programme, which was probably something of a conflation of these two theories, and which took the form of a proposition that all private property, even that of the Church, might be resumed in ownership by the government for the public defence, was floated into English politics at the Parliament of 1371. In the general crisis of that year, brought about by the dragging war and inefficient government, parliament was asked to vote £50,000 for the French wars, and the laity demanded that the clergy should bear an equal share in the levy.[3] The claim was resisted by the representatives of the great monasteries, but it was upheld by a group of

---

1 For an account of the sermons *v.* Gwynn, *op. cit.* 85–9.
2 For Conway and his treatises *v.* Gwynn, *op. cit.* 90.
3 For the well-known speech of a peer on the wealth of the clergy in 1371 *v.* Wyclif, *De civili dominio,* ed. Loserth, II, 7. Strictly speaking, the topic was not wholly new; it had been broached by the lay patrons of monasteries at the Parliament of 1307, and developed by William of Ockham in his treatise written to Edward III in 1339.

mendicants, of whom the spokesmen were two Austin friars, who petitioned Parliament that all possessions of the clergy should be regarded as national assets in all cases of necessity.[1] No direct notice was taken of the petition, and the clergy were successful in their demand that their contribution should depend upon a vote of convocation, but the corporate rights of the 'possessioners' (the current term for the non-mendicant religious orders) had been publicly challenged, and for the next forty years the monks were to be the object of a number of attacks, public and private. It is noteworthy that in the fictitious narrative of a session of parliament in 1374, where four religious were asked their opinion on the papal claims of complete dominion, spiritual and temporal, the black monk, Uthred of Boldon, maintained the dual lordship with the traditional arguments, while the Minor and the Austin friar denied the papal right to temporal dominion; the fourth, a Preacher, refused to commit himself to any opinion.[2] So far forth, it would seem, the friars were at this time willing to go with the revolutionary party.

The events of 1371 were sufficient to disturb the possessioners, and two of their leading theologians, Uthred of Boldon and William Binham, took occasion to attack in their public lectures at Oxford the secular master whose powers of mind and great reputation gave him the intellectual leadership of the radical party to which he had given his support.

Probably no character in English history has suffered such distortion at the hands of friend and foe as has that of John Wyclif. While no historian has yet been able to approach him with perfect sobriety of judgement, the events of his career, the authenticity of many of the works attributed to him, the degree of his speculative powers, and even the spelling of his name, have been, and still are, matters of controversy.[3] Here it is not

---

1 The articles of this petition have been printed with comments by V. H. Galbraith in *EHR*, xxxiv (1919), 579–82. For a discussion of the whole episode *v.* Gwynn, *The English Austin Friars*, 211–16. Cf. also M.V. Clarke, *Medieval Representation and Consent*, 31.

2 *Eulogium Historiarum*, ed. F. S. Haydon, iii, 337–9. It is difficult to see how this narrative can be received as authentic history. H. B. Workman, however, appears so to regard it (*John Wyclif*, i, 228–30), though he rightly (*ibid.* 236–7) treats the speeches of the seven lay lords 'in a certain council' as fictitious.

3 The fundamental misconception of Wyclif as the venerable originator of a beneficent reform and *Aufklärung*—the Abraham or Benedict of the Protestant churches—has vitiated all save the very latest studies of his life and thought, nor were the early revolts from this view, and the endeavours to make of him a great scholastic philosopher, more successful in giving a true picture than were those of Catholic and Tractarian controversialists who minimized his influence. Even Dr Workman, who is extremely candid in supplying evidence of Wyclif's intellectual and temperamental limitations, is occasionally betrayed into expressions of reverence. Dr Workman's study, the first to be based on a detailed study of contemporary sources and the recently published works of Wyclif, is invaluable for the mass of information it provides and for the numberless references to Wyclif's writings, but there is still room for a definitive examination of Wyclif's philosophical and theological position similar to existing studies of earlier English scholastics. Pending this, it will probably not be mistaken to regard him as a thinker not unlike Marsilius of Padua: perverse, that is, and even confused as a metaphysician or pure theologian, but abounding in radical views and new methods of debate, and with a capacity amounting to genius for propounding the germinal

necessary to enter into any of these discussions, as the main lines of his charges against the religious can be seen clearly enough in works which are certainly genuine.

The views of Wyclif upon the religious life and its contemporary practitioners underwent, as did his views on almost every aspect of religion, a considerable modification in the last fifteen years of his life. His adversaries, writing years after, attributed his hostility to the monks to his unfortunate experiences at Canterbury College, from the mastership of which he had been expelled by Simon Langham, whose action had been upheld on appeal by the pope.[1] It may well have been so: but his attitude to the possessioners was the logical outcome both of his early sympathy with the Spiritual friars, his later theories of grace and dominion, and his alliance with the opposition to Rome, and it harmonized with all the other developments of his thought at this time. In any case, the rift had occurred by 1374, and henceforward the monks, as one of the 'sects', are contrasted with the followers of the pure doctrine of Christ, though they are attacked far less violently than the Roman Curia on the one hand and the four orders of friars on the other.[2] They err in following the Rule of Benedict rather than that of Christ, and like all possessioners they depart from the Master's ideal and their own profession by enjoying secular rents and still more by appropriating the funds of parish churches.[3] They are, moreover, notoriously well found in every kind of cattle and provisions, which they squander and waste beyond all other men with intolerable carelessness.[4] Such accusations are made more than once, but despite the wide and exposed target presented by the monks, Wyclif devotes singularly little space to accusations against them. He had, however, once and for all broken with them in his reply to Uthred and Binham; in this, his first piece of publicist writing, the *Determinacio*, he argued that goods bestowed for spiritual uses should, if not used according to this purpose, be restored to their donors, and that in default of action on the part of the spiritual

---

ideas that were to dissolve the medieval church more than a century after his death. The text of this chapter and note were written before the appearance of K. B. McFarlane's *John Wycliffe* (1952); this is not a definitive biography, but it is a masterly and sober sketch.

1 So William Wodeford, O.F.M., in *Fasciculi zizaniorum*, ed. W. W. Shirley, 517. For the whole episode *v*. Workman, *John Wyclif*, I, 174–94, where the warden of Canterbury College is identified with scarcely any hesitation with John Wyclif rather than with Whitclif of Mayfield, and *supra*, p. 21.

2 The most elaborate attack is in *De quattuor sectis novellis* of ? June 1383, in *Polemical Works*, ed. R. Buddensieg, I, no. vi. *Obiter dicta*, such as the reference in the *Responsiones ad xliv conclusiones monachales* (*Opera Minora*, ed. J. Loserth, 219) to the religious as devil's nestlings: 'claustrum est nidus dyaboli a quo rapit multas animas ad infernum, in quo fovet pullos suos', are probably directed primarily to the address of the friars, though Wyclif had certainly no desire to limit the reference.

3 Cf. *De nova praevaricantia mandatorum*, ch. 5 (*Pol. Works*, I, 131 seqq.).

4 *De quattuor sectis novellis*, ch. 2, (*Pol. Works*, I, 246): 'Inter omnes homines magis habundant sua promptuaria cibariis et altilia cum bobus et ovibus crassitudine sive ping- wedine.' Cf. the tract on the seven deadly sins (probably not by Wyclif, but certainly reflecting his ideas) in *Select English Works*, ed. T. A. Arnold, III, 157–8. 'No folc in this worlde maken more waste.'

authorities, the heirs of the original donors might resume possession.[1] Such arguments, though calculated to rouse hostility to their author among the older orders, were calm and academic in comparison with those directed against the friars.

Yet with these, also, the relations of Wyclif had not always been unfriendly. There is no record of any serious quarrel during the first twenty-five years of his residence at Oxford; he had translated the Rule and Testament of St Francis, and when warden of Canterbury College is said to have worn a rough gown similar to that of the Minors.[2] In later years he had the support of the friars—or at least of the Minors and Austin friars—in his early opposition to papal demands and to clerical dominion, and there is an interesting record of a friendly interchange of lecture notes between him and William Wodeford, a leading Minorite doctor at Oxford, as late as c. 1370.[3] Even when the break occurred he did not feel it useless to issue a last appeal to those of the friars who had fought with him in the past.[4] When, however, he openly rejected transubstantiation and broke with the papacy, he drew upon himself opposition from all the four orders, in particular the Minors and the Carmelites, while he himself, with ever-increasing bitterness of feeling, launched a series of counter-attacks which far surpassed in virulence any assaults of which he had been the object.

In these treatises and pamphlets, which issued from the rectory of Lutterworth in journalistic profusion during the last three years of his life, Wyclif abused the religious of England, monks, canons and friars, through all the moods and tenses. Not since the days of Gerald of Wales had any body of men received such a drenching. There is, indeed, a certain superficial similarity between the writings of the two men. With both, the mention of their *bête noire* released an inexhaustible stream of words; neither writer achieved or even aimed at economy or compression, and both were prepared to repeat the same charges and arguments and turns of phrase *usque ad nauseam*; with both there is a note of personal anger, and in both the fixed idea is betrayed by the tireless iteration. There, however, the resemblance ends. There is between the two an essential difference of aim and method. While Gerald's purpose, so far as he had one consciously in mind, was to mend monasticism, Wyclif desired nothing but to end it. Gerald's normal method was to support a series of sweeping general

1 *Determinacio ad argumenta Johannis Outredi* (*Opera Minora*, 410). For the view that gifts to churches should revert to the donors, cf. earlier instances in *Statutes of the Realm*, 1, 91–2; *Chronicles of Ed. I and Ed. II*, 1, 164–5, and K. L. Wood-Legh, *Church Life in England under Edward III*, 8.

2 Cf. *English Works*, ed. F. D. Matthew, 39–51 and Workman, *John Wyclif*, 11, 98.

3 See the quotation from Woodford's treatise on the Eucharist in Little, *The Grey Friars in Oxford*, 81; and for the friendship with the Austin friar, Thomas Winterton, v. Gwynn, *The English Austin Friars*, 225–6.

4 This is the preface (*De apostasia*) to his Eucharistic treatise of 1381 (ed. Dziewicki, 1889). For an analysis v. Gwynn, *op. cit.* 262–7. In it Wyclif refers to 'my dear sons in the mendicant religion'.

charges with a limited number of examples drawn from his own experience; Wyclif devoted his energies to demolishing the whole system by *a priori* reasoning based on Scriptural, theological and historical considerations. Finally, while Gerald retained a sympathy with the ideals of monasticism and a fond memory of individuals from the golden past, Wyclif, in the impersonal manner that distinguishes all his writing and that seems to reflect a mind to which personal affection was a stranger, omits all mention of the misdeeds of individuals, as he omits also any reference to the more amiable qualities of those who had once been his friends.

The pamphlets directed against the friars belong, as has been mentioned, without exception to the last few years of Wyclif's life and principally to the period when, exiled from Oxford, he had seen his teaching publicly condemned and his itinerant followers harassed and obstructed, and when, warned by a first stroke that his days were numbered and conscious at the same time of his teeming brain, he worked with feverish haste before the night should fall, with an embittered spirit and a mind, perhaps, pathologically obdurate and inflexible,[1] to leave a mass of seed to be drawn upon and broadcast by his disciples after his death. This sour legacy of hatred, passed from mouth to mouth in England for a few years only, and then slumbering for centuries in the libraries of central Europe, has within the last seventy years been made public property for the first time. The reader who endures to pass through its parching expanse may indeed be repelled by the total lack of spiritual warmth, but he can scarcely fail to recognize the mental power and single-minded purpose with which it is animated.

Wyclif's central thesis is simple and radical enough.[2] All organized bodies among the Christian community, all set forms of life and government, are 'sects', at best superfluous, at worst infernal, in any case opposed to the one true sect or way of life instituted by Christ. Four sects in particular stand condemned: the pope, together with his cardinals and prelates; the orders of monks; the orders of regular canons; and the four orders of friars. All receive summary judgement. The pope, whose claim to be the Vicar of Christ is inconceivably preposterous, is unsurpassed for open and shameless transgression of the Ten Commandments; he is not only mendacious, but is quintessential mendacity itself; he is the Antichrist *par excellence* of the western world;[3] the monks, long since unfaithful to whatever good there may have been in their Rule, have absorbed so much land and wealth that all the poor of England could live on the

---

1 Restlessness and irritability are familiar symptoms of advanced arteriosclerosis.

2 The two tracts *De fundatione sectarum* (? August 1383) and *De quattuor sectis novellis* (? July 1383) both in *Pol. Works*, i (nos. i and vi), give the clearest summaries.

3 *De nova praevaricantia mandatorum*, ch. 4 (*Pol. Works*, i, 127): 'Fingit enim quod sit immediatus Cristi vicarius in terris...nullum est manifestius mendacium in hoc mundo.' *De oratione* (end of 1383), ch. 4 (*Pol. Works*, i, 349): 'sicut papa perversus est anticristus atque dyabolus, sic est mendacium in abstracto [!] et pater mendacii.' *De solutione Satanae*, ch. 1 (*Pol. Works*, ii, 396): 'Papa, qui est nobis occiduis precipuus anticristus.'

rent;[1] the canons' relationship to the father of lies is sufficiently shown by their claim to have Augustine for their founder;[2] and finally the friars, compact of lies from the sole of the foot to the crown of the head, have been launched upon the world in these latter days by the devil himself. The Scriptures, Wyclif urges, abound in types of these pests: the pope is Gog; the other three sects Magog.[3] As for the four orders of friars, all children of Cain who slew his brother, they may be seen in figure in the four beasts of Daniel: the bear, the leopard and the lioness stand for the Preachers, the Minors and the Austin friars; the fourth beast, with its ten horns and its teeth and claws of iron, bears a remarkable resemblance to the Carmelites.[4] All are apostates, idolaters, schismatics, heretics; their houses are strongholds of murder and rapine, Caim's castles;[5] it would be more tolerable for England to be ravaged by her enemies than to be secretly devoured by infidels of this kind;[6] poisonous vermin as they are, they should be smoked out of their nests and destroyed with all their brood like rats or vipers.[7] And Wyclif concludes with a verse from the liturgy in which all angels and saints are implored to drive the demons out of christendom.[8]

Such passages, in which the most distinguished theologian of his generation at Oxford rails at the friars like a drab, abound in Wyclif's polemical works. They are an early and melancholy example of a type of literature that was to remain only too common throughout the religious controversies of succeeding centuries. Wyclif, however, had a mind capable of a higher flight than this, and if in the realm of mere abuse he helped to found a genre of English writing, he also laid down, with singular fullness of detail, the main lines along which all future attacks upon the religious moved.

With dogged insistence he beats home, throughout his tracts, a series

1 *De quat. sect. nov.* ch. 2 (*Pol. Works,* 1, vi). Wyclif's reiterated opinion that if the wealth of the clergy were transferred to the king and nobles there would be no poor men left in the land would seem to do little credit to his perspicacity; unless, indeed, it is candour that is wanting.

2 Wyclif himself attributes their foundation to another agency; cf. *De oratione,* ch. 4 (*Pol. Works,* 1, 351): 'tertia secta que noviter ex impetracione a patre mendacii impetravit habitum atque claustra.'

3 *De solutione Satanae,* ch. 1 (*Pol. Works,* 11, 396).

4 Cf. Wyclif's *ep.* ix, *De fratribus ad scholares (Opera Minora,* 16–17).

5 *De fund. sect.* ch. 7 (*Pol. Works,* 1, 40): 'castella caimitica'. Wyclif relished the phrase and repeated it frequently, even if he did not originate it. Thinking that the correct spelling of the name of the first murderer was Caim he took the letters as initials of the Carmelites, Augustinians, Jacobites (i.e. Dominicans) and Minors.

6 *De detectione perfidiarum Antichristi (Pol. Works,* 1, 383): 'Tolerabilius esset regno predari per publicos hostes quam sic corrodi subdole per huiusmodi infideles.'

7 *De oratione,* ch. 5 (*Pol. Works,* 1, 353): 'Sicut enim nidus animalium nocivorum debet destrui in radice, ut patet de muribus, serpentibus et aliis...sic debet esse de istis sectis nocivis.'

8 *De fund. sect.* ch. 16 (*Pol. Works,* 1, 79):

> 'Gentem auferte perfidam
> Credentium de finibus.'

The lines occur in the hymn for vespers of All Saints.

of accusations against the friars that became commonplaces of all future controversy. There is, first, the charge that the mendicants, armed with special powers, using every blandishment, and appearing from time to time as birds of passage, were able to attract penitents away from the parish priest; the latter in consequence lost the knowledge of souls to which a pastor has a right, in addition to losing the gifts which a natural generosity might prompt or less worthy considerations extract. The penitent, for his part, having thus the opportunity of approaching a series of confessors personally unknown to him, lost the care of a single spiritual physician who might be supposed to understand his case, besides avoiding an occasion of natural shame which might act as a deterrent.

Next, the friars were accused of beguiling widows and young people, of living upon them and of cajoling them into parting with every kind of commodity. No bolt or bar was proof against a friar.[1] Moreover, they used their privileged position at the university and elsewhere to induce boys of promise, or those who were heirs to property, to become friars; chicanery and even violence were employed when more straightforward methods failed. These accusations led naturally on to that of immorality, which Wyclif often makes by way of apophasis.[2] While the young friars intrigued with servant girls, the more experienced were accused of corrupting even ladies of noble blood.[3] Finally, from the proceeds of begging and unscrupulous dealing of all kinds, the friars built magnificent churches, sumptuously decorated and furnished, and provided themselves with spacious and comfortable homes.

In addition to these and other charges, common to all critics of the age, there are two which recur, and are peculiar to Wyclif: the charge that the friars by begging and dispatching money abroad are ruining the realm, and that they are heretical on the subject of the Eucharist. To the first Wyclif returns several times, and with characteristic thoroughness supplies again and again calculations of the gross sum thus lost either by dispatch overseas or in the construction of Caim's castles. A conservative estimate, he says, puts the number of English friars at four thousand; if £5 a year be allowed for the keep of each and another £5 per head for building and other overhead costs, some £40,000 is taken from the wealth of England by drones every year; they do nothing in return but corrupt the gospel teaching.[4]

The charge of heresy against the friars was a necessary rejoinder to

---

1 *De fund. sect.* ch. 8 (*Pol. Works*, I, 44): 'Sunt qui penetrant domos viduarum propter subtilitatem sue ypocrisis, non solum ad fortiter manducandum aut subtiliter mendicandum, sed ad feminas eciam nobiles deturpandum. Nec sera vel repagulum obstat illis.' Elsewhere (*Sermons*, III, 194) Wyclif remarks in questionable taste that if a friar blesses a cask in the cellar he turns it into accidents without substance.

2 *De fund. sect.* ch. 7 (*Pol. Works*, I, 40): 'taceo autem de corporali incontinencia.'

3 *Ibid.* ch. 12 (*Pol. Works*, I, 55): 'Numquid credimus quod sit fratribus juvenibus meritorium et securum sic habitare noctibus et diebus cum domicellis juvenibus dominarum?'

4 *Ibid.* ch. 4 (*Pol. Works*, I, 28): 'Calculant autem speculatores discreti', etc. Cf. *Triplex vinculum amoris*, ch. 9 (*Pol. Works*, I, 192–3). The number 4000, which would have been roughly correct for 1348, should certainly be almost halved for 1380 (v. Knowles, *Medieval*

their attack on Wyclif. His polemics against them date without exception from the last years of his life, and undoubtedly owe their origin to the firm stand taken by them against his doctrine on the Eucharist. In response, he retorts the charge: the friars are heretical in their incomprehensible and novel teaching of transubstantiation; faithful to the pope and holding him for infallible, they maintain a preposterous theory of accidents remaining without substance, which they dare not put in plain English for ordinary Christians, but shuffle and evade the issue as to what is present in a consecrated Host.[1]

These individual charges, however, are such as any critic might make. It is not these which make the assaults of Wyclif on the religious life something new and formidable. The capacity of his mind to penetrate the surface and touch the springs of life below, the unshrinking logic with which he draws conclusions from his accusations, the cold and drastic purpose behind his words, all of which were to bear fruit in due season, are more clearly seen in the frontal attack which he makes on the whole system, and the radical and unflinching campaign of extermination which he proposes. While others, before and after, were content to abuse the friars, Wyclif drives hard against their origins, ideals, pretensions and methods. While others were content to reform, Wyclif's hatred could be satisfied only with the complete extinction of his opponent. *Ecrasez l'infâme.* It is in this, and in his appeal to the alleged purity and utter simplicity of a primitive age, that his significance consists. By proceeding thus, he gave the go-by to all the elaborate framework of ethics and apologetics, to all the mass of speculation and tradition, that had gone to make the *Summa theologica*, and threw the *onus probandi* back upon those who for centuries had scarcely felt the need to expound their ideals, still less to defend them and prove their truth.

With a lucidity and precision which contrast strongly with the diffusion and apparent disorder of many of his treatises, Wyclif lays down the broad lines of attack which future generations did little more than develop. Originally, so his theory has it, clergy of the apostolic model had ministered to a Church in which the only religious way of life had been that of Christ and His gospel. When a decline set in:

It is licly that Cristis preestis, that stooden til that monkes comen, turneden to myche from Cristis love, and monkes lyveden than wel beter. But thes monkes stoden awhile and turneden sonner to coveitise; and aftir monkes camen thes chanouns; and after chanouns camen freris.[2]

Religious Houses, 364); that of 20,000 (*Sermons*, II, 435) is a fantastic overstatement. There were at the time some 200 friaries in existence, but many of these must have been small houses with less than ten inmates, inclusive of lay brothers.

1 Cf. *De detect. perfid. Antichristi* (*Pol. Works*, I, 382), and *The Church and her Members* (*Sel. English Works*, III, 352–3), etc.

2 *The Church and her Members* (*Sel. English Works*, III, 345–6). The appeal to primitive simplicity was, however, in the air at the time. Cf. Uthred of Boldon's treatises on primitive monasticism.

All these deformed public and private worship and put their private Rules above the law of Christ, and obedience to superiors (often against the claims of charity and reason) above obedience to the Gospel. As for these founders of theirs, Augustine is undoubtedly a saint in heaven, for Wyclif has read his works, which give certain evidence of sanctity; Benedict may be there, also, though Wyclif would not be too sure of this; as for Francis and Dominic, *credat Judaeus Apella.*[1] All have now grown rich and useless; but worst of all are the mendicants, who suck the blood of the nation and scatter heresies:

And here men noten many harmes that freris don in the Chirche. They spuyles the puple many weis by ipocrisie and other leesingis,[2] and bi this spuyling thei bilden Caymes Castelis to harme of cuntreis. Thei stelem pore mennis children, that is werse than stele an oxe; and thei stelen gladlich eires, Y leeve to speke of stelyng of wymmen...Thei moven londis to bateiles,[3] and pesible persones to plete;[4] thei maken many divorsis, and many matrimonies, unleveful,[5] bothe bi lesingis maad to parties, and bi pryvelegies of the court. Y leeve to speke of fighting that thei done in o lond and othir....And sith coventis of freris ben shrewis[6] for the more part or moche, no woundir if thei envenyme men that comes thus unto hem.

A good friar, indeed, is as rare as the phoenix.[7]

As all such private rules of life, even when not so clearly vicious, are superfluous and harmful to the spread of the spirit of the gospel, the orders one and all must be suppressed, Caim's castles sacked, and parliament should advise the king to confiscate their possessions, which may be given back to the donors or their heirs, or used by the king for the defence of the realm. Such friars as are not wholly abandoned or heretical may find employment as parish priests or schoolmasters.[8] Wyclif, indeed, had his programme so clearly defined in his imagination, that he more than once proposes simple tests by which the iniquity of the friars may be ascertained. The easiest way, he says, is to oblige them under penalties to put on paper, or to depose under the convent seal or before fit witnesses, exactly what their belief in the Eucharist is. Those who fail to write correctly (that is, in Wyclif's sense) or at all—and if they are faithful to the pope, they are bound so to fail—must forfeit their possessions and be avoided as heretics.[9] A second test of the *ad hominem* kind, and simpler

---

1 *Tripl. vinc. amoris,* ch. 5 (*Pol. Works,* I, 177): 'De Augustino evidenter suppono quod sit beatus in patria propter evidencias quas ex scripturis suis elicui. De Benedicto autem hoc idem suppono plus leviter. Et hoc idem qui volunt possunt supponere de Dominico et Francisco.'   2 Leesingis: lies.

3 This is a reference to the Flanders crusade of Bishop Spenser of Norwich in 1383; it was preached by the friars and is a frequent topic in Wyclif's tracts.

4 Plete: plead in the courts.   5 Unleveful: loveless.

6 Shrewis: malicious.

7 *Ep.* ix *De fratribus ad scholares,* 16: 'Bonus enim frater rarus est cum fenice.'

8 *De quat. sect. nov.* ch. 10–12 (*Pol. Works,* I, 279–85).

9 *The Church and her Members* (*Sel. English Works,* III, 352–3). Cf. *De quat. sect. nov.* ch. 11 (*Pol. Works,* I, 282); *De detect. perfid. Antichristi* (*Pol. Works,* I, 382–3).

to apply, is to ask a Carmelite or Austin friar when his order began and then ask a Preacher or a Minor whether he agrees. This will infallibly set them by the ears, and consequently all Christians should avoid them till they all agree on the truth.[1]

In this way, by God's help, the realm might be disembarrassed of the whole brood,[2] and while the good work is in hand, continues Wyclif, all minor sects may be sent the same way. Hospitals would not be missed, nor chantries nor guilds; and, with a sense of Thorough that verges on the sublime, Wyclif throws them on the fire.[3] What, then, of Oxford colleges? Wyclif had loved Oxford dearly—it is perhaps the only deep personal emotion he ever reveals—and in a passage, which must be the earliest of all the many tributes that have been paid to the beauty of a city that has cast her spell over so many minds, he writes of her fresh meadows and pleasant streams, her verdure 'branchy between towers', the soft airs that make of her a dwelling fit for angels, a very house of God and gate of heaven.[4] Yet even this sweet Oxford had been deflowered by the friars; they had cast its prophet forth; he was an exile who would never see its spires again. Rue, not snapdragon, clung to the walls of Balliol, and the rector of Lutterworth swept his earliest home, along with Caim's castles, out from the new Jerusalem.

There alone did his prophetic spirit see false. To those who lived in the age that was dawning, Wyclif's diatribes and schemes may have seemed the outpouring of a mind warped by heresy or soured by disease. Caim's castles, unshaken by the distant drum, grew more splendid still. Yet medieval monasticism might well have felt a premonitory tremor throughout its frame in the years when both Wyclif and Langland were walking over its grave. With an appalling precision the fate which they foretold came upon the religious, and the programme which Wyclif had outlined was carried through to the last detail. They might scatter his ashes in the Swift, but he had not failed to be beforehand with them. He had cast his bread upon the running waters, and it returned after many days.

Wyclif left no successor of influence and ability comparable to his own. His mantle—or a large part of it—fell years later, and in Bohemia. Of his followers and supporters from the schools several of the ablest and most intelligent, such as Philip Repyndon, future abbot of Leicester and bishop of Lincoln, recanted under the pressure of persecution or the more in-

---

1 *The Church and her Members* (*Sel. English Works*, III, 353): 'Carmes seien that thei were bifore the tyme that Crist was born. Austyns seien that thei weren many hundred wynters bifore other freris. Prechours and Minours seyn the reverse.'

2 *De detect. perfid. Antichristi* (*Pol. Works*, I, 383): 'Posset regnum exonerari de istis sectis.'

3 *De quat. sect. nov.* ch. 8 (*Pol. Works*, I, vi).

4 *De fratribus ad scholares*, 18: '...loco congrue situata, fontibus et fluviis irrigata, pratis et pascuis circumdata...arbustis virentibus et locis nemorosis vicina...locus amenus fertilis et optimus...domus Dei et porta celi congrue vocitata'. Was Wyclif thinking of the panegyric on Paris of John of Salisbury (*PL*, CXCIX, col. 113)?

sidious arguments of self-interest, while the country knights and small landowners, whose sympathy with Lollardy is a curious and not fully investigated feature of the times, gradually dwindled in number and influence when deprived of a leader and exposed to the conservative forces that grew in strength during the later years of the reign of Richard II.[1] The most persistent element was that of the poor priests and their supporters among the small men and country people, and it was here that Lollardy hibernated, as it were, in London and in the woodlands of Essex and Buckinghamshire, till the climate became more suitable to its growth in the sixteenth century.

For a few years after Wyclif's death his immediate followers, such as Hereford and above all Purvey, continued to produce anti-Mendicant tracts, many of them more reckless in tone even than anything Wyclif wrote, freely accusing the friars and clergy generally of adultery and unnatural vice, and advocating marriage as a prophylactic.[2] Their activities were to a certain extent checked, or at least driven underground, by the repressive measures of 1388, and defections were numerous. There was, however, a revival in 1394–5, when an attempt was made by the Lollard small landowners to bring on a full discussion of the ills of the Church in parliament. The attempt failed, but a manifesto of Twelve Conclusions was nailed to the door of St Paul's[3] and Povey succeeded in getting into the king's hands[4] a programme of ecclesiastical disendowment, by which the income of bishops and religious houses was to be diverted to support fifteen earls, 1500 knights, 6200 squires and 100 almshouses, not to speak of £20,000 per annum which was to go to the king for national defence. Furthermore, wealthy secular clerks were to be mulcted of £100,000 a year for the benefit of poor and deserving priests and fifteen universities. In this sweeping transference of funds it is noteworthy that Premonstratensians, alien monks, Carthusians, Bonshommes and the quasi-regular communities serving hospitals or inhabiting hermitages were not to be touched.[5] Though this scheme anticipated in the strangest manner both the velleities and the actual achievements of Henry VIII it was—even apart from intrinsic miscalculations and economic obstacles—no more practical politics than was Wyclif's method of weeding out the friars by means of an essay on the Eucharist.

1 For this, the valuable chapter of Workman, *John Wyclif*, II, 325–404, may be consulted. He significantly entitles it 'Broken Reeds'.

2 Many of these tracts are printed in the volumes already published of Wyclif's English works. T. Arnold and F. D. Matthew discuss the authorship of several in their editions, and Workman has an Appendix on the subject (*John Wyclif*, I, 329–32). In any case, there is very little original matter that might make the question important for a historian. The voice, as Dr Workman truly remarks, is the voice of Wyclif, however hairy the hand, he might have added, and strong-scented the garments may be. It may be noted that Hereford ultimately became a Carthusian.

3 *V.* Workman, *op. cit.* II, 390 *seqq.*

4 Cf. *Fasciculi zizaniorum*, 364: 'Fuit probatum in uno libro quem rex habuit.'

5 *V.* Walsingham, *Hist. Anglicana*, ed. H. T. Riley, LI, 282; C. L. Kingsford, *Chronicles of London*, 67; and Workman, *John Wyclif*, II, 397–9 and Appendix Z, 420–1.

No public notice was taken of the proposal at the time, but fifteen years later, in 1410, there was another wave of anti-monastic and anti-clerical feeling among the knights of the shire of Lollard sympathies, and a monastic chronicler relates that Purvey's scheme was served up again as a petition in parliament.[1] It is difficult to believe that this was so, and no official record exists of any such petition, though there was certainly Lollard and anti-clerical activity in that year, and the suppression of the alien priories, though due to other causes,[2] may well have caused a land-hunger among founder's kin of other religious houses, and a corresponding hyperaesthesis in monastic circles. Whatever the exact truth of the matter, it was the last time that the Lollards were strong enough to make a quasi-public attack upon the possessioners. The monks, however, then as always, had the long memories of an undying family, and it is no matter for wonder that they and the friars took a leading part in the suppression of Lollardy in the early fifteenth century.

II. WILLIAM LANGLAND

During the decades of crisis in England preceding the Peasants' Revolt, and in the very years when Wyclif's mental development was leading him towards a collision with the friars and to an attack on all religious, another Englishman of keen mind, as critical of the existing state of things as Wyclif, but possessed of what Wyclif entirely lacked, a deep fund of love and compassion, was moving unknown and unnoticed through the Malvern bracken or along Cheapside. The points of contact between the two, which are as striking as the profound difference of outlook which separates them, show beyond reasonable doubt the problems and abuses that were troubling all reflective minds.[3]

Langland, for all his sympathy with the common man, shares Wyclif's abhorrence at the evil use made of the legacies of great men by the possessioners. If layfolk were wise, he says, they would ponder long before they deprived their heirs of their ancestral lands for the sake of monks or canons

1 Walsingham, *Hist. Anglicana*, II, 282. It is not among other petitions in the *Rot. Parl.* and there are a number of small difficulties regarding the transmission of the text. W. T. Waugh in his article on Sir John Oldcastle in *EHR*, xx (1905), p. 440, is of the opinion that Walsingham either invented or at least grossly exaggerated the whole incident. Workman, *John Wyclif*, II, 421, accepts Walsingham's account as substantially authentic, but it must be confessed that there are serious objections to this, and knowing the methods of Walsingham and some previous chroniclers of his house, it would seem better to suspend judgement.

2 For this *v. infra*, pp. 162–5.

3 The orthodox view, first propounded fully by Skeat in his edition of *Piers the Plowman*, is that the three recensions, known as the A, B and C texts, are all the work of William Langland and date from *c.* 1362–3, 1377 and 1393 respectively. Others have seen in the whole the work of two, three or even more poets. Whatever may be thought, the dates of the three versions are fairly certain, and to the present writer it seems unquestionable that the A and B texts, at least, are by the same author, Langland. The quotations are from Skeat's monumental edition, and are mostly taken from the B text, quoted by *passus* and line. For purposes of comparison, it may be noted that Chaucer's *Prologue* and his most racy Tales date from 1386 to 1389.

who are rich enough already;[1] it would be as wise to moisten the Thames with a cask of drinking water.[2] The thought recurs elsewhere of the injustice done to heirs of donors by the rich, heartless religious:

> Litel had lordes to done . to gyve londe fram her heires
> To religious, that haue no reuthe . though it reyne on here auteres![3]

And Langland does not shrink from the logical deduction; like Wyclif, he urges a resumption of church lands by the heirs of the founders.

The poet, indeed, paints a more vivid picture than the controversialist of the luxurious possessioner, and in words which exactly anticipate Chaucer, if indeed, they did not inspire the familiar lines in the *Prologue*, he describes the monk out of the cloister, restless, rich and haughty:

> A ryder . a rowmer bi stretes,
> A leder of louedayes[4] . and a londe-bugger,[5]
> A priker on a palfray . fro manere to manere,
> An heep of houndes at his ers . as he a lorde were.
> And but if his knaue knele . that shal his cuppe brynge,
> He loureth on hym and axeth hym . who taughte hym curteisye?[6]

It is after a detailed description of such a monk that Langland utters his celebrated prophecy of the fate of the great abbeys, which was to receive in due time an exact fulfilment usually denied to such utterances. It is here also that the poet, again resembling Wyclif, foretells the destruction of Caim—the rich Church—with all its works.

> Ac there shal come a kyng . and confesse yow religiouses,
> And bete yow, as the bible telleth . for brekynge of yowre reule,
> And amende monyales[7] . monkes and chanouns,
> And putten hem to her penaunce . *ad pristinum statum ire,*
> And barounes with erles beten hem . . .
> And thanne shal the abbot of Abyndoun . and all his issu for euere
> Haue a knokke of a kynge . and incurable the wounde.[8]

If in the first redaction of the poem the wealthy possessioners are the object of Langland's strictures, in the two later versions it is the friars who receive harder treatment. The charges are the familiar ones: the friars

1 B, xv, 316–19. Cf. Chaucer, *Somnour's Tale*, ed. Skeat, 1721–3.   2 *Ibid.* 331–2.
3 B, x, 312–13. Skeat in a note *ad loc.* quotes a parallel from Wyclif, *Select English Works,* ed. T. A. Arnold, III, 380, where it is said that people give to the friars 'though it rain on the auter of the parische churche'.
4 Loueday: a day for settlement of disputes by arbitration, and therefore an opportunity for acquiring and exercising influence. Cf. Chaucer, *Prologue,* 258 (of the Friar): 'In love-dayes ther coude he muchel helpe.'
5 Londe-bugger: a land buyer.   6 B, x, 306–11.   7 Monyales: nuns.
8 B, x, 317–21; 326–7. The phrase 'abbot of Abingdon' has exercised commentators; no doubt it is due purely to the exigencies of alliterative metre, but it is far more effective than 'the abbot of Engelonde . and the abbesse his nece' to which it is changed in C, vi, 177. Possibly the original version had given offence. [Since writing this note I have read N. Coghill's article, 'Two Notes on Piers Plowman: The Abbot of Abingdon', where he shows that in 1392–3 (the date of the C text) the then abbot was engaged in prosecuting some of his tenants with a severity that provoked comment; the poet might well have felt that the times counselled discretion.]

obtain faculties through favour of the great, and by backbiting the clergy and flattering the people they supplant the parish priests and entice their penitents away from them.[1] They cannot rest at home, but go from house to house like street musicians;[2] no home is secure against their infiltration; they profess to come as physicians; actually, they dishonour the women.[3] The tone grows more bitter as the poem proceeds; the ubiquity of the friars, swarming like ants, seems to have acted as an irritant upon Langland. Everything else in nature, he complains, even monks and nuns, keep to a fixed number—everything, save only friars, who are prolific beyond counting, and he adds coldly that heaven has a fixed and even number of inhabitants, but there is no known limit to those of hell.[4] And in the very last lines of the poem a friar is introduced as offering himself as confessor to the dying Contrition, to whom he gives letters of fraternity for a small sum, and thus flatters him out of all sorrow for sin:

> The frere with his phisik . this folke hath enchaunted,
> And plastred hem so esyly . thei drede no synne.[5]

It is in a sudden outburst of wrath at this that Conscience starts up and goes forth over the wide world to seek Piers the Plowman, and the poet awakes.

Langland's fierce indignation with the friars is indeed in some respects more savage than Wyclif's. It is also far more impressive, for it lacks the notes of egoism and extravagance which give to some of Wyclif's tirades a touch of tedium and even of the ridiculous. It is, in fine, more genuine. Langland, whatever we may think of his judgements and ideals, was clearly a man of deep personal religion, with a humility and sense of reverence altogether lacking in his more celebrated contemporary. In addition, his thoughts ran completely along the lines of the traditional spirituality of the Church. While Wyclif, though expressing himself in scholastic terms and categories, was in fact cutting himself loose from all links with the immediate past, Langland, rebel though he may have been, held fast to tradition, as well in the doctrine of the active and contemplative lives as in that of the primacy of Love, derived originally by the mystics from the schools, and given a new extension and depth by Richard Rolle.[6] Langland, in short, is on the right wing of the army of reform, orthodox and

---

1 B, xx, 322 *seqq.*
2 B, x, 92–3:
> 'Nought to fare as a fitheler or a frere . for to seke festes,
> Homelich at other mennes houses . and hayten her owne.'
3 B, xx, 338–45. 'Sire *Penetrans-domos.*'
4 B, xx, 262 *seqq:*
> 'Of lewed and of lered . the lawe wol and axeth
> A certeyn for a certeyne . save onelich of freres.'
5 B, xx, 376–7.
6 Cf. the magnificent passage on theology in B, x, 180–8:
> 'A ful lethy [=useless] thing it were . yif that love nere [=were not]
> Ac for it let best by [=thinks most highly of] love . I love it the bettre.'

heretical, in which Wyclif, the unspiritual polemist, stands on the extreme left.

The author of *Piers Plowman*, therefore, however severe his judgements on the friars he knew, did not, as did Wyclif, include St Francis and the whole Minorite ideal in his condemnation. He had seen Charity running and singing in ragged weeds, and wearing a friar's habit, though it was long ago, and in St Francis's time,[1] and in a passage of unusual beauty he recalls the tales of saints who had been fed by the fowls of the air, and bids the friars refuse money that has been unjustly extorted by lords from the poor, and wait in trust for heaven to send them gifts, content meanwhile with the simple fare of their Rule:

> For we ben goddes foules . and abiden alwey,
> Tyl briddes bringe us . that we shulde lyuve by.
> For had ye potage and payn ynough . and peny-ale to drynke,
> And a messe there-mydde . of o manere kynde,
> Ye had right ynough, ye religious . and so yowre reule me tolde.[2]

Indeed, we may think that Langland, whether or not he was actually a 'stickit priest', was certainly in spirit a *vocation manquée*. Of a truth he had a kind of nostalgia for the cloister, or for a golden phantasm of the cloister that had never wholly faded from his imagination:

> For if heuene be on this erthe . and ese to any soule,
> It is in cloistere or in scole . be many skilles I fynde;
> For in cloistre cometh ne man . to chide ne to fighte,
> But alle is buxumnesse there and bokes . to rede and to lerne.[3]

But these traits, while they soften the picture the poet paints, render his stern judgement on the religious and especially on the friars all the more impressive. They were to him corrupting what had been of the best; they had taken Love out of the cloister:

> For there that Loue is leder . ne lacked neuere grace.[4]

III. CHAUCER

For one reader conversant with Langland and Wyclif, probably a hundred are familiar with the *Prologue* to the *Canterbury Tales*. For the mass of educated Englishmen, therefore, the unforgettable portraits of the monk and the friar remain fixed in the memory as typical of the classes described during the whole of the later Middle Ages.

After studying the charges brought against the religious by Chaucer's two older contemporaries, the first impression on re-reading the *Prologue* is one of surprise at the moderation of tone. Biting as the irony may be, it stops far short of the vitriolic outpourings of Wyclif, and is at first blush less damning than Langland's accusations. Certainly Chaucer, man of the world and court poet as he was, tolerant by nature and permitting himself

---

1 B, xv, 219–20; 225–6.   2 B, xv, 308–12.
3 B, x, 300–4.   4 B, x, 186.

extreme liberty, if not libertinage,[1] of speech, is an excellent example of the conventional and orthodox party which gained influence during the latter part of the reign of Richard II, and remained dominant for half a century. He is, in fact, in many ways the typical easygoing *croyant* of an age of religious decline, who laughs at the failings of the clergy without indignation and without repulsion, who sits loose to moral standards through life, but makes his peace with God as years advance. Nevertheless, the very absence of moral indignation serves only to deepen the melancholy impression given by his devastating satire, and the final judgement will probably be, for those readers at least who have traversed the whole extent of the *Canterbury Tales*, that Chaucer's wit is as keen a solvent of religious pretence as is Wyclif's anger.

His method throughout the *Prologue* is to paint in strong primary colours a gathering of men and women who excel in the tricks or legitimate exercise of their professions. The rogues, indeed, outnumber the honest men, but a few of the outstanding characters are so blameless that the casual reader sometimes fails to note all the insinuations with which the poet undermines the honour of those who are less admirable. The Clerk and the Parson, on this division, become the purest of their kind, while the Monk and the Friar embody all the self-indulgence and versatile hypocrisy of their respective classes. The Monk, well-bred, full-blooded, capable, worldly and frankly dismissing the Rule as a code of the Dark Ages, is a figure drawn with a most skilful combination of suggestion and reticence. Nowhere, perhaps, is Chaucer's irony more subtle than when he assents to the Monk's candid disavowal of any love for an ascetic life; the passage has certainly divided the commentators, nor can it be said that the poet himself, by leasing from the monks of Westminster a home under the shadow of their abbey, and by electing to lie in death near their choir, has strengthened the case of those who would see in him a *Malleus monachorum*. It has surprised some readers that the Monk, when his turn comes to tell a tale, should have produced, instead of a story of gallantry, a series of lamentable happenings to illustrious historical personages from an inexhaustible store,[2] which is interrupted by the Knight when the whole company has become depressed or bored. There is, however, both moral and historical suitability in this; patchwork chronicles and encyclopaedias abounded in the religious houses of the time, and the Monk, like his counterparts in all walks of ecclesiastical life in every century, combined a worldly life with outward respectability and cultured interests.

---

1 Chaucer repented of this; *v.* his 'retracciouns', which include 'The tales of Caunterbury, thilke that sounen in-to (= tend to) sinne' at the conclusion of the *Parson's Tale*, ed. Skeat, § 1085, where he prays 'that Crist for his grete mercy foryeve me the sinne'. It may be noted that he does not retract his criticisms of friars and monks.

2 Cf. the words of the *Monk's Prologue*, 3161–2:

'Tragedies wol I telle
Of which I have an hundred in my celle.'

There is considerable likeness between the Monk's stanzas and some of those of Lydgate.

Unlike Shakespeare, Chaucer had no capacity for depicting fine shades of character, and when he has occasion, in the *Shipman's Tale*, to portray another monk, there is a strong family resemblance between the well-mannered, ingratiating, efficient and unprincipled Daun John and the older and more outwardly blameless Dan Piers.[1]

The Friar, who follows immediately after the Monk in the *Prologue*, and to whom more space is devoted than goes to any other character, is treated indeed with that mixture of irony and geniality that is as peculiar to Chaucer as is a somewhat different blend of the same ingredients to Sir Thomas More, but no doubt is left as to his basic rascality. Though we are never expressly told that the Friar is a Minor, there can be no doubt of this, and all the old charges come forward—the enticing of penitents, the extraction of money and gifts from them, from unprotected widows and from the sick, the varying roles of boon-companion, arbitrator, entertainer and district visitor among the older citizens, and of mentor and matchmaker among the young people.[2] Incidental references up and down the tales complete the picture, for whenever friars are mentioned the impression given is the same, whether the speaker be the Wife of Bath, telling with racy irony flavoured with compliment how the ubiquitous friars, by blessing every object in sight, have driven the fairies out of the country,[3] or whether it be the Somnour, sworn enemy of the Friar, who gives a full-length portrait of Frere John of Holderness on his rounds, ejecting the cat from the warmest corner as he settles himself down, ordering his dinner from the lady of the house, whose maternal grief is assuaged by the story of a vision of her lately dead child seen by the brotherhood on his way to heaven, and proceeding with a mixture of hypocrisy and flattery to solicit further benefactions.[4]

Chaucer agrees with Wyclif and Langland on the prodigious number of friars in the country

> As thikke as motes in the sonne-beem.[5]

He agrees also on a point of greater detail: that the money the friars beg goes towards their magnificent buildings. Thus Frere John of Holderness exhorts his audience

> to yeve, for goddes sake,
> Wher-with men mighten holy houses make,

---

1 Cf. the *Shipman's Tale*, 1215:
> 'Ther was a monk, a fair man and a bold,' etc.

also 1252 *seqq.*, especially 1258-9:
> 'Who was so welcome as my lord daun John,
> Our dere cosin, ful of curteisye?'

2 *V.* the *Prologue* for young women, franklins, housewives, innkeepers and widows. The *Somnour's Tale* adds an interesting account of the friar's behaviour first at the house of an ordinary well-to-do townsman, and then at the house of the local lord. The reference to marriages made by the Friar (in the *Prologue*) no doubt implies that the young women had been his mistresses, though loveless matchmaking by special dispensation had been one of Wyclif's charges against the friars.   3 *Wife of Bath's Tale*, 859-81.

4 *Somnour's Tale*, 1765 *seqq.*   5 *Wife of Bath's Tale*, 868.

that is, to the friar, and not

> As to possessioners, that mowen live
> Thanked be godde, in wele and habundaunce.[1]

How far the poet would have agreed with one of his characters that friars pester with their importunities like flies landing in one's plate may be a matter of opinion,[2] but the Somnour would have found Wyclif to agree with him in another forcibly expressed opinion.[3]

Chaucer, unlike his two contemporaries, was conscious of no mission or desire to reform society. If his testimony stood alone it might be permissible to regard it as the exaggeration of one who is writing to catch the attention of his public. There are indeed many traits in common to Chaucer and Dickens; both, with the keenest eye for the colour of men's clothes and for the foibles and eccentricities of their fellows, know nothing of the subtle texture behind the bright colours and still less of the spiritual heights and chasms that Langland and Dame Juliana of Norwich were exploring in their different ways. The close agreement, however, between Langland, Wyclif and Chaucer as to the worldliness of the monks and the rascality of the friars is too remarkable to be dismissed.[4] It is, we may feel, only a partial picture. While they were writing, Walter Hilton at Thurgarton and Prior John at Bridlington, possessioners both, were attaining to the vision of peace, the revelation of the Word, which is the final goal of all Christian strivings; on a lower and more visible plane such men as Thomas de la Mare and Uthred of Boldon were worthy, if not eminently holy, representatives of their profession; nor were all the theologians who opposed Wyclif and the preachers who delighted Margery Kempe entirely unworthy of their vocation. Nevertheless, it is hard to escape the conviction that the three writers who have just been reviewed are in their different ways witnesses to a corruption among the Mendicants, and a worldliness among the black monks, which were only too real, whatever limits we may put upon their extent and the severity of their incidence.

---

1 *Somnour's Tale*, 1775 *seqq.* Cf. the friar's words in the same tale, 2099–106:
> 'Yif me thanne of thy gold, to make our cloistre...
> By god, we owen fourty pound for stones.'

2 *V.* the Somnour's outburst when the Friar addresses the Wife of Bath:
> 'A frere wol entremette [=meddle] him evermo.
> Lo, gode men, a flye and eek a frere,
> Wol falle in every dish and eek matere.'
> *Wife of Bath's Prologue*, 834–6.

3 *V. Somnour's Prologue*, 1674:
> 'Freres and feendes been but lyte a-sonder.'

4 Further variations on the themes found in Chaucer and Langland are to be found in the popular verses of the next generation, printed by T. Wright, *Political Poems and Songs*, Vol. I, has (20) a 'Song against Friars' and (21) 'On the Minorite Friars' but the fullest and liveliest are the attack of 'Jack Upland' and the 'Reply of Dom Topias' in vol. II, nos. 3 and 4, composed *c.* 1401.

CHAPTER VIII

THE SPIRITUAL LIFE OF THE
FOURTEENTH CENTURY

The calamities and controversies of the times, the crisis of the Roman Church and the symptoms of decline in the external life of the religious orders, real though they are and arresting to the mind, must not be allowed wholly to obscure the glimpses of an inner life caught here and there in the fourteenth century, the more particularly as the outward manifestations of this life are of a different character from what had gone before.

The outstanding examples of sanctity in the twelfth century were for the most part found among the founders of religious orders and eminent abbots and monk-bishops; the secular prelates, such as St Thomas of Canterbury and St William of York, who received formal recognition, owed it to a violent death. In the thirteenth century, by contrast, the type of sanctity is to be found most frequently in the zealous diocesan bishop who had previously been a master in the schools. The three Englishmen to achieve canonization, Edmund of Canterbury, Richard of Chichester and Thomas of Hereford, were all of this class, as were several others, such as Grosseteste of Lincoln, William Button of Bath and Wells, Roger Niger of London and Walter Cantilupe of Worcester, who left behind them a reputation for sanctity. The last of this generation were perhaps Winchelsey of Canterbury and Dalderby of Lincoln, for whose canonization repeated efforts were made. The episcopate of the fourteenth century was in general of a somewhat different type, drawn more largely from clerics who had previously served the king in an administrative or diplomatic capacity. Of this class Simon Langham and William of Wykeham are eminent examples, and though a few, such as Grandisson of Exeter, were of a more spiritual temper it was not among them, as it was not among the prelates and provincials of the mutually hostile possessioners and mendicants, that sanctity was as a rule to be looked for. Rather, the examples of unusual holiness of life, which are not lacking in the fourteenth century, are almost all given by private individuals, unknown in their lifetime to any save a narrow circle of acquaintances and often unconnected with any organized religious institute within the Church. Rarely, if ever, after the twelfth century is it possible to find and follow in all the events of his life a monk of unusual holiness of life.

Once at least, however, the veil is lifted for a moment by a monk of Durham.[1] On the island-group of Farne, on a few acres of wind-swept,

---

1 The rediscovery of this monk is, like so much else, due to the untiring researches of W. A. Pantin, who found the Meditations in MS. B.iv.34 of the Library of the Dean and Chapter at Durham, and printed extracts with a commentary in an article, 'The Monk-Solitary of Farne: a Fourteenth-Century English Mystic'.

storm-beaten turf, the traditions of St Cuthbert had been lovingly preserved by monks of Durham who had heard and followed the call to the
desert, and had left the great priory with its noise and wealth for a life of
hardship and solitude, with creatures of the deep and sea-birds for their
only companions, and the sound of the surf always in their ears. For some
time at least in the thirteenth century the cell on Farne had had two inmates; of one of these, or it may be of a sole inmate, a memorial has been
preserved in the form of meditations or soliloquies. The writer would
seem to have been one Brother Peter of Durham, who was professed in
1345, and his work was written when the ravages of the Black Death were
still fresh in all minds. Brother Peter had been a student at Oxford, where
he had an escape from drowning in the Cher which he regarded as pro-
vidential, if not miraculous,[1] and when he wrote he had been for some
time on the island.

His meditations, half prayers, half spiritual reflections, are a latecomer
to that great family of writings beginning with the soliloquies of St
Augustine and including the prayers of Peter Damian, John of Fécamp
and St Anselm. They are likewise in the tradition of Bernard and Bonaventure, and are on the whole a prolongation of the monastic spirituality,
untouched by scholastic argument or by the new school of German and
Dutch mysticism. There is nothing of doctrinal note, and nothing that is
strictly mystical.[2] The writer can on occasion give a picture, simple and
arresting, of common human incidents rarely seen on Farne, as when he
compares the outstretched arms and bowed head of Christ on the Cross
to the loving gesture of a mother:

Thus do mothers in their tender love for their little ones. When they see them
afar off, and would have them run quickly back, they straightway stretch wide
their arms and bow their head, and the children, taught by nature and eager for
kisses, run and leap into their mother's embrace.[3]

The monk of Farne, like Ailred and John of Bridlington, had a particular
devotion to St John the Evangelist, not only as the beloved disciple but
as a fellow-solitary on an island, and St John enters into a passage which
is more directly personal than any other:

O Lord of Hosts, love-worthy Jesus, what was it that stirred thee to be so
full of care for me, that over and above thy most desirable hidden presence in
the Eucharist...and over and above that hope which thou hast willed to give
me in common with the other sons of Holy Church, by patience and the con-
solation of the Scriptures—why did not this suffice thee, but that thou must

---

1 The passage is quoted by Pantin, *art. cit.* 163.
2 Pantin, with an enthusiasm natural to an excavator who has made a valuable find,
perhaps rates the spiritual interest of the monk of Farne too highly. So far as his writings
go, there is no evidence of a mystical experience in the strictly theological sense of the term,
and his single 'vision-locution' can scarcely be compared (as on p. 169) with the 'shewings'
of Dame Juliana of Norwich, which were the external occasion of a deeper illumination
which only reached its term after many years.
3 The Latin is in Pantin, *art. cit.* 168.

teach me with thine own lips, and not by means of him who had told thee of my petition, John the Evangelist, thy dear one—to teach me what I had sought to know, how I might be saved in the day of judgment. With calm and joyful countenance thou didst answer: 'Love, and thou shalt be safe.' This thy delightful visitation, and this thy health-giving teaching made me perforce love thee, but beyond this I am full of happiness when I remember the winning kindliness with which thou didst pronounce these words, for thou didst speak them as it were with a smile. Help me then, Jesu, that I may be able to do what thou didst command, so that I may love thee, Lord, in all and above all, with that measure that knows no measure.[1]

This experience, however genuine, is not that of a mystic who has gone far in the ways of the spirit, but the words are those of an earnest and sincere man, who, like Rolle and the author of *The Cloud of Unknowing*, had mingled with the life of his age and then turned away, and who had followed to the letter the call to the wilderness, where God might speak to his heart.

While the monks, black and white, and the friars black, white and grey, exhibit no groups and few individuals of unusual holiness, it is noteworthy that such should have existed in the two orders, of canons and friars, who claimed St Augustine as their founder. The houses of canons were too numerous, too unequal and too unorganized to have a common spirit or to exercise mutual influence, but it is remarkable that the last Englishman to be canonized until our own day and the most notable spiritual writer of his time should both have been Austin canons and should have been contemporaries. Of Walter Hilton (*c.* 1330–96), canon of Thurgarton in Nottinghamshire, something will be said later; of John Thwenge of Bridlington there is all too little to be told.[2] By birth a Yorkshireman from Thwing in the uplands of the East Riding, he studied at Oxford for two years as a boy, but returned north in 1340, at the age of twenty, to become a novice at Bridlington, not far from his home, where he became in due course precentor, almoner and subprior. When the superior died in 1360 he would have been elected but for his refusal which, unlike that of others in similar circumstances, was resolute and final. The second choice of the community, however, died of the plague within a twelvemonth, and this time John Thwenge felt it his duty not to refuse.[3] Of his intimate life and personal characteristics little is known; the marvels related of him are few and not extravagant, and bear signs of direct trans-

1 *Ibid.* 170.
2 For St John of Bridlington *v. DNB*, XXIX. For the oldest surviving life, which is apparently sub-contemporary, *v. Nova Legenda Anglie*, ed. C. Horstman, II, 64 *seqq.*, and for a notice by a contemporary chronicler *v. The Kirkstall Chronicle, 1355–1400*, ed. by M. V. Clarke and N. Denholm-Young. J. S. Purvis, *St John of Bridlington*, and P. Grosjean, S.J., 'De S. Joanni Bridlingtoniensi Collectanea', may also be consulted. For the process of canonization *v.* also *Papers and Letters from the Northern Registers*, ed. J. Raine, 420–1, and for the bull of canonization of Boniface IX, dated 24 September 1401, *C.P.L.* V, 458–60. For the *cultus v.* 'The Liturgical Credentials of a forgotten English Saint', by J. O. Twemlow.
3 *Vita*, ed. Horstman, II, 66–7.

mission. It was told of him that as prior he slept in the common dormitory and on the bed which had first been assigned to him as a novice; he kept to the ordinary round and diet of the community, avoiding all ostentatious asceticism. When asked why he did not join a stricter order he replied that all Rules approved by the Church could lead a man to perfection, and that as for himself, he did not as yet keep his own Rule in its essentials. Asked on another occasion what Rule was the best, he gave the revealing reply: 'The Gospel of St John.' It may have been his predilection for the Evangelist, added to a knowledge of his character, that shaped the vision of the ancress of Richmond who saw an eagle approaching her bearing a scroll with the words 'Jesus is my love'.[1]

John Thwenge would seem to have spent all his life at Bridlington; he took no share in the public life of his day and no writings of his are known to have existed. After almost twenty years of rule he died of the plague in 1379; his influence is recorded upon at least two canons of saintly life;[2] one of these, William Sleightholm, his chaplain and confessor, who furnished details of his life and miracles, lived till 1421, and was visited by the erratic Margery Kempe; he died in the odour of sanctity.[3] Despite his retired life, the reputation of the prior of Bridlington was great and his contemporary, Archbishop Neville, took early steps in 1386 to initiate the process of canonization; this had a speedy issue and St John of Bridlington received in 1401 the title which all the efforts of kings and chapters had failed to secure for Dalderby, for Winchelsey and for Robert Grosseteste.

The Austin friars, like the Carmelites, had been in origin hermits. In the fourteenth century, owing perhaps to their relatively small numbers in north-western Europe, they were subjected to a stricter control and more direct supervision from the prior-general than were the Minors and Preachers of the same date. They had, moreover, at the middle of the fourteenth century, a succession of notable priors-general (William of Cremona, 1326–42; Thomas of Strassburg, 1345–56; Gregory of Rimini, 1357–8) who interested themselves both in the theological discipline of their order and in the personnel of the houses of studies at Oxford and Cambridge, which were for a time (1355–65) the only recognized *studia generalia* of the Austin friars.[4] Moreover, incidents such as the entry in 1361 at the friary of Huntingdon of a young nobleman of blood royal,

1 *Vita*, ed. Horstman, II, 71–2.

2 *Ibid*. 77: 'Hic [Johannes] Abraham per repromissionem eterne felicitatis duos filios enutrivit, idem monasterium perlustrantes imitatoriis ejusdem patris vestigiis per miraculorum choruscationem.'

3 *Ibid*. 70: 'Willelmus Sleghtholme...sanctitatis eminentia choruscus miraculis'. Margery Kempe asked leave of the archbishop of York to go to Bridlington to speak with her confessor, 'a good man, who was the good prior's confessor that is now canonized.' (*The Book of Margery Kempe*, chs. 52, 53; ed. Butler-Bowdon, 188, 193.) Sleightholm's reminiscences are referred to in the *Vita*, p. 70.

4 For the Austin friars of this period *v*. Fr A. Gwynn, S.J., *The English Austin Friars*. This book, a mine of information not to be found elsewhere, is illuminated by careful judgements and living appreciation of spiritual values. It cannot easily be absorbed at a single reading; it is a book which will bear repeated examination.

possibly heir to the earldoms of Hereford and Essex, in spite of the violent opposition of his relatives,[1] and tributes such as that paid by William Flete to his sometime provincial, William of Lincoln[2] (elected 1357), certainly imply that there was in the province a store of virtue sufficient to inspire both sacrifice and enthusiasm. The praise of William Flete has peculiar value, for it was given after he had spent twenty years in Italy in the solitude of Lecceto and had become the intimate of Catherine of Siena and of more than one other saint of her acquaintance. That a young Bachelor of promise, lecturing at Cambridge, together with two companions, should have sought and obtained permission from the prior-general to retire to Lecceto, a convent lying among ilex-groves near Siena, there to follow his hermit's vocation more purely, is another indication that there was a leaven of fervour in the English province.

Flete was more fortunate than he knew in seeking Lecceto, for in the rigid and almost morbid seclusion into which he withdrew he found, or was found by, a company of saints, Giovanni Colombini, founder of the Gesuati, Raymund of Capua, soon to be Master of the Preachers, and the incomparable Catherine of Siena.[3] The story of his chequered relations with Catherine, and of her wise and gentle treatment of his wayward obstinacy, are scarcely a part of English religious history, though the glimpse there given of fresh and delicate affection, of confident approach to God, of unhesitating resolve to renew all things in Christ, is inexpressibly welcome as a foil to the parching controversies of England and the lurid incidents of the Schism. There are signs that the learned English hermit, *il bacelliere* as he was known to Catherine's *famiglia* and to herself, who had left a career to find solitude, came to love seclusion as an end and not a means only; that (to use his own phrase of warning to others) he chose accidents rather than the substance[4] and, in spite of the love and counsel of such a saint as Catherine, refused to follow the call to action and judged others whose liberty of spirit was greater than his own. He certainly failed Catherine at a crisis, and drew from her two letters of poignant reproach, though on her deathbed she may have left him, next to Raymund of Capua, in charge of her 'family. In any case, Flete's reputation and influence in spiritual circles of Tuscany was very great; he was the correspondent of St Raymund, the apologist of Catherine, a spiritual writer of note.[5] With those who had been his brethren in England, however, he had broken all links; no visit had been exchanged, no letter passed. The silence was broken only after Catherine's death when Flete,

1 Gwynn, *op. cit.* 107 *seqq.*
2 *Ibid.* 143, n. 3: 'Sitis vos perfecti sicud magister vester celestis perfectus est: saltem sicud magister Willelmus de Lincoll' in hac parte perfectus fuit.'
3 *Ibid.* Part IV, 'William Flete at Siena'; and R. Fawtier, *Ste Cathérine de Sienne*, I. An Irish scholar, B. Hackett, is engaged on further research on Flete and St Catherine.
4 Cf. his letter, quoted by Gwynn, *op. cit.* 97. The phrase was a favourite one with Uthred of Boldon; *v.* p. 53 *supra*.
5 His *De Remediis contra Temptaciones* is extant in fifty MSS. in the British Isles.

acting, as he says, under irresistible influence, wrote three letters to England: one to all the Austin friars, one to the prior provincial, and one to the theological masters of the province.[1] These contain interesting references both to the Schism and to affairs in England, but their burden is purely spiritual. He exhorts his brethren to keep their Rule and love solitude: even if other friars leave their convents the Austin friars, with their tradition of contemplation, should keep to their cells whether they be celebrated scholars and doctors or unlettered. He speaks of the dangers and relaxations of the age; he was writing, though he did not know it, at the very moment when Wyclif and Langland were lashing the four orders and, introspective and self-opinionated as he was, he may have failed to gauge the temper of a country he had left so long before. Nevertheless, that he should have written in this strain, and that his letters should have been copied and preserved, is some indication that the ground was not wholly impervious to good seed. The letters were written in the summer of 1380; they are the last chapter in an episode over which the imagination lingers, a shaft of spring sunlight falling across the cold winter of the English scene; with them William Flete passes out of sight, one more Englishman and lover of England to find a second home and a grave in Italy.[2]

Within the limits of the fourteenth century, as is well known, there flourished in England a group of religious writers of great originality and spiritual wisdom, known by the convenient name of 'the English Mystics'[3]. They form a group of which each individual has an independent point of view, though the later among them knew, and owed much to, the earlier. They are separated from their predecessors and immediate successors by a number of characteristics: they all wrote in a private capacity and with an intensely individual outlook; they are all in some degree mystical writers, that is to say, they record or prepare for a direct perception of divine action upon the soul outside the limits of ordinary experience; and all wrote at least a part of their works in English. The last circumstance was

---

1 The letters have been edited by M. H. Laurent, O.P., in *Analecta Augustiniana*, XVIII (1942), 303–24.

2 For his abiding love of his country *v.* his letter to the masters (Gwynn, *op. cit.*, 203, notes): 'Orate, orate pro Anglia...Bene habeo Angliam in mea mente, et regem Anglie [*sc.* Richard II].'

3 Strictly speaking, they are only four in number: Richard Rolle (*c.* 1290–1349); the author of *The Cloud of Unknowing* (*fl. c.* 1360); Walter Hilton (*c.* 1330–96); and Dame Juliana of Norwich (1342–*c.* 1420). The unknown reviser in English of the *Ancren Riwle* (*c.* 1230), however, deserves a place beside them, while Margery Kempe, whose ambiguous figure has recently emerged from the waters of oblivion, must also be reckoned with, though she is of a very different temper.

From library catalogues and surviving MSS. we can trace Rolle at Witham, London, Beauvale and Sheen (2); *The Cloud* at London, Sheen and Mountgrace; and Hilton at London (2), and Sheen (2). Syon had at least two copies of Rolle and five of Hilton; probably many more were there. (*v.* E. M. Thompson, *The Carthusian Order in England*, ch. ix, 'English Carthusian Libraries', and the individual houses in N. R. Ker, *Medieval Libraries of Great Britain*.)

not without consequences: it excluded them from all share in the academic controversies of their age and has in our own day given at least several of them a celebrity far greater than that enjoyed by the theological notabilities of their day.[1] As one of them, Walter Hilton, was an Augustinian canon, and another, the writer of *The Cloud of Unknowing*, wrote for a religious, even if he was not one himself,[2] they cannot be left wholly out of sight in a study of English religious life.

The English mystics, though so original in temper, owe the main lines of their teaching and its external form in large part to two traditions, the one native and the other foreign. As Englishmen they inherited the eremitical spirit of the country; Rolle was himself a hermit and Juliana a recluse, while the author of *The Cloud* and Hilton wrote their chief treatises for a solitary and for an ancress. England had a long literary tradition of rules, half disciplinary, half devotional, for such, from Ailred's *Regula inclusarum* for his sister and the admirable *Ancren Riwle* down to more than one contemporary *Speculum inclusarum*.[3] On the other hand, two at least, the two with whom these pages are principally concerned, owed much either at first or second hand to the mystical theologians of the past, and in particular to the profoundly theological teaching of the Dominican school.[4] The precise point of contact with this school is not

---

1 Rolle's place in English literature and hagiology does not concern us here; and *The Cloud* and Dame Juliana's *Revelations*, though abounding in passages of very great beauty, were never widely known. Hilton, on the other hand, was continuously read by religious and layfolk; his place among the moulding influences of English prose has been signally vindicated by the late R. W. Chambers in his essay *On the Continuity of English Prose from Alfred to More and his school* (Oxford, 1932).

2 *The Cloud of Unknowing* was first printed from a defective original in 1871; the first edition from a good MS. was that of Evelyn Underhill in 1912. A critical edition of *The Cloud* and the *Epistle of Privy Counsel*, by Miss P. Hodgson (*EETS*. o.s. ccxviii) appeared in 1944, but perhaps the best edition for the general reader is that of Dom J. McCann (1924; re-edited 1942) in which the *Epistle of Privy Counsel* appeared in full for the first time.

The studied anonymity of the writer has hitherto successfully baffled all research and no conjecture as to his status has found universal favour. The dialect is East Midland. In the past he has been identified (certainly in error) with Hilton; others have supposed him an Austin friar (so Fr A. Gwynn) or an East Anglian secular priest (so Dom McCann). From his treatises all that can be inferred is that he had had a full theological training and was therefore a priest; his Thomist outlook would be compatible with his having followed the schools of the Dominicans, Carmelites or Austin friars; the young disciple of twenty-four (ch. 4) was also formed in the schools and had till recently been 'a servant among the special servants of God' and has now become a solitary (ch. 1); this might well imply that he had been a clerk *redditus* among the Carthusians and was now becoming a monk with them. In this case the home of the writer would almost of necessity be Beauvale, the only house in existence outside Somerset.

3 Ailred's *Regula Inclusarum* is in *PL*, xxxii, 1451 *seqq*. The *Ancren Riwle* is in *CS*, 56; the literature upon it has swollen beyond the limits of a footnote. For other English Rules v. 'Regulae tres reclusorum et eremitarum Anglie saec. xiii–xiv', by P. Livarius Oliger, O.F.M., in *Antonianum*, iii (1928), 151–90, 299–320; and *ibid*. ix (1934), 37–84; 243–65. Yet another *Speculum Inclusarum* has been edited by Père Oliger in *Lateranum*, n.s. ann. iv, no. 1 (Rome, 1938). Cf. also an Oxford thesis by Mrs L. E. Rogers (1933), which edits the *Advice to Recluses* from B.M. MS. Harl. 2372.

4 Cf. D. Knowles, 'The Excellence of *The Cloud*', for a discussion of the technical accuracy of the work.

clear. Both in the Rhineland, where the preaching of Eckhart and Tauler had been such a force, and in Italy, where Dante at the beginning of the century and St Catherine of Siena fifty years later had reflected the teaching of St Thomas in their different ways, the traditional doctrine of the mystical life was drawn out with growing precision. In England, no great master of this life is known to have existed among the Preachers in the period 1300–50, and it is perhaps to Germany that the line should be traced. The search, however, has hitherto yielded no results. Neither the author of *The Cloud* nor Hilton shows the slightest trace either of the pantheistic and extravagant language of Eckhart or of the great emphasis laid by Tauler on the moment of conversion and on the extreme mental sufferings which in his scheme precede the illumination of the soul, and as nothing is known of the early life of either writer, the student of their teaching has nothing but the content of their works to guide him in the search for their sources. Both are clearly men of education, and probably of theological training also, and their theology is not that of the contemporary English universities, with its admixture of Scotist and Nominalist thought, but is strongly, though not confessedly, Thomist, and though they use some of the terms of the pseudo-Dionysius, whose *Mystical Theology*, indeed, the author of *The Cloud* translated into English from Latin, they interpret them, as did St Thomas, in a wholly Christian sense. Similarly, if they derive from the German school, they have been singularly successful in retaining the firm lines of their originals while omitting altogether the equivocal Neo-Platonist and pantheistic expressions which marred the reputation of Eckhart. It is pleasant to think that the purity of their doctrine can be explained more simply; that as men of clear mind and personal experience in the ways of the spirit they adopted without question the sane traditional outlines of the Thomist system. No doubt this is in part what happened; but spiritual writers, and those of the Middle Ages in particular, are as a class extremely fearful of novelty, and the clear traces of borrowing from Dionysius, the Victorines and other sources in Hilton and *The Cloud* make it more than probable that the accurate technical expression of their thought is derived from an unknown original.

However that may be, by clearing the notion of contemplation both from meditative, quasi-intellectual associations of the Augustinian school of earlier centuries and from the unsound speculations of Neo-Platonism, as well as from the emotional, ecstatic and visionary accompaniments that have always bulked so large in religious literature, they achieved a clear distinction between the sphere of human cognition and endeavour and that in which God moves and illumines souls who have removed all obstacle to union with Him.[1] The nights of sense and spirit, the rejection of all that can be clearly perceived by the mind or can give pleasure to the will, the consequent reliance upon faith alone and the adherence to God

1 Cf. St Thomas, *Summa theologica*, IIa, IIae, Q. 52 a. 2 ad 1: 'In donis Spiritus Sancti mens humana non se habet ut movens, sed magis ut mota.'

above all creatures in the memory and will, the desire for union with the second Person of the Trinity, the Word who is also Christ Jesus, the signs by which true prayer of the spirit may be known: all these, which were to be the main topics of the Carmelite saints of the Counter-Reformation, are present in their main lines here. In this the English mystics, though limited in scope, are superior to all their contemporaries, not excepting Suso and Ruysbroeck, and anticipate to an extraordinary extent all the chief principles of the teaching of St John of the Cross. Perhaps in no writing of any language is the initial stage of mystical prayer defined and described with such accuracy and fire as in *The Cloud* and its accompanying treatises.[1] Certainly they are unsurpassed among English writers of any age for clarity and precision in their enunciation of the traditional doctrine of mystical union which can be traced back through the Fathers of the Desert to the words of Christ recorded by St John.

Both Hilton and the author of *The Cloud* are concerned in their most important treatises with guiding a single disciple through the early stages of the mystical life, though Hilton wrote on other occasions for those in secular life.[2] Both speak magisterially, with a certainty of touch that must imply experience of the hidden way to which they act as guides, though no direct personal confession ever breaks through the dignified reticence. Secure in their possession of the amplitude of revealed truth, and therefore at once unerringly orthodox and yet completely free with the liberty of spirit that can only come to one with a contemplative's knowledge of God, they are, as has been said, admirably sane and sober, though they treat of things that transcend the limits of ordinary experience. In neither is there a shadow of illuminist, quietist or antinomian sentiment; each had had experience of fraud, hysteria and enthusiasm, yet had lost nothing of his belief in spiritual reality and in the goodness of some, at least, of those who began to seek Christian perfection. Both, though living in an age of controversies and scandals, the age of Wyclif and the Great Schism, are so occupied with the central truths of revelation that they neither need nor care to attack the peripheral heresies of the day. Their enemy is sinful man, carnal man, man spiritually blind; they are concerned with the battle between darkness and light in the conscience of every man, the same then as now and as in the days of Christ. Hilton[3] in particular, as we picture

1 Dom John Chapman wrote of it in Hastings's *Encyclopedia of Religion and Ethics*, article 'Mysticism, Roman Catholic', that it is 'a marvellously clear and practical little treatise.... It seems to sum up the doctrine of St John of the Cross two hundred years beforehand.' An eminent Dominican theologian of our own day, Père Garrigou-Lagrange, O.P., writes (*L'Amour de Dieu*, 596) of this 'mystique anglais...qui annonce S. Jean de la Croix'. Dom Augustine Baker, the author of *Sancta Sophia*, wished his nuns at Cambrai to read it 'at least once in every two years...twice or thrice over'. (*Fr Baker's Commentary on the Cloud*, ed. J. McCann, in his edition of *The Cloud*, p. 154.)

2 Thus he wrote a treatise for Adam Horsley, a former baron of the Exchequer, who ultimately became a Carthusian at Beauvale.

3 Hilton's *Scale of Perfection* was printed in 1494 by Wynkyn de Worde at the request of the Lady Margaret Beaufort; it was reprinted by Dom Serenus Cressy in 1659, again in 1869 and again by Dom Roger Hudlestone in 1927. All these editions confuse the arrange-

him in the quiet priory of Thurgarton, secure in the possession of the pearl of price, unhindered by the troubles of Christendom and the corruption of the Church, setting down for a 'ghostly sister' in a neighbouring anchorhold the age-old way to union with Christ which would survive all decay and revival in the external fabric of religion, is able to make the noisy years of Wyclif and the friars vanish in the vision of peace:

Set in thy heart wholly and fully [he wrote] that thou wouldest nothing have but the love of Jhesu, and the ghostly sight of Him as He will show Him; for to that only art thou made and bought, and that is thy beginning and thy end, thy joy and thy bliss. And therefore whatsoever that thou have, but if thou have that, and know and feel that thou hast it, hold that thou hast right nought.[1]

And again:

Thou shalt cast out of thy heart all sins, and sweep thy soul clean with a besom of dread of God, and with water of thine eye wash it; and so shalt thou find thy drachma Jhesu. He is drachma, He is penny, and He is thine heritage. This drachma will not so lightly be found as it may be said; for this work is not of one hour or of a day, but many days and years with mickle sweat and swink of the body and travail of the soul. And if thou cease not; but seek busily, sorrow and sigh deep, mourn still, and stoop low till thine eye water for anguish and for pain, for thou hast lost thy treasure Jhesu, at last when that He will, well shalt thou find thy drachma Jhesu. And if thou find Him as I have said, as a shadow or glimmering of him, thou mayest if thou wilt call thy friends to thee for to make mirth with thee and melody, for thou hast found thy drachma Jhesu. . . . For in that sight and in that knowing of Jhesu is fully the bliss of a reasonable soul, and endless life. Father, this is endless life; that Thy chosen souls know Thee and Thy Son whom Thou hast sent, one soothfast God.[2]

ment of the MSS. The first edition to give the original division into two books was that of E. Underhill in 1923; a number of MSS. were used for this, but the edition is not in its form fully critical. Nevertheless, it shows clearly the development of Hilton's doctrine in the interval between the books, although Miss Underhill's contention that Hilton became 'Christocentric' from being 'Theocentric' is scarcely borne out by the manuscript evidence she herself adduces. Her introduction contains interesting notes on, and a pleasant description of, Thurgarton Priory. An edition of Hilton's works is at present in preparation for the E.E.T.S. In his opuscules, though not in the *Scale*, Hilton does attack the Lollards.

1 *Scale of Perfection*, ed. Underhill, 308.
2 *Ibid.* 117–18.

CHAPTER IX

DEVELOPMENTS WITHIN THE ORDERS: I

I. THE CISTERCIANS

During the fourteenth century a change occurred in the domestic life of the white monks which profoundly modified the character and activities of the Cistercians in England and Wales. This was the virtual disappearance of the *conversi*, who in the twelfth century had not only greatly outnumbered the choir monks in many abbeys, but had also been an essential factor in the Cistercian economy and the cause of its phenomenal success. It is scarcely too much to say that the perfecting of the converse-and-grange system had revolutionized both arable and pasture farming for the white monks, and when the *conversi* went or were no longer desired it was a sign that the influence of that revolution had passed.

Half a century ago this great change, like so much else, was attributed to the Black Death. The pestilence, so the argument ran, went far to eliminate the existing families of lay brothers, and in the decades which immediately followed the demand for labour and the rise in wages effectually prevented recruitment on a large scale. That many abbeys were hard hit is likely, and in one or two cases the actual figures of the losses are known, but it is clear from other evidence that the decrease of *conversi* had taken place very generally before 1350, while on the other hand rural conditions in the succeeding fifty years had not altered sufficiently to account for the virtual non-existence of the class throughout England.

In reality, two other important factors were involved, both of which preceded the Black Death in time. The first, which had been operative for at least a century, was inherent in the very nature of the life of the *conversi*, which depended far more closely than did the life of the choir monks upon a high level of moral worth and practical ability in the community. The granges, often numerous, were staffed entirely by the *conversi*; a monk was nominally in charge, but it is not clear that he was always in residence, and it must have required more than a little ability to control and maintain in contented employment the large numbers concerned. Often the *conversi* were left to look after themselves, or a single brother was entrusted with a grange as a bailiff.[1] Moreover, the two groups within the monastery had steadily drawn apart: for the choir monks reading and study were taking up more of their time and interest, and agricultural labour less, while on the other hand the class of lay brothers no longer contained as its strongest leaven the numerous responsible ex-freeholders and more substantial men who had eagerly joined the ranks of the *conversi* in the early days. When once the strength and simplicity of the spiritual purpose had gone the

1 For a fuller treatment of this *v. RO*, I, 74.

system was doomed. From the first there had been trouble in Wales, where the *conversi* were drawn from a wilder and more shiftless population, but in the thirteenth century the gangs of uncouth and often unruly lay brethren were getting out of hand even in Yorkshire and Lincolnshire. At the same time, the abbeys, now grown wealthy, were finding it simpler, and not on the whole more expensive, to exploit their distant granges with hired labour which had always been allowed by their statutes.

In addition, the white monks, like all other landowners and for the same reasons, were from *c.* 1300 onwards gradually going over from a regime of direct exploitation to one of leases and rents.[1] Here the Cistercians probably moved less fast and less far than the old orders, but the movement was there. For all these reasons, *conversi* were becoming more of a liability than an asset, and it seems certain that in England, as on the Continent, it was desire on the part of the monks to limit their intake rather than a failure in the springs of supply, that led to a gradual decline of the class. The white monks never attempted, at least in England or Wales, to develop craft work or industries such as weaving or fulling, which might have given useful and lucrative employment to numbers of lay brethren within the abbey precinct. Nor did they endeavour, as have religious orders in the modern world, to attract by a slight change of training and appeal the new class of urban artisans to a life of service within the monastery, and the Cistercians soon came to employ domestic servants like the black monk abbeys. For long, however, a small number of *conversi* are found at many houses,[2] and even when, at the end of the fifteenth century, Henry VII is found wondering at the absence of lay brothers and suggesting their revival,[3] there were probably isolated individuals here and there as there are at some English Benedictine houses at the present day. As a characteristic feature of the Cistercian life, however, they had disappeared before the end of the fourteenth century, and thenceforward the economy within and without the Cistercian monastery became less markedly different from that of the black monks,[4] though the unity of financial and administrative control under the bursar, and the

---

1 This has been dealt with in some detail as regards the Continent by J. S. Donnelly in his *Decline of the Cistercian Laybrotherhood*. There is room for a study of the changes in the English Cistercian economy in the fourteenth century. In 1363 Fountains is found petitioning Clairvaux for permission to convert granges ruined by wars into normal estates and to farm them out to seculars; cf. *VCH, Yorks*, III, 136, and *Memorials of Fountains*, I, 203–4.

2 In 1380–1 Jervaulx had 6 *conversi*, Rievaulx 3, and Roche 1 (Subsidy Roll 63, no. 12, cited in *VCH, Yorks*, III, 144, 151, 154).

3 This information comes from a letter of the distinguished abbot, Marmaduke Huby, to the equally distinguished abbot, Jean de Cirey of Cîteaux, in the Cistercian archives preserved at Dijon (*v. infra*, n. 1, p. 127). Henry, so he says, 'miratur...quod conversos non habemus,' and offers to get six or eight skilled in some craft, so as to attract others.

4 Miss R. Graham noted (*VCH, Glos.*, II, 101) that at Kingswood in 1402 the land was uncultivated through lack of lay brothers (*CPL*, v, 514), and added that in the fifteenth century 'manors and granges were let on lease and shortly before the dissolution the convent only cultivated at their own expense a small portion of their land around the monastery' (cf. *Monasticon*, v, 428).

relative homogeneity of the sources of income, as well as the compact area of property, made the white monk organization far simpler to the end.

Throughout all the stresses of the later Middle Ages the *Carta Caritatis* retained, both as a code and as a symbol, a greater strength than did the statutes and decrees of the Cluniacs and the Premonstratensians. The very fact that the bond was not one between the abbey and a person or an authority, but (at least for several centuries) to a mother-abbey and to a common gathering of fellows probably strengthened the moral tie. It is in any case certain that the links established by the *Carta Caritatis* survived in great part in England till the Dissolution; the Cistercians here never attempted—as the Cluniacs and Premonstratensians attempted with success—to cut themselves loose from overseas control.

Nevertheless, they too felt the strain, peculiar to the English and Welsh religious houses, of the financial policy of a succession of English kings and of the long wars between England and France.[1] As early as 1328 the general chapter notes that the king of England has prohibited visits and contributions to general chapter, and decided that the abbot of Cîteaux and the four 'elder daughters' shall send envoys to England to treat with him.[2] What happened does not appear, but connexions with Cîteaux were temporarily suspended and the English abbots seem to have taken matters into their own hands; in 1341 or 1342 the abbots of Waverley, Tintern and Quarr convoked a provincial chapter and passed decrees which the general chapter revoked.[3] Nothing more is heard of such attempts before the Great Schism, when the Cistercians, in common with the other centralized orders, passed through a period of shifts and disturbances of which an account is given elsewhere.[4]

When communications with Cîteaux were resumed, we find the English abbots in 1410 asking that two of their number, one from each province, should be allowed to represent the whole body at general chapter, bringing with them the contributions of all their houses to the expenses of general chapter, and of the abbot of Cîteaux when engaged on business of the order at the papal Curia.[5] The request was granted, and in 1411 the abbots of Waverley and Fountains were empowered to convoke all the abbots for an election of two of their number: the abbots of Rievaulx and Dore seem to have been chosen.[6] The arrangement apparently did not work; in

---

1 The publication of the statutes and acts of the general chapter for the whole of the later Middle Ages by Dom J. M. Canivez (*Statuta Capitulorum Generalium Ordinis Cisterciensis*) has thrown considerable, if fitful, light over the activities and shortcomings of the English white monks, as also over their relationship with Cîteaux. How close this was can be seen also in the correspondence preserved at Dijon, and I have been able to use, through the kindness of Dr C. H. Talbot, his transcripts of letters that passed between England and Cîteaux in the fifteenth and early sixteenth centuries; they are particularly numerous during the abbacy of the eminent reforming abbot Jean de Cirey, abbot of Cîteaux from 1476 to 1503.

2 Canivez, *op. cit.* III, 384.   3 *Ibid.* 469.
4 *V. infra*, 167–70.   5 Canivez, *op. cit.* IV, 132.
6 *Ibid.* 158, 190.

1417 the chapter notes that no English delegate has been destined for Constance; the fathers therefore appoint William Sulbury, a monk of Woburn, who had presumably found his way out to Cîteaux.[1] Nine years later the chapter has learnt from credible sources that all the English houses badly need visitation and reformation, and the abbots of Clairvaux, Ourscamp and Beaulieu are forthwith deputed.[2] Either through lack of energy or hesitation in the face of protest they failed to act, and in 1427 the need for reform is again noted, and the abbots of Beaulieu, Byland and Waverley are deputed for five years.[3] As Englishmen, they could not reasonably be resisted, and they seem to have acted with energy; for in 1433 the chapter noted that four English abbots had resigned in visitation.[4] The same chapter decided that as war has prevented the English and Welsh abbots from coming to chapter, they are to meet yearly during the next quinquennium at Northampton on 24 June for three days, during which meeting they are to choose two of their number to go to chapter.[5] Their contributions, which are not allowed to pass to France, are to go to support the representatives of the order at the Curia. To make assurance doubly sure, a bull was obtained in 1437 from Eugenius IV, giving the English and Welsh abbots leave of absence from general chapter, with permission to hold triennial general chapters of their own.[6]

Nevertheless, visitors from overseas, whether representatives of general chapter or abbots of mother-houses, still visited England, for in 1447 the abbot of Morimond is found asking that his arrangements in England and Wales may be ratified by the abbot of Cîteaux.[7] In the same year some English abbots complained that their bursars were commonly abusing their position to buy indulgences and conspire against their abbot; they begged that they themselves might take over the office.[8] The chapter gave the abbots of Fountains and Waverley, who were apparently already the 'reformers' in office, the power to deal with the culprits, and gave them furthermore power, acting in concert with the chapters of the two provinces, to establish two other abbots (one appointed by themselves, the other elected by chapter), to act as commissaries for the abbot of Cîteaux, who by this time had acquired an executive and supervisory control of the order which he had not enjoyed in earlier days.[9] The system thus established functioned for some time; thus in 1455–6 the abbots of Fountains and Furness, Warden and Coggeshall were commissaries;[10] but the general chapter still retained power to modify the arrangement, for in 1456 the abbots of Warden and Furness were detailed to reform St Bernard's College at Oxford, and the same two, with the addition of the abbot of St Mary's, Dublin, were appointed for nine years visitors of all houses in England, Wales and Ireland.[11] In 1463 the abbots of Fountains and Warden

1 Canivez, op. cit. IV, 212–13.   2 Ibid. 308.   3 Ibid. 312.
4 Ibid. 388.   5 Ibid. 391.   6 Ibid. 420–1.
7 Ibid. 604.   8 Ibid.   9 Dijon transcripts.
10 Canivez, op. cit. IV, 724.   11 Ibid. 749, 750.

were visitors;[1] in the following year the chapter had heard that the English white monks were changing the form of their habit, and adopting one not unlike that of the black monks; a sample of the traditional dress was sent to them by the abbot of Cîteaux, with instructions to conform.[2] In the next year the abbot of Cîteaux was himself in England, presumably for the purpose of coming to an understanding with the king over the church of Scarborough, which had been an object of contention for some two centuries. While in the country he appointed the abbots of Warden and Jervaulx visitors, and those of Woburn, Rievaulx and Beaulieu collectors.[3] Meanwhile the provincial chapters were still being held, and their decrees were ratified at Cîteaux. A little later, in 1476, three abbots in each province were visitors.[4]

II. THE CARTHUSIANS

The Carthusian order, despite its distinguished beginnings, had failed to multiply in England before the middle of the fourteenth century. The small priory of Witham in Selwood Forest near Frome, far from towns or trade routes, had remained alone till 1226. In that year William Longespee, Earl of Salisbury, a natural son of Henry II, gave to the order his manor of Hatherop in Gloucestershire together with other possessions. Unlike other monasteries, a Charterhouse could not enlarge its numbers beyond the existing number of cells; Witham therefore can hardly have supplied all the colonists for Hatherop; the others no doubt came from France. The new site proved unsuitable and a move was made some time before 1232 to some land given in exchange by the founder's widow, Ela, who is said to have presided at the beginning of conventual life at Lacock, her own foundation for Austin canonesses, on the morning of the day on which she proceeded to Hinton, ten miles away, for a ceremony of a similar kind.[5] Forty years later, Witham and Hinton together appear to have supplied colonists for a house in Ireland, possibly situated in the diocese of Clonfert. This was not a success, and by 1321 the process of winding up there was complete.[6]

More than a century separated the foundation at Hinton from that of the next English house, at Beauvale a few miles north-west of Nottingham. This was founded by Sir Nicholas de Cantilupe in his park at Gresley, presumably with monks from Witham and Hinton.[7] These three Charter-

1 Canivez, *op. cit.* V, 131.   2 *Ibid.* 149.   3 *Ibid.* 154.   4 *Ibid.* 340.

5 For Hinton, *v.* E. M. Thompson, *A History of the Somerset Carthusians*, and *The Carthusian Order in England*, 147 *seqq.*, with references. The site is now (1953) the property of Major F. Fletcher, and has recently been excavated by him with repairs to existing buildings; *v.* his article in *Proceedings of the Somerset Archaeological Society*, XCVI, 160–5, and *Monastic Sites from the Air*, by D. Knowles and J. K. St Joseph, 240–1.

6 Thompson, *The Carthusian Order in England*, 156–7.

7 Thompson, *op. cit.* 158. There is a full account of the site and buildings in *Transactions of the Thoroton Society*, XII (1908), 69–94. The writer there mentions the discovery of ecclesiastical remains in a farm at some distance, but fails to see a connexion with the Charterhouse. It would seem probable that this was the site of the 'fratry', which might be at some distance (at Hinton almost a mile) from the priory.

houses appear to have been of the primitive type, in which the converses had their quarters and chapel at a distance from the monks. At all subsequent foundations the entire community was housed within a single enclosure.

Thus in two hundred years (1170–1370) three English Charterhouses had come into being. In the fifty years that followed double that number were founded, three of which held communities twice or thrice as large as any of the earlier houses. Such a phenomenon, in an age which saw few, if any, additions to the numbers of the older orders, demands some consideration. The principal reason why the Carthusian order continued to find both recruits and benefactors was doubtless the persistence among its members of the primitive spirit of austerity and seclusion. Whether or no the Carthusians as individuals were of unusual sanctity of life, at least no accusations of vagrancy or dissolute living could be brought against them, and the concessions to a spirit of relaxation in this small matter or that, which the acts of the general chapters reveal to exacting critics of to-day, were either unknown to contemporaries or readily accepted by them. Next, a Charterhouse satisfied very well the needs of the devout founder in an age which more than ever demanded a *quid pro quo* for its alms, and which laid down the terms of its agreements with more detail and precision than before. Moreover, a Charterhouse could be, as it were, parcelled out among many founders. It was customary, after the site and a certain endowment had been given by the first promoter, for other individuals to come forward with funds for the construction of a single cell, thus ensuring for themselves the prayers of an individual monk.

Such may have been among the motives actuating founders and benefactors; there must also have been motives attracting recruits, for whatever may have been the case with other orders, the Carthusian life was not a career into which a portionless or feckless youth could drift *faute de mieux*, nor would the mere provision of buildings and endowment attract local recruits as might the prospect of an assured livelihood in a priory of Austin canons. Rather, the explanation of the steady, if small, stream of vocations is to be found in the new emphasis and outlook to be seen in the devotional literature of the time, which directed aspirants to the contemplative and mystical life, and to personal ascesis rather than to the more general conversion from the world and liturgical service of the older monastic orders.

The first and most celebrated of the new group of Charterhouses had an unusual origin. The story of the foundation of the London Charterhouse has features both interesting in themselves and significant of contemporary religious sentiment.[1] Sir Walter Manny, later Lord Manny,

---

1 The story of the London Charterhouse has been told so often that detailed references will not be expected. For the student Sir W. H. St J. Hope's posthumous *History of the London Charterhouse* is indispensable, as Hope printed there for the first time the historical portions of the fifteenth–sixteenth century register, together with other documents. Hope's

a distinguished soldier and courtier, had in 1349 bought a piece of land a little to the north-west of the city wall to serve as an overflow burial ground for the victims of the Great Pestilence. He erected a chapel, dedicated to the Salutation of the Mother of God, that is, the Annunciation, and his original intention was to establish a college of priests; this fell through, and the chapel was served by two recluses. Things remained thus for eleven years; then the Bishop of London, Michael de Northburgh, who when returning from Rome had been greatly impressed by the Paris Charterhouse, proposed to Manny that they should found jointly a similar monastery in the existing burial ground. Manny agreed, and the bishop approached the priors of Witham and Hinton, and succeeded in removing their original prejudice against an urban site. Before any practical steps could be taken, however, Northburgh and the two Carthusians died, and the project languished. It was revived some years later by a chance encounter between Manny and the then prior of Hinton, Dom John Luscote, who was in London on business.

This monk stands out from the records more clearly than any other of his order between Hugh of Lincoln and Prior Houghton. He was prior of Hinton when, in 1367, the general chapter, for reasons that do not appear but may have been connected with the projected foundation by Northburgh and Manny, decided to create an English province, and in the following year he was appointed its visitor and subsequently charged with the responsibility of founding the London house, for which he summoned recruits from the three existing monasteries.[1] Not only was he successful in this task but also, as will be seen, he took the initiative within a few years of founding a Charterhouse at Coventry. He had a reputation for holiness and could clearly inspire devotion; a monk who had originally been his clerk, and was himself noted for a long life of devotion, asked to be buried at Luscote's feet when he himself died, more than half a century after his first prior.[2]

The House of the Salutation was founded for a double community, perhaps because of its two founders (for Northburgh left in his will endowments for the house he had not lived to see) and therefore required a large cloister to accommodate some twenty-five cells. Records in some abundance have survived, and we can trace the gradual development of the buildings and learn the names of the chief benefactors, several of whom gave funds for one or more cells. These names are of considerable interest,

book, however, which consists of notes and passages left by him unco-ordinated, is very difficult to work with, and some of its architectural descriptions have been antiquated by recent (1948–9) discoveries, consequent upon the rebuilding of the Charterhouse after war damage. For an account of these v. D. Knowles and W. F. Grimes, *Charterhouse* (1954). Those who need only a straightforward narrative, with full references, will find it in Thompson, *op. cit.* 167 *seqq.*

1 Thompson, *op. cit.* 259.
2 Cf. Register in Hope, *op. cit.*, 82–4. In the recent excavations graves were found in the position indicated in the Register; v. Knowles, *op. cit.* pl. viii A.

as showing clearly the social types to whom, in the disturbed and revolutionary age of Wyclif and Oldcastle, the austere piety of the Carthusians made appeal.[1] Most notable among them are the eminent knights. It was an age of warfare, in which a highly coloured and often superficial chivalry disguised a ruthless and mercenary personality. The romantic ideal is seen in the knight who could impress and control Chaucer's Canterbury pilgrims; a less amiable type can be studied in the accounts of the doings of Sir Robert Knollys or Sir John Hawkwood. Manny himself was an outstanding representative of the class at its most respectable;[2] though responsible in his long and varied career for some acts of unnecessary savagery and questionable probity he was on the whole not only a brave, but a capable, honourable and devout man. Another warrior of good fame who gave money to the Charterhouse was William Ufford, Earl of Suffolk. It is more surprising to find the notorious Robert Knollys as the donor of a cell; the knightly tradition was maintained fifty years later by Sir John Popham.

Beside the knights were the devout aristocrats—Suffolk was in this class also; another generous benefactor was the long-widowed Countess of Pembroke, already foundress of a college at Cambridge and of an abbey of Minoresses not far away at Denney. It is more surprising perhaps to find bishops, whose enthusiasm for the religious orders was less now than in the days of Thurstan or Grosseteste, recognizing the claims of the Carthusians. In addition to Northburgh, the wealthy bishops of Durham and Lincoln gave cells. Finally, alongside of these magnates were the rich merchants of the city companies—Sir William Walworth and Adam Frannceys, fishmongers and mayors, William Symmes, grocer, and the rest. These, reinforced by a number of lawyers and civil servants, remained to the end the chief benefactors; one of the last, early in the sixteenth century, was Sir Robert Rede, goldsmith, whose chantry was served for a bare quarter of a century.

The proximity of the great city, the benefactions that came from it, the importunity of the lower classes of the citizens to maintain access to the ground, and the desire of the city notabilities to benefit in life and in death from the monks, led to close contacts and to a certain infringement of solitude. We read of visits, even to cells; of hospitality, of sojourns and of burials within the walls. Similar relations, on a lesser scale, obtained in the two other urban houses of Coventry and Hull.[3] The prior and convent became trustees for schools and hospitals, and personal gifts were frequent enough to become the occasion of animadversion in general chapter.

---

1 There are lists of the donors of cells in the Register (Hope, *op. cit.* 80; and Knowles, *op. cit.* 25).

2 Histories of the Charterhouse naturally tend to stress Manny's virtues. His career has never been treated in detail by a modern historian; the only critical account is that of T. F. Tout in *DNB*.

3 For these see Thompson, *op. cit.* 199–218, and articles in *VCH, Warwick,* II, 83 and *VCH, Yorks,* III, 190.

Serious as some of these may have been for the spiritual life of individuals, they did not essentially debase the Carthusian ideal. When a superior of unusual holiness appeared, they could be abandoned and forgotten.

While negotiations for the House of the Salutation were in train, a very similar series of proposals was leading to a foundation at Kingston-on-Hull.[1] Here those responsible were the successive heads of the wealthy family of the de la Poles—the first English mercantile family to be ennobled—and the monks came in, only after two earlier proposals for a college and a nunnery of Minoresses had been rejected, in 1378–9. Three years after the beginnings of Hull yet another urban Charterhouse came into being at Coventry.[2] Here the principal founder was Lord Zouche, supported by Richard II, and the founding prior of London, John Luscote, took a leading part. That he was able, as provincial visitor, to encourage the venture and to send three of his best monks from London, including his second-in-command or vicar, and his procurator, is a testimony both to his enterprise and to his trust in his young community in London.

The seventh English Charterhouse came into being less than twenty years later as a foundation of Thomas Mowbray, Earl of Nottingham, at Epworth in the Isle of Axholme,[3] a district celebrated in later religious history as the home of the founder of Methodism.[4] Almost simultaneously the eighth house was being founded by Thomas Holland, Duke of Surrey and nephew of Richard II, on land of his at the foot of the north-western slopes of the Cleveland Hills; the monastery became known as Mount Grace.[5] Surrey perished a few years later, in 1400, in an abortive revolt against Henry IV, and it was some time before Mount Grace found its feet, assisted by Henry IV and his three successors. When, a quarter of a century later, there was a proposal to found a Scottish house, recourse was had to Mount Grace, and two monks were sent to survey the prospects and help in the foundation; one of them became the rector, or superior of the organization, of the new house, and later its second prior, and for four years (1456–60) during the fifteenth century Perth was part of the English province. National rivalry, however, made English connexions undesirable; the majority of the founding community came from the Continent, and after 1460 the connexion with England was limited to an extraordinary visitation at the command of general chapter.[6]

Besides benefactions to other Charterhouses, and his own foundation at Syon, Henry V in his short reign founded also a Charterhouse of his

---

1 Thompson, *op. cit.* 199.

2 Thompson, *op. cit.* 207 and *VCH, Warwick*, II, 83.

3 Thompson, *op. cit.* 218 *seqq.*

4 John Wesley's father was rector of Epworth, in which parish the Charterhouse was still in part standing in the early eighteenth century.

5 Thompson, *op. cit.* 229. There is an elaborate description of the site and buildings, by W. Brown and W. H. St J. Hope in *Yorkshire Archaeological Journal*, XVIII (1905), 252–309, and another by A. W. Clapham in *VCH, North Riding*, II (1923), 24–7. Cf. also Knowles, *Monastic Sites*, 234–5.   6 Thompson, *op. cit.* 246–8.

own on a scale of royal magnificence at Sheen on the south bank of the
river almost opposite Syon. This house, originally planned for forty
monks, and constructed to house at least thirty, was both in numbers and
endowment the largest of the English Charterhouses.[1]

Thus within less than thirty years the number of Carthusian monasteries
in England, which after two centuries stood only at three, had suddenly
risen to eight, with a more than equivalent increase in celebrity. Moreover,
this had occurred in the very decades when the fiercest attacks had been
made on the religious life and on the possessioners by Wyclif and the
Lollards. When the circumstances of the foundations are considered more
closely, certain common characteristics appear. The increase was not
primarily due to the necessity of relieving pressure of numbers, or of
providing accommodation for would-be novices. Rather, the Charterhouses came into being at the will of the founder, and it is noteworthy
that in every case either the king, or someone in close relations with the
court circle, was responsible. In other words, the impulse towards the
multiplication of Charterhouses came from without, and from the highest
quarters; it was perhaps a reaction, however indirect, in the king and the
great nobles to the anti-monastic propaganda of the time.

It is too easy, however, by regarding the mystics in isolation and by
looking only at the growth of the Carthusian order, to exaggerate the
influence of this flowering of the religious life in its most spiritual form
at the end of the fourteenth century, just as it is perhaps even more easy
to exaggerate the significance to their contemporaries of Wyclif and his
followers. All the new Carthusian foundations put together implied
considerably less than a hundred new vocations at their origin; the population of the whole group was less than that of a single great abbey of black
or white monks in the twelfth century. As for the mystics, when we have
mentioned half a dozen names we are at the end of the list, even though we
may presume the existence of others who have left no memorial. An
estimate of value, however, as well as one of numbers, must accompany
all judgements on spiritual issues. The new Charterhouses undoubtedly
attracted or inspired vocations of a high type; they stood above the level
to which satire or contempt could attain; they preserved, and were
nourished on, the writings of the mystics; they were to form a core of
resistance, small but adamantine, to the dissolvent forces of a later date.

The Carthusian order had early been centralized on the Cistercian model,
though with certain peculiar features. General chapter was held yearly at
the Grande Chartreuse on the fourth Sunday after Easter; the prior of the
mother-house was *ex officio* president, and also the ruler of the order
between chapters, and the monks of the Grande Chartreuse had seats in
chapter. The prior of every house (or his procurator) had a seat, but, as

---

1 Thompson, *op. cit.* 238 *seqq. V. infra*, p. 175, and W. Wylie, *The reign of Henry V*, I,
214–20.

with the Cistercians, those from the more distant provinces, of which England was one, were bound to an appearance only every leap year. Though the order was divided into provinces, there were no 'provincials' with direct jurisdiction, as with the later friars, but the 'visitors' chosen from among the priors of a province, who were responsible also for applying capitular decrees and for reporting defaulting priors to the mother-house, fulfilled some of the functions of a provincial.[1] The Carthusians thus stood as it were half-way between the unarticulated Cistercian polity and that of the fully articulated orders of friars. Owing to the relatively small number of houses, added to their jealous observance of all constitutions and traditions, the Carthusian order never became, if the phrase may be used, too heavy for its engine, as did the Cistercians and the Friars Minor, and the general chapter continued (save for the abnormal years of the Great Schism) to function effectively till the Reformation and to enforce its will throughout the body. For the same reasons the provinces, and in particular the English province, never became self-consciously nationalistic and independent. Throughout the fifteenth century transferences of monks from England to the Continent and vice versa, for reasons of discipline or health, were of frequent occurrence.[2]

At the same time the English houses, especially the urban houses, tended to take on a local colour that at times threatened to dishonour Carthusian tradition, and were taken to task for it by chapter. Thus the London Charterhouse, which had made an unfortunate start with make-shift buildings, and had occupied land hitherto used by the people of London, was long in securing an enclosure wall, and meanwhile allowed seculars and even women to visit its church and bring corpses there for burial. For this the prior was brought to book by visitors from the Low Countries in 1405.[3] Similarly, in 1473, Prior Storer was taken to task for undue compliance with the world in granting domestic hospitality and in allowing hunting in the grounds. Twenty years later again, in 1490, the then prior obtained permission for the bishop of London to build a house for himself within the bounds.[4] Besides these extraordinary exercises of authority, the general chapter is found throughout the fifteenth century assigning punishments to individuals and administering reproofs to priors. The Carthusians had their share of moral and psychological misfits and difficult cases. There is also some evidence that minor relaxations, especially in the matter of poverty, had taken place. The hermit life of the individual monk, with a cottage and occupations of his own, tended to attract from relatives and clients presents of books and small comforts and

1 For this see Thompson, *op. cit.* 249 *seqq.*, based on *Statuta Antiqua Ordinis Carthusiani*, in *PL*, cliii, coll. 1125 *seqq.*

2 Many instances of the activity of the general chapter may be found in Thompson, *op. cit.* 263 *seqq.*, and 299 *seqq.*

3 Register, in Hope, *London Charterhouse*, 50–1.

4 Thompson, *op. cit.* 310, 311, citing unpublished MSS. Could this have been the prior's new cell referred to in Dissolution documents (Knowles, *Charterhouse*, 79)?

clothes, which could easily pass unnoticed in a community which met together rarely. Certainly there is record of such gifts, and of the rebukes of general chapter, and some personal documents have survived which show individual Carthusians to have had the use and practical possession of garments and articles which would certainly not have been tolerated in early days at the Chartreuse.[1] Similarly, when the day of dissolution came, some of the monks took away with them not only small movables but even the wainscot with which their cells were frequently fitted. On the other hand, serious moral lapses, and the even more lamentable tale of a slipshod, muddy existence such as the documents of some of the lesser rural houses of monks and canons disclose, were unknown in the Charterhouse. Till the end came the monks were living a life substantially in accord with their constitutions, and there is evidence that at London, if not elsewhere, the three last priors, whose rule covered the last forty years of the monastery's existence, brought about a return to the strictest observance, which had its reward in an access of fervent recruits and a last blossoming of sanctity.

Little as we know of the inner life of the Charterhouses, it is more than we know of any other group of religious in the century before dissolution, and two or three marked characteristics are evident. One of these might be expected in an observant contemplative order: it is a neglect of attention to external matters and an absorption in the details and demands of the purely monastic life. At every period of which we know anything in the relatively short life of the London Charterhouse, the chroniclers single out for praise monks who led exemplary lives of religious observance, and were scrupulously correct in their daily duties. Dom John Homersley, for example, whose employment was to write service-books for chapter and choir, left them without a word in the prior's cell when completed; and left there also without a word any gifts he might receive, covering the money with a tile outside the prior's cell when the weather was windy.[2]

A second characteristic, also to be expected, is an interest in books of mystical theology and in the writings of saints and saintly persons of the contemporary Church. It cannot be accidental that the few remaining lists of Carthusian books should contain several copies of various writings of Richard Rolle, together with *The Cloud of Unknowing*, the *Ladder of*

---

1 Cf. the list in *State Papers, Henry VIII*, vol. IX, fo. 170 (printed also in Thompson, *op. cit.* 327–8), of articles taken in 1519 by a monk of the London Charterhouse who had been sent to Mount Grace. They include 'a wyde sloppe furryd...of the gyfte of my Lody Convay...a newe pylche of the gyft of Mr Saxby...a new mantell by the gyfte of Sir John Rowson knyght of the Roodes...a lytell brasyn morter with a pestyll gevyn by the gyfte of a frende of myne...ii new tyne botylles gevyn by a kynsman of ours...a printed Portews [i.e., book of Hours] by the gyft of Master Rowson...a printed prymer gevyn by Master Parker'. These by no means exhaust the list of paraphernalia which went north with Dan Thomas Golding; he took with him also a 'complete frame for to wefe' and 'a doubyll styll to make with aqua vite'.

2 Register, in Hope, *op. cit.* 82.

Perfection of Walter Hilton, and the writings of St Catherine of Siena and St Bridget of Sweden.[1] We know that *The Cloud* in particular, a technically 'mystical' work, was put into the hands of the young monks in the last years of Carthusian life.[2] In the last years, also, we find Prior Houghton endeavouring to procure from abroad the complete works of Denis the Carthusian. The monks of the Charterhouse were therefore, we may suppose, familiar with what was then the standard literature of the contemplative life,[3] and we shall see on a later page how one, at least, made use of this teaching. Yet over all the records of the late fourteenth and early fifteenth centuries, even in the Charterhouse, there hangs that scent of cloth and leather, that flavour of the commonplace and of the limited, that makes the age seem one of bourgeois tastes, and lacking in spiritual aspiration. Yet in the Charterhouse, if nowhere else, it has always been the practice to be silent under the hand of God: *Secretum meum mihi*; and here, if nowhere else, the supposition, often dangerously invoked by apologists, is legitimate. There may well have been silent contemplatives there whose life was hidden with Christ in God.[4]

A third characteristic, less pleasing than the others, may be regarded as a consequence of a life passed in seclusion and, in some cases, introspection; it is a love of the marvellous which sometimes extends beyond the bounds of good sense. The stories that the fifteenth-century chronicler tells of early days follow the normal pattern of edifying narrative;[5] and the incidental intrusions of the marvellous are such as may be found in the monastic records of every age, and are not without a certain gracious simplicity. Maurice Chauncy, however, passes all bounds when he relates the story of the miraculous transference of the young William Tynbygh from Palestine to Ireland, and in his short narrative there are several references to signs and wonders.[6] This fondness for the marvellous is noticeable even in his well-known account of the Mass of the Holy Ghost in which the London Carthusians dedicated themselves to the sacrifice. Here, however, the recent date of the happening and the sobriety of Chauncy's personal claim do much to strengthen his credibility as a witness. In any case, his brethren proved themselves capable of holding fast, in the darkness of faith, to the teaching of Christ.

A natural result of the high level of Carthusian observance was a steady influx of recruits of worth and distinction. While the monks and canons and friars received their novices as a general rule from their own estates or from the town at their doors—boys who came sometimes for a career,

---

1 Thompson, *op. cit.* 313 *seqq.* Four of the extant MSS. of *The Cloud of Unknowing* are of Charterhouse provenance.
2 One of the MSS. of *The Cloud* was written by Dom William Exmewe.
3 For this, cf. R. W. Chambers, *On the continuity of English prose.*
4 The instance of Richard Methley, hitherto unknown, may be mentioned (*v. infra*, p. 224).
5 Register, in Hope, *op. cit.* 82–4.
6 Chauncy, *Historia aliquot martyrum...Cartusianorum*, ed. V. M. Doreau.

often simply to a life where livelihood was assured—entry to the Charter-house remained normally impossible without a real sense of vocation, and thus recruits were from the first (as they remain to-day) often men of years and of formed character. In the first decades at Witham the distinguished abbot, Adam of Dryburgh, came as a novice, and till the Dissolution such rare notices as survive show parish priests, distinguished clerks, monks and canons of every order passing into the Charterhouse. Prior Houghton was the last of a series of parish priests; he had been preceded by Sir Thomas More's parish priest and confessor in the city. Examples of distinguished men of learning may be seen in John Blakman, fellow of Eton and Merton Colleges, and warden of King's Hall, Cambridge,[1] who entered the remote Witham, as if with a desire to break entirely with his past, and Houghton himself.

III. THE PREMONSTRATENSIAN CANONS

Mention has been made in a previous volume of the settlement and early years of the Premonstratensian or 'white' canons in England.[2] The book in which those pages occurred was concerned only incidentally with the regular canons, and their early history was still suffering from the neglect with which modern research had treated them, but they have recently been studied with considerable fullness, especially in their first beginnings. For all details, therefore, of their origins and constitutional dispositions the reader may be referred to Colvin's monograph,[3] but the picture of the English medieval orders in the later centuries of the period would be incomplete without a brief account of their later fortunes.

The white canons or, to give them yet another name, the Norbertines, resembled very closely the white monks of Cîteaux in their constitutional framework, their domestic organization, and their religious ideals. Centralized upon Prémontré, with all the Cistercian emphasis upon simplicity, uniformity and disciplinary visitation, they were in a few points even nearer than the white monks to the organization of a fully developed order; the abbot of Prémontré had a pre-eminence which the first fathers had of set purpose withheld from the abbot of Cîteaux. Not only did he preside over general chapters, but he had the right of visitation of any house of the order. Moreover, though the annual visitation had originally been, as it was among the Cistercians, the task of the abbot of the founding house, the problem (which the Cistercians also recognized, but did not attempt to solve) of the house whose daughters were many and widely

---

1 Thompson, *op. cit.* 320.   2 *MO*, 360–2.

3 H. M. Colvin, *The White Canons in England.* This account, especially valuable when dealing with the origins of the order and the circumstances of each foundation, does not carry the story in any detail beyond the early years of the fifteenth century. There has recently been a welcome revival among the Premonstratensians of the study of their order's history, which finds expression in *Analectes de l'Ordre de Prémontré* (Brussels, 1905–14), continued as *Analecta Premonstratensia* (Tongerloo, 1925–).

dispersed led the Premonstratensians, before the end of the twelfth century, to take the practical step of establishing regional 'circuits' (*circariae*) for which visitors were elected by general chapter, though the right of the founding abbey to visit was left intact and was in fact exercised, at least sporadically, to the end. As a result, the abbot of Prémontré, who demanded from all his abbeys a fairly substantial tax to cover the expenses of general chapter and other administrative work, incurred a resentment which was scarcely deserved and which led ultimately to the disintegration of the order. Thus the wisdom of the first fathers of Cîteaux, who had set themselves resolutely to eliminate any resemblance to the abbot of Cluny, was once more demonstrated by the event.

In the domestic economy of the white canons the resemblance to Cîteaux was no less marked. Manual and agricultural work were practised by the canons, they received *conversi*, they adopted the grange system, and the similarity of situation between so many of the houses of the two orders —Kirkstead and Barlings, Byland and Easby—made the Premonstratensians sheep and corn farmers on the same scale and with the same results. For some reason, however, possibly to be found in the interval of forty or fifty years that separated the English foundations of the white monks from the white canons, the latter never rose in numbers, either of choir monks or lay brothers, to a rivalry with great abbeys such as Rievaulx or Fountains. The ruins of their abbeys, indeed, and their plan as revealed by excavation, give an impression of awkwardly arranged and comparatively modest buildings which are in strong contrast to the well devised and spacious domestic buildings of the Cistercians. In particular, the layout of no house hitherto excavated shows any large range that might have accommodated the lay brothers, and though several suggestions have been made as to the possible adaptation of their quarters for other purposes in the fifteenth century, these attempts only serve to emphasize the difference between the normal Cistercian and the normal Premonstratensian plan.

The ideal of the white canons, at least in western Europe, had from the beginning been monastic rather than apostolic. There was never any trace of missionary activity in England, and in early years they refused, again like the Cistercians, to receive churches as property, unless one was given to form the nucleus of an abbey. This very proviso, however, indicates a radical, if latent, difference between the monks and the canons: the latter might wish to avoid possessing churches as property, but there was nothing in itself unfitting in their ownership of a parish church. Very soon they became accustomed to profit from their status and to make use of a privilege granted as early as 1188 by Clement III to the order, enabling them to present canons as vicars in their appropriated churches.[1] There is, however, no evidence to show that English canons did in fact normally act as vicars of their own churches till late in the reign of Henry III. The

1 J. Le Paige, *Bibliotheca Premonstratensis Ordinis* (Paris, 1633), 642, cited by Colvin, *op. cit.* 277, n. 3.

practice then became frequent, but by no means universal. According to their statutes, a canon-vicar was required to have at least one confrère in residence with him, and few of the smaller abbeys could afford to dispense in quasi-permanence with four or even with two members of their body. Nevertheless the rule, awkward in practice though it was, would seem to have been honoured until the fifteenth century: by *c.* 1475 a single canon was common practice.[1]

Of the parochial, or as we should call it, the pastoral work of the white canons there is no record, but there is no reason to suppose that as a class they were more devoted to their people or more enlightened than their neighbours among the secular clergy. Certainly there is no evidence from the later Middle Ages to show that they regarded themselves as having a vocation to minister to the neglected or to raise the level of spiritual life in their parishes. Such few indications as exist are indeed not reassuring. Thus it is clear that the Premonstratensians, like almost all their contemporaries, regarded a church principally as an economic asset to the owner. They were as eager as others to appropriate churches for financial reasons and, more significantly still, they exploited their privileged status by impropriating even their vicarages, serving the churches thus vacated either by one of their own body or by seculars removable at will, thus undoing the work and legislation of the great reforming bishops of an earlier century. Despite efforts of parliament to put a stop to this practice it continued, and in 1475 Tupholme in Lincolnshire had canons removable at will in all its churches.[2] This arrangement, indeed, whatever its disadvantages for the parishioners, was more in accord with the principles of the religious life than what had gone before. The beneficed canon, once installed as perpetual vicar, was as fairly fixed as a secular, and if he lived at any distance from his monastery he was to all intents and purposes lost to community life, even if he returned for elections, visitations and similar canonical occasions. The removable vicar, on the other hand, remained at his church only during the good pleasure of his abbot, though here again the temptation to leave a difficult or recalcitrant subject alone must have been very great. Removable or not, the canons serving churches were bound by stricter regulations than the secular clergy, and the fruits of their benefices were in large part returnable to the abbey. It is therefore possible, and the evidence of Bishop Redman's visitations makes it probable, that they remained to the end a tolerably well disciplined, if small, element in English parochial life.

As the summary given above will have implied, the story of the relationship of the English white canons with Prémontré is on the whole one of the gradual loosening of ties both of sentiment and control. Though regrettable in its wider religious bearings, the course of events is instructive as showing that the clash of interests occurred on the economic level

1 Colvin, *op. cit.* 280.   2 *Ibid.* 283.

and was due primarily to political and social changes quite outside the realm of the regular life, though it may perhaps be felt that only when material preoccupations had obscured spiritual values could such interests have become paramount.

At their foundation, and for a century afterwards, the abbeys of the new centralized orders, founded in frankalmoin, were regarded as free, not only of tenurial service and incidents, but also of tallage and taxation. The demands made by Richard I and John were regarded as acts of violence which set up no precedent. The houses did not indeed avoid all contributions, but these were at first disguised as gifts and later, in the mid-thirteenth century, arrived at by a composition between the authorities of the order and the king; in any case the total was considerably less than that paid by the directly taxable subjects of the Crown.

On the other hand, from fairly early times the custom had come in (and had been erected into a statute of general chapter in 1290) that the abbeys should subscribe a considerable sum to Prémontré for the expenses of the order.[1] These subscriptions, not in themselves unreasonably large, tended (as is the way of taxes) continually to fall into arrears and therefore to appear as a formidable sum when the day of reckoning came; in 1238, for instance, the arrears of the English abbeys were assessed at £240. Thus constant demand on the one part and grudging payment or evasive tactics on the other had created an attitude of mind hostile to any friendly agreement.

At the same time, domestic taxation in England was becoming more and more a living issue. As is well known, the demands of Edward I and his efficiency in realizing them had far-reaching consequences in English constitutional history. Part of his programme consisted of a determined drive for the taxation of the clergy, and the Premonstratensian abbots found themselves summoned to Parliament along with other superiors holding in frankalmoin, and were forced to agree to very heavy taxation, amounting to half their revenues, in September 1294, and a tenth in the following December. The controversy following upon the issue of the bull *Clericis laicos* in the following year still further embittered the issue. The Premonstratensians compounded with the king, thus becoming liable to excommunication, while the campaigns of Edward in Gascony and Scotland, which followed immediately, led to still sharper demands; sorely in need of money, the king forbade the Premonstratensians to send funds out of the country to their head house. This prohibition, supported as it was by patrons of religious houses who professed indignation at the disappearance overseas of revenues bestowed for charity at home, was given statutory sanction at the Parliament of Carlisle in 1307, which forbade the abbots to visit Prémontré as well as prohibiting the export of money.[2]

---

1 P. F. Lefèvre, *Les Statuts de Prémontré*, 91. The sources of what follows are in Colvin, *op. cit.* 202 seqq.

2 The statute *De asportis religiosorum* is in *Statutes of the Realm*, 1, 150.

The financial restrictions were probably not unwelcome, and the English abbots acquiesced with a good grace, but the contemporary abbot of Prémontré was unwilling to accept their excuses. The English therefore appealed to the Holy See in January 1311; in October of the same year they were excommunicated as defaulters by the general chapter at Prémontré. Formal judgement, it would seem, was never given at Avignon on their appeal, but after much negotiation an arrangement was effected at the general chapter of 1316 which remained in force for more than a century. By its terms, the obligation on the English abbots to attend general chapter was restricted to the two annual 'visitors' of the province; the payment of fees to the abbot of Prémontré or his deputy, should he 'visit' the English houses, was disclaimed; and it was decreed that no taxes were to be levied on the English houses save for purposes expressed in the statutes of the order. These relaxations of the statutes were never revoked, and the French wars and the Great Schism effectually hindered any later attempts to draw closer the bonds of union. The visitors continued, at least intermittently, to travel out to Prémontré, and an occasional contribution in cash was conveyed, with or without leave, to its abbot, but war often severed the tenuous connexion, and with the outbreak of the Great Schism the break was complete. The abbot of Prémontré owed allegiance to the French king and the anti-pope Clement VII, and the white canons, in common with other centralized orders, set up for the time an autonomous organization, at first under the abbot of Welbeck, and later under the abbot of Bayham.[1]

When unity returned to the Church a compromise was reached, following upon petition to the pope on the part of the English abbots for a continuance of the *status quo*. They failed to receive complete satisfaction, but all visits to Prémontré were excused, no contributions were to be sent, and the abbot of Prémontré was to appoint as his commissary an English abbot to govern the order in his name. This commissary was at first appointed for three years, but the period soon became indefinite, and it was with these powers that the most distinguished of all the English Premonstratensians, Richard Redman, guided the destinies of his brethren from 1459 to 1505.

It may be well to follow the constitutional issue to the end, as it had no direct connexion with the critical situation of the white canons in England in the reign of Henry VIII. In the first years of the sixteenth century the abbot of Prémontré, fearing the consequences of the bankruptcy that threatened the central organization of the order, decided to attempt once more to catch the English abbots in his net. They retaliated by again petitioning the pope for complete independence, and, owing largely to the diplomatic maladdress of their opponents, succeeded in 1512 in winning their request from Julius II. As a result, the abbey of Welbeck was given the headship of the order in England and Wales. Even so, the end of the

1 For this *v. infra*, p. 169.

chapter had not been reached. Stricken once more by financial embarrassment, the general chapter of 1515 petitioned Leo X for the restitution of the English province to its obedience and liabilities. The case dragged on for sixteen years, and it was only in 1531 that a decision was given by papal judges-delegate against the English abbots. The decision had no effect. It was one more instance of that utter lack of contact with the urgent concerns of England that appears so often in the Continental records of the centralized orders at this time. Within nine years the abbey of Welbeck and the English Premonstratensians had ceased to be.

While certain aspects of the religious and economic life of the Premonstratensian abbeys are illuminated by the visitatorial documents of Bishop Redman, and will be noticed in a later volume, the activities of the white canons in general have left very scanty traces in the records of the later Middle Ages. It was in fact of all the large religious orders the most undistinguished in external achievement, and there is no reason to suppose that it maintained in its inner life anything of the intensity of the Carthusians or Bridgettines. Alone of all the orders (save the Carthusians) the English province founded neither house nor hall nor college at Oxford or Cambridge. So far as the law went, they had no need to do so, for Benedict XII had never legislated for them in this regard, and the modest numbers of their abbeys and their existing liability to taxation from Prémontré would have made the collection of a tax for a house of studies unpopular. Nevertheless, it is remarkable that they did not feel the impulse towards the schools. Individual canons, however, found their way to the university, and in the late fifteenth century Bishop Redman encouraged abbots to find suitable canons and pay for their studies.

The paucity of graduates helps to explain the dearth of men of distinction among the white canons. The only English diocesan bishop in the whole history of the English province was Richard Redman, though in the early sixteenth century at least four Premonstratensian abbots acted as suffragans for English diocesans. Besides Redman, almost the only white canon of note was John Wygenhale, abbot of West Dereham from c. 1430 to c. 1459, a trained canon lawyer who became vicar-general to the bishop of Norwich, and to whom as 'the good Jon Wygnale' John Capgrave dedicated his metrical life of St Norbert in lines which speak of the abbot's affability and hospitality.[1]

The order produced no chronicler, and no spiritual writer after Adam of Dryburgh. The library lists that survive show collections indistinguishable from those of the monks, with a notable catalogue from Titchfield containing English chronicles and parliamentary and legal records.

1 For Wygenhale v. Colvin, *op. cit.* 320–3.

CHAPTER **X**

DEVELOPMENTS WITHIN THE ORDERS: II

I. THE CARMELITES

The third order of friars, that of the Blessed Virgin Mary of Mount Carmel, had, as has been seen, particularly close associations with England.[1] The English province, therefore, which was the largest in the order, stood to the rest of the body in something of the same relation as did the Italian provinces to the rest of the order of the Austin Hermits; each, as nursing mother, held a special place in the affections of all. This place of honour carried with it a certain precedence: thus both Scotland and Ireland were treated as appendages of England; the provincial chapter had the right (elsewhere reserved to the prior-general and general chapter) of appointing lecturers in the schools of Oxford, Cambridge and London; and English friars were frequently elected vicars-general.

In contrast to the three other orders of friars, the province long remained without internal administrative divisions. Their creation, perhaps early in the fourteenth century, was due to an academic inconvenience, and is an interesting indication of the importance attached to a degree in divinity, at least among the mendicants. It had been found that one region (no doubt that of East Anglia, where the Carmelites were always in strength) had secured a preponderance of students at the university; to remedy this, four 'distinctions' had been established, taking their names from London, York, Norwich and Oxford; each of these was to choose four diffinitors to send to the provincial chapter, and from each an equal number of friars was to pass each year to the university, where they were to proceed in rotation to their degrees. By the end of the century, however, these rules were being disregarded; one distinction was again securing advantages for its own friars at the university, with the consequence that for thirty or forty years the office of provincial had become the perquisite of that district. Pope Boniface IX, therefore, in 1396 decreed that the system of rotation, applicable by the old statute to candidates for the doctorate, should now be applied also to the office of prior provincial, so that each distinction should in turn provide the supreme authority in the province.[2] It may have been with the idea of regularizing

1 *RO*, I, 196–9. Save for the critical studies of Fr Benedict Zimmerman, which were chiefly concerned with Carmelite origins and early days, scarcely any work has appeared on the English Carmelites, who appear to have left few records. In what follows some use has been made of an unpublished M.A. thesis of Manchester University, 'Some aspects of the English Carmelites in the first half of the Fifteenth Century', by Miss M. E. Turner.

2 *CPL*, 5 (1396–1404), 1. Though it is not specifically stated in the papal document, no doubt the doctors of theology, as with the Dominicans, had the right of voting in the provincial chapter. Once, therefore, one district had secured a majority among the doctors, it could control elections in its own interest.

still further the *cursus honorum* that the pope in the following year decreed a strict order in the duration of the studies of a would-be Carmelite doctor of divinity.[1]

Within the province schools of grammar and logic existed at Hitchin and Maldon, of philosophy at Winchester, and of theology at Coventry and London, with *studia generalia* at Oxford and Cambridge; in *c.* 1377 there were some sixty friars in the Oxford house. The Carmelites had a period of prosperity in the late fourteenth century, and their numbers came near equalling those of the era before the Black Death; the English province, which had probably never contained eight hundred friars, counted more than six hundred even in the middle of the fifteenth century.[2] As has been seen, the Carmelites did not attain to distinction in the schools till the beginning of the fourteenth century, when John Baconthorp rose to a position among the most eminent doctors of his age. He had no rival in the two generations that followed, but Carmelites were much in evidence in the schools when Wyclif entered upon the controversial phase of his career and, led by Wyclif's 'white hound', Peter Stokes, they took their full share in attacking him.[3] Towards the end of the century again, for reasons that are obscure, the Carmelite friars ousted the Preachers from the position they had held for a century as royal confessors and ambassadors. The connexion with the royal house seems to have begun with John of Gaunt, who had Carmelites about him and counted among his confessors Walter of Diss, Richard Mardisley, the preacher and controversialist, and John Kenningham of Ipswich the prior provincial. Henry IV in the early part of his reign had Robert Mascall, and in his later years Stephen Patrington, who was also confessor to the young Henry V. There was, therefore, sincerity as well as enthusiasm in the letter which Thomas Netter, recently elected provincial, sent to his friars asking prayers for the king. 'Indeed', he remarks, 'he is ours in a very special way. He is now our king, and he was in the past our own prince and our own little child—ours even from childhood. And beyond this he was ours from his grandfather and great-grandfather; indeed he is ours by prescriptive right, always ours to the present day. Yet perhaps I should have spoken more respectfully, and said: "we are his", for so it was. But my love has made me bold'.[4]

---

1 *Ibid.* 19–20. The curriculum laid down is: seven years in Arts; seven years as bachelor in theology; one year as lecturer on the Sentences; two years as principal lecturer on the Sentences; one year as lecturer on the Bible; only then, after eighteen years of study, at the age of thirty-two upwards, was the doctorate attained.

2 Knowles and Hadcock, *Medieval Religious Houses*, 198, 363.

3 For this *v. supra*, p. 72; there is an interesting pictorial record of this in the Carmelite Missal (*v. infra*, p. 279), where the consecration of the Host is represented; in two of the corners of the picture two white dogs are looking attentively at two sprawling clerks in the opposite corners; the editor regards these as heretical Carmelites; could they be simply Lollards?

4 Netter's letters were edited by Fr B. Zimmerman as 'Epistolae Waldensis' in *Monumenta Historica Carmelitana*, I, 444–82. The letter quoted is no. ix, pp. 447–8.

The writer of this letter—the only English friar of his age whose letters in part survive—was perhaps the most distinguished friar of any order between the age of Ockham and the Dissolution.[1] Thomas Netter was born at Walden in Essex *c.* 1372. He entered the Carmelite order as a boy and studied at Oxford, where the Franciscan, William Wodeford, was his master in 1389–90. Stephen Patrington took an interest in him, and he soon became one of the friars most prominent in public life. He took part in the trial of Oldcastle and was present at the Council of Pisa in 1409; he preached at the funeral of Henry IV. In 1414 he was chosen provincial and remained in that office till his death sixteen years later. Henry V took him as his confessor, and he remained on intimate terms with the king for the rest of the reign; indeed, it was said that his remonstrances had a great part in stimulating Henry to take action against the Lollards. Though the letters of Netter that remain are mostly formal, and in any case are not numerous, they nevertheless give the impression that their writer is a sincere, earnest and estimable man. We see him acceding to a request from Henry V for an English colony for the Carmelite house in the recently captured town of Caen; the group must be large enough to sing the divine office.[2] Four years later he acts in concert with the provincial of the Minors in forbidding the subjects of the two orders to ventilate controversial topics, such as the Immaculate Conception, the need for absolute poverty, and the authenticity of the traditions which attributed to Elias and St Augustine the foundation of the orders of Carmel and the Austin Hermits.[3] He is always on the side of reason and moderation, deploring the conduct of a friar who has declared that offerings made on a festival day need not go to the parish priest.[4]

His rule as provincial was efficient and just, though he was accused of severity; he certainly made a determined and apparently successful attempt to restore a good standard of discipline and observance in the province, and he is found remonstrating with the prior-general for lightly giving favours and dispensations to English friars. The general, John Grossi, for his part, esteemed Netter highly and refused to allow him to resign his charge.[5]

Henry V appointed him as envoy to Lithuania, to Duke Alexander and Ladislas king of Poland. The tradition that he made peace between them is, however, not easy to reconcile with the known course of events.[6] He was with the king at his death in 1422, and preached at his funeral.

1 For Netter *v. DNB*; H. B. Workman, *John Wyclif* (index); and J. H. Wylie, *Henry IV* and *Henry V* (index, and especially I, 238–41). There are short articles in *DTC* and *DHG* but, as the writer of the latter remarks, Netter has not yet received the attention he deserves. Most of the scanty personal details about him come from his *Doctrinale de sacramentis* (ed. Venice, 1571), e.g. I, 2, 516b; II, 85d; 95d; 187d; III, 81a. He refers to 'pater meus et magister devotus Frater Guilielmus [*sc.* Wodeford]' *ibid.* II, 85d, 87d, 95d.
2 'Epistolae Waldensis', nos. x–xi (*Mon. Hist. Carmelitana*, I, 448–9).
3 *Ibid.* nos. xxxii–xxxiii (*Mon. Hist. Carmelitana*, I, 469–70).
4 *Ibid.* no. xxxviii (*Mon. Hist. Carmelitana*, 474–5).
5 *Ibid.* nos. xxvii–xxviii (*Mon. Hist. Carmelitana*, 459–64).
6 C. L. Kingsford in *DNB*.

Netter's activities as provincial, as royal confessor and as diplomat made him something of a figure in the public life of his own day. To later generations he was a figure of notoriety as the fanatical mallet of the Lollards; modern historians have regarded him with a certain gratitude as the annalist, or even perhaps the archivist, of Wyclif and early Lollardy.[1] To his immediate posterity, on the other hand, he appeared as the theologian who had given a full and final answer to the Lollards, the Athanasius or the Augustine of their heresy.

His achievement as a theologian has been allowed almost to vanish. Though his great work was frequently printed in the fifteenth and sixteenth centuries, and reprinted at Venice as late as 1771, it has been lost to sight under the layers of anti-Lutheran and anti-Calvinistic apologetic, and has not yet been reached by the excavators of the late Middle Ages. In the great *Dictionnaire de Théologie catholique*, which devotes many pages to medieval and modern writers of minimal importance, Netter receives a bare half-dozen lines, and the English reader has to search far for an account of his works. Yet if a volume of apologetic may be judged by its external effect, that of Netter must receive a full meed of praise. As the judicious historian of Lollardy remarks, 'the work was authoritative, and no reply to it was even so much as attempted'.[2] Lollardy, in fact, great as was its moral, its emotional and its social appeal, could not stand up to logical thought and traditional theology clearly expressed. The extinction of the sect in all save the lowest levels of ecclesiastical life in the mid-fifteenth century, which is usually ascribed solely to the drastic coercion and stifling of thought practised by Courtenay and others, may in great part have been due to the simple, sound and effective attack of Netter.

The first part of his exposition of traditional Catholic doctrine on the points at issue was begun towards the end of the reign of Henry V, and completed after the king's death. In it Netter takes the Lollard theses one by one, explains and defends the orthodox position, and attacks its contrary. A copy of the work was sent to Rome, where it was examined by theologians and received the approval of Martin V, who called upon its author to write a second book on the sacraments. This was completed in 1427 and received similar papal commendation and official approval; the pope then asked for a third volume on 'sacramentals', the rites and devout practices of Catholics. Together the three parts make up a methodical account of many of the chief doctrines of the Church, considered in reference to those of the early Lollards. In form and treatment the work stands midway between two epochs, looking forward rather than backward. In its diffuse methods and its choice of topics and arguments it is medieval, but in its apologetic tone and its direct approach, which abandons the dialectic framework of the *quaestio* for the more direct

---

1 The *Fasciculi zizaniorum Magistri Joannis Wyclif*, ed. W. W. Shirley, was probably the work of Stephen Patrington as far as p. 359, when Netter took up the tale.
2 J. Gairdner, *Lollardy and the Reformation in England*, I, 200.

method of answer and proof, it anticipates the Counter-Reformation treatises of the following century.

Besides attacking the tenets of Lollardy by argument, Netter also took steps to preserve the early history of the sect. The *Fasciculus zizaniorum* is a fully documented account of the rise and development of Lollardy. As a collection of original sources it has few rivals in the fifteenth century. The narrative, which begins bravely enough, dwindles into a short connecting tissue and ultimately ceases altogether, but the documents and annexed treatises and sermons form a most valuable framework for the years that follow. As the story begins several years before Netter was old enough to be aware of the controversy, it has been suggested with great plausibility that the work was begun by Stephen Patrington, and handed over by him to his successor in the provincialate when he was called to higher office. Whatever Netter's share in the early parts, credit for the completion and transmission must rest with him, and we owe it to him that the events and the issues of early Lollardy can be related so fully and so accurately, with the names of the participants and the dates of the events recorded with some authenticity. He died near Rouen *c*. 1430.

The connexion of the Carmelites with the royal house continued for a time. Netter had been confessor to Henry VI when a child, and he was succeeded by John Stanbery. Richard, Duke of York, had John Kenynghale, and the Duke of Clarence, John Upton. After them, the Dominicans returned. The Carmelites also had at least five bishops in the early fifteenth century: Patrington (Chichester), John Swaffham (Bangor), Thomas Peverell (Llandaff and Worcester), Robert Mascall and John Stanbery (Hereford). In 1432, at the command of Eugenius IV, the order in England was reformed after the grant of the mitigated rule. But of this, and all other events in Carmelite history, scarcely anything is known; it is only with the end of the century that information again is given.

II. THE AUSTIN HERMITS

The fourth order of friars, that of the Hermits of St Augustine or, as it was generally called in England, that of the Austin friars, derived like the order of Carmel from a number of eremitical groups and, in this also like Carmel, retained something of the eremitical tradition in its first English foundations which, like those of the older monastic and canonical houses, but unlike those of the two first orders of friars, were founded as communities by royal or noble benefactors in remote and even wild surroundings in Suffolk, Shropshire and Kent. The tradition, indeed, remained, and for some years similar sites were chosen as at Shuttington in Warwickshire and Whittleseymere in the county of Cambridge. As with the Carmelites once more, however, the pull of the mendicant ideal and of the schools was too great to resist, and gradually the Austin friars fell into place as one of the 'ordres foure' with houses in the principal cities and towns and large convents at the two universities.

While this was happening in England the Austin friars abroad were beginning to build up a theological tradition of their own.[1] Looking as they did to St Augustine as their founder, it was natural that much of their teaching should have a strong Augustinian bias, but the peculiar character was largely due to the first great master of the order, who was adopted, while still actively teaching and comparatively young, as the norm to be followed by all the friars in their schools. Giles of Rome, who had been a pupil of St Thomas in his second Paris regency, was at that time a fairly orthodox Thomist, and the Austin friars long remained at once nearer in spirit to Thomism and less receptive of the theological and philosophical tendencies of Ockhamism than either Franciscans or Carmelites. It was in his Paris days, when he was tutor to Prince Philip of France, that Giles wrote the wholly Aristotelian treatise *De regimine principis*, but in later life, when archbishop of Bourges, he threw himself with ardour into the controversy between Boniface VIII and his old pupil, Philip the Fair, and produced the treatise *De potestate ecclesiastica*, a piece of extreme papalist propaganda, which served as a source, both in argument and language, for the writer of the bull *Unam sanctam*. In this work Giles adopted, in contrast to his earlier teaching, the extreme 'Augustinian' view of society, seeing in the visible Church the only authority entitled to rule mankind or dispose of property: in this Giles has been recognized as the immediate father of the doctrine of Dominion and Grace.[2] The papalist tradition was long cherished by the superiors and doctors of the order, most of whom were Italians, such as James of Viterbo, Agostino Trionfo, William of Cremona and the great theologian and prior-general of the mid-fourteenth century, Thomas of Strassburg, who was strongly Thomist in outlook and succeeded in obtaining the assent of the general chapter of 1345 to a decree aimed directly against Ockham; the decree was strengthened in the general chapter next following (1348).

Meanwhile in England the Austin friars, after slow beginnings, prospered under Edward I and still more in the reign of his son. It was then, in 1318, that the general chapter decreed that at Oxford and Cambridge, as at Paris, there should be two masters of theology, with the result that during the next sixty years friars from Germany and Italy, where the order was strongest, frequented the English universities and in particular Cambridge.[3] It was not, however, till the second half of the century that the Austin

---

1 For this *v.* Fr A. Gwynn, S.J., *The English Austin Friars*, ch. III, and authorities there cited. The early history of the Austin Hermits has recently formed the subject of an important series of articles by Fr F. Roth, O.E.S.A., under the title 'Cardinal Richard Annibaldi, First Protector of the Augustinian Order', in *Augustiniana*, II, 1–60, 108–49, 230–47; III, 21–34. It is understood that Fr Roth is shortly publishing the results of his researches on the English province of the order.

2 Gwynn, *op. cit.* ch. IV. *V. supra*, p. 61.

3 For the decrees of the general chapter in this matter, *v. Analecta Augustiniana*, IV.

friars took a leading part in ecclesiastical affairs. The first occasion was the controversy with the mendicants in which Archbishop Fitzralph embroiled himself. Here it was the prior of the London Austin friars, recently enriched with a magnificent church, who acted as agent for the four orders in delivering their list of reputed errors in his writings to the archbishop of Armagh (1357).[1] Some years later Geoffrey Hardeby, then regent master at Oxford, answered the archbishop's charges against the friars in his treatise *De vita evangelica*; it was by way of appendix to this that he trespassed upon another field of controversy by arguing the claim of his order to St Augustine as founder.

Thomas of Strassburg, as has been seen, reorganized the studies of the order, and his successor, Gregory of Rimini, sent some of the most promising friars to the English universities. As a result, something of an intellectual revival is visible in the English province between 1350 and 1390, and is reflected in the activities of a number of Austin friars. The earliest of these, John Waldeby, was a northerner, and a preacher and devotional writer of note, who became provincial in 1354. Bale, whose judgement on the friars of a bygone age is often generous and usually discerning, speaks of him as 'exceedingly pious and learned',[2] and his most recent historian writes of his sermons as those 'of an exceptionally zealous and able friar'. He was the friend of Abbot Thomas de la Mare, to whom he dedicated his series of twelve homilies on the Apostolic Creed, and whom he had often met when de la Mare was prior of Tynemouth. John Waldeby was succeeded as provincial in 1357 by William of Nottingham, whom twenty years later William Flete was to recall as a model of observance. Some time before 1361 Geoffrey Hardeby was provincial and in high favour with the old king Edward III. Another eminent Austin friar, associated not with the king but with the rival group surrounding the Black Prince, was John Erghome. This friar, like Hardeby associated with the York convent, was distinguished enough to become regent master at the papal court near Naples in 1386 when competition for the post was reduced by the ineligibility of the French friars during the Great Schism. It was he whose books, as is noted elsewhere, came to be entered in the catalogue of the library of the York convent;[3] here it is enough to remark that they mirror the mind of an exceedingly alert, versatile, inquisitive, up-to-date, and at the same time restless, shallow and worldly friar. They include the so-called *Vaticinia canonici Joannis Bridlington*, an obscure political satire on contemporary court life as seen from the angle of a supporter of the Black Prince's party, written by Erghome under the pen-name (so it would appear) of his contemporary, the saintly prior of the Austin canons at Bridlington.[4]

1 Fr A. Gwynn, *The English Austin Friars*, 86.
2 Bale, *Illustrium...Scriptorum Catalogus*, I, 499. 3 *V. infra*, p. 347.
4 Printed in T. Wright, *Political Poems and Songs*, I, 125–215. For the ascription, originally made by M. R. James, *v.* Gwynn, *op. cit.* 135, and James, in *Fasciculus J. W. Clark dicatus*, 12.

Such was the background of the activities of the Austin friars at the time of the controversy as to the right of the religious to possess wealth and avoid taxation. At the crisis of that dispute in 1371 it was two Austin friars, John Bankyn and another (perhaps Thomas Asshebourne) who presented Parliament with a petition in which it was argued that the clergy should contribute to the country's needs out of the wealth given them in the past. Three years later Thomas Asshebourne, perhaps then prior of the London convent, was the only one of the four religious doctors who, in the anonymous and probably fictitious account in the *Eulogium Historiarum*, advised the Black Prince in downright fashion at a parliament at Westminster to act boldly against the claim of the pope to be lord in temporal matters.

III. THE FRIARS: PREACHING

Among the various external employments of the friars the first place in theory, and to a large extent in practice also, was taken by preaching. The simple, extempore preaching of the early, evangelical days has often been described with enthusiasm, and has already received notice. Within recent years, also, the whole field of the preacher's activities in the fourteenth century has been traversed with a wealth of detail.[1] There is therefore no need to touch at all fully upon a subject of which the unpublished sources are so numerous, and are still occupying the attention of scholars.

Besides the apostolic preaching, at first by the wayside and in the market place, and later in churchyard or friary yard, by parish cross or from pulpit, the friars gradually came to meet a number of special calls. Many, indeed, of the occasions which in the modern Church are regarded as the peculiar province of members of the religious orders, such as the preaching of missions to a parish, and the giving of annual retreats to the clergy and religious of both sexes, are features of the life of the post-Tridentine Church which did not exist in the Middle Ages, but from the first the friars acted as special preachers to bishops on visitation, in parish, collegiate and capitular churches and in nunneries and the smaller houses of men; somewhat later, perhaps, they were the normal preachers at synods, to which previously monastic preachers had been invited.[2] They were besides not infrequently called upon to preach in a cathedral, before a university, or at court before the king, as well as to deliver a sermon on some topic of the day at Paul's Cross, while in the fourteenth century the custom, common all over western Europe, of providing a preacher for every day of Lent in the larger town churches gave further regular employment.

1 G. R. Owst has made the subject peculiarly his own by his two attractive books, based on a very full study of the sources: *Preaching in Medieval England*, and *Literature and Pulpit in Medieval England*. Besides the sources listed therein, a very full bibliography of the subject will be found in the *Cambridge Bibliography of English Literature*, I, 170 *seqq*.

2 For monks as preachers at synods *v*. Owst, *Preaching*, 52–3.

Their typical activity, however, remained the preaching journey from town to town, with its sermons on Sundays and the frequent festival days;[1] to these may be added the regular sermons in their own churches, which in the later Middle Ages were perhaps the principal theatres of the friars' oratory. These friary churches became in the fourteenth century a new model in church building; they were designed as spacious halls to accommodate the maximum number of auditors within sight and earshot of the pulpit.[2] The typical large cruciform church of the Early English or Decorated periods affords surprisingly little room for a massed congregation; the pillars, aisles and crossing, to say nothing of screens, tombs and chantry chapels consume a large area, and the central nave is usually narrow, long, and acoustically faulty. The friars' churches, by contrast, are little more than great barns, capable of seating a very large congregation, and it is possible, though not certain,[3] that it was their example, and the popularity of the Sunday afternoon sermon among the richer townsfolk and villagers, that brought into fashion the wide naves and 'aisled chapel' type of large parish church in the late fourteenth and early fifteenth centuries. Besides the Lenten course, there was an occasion for a special sermon in parishes on Palm Sunday, when the procession with the Host halted at the Cross in the churchyard, and, some weeks later, the Rogation days were similarly marked.

It does not seem possible, with the material at present available, to distinguish between the methods, topics and clientele of the various orders. All four families of friars produced both well-known popular preachers and compilers of manuals and *exempla* of pulpit oratory. Thus among the Preachers the unfortunate Thomas Waleys, in his more peaceful years, made a name for himself in the pulpit, and at about the same time the ablest sermon-writer of all, the Dominican John de Bromyard, who should be distinguished from his namesake, the anti-Wyclifite theologian and chancellor of Cambridge (1383), was perhaps the most celebrated preacher of his day, who, besides his preaching tours and polemics, composed a *Summa predicantium*.[4] The Minors had surprisingly few celebrities at this time, but there are records of many ordinary touring preachers and of the compilers of at least three *Summae*. The Carmelites were perhaps the most active of all the orders in the second half of the century. Many names of sermon-compilers have been handed down, among them the prince of classifiers, Dr Alan of Lynn, who provided a table of contents to

---

1 For samples of such journeys, taken from sermon notes, *v.* Owst, *Preaching*, 58 *seqq.*
2 Strangely enough, no great friary church has survived *in toto*; an idea of the preaching nave could be gained, before its destruction by enemy action in 1941, from the church of the Austin Friars (now the Dutch Church) off Throgmorton Street, E.C. 4 (plan and description in *Royal Commission on Historical Monuments: London: City*) and from that of the Preachers at Norwich, now St Andrew's Hall (plate in Jarrett, *The English Dominicans*, 66). *V.* also A. R. Martin, *Franciscan Architecture in England*.
3 Cf. the remarks of Owst, *Preaching*, 159.
4 *V.* references in Owst, *Preaching*, 68 *et al.* and *DNB*, and for Waleys *v.* B. Smalley, 'Thomas Waleys, O.P.'

a vast French sermon-encyclopaedia, and who was to examine an episode in the life of Margery Kempe.[1] Three court preachers of the time were white friars, and two of their number obtained bishoprics largely on the strength of their success in the pulpit.[2] Among the Austin friars the three Waldeby brothers or cousins attract notice; the second, John, was provincial prior and composed a collection of popular sermons for all the Sundays and holidays of the year, as well as numerous homilies, while the third, Robert, after a distinguished career as preacher, became in turn archbishop of Dublin, bishop of Chichester and (for a few months) archbishop of York.[3]

The golden age of the popular sermon in medieval England appears to have been the middle and latter half of the fourteenth century, when the towns, grown large on a period of prosperity, and the parish churches, rebuilt with more spacious nave and aisles, gave audiences to the preacher, and when social troubles, plagues, war and Lollardy opened a field for evangelists, orthodox or heretical. It was at this moment that such a fashionable and sophisticated friar as the Carmelite court preacher William Badby could attract hearers as to a show.[4] There was, however, no saint among the evangelists, and preaching could no longer stir the masses to follow the good tidings into desert places or to a crusade, as it had done more than two centuries previously in the days of Bernard and Norbert, of Vitalis and of Robert of Arbrissel, and as it was to do many centuries later with Whitfield and Wesley. The successes of Wyclif's Poor Priests were not comparable to those of the early days of Methodism, and in fact their unchartered activities hastened the ruin of the art. Although Margery Kempe bears witness that sermons were still an important element in the religious life of the devout in her day, recent investigation appears to show beyond a doubt that originality and the discussion of actual topics and the denunciation of abuses vanished from the orthodox pulpit as a result of the precautions taken against heresy in the early decades of the fifteenth century.

IV. FRIARS AS BISHOPS

In the course of the thirteenth century the friars, in the Church at large, had come to replace the Cistercians and Premonstratensians as the nominees to bishoprics of both popes and princes eager for discipline or reform. In England, however, owing partly to the freedom of election which was one of the provisions of the Great Charter, and partly to the growth of

1 B.M. MS. Royal 3.D.iii; for him, *v*. Owst, *Preaching*, 307. As 'a worshipful doctor of divinity, named Master Aleyn, a White Friar' he figures in an inquiry into the alleged miraculous escape of Margery Kempe from a falling roof-beam (*Book*, ed. Butler-Bowdon), ch. ix, p. 45; EETS, CIX, 21.

2 The three were John Swaffham (bishop of Cloyne 1363–76, Bangor 1376–98), Thomas Peverel (bishop of Llandaff 1398–1407, Worcester 1407–19) and Stephen Patrington.

3 For the Waldeby brothers *v*. Owst, *Preaching*, 64–6 *et al*. and Fr A. Gwynn, S.J., *The English Austin Friars*, 114–23.

4 For the manuscript reference, *v*. Owst, *Preaching*, 221.

a strong, energetic and class-conscious hierarchy, many of the members of which were secular university-trained bishops, the fashion had not been followed: the two friars who were in succession the first and only members of their respective orders to rule at Canterbury were appointed directly from Rome, and instances of friars ruling English dioceses before 1350 are very rare. During the fourteenth and fifteenth centuries the sees of England and Wales were, with few exceptions, filled by candidates acceptable to both pope and king who had usually been first proposed by the latter. This system led to the appointment of a number of friars, not precisely as a tribute to their sanctity of life or pastoral zeal, but as the natural reward of a trusted counsellor or confessor. Rarely did they attain to the wealthiest and most influential sees, but they were frequently appointed to one of the three Welsh dioceses, which came to be regarded as stepping-stones to the lesser English sees. During the same period a considerable number were appointed to Irish sees and that of Sodor and Man, but whereas in the fourteenth century an Irish appointment was often also a papal provision for a friar who had done good service at the Curia, in the fifteenth the primary purpose was to secure an energetic man in episcopal orders to act as suffragan for an overworked or absentee English diocesan. A similar end was achieved by an appointment to Sodor and Man or (especially in the fifteenth century) by papal provision to an oriental title *in partibus*. Thus between 1350 and 1535 some forty-four English Dominicans received episcopal consecration; between them they occupied six English, ten Welsh and eighteen Irish sees, and in addition five took the title, without fulfilling the functions, of bishop of Sodor and Man, and eight were provided to sees in France or *in partibus*.[1] Similar use was made of the Minors, but as these were employed in diplomacy by English kings less than the Preachers and Carmelites, appointments to English sees were not in question, and it is a notable fact that save for John Pecham and the almost contemporary Walter of Gainsborough, no Franciscan friar ever held an English see. Six Welsh, one Scottish, sixteen Irish and seventeen bishoprics *in partibus* were, however, held by Franciscans; the Irish sees concerned were usually small, poor and unimportant, and the friars concerned rarely resided in, or even visited, their diocese, but acted as suffragans in England.

The numbers of friars from the other two orders in episcopal orders have not been established with the same accuracy; they were certainly not so large, though the Carmelites, at the turn of the fourteenth century, supplied more than one English bishop, including Stephen Patrington, who reached Chichester by way of St David's, and Thomas Peverel, who climbed from Ossory to Llandaff and thence to Worcester. Somewhat earlier the Austin friars in the person of Robert Waldeby reached the metropolitan see of the north.

The English friar-bishops, taken as a whole, made little mark in their

---

1 For a list of these from *c.* 1330 to *c.* 1480, *v.* Appendix III.

dioceses; as has been suggested, they were usually royal servants who attained episcopal rank only at the end of their career. Those appointed to Welsh sees may have fulfilled their difficult pastoral task more conscientiously; the Irish nominees certainly did not. In so far as these friars made any contribution to the religious life of the country it was chiefly in the unassuming but necessary routine tasks of confirming, consecrating and ordaining performed by the suffragan in districts which for decade after decade might never see the face of their ordinary.

v. THE FRIARS AND THE UNIVERSITIES

The early opposition of the secular masters to the mendicants, which had come to a crisis owing to the insistence of the friars on their right to proceed to a course in theology without having passed through the arts school and acted as regents in arts, had been lulled to an uneasy rest by the award of the papal arbitrators in 1314. By this the statute of 1253 was upheld, which had made the career of every friar dependent upon a grace in congregation excepting him from the normal rule, but whereas hitherto power of refusal had been vested in the individual members of congregation, it was now to rest only with a majority of masters of theology who were actually regents at the time.[1] As the majority of masters would be friars or religious (who were all equated with the friars on this point) this clause gave the religious candidate the necessary safeguards. Those, however, who had not ruled in arts, had to take a solemn and public oath before being admitted to oppose in theology that they had studied philosophy for eight years, and theology for six more.

This settlement put an end to essential grievances, though the mendicants found watchfulness a necessity in order to ensure that its terms should be safeguarded, while the university jealously preserved its rights from infringement by 'wax doctors', as those (usually religious and often foreigners) were called who came before congregation supplicating a grace with no further qualification than the letters of some influential lay or episcopal patron. Whenever friction of any kind, however, occurred between mendicants and seculars, academic strife recommenced. One such occasion was the attack on the mendicants by Archbishop Fitzralph. One of his principal grievances was the alleged kidnapping of promising boys at Oxford and elsewhere by the mendicants which, according to the secular masters, caused parents of the upper class to be fearful of allowing their sons to attend the university. A statute was passed in consequence in 1358 forbidding the mendicants to receive any recruit under the age of eighteen; the members of any offending community were deprived for a year of the right of giving or attending any lectures.[2] A similar statute was

1 H. Rashdal¹, OHS, *Collectanea* II, 193–273, and A. G. Little, 'The Dominicans versus the University of Cambridge'.
2 *Munimenta Academica Oxon.*, ed. H. Anstey, 205–6.

enacted at Cambridge,[1] though no record of it survives. The friars after a short delay appealed to Rome, not confining themselves to their latest grievance but opening up again the whole question of the need for an arts degree and the existing ban on the activities of more than one regent in any one religious house. Urban V replied in 1365 by issuing mandates suspending the offending statutes for a year and ordering the universities of Oxford and Cambridge to appear at the papal court to show reason why the repeal should not be perpetual.[2] This drew the king into the controversy and the four provincials were instructed to lay their case before him (May 1366). As result, the statute as to age was annulled on condition that the mendicants withdrew their action in the papal court. Despite this experience the secular masters continued to make difficulties from time to time, and in 1388[3] and again in 1421 the king intervened on behalf of the friars.[4]

---

1 J. R. H. Moorman, *The Grey Friars in Cambridge*, 108, where other restrictive measures are noticed.

2 *CPL*, IV, 52, 91.   3 *Cal. Close R.* (*1385–9*), 2 Ric. II, 378.

4 Wilkins, *Concilia*, III, 400.

CHAPTER XI

THE FORTUNES OF THE CLUNIAC HOUSES
AND THE ALIEN PRIORIES

Besides the autonomous black monk houses and their dependencies, there existed in England a large number of monastic bodies, some relatively important, the majority insignificant, who were controlled either directly or mediately by abbeys in France and Flanders. These, both by contemporaries in the later Middle Ages and by recent historians, have often been grouped together under the designation of 'alien priories'. Actually, they fall into two distinct classes: the family of Cluny and the dependencies of autonomous foreign houses. The former had from the beginning the capacity, or at least the potentiality, for fruitful individual activity; the latter, so long as their status remained unchanged, enjoyed at the best a derivative life. In the twelfth century, when intercourse between these islands and the Continental dominions of the kings of England was close, the personnel of these houses differed little, if at all, from that of other English monasteries, but in the thirteenth century matters altered: the Cluniac houses, though often ruled by a French prior and containing a group of foreign monks, tended to draw their recruits from the countryside; the priories and cells depending directly on individual French houses, being for the most part too small to receive novices, came to be manned largely by foreigners. All of them remained entirely outside the jurisdiction of the presidents and provincial chapters of the black monks, and the Cluniac family was exempt also from episcopal surveillance, depending as it did, through Cluny, immediately upon the Holy See. As the Cluniacs paid a small regular tax to their mother-house, and occasional larger grants, while the others sent all their revenues abroad, they naturally became an object of suspicion to the growing national feeling and an attractive spoil to the Crown, and when enmity to France became endemic they were seen as a financial asset to the enemy, and a potential source of danger to England. The hostility thus aroused was often increased, especially in regard to the smaller houses, by the irregular and disedifying conduct of the inmates, who were often *mauvais sujets* or restless individuals sent across the Channel as a good riddance.

The Cluniac family, at the opening of the period, consisted of some thirty-eight houses of which eleven or so were large, fully organized monasteries, almost all with dependencies of their own, while of the others the majority were priories in miniature, depending on a larger house, and the rest cells holding three or four monks without the full monastic life.[1]

1 For the English Cluniacs in the later Middle Ages the richest collection of sources is that of Sir G. Duckett, *Charters and Records of Cluny*. Miss R. Graham has long made a special

The main lines of Cluniac organization have been set out elsewhere;[1] they endured unchanged, at least in theory, during the thirteenth century, but in practice the subjection of the residents in the English houses to Cluny, La Charité and St Martin des Champs entailed little besides a small tax, the obligation of receiving a nominated prior and the necessity of visiting Cluny in the person of their prior for the annual general chapter. As individuals, they were in principle completely at the disposal of the abbot of Cluny; how far his right was exercised in distant provinces is not clear, but it would seem that simple monks were, on the whole, left undisturbed. The indirect consequences of this subjection were, however, considerable; besides the prior, who in the case of the major houses was almost invariably a foreigner in the thirteenth century, and sometimes entirely without experience of English ways, there were always a number —sometimes a majority—of foreign monks. As the fourteenth century proceeded, and war with France became almost the norm, feeling both inside and outside the communities concerned stiffened against this foreign element, especially when in authority.

The organization of the Cluniac family was in origin patriarchal and quasi-feudal. Authority rose by steps from daughter to mother up to the abbot of Cluny, who possessed and exercised almost exactly the powers claimed by the fourteenth-century popes as 'universal ordinaries' over all the members of the Church. There was originally no legislative body, nor was there any system of counterchecks. In the thirteenth century, however, the decrees of the Lateran Council and perhaps also the new mendicant organization influenced the practice of Cluny. The family was divided into ten provinces, of which England was one, and the annual visit of all the priors to Cluny became a general chapter at which statutes were approved and published and visitors appointed by the meeting to examine the state of all the houses.[2] These visits, it would seem, were regularly carried out until the French wars began at the very end of the thirteenth century.

With the outbreak of these wars, which continued at first intermittently and then almost without cessation for more than a century and a half, national feeling against foreigners grew, creating grave disabilities for the

study of the Cluniac houses in England, and reference may be made to her articles and papers (v. bibliography to date 1949 in *Medieval Essays presented to Rose Graham*) on various aspects of Cluniac history, especially to those collected in *English Ecclesiastical Studies*: 'The Papal Schism of 1378 and the English Province of the Order of Cluny'; 'The English Province of the Order of Cluny in the Fifteenth Century', and 'The Priory of La Charité sur Loire and the Monastery of Bermondsey'. The same author's 'The History of the Alien Priory of Wenlock' may be added to the foregoing.

1 *MO*, 145–50.

2 A. Bruel, 'Les Chapîtres Généraux de l'Ordre de Cluny', was the first to sketch the history of these chapters and indicate the sources where *acta* may be found. The first chapter of which an account survives is that of 1233. Occasionally in the twelfth century, even as early as 1132, the abbot of Cluny had called a special meeting of all priors at Cluny, and had promulgated statutes (v. *MO*, 157), but these were not deliberative chapters, nor were any officers or visitors appointed in them.

foreign houses. In 1289 Edward I forbade the forwarding of sums of money abroad, and in 1295, when the king of France had invaded the English territory, he seized the temporalities of all alien houses. The procedure was identical with that originally adopted in the case of vacant abbacies of which the holder was a tenant in chief. A royal official received all revenues and allowed a bare maintenance to the monks, whose activities were now further curtailed by an order in Council which anticipated with curious exactness the measures taken with regard to the movements of aliens in 'restricted areas' during the threat of German invasion in 1940. All foreign monks living within thirteen miles of the sea or a navigable river were to be transferred inland; a guardian was appointed in each county to supervise them; they were confined to the monastic precincts, their correspondence was suspended and strict regulations governed all their intercourse with others.[1]

Only a few years later, the sending of a tax overseas was forbidden by statute; in 1324 the priories were again seized, as also from 1337 to 1360 and from 1369 onwards. In 1376 Parliament endeavoured to remove foreign agents by demanding that superiors overseas should appoint English vicars general with powers to nominate English priors and banish foreign monks. The petition was without formal effect, but the papal schism which occurred two years later severed ecclesiastical relations between England and France and thus effected in practice what had been asked.

Not all these oppressive measures were fully enforced upon the Cluniac family. In some cases the personal influence of a prior or powerful patron secured the house from molestation, and in general the authorities of all the larger priories soon began to work towards a *modus vivendi*. This took one of two forms. The less important houses bought off the royal control by the payment of a lump sum, followed by a heavy annual tribute. This, though less overwhelming than direct financial control, was extremely onerous, and in consequence the larger priories, when war with France dragged on indefinitely, took the step of petitioning for a charter of denization, a process which corresponded to the naturalization of an individual. For this an English prior and powerful advocacy were necessary; a large money payment was then made, and the house was thenceforth reckoned as fully English, with no obligations of paying tribute overseas. Denization, however, did not of itself involve total separation from Cluny.

The first to move thus was Lewes in 1351; it was followed in due course by all the remaining ten major priories, the last to make the change being Northampton and Montacute, in 1405 and 1407.

Meanwhile, the English Cluniac province had adopted a novel and interesting constitutional experiment. When the Papal Schism began in 1378 France followed the popes of Avignon, England those of Rome, and

---

1 *Cal. Fine R.* I, 362–4. For this measure and its effects *v.* R. Graham, 'The History... of Wenlock', 132–3.

Urban VI severed connexion between Cluny and England, setting up an English chapter to act instead of the general chapter of Cluny and to elect two presidents to replace the abbot of the mother-house. After some dissension, due largely to rivalry between the lines of Cluny and La Charité, the priors of Thetford and Bermondsey were chosen, but a few years later, in 1389, Boniface IX altered the arrangement by setting Archbishop Courtenay of Canterbury, who was conservator of the privileges of Cluny in England as well as papal legate, alongside of the two priors as administrators of the province. This unpromising arrangement worked smoothly enough under Courtenay and Arundel, who had a family interest in Lewes; priors and visitors were appointed regularly, and some statutes of the meetings survive, including one enforcing the sending of a monk to the university from each conventual priory.[1]

The Papal Schism ended with the election of Martin V in 1417, and with it the *raison d'être* of the English organization. Denization had not canonically affected the relations between Cluny and England, and the abbots of Cluny began an attempt to regain all their lapsed rights. National sentiment had, however, grown very strong, added to a natural desire for self-determination. Already some of the houses had proceeded to work for complete independence by means of papal or royal privileges. Bermondsey had become an autonomous abbey in 1399, though Cluny refused to recognize the change; others had secured freedom of election by papal or royal grant. As a compromise on the main issue, the prior of Lewes had in 1410 been appointed by the abbot of Cluny as vicar-general in England, but the daughters of La Charité did not relish the arrangement, while the prior himself, John Burghersh, came near having the abbatial dignity put upon him through the good offices of the countess of Arundel. He was, however, of small administrative ability, and it was left to the historian Thomas Elmham, a better known figure, to work towards a permanent settlement. At a provincial chapter in London in 1414 a series of proposals was drawn up for presentation to the abbot of Cluny; they amount to a complete devolution of powers, establishing a kind of 'dominion status'. An English vicar-general was to replace the abbot of Cluny as receiver of monastic professions, confirmer of elections (which were to be free) and president of the triennial chapter. This, while ostensibly retaining the dependence upon Cluny, would in practice have removed all necessity for individual English monks to go overseas, and would have given the abbot of Cluny little more than titular supremacy. The petition may be regarded as the work of Elmham, and it was accompanied by a covering letter from Henry V, this also probably drafted by the same hand, in which he warmly supported the various clauses of the document.[2]

---

1 *V.* R. Graham, 'The Papal Schism...and the English Province of Cluny', with references.
2 *V.* R. Graham, 'The English Province...in the Fifteenth Century'. It should, however, be noted (p. 67) that V. H. Galbraith, *The St Albans Chronicle*, p. xxiii, goes far to disprove the identification of Elmham with Henry's biographer.

The abbot of Cluny not unnaturally lacked enthusiasm for the scheme, which he refused to endorse. He did, however, give Elmham shortly after full powers as vicar-general, and henceforth the office was a regular institution, being held from 1419 to 1464 by the priors of Lewes save for two brief intervals in 1431–2 and 1458, when abbots of Cluny sent special representatives to England in an endeavour to recover their old control.

Meanwhile, the centrifugal process was continuing. Bermondsey had already escaped from the system for all practical purposes in 1399, though both Cluny and La Charité refused to acknowledge the transaction and endeavoured even fifty years later to reassert their rights. Thetford had secured freedom of election previously, and was soon followed by Northampton and Montacute. In another direction, Cluniac houses abroad lost finally in 1440 several of their priories in England which had long been in the king's hands along with the other alien priories.

The final stage was reached at the end of the fifteenth century, when the Cluniac priories began one by one to secure papal bulls exempting them from all jurisdiction of Cluny and setting them immediately under the Holy See. Lewes acted thus in 1480, Lenton in 1484 and Wenlock ten years later. Finally, in 1490, at the request of Henry VII, Innocent VIII put the whole family of Cluny in England, along with the exempt black monk houses of the realm, under the visitatorial jurisdiction of the arch-bishop of Canterbury, and for the last fifty years of their existence they remained, both juridically and practically, independent of the great abbey whose fame and observance had prompted William de Warenne, more than four hundred years before, to introduce them to English skies under the shadow of his castles in Sussex and Norfolk.

In addition to the family of Cluny, the class of 'alien priories' included a very numerous and widely scattered body of baillivates, cells and priories depending upon almost every important abbey of Normandy and north-western France. The circumstances of their origin, religious development and general characteristics belong to the history of an earlier century and need not be recapitulated here.[1] During the later Middle Ages they experienced little internal change, save that a number of those originally conventual became mere cells. Their number, though large, was certainly by no means as great as the lists of past generations of medievalists might suggest, for the hundred and fifty 'alien priories' listed by more than one historian have among them very many establishments that were no more than cells where one, two, or three monks resided, or even mere baillivates which served as headquarters for the monk appointed from time to time to oversee his abbey's distant estates. It may be accepted as certain that not more than seventy were at any time fully conventual houses, monasteries in miniature, and at the end of the fourteenth century there were probably

1 *MO*, 134–6.

no more than forty such in being.[1] Of these priories almost all, excluding the Cluniacs, were the property of autonomous black monk abbeys; the only notable exceptions were a small family of three Grandmontine priories and another of the dependencies of Tiron. Of the black monk priories some fifteen or twenty were of considerable size; houses such as Blyth (Notts), Boxgrove (Sussex), Folkestone (Kent), St Neot's (Hunts), Spalding (Lincs) and Totnes (Devon) were, for most of their existence, regular, if small, monasteries with churches and conventual buildings modelled in plan and design upon the greater abbeys.

As England became more and more a nation separate from France, a twofold process developed. While the larger priories one by one severed connexion with the owning abbey and became autonomous, the smaller tended to decrease in personnel and often to lose their conventual character. Both tendencies were accelerated by the confiscations following on the French wars. When the 'alien priories' were from 1295 onwards repeatedly seized into the king's hands, the larger ones were able in many cases to purchase denization or at least, by the payment of heavy farms, to retain control of their affairs; the smaller often passed completely out of the control of their owners and lost their inmates, since a royal permit, often difficult to obtain, was needed in order that foreign abbeys might reinforce their communities. The feeling of hostility to France, which heralded a new era in European politics, became endemic about the middle of the fourteenth century, and was stronger among the land-holding and merchant classes than in government circles. There was a short interval of peace during which the mother-houses resumed control, but conditions worsened after the resumption of war in 1369, and in 1377 the Commons presented a petition demanding the expulsion of all aliens including monks. As a result, the government decided to expel all save for conventual priors and proctors-general, and all isolated properties were to be farmed to the highest bidder.[2] In the event, as happened with so many regulations, royal and papal, of the age, personal exceptions were immediately granted on a fairly large scale, but the restrictions on immigration gradually resulted in the devolution of many properties to lay farmers and in extinction by death of the communities of small priories. From 1377 onwards, there-

---

1 For various estimates, see J. H. Wylie, *The reign of Henry V*, I, 338, n. 8. The *Monasticon* has 141, Reyner, *Apostolatus Benedictinorum*, 110, etc. The present writer and R. N. Hadcock, in their lists in *Medieval Religious Houses*, include under various orders (not counting Cluniacs) some sixty alien priories and some forty alien cells (i.e. houses of three religious or less). The alien priories as a group have received too little attention from historians, who have been content to repeat commonplaces on their number, decadence and suppression. The work of A. C. Ducarel, *Some Account of the Alien Priories, etc.*, is of little value, and the articles in the volumes of the *VCH* make no attempt at synthesis. C. H. New, *History of the Alien Priories to the Confiscation of Henry V* (University of Chicago, privately distributed, 1914), is not wholly reliable. By far the best short account is by Miss M. M. Morgan (Mrs Chibnall), 'The Suppression of the Alien Priories', a fuller account of some aspects is in the same writer's 'The Abbey of Bec-Hellouin and its English Priories'.

2 *Rot. Parl.* III, 22–3.

fore, the alien priories began to dwindle seriously in number; the normal process was a sale with the consent of the owning house, payment being deferred till the end of the war.[1] Few priories, however, passed permanently into lay hands. Patrons and benefactors naturally wished for a continuance of the prayers which had been one of the purposes of foundation, and the Church showed active disapproval of the alienation of dedicated property. Consequently, such of the priories as were sold went for the most part to such beneficiaries as William of Wykeham's colleges or the royal chapel of St George's, Windsor.[2]

Henry IV on his accession restored the unsold alien lands to their owners; a great number of the priories were without superiors, and the king allowed the long overdue appointments to be made; eight or ten of the largest had by this time become denizen, but in all some twenty-five, exclusive of Cluniac houses, received priors.[3] It seemed, indeed, for a moment that the *status quo ante bellum* might be restored, but national feeling was definitely hostile to the drain of money overseas, and the minority, strong and vocal, who were partially in sympathy with the anti-monastic agitation of the Lollards, swelled the protest, though the alien priories as such were not an object of attack. The Commons therefore again petitioned for seizure, which was granted in 1402,[4] and the remaining priories reverted to what had for more than half a century been the normal state of things. The king made use of the situation, and at a Great Council at Westminster in 1408 it was decreed that the income of the farms of alien priories or cells should be appropriated to the income of the royal household. This, though it was an adminstrative act of some significance, was not, as has been sometimes stated, the final act of confiscation, but merely a diversion of funds hitherto accruing to the Exchequer.[5] The greater houses were allowed to continue existence on the old terms of a stiff yearly payment, while the cells or baillivates were retained by the king as separate entities, and for the most part given in farm to individuals from whom they might be recalled at will.

Matters remained in this condition for some years, but in 1414 a majority in the parliament, fearing that the alien priories might be restored to their former owners, petitioned that all foreign religious should be expelled, and that all their possessions hitherto confiscated should be retained in the king's hand, with the right of pre-emption secured to the actual farmers. Henry agreed, though he excepted conventual priories, and as denization was still permitted, few of these were in fact affected. The Act of 1414 was, nevertheless, the one which gave statutory sanction

---

1 New, *History of the Alien Priories*, 80–1.
2 For authorities, *v.* M. M. Morgan, 'The Suppression of the Alien Priories', 207.
3 Wylie, *Henry IV*, I, 79.
4 *Rot. Parl.* III, 499.
5 *Rot. Parl.* III, 586; Rymer, *Foedera*, VIII, 510. The view of Wylie in *Henry IV*, III, 142, and *Henry V*, I, 338, was convincingly refuted by Miss Morgan, *art. cit.* 208. *V.* also Stubbs, *Constitutional History*, III, 283–4.

to the suppression of the alien priories.[1] The small properties affected remained mostly in the hands of lay farmers, though shortly before Henry's death he gave an undertaking to Pope Martin V that all such possessions should be converted to endow churches, colleges and religious houses, with some compensation for the Continental owners.[2] No compensation was in fact given, either before Henry's death or after; a few of the estates were during his lifetime given to his new foundations of Sheen, Syon and Mount Grace, but the remainder continued to be held by farmers. Finally, Henry VI, after the matter had been made the subject of a protest at the Council of Basel in 1434,[3] transferred the bulk of the confiscated property to religious houses or colleges, in particular to the royal foundations of Sheen, Syon, Mount Grace, Windsor, Eton and King's College, and to the two foundations of William of Wykeham at Winchester and Oxford.

Such was the so-called 'suppression' of the alien priories. The whole transaction has often been misunderstood, and its importance, both in itself and as a precedent, exaggerated. The number of fully conventual alien priories in existence in 1414, by which date practically all the more important had become denizen, almost certainly did not exceed thirty, and may well have been less; few of these had a numerous community, and in fact a number subsequently became denizen or were allowed for decades to continue their existence. The remainder, whether cells or baillivates, had little that was specifically monastic or even ecclesiastical about them; they were simply manors or churches of a foreign proprietor.

It is natural that a measure of this kind, undertaken, at least in its beginnings, on the royal initiative, should be regarded by historians as an interesting precedent for the complete suppression of 1536–40. When closely regarded, however, the differences are more apparent than the resemblances. The elimination of the alien priories, in the first place, was a long and tentative process, covering almost two hundred years, not a sudden blow, and was due throughout primarily to considerations of supposed national interest such as have prompted governments by no means hostile to the religious life, and in countries and centuries widely separated, to confiscate during a war religious or educational establishments controlled entirely by 'enemy aliens'. At every stage protests were raised against the complete secularization of the properties concerned, and these protests were in the event successful. The final Act of Suppression was only the culmination of a long process, which it did not in fact terminate, and the final alienation, in almost every important instance, benefited neither private individuals nor the Crown, but some new and flourishing religious house or collegiate establishment while, as has been noted, the

---

1 Morgan, *art. cit.* 209. The Act is in *Rot. Parl.* IV, 22, and is reprinted in Lodge and Thornton, *English Constitutional Documents*, 318–19.
2 *Henry VI, Memorials*, ed. G. Williams, I, xc; II, 263–5.
3 *Ibid.* II, 264.

majority of the fully developed monasteries escaped suppression by denization. The coincidence of an active, vociferous outcry against monastic possessioners and the whole monastic ideal during the final decades of the process should not be allowed to confuse the issue. The alien properties, in the majority of cases, went to institutes that would have been among the first to go in any revolution carried through by the Lollards. The history of the disappearance of the alien priories is indeed, especially in its last phase, one more instance of the change in the religious climate between the reign of Henry V and that of Henry VIII, and a comparison of the Act of 1414 and its execution with that of 1536 and its sequel hinders, rather than helps, any interpretation of the work of Cromwell as the continuation of that of Henry V.

Midway as regards organization between the hierarchical 'order' of Cluny and the isolated dependencies of individual foreign abbeys stood three groups of priories, those depending upon Tiron, Grandmont and Bec-Hellouin. Tiron, besides its autonomous abbey of St Dogmael's, had four small priories and other properties, chiefly in Hampshire and the Isle of Wight, directly dependent upon itself, and we know from a casual reference that the abbot, as early as 1301, had appointed a proctor-general, in this case, at least, the prior of St Cross, to act for him in all relations with the government and the courts of law.[1] The Tiron group of priories, Andwell and Hamble (Hants), St Cross (Isle of Wight) and Titley (Hereford) were among the earlier (1391) sales of alien houses, and passed as a group to the endowment of Winchester College.[2]

Grandmont had three priories in somewhat remote situations; it was in origin quasi-eremitical and independent, but the small dependencies gradually came to resemble those of the black monks or Austin canons, by both of which bodies they were claimed as members. Of the three priories, one, Grosmont in Yorkshire, became denizen; another, Craswall (Hereford) survived till 1462, when it was granted to Christ's College, Cambridge; the third, Alberbury (Salop) was confiscated in 1414.[3]

As for Bec, although this was a normal black monk house with customs similar to the other houses of Normandy, the circumstances of her origin gave her a place apart, at least in early years, and the priories founded by and depending upon her formed a group, following her customs and wearing her grey variety of the monastic habit and known sometimes as an 'order', though they differed little in their relations with the mother-house from the group of priories depending upon such a monastery as, for example, St Albans or Durham.

1 *Reg. Ricardi Swinfield*, ed. W. W. Capes, 379 (14 April 1301). The prior of St Cross, presenting a prior of Titley to the bishop, writes as 'procurator abbatis et conventus s. Trinitatis de Tyronio... in partibus Anglicis constitutus generalis'.

2 New, *History of the Alien Priories*, 80–1. *Medieval Religious Houses*, under houses concerned.

3 R. Graham, 'The Order of Grandmont and its Houses in England'; *Medieval Religious Houses*, as above.

Bec, early rendered famous by its saintly founder, Herlouin, and his first and second priors, Lanfranc and Anselm, gave more than any other abbey of its sons to the service of the Church in England, and received in return many gifts of land from the new owners.[1] It so happened that the son of Herlouin's overlord and patron became founder of the great house of Clare, and he and his kin were founders of two of the Bec priories, Stoke-by-Clare (Suffolk) and St Neot's (Hunts), and patrons of the third, Goldcliff (Monmouth). Besides these priories, which were fully conventual autonomous economic units, Bec became possessed of some forty manors scattered over England from Warwickshire southwards. These were exploited by the mother-house, but were too numerous to be managed by a single monk-bailiff. Consequently, small groups of six monks or less were set up at three of the manors, Cowick (Devon), Steventon (Berks) and Wilsford (Lincs), while the rest were consolidated at first under two monk-bailiffs at Ruislip (Middlesex) and Ogbourne (Wilts), which were nominally priories, and later, when Ruislip lost its status, under one at Ogbourne alone. The prior of Ogbourne became also, in the early thirteenth century, the abbot's proctor-general for all suits affecting the English properties of the order.

Over this disparate family the abbots of Bec did their best to maintain control, partly by the vow of obedience taken by the monks to Bec, partly by occasional visitations, but more effectively by summons to the annual chapter at Bec, and by the small pension paid by each priory. The connexion was maintained with some success till the French war at the end of the reign of Edward I, when all property belonging to French houses was seized, and the monks near the sea or a navigable river (such as the Ouse at St Neot's) moved to another priory or one of their manors. The property was restored in 1296 for the payment of a heavy annual farm, but in 1324 it was again seized by Edward II and a still higher farm exacted. Henceforward, the abbot of Bec, in common with other French owning houses, was fighting a losing battle with circumstances. The priories were repeatedly taken into the king's hand, and it was difficult to get permission for French monks to be drafted to England; the difficulties were accentuated by the Schism, and the ties with Bec gradually broke. The group of priories splintered: Stoke and St Neot's became denizen; Goldcliff, protesting, became a cell of Tewkesbury.[2] Steventon was sold in 1363, and Wilsford granted away as an alien priory in 1401. Cowick remained under the abbot of Bec till the middle of the fifteenth century. Ogbourne and its appurtenances was divided among various colleges and religious houses.

1 The two paragraphs on Bec priories follow very closely Miss Morgan's article on the subject (v. supra, p. 162, n. 1).
2 For Goldcliff, v. R. Graham, 'Four Alien Priories in Monmouthshire'.

CHAPTER XII

THE LOOSENING OF DISCIPLINE

I. THE GREAT SCHISM

The Great Schism of 1378–1409 inevitably affected all those religious who were dependent upon mother-houses situated in the dominions of the French king, or who belonged to international orders. News of the election of Urban VI, the first Italian pope for a lifetime, was received enthusiastically in England, and when reports of the controversy and schism arrived they were too late to cause a transfer of allegiance, which in any case would not readily have been given to a Frenchman. The severance of relations with all who acknowledged Clement VII, however, entailed serious consequences in many quarters.[1]

Among the black monks those of the family of Cluny were seriously affected; the monks made profession to the abbot of Cluny; the priors attended chapter either at Cluny or their immediate French mother-house; and priors were appointed from overseas. This machinery was now thrown out of gear even more seriously than during the periods of active war with France.[2] A bull of Urban VI ordered the priors of Thetford and Bermondsey to hold a general chapter of all those who usually went to Cluny, wherein they might elect two monks with all the powers of the abbot and general chapter of Cluny. This proposed scheme of government met with opposition when the chapter assembled, for three of the four priors of the direct foundations of Cluny—Lewes, Montacute and Lenton[3]—maintained that they, together with the fourth, the prior of Thetford, should have replaced the general chapter. They refused to take part in the election as ordered, and the two priors of Thetford and Bermondsey, both of English birth, were chosen to rule the body. The appeal of the three dissenters to Urban VI was nevertheless rejected, and the two priors, together with the archbishop of Canterbury, were given full authority, with the curious consequence that in the years that followed the exempt Cluniacs were governed by archbishops of Canterbury. As both Courtenay and Arundel had personal links with the monks the arrangement worked well enough. The three prelates appointed all superiors and summoned chapters to Bermondsey in which definitions for the whole province were published. The harmony was finally disturbed by the prior of Bermondsey, John Attleborough, an ambitious and domineering man, who fell foul of

1 For the general effects of the Schism in England, v. É. Perroy, *L'Angleterre et le Grand Schisme d'Occident*, 76 seqq.
2 *V.* R. Graham, 'The Papal Schism of 1378 and the English Province of the Order of Cluny'.
3 The slip of 'Thetford' for 'Lenton' in Graham, *art. cit.* 484 (ten lines from foot) is corrected in the reprint.

his colleagues and succeeded, no doubt at heavy expense, in procuring the erection of his house to abbatial rank in 1390, thus severing for good its dependence upon La Charité. He enjoyed his dignity for a few months only, and was then driven into resignation after a charge of maladministration; he was finally consoled by papal provision to the bishopric of Ardfert in Ireland. In other respects the machinery set up in 1389 worked well. Meanwhile, the practical severance from Cluny had emphasized the disadvantages of a foreign connexion, and there was a general move to follow Lewes (1351), Thetford (1376) and Bermondsey (1381) in seeking denization. Lenton (1392), Pontefract (1393), Wenlock (1395), Barnstaple (1403), Northampton (1405) and Montacute (1407) fulfilled the requisite conditions by putting up sums of varying magnitude and providing English priors. When unity returned to the Church, Cluny and the other French houses never recovered effective control, and the prior of Lewes was appointed vicar-general for all Cluniacs.

All other groups of aliens were small in comparison with the family of Cluny, but it is interesting to find Boniface IX basing his treatment of the four Bec priories on the model just described. The priors of the two largest—Ogbourn and Cowick—acting in concert with the bishop of London were to make all appointments and hold miniature chapters.[1]

Of all the religious families the Cistercians were the hardest hit by the Schism.[2] Quite apart from the ultimate dependence of the seventy-odd abbeys upon the general chapter at Cîteaux, twenty houses depended immediately upon mother-houses in France, as did also the twelve daughters of Savigny. The first step of Urban VI was to release the white monks from obedience to the then abbot of Cîteaux, and to appoint a vicar-general for the order from among his own supporters; this was followed by the provision of 'shadow' abbots of Clairvaux and Morimond, to have jurisdiction over the daughter-houses of those abbeys within the Roman allegiance. As for England, the pope, some time before 1381, ordered the abbots of Rievaulx and Warden to summon a chapter of the province and set all the machinery of government in action. Rievaulx in the north was the eldest daughter of Clairvaux; Warden, in the southern province, was firstborn of Rievaulx. The new system functioned without a hitch for a time, though difficulties arose when general chapters of the Cistercians of the Roman obedience demanded a subsidy from England; this was refused, as forbidden by the statute of Carlisle of 1307, and the English monks were in consequence threatened with excommunication. In or before 1394 Boniface IX reorganized the English system by ordering the abbots of Boxley, Stratford Langthorne and St Mary Graces to summon the annual general chapter and appoint president and visitors. The choice of an abbot of the new royal foundation and of the heads of two small

1 Perroy, *op. cit.* 91–2; M. Morgan, 'The Abbey of Bec-Helluoin and its English Priories'.

2 R. Graham, 'The Great Schism and the English Monasteries of the Cistercian Order'.

houses distinguished only by their proximity to London suggests royal influence; it ran counter to all the jealous Cistercian traditions of seniority. This may have been the reason why the new general chapter, though working smoothly on most occasions, ran into a series of disorderly quarrels connected with elections: those at Dore, Meaux (1396) and Beaulieu were scandalous in their violence, though the dispute at Meaux had the happy result of giving the unsuccessful candidate, the studious Thomas of Burton, leisure to compile his chronicle.[1] News of these and other quarrels reached Boniface, and he revoked the powers of the three abbots, apparently without immediate effect. Later, however, in 1401, he gave similar jurisdiction to the abbots of Waverley and Furness, the two earliest foundations. This arrangement worked well enough until in 1409 the Schism ended and the English white monks were once more united under the abbot of Cîteaux.

The English Premonstratensians had long been at sixes and sevens with the central government of the order, and could thus view without apprehension the severance of the bonds between themselves and one who was now an adherent of the antipope Clement VII.[2] The situation, as careerists in all the orders concerned realized, could be exploited by swift action, and the abbot of Welbeck, John Baukwell, obtained letters from Urban VI giving him power to act as the abbot of Prémontré in England: to summon a biennial chapter, appoint visitors and confirm elections. The abbot of Newhouse, however, who had undoubted rights of seniority as abbot of the first English foundation, was not prepared to accept the abbot of Welbeck, and in 1406 succeeded in obtaining fresh bulls cancelling the previous issue and substituting himself for the abbot of Welbeck as acting head of the order. A prolonged controversy followed which had not reached an issue by 1411. By that year communications between England and Prémontré had been reopened, and the abbot of Prémontré had appointed the abbot of Bayham as his own commissary. Abbot Baukwell of Welbeck refused to acknowledge him, and was supported by the abbots of Croxton, Sulby, Newbo and Beauchief. Unfortunately for himself, the abbot of Welbeck passed under a political cloud, possibly owing to implication in the northern rising of 1405, and found it necessary to go into exile in Scotland. This enabled the abbot of Newhouse to visit Welbeck, declare Baukwell contumacious for failing to obey a citation, and, in spite of threats of violence on the part of his supporters, to elect a new abbot in his room. Soon after this, however, the abbot of Bayham was granted a fresh commission by the abbot of Prémontré, and although the abbots of England made a bid for independence, an equilibrium was reached in which successive abbots of Bayham acted as commissaries for the abbot of Prémontré until, in 1459, a permanent commission was granted to abbot Redman of Shap.

1 *Chronicon monasterii de Melsa*, ed. E. A. Bond, III, 271, 274.
2 *V*. H. M. Colvin, *The English White Canons*, 219, 232.

The Carthusians, though few in number, were at the time of the Schism in their period of modest expansion, but from the nature of the case were less affected.[1] The order was split in twain, and the Roman allegiance established Seitz in Austria as the head house. The English priors were excused attendance at the meeting owing to the long and roundabout journey required, but ordinances were made affecting, and in some cases even demanded by, the English monks.

The friars were less affected than the monks. The central government in all cases, being based on Rome and the Curia, accepted the election of Urban, and a dissident general was removed.[2] Consequently, the English provinces could go forward without new arrangements, and there is evidence that their life continued in its normal rhythm.[3]

II. PAPAL PRIVILEGES

Towards the end of the fourteenth century a considerable change is visible in the dealings of the Roman Curia with individual religious. In the twelfth century and, as a general rule, in the early thirteenth century also, negotiations or requests for privileges of any kind had normally to pass between the abbot or prior, or the prelate and his community acting as a single person, and the pope, and the privileges granted were most frequently corporate in their scope: papal protection or confirmation, the bestowal of exemption or of the *pontificalia*, the granting of indulgences or the remissions of papal taxes and suchlike. This way of proceeding was in accordance with the ancient monastic principle, embodied in early canon law, that the individual monk, even as petitioner for spiritual favours, had no standing save in association with, or acting with the consent of, his religious superior. Gradually, however, we can see this tradition being broken, partly owing to the proliferation and mechanization of all the administrative departments of the Curia during the period of residence at Avignon, partly owing to the increasingly materialistic outlook of the papal bureaucracy, by which the granting of a petition came to be regarded somewhat as a modern administrative department regards the issue of a licence, and partly as one of the deplorable effects of the Great Schism, which could not help but lead the rival pontiffs to encourage clients and augment their revenues by every available means. Fighting for support, both political and material, as they were, they found themselves in no position to take a high line with their petitioners. Knowledge of this must in its turn have encouraged the latter to try their fortune, as it must also have paralysed the local superiors in their endeavours to preserve the old regularity of discipline, breaches in which, especially in the matter of

---

1 *V*. E. M. Thompson, *The Carthusian Order in England*, 259.

2 In the case of the Dominicans St Raymund of Capua was substituted for the Clementine master-general. Cf. N. Valois, *La France et le Grand Schisme d'Occident*, I, 238.

3 Perroy, *L'Angleterre et le Grand Schisme d'Occident*, 94, n. 3, notes visits to the English houses by the master-general of the Carmelites.

private ownership of funds, were, as we shall see, precisely what gave individual religious the wherewithal to implement their supplications. Whatever may have been the relative weight of these various factors, the papal registers make it abundantly clear that it was when the Great Schism broke the Western Church into two sections that the issue of these various privileges to individuals attained proportions hitherto without precedent.

These privileges may be divided into two main classes: the purely spiritual, satisfying personal convenience or devotion; and those which in one way or another exempted the individual from some of the obligations or canonical disabilities of the religious life, sometimes to his material benefit and always to the detriment of the spirit of obedience.

Among the spiritual privileges three stand out beyond all others: the privilege of the portable altar—the permission, that is, to offer Mass outside a church or chapel; freedom of choice of a confessor; and the grant of a plenary indulgence at the hour of death. All these, from 1378 onwards, were granted with a liberality that suggests a purely routine issue, if not a preoccupation with financial returns, and none of them, save the first, was restricted to religious or clerics. In themselves they were not objectionable; the fault, where it existed, lay in the manner in which they were solicited, for in many cases they would seem to have been given in answer to the unsanctioned initiative of the individual, implemented by his own private funds.

Far more destructive of monastic principles were two privileges that cut at the roots of the religious life: appointment as papal chaplain, and permission to hold a benefice. The papal chaplaincy, besides its honorific value and certain spiritual advantages obtainable by its holders, carried with it, in its complete form, exemption from regular life and obedience, and could therefore serve a religious as a gateway to a career or (as often happened) to the acceptance of valuable preferment.[1] The two grants, 'with' or 'without' privileges, are often distinguished in the papal registers solely by a note of the fee paid, ten or twenty *grossi* as the case might be, and this practice may give some indication of the attitude of the Curia towards such petitions. Before the Schism these grants were so rare as to be negligible; they were given occasionally to distinguished prelates, and there were only three to English religious in the seven years (1371–8) of the pontificate of Gregory IX. Under Urban VI their number, seventeen in nine years, was still not remarkable, though it was in this pontificate that the Carmelite, Walter of Diss, was allowed in 1383 to bestow fifty chaplaincies in England in aid of the Flemish crusade of the bishop of Norwich.[2] Under Boniface IX, however, the practice passed all bounds: in the fifteen years of his reign more than two hundred and sixty such

---

1 The superior concerned sometimes counter-insured himself. Thus in 1402 Abbot William of Peterborough obtained an ordinance that monks of his house who were papal chaplains should nevertheless obey him (*CPL*, v (1396–1404), 546).
2 Walsingham, *Hist. Anglorum*, II, 157; *GASA*, II, 417.

privileges to English religious were entered in his register, and in the three short pontificates that followed, covering in all eleven years, some seventy-five were issued. With the accession of Martin V in 1417 the practice all but ceased, the pope issuing only two privileges of the kind in fourteen years.[1]

All orders were represented among the recipients, but the number of Austin canons greatly exceeded those of any other body, being almost double those of the Cistercians, Minors, Preachers and Carmelites, which in their turn were all notably more numerous than the black monks. This preponderance of the black canons, many of whom came from small houses, suggests that the privilege could easily be acquired on the initiative of an undistinguished individual, and perhaps also that a regular agency existed in England, possibly in the office of papal collectors or bankers, where the petition could be filed and to which the privilege could be expedited. It is not surprising, therefore, to find the general chapter of the Augustinian canons in 1401 imposing a tax to raise funds to fight this abuse, presumably by challenging the applications when they reached the Curia,[2] and the St Albans chronicler still earlier records the evil consequences of the faculties granted to Walter of Diss, whereby several of the monks of the abbey had been seduced.[3]   Concurrently with the rise of the rate of frequency in the bestowal of papal chaplaincies went that of granting permission to religious to hold benefices with or without the cure of souls, though this privilege spread more slowly and continued to be given for considerably longer. Such a privilege not only broke the ties of the religious life, but reversed the secular policy of the papacy, which had indeed often permitted and even encouraged monks to evangelize a pagan country, but which had hitherto consistently distinguished between the monastic orders and the benefice-holding secular clergy. It is, indeed, remarkable that this practice developed at the very time when the monks and canons were coming under the fire of the Lollards and satirists as 'possessioners'. Here Boniface IX began the practice, though only ten English cases occur in his registers. His three short-lived successors were more generous with a total of some fifty grants in nine years. Unlike the grant of papal chaplaincies, this privilege, far from disappearing when the Schism ended, increased greatly and maintained a very high level of frequency throughout the fifteenth century. Martin V, indeed, was restrained, but Eugenius IV, with sixty-one, and Nicholas V, with seventy such grants, passed all reasonable bounds, to be exceeded in turn by Pius II (1458–64) with some ninety cases in his register.

This dispensation could rarely have been justified on religious grounds, and what is known of the petitioners indicates that they were in general restless subjects. Sometimes, indeed, a real economic pressure lay behind

---

1 These figures have been obtained by combing the volumes of Papal Letters, and do not claim to be absolutely complete.

2 *AC*, 79.   3 *GASA*, II, 417–18.

a request. Thus superiors in office made the application on the score of the poverty of their house, or as an insurance against their day of retirement, while sometimes, as at Hailes, the monks proposed to serve a church of their own which was too poor to attract an incumbent.[1] Usually, however, the request was purely personal, and was often accompanied by a claim to noble birth, distinguished kinship or eminent patronage on the part of the petitioner. The friars in particular often applied as chaplains of a nobleman, in whose gift no doubt the wished-for benefice lay.[2] As with papal chaplains, so with this privilege, the petitioners came from every religious order, not excepting the Carthusian, and here also the Austin canons are numerous. They are, however, run close by the black monks, whereas the Cistercians have only half, and the Preachers only a third, of their numbers. Only by prolonged research among the bishops' registers, and perhaps not even then, could it be ascertained how many of the satisfied petitioners in fact secured benefices, but many undoubtedly did so, though still further research would be needed to discover what proportion, if any, actually resided in their parish or chapter. Although the provenance of the applicants is very varied certain houses appear far more frequently than others; among such are Glastonbury, Canterbury, Christ Church and St Albans among the black monks, and among the Cistercians Fountains and Meaux.

These two, though the most common, were far from being the only type of papal privilege sought. Another frequent petition was that a monastery might have leave to farm out all its possessions, including its churches, without reference to the bishop of the diocese. A rarer type, sought by individuals, was for security of tenure of office. Thus William Albon, prior of St Albans and 'subject to great illnesses' was made irremovable,[3] as was also a prior of St Augustine's, Canterbury, a prior of Bedemansberg, a cell of Colchester, and the aged chamberlain of Glastonbury,[4] while a monk of Thetford[5] and a canon of St Osyth's obtained guarantees that they would never be sent away from their houses against their will. Any kind of grant could be guaranteed in this way; William Sudbury, a monk of Westminster, obtained possession for life of such books, jewels, money and the rest as came into his hands,[6] while a

---

1 *CPL*, VI (1404–15), 80.

2 This is particularly noticeable in the great days of patronage and so-called 'bastard feudalism'. Many cases occur in *CPL*, VI (1404–15), when the nobility are found patronizing the mendicants, e.g. Dominicans (Duchess of Gloucester; Thomas Courtenay, Earl of Devon), Franciscans (Humphrey, Duke of Gloucester), Carmelites (Henry, Earl of Northumberland; John, Duke of Norfolk), and Austin friars (Henry, Earl of Northumberland; Humphrey of Gloucester). Cf. also forty years later the Registers of Nicholas V, *CPL*, X (1447–55), *passim*.

3 *CPL*, XI (1455–64), 88.   4 *CPL*, V (1396–1404), 202.

5 *Ibid.* (1402), 546. Robert Willingham receives indult to remain in Thetford priory for life 'because divine offices are there by day and night solemnly and devoutly performed, and because the priory possesses a copy of divers books in which he desires to study, and he fears the prior may send him to another place where perhaps divine worship is less devoutly performed and such copies do not exist'.   6 *Ibid.* 197.

prior of the same abbey obtained a papal guarantee of the corrody he had been given, and a monk of Evesham was confirmed in his private apartment.[1] Finally, there was the papal licence to transfer to another house or order, a proceeding which in earlier times needed no external licence and which was not necessarily an abuse, much as the domestic chronicler might lament the inconstancy of its beneficiaries.

Meanwhile the normal applications at the Curia on behalf of the house as a whole continued. Grants of *pontificalia*, appropriations of parish churches, and suchlike, though perhaps rarer than before, occur intermittently.

As for individual monks, the possibility of obtaining such privileges undoubtedly had a relaxing effect. Even though the total number of privileges obtained over a hundred years was small in comparison with the total number of religious in the country, the comparative ease with which they could be obtained was a standing evidence that the Curia regarded its supreme power over all ecclesiastical law not as a means of advancing the kingdom of God, and the reign of evangelical perfection, but as a right to be exercised at will or mechanically, if not actually exploited as a source of income. At the same time it would be unwise to assume, from the prominence given to the matter by the laments of the would-be reforming abbot Whethamstede of St Albans, that it bulked as large in the minds of all abbots or of the monks of all houses.[2] To the friars, at least, who lived normally so much in the world, and to the canons, who already undertook parish work here and there, the permission to hold benefices would not always have seemed a complete change of life.

---

1 *CPL*, XI (1400), 335. This, however, was resisted by the abbot and convent and revoked in 1403 (p. 551) 'as contrary to the rule of the order against private property, as disturbing obedience, and being a pernicious example'.

2 *Reg. J. Whethamstede*, ed. H. T. Riley, I, 137–47.

CHAPTER XIII

KING HENRY V

I. THE MONASTIC FOUNDER

The short reign of Henry V, which in more than one respect marks an epoch in English church history, was distinguished by the establishment of two monastic houses notable both on their own account and because they were to all intents and purposes the last monasteries to be founded in medieval England. Each owed its existence directly to the king, and their endowment and subsequent fame were not unworthy of the royal munificence.

When Gregory XII in 1408 officially exonerated Henry IV from responsibility for the execution of Archbishop Scrope of York, the king undertook, so the report went, to found three religious houses of strict life in expiation of the 'martyrdom'.[1] He himself, either from lack of funds or from lack of zeal, got no further than the first movements in the matter, but his son took up the liability, and from 1414 onwards pressed on with the work. Recent experience in the country and contemporary opinion in general would have led anyone in quest of strictly-living religious to turn to the Carthusian order; this Henry did, and his application to the German (i.e. Low Countries) province for seven monks showed that he was alive to the good report of that region for fervent piety. One of the seven was, however, an Englishman specified by name, and the first prior was English.[2] The community was to number forty, and the foundation charter was signed on 1 April 1415;[3] the site was in what is now the Old Deer Park, near the Observatory, on the south bank of the Thames near West Sheen or, as it is now called, Richmond, where Henry IV had built himself a palace. The house, designed to be the largest Charterhouse in England, was called the house of Jesus of Bethlehem, and was richly endowed with land formerly belonging to alien priories, and furnished with books drawn chiefly from Mount Grace. It prospered in the century of life that remained to it, and John Colet and Reginald Pole were not the only earnest churchmen who found refreshment of spirit within its walls.

The second royal foundation was destined to still greater celebrity and a longer life, and is in itself of very considerable interest. It was a house of the new and fervent 'double' order of the Bridgettines, founded only forty years previously by the noble Birgitta or Bridget of Sweden, and governed by her daughter Catherine as abbess; the mother had already

---

1 J. H. Wylie, *Henry IV*, II, 352; *Henry V*, I, 214 *seqq.*
2 His name was John Widrington, possibly the *dominum Wynenarm* (?) asked for by the king, *v.* B.M. Add. MS. 24,062, fo. 145, and other references given by Wylie, *Henry V*, I, 215.   3 *Monasticon*, VI, 33.

been canonized, the daughter in due time joined her among the saints of the Roman martyrology.[1] The story of the foundation of the house has some unusual features, and since the story is a complicated one, and has never been set out in brief, a few pages may be devoted to its exposition.[2]

The introduction of the order into England was simplified, and had in fact first been suggested, as a result of the personal relationship between the royal houses of England and Sweden. The king's younger sister, Philippa, had been betrothed as an infant and married as a child, at Lund in 1406, to Eric, King of Denmark and Sweden.[3] The lady in charge of the young queen's new household was a granddaughter of St Bridget, and Philippa herself wasted no time in visiting the celebrated convent of Vadstena, the mother-house of the order, where she was admitted as *consoror*. In addition, towards the end of the year in which Philippa had arrived in the country, one of her suite, Sir Henry (later Lord) Fitzhugh, a nephew of Archbishop Scrope and later to become the king's chamberlain, had visited the place. Fitzhugh, whose reputation for earnest piety may perhaps be indicated by a legacy of two works of Richard Rolle in the will of a relative and fellow-peer, Henry, Lord Scrope,[4] told the community on the eve of St Andrew, 29 November 1406, that he was come to announce his intention of devoting property at Hinton Uppehall (Cherry Hinton) near Cambridge towards the foundation of a convent of their order, and had in fact already made it over to a group of English trustees.[5] All the circumstances of Fitzhugh's visit to Vadstena suggest that he was endowing a house of which the foundation had already been determined upon, and there is little doubt that Henry IV had cherished, or at least toyed with, the project as part of the satisfaction due for the murder of

---

1 For SS. Bridget and Catherine *v. DHG*; for the cult of St Bridget in England *v. infra*, p. 277.

2 For Syon, *v.* G. J. Aungier, *History and Antiquities of Syon Monastery*. This work, which is largely concerned with the topography of Isleworth, contains only a brief and incomplete account of Syon; it is, however, carefully done, and there are useful appendices of original sources. The *Martiloge* (B.M. Add. MS. 22, 285) contains an account of the foundation, together with lists of abbesses, confessors, etc. For early days *v.* also Wylie, *Henry V*, I, 220–9. The first really exhaustive study of the foundation, making use of published and unpublished documents in Sweden (but overlooking some English material) was that of Torvald Höjer, *Studier i Vadstena Klosters och Birgittinordens Historia*. Among original sources are the annals of Vadstena, *Diarium Waʒstenense*, ed. Benzelius, reprinted in *Scriptores rerum Suecicarum medii aevi*, ed. E. M. Fant., I. Numerous letters from Vadstena to England and the Curia, as also Fitzhugh's gift, are in *Diplomatarium Suecarum*, ed. C. Silfverstolpe, II, iii, 1415–20. All these were used by Miss M. Deanesly for an excursus on the foundation of Syon Abbey in her edition of *The Incendium Amoris of Richard Rolle of Hampole*, 91–144, to which the following pages are greatly indebted. The account there given, however, is long and somewhat complicated, with some disputable points; hence it seemed best to give a fresh survey.

3 Wylie, *Henry IV*, II, 458.

4 Deanesly, *op. cit.* 97, citing Rymer, *Foedera*, IX, 276. The MS. may have been the holograph of Rolle himself.

5 *Diarium* in *Scriptores rer. Suec.* I, 128. In 1415 the Vadstena superiors refer (*Diplom. Suec.* III, no. 2082, pp. 38–9) to the previous request from Henry IV. *V.* also Deanesly, *op. cit.* 97–8.

Fitzhugh's uncle, the archbishop. The king had indeed actually applied for the papal sanction to use for this purpose the decayed hospital of St Nicholas at York.[1] The abbess of Vadstena, therefore, duly acknowledged the gift, and sent, on 6 April 1408, two brothers of the monastery, a priest named John Petersen and a deacon named Katillus, to view and take possession of the property. The design, however, miscarried and the two Bridgettine monks, though they remained in England, were for at least seven years without a regular home. No foundation at Hinton was ever made, and probably none was ever intended there. The property was devised to the king, and not formally made over to Syon till 1444.[2]

Henry V, however, revived his father's project in all seriousness and on the grand scale, and the first stone of the monastery of the Holy Saviour, St Mary the Virgin and St Birgitta, was laid by the royal hand at Twickenham on 22 February 1415.[3] The king, no doubt, wished to have this good deed, together with the foundation of the House of Jesus of Bethlehem, behind him when he sailed for France, and he was speaking truly, if proleptically, in the autumn of that year before Agincourt, when he referred to his foundation of

> Two chantries, where the sad and solemn priests
> Sing still for Richard's soul.[4]

There was, however, much in fact yet to be arranged. Although a foundation charter was issued in March,[5] in which the appointment of an abbess and confessor (the title in the order for the superior of the brethren) was announced, as if the community was already in being, this was not in fact the case. A number of would-be sisters and brothers of varied provenance had, so to say, given in their names for the venture, but they could not undergo training or make their profession until Bridgettines had come from Vadstena to instruct them, and as yet the only members of the order in England were the two brethren who had arrived in 1408. Henry therefore, in April 1415, applied for nuns from Sweden, and in May four consecrated and two unconsecrated sisters, with another brother, set out[6] and, on arrival, began the task of instructing the little company, gathered from various existing orders, who had volunteered to join the new house.

Difficulties now multiplied, chiefly of a canonical nature. It was the king's original intention to found more than one house of Bridgettines; a firm constitutional framework was therefore necessary. But owing to the dislocation of normal procedure due to the Schism and the Councils,

---

1 Wylie, *Henry V*, I, 221.
2 Deanesly, *op. cit.* 104–5; Miss D. M. B. Ellis, *VCH, Cambs*, II, 303.
3 Syon *Martiloge* (*supra*, p. 176, n. 2), fo. 14, cited by Deanesly, *op. cit.* 105.
4 Shakespeare, *Henry V*, IV, i, 306–7.
5 *Monasticon*, VI, 542; *Charter Rolls, 2 Hen. V*, part 2, n. 28. The witnesses fit the date, one or two with comparatively narrow margins, and there seem no grounds for supposing it to be, like many earlier foundation charters, merely an (interpolated) recital of things done.
6 *Diplom. Suec.* I, no. 2082, pp. 38–9 (16 May 1415); *Diarium* in *Scriptores rer. Suec.* III, 136.

the Bridgettine Rule had not yet been solemnly confirmed by the pope, while, to complicate the issue, additions made to the original Rule by its compiler, Peter Olafson, the saint's confessor and first confessor of Vadstena, were causing disagreement even in Sweden.[1] This unsettled state of things not only retarded the foundation, but had direct repercussions in England. Among the additions made by Olafson were, it seems, directions that the sisters should work in the brewery, bakery and kitchen; these the Vadstena nuns accepted, though with some hesitation, but the Swedish sisters in England and their new recruits were apparently unwilling to do so. At the same time the abbess appointed by the king was, according to the terms of the foundation charter, to rule the whole house in spiritual as well as temporal matters, whereas in the Bridgettine rule the confessor was to have control of the brethren *in spiritualibus*. To find a settlement for these difficulties the king, in January 1416, called a conference of monks and theologians under the chairmanship of his official confessor, the Carmelite bishop of St David's, Stephen Patrington. Among the members of the conference were two monks of St Albans (one being William of Alnwick), a monk of Bermondsey, and the abbots and priors of the Cistercian houses of Stratford Langthorne and St Mary Graces.[2] They decided against the abbess and the sisters on the points mentioned above, and either at this or a subsequent meeting made, from the Rule of St Benedict and the Cistercian constitutions, additions of their own to supplement the Bridgettine rule for England only. These were embodied in the directory of Syon and remained in force even after the dissolution of the house.

The anxieties of the mixed group of religious and postulants at Twickenham—eight Bridgettine sisters, four (later three) Bridgettine brothers, a number of English nuns and ex-recluses and a smaller number of English monks and ex-anchorites—were not yet at an end. Henry's preoccupations in France and the unsettled state of the Curia doubtless prolonged the time of uncertainty, and at the end of 1417 there was still no organization in the house. As there was no duly professed superior, the novices could not take their vows, while the English sisters were unwilling to confess to a Swede and the Swedish sisters considered it against their original vows to confess to an unprofessed Englishman.[3] Finally, late in 1417 or early in 1418, the king sent to Vadstena, in answer to requests, a petition, to be completed in due form by the Bridgettine authorities and sent to the pope, in which he asked for papal approval and confirmation of all arrangements at Twickenham, and for licence for the English recruits already in religion to transfer to the Bridgettine order and exercise full

---

1 Deanesly, *op. cit.* 110–13, citing T. Höjer, *op. cit.*

2 For this, *v.* the *Additiones* to the Syon Rule, introduction, printed by Deanesly, *op. cit.* 122, and confirmed by an Uppsala MS. printed by Höjer and cited by Deanesly, *op. cit.* 111. It is the latter source that supplies the name of Patrington.

3 See the sheaf of letters sent to Henry, Fitzhugh and the Syon community, in *Diplom. Suec.* III, nos. 2519–22 and 2524 (pp. 359–68).

authority therein.[1] The request was granted on 18 August 1418,[2] and when all preparations had been made the first profession took place on 1 April 1420, when twenty-seven sisters, five priests, two deacons and four lay brothers took their vows.[3] This was in truth the real foundation day of the abbey.

It is now necessary to go back a little to consider who were the superiors of the new community. The foundation charter of 1415 names as confessor William Alnwick, and as abbess Matilda Newton, and states that both were professed members of the order. At this early date, only a winter month after the first stone had been laid, and three months before the arrival of the Swedish sisters, these arrangements must be regarded as no more than forecasts. William of Alnwick can certainly be identified with the monk of that name who had for some time been a recluse at Westminster,[4] while the subsequent actions of Matilda Newton, a nun of Barking, show that she felt drawn to a life of retirement. She was probably in effective control by the end of 1415, for her claim to complete jurisdiction was one of the matters on the agenda at the conference of January 1416.[5] As William Alnwick was one of the committee on that occasion he can scarcely as yet have been confessor at Syon,[6] and the absence of an effective head of the brethren may have been part of the trouble. The claim of the titular abbess (she had not yet been regularly elected and confirmed) was disallowed, and she resigned after a time, perhaps early in 1417, and retired as an ancress to her old home at Barking.[7] She was succeeded, perhaps after an interval, by Joan North, a nun of Markyate near St Albans.[8]

As for William Alnwick, the length and date of his residence and rule at Twickenham cannot be ascertained with certainty. As has been seen, he appears as confessor both in the foundation charter of 1415 and in the petition to the pope of 1417–18, but so also does Matilda Newton appear as abbess; in other words, both documents aim solely at supplying for

1 Printed by Deanesly, *op. cit.* 130–7, from MS. A26 Royal Archives, Stockholm. It is noteworthy that William of Alnwick and Matilda Newton still appear as 'father' and 'mother' of the community.

2 Deanesly, *op. cit.* 137–44 from MS. A23, Royal Archives, Stockholm. Cf. *Monasticon,* VI, 544.

3 B.M. Add. MS. 22,285, fo. 14, cited by Deanesly, *op. cit.* 124.

4 *Amundesham,* I, 27: 'Willelmus Alnwick, reclusus monachus Westmonasterii...in custodiam feminarum prefectus est.'

5 Deanesly, *op. cit.* 110–11, citing foundation charter in *Monasticon,* VI, 540.

6 In the document printed by Deanesly, *op. cit.,* listing those present at the conference of 1416, he appears as 'Gulielmum Anroyt, monachum S. Albani' (for his provenance *v.* Appendix II, p. 367), but the addition 'confessorem...Henrici quinti' makes the identification with the Westminster recluse almost certain.

7 Miss Deanesly points out that the reading of the Rolls editor's text of *Amundesham,* I, 27, *prima abbatissa monialium,* should read *p.a. monialis* (i.e. Matilda was a nun, not abbess, of Barking). Her date of retirement seems clearly fixed by her pension, which was granted 8 May 1417 (*C.P.R. Hen. V,* 1416–22, 103), confirmed on 24 April following, with arrears (*C. Close R. Hen. V,* I, 463), and renewed again 23 January 1423 (*C.P.R. Hen. VI,* 1422–9, 43).

8 *Amundesham, loc. cit.,* gives her provenance, the Syon *Martiloge* her name.

legal and canonical purposes the essential *personae* of the new establishment. On the other hand, the St Albans chronicler, who was well placed to receive information, states that William Alnwick was in office for a year only, during which period Matilda resigned and the pope assented to the foundation;[1] if pressed, this statement must indicate a period within the years 1417–18. With the evidence at present available no more can be said; in any case, before the house began its fully regularized life Alnwick was back in his cell, and when all constitutional matters had been settled new superiors were in office. The abbess, as has been seen, was Joan North; the confessor was Thomas Fishbourne.

Fishbourne was another ex-recluse, but of a different type. Like Alnwick, he was a northerner, but he had been a landed gentleman who had acted as steward to Abbot William Heyworth (1401–20) of St Albans.[2] He had subsequently obtained permission to receive priest's orders, and had retired to the hermitage of St German's near St Albans, where he had acted as director to some of the nuns and boarders at the fashionable nunnery of Sopwell.[3] This had brought him to the notice of the king, who was on occasion his penitent, and he also, like William Alnwick, took an interest in the projected Bridgettine house. As a relative of Bishop Clifford of London, who had had a share in the promotion of Martin V, he would be *persona grata* at the Curia, and no doubt it was for this reason that he was chosen to visit the pope in 1418 and obtain the bull of approval.[4] He was already recognized by the authorities at Vadstena as the spiritual guardian of the Twickenham community,[5] and when professions had been made and elections were pending, he was duly elected first confessor.[6]

The house was royally maintained, at first by an annual charge of one thousand marks on the Exchequer, and later by the revenues of a number of alien priories and gifts of private benefactors. The original site was in the park of Twickenham, across the river from the palace which Henry had built between what is now Richmond Green and the Thames, but this proved too damp and too small, and in 1431 the community moved a short distance down the river to Isleworth, and finally settled on the site where

1 *Amundesham, loc. cit.* William departs 'post anni circulum', and 'in tempore Willelmi Alnwick' Matilda resigns, while 'medio vero tempore' [= 'meanwhile'] Fishbourne goes to Rome.

2 *Amundesham, loc. cit.:* 'Primo dapifer domini abbatis Willelmi'.

3 Amundesham instances Elizabeth Beauchamp and Alienora Hulle. The former was probably Elizabeth, wife of Richard, earl of Warwick; the latter, who was in the service of Queen Joan in 1417 (*C.P.R. Hen. V, 1416–22,* 304), was the object of attack when the priory was raided by the brigand William Wawe in 1428 (*Amundesham,* I, 11). Fishbourne first appears in the king's service as 'chaplain' in 1413, when on 13 December he receives ten marks p.a. for life, with six months' arrears (*C. Close R. Henry V,* I, 46). On 20 April 1416, he was one, along with Fitzhugh, of the trustees to whom property at Twickenham was devised for transference to the new foundation (*C.P.R. Hen. V,* 1416–22, 34–5).

4 *Amundesham, loc. cit.:* 'Romam...proficiscens...fundationem Domus sancti Sion... papalibus communiit scriptis.'

5 *Diplom. Suec.* III, no. 2522, pp. 365–6.

6 Ellis, *Original Letters,* 2nd ser. I, 91. The bishop's visit took place on 5 May 1421. He refers to Fishbourne as 'my welbelovyd cousin'. Fishbourne died in 1428.

the mansion named after the monastery still stands in the water-meadows. The abbey was dedicated to the Saviour and St Bridget, but was from the first called Syon or Mount Syon of Sheen—Syon, the vision of peace, being chosen as its name by the founder, 'a true son of the God of peace, who gave peace and taught peace and chose St Brigit as a lover of peace and tranquillity'.[1]

Syon and Bethlehem of Sheen, which after the Bridgettines had moved stood almost opposite one another across the water and kept alive an almost unceasing round of prayer with nightly signal-bells across the river flats,[2] were to have the fate, without parallel among English religious houses, of surviving as communities long after every trace of their material presence had passed from the site of their dwelling. The Carthusians of Sheen survived in exile until the French Revolution; the Bridgettines, after centuries abroad, returned to their motherland and still live. Their houses on the other hand, unlike multitudes of less celebrated convents, have wholly passed from view. Syon House preserves the name and a few fragments of the one, and of the other every vestige has disappeared so that even the exact site of the elaborate building cannot be identified. One who walks in spring along the quiet river-bank under the scented boughs of may, by what is still one of the most placid and beautiful reaches of the lower Thames, may chance to think of the two eminent men of letters whose memory still survives at Twickenham, and perhaps also of the four, scarcely less celebrated, whose lives, so diverse in genius and fortune, mingled their streams for a short space where now is open parkland.[3] Few will give a thought to those who for little more than a century filled the cloisters of two royal monasteries, and whose bones now rest in an unknown grave somewhere beneath the expanse of green from which every trace of their habitation has vanished.

The third foundation, also, it would appear, destined to be near Sheen,[4] was to be of the strict and eremitical order of monks following the Rule of St Benedict, which had been founded in Italy rather more than a century before by the canonized pope who made the great refusal. Henry had early been in negotiation with the Celestines in Paris, and in 1414 two bishops, Courtenay and Langley, visited the convent there, examined its Rule, and brought three monks back to England. A start may actually have been made with the buildings, but the scheme foundered first, it would appear, on a question of finance, and then, irrevocably, in the general hostility to France in the summer of 1415. The failure is to be regretted, as the introduction of these strictly living monks following the Rule of

1 *Monasticon*, VI, 542.
2 *Brut* (ed. J. Williams ap Ithel), II, 496; Wylie, *Henry V*, I, 229.
3 Sir William Temple and Lady Temple (*née* Dorothy Osborne) had a villa among the ruins; here Swift acted as Temple's secretary, while his Stella, Esther Johnson, was the daughter of one of Temple's servants.
4 For an assemblage of all the pieces of evidence, the sum total of which is inconclusive, *v*. Wylie, *Henry*, *V*, I, 230, n. 8.

St Benedict would have opened another interesting chapter in English religious history, even if it is improbable that the order would have spread in this country.

II. THE MONASTIC REFORMER

It was remarked on an early page of this volume that after the distinguished presidency of Thomas de la Mare, no attempt was made for many years to frame new legislation for the black monks. Nor, in all probability, would any further activity have been forthcoming in the early fifteenth century had it not been for an external stimulus from an unexpected quarter. We know from many sources that *c.* 1420 criticism of the black monks was once more becoming a living force, this time chiefly in ecclesiastical circles. Reforms had been mooted by the Council of Constance in 1417, and English abuses were brought before the Council of Pavia-Siena in 1423; previous to this there had been representations in England.[1] King Henry V had already shown himself, in the matter of the alien priories, an energetic and practical moderator. Early in 1421 he landed at Dover after an absence of four years, and after the coronation of Queen Katherine made an extensive tour of the chief towns and shrines of England. While on this progress he was asked to undertake the reform of the black monks.

It is not clear who were the prime movers in the affair.[2] The St Albans chronicler states that allegations had been made by 'false brethren'. These, he says, were justified in part, since a number of prelates and ancients of the order had recently passed away, whose places had been taken by a younger and less restrained generation.[3] The well-informed Croyland annalist gives more definite information by pointing to Robert Layton, the Carthusian prior of Mount Grace, himself once a black monk, as the chief accuser. It is certainly significant that he should be found in attendance at Westminster when the charges came to a head.

Whatever the sources of the complaints, Henry acted with remarkable speed and vigour.[4] Despite his constant shifting from place to place, and the multifarious matters which were demanding, and receiving, his attention, he wrote at once (16 March) to the abbot of Bury, desiring him to convoke a general chapter at Westminster on 5 May, when parliament and convocation would also be entering into session. Upon the abbot's

1 Cf. *J. Amundesham, Annales*, I, 73–81.

2 For the whole episode, *v.* the editor's valuable note in *MC*, II, 98–101, and [J. H. Wylie and] W. T. Waugh, *The reign of Henry the Fifth*, III, 270–2, 283–5. The sources, apart from chapter records, are Walsingham, *Hist. Anglicana*, II, 337–8 and the Croyland Continuator (ed. Fulman) in Gale, *Rerum Anglicarum scriptores veteres*, I, 513. As the abbot of Croyland was one of the first six monastic delegates, this writer had every opportunity to be well-informed.

3 Walsingham, *Hist. Anglorum*, II, 337. So I understand 'major pars prelatorum ac seniorum…defecisset, et effraenata juventus ejus tempore successisset'. Prof. Waugh, *op. cit.* 284, perhaps misunderstands Walsingham's *falsi fratres* when he states that the charges originated with 'certain friars'.

4 Waugh, *op. cit.* 285, justly remarks: 'Henry's amazing energy and industry were never more strikingly illustrated than during this visit of his to England.'

replying with caution that the next chapter was not due for two years, and that further correspondence should be addressed to the presidents, Henry wrote at once (25 March) to these latter, ordering a gathering of prelates and as many notabilities as possible.[1] This time the prelates concerned allowed nice customs to curtsey; there was no talk of the chapter of 1423, and a summons was sent out to each house bidding the superior come up to London with his dependent priors and two or three theologians. The summons was effective; sixty prelates and more than three hundred proctors and theologians arrived, and in consequence there lay in or around the precinct of Westminster all the leading black monks of the country, in addition to the entire peerage and episcopate, the knights and burgesses of parliament, and the members of convocation.

While Parliament was sitting in the Painted Chamber the monks met in the Chapter House. The king, accompanied by only four others, entered and after an appropriate sermon by Edmund Lacy of Exeter, who appears to have had a particular zeal in the matter, himself addressed the assembly, recalling to his hearers the primitive observances of their order and reminding them that his royal ancestors and other founders had made their benefactions from a sense of the value of the prayers of men of an austere and regular life.[2] Let them return to the old regularity, and their prayers, which he valued so highly, would once again be effectual.

It is unfortunate that no fuller report remains of this interesting and characteristic speech. Henry's reliance upon the intercessory prayer of the monks and his lively sense of the *quid pro quo* implicit in benefactions to religious is wholly in keeping with other utterances of his, while the recall to the past, echoing as it did a sentiment widespread at the time, must no doubt be attributed to the coaching of those who had urged reform upon the king.[3] After his speech, Henry appointed the bishop of Exeter, the prior of Mount Grace, and his own secretary[4] to confer with six delegates of the monks upon certain articles of reform that had been prepared. The monks then elected a distinguished committee which included the sole president (the prior of Worcester), John Fordam of the same house, who had represented the order at Constance, Thomas Spofford, abbot of St Mary's, York, and soon to be provided to the see of Hereford, who also had been at Constance, where in 1417 he had taken a leading part in the negotiations for reform among the German monasteries, and John Whethamstede, abbot of St Albans. To these was given power of reporting on the articles, not that of legislating, but after the articles had been handed over an additional twenty-four monks were appointed, with full powers of

---

1 The letters, which were written in English, are in *MC*, II, 104–5.

2 Walsingham, *Hist. Anglicana*, II, 337–8: 'Ipsemet alloquebatur de pristina religione monachorum...ac de modernorum negligentiis et indevotione.'

3 See references to contemporary tracts in *MC*, II, 99 and *infra*, pp. 270–2. Cf. also Henry's reference before Agincourt to the prayers of the English monks then at Prime.

4 This was presumably John Stafford, Keeper of the Privy Seal, 1421–2, later archbishop of Canterbury.

settlement. The articles, thirteen in number, contained nothing novel or of unreasonable severity; they dealt with familiar topics: the obligations upon superiors of residence and regular life; the accountability of all officials; uniformity of dress; regularity in the eating of meat and in the winter regime of a single meal; the discontinuation of money payment in lieu of the issue of clothing and other necessaries; the abolition of private apartments and the curtailment of visits in society. The most noteworthy points were the explicit reprobation of the abbot's separate establishment,[1] the earnest attempt to abolish the practice, now become common, of allotting private rooms to distinguished monks, and the straightforward attack on the *peculium*,[2] with the proposal that the issue of all clothing and personal supplies should be the task of a single trusted official. The articles were, indeed, a carefully devised and practical attack on recognized abuses.

Reasonable as they were, however, it was not to be expected that a large committee of black monks would swallow without ado the complete dose thus gratuitously offered for their consumption, the less so as the king had left England, never to return, on 10 June. They immediately divided into sub-committees which reported critically, if not captiously, upon the articles. Thus they asserted that the separation of establishments between abbot and monks had a basis in the Rule, that the assignment of private rooms to doctors, scholars and officials was only reasonable, while the practical proposal that a single official should issue all clothes was met by the unconvincing reply that no one person could be found in a house to meet the varying needs of individuals without fear or favour.[3]

More than one of these reports was handed in, but it was left to the abbot of St Albans who, though not president, appears to have commanded a general respect which his surviving writings do little to justify, to produce a positive list of seven articles based upon those of the king but dropping or mitigating all obnoxious matter. It is a pedantic and verbose document which, while sounding a recall to regularity, leaves the crucial issues undecided and everywhere respects current custom.[4] Its contents were accepted by the gathering, and were apparently ratified by the chapter of 1423.[5] The movement thus ended as had all previous attempts at a change: the first clear-cut proposals had been challenged, criticized and softened down till the resulting legislation took a form that did little to change existing conditions. It is interesting, but useless, to speculate upon the more drastic action that might have ensued had Henry V survived for ten or fifteen years.

1 *MC*, ii, 110: 'Cum hoc non sit fundabile in regula nec in intencione fundatorum.'

2 *MC*, ii, 113: '[Proprietas] maxime hiis diebus per recepcionem pecuniarum contra jura communia et statuta surrepit et inficit simplices conventuales.'

3 *MC*, ii, 116–17: 'Talis discrecio non est contra regulam, sed satis in regula est fundabilis.' *Ibid*. 120: 'Inconsonum esset racioni, quod doctores post emeritos in studio labores privatas cameras suas gradui congruentes non haberent.' *Ibid*. 119: 'Difficile valde foret... virum tam providum invenire, qui...justissime ministraret.'

4 *MC*, ii, 125–34.   5 So Pantin in *MC*, ii. 100.

CHAPTER XIV

MORE PORTRAITS OF MONKS

I. WILLIAM CLOWN

Rarely, after the years of the first fervour in the twelfth century, are we given a chronicler's portrait of the head of a house of Austin canons. For this reason, as well as for its intrinsic interest, we may for a moment glance at the career of Abbot Clown of Leicester.[1] The abbey of Leicester had in earlier centuries been a well-to-do but undistinguished house. It had prospered, especially from its sale of wool, and the abbot had for that reason been summoned to Edwardian parliaments. No doubt the fortunes of the abbey had also been influenced by connexions with the court that had begun when, from 1245 onwards, the earldom of Leicester had been held by the royal earls of Lancaster. Its period of greatest prosperity opened with the election of William Clown, a century later, in 1345. The new abbot, who probably took his name from a village in Derbyshire, was to hold office for more than thirty years, and the steady growth in the prosperity, and also, it would seem, in the good governance of the monastery, which coincided so nearly with the abbacy of Thomas de la Mare, is one more indication that the Black Death should not hastily be invoked as a catastrophic agent of universal scope. The pestilence ravaged the town of Leicester, and served as an excuse, or an occasion, for the appropriation of some churches, but it did not seriously affect the fortunes of the house.

Abbot Clown, perhaps even before his election, had won the friendship of Henry of Grosmont, earl of Leicester and earl (after 1351 duke) of Lancaster, whose influence was profitable to the abbey on more than one occasion. The abbot's record was one of steady gain: churches were appropriated, the convent was granted full enjoyment of all revenues during a vacancy, the abbot obtained exemption from attendance at parliament, and a number of manors and other possessions were added to its property. The abbot himself seems to have possessed most of the natural qualifications desirable in a ruler, together with a respectable piety. There is no suggestion that he had any distinction of mind, still less that he was a man of deep spirituality. His outstanding characteristic was a love of peace and concord, with tact and a sound judgement to match, and both inside the abbey and around it he was a peacemaker, and as such respected

---

1 The late-fourteenth-century canon of Leicester, Henry Knighton, devotes considerable space to the doings of Abbot Clown, and gives many personal details and characteristics as welcome as they are rare in chronicles of this epoch. A. H. Thompson in his monograph, *Leicester Abbey*, makes use of this and of unpublished material in his account of Clown's abbacy (pp. 28–39).

by good men.[1] He was also a man of great social charm, the intimate of Edward III, whose favour he had partly won by his taste for sport. Clown, we are told, had the name of being the most skilful master of greyhounds in the country, and the king himself and the Black Prince, as well as other great lords, anticipated the yearly exodus from town to the Quorn country of later hunting men by going down yearly to Leicester to follow him after the hare. He himself used to tell his canons (who may have believed him) that he engaged in these frivolous pursuits solely on account of the advantage he gained for his house from such social contacts.[2] Whether his order gained equally in prestige in a district that was a haunt of Lollards may be doubted. When Chaucer wrote his *Prologue* Clown was in his grave,[3] and the poet was no Dante to see him, like Orion, urging his shadowy pack over the stubble on the scent of a ghostly hare. Yet the Monk is a composite portrait; he cared little for the behests of Austin; and Chaucer, who knew London and the court, may well have heard stories of royal sport in Leicestershire.

It would, however, be unjust to regard Abbot Clown as no more than 'a manly man'. Leicester Abbey in his day clearly had a name for disciplined life. The chronicler records with satisfaction that four canons of the house were chosen to rule elsewhere, and if he records the departure of two of his brethren to benefices he notes also the retirement of two to anchorages at Chester and Leicester.[4] When Knighton ends his panegyric with an account of the abbot's death he notes that the lover of peace and quiet left this world at a time of peace and an hour of quiet, at midnight on a Sunday, and he describes his passing, surrounded and supported by his spiritual sons, in a rhythmic passage which seems to recall the antiphon commemorating the death of St Benedict.[5]

II. PHILIP REPYNDON

When Clown died there may have been present among those around him a young canon of very different character, destined to a less peaceful but even more distinguished career. Philip Repyndon, another Derbyshire

1 Knighton, *Chronicon*, ed. J. R. Lumby, II, 125–7: 'Hic quantae pietatis et patientiae, quantaeque discretionis et moderaminis erga subditos suos...lingua tabescit evolvere. Hic pacis et tranquillitatis amator erat.'

2 *Ibid.* 127: 'In venatione leporum inter omnes regni dominos famosissimus et nominatissimus habebatur, ita ut ipse rex, princeps filius ejus Edwardus, et plures domini de regno cum eo retenti erant sub annua pensione leporare. Ipse tamen saepius voluit asserere in secretis, se non delectasse in huiusmodi frivolis venationibus nisi solum pro obsequiis dominis regni praestandis, et affabilitate eorum captanda et gratia in suis negotiis adipiscenda.'

3 He died 22 January 1377. The date commonly accepted for the *Prologue* is *c.* 1386; *v.* also Appendix 1, p. 365.

4 Knighton, *Chronicon*, II, 126. Leicester gave an abbot to Missenden (1348), a prior to Mottisfont (1352), an abbot to Wellow (1373) and a prior to Tortington (?1376).

5 *Ibid.* 125. Thompson drily remarks that Knighton is in error either as to the day or as to the date (*op. cit.* 39).

man,[1] first comes into prominence as a young graduate at Oxford in 1382, when he was condemned, along with Nicholas Hereford and John Aston, on the occasion of the twice adjourned meeting of the synod whose first session is known as the Earthquake Council. Repyndon had already won notoriety by a sermon on the Eucharist at Brackley, a church connected with Leicester Abbey, and shortly after his condemnation he preached to the university on Corpus Christi day with a lively defence of Wyclif, in the near neighbourhood of Peter Stokes the Carmelite, who had been sent down by Archbishop Courtenay to publish the text of the condemned Wyclifian propositions. Repyndon was charged with heresy along with Hereford, and duly declared guilty by Courtenay, whereupon he made a full abjuration of all his errors.[2] Thenceforward his orthodoxy was unimpeachable. He was clearly a man of mental and practical ability, and seems to have made friends with the future Henry IV before his exile. Elected abbot of Leicester in 1394, he became counsellor and confessor to Henry on his return, and it is recorded that on the field of Shrewsbury the victor summoned a servant of the abbot's to his presence and sent the news of his success to his master: 'The King lives, having obtained victory over his enemies, thanks be to God!'[3]

Little is known of his term of office, though he appears as an active administrator of the properties of the convent. He retained his connexion with Oxford, and four times as abbot he was chancellor of the University (1397, 1400, 1401, 1402). In any case, he did not remain long at Leicester, for when Henry Beaufort was translated to Winchester in 1404, Repyndon, at the king's request, was provided by the pope to Lincoln. There he showed considerable zeal, though a zeal tempered with discretion, in bringing Lollards to book. He also succeeded in frustrating an attempt, which may have been initiated in a slightly different form by himself when abbot, to secure for Leicester the papal privilege of exemption from the diocesan. As finally worded, the Leicester petition asked for exemption only during the pontificate of Repyndon himself, which suggests that he may have shown an interest in his old home which was not appreciated by its inmates. In the event, he moved swiftly, and the petition was refused at his request.

His orthodox zeal, added to his friendship with the king, attracted the attention of Gregory XII, and in 1408 Repyndon was named cardinal, with the title of SS. Nereus and Achilleus. The pope, however, besides being under obligation to resign the papacy as a means of healing the Schism, had given an undertaking to create no more cardinals, and it is doubtful whether the bishop of Lincoln ever used his title. Considerable obscurity covers his movements in the years that follow. Owing partly

1 Repyndon = Repton. For him v. Thompson, *Leicester Abbey*, 54–60. There is an article on Repyndon by C. L. Kingsford in *DNB*, and a valuable unsigned article (by G. G. Perry) in the *Church Quarterly Review*, XIX (1884), 59–82. See also Bibliography, s.v. Archer.
2 For all this v. *supra*, p. 72 and H. B. Workman, *John Wyclif, passim*.
3 *Reg. Leycest.* in B.M. MS. Cott. Vit. F 17, fo. 73.

to the upheaval of the Schism, the old discipline that a cardinal must reside in the Curia, and thus resign his bishopric, was becoming relaxed, but the evidence of his register seems to show that Repyndon was absent for a considerable space in 1408–9, and it has been suggested[1] that he shared the wanderings of the pope and took part in the Council of Constance. Unfortunately, the rest of his episcopate at Lincoln has left few records. A happy accident, however, lifts the veil for a moment. When, in the summer of 1413, by a wayside cross on the road to Bridlington, that indefatigable traveller, Margery Kempe, had been successful in persuading her husband to join her in taking a vow of chastity,[2] she decided to give this a greater solemnity in order that she might be clothed with the white dress of one under vow, and for that purpose to renew the vow and receive the new dress at the hands of a bishop. The see of Norwich, in which diocese her home of King's Lynn lay, was vacant, but neither time nor distance seems ever to have been an object with the Kempes, and they decided to repair to Lincoln.[3] Arrived thither, they had to wait for three weeks for Repyndon, but when he came he was courtesy itself. He sent for the pilgrims at once, welcomed Margery warmly, and told her he had long desired to see her. She in turn gave him a complete account of her spiritual life, which he approved as full of 'hy maters & ful deuowt maters & enspyred of the Holy Gost', and advised her to put the account in writing; this she declined to do. She then made her request, as coming from Our Lord, that he should give her the ring and white garment of a vowess; the bishop promised to do so if her husband agreed. John was willing, and Margery then had dinner with the bishop; before the meal began he gave with his own hands, as was his daily practice, an alms of one penny and a loaf to thirteen poor men. The sight brought on for Margery an access of 'hy deuocion' with 'plentuows wepyng'. By this time, however, the bishop had taken further counsel, and had been advised not to grant Margery's request, probably through fear of scandal, as some Continental heretics, clothed in white, had made their appearance a few years previously. Margery, who was never one to take 'No' for an answer, retorted with a 'massage' from Our Lord: 'Dowtyr, sey the Bysshop that he dredyth mor the schamys of the world than the parfyt lofe of God'. This rebuke, whatever its provenance, was probably deserved, for Repyndon went on to suggest that Margery should approach the archbishop of Canterbury, in order that he might authorize Repyndon to clothe one who was not of his diocese. Margery replied with some dignity that she would visit the archbishop (which she did) for her own reasons, but not for the purpose he suggested, whereupon Repyndon went still further towards justifying her judgement by giving her twenty-six shillings

---

1 By the writer in the *Church Quarterly Review* already cited.
2 *The Book of Margery Kempe*, ed. S. B. Meech and H. E. Allen, 24/7 *seqq.* Butler-Bowdon, 49.
3 *The Book of Margery Kempe*, ed Meech and Allen, 33/20 *seqq.* Butler-Bowdon, 60.

and eightpence to buy her clothes, with a request for her prayers. This was not her last meeting with the bishop of Lincoln, for in 1417 she visited Lincoln once more to secure letters of protection against the mayor of Leicester, who had imprisoned her as a heretic. These were duly provided, but Margery gives no details of the interview.

Repyndon resigned in 1419, but did not die till 1424. Though so little is known of his personality and opinions, once he had abandoned his youthful exuberance, his is an interesting career, typical of the age in its reaction from Lollardy and in its reliance on patronage, and we could have welcomed another Knighton to give us his reflections on the pre-abbatial and post-abbatial periods in the life of the only English Austin canon to enter, or at least to come near to the door of, the Sacred College.

III. THOMAS CHILLENDEN

Fifty years after the death of Henry of Eastry, the cathedral priory of Christ Church began to be aware of the presence of another great administrator and builder. Thomas Chillenden[1] first showed his ability to grasp and use power as one of the treasurers under the unworldly Prior John Vynch (1377–91), when he and his colleague in the treasury not only saved their house from any ill effects of the prior's neglect of administration, but built up a sound and firm economic basis for future expansion. Chillenden was a man of great designs, with a clear sight of ways and means. On becoming prior in 1391 he retained in his hand the treasurer's office, thereby transferring what had been a centralized and independent office of receipt and issue, working under the ultimate control of the prior and seniors, into an instrument of power in the hands of the head of the house. Thus secure in control of the finances, he proceeded to revolutionize the economic organization of the Christ Church estates by changing over from a regime of exploitation to one of leasehold. In five years all was accomplished, and in 1396–7 rent-paying farmers were in possession of the demesne on all the Christ Church manors save a few near home. Chillenden had been able to find men able and willing to take land up at a high rent; his income rose steadily and in the last year of his priorate the receipts of the priory reached the unprecedented figure of £4100.

The money was needed. Chillenden, 'the greatest Builder of a Prior that ever was in Christes Church',[2] had the insatiable thirst for building and replanning, that love of clean new stone and oak fresh from the

1 There is no modern study of Chillenden, who is not noticed in *DNB*, though materials for a study of his activities, if not of his personality, exist at Canterbury. Among printed sources may be noted the list of his works in *Lit. Cant.* III, 112–22; 'A Monastic Chronicle of Christ Church, 1331–1415', ed. C. E. Woodruff; C. E. Woodruff, 'Note on the inner life and domestic economy of the priory of Christ Church in the fifteenth century'; and R. A. L. Smith, *Canterbury Cathedral Priory*, 192–5.

2 Leland, *Itinerary*, ed. L. Toulmin Smith, IV, 41. Leland notes that Chillenden was a doctor 'of bothe the lawes or he was made a monche', and that according to Archbishop Warham, he had written legal works.

carver's tool, that so often accompanies and sometimes goes far to justify the acquisition of wealth. His monument is the nave of Canterbury Cathedral, that masterpiece of Henry Yevele in the new style which had not yet lost its first grace and purity.[1] We may, if we wish, imagine prior and designer watching the work along with Chaucer, whose pilgrims had made their journey to the martyr's shrine ten years earlier. Masons and carpenters were never out of the precinct while Chillenden governed the priory: the interior of the church was new whitewashed from top to bottom, a chapel and lodgings for the sacrists were built, together with part of the cloister, prior's lodging and chapter-house, and there was much reconstruction round the Great Court. Nor did he neglect the estates. Manor-houses and mills were repaired, new land and property in the city acquired, and Canterbury College at Oxford rebuilt entirely save for the hall and two chambers. Vestments and plate went to the sacristy, and books, with scarcely an exception texts and commentaries of canon and civil law, to the library. As was to be expected, expenses on building rose steeply from £739 in 1392 to £2522 in 1394; altogether, new constructions in Chillenden's first eight years as prior accounted for £13,056, exclusive of repairs and maintenance. Any attempt to express a modern equivalent of this sum is futile, but we should certainly be under the mark in thinking in terms of a quarter of a million pounds in present-day values. The buoyant rent-economy stood the strain, and when Chillenden died in 1411 he left a debt of no more than £1043. That Archbishop Arundel trusted him is seen by his presence as assessor or preacher during the metro-political visitations of 1389 and 1408.[2]

There is nothing by which we can gain a sight of Prior Chillenden's personality. Seen merely in his financial achievements, with the severely practical character of his books, he appears strangely similar to Eastry, and different alike from a Wessyngton and a Whethamstede. We have no means of knowing whether the nave of Canterbury was to him a vision of beauty, or simply a satisfactory bit of building.

IV. JOHN WESSYNGTON

It would be strange if this group of monastic heads of houses contained no representative from the great establishment at the shrine of St Cuthbert that dominated a whole region to a degree unknown in the south. Durham, indeed, had many notable priors, but whether on account of some streak of harder grain in the northern character, or whether because the prior of Durham, like the priors of other cathedral monasteries, was felt

1 Cf. J. H. Harvey, 'Henry Yevele, Architect, and his works in Kent', where the relations of Chaucer with Yevele are noted. W. P. Blore, 'Recent Discoveries in the Archives of Canterbury Cathedral', remarks that Yevele's name occurs in the only surviving Prior's account roll of this period.

2 *LV*, I, xxviii (Spalding); *Reg. T. Bekynton*, ed. H. C. Maxwell Lyte and D. C. B. Dawes, II, 1792 (Glastonbury).

to be the representative, rather than the father, of his community, identified with it rather than its potential opponent, it is certainly a remarkable fact that, although the house never lacked historians, there was no tradition of purely domestic chronicling, still less any attempt to compile a *Gesta priorum* similar to the history of the abbots of St Albans. It was as if the priors of Durham did their life's work as administrators in office without the faults, the idiosyncracies, and the power of inspiring devoted affection or sullen opposition that was possessed by many an abbot of the black monks.

Of all the long line of priors one of the most notable was certainly John Wessyngton, who held office for the remarkably long space of twenty-nine and a half years. Wessyngton, who hailed from a village known in later centuries as Washington, bore a name the fame of which a future scion of the house was to carry to the ends of the earth, and was entitled to a blazon—gules, two bars, in chief three mullets or—which was in a derivative form to have a fortune greater than that of the eagle of the Habsburgs. He was sent as a young monk to Durham College, of which he appears as bursar in 1398, and for which he wrote a tract vindicating its exemption from the control of the *prior studentium* appointed by chapter, on the grounds that it had been in existence before the office of prior had been instituted.[1] He must therefore have been born soon after 1370. He returned to Durham in or before 1400 when he is found as (the prior's) chancellor of the cathedral; it is probable that this recall took place before he had incepted in divinity. In the years that followed he spent much time in legal and historical research among the archives, and the results of his labours survive in large part in manuscript. Appropriately enough it was he who as prior built Durham's first library. Among his tracts were a defence of the rights of the prior's archdeacon, a collection of miraculous happenings connected with St Cuthbert, a version of the history of the origins of monasticism that was in circulation, and the short biographical sketch of Uthred of Boldon, whom he may have known as a young monk when he visited Finchale.[2] The most remarkable of his historical composi-tions was a narrative of the origin and history of the bishopric and monastery from the earliest times, brought down in detail to 1195 and continued to 1356; a summary of this has been printed.[3] The interest of the work lies chiefly in the evidence it provides of long research among the books and muniments of the priory, and the care given to the drafting and revision of the manuscript. It is, as has been pointed out, an example of a class of writing which was in vogue in the greater monasteries at the beginning of the fifteenth century, and which can be seen in its most developed form in Thorne's great history of St Augustine's abbey at

---

1 Printed in OHS, *Collectanea*, III (1896).

2 A skeleton list of his writings is in *Hist. Dunelmensis scriptores tres*, ed. J. Raine, app., no. ccxxviii. For the tract on monastic origins *v. infra*, p. 270–1, and for the *Vita compendiosa* of Uthred *v. supra*, p. 48.

3 This is discussed in all its aspects in an important article by H. H. E. (later Sir Edmund) Craster, 'The Red Book of Durham'. The summary is in *Scriptores tres*, beginning p. ccccxxii.

Canterbury: the long, fully documented history of a house. In the same way, Wessyngton's legal tracts are an example of another contemporary activity: the clear enunciation of all the feudal and other rights in an age when claims of every kind on the part of a landlord were liable to go by default unless they could be upheld by flawless legal proof. By a happy chance we can follow Wessyngton at work, not only in his various revisions and corrections, but in going beyond any of his predecessors in opening before notarial witnesses the ancient *Liber majoris altaris*, the chained and locked golden gospel book which, along with the *Liber vitae*, stood upon the high altar of the cathedral, and which was found to contain a number of ancient muniments relating to the history and possessions of the church.[1] Wessyngton was not a great historian; he had little interest in the presentation of his findings, or in the criticism of his documents, or in the motives and characters of men of the past, still less had he anything to do with the lively and personal detail of a Malmesbury or a Paris; he is far inferior to the earlier writers of his own house. Nevertheless, it is a masculine, accurate, trained mind that we can see at work.

In 1416 Wessyngton was elected prior and entered upon one of the longest and most fruitful reigns in the Durham annals. He filled the office of president (1426–32), took a leading part in the negotiations with Henry V in 1422 and accompanied the bishop of Durham on visitation besides often acting as visitor from the general chapter to the other houses of the northern province. When he came to lay down his charge his brethren, in enumerating his good works,[2] noted his zeal for the rights and dignities of the cathedral, his gifts and purchases of vestments and jewels, and his various attentions to the fabric, including particularly repairs to the central tower, the construction of a new infirmary, and a rebuilding of the prior's quarters. They recalled with emphasis the toil that he had endured and the ceaseless vigilance with which he had served the interests of his flock.[3] There is no word of his human or spiritual characteristics, nor of the affection of his brethren; such expressions would perhaps have been out of place in this context, and they were in any case alien to the Durham manner. A wise steward of a great household Wessyngton certainly was; the warden of a precious inheritance of beauty; but like others of his line, he seems to have shunned the role of father and leader. The priors of Durham are scholars turned administrators; they have neither the faults nor the personal virtues of the great abbots.

Wessyngton retired from office in 1446, when he must have been well over seventy years of age, and an account of his works was recorded for the sake of posterity.[4] Numerous and costly as they were, they represent expenses far smaller than those of an Eastry, a Chillenden or a Whetham-

---

1 For the notarial visit *v. Scriptores tres*, app., no. ccv, and Craster, art. cit. 521.
2 *Scriptores tres*, app., no. ccxxvii (pp. cclxvi–vii).
3 *Ibid.*: 'Prior noster et pastor egregius, indefesso studio et jugi vigilancia, &c.'
4 *Ibid.* pp. cclxviii–xxvi: The sum total (not reckoning repairs to properties outside the priory) was £2321. 13s. 4d.

stede. A grateful community, mindful of his own care for the sick and aged, made careful and generous provision for his comfort, in 'a chamber called Coldingham' and elsewhere, with a chaplain, a man-at-arms, a clerk, a valet and a lad to attend him, and in this dignified leisure he survived for some six years, dying in 1451, a few months after the Wars of the Roses had begun, and a few months before the birth of Leonardo da Vinci.

V. JOHN WHETHAMSTEDE OF ST ALBANS

No gallery of monastic portraits of the fifteenth century would be complete without one of John of Whethamstede, who had the distinction, unique in the annals of his own abbey of St Albans, and hard to parallel elsewhere, of being twice elected abbot. His name, indeed, occurs on more than one page of this book in connexion with particular aspects of his life and work, but he deserves to be seen also at full length.[1]

John Bostock was the son of a man of the yeoman class who had come to Hertfordshire from Cheshire and had prospered, becoming the owner of a small manor, Mackery End. He found a wife in the south, a daughter of the wealthy Thomas Mackery, two of whose sons had become monks at St Albans and held office at Tynemouth.[2] John was born c. 1393[3] and became a novice presumably round about 1408. Unusually intelligent, his gifts marked him out for the career of a student, and as early as 1414 he was prior of the students at Gloucester College, where he incepted in theology unusually young in 1417.[4] Soon after, he returned to St Albans, where he was appointed prior, and when in 1420 Abbot William Heyworth was appointed to the bishopric of Lichfield, the young prior was elected abbot. It was an extraordinarily rapid rise in a community as numerous and as talented as that of St Albans, though the house could point to more than one precedent in the fourteenth century. Yet although the monks had more than once in the past given their votes to a brilliant young student, there must have been in Whethamstede a great charm of personality and a promise, at least, of wise governance. His subsequent career was to show him sensitive indeed to the climate of opinion around him, but without the qualities of leadership and the grasp of principle that might have given a new spiritual impulse to his abbey.

Immediately after his election he was drawn into great affairs. In 1421, when the black monk abbots were assembled at Westminster to hear the king's projects of reform, Whethamstede was chosen as one of the six

1 For Whethamstede v. *DNB* and details in John Amundesham (*Annales Johannis de Amundesham*, ed. H. T. Riley) and the early part of *Reg. J. Whethamstede* (ed. H. T. Riley). I have also received much help from the valuable thesis of Miss C. E. Hodge (v. infra, p. 267), 'The Abbey of St Albans under John of Whethamstede'.

2 Some facts about Whethamstede's family and early life are given in B.M. MS. Harl. 139, fo. 98, a transcript of Cheshire documents made by Sir Simon d'Ewes and cited by Miss Hodges. Cf. also *Amundesham*, I, 220–1.

3 He is described as 'in about his fiftieth year' in 1442 in *CPL*, IX, 266.

4 Westminster Abbey Muniment 12399. This reference is from Mr W. A. Pantin.

representatives of the monks to confer with the king's three commissioners.[1] Although his colleagues were men of seniority and distinction, such as Prior Wessyngton of Durham and Abbot Spofford of York, it was Whethamstede who drew up and read to the assembly the counter-proposals which the monks put up against the more radical programme of the king's advisers.[2] Two years later he was chosen a member of the English delegation to the Council of Pisa-Siena, appointed as proctor for the black monks, and commissioned by Archbishop Chichele to write to the pope on behalf of the clergy of the kingdom.[3] At Pavia he served his order by opposing the bishop of Lincoln, who was attacking the exemption of certain abbeys.[4] He returned in 1424 and at the following chapter of 1426[5] he was elected president, with Wessyngton as one of his colleagues. He was re-elected at the three following chapters, thus holding office from 1426 to 1438.[6] In 1432 he was nominated proctor for the black monks at the Council of Basel, but seems to have acted by deputy owing to pressure of important business at home.[7]

Meanwhile, he had been active at St Albans. Already in 1423 he had 'visited' his abbey and promulgated a set of gently reforming ordinances.[8] On his return from Italy he toured the dependent cells on a visitation in 1425–6, and when back at St Albans he held a synod of vicars of the exempt churches within his territory and proceeded severely against Lollardy.[9] Two years later he reorganized the finances of his abbey by instituting a *magister operum* with charge of the fabric of the church and neighbouring buildings, and setting up a chest for emergency funds with regular sources of income.[10] During all this period he prosecuted an energetic policy of building at St Albans and on his manors, and kept up a lively, persevering and often successful war of litigation against all who threatened to encroach upon the rights or preserves of the house. Along with his activity he entertained a succession of magnates at home, won and retained the friendship of Duke Humphrey and others, and compiled a series of literary works, including the four volumes of the *Granarium* and the *Palearium Poetarum*, which alone would have seemed a tolerably adequate contribution to the abbey's output of work. Indeed, there is some evidence that Whethamstede, in the last years of his first term of office, drew criticism upon himself by his preoccupation with his studies.[11]

1 For this *v. supra*, p. 183. The fullest account is that of the Continuator of the *Historia Croylandensis* in T. Gale, *Rerum Anglicarum scriptores veteres*, I, 513–14. The abbot of Croyland was one of Whethamstede's five colleagues.

2 *Hist. Croylandensis* (*Rerum Anglicarum Scriptores Veteres*, 514): 'Una tamen prae omnibus omnium consensu per abbatem S. Albani modificatio et responsio finalis summarie est conclusa.' Cf. Walsingham, *Hist. Anglorum*, II, 338.

3 *Amundesham*, I, 17.   4 *Ibid.* 73–81, 142–3.   5 *MC*, II, 175.

6 *MC*, III, 104–5.   7 *Scriptores tres*, pp. ccxxvii, ccxxxviii.

8 *Amundesham*, I, 101 *seqq.*   9 *Ibid.* 205 *seqq.*, 222 *seqq.*   10 *Ibid.* 275.

11 Miss Hodge notes that a reference in the article *Concilium* in part I of the *Granarium* is dated 1438, and since Amundesham (II, 270) says that that work and the *Palearium* were completed in Whethamstede's first term of office, the output during the last three years was considerable.

In view of all this display of energy, much of it externally fruitful and apparently accompanied by the approval and even the admiration of his community as a whole, it is surprising to find the abbot in 1441 taking the decision, rarer in the Middle Ages than in more modern times, to resign his office, a decision which he carried into effect despite the appeals of some at least of his monks.[1] Ostensibly we are not left ignorant of his reasons: all is well and at peace; the repute of the abbey is great; he can therefore drop easily and gratefully away, a course he is all the more ready to adopt in view of the many exhausting and trying difficulties he has had to face, of his complicated ailments, and of his distressing proclivity to blush in public when he hears or sees anything unseemly.[2] Historians have not found these reasons entirely convincing; they are indeed in some respects mutually incompatible; the last is trifling, if not absurd, and the abbot's constitution did in fact carry him through another quarter of a century, which included fifteen years more of office. It has been urged that the resignation was in fact due to motives of political expediency; Whethamstede is said to have foreseen the eclipse of his fortunes with the waning of those of Humphrey of Gloucester. This, however, cannot be proved or even persuasively argued. All was not, in fact, well at St Albans. Shortly before resigning, Whethamstede had endeavoured to reform Redburn, the holiday villa of the abbey, without success, and besides this failure to enforce reasonable regulations, there is evidence that serious irregularities had been allowed to develop, which indicates that the abbot no longer had his community under control.[3] We may therefore think that Whethamstede, never a strong character, and never willing to see and to admit unpleasant truths, had for long succeeded, by a combination of great intelligence with a desire to please, in seeming to lead public opinion while he was in fact only interpreting it, giving his monks what they wanted rather than moulding them by precept and example. Faced at last with the need for strong action he retreated into his literary pursuits and then, when reasonable disciplinary action was resisted, decided to resign rather than attempt to deal with a crisis. It may be added that Whethamstede's own words, if correctly reported, make it hard to avoid the conclusion that he was a neurotic, with the combination of energy, obstinacy, and avoidance of reality that is so often found in such a one.

His resignation was accepted, after the cumbrous process had been completed which was necessary when the head of an exempt house retired from office, and he betook himself to what he hoped would be a dignified

---

1 The almost contemporary resignation of Abbot Harwden of Westminster is scarcely a parallel; still less the withdrawal of Abbot Kirton of Westminster.

2 *Amundesham*, II, 234. (The reasons are given as the abbot's own): 'Erat enim spiritu multum pusillanimis, et propterea ex occasione levissima invaserat timor ac tremor viscera ejus...[his diseases were] in splene in renibus in hepare in visceribus...erat enim plusquam puellaris erubescentiae de facilique nimium prorumpens in ruborem quotiens contingeret ipsum aliquod aspicere obscoenum vel audire.'

3 *Ibid.* II, 208–11.

and well-found leisure.[1] His successor, John Stoke, however, was less
tactful and more domineering than he had been. Whethamstede's income
was threatened, and he was forced to enlist the support of Humphrey of
Gloucester to safeguard his promised pension. Moreover, under Stoke the
enigmatic figure of William Wallingford began to overshadow the scene
and to be the centre of cliques and complaints. When, therefore, after ten
years' rule, Stoke died, Whethamstede was pressed (or himself offered) to
become a candidate. We are not told why the arguments of ten years since
were no longer valid; possibly the ex-abbot found that leisure palled, or
that St Albans needed his presence, at least as a safeguard against something worse, for Wallingford's name was mentioned as that of a possible
choice. In any case, he was elected, apparently without contradiction.[2]

His second term of office, which lasted for fifteen years, was less
spectacular than the first. Times were difficult; there was a legacy of
financial stringency and possibly serious malpractice on the part of the
brothers Wallingford; civil war demolished many old relationships, and
in 1461, after the victory of the northern army at the second battle of
St Albans, the town and the abbey's territory (though not its precinct)
were ravaged by the victors. The house was reduced to such straits that
some, at least, of the monks were temporarily dispersed, and the abbot
retired to a country manor to ride out the storm. He was not idle, however, and succeeded before his death in obtaining a renewal of privileges
from the new king. He died, apparently beloved and lamented by his
monks, in 1465, at the advanced age of seventy-two.[3]

No account of Abbot Whethamstede would be complete without some
mention of his works and purchases. St Albans was a wealthy house, but
Whethamstede, coming as he did from a race of successful yeomen, must
have been a more than usually able administrator to realize such profits
during his first term of office and to restore the finances of the abbey
during his second term. If he knew how to gather he had also a magnificence in spending. The list of his outgoings and purchases is an impressive
one, recalling that of Chillenden and surpassing that of Wessyngton. In
his first term of office of twenty years he spent some £2334 on buildings
and furnishings in church and monastery alone: this included some £891
on repairs and additions to the monastery, £142 on repairs to the church
and £641 on church vestments and plate; £231 went towards the rebuilding
of the abbot's own lodging, guest-hall and chapel. A sum of almost equal
magnitude (£2372) went to repairs and new buildings in the abbey's
property, both in the town of St Albans and on the abbot's manors, with
£108 towards an almost complete rebuilding of the students' quarters at

1 He retired to his native village, where he rebuilt the manor house and acquired property;
so B.M. Harl. 139, fo. 91ᵛ, cited by Miss Hodge.
2 According to his Register (1, 5) rival factions favoured William Albone and Wallingford. Both retired, leaving Whethamstede as *tertius gaudens* to be demanded by all. He
pleaded illness and old age, but finally gave in.
3 *Reg. J. Whethamstede*, 1, 473.

Gloucester College. Another £1362 went on purchases of new property, £326 on presents to royal visitors, christening gifts, and *douceurs* to counsel and sheriffs, while £170 went to purchases of books for library and choir. During the same period the obedientiaries were able between them to put up more than £1000 for additions to church and monastery, and for various precious objects, while monks in private station contributed some £400.[1] The surviving list of treasures and vestments in the possession of the abbey at the middle of the fifteenth century is one of extraordinary richness. Even in his second term, when conditions were far more difficult, Whethamstede was able to spend £500 on the monastery and church, besides purchasing the great manor of La More for £2000.[2] When we consider all these achievements, together with his success in righting the ship after the storm of 1461 and the literary reputation which impressed not only Duke Humphrey, but the Italian humanist Pietro da Monte, we feel that this must have been no ordinary abbot.

Yet it is impossible to regard John of Whethamstede as a great man. Had we only the bare record of his works and gifts, such as the Glastonbury and Croyland chroniclers give of their abbots, he would appear as an energetic and magnificent ruler. In fact, however, the picture is complicated both by the survival of his letters and verses and by the light thrown by the St Albans chroniclers and his own comments on the state of the abbey and his own actions. As regards his writings of every kind, while great allowance can be made for the maladjustment of the monastic and university training to the humanist studies on the one hand and to vernacular literature on the other, it is still true that style and taste reflect personality. The writer of Whethamstede's letters and verses cannot have been a man of true simplicity, or even a man of powerful and direct intelligence. Nor do the reforming ordinances and the personal interventions of Whethamstede give an impression of massive benevolence and of an ability to utter an effective 'word of command' such as is given by Thomas de la Mare. Whethamstede was the spokesman of his order in early manhood, but he never became its leader, the patriarch and father of monks. He saw the Italy of the early Renaissance without giving any sign that he was seeing something unfamiliar and new. He understood the external life of his times, but neither in mind nor in spirit did he rise above it.[3]

1 *Amundesham*, II, appendix A. These pages might serve as a *locus classicus* for an account of a great abbey's treasures and purchases.

2 *Reg. J. Whethamstede*, I, 423–33, 455–9.

3 His panegyrist (a contemporary) exclaims (*Reg. J. Whethamstede*, I, 474): 'Prospice Abbatum Gesta, revolve patrum nostrorum annalia, nec invenies huic Patri vel in hiis quae cleri sunt consimilem, vel in politicis aequalem.' For recent estimates of Whethamstede as a literary figure *v.* W. F. Schirmer, *Der Englische Frühumanismus*, 82–98, and R. Weiss, *Humanism in England during the 15th Century*, 30–8. Professor Weiss gives as his final judgement (p. 38): 'Whethamstede was one of the last of the English medieval polygraphers rather than one of the early English humanists.'

VI. FRIENDS AND FOES OF MARGERY KEMPE

Through a fortunate accident of survival and discovery we are not wholly dependent, as were earlier historians, upon satirists and controversialists for a contemporary picture of the monks and friars in the first decades of the fifteenth century. For more than a quarter of a century (c. 1412–c. 1438) after her conversion Margery Kempe[1] was living in the busy port of Lynn or moving about the country. It is no part of our present task to pass judgement on the spirituality of that remarkable woman, but one who reads her autobiography with attention cannot fail to be impressed, not only by the capacity and substantial accuracy of her memory, which can often be controlled from other sources, but with the good sense and restraint—if indeed charity is not a better word—of her personal judgements even on those who criticized and opposed her. Outspoken to their faces, she was never malicious behind their backs. A woman such as she, reputed alternately a saint and a heretic, who combined great determination and native wit with the psycho-physical characteristics of an hysteric, and a liability to fits in public of loud sobbing and crying, could not but act as a magnet to religious authorities and spiritual directors in a society still permeated with a sense of spiritual reality. Different though the two may be, it is nevertheless instructive to compare this aspect of the fortunes of Margery Kempe with the early career of St Teresa of Avila, as seen in her autobiographical writings. Certainly Margery, like Teresa, made contact with some of the most eminent prelates and many of the distinguished theologians, preachers and holy persons of her day, and the encounter was usually such as to reveal the characters of both parties. Speaking very generally, we can say that Margery does much to restore our view to what we cannot help feeling is a true focus. We see the ordinary folk of the day, full, indeed, of gossip and curiosity and instability, but also fundamentally kindly, hospitable and respectful of religion, easily roused both to fury against a suspected heretic and devotion to a reputed saint, flocking in admiration to the sermons of a friar and reverencing a good priest or anchorite.

Friars, indeed, appear at every stage of Margery's career. One of the first, if not the first, of her directors was the 'holy ankyr' at the Dominican friary of Lynn. He was a learned man, an inceptor in divinity, and ac-

---

1 Margery Kempe (c. 1373–c. 1438) came of a well-to-do family of King's Lynn; her father, John Brunham, was repeatedly mayor, and her husband chamberlain, of the town, where she spent all her life, save for pilgrimages and a year or so in Danzig. Her *Book*, the autobiographical record of her wanderings and experiences, came to light only in 1934. An abridged version in modern English was published by the owner, Colonel W. Butler-Bowdon, in 1936, and the whole was edited with admirable care by S. B. Meech and Miss H. E. Allen for the EETS (o.s. ccxii, 1940). This is cited by page and line. An introductory volume, to treat in greater detail of Margery's character and spirituality, has been promised by Miss Allen, but has not yet (1954) appeared. The manuscript, which is not the archetype, though it is the only one known to exist, belonged to the Carthusian priory of Mount Grace, and has marginal notes referring to inmates; cf. *infra*, p. 225 n. 2.

cording to his penitent a holy man, filled at times with the spirit of prophecy.[1] He was loyal to Margery in all her difficulties and trials; she was
(so she says) directed to him by divine command, and his death was a
severe trial to her. For better or for worse he must be held responsible
in part for her spiritual development. Second only to the Dominican
anchorite was the distinguished Carmelite Master Alan of Lynn, a doctor
of divinity of Cambridge and an author of note, with a notable interest in
spiritual literature.[2] He was a man of fifty or more when he first came into
Margery's life, and he too remained her friend in difficulties and times of
opposition. A temporary separation occurred owing to the direct prohibition of the Carmelite provincial, the eminent Thomas Netter, who had
issued a general condemnation of the publicity given to women of the
world claiming spiritual gifts.[3] The prohibition was directed against the
vagaries of Lollards, but Margery's confessor bade her observe it, even
though she was inwardly admonished that no separation should take
place, and they passed in the street without a word. They met again later,
however, with Netter's permission, and Master Alan reiterated the expression of his faith and loyalty.[4] A third supporter was another Carmelite of
note, William Sowthfeld of the Norwich friary, 'a good man and an holy
leuar', who himself left behind him a reputation of sanctity and who was
reputed to work miracles after his death in 1414.[5] Somewhat later, she
received encouragement and good advice from a grey friar at Norwich,
a doctor of divinity,[6] and a visiting Preacher, a doctor of the name of
Constans, gave her confidence when in distress concerning her 'cries'.[7]

Friars, however, were not always on her side. At her meeting with
Archbishop Bowet of York in 1417/8 several Preachers, one of them
suffragan to the archbishop, opposed her, though on untrue and hearsay
evidence.[8] More serious was the opposition of an unnamed friar, a

1 *Book*, 17/31 and notes. *V.* also index *s.v.* 'ankyr'. Miss Allen's description of him as
'a fanatical type of mystic' is perhaps a little severe without further definition. A successor
(perhaps the immediate successor) in the anchor-hold compiled the well-known *Promptorium
parvulorum* in 1440. The learning and literary work of these two anchorites throws a welcome
light on the occupations of anchorites in general.

2 *Book*, index *s.v.*, esp. 22/11–12 with note. Butler-Bowdon, 45. Cf. Bale, *Scriptorum
Illustrium Maioris Britanniae*, I, 552–3. His age is given in a document cited by F. Blomefield,
History of Norfolk, VIII, 525. He is probably the White Friar who counselled Margery to
write in early years: 'Sche was warnyd in hyr spyrit that sche shuld not wryte so sone.'

3 *Book*, 168/5 and note *ad loc.* and on 170/7; also introd. lvii. Butler-Bowdon, 246.
Netter had no animus against devout women who were orthodox, and indeed encouraged
Carmelite tertiaries to become anchoresses.

4 *Book*, 170/7. Butler-Bowdon, 249.

5 *Book*, 41/2 and notes. Butler-Bowdon, 71. Bale's account of Sowthfeld is printed in
Appendix III, viii, of *Book*, pp. 374–5. 'Leuar' = 'liver'.

6 *Book*, 227/33. Butler-Bowdon, 310.

7 *Book*, 165/32. Butler-Bowdon, 242. The friar consoled her with the example of Mary
d'Oignies.

8 *Book*, 129/18: 'Too Frer Prechowrys.' Cf. *ibid.* 132/6; and for the suffragan, *ibid.*
133/17. Butler-Bowdon, 200. Several Dominicans were assisting English bishops at this
time, but the York suffragan has not been identified. John Greenlaw (suffragan 1401–21)
has been suggested.

celebrated preacher, who was apparently stationed for some time at Lynn. In view of the sequel, it is noteworthy that his excellent reputation and the great success of his preaching are known to us from Margery herself, so we may accept her statement that he was not at that time either bachelor or doctor of divinity.[1] His hostility was, in origin at least, pardonable, for it arose out of the interruptions caused to his sermons by Margery's 'cryings'. These were in fact a tribute to his unction; he 'seyd ful holily & ful devoutly & spak meche of owr Lordys Passyon that the seyd creatur myth no lenger beryn it. Sche kept hir fro crying as long as sche myth, and than at the last sche brast owte wyth a gret cry & cryid wonder sore'.[2] The preacher took this well enough, but when the performance was repeated on further occasions he was less tolerant, and forbade her to hear his sermons. This she took very hardly, but though her friends defended her and interceded with him he stood firm, and ultimately denounced her and her supporters from the pulpit, to her no little distress. As he remained for some time at Lynn, and continued his opposition, this came to be one of the most serious trials of her career.

Monks, as distinct from friars, naturally play a smaller part in Margery's spiritual Odyssey, for they were neither public preachers nor available in general as confessors. The only exception of which she tells us was a monk-anchorite of some note, Thomas Brackley of Norwich, who had come from afar to the anchor-hold there. She tells us that 'he bar a name of gret perfeccyon and be-for-tyme had lowyd this creatur ryth meche'. He turned against her through giving credence to a gross slander; she convinced him of his mistake, whereupon he offered to undertake her direction. She declined, again (so she says) by divine inspiration.[3]

Another contact with monks came about through her parish church. This, the church of St Margaret, belonged to the priory of Lynn, a cell of Norwich cathedral monastery, but the 'parisch preste', Master Robert Springold, a bachelor of law and another faithful confessor and director, was of course a secular, as was the keeper of the Lady Chapel, another friend.[4] The monks, however, ultimately came into the story, for her 'cries' at one period increased to such an extent that these priests were unwilling to give her the frequent Communion, for which Archbishop Arundel had given permission, in the church itself; they therefore used the

---

1 *Book*, 148/28–9. Butler-Bowdon, 224. The identification of this friar with Melton is based upon annotations by a later hand on the Mount Grace MS., but the Melton of these notes is probably the sixteenth-century chancellor of York. For Melton, *v.* Owst, *Preaching in Medieval England* and Little, *Franciscan Papers*, 245. Margery does not give his name; it seems to have been her habit never to mention by name those hostile to her.

2 *Book*, 149/14–7. Butler-Bowdon, 224.

3 *Book*, 103/1–3 and notes. Butler-Bowdon, 152.

4 For Springfold, *v. Book*, index *s.v.* Margery uses the term 'parish priest' in its normal medieval significance, for a priest supported by the parson and employed in parish work. It never bears the meaning, as it does to-day, of the canonical *parochus*, which appears to have been introduced from Ireland in the early nineteenth century. At St Margaret's the *persona* was the Norwich community, represented at Lynn by the prior (*Book*, 58/33).

neighbouring chapel of the prior, Dan Thomas Hevyngham, who was well disposed to her.[1] A contretemps occurred when a new arrival from Norwich, unused to Margery's ways, objected to her laments and refused to enter the chapel while she was there. The matter was adjusted, and the two successive priors of Lynn remained well disposed. It is interesting to find Margery mobilizing all her spiritual resources to resist the attempts of interested parties to secure the privilege of all the sacraments for two dependent chapels.[2]

Apart from the religious who played a part in her life Margery had two or three noteworthy experiences in monasteries she visited. One was at an unnamed house where a monk holding an important office behaved at first uncourteously towards her. When, however, dining at the abbot's table she edified the company with her conversation, this monk approached her in the church and asked her to tell him if he would be saved. Margery, after a space of prayer during his Mass, told him of his sins: unchastity, despair, and the holding of property, and warned him to give up his external duties. The monk, after a moment of surprise, 'led hir into a fayr nows of offyce, made her a gret dyner, and sithen yaf hir gold to prey for him'. On a subsequent visit she found that he had taken her advice, and was now a respectable subprior, and duly grateful to his mentor.[3]

Still more vivid is her account of a visit to Christ Church, Canterbury. Here she fell into disfavour with the monks owing to her continual weeping, so much so that her husband, overcome by shame, left her in the lurch and retired to his inn. In this predicament, and apparently surrounded by monks and others, she was accosted by a distinguished inmate, the elderly Dan John Kyngton, sometime chancellor of Queen Joanna.[4] He asked her if she could speak about God, whereupon Margery 'rehersed a story of Scriptur'. This was unfortunate, for Dan John, smelling a Lollard in the wind, expressed a wish that she might be put in prison. A young monk then ventured the opinion that she was either a saint or possessed by the devil. Margery, in the spirit of Sir Thomas More, countered by offering to tell them a merry tale: there was once a man, she said, whose confessor enjoined upon him as a penance that he should hire others at a price to speak evil of him to humble him. One day it happened that 'he cam among many gret men as I do now among yow, despysyng

---

1 For Hevyngham v. Book, index s.v., and Appendix III, iv and vii.

2 Book, 58/25 seqq. Butler-Bowdon, 93. Col. Butler-Bowdon (note ad loc.) suggests that the priest who wrote the Book for Margery was Prior John Dereham or one of his monks. Meech and Allen nowhere adopt or even mention this suggestion, but to the present writer, after repeated reading of Book, 57–9 and 170–1, the identification appears most probable. Dereham was a monk of some note, and a doctor of divinity (cf. MC, II, 155; III, 319).

3 Book, 25/28 seqq. Butler-Bowdon, 51. The subprior was normally in charge of the internal discipline of the monastery.

4 For Kyngton v. infra, p. 231, with references. Again Margery does not name him, but her facts are correct. He died 18 October 1416. As the Book was not formally written till 1431 this passage (among others) would seem to show that Margery had either dictated notes much earlier, or had memorized some of her adventures.

hym as ye do me, the man lawhyng er smylyng & havung good game at
here wordys'. When asked by their leader why he laughed at the treatment
he was receiving he explained that for one day at least it would cost him
nothing to be despised, 'I thank yow alle'. So it was with her, continued
Margery; at home she wept because none scorned her, here she had scorn
in plenty, and so 'I thank yow alle serys heyly what fore-noon and aftyr-
noon I have had resonably this day, blyssed be God thereof'. She then
swept out of the cathedral, followed by the monks and crowd shouting,
'Thou shalt be brent, fals lollare. Her is a cartful of thornys redy for the
and a tunne to bren ye wyth'. She was only rescued by the surprising
appearance of 'tweyn feyr yong men' who took her home to her inn, where
she found her husband waiting.[1]

Yet a third experience was at the Cistercian abbey of Hailes, where she
had venerated the Holy Blood on her way back from Bristol, '& had
lowde cryes and boystows wepynges'. The monks were impressed, had
her in, and 'mad hir good cher', but none the less 'sworyn many gret
othys and horryble' in her presence, whereupon she lectured them with
suitable texts from Scripture. This the Cistercians took in good part.[2]

Trifling as all these incidents are, they are precious vignettes of a passing
moment in a monastery: the free conversation with women, the well-
supplied board, the group of rustic Cistercians swearing and guffawing,
the sudden outbreak of fury at the gate of Canterbury. If these only
supplement the picture given by visitation records, yet the respect of the
friars for an earnest soul, together with their knowledge of spiritual
literature, and the firm loyalty of Master Alan and the Dominican anchorite
must be set against the coarse and worldly character portrayed by Chaucer.

VII. FRIAR BRACKLEY

In the great collection of letters amassed by the Paston family we make
the acquaintance of a friar who bears an unmistakable family likeness to
Chaucer's worthy limiter.[3] This is Master Doctor John Brackley, *Minorum
minimus* as he signs himself, who contributes some of the most racy
numbers to the correspondence, appearing throughout as a henchman,
intriguer and violent partisan on the side of John Paston, senior, and of
Sir John, the elder of the two sons of Margaret Paston to bear that name.

Master Brackley was a celebrated preacher, not unaware of his gifts, in
demand not only in East Anglia to preach before the justices, but even at
Paul's Cross, the Broadcasting House of that age, on the eve of the
coronation of 1461, and if the sample of his eloquence that has been

1 *Book*, 27/18 *seqq.* Butler-Bowdon, 54. A 'tunne' or cask was used to enclose the victim
for burning; cf. the well-known account of the death of Badby.

2 *Book*, 110/34 *seqq.* Butler-Bowdon, 163.

3 The references are to *The Paston Letters*, ed. J. Gairdner (1904). This was the last and
fullest edition, but it contains no table of concordance which would simplify the task of
verifying references to one of the previous editions; the numeration of the letters is wholly
different.

preserved in the form of a Whitsun sermon[1] does not wholly explain his reputation, we may well imagine that such anecdotes as that of the white owl, herald of Fastolf's death, that whooped from the belfry and blundered between the legs of William of Worcester's horse, might have served as *exempla* to stimulate the drowsy.[2] Brackley had a talent for vituperation, and seems to have been strongly anti-Irish in his sympathies;[3] William of Worcester, his adversary for many years, came in for some vivid abuse, and it is not surprising that he was equally outspoken in return.[4] Friar John never tired of urging his patrons to make friends of the mammon of iniquity,[5] but despite their best efforts John Paston and his son were never wholly successful in carrying out the advice.

Friar Brackley's chief significance in the letters comes from his central position in the great Fastolf case. He was present at the deathbed of Sir John Fastolf, from which he wrote to beg John Paston to come with all speed: 'It is hey tyme; he drawyt fast home ward.'[6] Paston's presence was solicited to make assurance doubly sure in the matter of Fastolf's will, one version of which, giving in effect the inheritance of his estates to John Paston, had been drawn up and engrossed and authenticated by Dr Brackley himself, if indeed it had not been, as his enemies suggested, forged by the legatee and the Doctor.[7] The friar became in consequence a key-witness in the hard-fought probate suit that followed, and one of the documents among those bearing on the process is an account of his last hours, in which Brackley is seen, true to himself, asserting with his dying breath the justice of Paston's claim.[8]

1 *Paston Letters*, III, no. 436, pp. 256–8.   2 *Ibid.* III, no. 418, p. 231.

3 *Ibid.* 229: 'Pensetis...instabilem virum, utinam Hibernicum non ingratissimum, cujus nacionis aliquales proprietates sunt istae—animo saeva, vultu ferox, torva affatu, versupellis moribus et inconstancia in omnibus bonis viis suis...nunc in promptuario propter Jhesum Christum deleantur de libro vertuose et unanimiter viventium et a modo cum justis nequaquam scribantur, &c.' The '&c.' is Brackley's.

4 William of Worcester writes to Margaret Paston of the 'malycouse contryved tales of Frere Brackley'. (*Paston Letters*, IV, no. 681, p. 293.)

5 *Ibid.* III, no. 355, p. 196.   6 *Ibid.* III, no. 383, pp. 144–5.

7 For the whole business of Fastolf's will, *v. Paston Letters*, introd., and I, 234–6.

8 *Ibid.* IV, no. 666, pp. 275–6.

CHAPTER XV

THE SECOND CENTURY OF VISITATION,
1350–1450

The bishops' registers, with scarcely an exception, yield little or no information for the second half of the fourteenth century. For the most part they are less comprehensive than before, and contain little more than records of ordinations and institutions. By way of compensation, however, the activities of the monastic visitors, hitherto almost without record, can be studied in greater detail between 1360 and 1390 than at any other time before or after. Yet it is not the regular visitors from chapter that have left most traces, but a series of extraordinary visitations by Abbot Thomas de la Mare of St Albans.[1]

That eminent man, by far the most distinguished abbot of the century, had been one of the abbots president almost without a break from shortly after his accession, c. 1351, and soon acquired a unique reputation as patron and reformer. It was his personal prestige, and not strictly his official position, that led Edward III, c. 1362–5, to call him in to deal with the affairs of half a dozen monasteries in which the king took interest as hereditary founder or patron, and which, owing it may be to abnormal years after the great plague, stood in urgent need of reform. The first of these was Eynsham where, we are told, de la Mare effected a wonderful change for the better. Part of the process of this visitation appears to have survived in a long examination of the abbot which reveals much of the domestic and economic structure of the place.[2] The abbey had shortly before been the scene of *émeutes* in which the deposed Abbot Nicholas had come back at the head of an armed band. Fighting had ensued, but the exile was victorious and the bishop of Lincoln, influenced by the great mortality in the house in 1349, had acquiesced in a *fait accompli*. Whatever may have been the measures of reform the abbot, who put up a spirited defence against his critics, survived the storm securely. Next came Abingdon where no record survives, and Battle, at both of which houses abuses were removed and customs contrary to the Rule abolished. From

---

1 There is a summary account of this in *GASA*, II, 405: (at Eynsham) 'religionem mirifice reformavit'; (at Abingdon and Battle) 'abusiones quasdam eradicavit, et inolitas consuetudines introductas contra Regulam explantavit, et pro illis inseruit bonos mores'. *Ibid.* 406: (Reading) 'adivit audacter, visitavit efficaciter et personas inflexit subtiliter et modeste ad religionis observantiam et amorem'; (Chester) 'non veritus atrocitatem vel inconstantiam gentis Wallicae, adiit animosus'. The dates and other circumstances of de la Mare's visits are discussed by Pantin, *MC*, III, 34–5, who also prints other documents cited below. For the disturbances at Eynsham *v.* H. E. Salter, *Cartulary of Eynsham*, I, xxiv–vi, with sources cited. The charges against Abbot Geoffrey, who was one of those originally driven out by the *revenant* Nicholas, were presumably the hot ashes of old feuds. Salter (*loc. cit.*) quotes injunctions of a bishop's visitation c. 1380.

2 *MC*, III, no. 209, pp. 36–51.

Battle a valuable piece of evidence is extant in the form of a letter from the new abbot to de la Mare in which, after alluding to his zeal for the well-being of the order, he informs him that since his visit all has been peace and order at Battle.[1] Reading next received his attention: some monks had conspired against the abbot and were removed to cells of Reading and St Albans; the rest were tactfully dealt with.[2] Finally, he undertook what was regarded as his boldest venture when he risked an encounter with the 'fierce and fickle' Welsh to depose the abbot of Chester, a vicious and wasteful superior who was actually one of the abbots president, and to bring back with him some monks to be trained in good observance at St Albans.[3] Still more gratifying, in view of the past, was his reception at Bury St Edmund's which he did not, indeed, visit in formal manner, but where he helped to compose the differences that were distracting the abbey at the time.[4] His domestic chronicler, by whom these facts are recorded, might be suspected of partiality, but the letter from Battle and the title Patriarch of the English Monks by which de la Mare was known even in the Curia[5] are unexceptionable evidence of his success. A still more striking compliment is paid him by a nameless monk of York, writing in 1366 to Uthred of Boldon of the hopeless impasse in Whitby affairs after the two visitations from chapter. He can see no remedy, he says, save in a visit from the abbot of St Albans, with the king's authority behind him.[6] Here, indeed, when de la Mare was in his prime, we can see all the conditions verified for fruitful visitation: the personal resolution and prestige of the visitor; the support of competent authority; the desire to do good to souls and a reserve of good traditions from which to draw. However extra-canonical the procedure may have been, we have here, for almost the first time since the days of Lanfranc, the classical *mise-en-scène* for black monk reform: a great abbot supported by the monarch. The happy collocation of circumstances was not to recur.

The comparative inefficiency of the visitors from chapter, even when they were men of zeal and ability, is well seen in the contemporary case of Whitby.[7] There the community had for some time been split into two parties; that of the abbot, a high-handed, avaricious and extravagant man of personal integrity, and a larger body led by the prior and subprior and including several accused with justice of incontinence and of amassing

1 *MC*, III, no. 221, pp. 62–3. The writer refers to de la Mare's 'innata bonitas et grandis affecio...ad augmentum religionis monasticae', and adds: 'locus noster posset dici verius Pax quam Bellum'.

2 A short document survives, printed in *MC*, III, no. 210, p. 52.

3 This visitation can be dated 1362 (?1363); cf. Pantin's note, *MC*, III, 35.

4 *GASA*, II, 406: 'Rogatu Regis recessit ad monasterium praecipuum totius regni... ubi invenit omnes paratos ad se submittendum suae visitationi.' This is perhaps wishful thinking.

5 *Amundesham*, App. E, p. 304: 'Propter notabilem religionem et zelum regularis observantiae...Patriarcha Monachorum Angliae appellatus.'

6 *MC*, III, no. 354, p. 309: 'Nec video quin omnino expediat quod dominus abbas S. Albani accedat personaliter...cum potestate...regia.'

7 *MC*, III, nos. 222, 350–4, pp. 63–8, 277–309, with the editor's notes.

private property. Foremost among the latter was one Thomas of Hawkes-garth, a peculiarly turbulent spirit, whose friends had on one occasion gone so far as to make an assault upon the abbot by night with swords and clubs,[1] and who utterly refused to come within the abbot's reach, alleging, when charged with disobedience, that there were situations in which even a stout heart might pardonably quail.[2] From the voluminous information supplied by both sides to the quarrel the impression is received of an incorrigibly factious and unhappy, rather than of a completely degraded, community. The troubles came to a head *c.* 1365, and Archbishop Thoresby at a visitation did something to punish the moral faults.[3] The internal feud, however, which was largely concerned with points of administration, showed no signs of dying away, and in 1366 Whitby was visited by commissioners of the abbot of Bardney, one of the presidents. Apparently they did little but report to chapter that things were desperate, and in consequence a special visitation was decreed, and within a few days the abbot of St Mary's and Uthred of Boldon, warden of Durham College and the most distinguished private monk of his age, arrived at Whitby. Much of the dossier they compiled has survived, and the *detecta* are accompanied by short and often very acute observations, probably by Uthred himself. After hours of listening and questioning a series of articles was drawn out against both the abbot and several monks. All nominally submitted and offered defences or canonical purgations; penances were assigned, and the abbot made a number of undertakings. Mutual distrust, however, per-sisted, and the community refused to endorse the abbot's presentation of the accounts.[4] It was at this juncture that Uthred's nameless correspondent considered that matters had reached an impasse.[5] In the sequel, Thomas de la Mare was certainly consulted, though there is no evidence of his intervention; the patent rolls, however, show that the king took a hand, examining the finances and ordering the arrest of the apostate Thomas of Hawkesgarth.[6] As for the abbot, he remained in office till his death eight years later.

Apart from the Whitby documents the solitary account of a chapter visitation of this period is a colourless set of *comperta* from Durham *c.* 1390.[7] For the canons there are equally scanty records, but such as exist do not inspire confidence in the system. At Stoneley in 1368 the

1 *MC*, III, 305: 'Noctanter cum gladiis, baculis et aliis armis invasivis insultum eidem abbati ad hostium camere sue dederunt ad interficiendum eundem.' *Ibid.* 300. Thomas Hawkesgarth secured six friends to support his absolute innocence in the affray though elsewhere (*ibid.* 302) the fact of the brawl is admitted.
2 *MC*, III, 300: 'Dixit quod hoc fecit propter justum metum, qui possit cadere in con-stantem virum.' This was a technically excusing circumstance in canon law.
3 For the archbishop's visitation, *v. MC*, III, 284, 287 and *Chart. abb. de Whiteby*, II, 657.
4 *MC*, III, 308. The financial statement is *MC*, III, no. 222, pp. 63–8.
5 *Ibid.* 309 and references on p. 278.
6 References in *MC*, III, 277–8. For other examples of royal intervention in monastic difficulties I may be allowed to follow Pantin in referring to K. Wood-Legh, *Studies in Church Life under Edward III*, ch. 1.
7 *MC*, III, no. 236, pp. 82–4.

abbot of Oseney and the prior of Bicester confess that the situation is beyond them; the house has funds enough, but the prior is old, infirm and quite incompetent, and the community do as they please like seculars. Forty years later, some innocuous injunctions for Plympton and St German's given by the prior of Launceston will not reassure those who have gathered from other sources, such as Grandisson's register, material by which to judge of the west country canons of the time.[1]

With the turn of the century, a fresh batch of documents becomes available for the study of episcopal visitations. Pre-eminent among them is the rich deposit that has been extracted from the Lincoln archives, but there is fairly adequate evidence from Hereford and Wells, chanceries so well represented in earlier records, and these, together with a few more isolated notes, enable us to make a survey wide enough to provide comparisons with the previous evidence.

In the century between 1325 and 1425 the conditions of English church life had profoundly changed. Externally, the great pestilences had undoubtedly thinned the numbers of the monks and canons, while the social upheavals and the economic changes had changed their methods of exploiting their lands; in addition, the long wars had brought decay to many of the alien priories. In the realm of ideas, the attacks made by Wyclifites and satirists upon the religious life had helped to isolate the possessioners and to break the harmony of the Church; no corresponding reform or revival had taken place, and the religious orders, therefore, like an ageing tree, had lost something of strength and elasticity by the mere passage of the years. The episcopate also had changed. Though still powerful and entirely orthodox, and even more closely connected with government than before, it was undoubtedly less efficient as a spiritual force. The office was now used to reward servants of the Crown, who continued to fill high offices of State and perform important duties which entailed frequent and prolonged absences from the diocese. While the typical bishop of 1280–1320 was an eminent diocesan official or the ex-superior of a cathedral priory, his counterpart a century later was a clerk who had long served the king, often without proceeding to Orders. Papal provision, extremely common during both periods, had little or no influence upon the character of the bench. The pope appointed one who was *persona grata* to the king in order to secure the latter's financial and diplomatic support. As a consequence, visitations were performed more rarely, and were often delegated to the bishop's Official or commissioners appointed *ad hoc*. In short, on this side and on that there was a sensible decrease in enthusiasm and receptivity.

The Lincoln records, which form an unbroken series covering thirty years (1420–49), and three episcopates, are unique in the fullness of

1 *AC*, App. I, pp. 166, 170–3.

information they provide.[1] For the reign of Richard Flemyng (1420–31) and William Gray (1431–6) the registers contain injunctions of the type familiar in earlier days, but for the days of William Alnwick (1436–49) the actual dossiers of visitations have been in large part preserved, the raw matter, that is, which formed the basis for injunctions and decisions. Thus while the registers preserved only such features as seemed to the registrar worthy of permanent record, Alnwick's documents are the material accumulated on the spot and used by the bishop in the actual discharge of his business as visitor. By giving us both the copious *detecta*, the shorter *comperta*, and in some cases the final injunctions as well, they allow us to see the relationship of the bishop's formal commands to the evidence previously put before him, and to form an idea of the method of the whole.

The great diocese of Lincoln, the largest in medieval England,[2] held also within its limits a greater number of religious houses than any other. Even when the exempt orders are left out of the reckoning, there remain more than half a dozen important black monk abbeys, including Peterborough and Ramsey, houses of the first rank, and a very great number of Augustinian houses great and small, including a number of abbeys and important priories such as Dorchester, Dunstable, Leicester, Northampton, Oxford (St Frideswide's), Thornton and Wellow. For the majority of these there are one or more sets of injunctions or (when Alnwick is concerned) a detailed *procès-verbal* of the examination. Taken as a body, therefore, they allow us to form a considered judgement on the state of the black monks and the black canons of the Midlands.

Of the three prelates Richard Flemyng, the first, was a Yorkshireman and a distinguished Oxford theologian. In his youth he had had Lollard sympathies, but these had long vanished and he was a papal chamberlain at the time of his provision to Lincoln. When bishop, he was employed as ambassador to Germany for most of 1421 and was at the Council of Pavia-Siena for many months of 1423–4; while there he was provided to York and it was almost two years before the imbroglio was cleared up and he could be re-translated to Lincoln. Gray had been an agent of Flemyng, and was provided to London in 1426; during his short tenure of the see of Lincoln he was frequently called away on public business. Alnwick, who had been for ten years Treasurer, and since 1430 confessor to Henry VI, held the see of Norwich from 1426 to 1436. He was on the whole less

---

1 Edited in three volumes, with notes and admirable introductions, they are perhaps the most outstanding item of the many that go to make up the heavy debt that all students of medieval religious history owe to the industry and judgement of the late A. H. Thompson. Moreover, their format, as analysed by their editor, has made clear once and for all the significance of the various stages and documents of a visitation. In addition, they are a mine of information on the daily life and organization of the monasteries and on the social life of the times.

2 It stretched from the Humber to the Thames, and comprised the counties of Lincoln, Leicester, Northampton, Rutland, Buckingham, Oxford, Huntingdon, Bedford and part of Hertford. If the medieval diocese of York had an area almost as great, much of this was wild moor and crag; both population and the number of churches were smaller.

distracted from his pastoral duties than the others; he had been energetic in visitation at Norwich, and showed the same characteristic at Lincoln.[1] He had the assistance of a small group of trained clerks, some of whom are found at almost every visitation.

In addition to their continuity and bulk, the records of the three bishops are complementary to a remarkable degree. Whereas from Flemyng and Gray it is the injunctions that have survived among the documents of their registers, that of Alnwick contains only a single set of injunctions, while the original minutes of his visitations have survived separately. These comprise in the majority of cases the depositions of the monks, the inquiries based upon their evidence, and the notes (*comperta*) of the bishop deriving from these, from which in due time the injunctions were to be framed. Sometimes, also, the injunctions (which are not in the register) themselves follow, either in the form in which they were delivered verbally in chapter,[2] or in their final shape as dispatched later by the bishop. Taken as a whole, this is by far the richest collection of actual minutes in existence; as we read it we sit in the chapter-house with the bishop and his officials and listen to the grievances, rancours and hopes of the religious. For certain aspects of the life in monasteries and nunneries of the early fifteenth century it is an invaluable witness.

As hitherto, no essential difference is discernible between monks and canons, and very little between great houses and small. At almost all certain faults are noted. Most common, perhaps, is neglect to observe the monastic enclosure: hence, on the one hand, the practice of frequenting houses in the neighbourhood of the monastery, and particularly in the adjoining town, and on the other, a neglect to close the doors of church and cloister against promiscuous visitors. The former fault led to unlawful entertainment and pastimes, either in the houses of townsfolk or taverns, and hence often to scandal and grave moral faults. The latter resulted in the intrusions of miscellaneous visitors and animals into the most private parts of the monastery, and to gossip and assignations which again were the occasion of grave faults. Next, there was the almost universal practice of breaking the great silence by social drinking after compline: when the Office was over the night was still young; some of the obedientiaries had been out all day and would not in any case rise for mattins; this, and the reluctance common to all ages and callings to leave the warm precincts of the cheerful day, led to gatherings which at best were irregular, and usually ended in excesses, caballing and slackness in attendance at Office. Thirdly, there was an almost universal carelessness in keeping choir and refectory, due partly to the age-old freedom enjoyed by the obedientiaries, and

---

1 Thompson justly remarks (*LV*, III, 409): 'the thoroughness with which in later years he perambulated the wider area of the diocese of Lincoln was a continuation of the conscientious diligence which gives him a remarkable eminence among the prelates of his age.'
2 E.g. *LV*, II, 87, 180.

partly to the more recent institution of frequent periods of recreation, which, besides taking batches of the community in turn to a grange or cell for rest or bleeding, led also to a large section dining each day on meat outside the refectory. This last custom entailed the maintenance of at least three distinct households—that of the abbot, that of the community, and that of the misericord, which was often a department of the infirmary.

On the administrative side, the most common cause of trouble was the incompetence or self-will of the superior. The canonical safeguards giving advisory or controlling powers to the community were everywhere neglected in an age when canonical discipline was everywhere in decay. Accounts were not given, the permission of council or chapter was not asked, while, in addition, the level of ability among superiors had apparently fallen, for the number of houses, great and small, where the prior or abbot was manifestly extravagant or incompetent is to all appearances greater in Lincoln *c.* 1420 than it was in Yorkshire or Gloucestershire *c.* 1300. Greater, also, appears to be the number of cases in which the good fame of a superior is tarnished. Statistics here are all but valueless, for in the last resort each student must form his own judgement on the precise degree of culpability incurred when the accused was technically acquitted of the full crime, but cases where some degree of guilt existed are unquestionably numerous.

Some houses have a peculiarly bad record. Bardney, never a home of fervour, was desperately in debt and irregular in discipline in *c.* 1430 and 1439/40, largely owing to an inefficient abbot.[1] Eynsham, another permanently unsatisfactory house, was in still worse case. A series of visitations and commissions under Gray was concerned with ordering the finances and examining into the delinquencies of an abbot guilty of incontinence in many forms.[2] At Peterborough, one of the wealthiest abbeys of England, the incompetence of the abbot necessitated a commission of administration in 1432 and his total withdrawal from all effective control in 1437 in favour of the prior, though the latter, so complaint had said nine years earlier, was incompetent from illness, while the subprior was a simpleton.[3] Five years later a new abbot appeared to have the place under control, but in 1446 he, too, was under a cloud, accused of incontinence and certainly guilty of ostentatious and worldly behaviour on his manors and in the chase, and of gathering round himself a clique of disorderly young monks. He appears, however, to have pulled himself together, and continued in office till his death thirty years later.[4]

Two smaller houses, the sometime alien priories of Daventry and St Neot's were among the most dissolute. To both Gray addressed the

1 *LV*, I, 1–4; II, 9–31.   2 *Ibid.* I, 54–63.
3 *Ibid.* I, 100–3; III, 269–82. Cf. *ibid.* III, 276: 'Camerarius dicit quod, quid per senium abbatis et infirmitates ejus et prioris et simplicitatem supprioris, quasi perit religio.'
4 *Ibid.* III, 283–302; cf. 296–7 especially.

fearful indictment reserved for houses almost beyond hope.[1] At Daventry in 1433 the numbers were down, monks were in apostasy, accounts were neglected, and church and cloister lay open to all comers.[2] Nine years later the injunctions made on all these heads had borne no fruit. Regular life did not exist; the monks frequented taverns in Daventry and all had hounds of their own; women penetrated into frater and infirmary and soiled the conduit in the cloister by coming thither with their washing-pots. The prior's administration was a disgrace, and he defaulted in his attempt to clear himself from a charge of adultery.[3] St Neot's was equally disorganized; in 1432 there was no refectory and no accommodation for readers in the cloister; women and seculars haunted the precincts and the monks the town.[4] Seven years later Alnwick found things even worse. The place was in debt, the church and other buildings failed to keep out the weather; the subprior was weak in the head; the prior, who never celebrated Mass and regularly disappeared for the day, was accused of maladministration, of procuring the resignation of his predecessor and his own election by heavy bribes, and of adultery; the first charge was obviously just; the second seems to have been well-founded, and the third was tacitly admitted, though the accused denied immoral relations since his election.[5]

Among the canons two large houses, Dorchester and Huntingdon, were in chronic trouble. Dorchester was perhaps the most distressing house of the diocese. In 1441 its possessions were wasted, the cloister was a public passage, and the canons hunted and hawked, or drank in the neighbouring taverns. In the evening after compline, we are told, they repaired to Thomas Tewkesbury's room, to which women resorted, where they called for good ale and settled down to chess, that universal solace of the reprobate. Several were incontinent, while the abbot was accused of keeping at least five mistresses at the common expense.[6] Four years later

1 This occurs in full in the injunctions to Huntingdon, *LV*, i, 76; elsewhere a brief cross-reference is given, which the reader might well miss but for the editor's warning. The severest passage runs: 'Observancie regulares et regula...quasi totaliter obliviscuntur; divinum officium nocturnum pariter et diurnum necgligitur; obediencia rumpitur; elemosina consumitur; hospitalitas non observatur; sed et tota providentia temporalis...penitus adnichilatur. Non est hic aliud nisi ebrietas et crapula, inobediencia et contemptus, proprietas et apostasia, sompnolencia, non dicimus incontinencia, sed torpor et omne aliud quod in malum declinat et hominem trahit ad gehennam.' This resonant commination, it must be recalled, was not the molten lava of Gray's indignation, but common form, copied out of the file by the registrar. Nevertheless, such a sweeping condemnation could not have been served on any tolerably respectable community.

2 *LV*, i, 43–4.

3 *Ibid.* ii, 60–7; esp. 63: 'Mulieres habent commune accessum ad coquinam et ad lavatoria in claustro, ubi ascendunt merginem [plinth] ut impleant ollas [pots] suas in lavatoriis; sicque pedibus ipsam merginem coinquinant.'

4 *Ibid.* i, 109–11.   5 *Ibid.* iii, 320–7.

6 *Ibid.* ii, 68–78: (71) 'Quidam [canonici] intendunt aucupacionibus, quidam venacionibus, quidam publicis tabernis.' (72) 'Fit concursus canonicorum...post completorium, et ibidem mittunt post bonam servisiam et ludunt ad scaccos et cetera alia agunt que sunt inhonesta.' It is noteworthy that while four canons opined that all was well (*omnia bene*) at Dorchester, three of the four were accused of flagrant incontinence by others.

there was a new abbot, and things were somewhat less scandalous, though the old abbot was still in residence and *sibi constans*. The principal remaining source of trouble was canon Ralph Carnelle, who added to incontinence the qualities of a desperado. He carried weapons, wore a 'jacket of fence', carried the younger canons to drink with him in the town, and brought up students from Oxford to his assistance when attacked. On one occasion, in the course of a difference with the prior, he had fetched him a clout on the ear that left him permanently deaf. Ralph, for his part, accused the new abbot of disedifying life and applied for leave to devote himself to study at Oxford.[1] Unfortunately there is no record of the outcome. Huntingdon had merited in 1432 the scathing preamble addressed to Daventry and St Neot's; regular life could scarcely be said to exist, and the canons resorted to the town to drink and gamble.[2] Seven years later Alnwick found no improvement; there was general decay; the prior was accused of inattendance at Office, of omitting the words of consecration in the Mass, of absence by night in secular dress, of common brawling, and of sin with half a dozen women.[3] Of the smaller houses Caldwell received the same indictment as Huntingdon, and Markby another as stern from Alnwick;[4] Canons Ashby was in a bad way in *c.* 1432, with an absentee prior, and in 1442 only four out of eleven canons attended choir.[5] Finally, at Bradwell, Gray could observe that only the shadow or image of the religious life remained, a mere token to which nothing deeper corresponded.[6]

From the nature of the case it is less easy to select houses deserving praise, but bearing in mind the copious complaints and accusations forthcoming elsewhere, it is fair, at least in Alnwick's records, to accept at their face value any declarations that all is well. Judged in this way, Missenden, Northampton (St James), Owston, Wellow and Wymondley among the canons were respectable, and of the black monks, Croyland and (at its last visitation) Eynsham.

It is natural to ask whether any observable good was effected by these visitations. Unfortunately, it is only in the rarest cases that we have a sequence of three or four visitations for a single house. As has been seen, some of the worst show little sign of improvement; Dorchester, Daventry, Huntingdon and St Neot's are examples. At others, such as Eynsham and Peterborough, there is evidence of a change for the better, or at least of an ebb and flow, and it is difficult to suppose that such a turning over of

1 *Ibid.* II, 78–83: (79) 'Radulphus vestitus est multociens deploide defensionis et gerit secrete sub habitu suo longos cultellos.' (81) 'Petit igitur idem Radulphus ut dominus... ordinet ut...studium exercere possit'.

2 *Ibid.* I, 76–9.   3 *Ibid.* II, 148–55.

4 *Ibid.* I, 27–8; III, 219–27 (Markby), esp. 225: 'nec eciam vix effigies religionis nisi tantum signum cui signatum minime correspondet.'

5 *Ibid.* I, 30–2; II, 43–6.

6 *Ibid.* I, 22–3: 'Tantum quasi umbram vel effigiem religionis et signum cui signatum non correspondet.' This is a variation of the common form used later by Alnwick.

soiled linen as took place elsewhere failed to shake out at least some of the vermin. Two points, however, must strike the reader of the Lincoln visitations as disquieting, when he recalls the earlier York series: the rarity of depositions of a superior and the almost complete absence of any record of the punishment of individuals.

An inflexible resolve to get rid of a scandalous superior must always be the acid test of a visitor's sincerity. While it should be remembered that complete materials for a judgement are often wanting and that in some cases the bishop may have taken action after the visitation had been completed, as also that gross dilapidation or a criminal breach of the vow of chastity were needed as canonical grounds for deposition, it is nevertheless true that on at least twenty occasions in this collection the removal of a superior seems to modern eyes to have been an essential condition of reform, and that in only three or four of these did the bishop proceed to extremities, while on four or five other occasions he established some kind of committee or coadjutorship. Assuredly, past experience had shown that very great difficulty might be found in getting out of the way an unscrupulous man who had a canonical foothold to grip, but it is natural to suppose that a firm visitor could put very severe pressure on a really incompetent or morally weak superior, even where the canonical case against him had flaws, and, whatever the issue, the bishop, had he taken his stand firmly by truth and justice, would have kept his own hands free from stain against the day when shepherd and sheep came up for judgement in the light of eternal truth. It must, therefore, be said that all the bishops concerned acted with an extreme leniency.[1] Thus Gray at Canons Ashby in 1422, after serving such a fearful indictment on the priory, allowed the prior to remain in office although, besides other grave shortcomings, his relations with three women formed the subject of a special injunction. In the event, he abandoned his post altogether.[2] Similarly, when Alnwick was at Dorchester in 1441 the abbot, in addition to maladministration and a general irregularity and lack of control, was accused, as has been noted, of keeping five married women as mistresses. Yet he apparently escaped immediate judgement and though four years later another was ruling, the old abbot was enjoying private quarters and a comfortable pension, together with a considerable share in the convent's affairs, while remaining faithful to his malpractices.[3]

At Leicester, in 1440, the abbot, besides making personal use of the revenues and treating his subjects in the harshest manner, was accused of incontinence and still more forcibly of witchcraft and divination. Yet he kept his office, and nothing is said of any acquittal of the former charge,

1 The editor's observation (*ibid.* II, lix), that 'in the prescription of penalties and in the admission of purgations Alnwick was merciful and easy', is certainly no overstatement, but his judicious remarks on the difficulties in the way of a reformer (*ibid.* lx–lxii) deserve careful attention.

2 *Ibid.* I, 30–5.

3 *Ibid.* II, 68–83. The last phrase of the above paragraph is Thompson's (p. 78 n.).

while he was allowed to exculpate himself of the latter on his own un-supported oath.[1] At Peterborough in 1446, where the abbot was charged, not only with worldliness, laxity and partial government, but with grave maladministration and adultery with three women, he was allowed to clear himself on his own word of two parts of the last charge and to expurgate himself on the last head, and although the bishop at first superseded his temporal administration in favour of a committee of four, he made so skilful an appeal for mercy that he was allowed to conduct affairs with the four as assessors only.[2] Again, at Humberstone in 1440, where all dis-cipline was in a state of advanced decay, and where the few brethren who remained were equally ready to accuse and support one another, the cul-prits were given small penances and allowed to clear themselves by their own word alone.[3] Nor do these examples exhaust the list of such cases.

In the matter of penances, also, there is a seeming relaxation of severity. In the visitations of c. 1300 the monk or canon convicted of, or confessing, notorious incontinence was put upon an extremely severe penance, which he was usually required to undergo in exile. In the Lincoln visitations it is hard to find a single case of exile, and remarkably light punishments are inflicted; thus a canon of Markby, convicted of a long-standing criminal intercourse with a woman by whom he had two children, escaped with a mild dietary penance and some vocal prayers, while an extremely dis-orderly fellow-canon, suspected of homosexual practices, got off with a caution.[4]

In matters of religious observance the principal change from earlier times is in the matter of private funds. At the end of the thirteenth century almost every visitor was concerned to check the practice of issuing clothes and pocket-money, and to insist on the delivery of garments, like food, from the common store. In this they were supported not only by the Rule and decrees of chapter, but by papal constitutions. In the fifteenth century the bishops no longer tried to stop the practice; they were concerned instead with assuring the community of a fair allocation of pensions for clothes and private expenses, and by a strangely irregular turn of discipline they set up a scale of fines to be paid out of pocket-money for non-attendance in choir and similar failings.[5]

---

1 *Ibid.* II, 206–17.   2 *Ibid.* III, 285–302.
3 *Ibid.* II, 139–48.
4 *Ibid.* III, 224. The former canon was put on bread, beer and vegetables on two days of the week for three months. The vocal penance was 'dicere ad duodecim vices sex psalteria Davitica equaliter.' It is not clear whether *psalterium* here signifies 150 psalms (a heavy task) or a nocturn of six psalms.
5 Thus clothes-money is fixed for Bardney at £2 p.a. (*LV*, II, 15), for Kyme at 16s. (*ibid.* II, 169), for Eynsham at £1. 6s. 8d. (*ibid.* III, 55), for Thornholm prior £1. 6s. 8d.; others £1 (*ibid.* III, 367) and for Wellow £1. 6s. 8d. (*ibid.* III, 391). For fines v. Ramsey, I, 104, where a breach of silence or absence from choir is assessed at a penny, and drinking after compline at sixpence for a private monk and 3s. 4d. for one of the presidents. The takings are to go to flooring the cloister, etc. In *Cartulary of Eynsham*, ed. H. E. Salter, I, xxvii, the total annual exhibition for a monk in clothes, meat and wine (bread and beer are excluded) is £4. 6s. 8d.

In these records, as in earlier ones, there is a singular dearth of reference to the visitations from provincial chapter. These, if made, can have had little effect upon the course of events, and only once does a bishop of Lincoln refer to the capitular decrees of the canons.[1]

From Hereford some registers have survived contemporary with the Lincoln records. That of Trefnant (1389–1404) contains a single set of injunctions which shows Chirbury in much the same state as of old, and which provides another instance of a tariff being set up for clothes-money.[2] The register of Thomas Spofford (1422–48) is fuller.[3] Spofford, sometime abbot of St Mary's, York, was a distinguished man who had represented England at the Council of Basel. He was certainly among the more zealous and conscientious of the prelates of his day. In his register Chirbury and Wigmore figure once more in their old roles. In 1423–4 both were in a state of spiritual and material collapse.[4] At Chirbury the prior, after being superseded, resigned; a canon of Llanthony took his place and in 1427 he and his small community seem to have been at peace.[5] Later, in 1441, some wild Welsh took advantage of a vacancy to put in a relative. He was, however, a respectable choice, a canon of London, and was subsequently approved by Spofford.[6] At Wigmore, twice visited by the bishop and his commissaries in 1424–5, much of the time was taken up in examining a charge of simoniacal election against the abbot; the outcome is unfortunately not recorded. On other matters also the abbot and community were at issue, the former painting an almost idyllic picture of their life, save for the state of the fabric, while the others lodged various complaints against the abbot in person and discipline in general.[7] Ten years later, the bishop found the canons roaming abroad at night and hunting and fishing by day, and the abbot was severely reprimanded.[8]

In the west we have the registers of Wells from 1425 to 1465. That of John Stafford (1425–43) gives little information.[9] He was a political bishop, Treasurer 1422–6, Keeper of the Privy Seal 1421–2, and Chancellor 1432–50; he passed from Wells to Canterbury. When at Wells he visited rarely and often sent a deputy. Bruton, often a troublesome house, had an irregular prior, defamed of incontinence. He was ordered to do nothing

1 Gray at St Frideswide's in 1422–3 (*LV*, i, 97).
2 *Reg. J. Trefnant*, ed. W. W. Capes. The Chirbury injunctions of 2 November 1394 are on pp. 22–4.
3 *Reg. T. Spofford*, ed. A. T. Bannister.
4 *Reg. T. Spofford*, 39 (Chirbury, August 1423): 'tam in spiritualibus quam in temporalibus multipliciter collapsus.' *Ibid.* 44 (Wigmore, February 1424): 'nimium est collapsum.'
5 *Reg. T. Spofford*, 78–9.
6 *Ibid.* 243: 'Quidam Wallici montani et feroces.'
7 *Reg. T. Spofford*, 44, 64–76. The abbot, we are told (p. 66): 'habet venatorem et i mut [pack] de canibus venaticis et iiii lepores causa recreacionis cum fratres exeunt ad Seynes.'
8 *Ibid.* 216 (? August 1436).
9 *Reg. J. Stafford*, ed. T. Scott Holmes.

without the consent of the community and his lay council, and to remove all suspect women. This was not done, but the defaulting prior is soon found in retirement and was banished to Poughley.[1] At Muchelney, where grave excesses and scandals had been reported, Abbot Frome of Glastonbury was deputed as visitor. His efforts, of which no record survives, were ineffectual, and two years later, having again heard of scandals, the bishop himself visited the place. Here, as all over England, the open gate of the enclosure was indicated as an occasion of mischief.[2]

Stafford's successor was, even more than himself, the perfect type of political bishop. Thomas Bekynton (1443–65), long a royal servant, was Keeper of the Seal during the first months of his episcopate and a frequent absentee in subsequent years.[3] Often called away by royal summons when about to engage on a visitation, he did much of his work through his vicar-general and commissioners. His dealings with Keynsham are typical. In June 1447 the abbot and convent were cited to visitation, report having reached the highest in the realm, and the king himself, that the abbey was the scene of wilful homicide, mutilation, perjury and other fearful crimes, while the canons wandered abroad or quarrelled among themselves. A fortnight later, however, the bishop, hindered by arduous business, deputed his vicar-general to visit. No record survives.[4] Two years later (27 August 1449) there is another citation, and again, less than a fortnight after, the bishop has been called away by the king and appoints commissioners.[5] Two years later yet another commission is sent, and this time their injunctions have been preserved. They are the same in almost every particular as those issued to Taunton by Bekynton a month before; those to Bruton in the following year are of the same model, and taken together with a second and still longer set given to Keynsham in 1451 enable us to gauge the condition of the canons' houses.[6] At all three there is extreme irresponsibility on the part of the superior; the canons frequent houses in the town; there are suspect women visitors, and undue familiarity between groups designated as 'senior' and 'junior' canons, the latter being apparently those in training in the house and not yet in orders. The canons have private rooms, which at Keynsham are noted as places of nocturnal drinking and song, an occasion of gossip and intrigues, and the extent to which the privacy of the enclosure had vanished may be seen in the injunction that canons are not to entertain women in their rooms without explicit permission. The fashionable vice of profane swearing also receives notice. At Bruton hunting is castigated as an occasion of scandal, and the canons are to abstain from it save at holiday time and with special permission. Precise as these injunctions are, they had little effect, and the abbot was accused of non-observance. They were reiterated almost in

1 *Reg. J. Stafford*, I, 80–3, 92, 96. 2 *Ibid.* II, 181, 209.
3 *Reg. T. Bekynton*, ed. H. C. Maxwell-Lyte and M. C. B. Dawes.
4 *Reg. T. Bekynton*, I, 78. 5 *Ibid.* pp. 116, 117, 165.
6 *Ibid.* 162–4 (Taunton); 165–7 (Keynsham); 180–3 (Bruton); 260–4 (Keynsham).

entirety at Keynsham four years later (1455), and in 1458 the house was
cited to a visitation for neglecting them. By this time Bekynton was too
old and weak to visit, and therefore sent commissioners; Keynsham passes
out of sight with a complaint in 1458 that the injunctions are not kept there
or at any other of the houses visited.[1]

A similar lack of success had accompanied the bishop's efforts to get rid
of Prior Richard of Bruton earlier in his reign. The prior and community
were accused of dilapidation and incontinence. Bekynton, who had
appointed 14 December for his visit, found himself hindered a week before,
and sent the Carthusian prior of Witham and two doctors, with full power
to depose and interdict the prior if necessary. After a month a second
commission was dispatched to deal with the prior, but when he died
eighteen months later he was still in office.[2]

No injunctions survive for the more important houses of Glastonbury
and Bath, but Muchelney and Athelney, visited by Bekynton in 1455,
received long sets, in great part identical, but showing by their variants
and references to individuals that the visitation had been a careful one, and
that the injunctions were based on *comperta*. At neither house is grave
laxity revealed, but there are the familiar prohibitions of night-drinking,
entertainment by friends in the town, and admission of women. Blasphe-
mous swearing receives attention, and the injunctions, as at Ramsey under
Alnwick, are sanctioned by a scale of fines and loss of holidays.[3]

In the opening years of the fifteenth century some light is thrown after
a long interval upon the monasteries of West Wales in the register of Guy
Mone, bishop of St David's (1397–1407).[4] Mone, another royal servant,
held the Privy Seal in 1396–7 and was Treasurer in 1398 and again in
1402–3, but found time to visit some of the small houses in his diocese.
At Brecon and Pylle, as in England, he found the priors of small communities acting as sole proprietors of the funds, and at Pylle the superior
had been for years living in adultery with a kept mistress. He received
a reprimand, but was not deposed.[5] At Carmarthen he found exactly the
same abuses among the canons as in Somerset, and at the Tironian abbey
of St Dogmael's, now reduced to an abbot, three monks and some lay
brothers, observance is clearly at a low ebb though no major faults are
castigated. Local colour is given by an injunction to Dom Howel Lange
to drink neither wine nor metheglin.[6]

While Mone was in West Wales, Archbishop Arundel was engaged on

1 *Ibid.* 302, 308. 2 *Ibid.* 52, 57.
3 *Ibid.* 252–4 (Muchelney); 254–6 (Athelney). These injunctions (e.g. 'no monk,
especially J. Styland, is to strike anyone with a knife') appear, when compared with those
of Lincoln, unskilful attempts to frame a decree of universal scope while ensuring that the
guilty individual should not miss the point.
4 *The Episcopal Registers of the Diocese of St David's*, 1397–1518, I (1397–1407).
5 *Reg. G. Mone*, 361 *seqq.*, 375 (Pylle); 231–7 (Brecon).
6 *Ibid.* 237–47 (Carmarthen); 247–53 (St Dogmael's).

a metropolitical visitation of his province. Some injunctions for Ely survive; the house was flourishing, and the primate was chiefly concerned to secure the attendance of officials in choir and to confirm the treasury system and the supervision of estates. It is noteworthy that he expressly forbids the issue of clothes-money.[1]

The general conclusions to be drawn from all these early fifteenth-century visitations may be summarized as follows.

The typical diocesan bishop had been succeeded commonly enough by a royal servant who had often to absent himself on public business or attendance on the king. These men had naturally less time to devote to the affairs of religious houses and, it may be added, little interest in the monastic way of life; consequently, the work of visitation was often deputed to officials, whose injunctions had often less moral weight and practical force than those of the prelate himself. Some bishops, nevertheless (Alnwick is a case in point), still devoted much time and great pains to visitation, though even among such men as these there is visible a tendency to refrain from drastic measures and severe punishments; they were, in other words, content to leave things much as they found them.

The religious houses, for their part, were undoubtedly several degrees more distant from fervour than they had been in 1300. At almost all the barrier which was their physical separation from secular life had fallen. In some cases complete decadence was manifest; at others only a general want of zeal, showing itself in individuals as a readiness to escape in every direction from solitude and silence, and in the neglect as a body of the essentials of common life. No doubt there were still a number of the greater monasteries—St Albans, Durham, Christ Church—where a dignified life was still lived, but it must be confessed that the picture given at Peterborough and Ramsey is not a bright one.

1 *Ely Chapter Ordinances*, ed. S. J. A. Evans, 52–56.

CHAPTER XVI

THE SPIRITUAL LIFE OF THE FIFTEENTH CENTURY

The fifteenth century gave birth in England to no one who might continue the line of spiritual and mystical writers that had given such distinction to the previous age. Margery Kempe, whatever judgement may be passed on her, and however great her familiarity with the English mystical writers, is clearly of another vintage. Yet there is abundant evidence, from the *Book of Margery Kempe*, from the survival of manuscripts, and from incidental references, that the three great writers of the fourteenth century—Richard Rolle, the author of *The Cloud of Unknowing*, and Walter Hilton—continued to form the standard reading of those who desired instruction in the ways of the spirit.[1] It is, however, remarkable that, with few exceptions, all the surviving manuscripts of these authors come either from the libraries of the Carthusians and Bridgettines, or from the collections of devout lay folk. It is as if the monasteries of black and white monks clung to the traditional writers of the past, Cassian, Bernard, the Victorines and the rest, even though the devotional climate of the age had changed so greatly.

Of the spiritual life of the older orders and friars, indeed, we know next to nothing in this century. There is, however, one somewhat enigmatic manifestation which deserves mention: the race of Westminster recluses. Here, at the heart of what must always have been one of the most distracted and least secluded of communities, provision was by long tradition made for a recluse who had been and indeed still was, a monk of the house. Nothing has as yet been discovered of the origin of the Westminster *reclusorium*. Though it might be regarded as a faithful attempt to implement a commonly neglected passage in the Rule of St Benedict,[2] there is no evidence to suggest that a domestic recluse was normal, or indeed found anywhere else in the monasteries of England in the later Middle Ages.[3] The institution had, however, a respectable antiquity at Westminster; it is alluded to in 1246 and 1248 in a way that suggests that it was

---

[1] This fact, already implicitly recorded by the editors of the works concerned, was first given clear expression by the late R. W. Chambers, in his essay, *The Continuity of English Prose from Alfred to More* (1932).

[2] *S. Benedicti Regula*, c. 1: 'Heremitae qui non conversationis fervore novicio, sed monasterii probatione diuturna, qui didicerunt contra diabolum multorum solacio jam docti pugnare; et bene extructi fraterna ex acie ad singularem pugnam heremi securi...contra vitia...pugnare sufficiunt.'

[3] There were undoubtedly recluses within the precincts of other monasteries, usually having their cells in, or adjacent to, the church, as at Durham, Sherborne and Worcester, but it is not clear that they were monks of the house. Cf. R. M. Clay, *The Hermits and Anchorites of England*, esp. 80 *seqq*.

already of some standing,[1] and a few years later the recluse and his lodging are referred to in the customary of the house.[2] After that, there is a long silence in the records which does not necessarily imply the absence of a recluse, though it may well do so. In any case from the last decades of the fourteenth century onwards occurs what may be called the golden age of the Westminster *reclusorium*.

The presence of these recluses is indicated not only by references in the general sources of contemporary history, but also in the domestic account rolls of the house, and from *c.* 1380 onwards there is evidence of a succession of six or seven recluses. Thus in 1381 Richard II visited the Conqueror's shrine, and confessed to the recluse there,[3] and a few years later this anchorite received a legacy from a city merchant,[4] while in 1397 Thomas, earl of Warwick, when accused of treason, pleaded that he had acted in good faith, trusting in the holiness and wisdom of the abbot of St Albans and of the recluse of Westminster.[5] King Richard's interview was probably with Dan John Murymouth, who died in 1393; the earl of Warwick may have built his trust upon him, but by 1397 he had been succeeded, as it would seem, by Dan John London, who, after filling the posts of treasurer of Queen Eleanor's manors and warden of the misericord, had retired into the *reclusorium* soon after 1390, as the St Albans annalist implies after recording his death in 1429, after forty years as a hermit.[6] This is not the only mention of Dan John. Lord Scrope of Masham, another conspirator, left his rosary and some money in his will to John, the recluse of Westminster,[7] and he may also be the recluse of Westminster referred to in the *Revelation respecting Purgatory* of 1422.[8] There is, however, another candidate for the last distinction. Elsewhere in this volume an attempt has been made to disentangle the various contemporary Williams of Alnwick, two of whom were monks of St Albans.[9] One at least was also a recluse at Westminster before and after a short term

1 The recluse is referred to in *C. Lib. R.* 1245–51, p. 78 (1246), and in 1248 Henry III transferred a maintenance grant hitherto given to him, presumably after his death had occurred; cf. *Close R. Hen. III*, 1247–51, p. 24: 'Rex concessit Alicie que fuit uxor Magistri David quondam sirugici (*sic*) regis…illos tres obolos quos frater Nicolaus reclusus apud Westmonasterium habuit de elemosina regis constituta.'

2 *Customary of Westminster*, ed. E. M. Thompson, ii, 20.

3 J. Stow, *Chronicle of England* (ed. 1631), 286.

4 *Cal. of Wills, Court of Hustings*, ii, 398. The Westminster recluse has been studied by others besides E. H. Pearce, *Monks of Westminster*, notably by Miss R. M. Clay, *The Hermits and Anchorites of England*, 153–5, M. Deanesly, *The Incendium Amoris of Richard Rolle*, 118–21, and Sir Charles Peers and L. E. Tanner, 'On some recent discoveries in Westminster Abbey'. The account in the text is indebted to all these, but supplements and revises each in some respects.

5 *An English Chronicle*, ed. J. S. Davies, p. 11. The abbot was presumably Thomas de la Mare, who died September 1396.

6 *Amundesham*, i, 33: 'Obiit Dominus Johannes monachus Westmonasterii, et ibidem heremita reclusus per quadraginta annos extiterat.'

7 Rymer, *Foedera*, iv, ii, 131.

8 Lincoln, MS. Thornton, in C. Horstman's *Richard Rolle*, i, 384–5, cited by Miss Clay, *op. cit.* 154–5.

9 *V.* Appendix ii, pp. 367–8.

of a year or so as superior of the new royal foundation at Twickenham. The existence of two recluses exactly contemporary with each other at the same house is remarkable, but the fact seems to be established, and a historian of Westminster has himself noted such an occurrence some twenty years later.[1] It is certainly curious at first sight that a recluse should have come into residence at Westminster without leaving any trace of his name in the abbey muniments, but it is possible that he was supported by royal and other alms.[2]

There remains, however, a difficulty as to his place of lodging. The original *reclusorium* would seem to have been near the infirmary, probably to the east of the chapel of St Katherine near the wall of the palace,[3] and the appearance of the recluse on the infirmarer's rolls of the late fourteenth and early fifteenth centuries suggests that he was still lodged there.[4] It is, however, difficult to imagine two recluses side by side, or to suppose that a stranger to the house, such as William of Alnwick, would have retired from his own monastery to the infirmary of another. This difficulty may have been resolved by the suggestion recently put forward[5] that a *reclusorium* existed in the angle between the wall of the south ambulatory and the east wall of the south transept of the Abbey. This site can be paralleled from other anchor-holds, and would have been readily accessible to strangers seeking shrift or counsel. On this hypothesis there would have been two *reclusoria* of differing types at Westminster. This, at least from the middle of the fourteenth century onwards, is not entirely inconceivable. We may indeed wish to think—and we may be right in thinking—that the monks of Westminster concerned, after a life of service with Martha, wished to end their days in seclusion and recollection with her sister. On the other hand, the entries in the accounts of pensions granted to deserving brothers, and the allowances of candles, coals and faggots, with an occasional payment in cash, for the recluse, taken together with what we know from other sources of life at Westminster at the time, suggest that the inhabitant of the *reclusorium* near the infirmary (if indeed it was there) may have been just one more of the honourably pensioned brethren, who had deserved well of the republic and who wished to spend his last years in quarters somewhat more secluded than the other *stagiarii*, but not necessarily in any remarkable austerity. Whatever the truth of the

1 Pearce, *op. cit. s.vv.* Southbrook and Ocle.

2 A Westminster recluse is recorded as having paid in 1420 £4 (? in alms) on behalf of the king (*Issue Roll of Exchequer*, cited by Clay, *op. cit.* 154), and for a private legacy (*v. supra*, p. 220).

3 The *Customary* of Abbot Ware (II, 20), who held office 1258–83, in describing the duties of the *custos ordinis*, decrees that in the course of his tour of inspection (cf. *The Monastic Constitutions of Lanfranc*, ed. D. Knowles, 79) he shall proceed 'per totam curiam ...eciam usque ad reclusorium fratris nostri atque ulterius per Tamisiam, si voluerit.' *V.* also H. F. Westlake, *Westminster Abbey*, II, 336–8.

4 In the convent accounts the infirmarer appears as supplying the recluse with the allowance (12 lb. per annum) of candles normally given to each inmate of the infirmary.

5 By Peers and Tanner, *art. cit.*

matter, the line would seem to have ended with Walter Coggeshall, recluse from 1435 till 1432/3, who had been cellarer, granator, and 'warden of the new work', and Richard Southbrook (1445/6–1458/9), who had been a scholar at Oxford and later precentor, though for some years of the latter's tenure a second recluse, John Ocle (1445/6–1448/9) is noted.

The Westminster recluses, though they are seemingly without exact parallel in the monasteries of their day, are not an isolated phenomenon. Readers of *The Book of Margery Kempe* will recall that a friar-recluse in the Dominican house at King's Lynn was one of her earliest and most trusted confessors and directors. He was a trained theologian, well read also in spiritual literature. A successor in the same cell was equally distinguished; he employed his leisure in learned lexicography. Another recluse in Margery's story was the black monk, Thomas Brackley, a recluse in the Chapel of the Fields at Norwich.[1] It is noteworthy that he was not a monk of Norwich, and lived at a distance from the cathedral priory, while on the other hand the Chapel of the Fields was the focus of a remarkable group of priests well abreast of the devotional life of their times.

These three instances of Westminster, Lynn and Norwich, to which may be added that of St Albans, in all of which we see recluses who are men of gifts and influence, are indeed very striking. They suggest, as do the new foundations of Carthusian monks, that there was a strong contemporary current setting towards the solitary life, that it was often felt most by those of learning or strong personality, and that it found no satisfaction in the normal claustral life. It is probable that if all records had survived we should find other examples in cities such as Bristol, Coventry and York. True as this may be, it is nevertheless worth remembering that in all ages like attracts like, and that a saint, real or reputed, comes into contact sooner or later with most of the leading figures in the spiritual life of his day. The fact, therefore, that a Thomas Fishbourne, a William of Alnwick or a Dominican recluse has a finger in many pies may well be an indication that they and their like were rare. Yet we should probably do well to remember that it is in the anchor-hold, rather than in the cloister, that the hidden saints of the fifteenth century are to be found.

The history of English spirituality between 1350 and 1500 has yet to be written.[2] We have glanced in an earlier chapter at some of the writers who make up the group of English mystics, and we have seen that the two greatest, the author of *The Cloud of Unknowing* and Walter Hilton, have an intellectual and emotional austerity, and a sense of the transcendence of supernatural reality, which are derived from some of the purest sources of theological and ascetical tradition. This stream continued to flow till the reign of Henry VIII, but there is some evidence that from the begin-

---

1 For these *v. supra*, pp. 198–200.
2 Miss H. E. Allen has long been engaged on a study of the influences from abroad that were at work in the devout circles where Margery Kempe moved, and Mr F. R. Johnston has studied the cult of St Bridget and her Revelations in this country.

ning of the fifteenth century onwards it was contaminated by another current, that of a more emotional and idiosyncratic devotion, manifesting itself in visions, revelations and unusual behaviour, deriving partly from one aspect of the teaching of Ruysbroeck and Suso and the other mystical writers, and partly from the influence of some of the women saints of the fourteenth century, such as Angela of Foligno, Dorothea of Prussia and Bridget of Sweden.[1] The most familiar example of this type in England is Margery Kempe, whose spiritual experiences lie outside our province, and it seems to have flourished chiefly in individual groups in the more important towns.

The corporate transmission of the spiritual teaching of the fourteenth century, both English and Flemish, was the work of the Carthusians. A glance at the list of the surviving manuscripts of the English mystics is enough to show this in their regard. Thus from the London Charterhouse come two copies of *The Cloud*, two of Hilton, and *The Mirror of Simple Souls*; from Sheen two Rolles and two Hiltons; from Beauvale a Rolle; and from Mount Grace *The Cloud*, *The Mirror* and *The Book of Margery Kempe*;[2] and this in spite of indications that the Carthusian spirituality had begun to admit elements less pure in tradition than Cassian and the writings of the early priors of the Grande Chartreuse. Moreover, we know from the evidence of manuscripts that *The Cloud* was copied more than once, and assiduously read in the London Charterhouse until the Dissolution.

From the Charterhouses, also, come almost the only indications of a life of unusual fervour in the monastic world of the time. At the London Charterhouse Dan John Homersley and others were models whom the next generation was to remember; from Hinton at the same time comes the story of Dan Stephen's vision of the Magdalen,[3] while Sheen from the first was an exemplary house. Above all others, however, the distant Mount Grace seems to have absorbed most fully both the old English teaching and the spirit of the Flemish mystics and the *devotio moderna*, with its direct, loving, almost pietistic approach to Jesus, the crucified lover of the soul. Already in the early decades of the century Prior Nicholas Love had translated and adapted St Bonaventure's meditative Life of Christ,[4] and towards the end of the century Mount Grace was the home of another translator who was also an ardent seeker after the pearl of price that could only be found in solitude. In his writings, at least for a moment, the veil is lifted which, as the historian of the English

1 Miss Allen in her Prefatory Note (pp. lix–lx) to *The Book of Margery Kempe* gives a list of the principal women saints whose writings and examples may have been known to Margery.

2 *V*. N. Ker, *Medieval Libraries*.

3 For a full account *v*. E. M. Thompson, *A history of the Somerset Carthusians*, 270–4. Visions, real or imaginary, are no proof of sanctity, but in their context they may on occasion indicate an atmosphere of spiritual endeavour.

4 *The Mirroir of the blessed lyf of Jesu Christ*. This is a free translation of St Bonaventure's *Meditationes*.

Carthusians lamented, seemed to hide from us all glimpses of the inner life of the monks.

Richard Furth, or Richard Methley as he was called,[1] came no doubt from the village of that name seven miles south-west of Leeds on the road to Pontefract; he would thus have grown up less than fifteen miles from Richard Rolle's Hampole. He has contrived in his short treatises to give us several interesting personal details. He was born in 1451/2 and became a Carthusian at the age of twenty-five.[2] He owed his vocation, so he liked to believe, to an aged and paralysed ancress to whom he had given a large alms a few days before her death; within three months he had entered the Charterhouse, and each year as the feast of St Leonard came round (6 Nov.) he remembered the ancress, whose cell had been attached to a chapel with that dedication.[3]

Methley spent much of his free time in writing in his cell. In the short autobiographical tract *Refectorium salutis*, which covers almost day by day the weeks between 6 October and 15 December 1487, he mentions two other works, one 'On the name of Mary and the Sacrament of the Altar', and the other, entitled *Trivium excellencie*, on the Compassion of the Blessed Virgin. There exist in addition the tract *Scola amoris languidi*,[4] a translation into Latin of *The Cloud of Unknowing* and a copy in his writing of *The Mirror of Simple Souls*. He was aware of his predecessors, and his writings contain echoes of Rolle[5] and *The Cloud*,[6] and perhaps also of Hilton.[7] His work was much on his mind, so much so that once when praying that he might be dissolved and be with Christ the reflection came that if his prayer were immediately heard he would leave some of his writings uncorrected for others to read. This and other passages[8] have a *naïveté* which suggests that Methley, at least at this period of his life, had not yet attained to the wisdom of the saints, but it would be wholly unjust to dismiss him as merely an emotional and excitable dreamer.

1 Methley's compositions were noted by M. R. James in his *Catalogue of MSS. of Trinity College, Cambridge*, III, no. 1160, pp. 176–8 (MS. O 2. 56) and *Catalogue of MSS. of Pembroke College, Cambridge*, pp. 197–9 (MS. 223). Miss H. E. Allen had a short notice of him in *Writings ascribed to Richard Rolle*, 416–17. My attention was directed to Methley by Dom Aelred Watkin; my thanks are due to him and to Dom Dominic Gaisford who transcribed part of the Trinity MS., who allowed me to use the transcripts.

2 Trinity College, Cambridge, MS. O 2. 56, fo. 30: 'Anno ejusdem 1485 etatis mee ut arbitror tricesimo quarto ingressionis in ordinem cartusiensem nono.'

3 *Ibid.* 59ᵛ–60.

4 This tract, though its immediate ancestry is Flemish, has distant echoes of Augustine in its opening sentence (fo. 1): 'Omnium creaturarum summum studium est amare et amari.' Cf. Augustine, *Confessions*, II, 2: 'Et quid erat, quod me delectabat, nisi amare et amari?'

5 *Refectorium salutis*, fo. 56: 'Sicut et ille almus Ricardus dictus de Hampol.'

6 The passage from the *Scola amoris* quoted below contains clear reminiscences of the instruction on prayer by the author of *The Cloud* (ch. xxxviii), as does the marginal reference on fo. 7ᵛ to St Gregory (cf. *The Cloud*, ch. lxxv).

7 As, e.g. in his use (*Scola amoris*, fo. 1) of 'amor sensibilis' with a mystical connotation which seems to reflect Hilton's favourite distinction between reformation in faith and in feeling.

8 E.g. the suggestion of diabolical agency (fo. 65), and his desire (fo. 66) to die *speciali miraculoso modo* (which in the context seems to mean by excess of mystical love). There are other passages of a similar character in the other treatises.

There are a number of autobiographical passages in which he describes experiences which, if not in the full sense mystical, are at least on the fringe and threshold of the contemplative life. Perhaps the most explicit is the following:

Ineffable is the yearning of love. But if naught were said of it haply some might say that it was a thing of naught; and so, following God's will, I will set out as best I can what I have experienced. And if I cannot tell it as it is, yet I do not doubt that what I am about to say is true. Since, then, one who has had experience bids thanksgiving be made to God, he who has not experienced it should not impugn it out of envy for the solitary.

On the feast of St Peter in Chains [1 August] I was in the church at Mount Grace, and after celebrating Mass was engaged upon thanksgiving in prayer and meditation, when God visited me in power, and I yearned with love so as almost to give up the ghost. How this could be I will tell you, my brethren, as best I can by the grace of God. Love and longing for the Beloved raised me in spirit into heaven, so that save for this mortal life nothing (so far as I know) would have been lacking to me of the glory of God Who sitteth on the throne. Then did I forget all pain and fear and deliberate thought of any thing, and even of the Creator. And as men who fear the peril of fire do not cry 'Fire hath come upon my house; come ye and help me', since in their strait and agony they can scarce speak a single word, but cry 'Fire, Fire, Fire!' or, if their fear be greater they cry 'Ah! Ah! Ah!', wishing to impart their peril in this single cry, so I, in my poor way. For first I oft commended my soul to God, saying: 'Into thy hands,' either in words or (as I think rather) in spirit. But as the pain of love grew more powerful I could scarce have any thought at all, forming within my spirit these words: 'Love! Love! Love!' And at last, ceasing from this, I deemed that I would wholly yield up my soul, singing, rather than crying, in spirit through joy: 'Ah! Ah! Ah!'[1]

Such experiences became frequent to Methley; whether they changed into a deeper and more truly mystical contemplation we do not know. The absence of any further record after 1491 might suggest that he died young.[2] However this may be, he opens for a moment for us the door of his cell. We see him praying before the stone statue of Our Lady above the altar

---

1 *Scola amoris*, fos. 7–7ᵛ. Cf. St John of the Cross, *Spiritual Canticle* (first redaction), stanza i, § 9: 'And at this season of love there takes place this stirring of these reins of the desires of the will, which is much like to a torture of yearning to see God, so much so that the rigour wherewith love treats the soul seems to it intolerable...because it is left thus wounded and grieving, and has not been wounded further, even to the point of death.' Also *Dark Night of the Soul*, Book I, ch. xi, § 1: 'At times...the yearnings for God become so great in the soul that...the natural powers seem to be fading away.' These passages, as their position in St John's scheme shows, refer to initial stages of the contemplative life.

2 The *Scola* was written in 1485; the experiences of the *Refectorium salutis* date from two years later, *sc.* 1487. Methley was living at least as late as 8 December 1491, when the transcription of the *Mirror of Simple Souls* was completed. (James, *Pembroke College, Cambridge, MSS.,* 198–9.) In her introduction to *The Mirror* (London, 1928), Clare Kirchberger states (p. xxiv n.) that he died as vicar (= subprior) of Mount Grace in 1528. She gives no references for this. That his memory was held in high regard is shown by marginal notes in the manuscript of *The Book of Margery Kempe* indicating similarities between Margery and Methley.

in his oratory, feeling the wind that entered through the new unfinished window he caused to be made to let in more light and air, thanking God each morning, as he put on his habit, for the gift of his Carthusian vocation, and bearing witness to the esteem in which the order was held by all.[1] It may be he had not fully learnt the strength that lies in silence; *secretum meum mihi* were words dear to the earlier saints of his order, whose numbers who shall tell? It may be also that he had not learnt that the darkness of faith is the nearest way to God. Yet at the least he was a sincere and earnest monk who had left all things for the treasure hidden in the solitude of that quiet cloister shadowed by the hanging oaks on the skirt of the high moors.

1 *Refectorium salutis*, fo. 57ᵛ: 'Cogitare cepi quanta cum aviditate solent homines petere pro caritate ut Carthusienses orent pro se eorumve carorum animabus ob ordinis sanctitatem.'

Part Two

The Institutional Background

CHAPTER XVII

RECRUITMENT, EMPLOYMENT AND
THE HORARIUM

Although biographical accounts and items of personal information are rare in the later medieval period, it is possible to arrive at a fairly clear estimate of the local origin, and at a less clear one of the social standing, of recruits to the monasteries of black monks. Detailed information about the Cistercians and the canons black and white is more scanty, but all indications tend to show that there was no great difference between them and the black monks in the provenance and class of their recruits.

From the end of the twelfth century it was common, and in the fourteenth and fifteenth centuries all but universal, for a monk to be known by his own Christian name specified by his place of origin: e.g. William of London. Only those of distinguished family, such as Thomas de la Mare, and, from the end of the fourteenth century onwards, a growing number of townsfolk, were known by a family surname, but even when, in the early sixteenth century, this custom was becoming more general, it was still common for a monk to be known by his place of origin, as can be seen when, for example, the William of Boston who appears at a visitation figures as William Perkins in a pension list a few years later. As we possess complete lists of the monks of Christ Church, Canterbury, Westminster and Durham[1]—three of the largest and most distinguished houses in the country—and numerous shorter lists and references to monks of many other houses, we can determine the provenance of a very large cross-section of the monastic population. For every house the conclusion is the same: the vast majority of recruits came from the manors and estates owned by the monastery and (in the case of urban sites) from the town or city and its environs; a smaller group came from other cities, London above all; only a small minority bore family names or were strangers from afar. The conclusion must be that a majority of the monks either entered the monastery from the town at its gates or were 'discovered', so to say, and sent up to the almonry school or noviciate by monastic officials on tour of the abbey manors and dependent priories. The number of recruits of standing from distant and even from foreign parts, which was appreciable in the century after the Conquest, was negligible in the fifteenth century.

The social status of these recruits is less easy to discover, but it is probably safe to say that a majority were sons of burgesses or of the

---

1 The Canterbury lists were published, with brief notes, by W. G. Searle in *Cambridge Archaeological Society Publications*, XXXIV (1902); those of Westminster, more elaborately annotated, by E. H. Pearce, *Monks of Westminster*; those of Durham have been collected, but not yet published, by Canon S. L. Greenslade. Searle's Canterbury list is far from complete, but this does not affect the case.

middle and lower ranks of rural landowners and freemen. No English house ever attempted, or was ever in a position to attempt, to make itself into a preserve for the sons of noble or at least knightly families, as did certain abbeys on the Continent at one time or another. St Albans was second only to Westminster in its close connexion with royal and noble patrons, but there are few known instances of monks of family there. We know the origins of four celebrated abbots of the period: Richard of Wallingford (1308–35) was the son of a blacksmith; Michael de Mentmore (1335–49) came of middle-class country stock; Thomas de la Mare (1349–96) was of distinguished, but not noble lineage;[1] John Whetham-stede (1420–65) was the son of a small landowner whose father had come south from Cheshire to better himself;[2] his mother was a Mackery of Mackery End in Hertfordshire. Early in the fourteenth century we hear of the sons of townspeople becoming monks at St Albans,[3] and at both Westminster and Canterbury the names of a large majority of the monks suggest a rural and therefore a relatively humble origin.

Whereas in the twelfth century members of the feudal families and even of royal blood are found in the monasteries, in the later centuries their presence is very rare. The familiar instance of the great abbot of St Albans must not mislead; it is hard to find a parallel in any house between his death and the Dissolution, even in an age when Beauforts and Scropes and Courtenays were giving their sons to the Church. It should not, indeed, be forgotten that one of his brothers was abbot of the Austin canons at Missenden, and two other brothers were monks in private station at St Albans and Thetford. With a sister a nun at Pré they were a remarkable family, but they were not typical of their age, still less of the age that followed.[4] There is no evidence that the aristocracy who fought in the French wars and the Wars of the Roses bred a race comparable to that of the great recusant families of the early seventeenth century, the Beding-fields, Jerninghams, Dormers and Welds, whose sons and daughters populated the colleges and convents of Douai, Ghent and Brussels. So far as can be seen, there are no aristocratic names at Christ Church, and at Westminster, which might be supposed to attract courtly recruits, only three names of note occur: Thomas Pomerai, said to be the illegitimate son of a nobleman; Thomas Clifford, probably fifth son of the Lord Clifford who was slain at St Albans in 1465; and Edward Bridgewater, possibly the son of Owen Tudor and Queen Katherine.[5]

While the vast majority entered as boys between eighteen and twenty,[6]

1 *GASA*, ii, 181, 299, 372.

2 *Monasticon*, ii, 199, n. e, and MS. cited by Miss Hodges in an unpublished Manchester thesis.   3 *GASA*, ii, 202.

4 For the relatives of Abbot Thomas within and without the cloister, *v. GASA*, ii, 371–3.

5 Pearce, *op. cit.* 138 (1421–2), 159–60 (1462–3), 161 (1465–6), 7; cf. M. R. James and J. A. Robinson, *The MSS. of Westminster Abbey*, 97 *seqq.*

6 The rule 'infra vicesimum annum [i.e. before the nineteenth birthday] monachi non recipiantur [*sc.* ad professionem]' was unchanged from the first chapter in 1218 till the end, three hundred years later, but the clause immediately following: 'nisi commendabilis

often after passing several years in the almonry school, there were a few late entrants. Occasionally they were men of note, with a career behind them, but it is not always clear that their motives were wholly spiritual. Thus a Master John Kyngton, a lawyer and chancellor of the Queen, who became a monk at Canterbury in 1408 and was seen there by Margery Kempe, showed in his comfortable quarters little of the monk's life, and enjoyed a leisurely retirement.[1] Another late arrival, Master Ralph Selby, took the habit at Westminster in 1398/9 after filling the offices of subdean of York and archdeacon of Buckingham, but here again the possession of a papal indult enabling him to visit the archdeaconry by deputy suggests no very sharp severance of ties with his previous life.[2] Yet another trickle of recruitment came from other orders; at Canterbury half a dozen ex-canons joined in a century and a half; at Westminster only one or two are noted.

The modern practice of taking a new name from a patron saint on entering religion had not begun in the true medieval period. The monk was known by his Christian name, and as the number of these in common use was extremely limited, the toponymic or surname of provenance was by no means superfluous. It has been reckoned that of the seven hundred-odd monks of Christ Church whose names are known, four hundred and fifty-one, or nearly two-thirds, bore one of the six names John, Henry, Richard, Robert, Thomas and William.[3] In the twelfth and thirteenth centuries the surname of origin was common without the monastery also, as so many of our present surnames witness, but in the fourteenth and fifteenth centuries family or occupational names became more common in the country at large, and were universal for the upper and middle classes by the middle of the fifteenth century. Many of these began to find their way into monastic lists, but the old custom persisted to the end, as may be seen by a comparison of lists of monks drawn up shortly before the Dissolution, with those of the same men compiled by the officials charged with paying their pensions; the family name almost always takes the place of the name of provenance, where this existed. Thus, to take a single example, the family name of the penultimate prior of Worcester was Peers, but in all the documents of his religious life he is William More, from the hamlet of his origin.

Round about the year 1500 a sudden change of fashion is noticeable. Many of the brethren now bear names which were clearly assumed on entering religion and in some cases follow their Christian names. These names are of two types. The one is made up of the names of saints, usually

---

utilitas vel necessitas aliud induxerit', left a wide loophole. The usual age for beginning the noviciate was eighteen, though there was a move in 1279 to exclude all under twenty-one. Cf. *MC*, I, 10, 118. Clothing at fifteen was common in the fifteenth century (*LV*, I, 32).

1 *Chronicle of John Stone*, ed. W. G. Searle, 7–8; cf, *The Book of Margery Kempe*, ed. W. Butler-Bowdon, 54 *seqq.*; ed. Meech and Allen, 27.

2 Pearce, *op. cit.* 128; cf. *ibid.* 34.   3 *Ibid.* 36.

either fathers of the Church or national figures. Thus at Westminster Gregory, Austin, Jerome, Ambrose, Bernard, Chrysostom, Laurence and Benet occur, and at Christ Church Ambrose, Clement, Jerome, Gregory, Benet, Alban, Wilfrid, Anselm and Becket.[1] At Glastonbury the collection has a more antiquarian ring and includes Arimathea, Arthur, Ceolfrid, Joseph, Dunstan, Edgar, Wilfrid, Alphege, Kentwin, Neot, Indract and Fagas; the list is echoed at the neighbouring Athelney with Alfred, Athelstan, Edgar and Ethelwyn.[2] The fashion even reached rustic Bardney, where in 1525, besides Austin, Jerome, Gregory and Ambrose are found Maurus, Botolph and Aidan.[3] More curious still is another group of names found at Westminster, harbinger of Puritan taste: Goodhaps, Vertue, Charity, Goodluck, Grace, Faith, Hope, Patience, Verity, Mercy and Meekness. At other houses old fashions persisted to the end.

The novice, usually between seventeen and twenty-one years of age, when clothed with the habit passed under the care of one of the senior monks who held no administrative office, and who was known in most houses as the master of the novices (*magister noviciorum*) and at Canterbury at least as the master of observance (*magister ordinis*).[4] At Christ Church certainly, and at Westminster probably, the master held office for a year at a time, having charge, that is, of the recruits of a single year from clothing to profession, but there is evidence that he returned to the same post a year or two later. The emphasis laid on spiritual training in the Rule, which in post-Tridentine religious orders was developed into something of a spiritual technique, rarely appears in medieval English documents of the black monks. They insist rather on the learning of the customs and liturgical observances of the house. In earlier centuries a large part of the novice's time had been taken up in learning by heart almost all the usual psalmody, lessons and chant, and examination in this preceded, and might delay, profession. These demands were gradually modified, partly owing to difficulty found in memorizing by the older recruits of the thirteenth century, and an unwillingness on the part of university-trained men to submit to such a discipline, but partly also because the elaboration of musical notation and the provision of adequate lights in choir removed the necessity for so much memory work.[5] Its place was taken, in a world that was rapidly developing its educational

---

1 See lists in Pearce, *op. cit.* and Searle, *op. cit.*
2 *Visitations of Somerset Religious Houses*, ed. H. C. Maxwell-Lyte, 211–13.
3 *DV*, II, 78–9.
4 That, at least, seems a permissible inference since the compilers of the Canterbury list, edited by Searle, insert each year the name of the *magister ordinis* before that of the novices. It is worth remarking that as late as 1517 the juniors at Eynsham are not to learn grammar or chant or anything else 'quousque psalterium cordetenus recordaverint et eciam impnos ac alia officia perfecte sciverint' (*DV*, II, 138–9).
5 *V. RO*, I, 285–6 and *MC*, index *s.v.* 'Novices'. The conservatives deplored the introduction of lights in choir: 'unde multi minus bene reddere servitium curaverunt et minus sciverunt' (*GASA*, II, 106).

resources, by instructions of the type given in the arts course at univer-sities. At the same time, the novice learnt the technique of formal writing and 'flourishing' and of preparing the materials for that and for illumina-tion. His 'school' was in an alley of the cloister, often the west, where the master had his official seat and where, as at Durham, a small collection of books existed and, as marks elsewhere on the stones still show, the novices played parlour games. The period of training and seclusion from the community lasted till ordination, which usually took place after some seven years.[1] During this time, at least at some houses, the novice received none of the regular or occasional payments given to the monks for clothes, spices and the rest, though he attended chapter, where as a professed monk he had certain rights. Ordination marked his emergence from tutelage, and the day of his first Mass was signalized by the reception of a present of money from the obedientiaries and a feast of congratulation.[2]

At ordination the monk passed fully into the life of the house, and became eligible for any of the various offices and employments of the community. Here his prospects were very different from those of his predecessors in the days of Lanfranc. Then, a monk could have looked forward to a long series of years, perhaps a whole lifetime, passed as a monk of the cloister; he would then have been occupied, when not engaged in community duties in church or chapter, partly in reading, and partly in copying or illuminating and binding all kinds of books. Only relatively few of the community were then engaged in administrative or whole-time official work. Gradually, as we have seen elsewhere, administration, and in particular the supervision of estates came to claim a large number of monks, while a century later the career of a student, with long years of residence at a university, opened up for another type of mind. It is there-fore natural to ask ourselves what proportion of monks at a large abbey would now remain for most or for all their lives without either academic or administrative occupations.

With many hundreds of houses, varying indefinitely in size and com-mitments and personnel, it is clear that a simple answer cannot be given. For one great abbey, however, the muniments are so extensive that a devoted scholar has been able to establish something approaching to reliable statistics for the fourteenth and fifteenth centuries. Of the forty-nine monks of Westminster in residence in 1297/8 twenty can be shown to have held office of one kind or another during their monastic careers; in 1399/1400 the corresponding figures are fifty-nine and twenty-seven.[3] These figures must be taken as considerably below the true numbers, for there were a number of offices or employments such as master of novices,

1 This was the period at Durham; cf. *Rites of Durham*, ed. (1) J. Raine, 81; ed. (2) J. T. Fowler, 96.
2 This present is an event which helped Pearce to date the careers of the Westminster monks.
3 Pearce, *op. cit.* introduction, 31–2.

master of the claustral school, second and third priors and confessors, to say nothing of assistants and deputies to many of the major officials, which do not appear in the Westminster accounts. In addition, there were the monks studying at Oxford and the unascertainable number who died young or who left the house for one reason or another. When allowance is made for all these eventualities, the chances were distinctly in favour of a monk receiving at some time in his mature years an administrative or official position.

Nevertheless, there were in a large house at any given time a considerable number of priest-monks—less than half the whole community, however—who had no office. How did they employ their time in the later Middle Ages? If we turn for guidance to the constitutions governing their life, we find the chapter of 1343 laying down the regulation that had long been traditional: abbots and priors shall see that the monks of the cloister are, in lieu of manual work, occupied according to their abilities in various tasks, such as studying, reading, and writing, correcting, illuminating and binding books.[1] This was reiterated without change in the statutes of 1444 and undoubtedly remained in force till the end.[2] It is a commonplace of recent writers on monastic history that manuscripts of the classics and general traditional literature were no longer copied as in the twelfth century, that illumination had passed from the monasteries and had become commercialized and that the need for manuscript books became progressively less after the invention of printing. All this is true, yet it would seem also true that writing, as well as bookbinding, continued to be a claustral occupation which at all large houses, and probably also at most smaller ones, was practised by at least several of the monks. Service books in particular were the work of monks to the end. Thus c. 1380 we have the name of a monk of St Albans who wrote six large books of the kind;[3] the writers of the Sherborne and Westminster (Litlington) missals were probably monks;[4] and in 1438 the monks of St Albans were at work on a series of great antiphoners.[5] At about the same time a monk of the London Charterhouse is seen 'incessantly writing sacred books for the church, for the frater and for the cell',[6] while in 1491 the presence of *scriptores* among the canons of a Premonstratensian abbey is taken as normal by Bishop Redman.[7] In the very last years at Worcester a monk is employed by the

1 *MC*, II, 51: 'Abbates...monachos suos claustrales loco operis manualis...certis facient exerciciis occupari, videlicet studendo, legendo, librosque scribendo, corrigendo, illuminando pariter et ligando.' The word *legendo* (i.e. reading with commentary to students; cf. the 'reader' at universities) is not in the corresponding decree of the chapter of 1277 (*MC*, I, 74).

2 *MC*, II, 205.   3 *VCH, Herts*, IV, 395.

4 James and Robinson, *op. cit.* 8; Pearce, *op. cit.* 120 and index, *s.v.* For the Sherborne Missal *v. infra*, p. 278.   5 *Amundesham*, II, 198.

6 Cf. the Charterhouse Register in W. H. St J. Hope, *The London Charterhouse*, 82: 'Pater domnus Johannes Homersley...sacros libros pro ecclesia pro refectorio et pro cella incessanter scribebat.'

7 *Collectanea Anglo-Premonstratensia*, ed. F. A. Gasquet, III, 113: 'qui ibidem scriptores sunt...'.

prior to write and 'flourish' his register, and to bind and repair books in the library, though it is worth remarking that the prior had the books of his chapel written and illuminated by a skilled secular priest,[1] and the circumstances both of the Worcester and of the Premonstratensian employments suggest that by this time such work was regarded as an unusual labour to be rewarded rather than as a daily task to be taken as a matter of course, though writing (which may, however, imply composition) is noted as a current employment of the monks of Durham at this time.[2]

Besides every stage in the production of books, other minor crafts continued intermittently to be monastic occupations. In the early fifteenth century those among the young monks of St Albans on holiday at Redburn who had no bent for study were to be taught some manual craft;[3] a few decades earlier we hear of the abbey clock and the church organ being repaired by the brethren.[4] Twenty or thirty years later a monk of Christ Church, Canterbury is noted for his unusual skill in embroidery and thirty years later still another monk there is gifted with the same talent.[5] On the eve of the Dissolution Wolsey's commissary, Dr Allen, is found somewhat unexpectedly recommending the practice of manual crafts at Wenlock, and it is noteworthy that one at least of that community was able to turn his hand with success to a whole series of very technical pursuits.[6] In the very last hour the commissioners of 1536 found at St James, Northampton, almost every member of the community practised either embroidery, writing, carving or painting.[7]

When a monk had no capacity for such quasi-manual employments or for professional theology there was the basic employment of reading and study. At Durham, so the account goes, all the monks 'studied upon there books every one in his carrell all the afternoon'.[8] This study was in intention on Scripture and theology and led to the 'writing of good and

1 *Journal of Prior William More*, ed. E. S. Fegan, 74, 79–80, 82, 116, 256–62, 322, 324.

2 *Rites of Durham*, (1), 74; (2), 88. The monks were 'alwaies most vertuouslie occupied, ...either writing of good and goddly wourkes or studying the Holie Scriptures'.

3 *Amundesham*, II, 210: 'aliquid vel alicujus liberalis scientiae vel aliter alicujus artis mechanicae'.

4 *VCH, Herts*, IV, 395.

5 *Chronicle of John Stone*, 10 (1419): 'Erat [Thos. Selmiston] in arte brudatoria artifex curiosissimus, in toto regno non habens sibi similem.' Cf. *ibid.* 47 (1449).

6 Rose Graham, 'Roland Gosenell, Prior of Wenlock, 1521–6', 142: 'In primis consulitur quod artes mechanice licite et honeste inter commonachos exerceatur.' Dr Graham cites (*ibid.* 144–5) the obituary notice of William Corfill, sacrist in 1520, where his talents as organ-maker, clock-maker, weaver, bell-founder, etc., are extolled. It is a curious coincidence, if no more, that in 1489 Abbot Estney of Westminster, in a testimonial letter for a monk of his transferring to Much Wenlock, notes that he is 'a faire writer, a florissher and maker of capitall letters'. Pearce, *op. cit.* 163.

7 *Letters relating to the Suppression of the Monasteries*, ed. T. Wright, no. lxii (George Giffard to Cromwell, 19 June 1536): 'Ther ys nott oon religious person thear butt that He can and dothe use eyther inbrotheryng, wrytyng bookes with verey ffayre haund, makyng ther own garnementes, karvyng, payntyng or graffyng [i.e. sculptor's work].'

8 *Rites of Durham* (1) 70; (2) 83. Even if the assiduity attributed to the Durham monks is open to question, the fact of their employment remains.

goddly books', but there is evidence that all through the later Middle Ages the friars and monks prosecuted private studies of various kinds, as numerous collections of books left to the library or mentioned in inventories of the effects of a deceased brother show.[1]

Medicine had in the early Middle Ages been a frequent subject of study, and in the early twelfth century monks who had as young men studied at a medical school, or at least absorbed the new learning on the subject, often had considerable reputations. Medical practice was repeatedly forbidden by councils both as a lucrative and therefore unmonastic occupation and also as leading to attendance upon women. Moreover, as medicine became one of the principal subjects of study at the universities it became impossible for a self-taught monk to compete with the experts. Nevertheless most monasteries had a collection of old medical classics, as well as a constant supply of clinical cases in the infirmary, and monks continued to acquire at least a book-learning on the subject. Although the black monks employed a medical practitioner, canons were, on occasion, allowed to try their surgical skill out on their confrères.[2]

Mathematics, as a part of the new education, especially at Oxford, continued for long to appeal to certain minds. In the early fourteenth century the young Richard of Wallingford had a passion for it, and later as abbot repented of his enthusiasm.[3] Mathematics led naturally to astronomy, for which the same abbot had a high reputation. It also led, in the late thirteenth and early fourteenth centuries, to the pseudo-science of astrology, in which also Wallingford excelled. This remained a favourite pursuit for long, and at the end of the fourteenth century the well-known theologian, Simon of Sutherey, monk of St Albans, was an adept.[4] Early in the same century another pseudo-science, alchemy, came into vogue. This was a peculiarly costly and absorbing pursuit, with a discovery of vast import lurking just out of sight, comparable in these respects, at least, with some departments of modern scientific research. As early as 1320 it had got William de Somerton, prior of Binham, into debts and troubles of all kinds.[5] Sixty years later it attracted the Augustinian friar, John Erghome, and in 1440 an abbot of Leicester was deeply involved.[6] Chaucer's canon, a contemporary of Erghome, was no doubt drawn from life. Beneath alchemy lay the occult sciences and witchcraft, which now and again leave traces in the visitation documents.

Finally, a word must be said of heavy manual work, the tasks of the unskilled labourer in the field or on a building. As regards the black

---

1 *V. infra*, pp. 340–1.

2 *MC*, II, 48; III, 84, 291. Cf. *LV*, I, 90 (Newnham), where John Rothwell is not to practise surgery save on his brethren.

3 *GASA*, II, 182.

4 *Amundesham*, II, 305. There is, however, some confusion here between astronomy and astrology.

5 *GASA*, II, 132.   6 *LV*, II, 211–12.

monks, one of the few references in the fourteenth and fifteenth centuries is that to the digging of the foundations of the Lady Chapel at Ely by John of Wisbech and other monks *c*. 1321.[1] No doubt there were similar happenings elsewhere, but work of this kind was occasional and voluntary, when the need for labour was urgent and enthusiasm ran high. At the same time, two casual references, preserved almost by chance, warn us that it may always have been customary in the houses deep in the fields for the monks, or at least the young monks, to lend a hand at harvest time. The one comes from Eynsham, where one of the charges against the abbot at a visitation *c*. 1363–6, was that of allowing the novices, when helping with the hay, to mingle with the common labourers.[2] The other, a century and a half later, is from the Lincolnshire house of Humberstone, and is again a charge against an abbot. Complaint is made that he works like a layman in the hay and grain harvests, and compels all his monks to do likewise, from eight in the morning till five or six in the afternoon. This visitation was held at the end of June, and one deponent, with painful memories still undimmed by time, and a surge of emotion that broke the bonds of a learned tongue, added that he had made the monks wade knee-deep in water to rescue the floating hay.[3] It is worth noting that in both these cases objection was taken to the manner of the employment, not to the work itself, and at Humberstone the visitor contented himself by saying that the monks should not be made to work more than two or three hours a day.

If agricultural work was occasional even with the black monks, it is hard to believe that it had entirely disappeared among the Cistercians, but the records are so scanty that no certain pronouncement can be made. Certainly it remained to the end with the Premonstratensians. Bishop Redman, visiting St Radegund's in 1482, ordered the whole community, then apparently only six in number, to work from morning till evening in the garden or elsewhere 'as is commanded in our statutes', and in the same year at Newbo, where there were thirteen canons, he gave orders for all to be instant at toil at all hours as commanded by their prior. Outdoor work is clearly intended, as he continues that when the weather is bad, they shall study in their books. Twelve years later at Lavenden, where there were thirteen canons, he orders two Masses to be sung daily save during the hay and grain harvests, or times of unusual work.[4] From these references we may perhaps deduce that while the normal heavy pastoral or agricultural work was done by labourers, garden work and harvest help was furnished by the canons.

1 *Historia Eliensis*, in H. Wharton, *Anglia sacra*, II, 651.
2 *MC*, III, 46.
3 *DV*, II (29 June 1525), 170: 'Abbas...laborat circa fenum et grana et facit omnes monachos suos ita laborare ab hora octava usque horam quartam vel sextam post nonam.. et compellat monachos suos in anglicis to [go] in the water to the calff of the legg or to the kne to fetche the hay owt off the water.'
4 *Collect. Anglo-Premonstr.* III, 97–8, 60, 40–1.

The liturgical and domestic framework of the monastic day was treated in some detail in an earlier volume and need not be reviewed here. In theory, and to a great extent also in practice, the skeleton of the horarium was the same in 1500 as it had been in 1200, though it may have affected a smaller proportion of the community as a regular round. Such small changes as had taken place were due to abbreviations of the extra-liturgical psalmody and prayers, and to a few minor adjustments made to suit changing conditions of study.

In the later period, as in the earlier, the chief difficulty is to calculate the horarium in terms of clock-hours. The mechanical clock did not exist during the period when directories were chiefly composed, and no full time-table has come down from the last phase of monastic life in which clock-time is consistently given. All that can be attempted is to mention a few of the data, some of which are difficult to reconcile one with another.

In the early Middle Ages the traditional time for beginning the night office was *c.* 1.30–2 a.m. In 1532 the hour at Norwich Cathedral priory seems to have been earlier than 2–3 a.m.[1] From Durham, however, comes the precise statement of the old conservative that the bells were rung for mattins at midnight.[2] As elsewhere he speaks in exact terms of clock-time it is difficult to take this indication otherwise than in an exact sense. It may be compared with the statement of the St Albans annalist that the nuns of Sopwell (who presumably followed a time-table based on St Albans) rose for the night-choirs at 11 p.m.,[3] and also had a regulation that on certain feasts in summer (when lauds would precede the early sunrise) mattins were to begin immediately after compline.[4] The Carthusians, who recited the Office extremely slowly, began well before midnight; at the London Charterhouse in Prior Houghton's day they rose on ferial days at 10 p.m., and on feasts still earlier, and the Office was not done till 3 or 3.30 a.m.[5] Other orders, by that time at least, began later. Thus the Cistercians of Thame in 1526 were exhorted to begin mattins at 3 a.m. on feasts and at 4.0 on ferias,[6] while the Premonstratensians were to rise at midnight on feast-days and at dawn on ferias[7]—an injunction which would seem to have meaning only in the midsummer months. The hour of rising for the Austin canons is nowhere stated.

There is a similar variety in the hour of retiring. At Durham the *Salve*

1 *Norwich Visitations*, 268. The deponent clearly considered this hour too late.
2 *Rites of Durham*, (1) 19; (2) 22: '[The] bells was runge ever at midnight...for the Monkes went evermore to theire mattens at that houre of the night.' Cf. the direction of the visitor at Bradwell, a small black monk priory, in 1430–6, that mattins are to be recited 'mediis noctibus secundum consuetudinem in aliis vestrae religionis monasteriis usitatum'. (*LV*, 1, 22).
3 *Amundesham*, 1, 11.
4 *GASA*, 11, 424 (Abbot Thomas's constitutions of 1351).
5 M. Chauncy, *Historia aliquot martyrum...Cartusianorum*, ed. V. M. Doreau, 69. Cf. Methley, *Refectorium salutis*, 68ᵛ (Mount Grace, 1487): 'Surrexi ad matutinas non media nocte sed duabus horis ante ut mos est cartusiensibus hodiernis.'
6 G. G. Perry, 'The Visitation of Thame', 713.
7 *Collect. Anglo-Premonstr.* 11, 102 (Blanchland, 1497), 104.

was sung at 6 p.m. and the monks retired forthwith; if they had a second period of sleep after mattins this early hour would harmonize with the midnight rising.[1] At Peterborough, however, the monks retired immediately after compline, at 8 in winter and 9 in summer.[2] The Premonstratensians were often exhorted to be in bed by 8 p.m., which would have given very little sleep before mattins,[3] and 8 o'clock was bedtime for the Austin canons also.[4] In the daytime, the latest Durham time-table seems to have departed from the traditional horarium by advancing all duties after the chapter by an hour or so. Chapter, followed by the Chapter Mass, took place between 8 and 9, but as dinner (presumably only on non-fasting days) was at 11 a.m., the High Mass must have begun at 10 o'clock, thus leaving little time for work in the morning. Vespers were at 3 p.m., supper at 4.30 and the *Salve* after compline, as has been said, at 6 o'clock.[5] The Austin canons of Huntingdon had vespers at 4 o'clock in the summer and 3 o'clock in the winter.[6] One of the few earlier attempts at a reform of the horarium shows Abbot Mentmore of St Albans *c.* 1340 transferring the Chapter Mass from 9 a.m. to *c.* 7 a.m., in order that the students might have an unbroken morning.[7]

1 *Rites of Durham* (1) 73; (2) 86.   2 *LV*, I, 102.
3 *Collect. Anglo-Premonstr.* III, 144 (Torre, 1478).
4 *Reg. T. Bekynton*, ed. H. C. Maxwell-Lyte and M. C. B. Dawes, I, 163, no. 17.
5 *Rites of Durham*, (1) 70–4, 82; (2) 82–8, 93–4.
6 *LV*, II, 150 (1439).   7 *GASA*, II, 306.

CHAPTER XVIII

THE WAGE-SYSTEM AND THE COMMON LIFE

Although the horarium and the basic official employments of the monks were in 1500 still very much what they had been four centuries earlier, the framework and balance of the religious life had undergone profound changes. These derived in the main from two developments: the obedientiary system and the wage system. The first of these occupied our attention in a previous volume;[1] it may be summarized by repeating that while at a house such as Christ Church, Canterbury, where there were well over a hundred monks, the vast majority c. 1150 were living the fully claustral life within the monastic enclosure, and only six or ten officials were in part exempt; two hundred years later, at the same house, now somewhat shrunken in numbers, there were among the priest-monks in active life two classes almost equal in size, those following the life of the cloister and those occupying one of the many administrative posts, with funds and often with estates to oversee. But in the intervening two centuries an internal disintegration or atomization had also begun to take place; the monks had begun to move in a journey that was to accomplish several stages before the last compulsory one; they were beginning to cross the space that separates a religious body with fully communal life from a college of clerks or a chapter of resident secular canons. This change had come about principally through the introduction of what may be called the 'wage system', accompanied by the appearance of a growing number of private apartments and even of private establishments within the monastic enclosure.

The early development of this system was briefly discussed elsewhere. A small issue of money for charitable gifts, a larger allowance for minor personal indulgences, and the institution of 'clothes-money' had begun the long process, and the total sum that ultimately passed into the hands of each monk was made up of several elements. They may be classed under four heads: clothes-money; spice-money; dividends and customary presents; and money for work or services done.

Clothes-money, the earliest major payment, had been long and earnestly resisted and condemned by all authorities from prior to pope. It had nevertheless become widespread and little short of universal among all monks and canons by the mid-fourteenth century. It varied considerably in amount from one house to another, and even at the same house at different times: the largest sum was perhaps that of £2 at Bardney in 1437, which appears as a very steep rise from £1 six years or so earlier;[2] Wellow

---

1 MO, 433–4.

2 LV, II, 15; cf. ibid. I, 4. But Bardney was always *sui generis*, and too much should not be made of this. V. infra, p. 245 n. 2.

had £1. 6s. 8d.,[1] Ely £1. 2s. 6d.[2] and Eynsham £1. 6s. 4d.;[3] Newhouse in 1482[4] and Durham at the Dissolution had £1, while the small Kyme in 1440 had only 16s.[5] Yet the practice was never fully accepted, and the most persevering attempts to check it came from bishops, not, as it would seem, from set policy of reform, but because the canon law that governed their visitations had never been altered, whereas the monks themselves had long custom and even some chapter pronouncements in the opposite sense. Thus Thoresby of Worcester at Gloucester in 1350, Archbishop Arundel at Ely in 1401 and Oliver King at Bath in 1500[6] insisted on the issue of clothes instead of cash, and the same was recommended by Wolsey's commissioner at Wenlock in 1526.[7] Moreover, at some houses, of which Westminster may have been one, the issue of a routine outfit every year seems never to have been superseded, while at other houses, such as Faversham, cash had been replaced by clothes as being in effect a more valuable allowance in times of rising prices or growing needs.[8]

Nevertheless, for the black monks as a body clothes-money was normal. The final and official capitulation to prevailing custom may be recognized in 1421. In that year the reforming commissioners of Henry V had reiterated briefly and firmly the monastic tradition and canonical doctrine.[9] Objections of all sorts were immediately voiced, and the final articles approved by general chapter contained what was in effect an approval of the wages-system, introduced and followed by a long and involved apologia for the decision. The operative clause ran: 'We allow and suffer, according to the ancient custom and use of various places, that our monks should receive and spend sums of money both for necessities and for comforts (recreaciones), not at their free pleasure, but only in the ways we have mentioned above and that with discretion.'[10]

In addition to clothes-money or the issue of clothes there was in most houses an allowance for spices. This was explicitly countenanced at least as early as 1338 by chapter which, after prohibiting allowances for food and clothing, added that it was permissible for money to be given as largesse (ex curialitate) for spices and other small necessaries which it was fitting that monks should have.[11] Two years later this was confirmed at St Albans by Abbot Mentmore.[12] At some monasteries spice-money was a charge on the chamberlain's funds, as at Abingdon, where each priest

1 LV, II, 391.   2 Ely Chapter Ordinances, ed. S. J. A. Evans, 55.
3 LV, I, 55.   4 Collectanea Anglo-Premonstr. ed. F. A. Gasquet, III, 77.
5 LV, II; Rites of Durham, ed. (1) J. Raine, 81; ed. (2) J. T. Fowler, 96–7.
6 VCH, Glos. II, 58; Ely Chapter Ordinances, 55; J. Britton, History and Antiquities of Bath Abbey Church, appendix, p. 141: 'Monachis solus victus et vestitus, non pensio aut proprium concedatur.'
7 R. Graham, English Ecclesiastical Studies, 143.
8 M. Bateson, 'Archbishop Warham's Visitations'.
9 MC, II, 113: 'Provideatur ut statutum domini Benedicti Papae duodecimi...Ne victualia ministrentur in pecuniis firmiter observetur et...ordinetur unus fidelis dispensator commonachus qui...provideat...de habitibus...non in pecuniis sed in ipsis rebus omnino.'
10 MC, II, 131–2.   11 MC, II, 11.   12 GASA, II, 307–8.

received the large sum of £1. 16s. 8d. a year for spices.[1] Failing clear indications, it is impossible to say what commodities were included within the term 'spices'; probably most of the personal purchases now made at a drug-store, confectioner's and grocer's shop formed its basis, but the word as a commercial term in the later Middle Ages covered a multitude of consumer goods, not all of them perishable, in something of the same way that the simple chemist of the last century has now attracted into his stock a long train of articles wholly unconnected with drugs or hygiene of any kind.[2] At some monasteries, it would seem, clothes-money and spice-money was given as a consolidated sum; thus at St Albans in the early decades of the fifteenth century Abbot Whethamstede increased the annual (unspecified) sum allowed to each monk by 6s. 8d., and ordered its distribution three times a year.[3]

A third source of income was by way of regular gift or distributed dividend. Besides the occasional presents given regularly by obedientiaries to a monk on one or two of the notable moments of his monastic life, such as his first Mass and his first presidency in the refectory,[4] many houses had a custom that the major officials should present each monk with a specified sum on certain days. As the accounts of all the obedientiaries concerned are seldom extant for a single year or neighbouring years, it is impossible to compute the total sum of all these presents, but it would certainly amount to £1 or more. Besides these official gifts, some houses had further sources of largesse. Thus Westminster had the three groups of manors, the gifts of Queen Eleanor, King Richard II and King Henry V respectively, from which the residual income, after the religious and charitable purposes of the bequests had been satisfied, was free for distribution among the monks. In good years, the dividend for priests from the three sources was £3. 10s., 13s. 4d. and £1 respectively; junior monks had less and the prior a double portion.[5]

Finally, the custom of paying monks for services of all kinds grew very considerably during the fifteenth century. The spiritual good offices of prayer, which could not be directly expressed in cash terms, might be made the occasion of a gift or legacy. Thus testators at St Albans bequeath sums to be divided amongst the monks, the infirm monks, and the novices, clearly in expectation of prayers, and the custom of bequeathing a dividend to all monks attending a funeral in the abbey church or a neighbouring churchyard was universal.[6] Monks were also paid individually for carrying

1 R. H. Snape, *English Monastic Finances*, 164, with details.

2 Cf. R. S. Lopez in *Cambridge Economic History*, II, 331: 'Pegolotti in the early fourteenth century listed no less than 386 items under the heading "spices". He included... such wares as copper, glue and cotton.'

3 *Reg. J. Whethamstede*, ed. H. T. Riley, I, 459.

4 E. H. Pearce, *Monks of Westminster*, introd., 22–5, where an account of the latter occasion (*primo sedere ad skillam*) is given.   5 *Ibid*. 16–20.

6 Miss C. E. Hodges, in her unpublished Manchester thesis, 'The Abbey of St Albans under John of Whethamstede', gives many references from unprinted sources. Other instances occur a century later in the Journal of Prior More of Worcester.

out chantry duties in the abbey church, as well as for saying some special Mass or acting for another official. Indeed, monks were even paid by their superior for work done for himself or for the house, as can be seen in the accounts of Prior More of Worcester, where he pays one of his monks for writing for him and another for binding books in the library of the priory.[1] Many houses, it is clear, were in a fair way to becoming an institution such as a college or hospital, where the inmates received their keep and certain allowances from the common fund, which they could in small ways supplement at will.

The total sum thus obtained annually doubtless varied greatly from house to house, but at the largest and richest it was very considerable, amounting to a sum perhaps equivalent in purchasing power to £100 or £200 of our money. That this is no exaggeration is seen by the gifts made by monks to the monastery, and by the books and valuables that passed into the hands of the house at their death. While it is difficult to be certain in every case that the gifts were not, partly at least, provided by friends or relatives of the donor, or purchased from a surplus of some office which he had administered wisely, it is certain that many were the fruit of the earnings or savings of individual monks and priors. The character of these gifts may be seen in a list of benefactions to St Albans under Abbot Whethamstede;[2] an almost contemporary papal indult to a monk of Westminster to possess for his life any books, jewels, money or other goods, providing that they go ultimately to his monastery, should not be taken as an exceptional privilege, but rather as a kind of additional insurance policy similar to many other papal indults safeguarding an existing right or custom.[3] Indeed, so natural was it to presume the possession of small sums of money by a monk that visitors in the early fifteenth century are found applying to large monasteries the system of fines customary in colleges: thus at Ramsey Abbey in 1432 a monk is to be fined 6d. for drinking after compline, and a president 3s. 4d. for a similar offence; absence from choir below a fixed quorum was fined a penny a head, breaking silence in the refectory at Wenlock cost twopence a day on ordinary days, and twopence for each course on feast days.[4]

Finally, a corporate sanction was given to the conception that possession of funds was a privilege by the bestowal of pensions upon members of the community who had done unusually good service in administrative positions. The ex-superior is perhaps in a class by himself. Resignations were so rare, and the legal conception of the abbot or prior as the proprietor of his estates was so widespread, that the endowment of a superior

1 *Journal of Prior William More*, ed. E. S. Fegan, 74, 256, etc. At St Albans *c.* 1423 the succentor was allowed 3s. 4d. for relieving the priest of the week from the task of leading the choir when the church was full of people (*Amundesham*, I, 104).

2 *Amundesham*, II, Appendix, I, 322–61.

3 *CPL*, V, 197. The monk was William Sudbury.

4 *LV*, I (Ramsey, 1432), 104; the refectory fine at Wenlock occurs in 1523 (R. Graham, *English Ecclesiastical Studies*, 134).

en démission was treated as natural and inevitable, but he was not the only one to be provided for. Though the clearest and fullest evidence comes from Westminster, there is no reason to suppose that abbey to have been unique in this respect. At Westminster the first to be given a pension in consideration of his good services to the house appears to be Richard Exeter, who was assigned £2. 13s. 4d. a year on his retirement in 1382. Thereafter pensions become more frequent, with an average of one every five years until the Dissolution. More rarely, a monk was awarded an allowance merely or chiefly on account of his physical infirmity.[1]

Yet another manifestation of the breakdown of the common life can be seen in the multiplication of private chambers and establishments. The gradual departure from community life began soon after the Conquest. First the abbot or conventual prior, and then, in spite of all attempts to prevent it, the second-in-command acquired first a private chamber and then a lodging which became gradually more and more elaborate. Early in the fourteenth century studies were provided at many houses for the theologians; and by 1393 priors, retired superiors and doctors are allowed rooms of their own. At about the same time, repeated provision against dividing the dormitory into cells seems to show that this, too, was not unknown.[2] In 1444 the old prohibition is repeated, with an additional decree that money is neither to be asked nor accepted by the prior in allotting the better cells.[3] Some time before this, in 1343, a certain number of private chambers are assumed to exist in each abbey, for certain classes, such as priors, retired superiors and doctors of theology are expressly allowed to have them.[4] Eighty years later, the abolition of private rooms was one of the main desires of the reformers; it was successfully resisted, and sacrists, doctors, and others of tried worth were excepted from the prohibition.[5] Finally, the serving of meals in such cells is allowed if permission is obtained.[6] In a less exceptionable form, the provision of sets of rooms in the infirmary for the aged had become a more or less general custom.

The visitation records here, as in the matter of clothes-money, show the bishops as endeavouring to maintain the traditional canonical ruling

---

1 Pearce, *op. cit.* introd. 33–4.

2 *MC*, II, 47 (1343): 'Cellas in dormitorio felicis recordationis Benedictus papa duodecimus esse prohibuit.' The beds are to be uncurtained and visible to all. This decree was frequently repeated. Contrast the arrangements at Durham in the sixteenth century, where every monk has 'a little chamber of wainscott very close' with window and desk (*Rites of Durham*,(1) 72; (2) 85). These windows are still to be seen in the Library of the Dean and Chapter at Durham.

3 *MC*, II, 199: 'Ne quis prepositus cellas in dormitorio munere, precio vel exactione vendat seu inhabitare permittat, neque aliqua exactio pro cameris superioribus deliberandis fiat pecuniaria ab hiis quibus incumbit disponere.' This is a far cry from the immediate paternal care of the abbot in the Rule of St Benedict.

4 MC, II, 36. 'Nullus claustralis exceptis prioribus et prelatis cedentibus aut doctoribus habeat cameram, armigerum vel ministrum.'

5 *MC*, II, 120.   6 MC, II, 208.

which the chapters had already breached. Brantyngham of Exeter in 1373 commanded the Tavistock monks to abandon the private chambers in which they were apparently taking meals.[1] Ramsey in 1439 had recently instituted a system of private establishments, as had Bardney, apparently with personal attendants, in 1437.[2] The Austin canons, as might be expected, had taken to the practice even earlier. Grandisson of Exeter found the canons of Launceston and Bodmin with private rooms in 1346 and 1347.[3] At Launceston, indeed, things had gone still further: the canons had not only private rooms, but a house, dog, boy, herb-garden and dove-cot apiece; these were to be abolished. Exactly a century later, in 1451, Bekynton of Wells accepted the rooms at Taunton and Bruton, but a canon was to lose the privilege if he entertained a lady without permission, or held a drinking-bout.[4] The canons, indeed, had the system till the end.[5]

Recreation, that is to say, a temporary but intentional relaxation of the normal monastic regime of silence, prayer, work and seclusion, had no explicit mention in early monastic legislation, as it has no part in the daily life of a Carthusian or Trappist at the present time. The daily period or periods of talking in the cloister, though in effect they tended to be recreative, were not devised as such, and endeavours were made to preserve the serious or official level of the conversation by barring English.[6] Gradually, however, a number of recreative occasions developed, and it may be well to review them as they were in the fourteenth century.

First and oldest, perhaps even existing in Continental monasteries before the Conquest, were the opportunities given by periodical blood-letting and by invitation to the abbot's table. Both survived to the end, though not unchanged. Bleeding times or seyneys were legislated for with increasing detail.[7] They implied absence from choir and cloister for about two days, a fortifying diet in the infirmary, with rest and conversation. Though presumably never abolished, they became relatively less important as other recreative occasions increased, and it may have been that as hygienic fashions changed bleeding was less practised.

---

1 *Reg. T. Brantyngham*, I, 312–15.

2 *LV*, III, 303; II, 12. The Bardney monks were apparently living in chambers each served by a valet. They were told to live together, either (*a*) each with his servant at the common charge, or (*b*) without servants, but each having a fixed income. They chose the former alternative.

3 *Reg. J. Grandisson*, ed. F. C. Hingeston-Randolph, II, 1007, 1011.

4 *Reg. T. Bekynton*, ed. H. C. Maxwell-Lyte and M. C. B. Dawes, I, 163, no. 11; 181–2, no. 14.

5 E.g. at Keynsham (SRS, XXXIX (1924), 216).

6 *MC*, II, 47. The statutes of 1343 (often repeated) lay down that the monks: 'in prandio et solaciis aliis, ac etiam in capitulo... aliisque colloquiis, necnon in claustro in parliamento loquantur duntaxat Gallicum seu Latinum.' As late as 1527 it was a charge at Malmesbury that chapter was held 'in lingua materna et non in lingua Romana' (*MC*, III, 127). This convention may not have been without effect upon the studies and reading of the monks in the later Middle Ages.

7 *MO*, 455–6; *RO*, I, 284.

Invitation to the abbot's table was primitive in the Benedictine tradition and is assumed, possibly with the corollary of meat-eating, in the familiar decretal *Cum ad monasterium* of Innocent III. From an invitation to dine it developed into a visit to one of the abbot's manors in the neighbourhood of the monastery. As time went on, a particular manor was selected and adapted as a rest-house for the monks. Thus St Albans had Redburn; Christ Church, Caldecote; Westminster, Hendon; Bardney, Suthrey; Durham, Finchale; Tewkesbury, The Mythe; Worcester, Battenhall.[1] Almost every house of the black monks may be found to have such a place, save for some, such as St Augustine's, Canterbury, and possibly Glastonbury, where several unspecified manors were used.[2] Once a stay outside the monastery was in question, a day-to-day summons to individuals by the abbot was no longer feasible, and gradually a system was evolved by which all in turn took recreation. This varied greatly between house and house: at the larger ones the period of holiday was often considerable, but a modified observance was maintained; at smaller houses a shorter and more frequent absence was often combined with the seyneys and entailed complete exemption from regular life. For a long time the abbot retained his patronage of these holidays. Abbot Thomas de la Mare not only made elaborate regulations for Redburn, but constantly visited the place himself and joined in the life of the brethren. At about the same time the abbot of Glastonbury, Adam of Sodbury (1323–34) refers to the brethren who stay with him in turns, while throughout the fourteenth century the *ludi* of the monks of Durham continued at the prior's manor of Bearpark. Gradually, however, the superior's connexion with the routine vanished; a fixed place was chosen to which monks went in order. At Durham, owing to financial stringency, the *ludi* of Bearpark were exchanged for a period of residence at Finchale.[3] If frequency of allusion is an indication, the holiday-houses ceased to be very significant in the later fifteenth century. Perhaps the holidays at home or with friends, already introduced in the fourteenth century, came to take the place of communal recreations. Certainly an annual visit home is countenanced even by the reforming commission of 1421, and still greater freedom is envisaged by its critics;[4] visits to friends and relations are assumed in all subsequent legislation.

Hunting has often been regarded as a common monastic diversion of the Middle Ages. Chaucer and Langland are no doubt primarily responsible for this impression, but it must be acknowledged that neither in visitation

---

1 A few other fenland rest-houses may be noted: Dousedalehouse (Croyland); Oxney (Peterborough); Wykeham (Spalding); St Ives (Ramsey).

2 Cf. *Secretum Domini* (Bodl. MS. Wood Empt. 1, fo. 259), where the abbot refers to brethren *infra xii hidas existentes* (? on holiday), and to those *qui cum eo per vices in solaciis fuerint constituti*. I owe this reference to Dom Aelred Watkin.

3 So Miss E. M. Halcrow, from Durham muniments.

4 *MC*, II, 123: 'Et si contingat...visitare...parentes et amicos, hoc semel in anno ad maius fiat.' The critics objected that this might prevent a second visit to a dying parent.

records nor in the decrees of chapter does it appear as one of the most formidable causes of laxity.[1] Indeed, for a monk of a large abbey, especially one lying in a town, it would have been almost as difficult to indulge in it as for his modern equivalent to indulge in pheasant shooting. The chase, never approved of by ecclesiastical authorities, was formally forbidden to clerics by Clement V at the Council of Vienne, but it did not need this sanction to make such an essentially mundane pursuit unmonastic. Hunting, as a social phenomenon, was probably never more in evidence than in the twelfth century. Privilege, abundance of waste and woodland, and economic necessity encouraged it. Subsequent centuries of agrarian progress and stock-raising restricted opportunities and removed needs, and towards the end of the Middle Ages it was tending to become an aristocratic sport save in hill country and heavily wooded districts. Abbots, however, resident for long periods on their manors, priors of dependent cells, and indeed all inmates of small and remote houses could indulge a taste for blood-sports to the full, but while the two former classes might, with Chaucer's monk, vie with the greatest in the breed of their hounds and the technique of venery, the others took to the saddle or the snare in the homely fashion of a Flurry Knox or a Will Wimble.[2] It was with this last class that visitors tried to deal—with the remote Blanchland or the 'derne' Ulverscroft,[3] or with the chronically irregular Wigmore, where the abbot had a mute of hounds for the entertainment of the brethren in their seyneys.[4] With the black canons, indeed, as those of Bruton, hunting was tolerated if it was done with permission and for recreation only, whereas at Glastonbury nearby hunting was prohibited, and only the abbot might keep hounds for his park.[5] Perhaps it happened that the more bourgeois the monks became the less they desired to hunt. Prior More of Worcester (1518–36) kept hounds to control all kinds of vermin, but took no interest in the chase himself.[6]

1 Chaucer's picture of the Monk in the *Prologue* to the *Canterbury Tales* is familiar to all. Langland has a similar passage (B text, x, 308):

> A priker on a palfray. fro manere to manere
> An heep of houndes at his ers. as he a lorde were.

An almost contemporary (*c.* 1378) monk writing from Rome, says that English monks have a reputation there for fowling and hunting (*MC*, III, 79). It may have been a passing phase, comparable to that of the hunting parson of 1750–1840.

2 Examples of this type are Brother John of Humberstone in 1440, who stayed up till midnight in August with the harvesters and then retired to bed when the bell rang for mattins, or went out fowling by night (*LV*, II, 145), and Brother William of Bardney in 1444 who went out hunting with the abbot of Peterborough (*ibid.* 32)—a raffish personage of irregular life who 'rode off last Lent to Stamford, where he shot at the butts in lay attire' (*ibid.* III, 286–7).

3 *Collect. Anglo-Premonstr.* II, 98; *LV*, III, 386.

4 *Reg. T. Spofford*, ed. A. T. Bannister, 66.

5 *Reg. T. Bekynton*, I, 181; II, 556. The latter was a metropolitical visitation by the archbishop of Canterbury in 1408.

6 *Journal of Prior William More*, 13, 97, 210, 270, etc.

CHAPTER XIX

THE ELECTION AND PRIVILEGES OF
THE SUPERIOR

Throughout the fourteenth and fifteenth centuries the normal way by which an abbot or prior with jurisdiction attained office was that of free election by all the professed members of his community. The organs of national government and the relative importance of the black monk abbots in the life of the country had changed profoundly since the days when, in the century and more after the Conquest, the abbots had rivalled the bishops in influence at meetings of the Great Council, and the king had often by direct or indirect action appointed the great feudal abbots. Now, save for an occasional attempt at influencing the choice of a *persona grata* at such a house as Westminster,[1] he no longer concerned himself with the election, though he jealously guarded all the rights connected with a change of abbots.

In any consideration of elections in general, a number of large orders, and several small groups, must be isolated from the rest. To begin with, the Cistercians, Premonstratensians, Gilbertines, Carthusians and a few other fully developed 'orders' followed precise regulations of their own, with which no external authority interfered. Very few records of their elections have survived, but it is certain that almost all proceeded without incident, according to their rule as modified by canonical legislation, as purely domestic affairs, normally guided by a visiting superior.

Among the black monks two groups stand in some respects apart. The first of these is the relatively small number of houses, made up of twenty-two abbeys of men and two of women, from which the Conqueror had exacted knight-service, and which therefore ranked as baronies held by tenants-in-chief. The abbots of these houses had as individuals a direct relationship to the Crown. It was incumbent upon the community to announce a demise to the king, to obtain his permission to proceed to an election, and to announce the election and obtain confirmation; after which the temporalities of the abbacy were restored, and the abbot blessed by the ordinary. Over these elections, therefore, the king retained at least a distant surveillance, though the material effects of escheatment had been neutralized first, by the separation of the estates of abbot and convent and later by the payment of an annual sum in lieu of the heavy distraint when an abbey was taken into the king's hand during a vacancy.[2]

A still smaller group, partly but not wholly contained within the other,

1 As, for example, at Westminster in 1386, when Richard II wished for John Lakyngheth as abbot instead of William de Colchester, who was elected. Cf. E. H. Pearce, *Monks of Westminster*, 104 with references.
2 For this *v. RO*, 1, 278–9.

was made up of those houses of monks and canons, some ten in number, which, by achieving papal recognition as exempt from diocesan super-vision, depended directly upon the Apostolic See. The abbots of these houses, in addition to their Crown connexion, had to proceed to the Curia for confirmation before they were blessed, either by the pope himself or by a prelate of their choice in England. This was a costly and harassing business, for the Curia, especially in the century before the Great Schism, often used all the ingenuity of its canonists to quash the election on technical grounds, thereby opening the way for the pope to 'provide' the elect or another to the vacant office. Here again, by the beginning of the fifteenth century, most of the houses concerned had commuted their obligations for a fixed annual payment to Rome, and were allowed to seek confirmation from bishops in England. The papacy, however, still retained its basic rights. When, for example, Abbot Harwden of Westminster resigned in 1440, the pope 'provided' Edmund Kirton to the abbacy, perhaps because the latter took the notice of the resignation out to Rome.[1]

The groups of abbeys just mentioned, though bulking large in the records of the age, formed only a small fraction of the whole body of autonomous houses. The remainder, monks and black canons alike, furnish fairly abundant material. With them, the election was a purely domestic affair. No external superior presided, as he does normally in modern elections; the formalities were guaranteed by notaries-public, with the occasional presence of a canon lawyer. After the full body of electors, composed of the professed members of the community labouring under no canonical disability, had been notified and convoked, and the pre-scribed religious and canonical procedure had been carried out, the chapter of the Rule (in houses of monks) *de ordinando abbate* was read, followed by the reading and explanation by a notary of the relevant decree of the Fourth Lateran Council *Quia propter*. This laid down the three alternative ways of proceeding open to the electors: that of the Holy Spirit, that of scrutiny and that of compromise. In the first way, a name was called, and the assembly received it with acclamation which, if recognized as universal, was accepted as an election as it were inspired by the Holy Spirit. In a large and varied community such an acclamation could only take place if an individual had long impressed the imagination of his confrères. It was, however, by no means unknown, and it was fairly common in very small houses. The second way, that by scrutiny of individual votes, which since the Council of Trent has been the canonical norm, was by no means common. The democratic or egalitarian outlook which accepts a majority vote as unquestionably decisive was foreign to the medieval mind. Early canonical tradition had always favoured a unanimous choice, and the Rule had expressed a similar preference. St Benedict, however, in a somewhat enigmatic phrase, which had been adopted by Gratian and had thus passed

1 CPL, IX, 105, 128; Pearce, *op. cit.* 130.

into current law,[1] had proposed as an alternative to unanimity, election by the sounder portion of the community—an expression which had been changed into the still more ambiguous 'weightier and sounder portion'.[2] This, which had given scope for many divergent interpretations, was given precision by the Lateran decree that an election by two-thirds of the voting body was binding, and at the Council of Lyons in 1274 a further step was taken by allowing a bare majority to carry the day. That in such circumstances the sounder as well as the larger part of the community had decided was explained in more than one way. Some argued that the larger part was *ipso facto* the wiser part, but the more usual procedure was to show subsequently that the electors and elect possessed, besides the *auctoritas* of a majority, the *meritum* and *ʒelum* which canonists had required as signs of soundness. In any case, when the way by scrutiny was adopted three scrutators, chosen by the convent, sat in the chapter-house and recorded the vote given in their presence *viva voce* by each member of the community in turn.

By far the most common way, however, was that by compromise. In this the whole body chose, normally by something approaching to acclamation, a group of delegates, usually seven in number, to act for them. These usually included in their body the most notable officials of the community, with something of a bias towards those who held quasi-religious posts, such as the various priors, theologians and confessors. Such a group would inevitably contain at many elections the monk regarded by his fellows as the favourite candidate. In theory these delegates could, as soon as they had come to a corporate decision, declare their choice, which the chapter had previously undertaken to ratify. Actually, however, they often preferred to inform and safeguard themselves by summoning the community one by one to declare their opinion, thus approximating to the method of scrutiny, though they were in no way bound to accept the candidate with a bare majority.

When, by whatever method, the decision had been made, it was in some houses customary for the elect to retire to another part of the monastery, where he was waited upon by representatives of the convent who inquired whether he would accept office.[3] After a decent interval of real or conventional hesitation he accepted, and then, if no royal or papal interests were engaged, all that remained (in the case of an abbot) was to secure benediction at the hands of the diocesan, followed by a ceremonial installation and a great feast to tenants and local magnates.

---

1 *Regula S. Benedicti*, c. lxiv: 'Hic constituatur [abbas] quem sive omnis concors congregatio secundum timorem Dei, sive etiam pars quamvis parva congregationis saniore consilio elegerit.' Gratian, *Decretum*, Dist. 61, c. 14. Cf. *Extra*. 1, vi, 22 and *Cod. Justin.* 11, lix, 2.

2 For the history of *major et sanior pars*, and the evolution of the 'majority principle' *v.* O. Gierke, 'Ueber die Geschichte des Majoritätsprinzip' and A. Esmein, 'L'unanimité et la majorité dans les élections canoniques'.

3 The chroniclers of St Albans have many full accounts of elections, e.g. *GASA*, 11, 183–4, 382; *Reg. J. Whethamstede*, ed. H. T. Riley, 9–20.

Precision may perhaps be given to the picture already drawn by a glance at three taken from among the many accounts of elections available which are unusually complete in their detailed story; indeed, two of the three are so full as to deserve to be regarded as *loci classici* for a fifteenth-century election in all its legalistic amplitude. Two are from Glastonbury and the third from the cathedral priory of Durham; all three are chiefly made up of long official letters informing the bishop of the result, and by a curious chance all three occur in the same year, 1456.

Glastonbury had its first election early in May (7–9) of that year. The community decided to proceed by way of compromise; nine delegates were chosen, who duly announced that one of their number had their unanimous support; then, when the convent had reiterated its undertaking to abide by their choice, one of their number, in the name of his colleagues and the community, formally elected William More. The new abbot, however, lived to enjoy his dignity less than six months, and on 13 November the community proceeded to make a fresh choice. This time their procedure was slightly different. For a reason which does not appear, but which does not seem, in the light of events, to have been due to the rivalry of faction, the preliminaries gave more trouble than the election itself. The chapter began by nominating two delegates, both of whom had served earlier in the year; these were to nominate seven others. The two, however, could not agree and after a time returned to the convent and resigned. The community then decided to proceed by way of scrutiny, and three scrutators were chosen to interrogate apart each member of the community and to record his vote. Before this process could be completed, however, the prior and convent changed their minds, withdrew their commission from the scrutators and appointed seven delegates, several of whom had acted in May, to join the two previously appointed. This panel, however, resigned in their turn, whereupon the convent chose three to take the votes of the community. The three, somewhat unexpectedly, speedily completed their task, and announced that the convent had elected John Selwode by a vote which was unanimous save for the suffrage of the elect himself.[1]

The contemporary Durham election[2] was conducted by the subprior and convent, who decided to proceed by way of individual suffrage. Three scrutators were chosen and the brethren proceeded to vote. In this case there was something of a close fight; John Burnby, sometime subprior and now head of Durham College at Oxford, had thirty-eight supporters while twenty-five favoured the existing subprior, Richard Bell, later bishop of Carlisle; six votes, including those of the two rivals, were scattered among three marginal candidates. Burnby was declared duly elected by a majority of suffrages, but it was felt necessary to satisfy the canonical requisites oi merit on the part of the elect and zeal on that of the electors. As both

1 For these two elections *v. Reg. T. Bekynton*, ed. H.C. Maxwell-Lyte and M.C.B. Dawes, II, 445–54.   2 *Durham Obituary Rolls*, ed. J. Raine, 91–102.

rivals had Oxford degrees and had filled the office of subprior, there was a certain artificiality in any external reckoning of merit, and the declaration as to the zeal and standing of the respective electors was perhaps not intended to be more than a formality.

In the following year an election at Bath showed yet another pattern.[1] Here, in the bishop's cathedral priory, a smaller electorate of twenty-three, after deciding to proceed by way of compromise, chose the bishop as sole compromissary with right to elect, while in 1448 thirteen electors at Bruton proceeded by way of acclamation.[2] The two last-mentioned methods were indeed usually preferred by moderately-sized and small houses in which, when opinions were divided, election by compromise or scrutiny may have been avoided as defining still more clearly the lines of division.

Once elected and confirmed, the abbot or prior of an autonomous house of any order remained in office till death, unless he were deposed for grave canonical faults or resigned of his own free choice. Depositions were always rare; resignations, which in the twelfth century were almost equally so, became somewhat less unusual towards the end of the Middle Ages, though the alternative method of allowing the administration to be put into commission was sometimes adopted, as at Westminster in 1467.[3]

If a superior resigned for reasons of health or age, or indeed for almost any reason including disciplinary pressure, it was understood that he should have for the term of his life an establishment of his own that varied from house to house in some relation to its wealth and amenities. The abbot of a large black monk abbey usually received as dower one of the large manors of the abbatial portion, with its chapel and hall and staff, and one or more monks to act as chaplain and companions. At smaller houses the 'quondam', as he was called, might have a set of rooms and a garden, together with a companion, a generous allowance of food and fuel, and a money pension. This practice, which was in part a concession to human weakness, and in part the result of the legal and social convention by which the abbot or prior was regarded as the *persona* and proprietor of his church and monastery, probably tended to reduce rather than to increase the number of resignations, as a long-lived quondam might well prove a financial as well as a personal liability to the new superior and his community.

All through the medieval centuries from the mid-twelfth to the Dissolution the abbots and priors of black monk houses spent much of their time on their estates. This practice, which had begun soon after the division of estates between abbot and convent, was in part the acceptance by abbots of the contemporary custom of all great landholders, who passed from manor to manor consuming the stores of the year. It spread, however, to houses which were not feudal baronies, such as the cathedral

---

1 *Reg. T. Bekynton*, II, 434–8.   2 *Ibid.* 438–40.
3 Pearce, *op. cit.* 141.

priories, where certain manors were earmarked for the support of the prior and his establishment,[1] and it continued till the Dissolution, though for a century or more economic developments had rendered such itineration unnecessary. Custom, which no one was prepared to change, had no doubt built up a system of economic administration which would have been thrown out of gear had an abbot, with his large household and numerous guests, been permanently in residence, but the continuance of the quasi-absentee superior was chiefly due to a general unwillingness to break away from a state of things which was incompatible with a fully spiritual conception of an abbot's responsibilities. Still more strange to modern ways of thought than itineration round distant manors was the practice of living for considerable periods at a house only a mile or two from the abbey, rather than in the abbey itself. Thus the abbots of Westminster, when in town, usually lived at their manor of La Neyte, the priors of Durham at Bearpark, and the priors of Worcester at Battenhall, though all these prelates had roomy quarters within the precinct of their monasteries. Their sojourn within the enclosure was indeed usually limited to certain seasons of liturgical solemnity such as Christmastide, the beginning of Lent, Easter and Pentecost. Thus it has been computed that the prior of Durham in the late fourteenth century spent some seventeen weeks, or about one-third of the year, in the priory itself, and the prior of Worcester, shortly before the Dissolution, only nine weeks.[2] If figures could be extracted from the account rolls of Westminster and other houses their tale would be very similar. At some houses, however, as for example St Albans, an impression is gained of more or less continual residence, but this may be an impression only, which the facts if known would contradict.

This habitual absence, however, was not common to all religious superiors. A few of the larger houses of black canons may have experienced it, but at all smaller houses, and at all the houses of the newer orders of monks and canons, the superior was normally in residence save when absent on business of the house or order. The occupation of separate quarters was, however, universal. As will be seen in the review of architectural development,[3] the abbots and priors first left the common dorter for small contiguous apartments, and then in turn abandoned these for lodgings complete with hall, chapel and kitchen. The smallest houses of canons, long before the fifteenth century, contained apartments for the prior with direct access to the outer court or outside world.

The abbot or prior retained till the end, at least in theory, the quasi-absolute and monarchical powers of monastic tradition as expressed in the Rule of St Benedict, which had influenced all subsequent codes and had

---

1 As, for example, at Worcester, where certain manors appear in Prior More's diary as his permanent sources of income (*Journal of Prior William More*, ed. E. S. Fegan, 357–75). At Durham, however, the prior never had particular estates allotted to him.

2 The Durham figures over several years were calculated from the account rolls by Miss E. M. Halcrow; those of Worcester by the present writer from Prior More's *Journal*.

3 This has been held back to appear in the final volume.

even been taken up into the *Decretum* by Gratian, thus becoming law for the universal Church. Canonical limitations to his untrammelled action, which had increased in the great days of the legislating papacy, had ceased after the Benedictine Constitutions, and the quasi-democratic movements visible in the chapters of large abbeys such as St Albans in the twelfth century had never developed or even continued, while the council of seniors, which was an active advisory body at some houses in the thirteenth century, is scarcely ever mentioned in our period. Its place was largely taken for a space by the abbot's own council composed chiefly of lawyers and magnates, with a few monks, but this in its turn passed, or at least ceased to be significant, long before the Dissolution. Yet in spite of the apparent freedom thus left to the superior, spiritual and disciplinary flexibility and the range of the abbot's initiative became in fact more and more restricted; for these were substituted a fixed routine governed by customs and conventions, and an unchanging framework within which the individual monk had many opportunities of freedom and change. The chapter, however, which continued its routine and business meetings, still existed as the body which could sanction new regulations and observances; it could also, by criticism and obstruction, hold up any measures of reform that seemed likely to press too hardly upon those used to old ways.[1]

1 Thus, for example, the Redburn regulations of Abbot Whethamstede *c.* 1430, were criticized when they were produced 'causa examinationis in domo capitulari, praesente Priore' (*Amundesham*, II, 211).

CHAPTER XX

THE NUMBERS OF THE RELIGIOUS

The strength of the monastic population of England has in the past been the subject of much speculation, and it had often been assumed till recently that nothing but speculation was possible. In fact, however, the material for fairly accurate statistics has for long been accumulating in print, and only the patient work of a careful scholar was wanting. Direct statements of numbers in chronicles or narratives are indeed very scanty, especially after the twelfth century, but in later times precise figures can often be found in the record sources. Thus the acts of an election or a visitation often give, either explicitly or by implication, the numbers of a community, while in the case of a few great monasteries—Christ Church, Canterbury, Westminster and Durham are perhaps the only examples—we possess what amounts to a complete list of the monks for two or more centuries. Elsewhere, and especially in the case of the mendicants, the numbers can often be deduced with some accuracy from the sums given by benefactors for a supply of clothing or one or more days' provisions. Yet another source is the records of the poll taxes of 1377, 1379 and 1380–1,[1] while for the last years there are abundant and detailed materials. These last, however, have their own difficulties of interpretation, and will be more fully considered on a later occasion. Such was some of the material available, and in recent years two scholars, working independently and unknown to each other, have examined these and other sources and applied to the figures elicited the technique of the demographical statistician. Many of their sources and estimates, indeed, differ considerably, but their broad conclusions are remarkably similar. What follows is largely based upon the figures they supply.[2]

1 Printed by John Topham, 'Subsidy Roll of 51 Edward III'.
2 Professor J. C. Russell, of the University of New Mexico, has devoted many years to the study of the population of medieval England; his book, *British Medieval Population*, is the fullest and most learned attempt yet made to compile statistics for this purpose. His findings of the numbers of religious, therein contained, are to be found also, with copious references to the sources, in an article, 'The Clerical Population of Medieval England'. While Russell was at work, R. Neville Hadcock was engaged in this country in collecting material bearing on the size of religious houses for his *Map of Monastic Britain* for the Ordnance Survey. When, in 1950, Mr Hadcock agreed to collaborate with the present writer in compiling data for *Medieval Religious Houses*, he assembled and analysed the results of his researches, of which the main conclusions are printed in an appendix (pp. 360–6) to that work. It was only then that he became acquainted with Russell's monograph, and a comparison of figures revealed a remarkable agreement, rendered still more significant by the absolute independence and difference of method of the two workers. Thus, to take a few of the most striking figures: the estimated total for the Austin Canons, 1200–50, was 2879 (Russell) and 2880 (Hadcock), and for the same order in 1537–40 there was exact agreement on a figure of 1620; for the Austin Friars *c.* 1350 Russell gave 611 and Hadcock 609, and for the same order *c.* 1536 Russell 288 and Hadcock 294. Hadcock, in addition to the tables referred to above, compiled statistical lists for every religious house, which he allowed the

In the centuries from 1066 to 1540 certain broad tendencies can be discovered. Thus, as has been said elsewhere,[1] the numbers of monks and
regular canons rose steeply from the Conquest for more than a century.
At the death of Edward the Confessor there were only some 850 monks
in England, distributed over some 50 houses; by 1150 their numbers had
risen to 5500 in 290 houses, and by 1216 to 6200 in 340 houses.[2] Within
the same period the number of regular canons of all kinds had risen from
zero to 3800 in 220 houses, and those of nuns and canonesses from 200 in
twelve nunneries to 3000 in 140. Thus the total number of religious men
and women in England (excluding the Cistercian and other lay brethren)
had reached the astonishingly high total of 13,000. This total, for the
orders concerned, was never exceeded. The great age of monasticism had
passed, and a stabilization, if not a decline, of numbers was to be expected,
but it was undoubtedly hastened by the arrival of the friars, who drew off
at least some of the potential recruits from the abbeys, and who in the first
century of their existence in England founded some 200 houses with a
population of 5000 friars. During the same period the number of monks
had fallen by some 600 to 5500 and that of the canons by a small number
also. The nuns, on the other hand, had not notably decreased, and many
houses had actually increased in the thirteenth century. Thus the increase
from the friars had more than compensated for any decline in the older
orders, and in the early decades of the fourteenth century the population
of religious men and women in England reached an absolute maximum of
some 17,500, to which must be added, in the years before the suppression
of the Templars in 1312, over 600 belonging to the military orders. This
date of maximum, it is well to note, coincided almost exactly with the
maximum growth of the total population of England, which had risen
from perhaps one million in 1066 to some three millions in 1300, when a
decline set in some decades before the Great Pestilence.[3] It is probable
that there was a corresponding slight decline in the numbers of religious,
but all normal trends were dislocated by the catastrophe of the Black Death
of 1348–9, followed as it was by several heavy attacks of the plague later
in the century. The first and greatest onset, it is now generally agreed,
reduced the total population by something more than one-third. The
religious population, on the other hand, appears to have decreased by
something nearer to one-half.[4] It should be remembered, however, that
the estimated total fall of the population is little more than conjecture,

present writer to use. What follows is based chiefly upon this material, supplemented and
checked by Russell's figures. Both Russell and Hadcock use the figures in Dissolution
documents with caution, as showing a state of things at the end of a lengthy period of unrest;
there will probably never be complete agreement as to the statistical value of surrender
documents and pension lists.

   1 *MO*, 713–14.
   2 For these totals *v.* Knowles and Hadcock, *Medieval Religious Houses*, 360–6.
   3 For the population of England, *v.* Russell, *British Medieval Population*. All authorities
now accept *c.* 1300 as a peak.
   4 The losses of individual houses have been considered in greater detail above, pp. 10–12.

while on the other hand the figures for the religious, which are precise, come from various years between 1350 and 1370, when numbers may well have fallen through lack of recruitment as well as from the initial major loss.

It has often been stated in the past that the monks and other religious never made good these catastrophic losses, and that in fact they declined still more in number before the Dissolution. Careful examination has shown that this was not so. The numbers of all the various orders rose steadily after the first shock till c. 1422, the increase being between one quarter and one third over the post-pestilence low-water mark. The rise in many cases continued more slowly till c. 1500, save for the black canons, who barely held the numbers they had reached in 1400; thus at the end of the reign of Henry VII there were probably more religious in the country than at any time since 1348, the total, which was over 12,000, being an increase of some 50 per cent over the post-pestilence total of 8000, which itself was perhaps one-half of the total in 1300. In other words, the total in 1500 was between one-quarter and one-third less than the maximum of 1300, and almost equal to that of the older orders in 1200 before the arrival of the friars. Numbers mean little in spiritual reckoning, but however we may interpret them, they go far to dispel the opinion that the religious orders in the early Tudor period were in a condition of rapid numerical decline. It is true that some decline had undoubtedly taken place by 1535, but it is the still sharper decline, which may have been in the order of 25 per cent, between 1535 and the dissolution of each particular house, that has been responsible for many hasty judgements. The lists of those who signed the instrument of surrender or who later were assigned pensions are numerous, and these show an aggregate almost exactly equal to that of the lowest reached after the Great Pestilence. But during the last few years of monastic life, both before and after the visitation of 1535, the future had been so uncertain that recruitment had languished and many doubters had defaulted, while the methods and decrees of the visitors, and the wholesale dismissal of those under a certain age, brought the totals far below the aggregate of ten years before.

The principal orders, if considered separately, show significant differences in their periods of greatest expansion. The black monks attained their maximum shortly before 1154; they remained constant for half a century and then fell slightly. The white monks reached their highest point in the last decades of the twelfth century, when all their abbeys had had time to consolidate their position; they seem to have declined little (conversi apart) during the thirteenth century, for although one or two of the very largest houses, such as Rievaulx and Fountains, had declined somewhat from their phenomenal expansion, and had besides sent out numerous colonies to new foundations, the late arrivals such as Beaulieu and Hailes were still attracting numerous recruits in the reign of Henry III.

The black canons, whose period of expansion accompanied that of the Cistercians, and lasted even longer, followed much the same rhythm as the white monks, and seem to have kept their strength throughout the thirteenth century. The Premonstratensians, who were later to arrive and to expand, probably increased till the middle of the century, though their numbers were never very large.

The friars increased steadily from their first arrival till *c.* 1320, declining very little before the Black Death. Of the four orders the Preachers were slightly more numerous than the Minors before 1350, and the Carmelites were considerably more numerous than the Austin friars; these two last taken together were less in number than either of the other two taken separately.[1]

Besides being most numerous in the aggregate, the black monks had in general by far the largest houses throughout the Middle Ages. The average size of the fifty largest black monk abbeys and priories was about fifty inhabitants between 1154 and 1200, and about 30 in 1500; for the Cistercians the corresponding figures were in the neighbourhood of 30 and 18, and of the Austin canons 10 and 7. The largest recorded number for a black monk house is 150 for Christ Church, Canterbury, *c.* 1150,[2] but Gloucester, Reading and St Albans[3] all reached or approached a total of 100 at one moment or another in the twelfth century, while Westminster reached 90[4] Bury and Ely some 80, and Durham 70.[5] In *c.* 1500 Canterbury was still the largest house with 70 monks, Bury had 60, St Albans 57, Gloucester 50, Westminster 46, Ely 42 and Reading 40.[6] No other order, taken over the whole period, could come within sight of such totals. It is true that even the largest were for a moment equalled by two or three Cistercian abbeys, but the celebrity attained by these must not obscure the fact that their period of bloom was brief, and that at any time the majority of Cistercian abbeys were small. In the early days four or five stood high above all others. Rievaulx housed 140 choir monks and 600 *conversi* for a brief spell under Ailred;[7] Fountains had 80 and 200,[8] Waverley 70 and

---

1 The totals *c.* 1320 were approximately: Preachers, 1760; Minors, 1700; Carmelites, 800; Austin friars, 600.

2 Cf. *MO*, 714.

3 For Gloucester, *v. MO*, 714; for Reading, *v.* Knowles and Hadcock, *op. cit.* 74; for St Albans, *v. GASA*, I, 234.

4 For Westminster *v. VCH, London*, I, 436 n. 29, 447, and Knowles and Hadcock, *op. cit.* 80.

5 For Ely *v.* F. W. Williamson, *Letters of Osbert of Clare*, 10; for Bury, *VCH, Suffolk*, II, 69; for Durham, *Gesta Dunelm.*, 8.

6 Seventy Canterbury monks subscribed to the oath of Supremacy in 1534 (*L & P.* xv, 453); for Bury in 1538 *v. VCH, Suffolk*, II, 69; for St Albans, *VCH, Herts*, IV, 413; for Westminster, *VCH, London*, I, 447; for Ely, *VCH, Cambs*, II, 205; for Gloucester, *VCH, Glos*, II, 59.

7 This figure is given by the contemporary Walter Daniel in his *Vita Ailredi*, ed. Powicke, 97. It has often been questioned, but there seems no valid reason for dismissing or amending it.

8 For Waverley *v. Annales Monastici*, II, 244; the Fountains and Furness numbers can be fairly deduced from the size of the two dorters; for Louth Park *v. Chron. Abb. de Parco Lude s.a.* 1246.

120, Furness 70 and 120 and Louth Park 66 and 150, but the great majority never exceeded a total of 30 monks and 40 to 60 *conversi*, and some totalled much less, while by the thirteenth century Rievaulx and her peers had shrunk to more normal proportions. The Austin canons' houses were smaller still. Unlike the monks, they were usually founded with a fixed complement, 13 being the norm for a moderate house and 26 for an unusually large one. A few, exceptionally well endowed, exceeded even this number, but Oseney with 50, Cirencester, Leicester and Plympton with 40, and Merton and Bridlington with 36 and 32 were exceptional.[1] The great majority never rose to twenty canons, and houses of less than ten were common from the earliest times. After the Black Death even these modest numbers were scaled down, and perhaps Bridlington, Guisborough and Nostell were the only houses with about 30 canons in 1500. The Premonstratensians likewise had a complement of 13, or rarely of 26, and scarcely ever exceeded the higher figure.[2] Similarly the Carthusians normally had a community of 12 monks and a prior, with a smaller number of lay brothers; London and Sheen were exceptional in being 'double' houses, with a nominal complement of 26, which in the case of London at least was slightly exceeded in the early sixteenth century.

The houses of friars varied very considerably in size. Unlike the monks and canons, the friars were a quasi-floating population, controlled within certain limits by centralized authority, which could remedy a shortage in one friary from a superfluity elsewhere, when such existed. Three convents, in all the orders of friars, stood out far above the others, those of Oxford, Cambridge and London. The two former, besides containing students from the whole province, had a considerable quota of foreign friars taking a degree in theology, at least till the end of the fourteenth century. The London convents also were centres of domestic study, in addition to being at the heart of the largest city in the land. In the days of plenty before the Black Death both Preachers and Minors maintained about 90 at Oxford[3] and 75 at Cambridge,[4] while London held an equally important position with 90 or more. After these three, Canterbury, Lincoln, Northampton, Norwich, Stamford and York often had 50 friars or so; some of these were undoubtedly provincial houses of study. With

---

1 The Oseney figures of 50 canons and 24 lay brethren seem unduly large, but they are explicitly given in an instrument of mutual exchange of suffrages with Worcester printed by H. E. Salter, *Oseney Cartulary*, III, 79. Waltham had 48 canons in 1273 (*CPL*, I, 446). Nostell had 29 in 1540 (*VCH, Yorks*, III, 234).

2 H. M. Colvin, in his *White Canons in England*, Appendix II, pp. 358–9, gives all available figures and concludes: 'to find as many as thirty canons in an abbey would have been exceptional at any time [His only instances of such a number are Barlings, 33 in 1377, and Croxton, 30 in 1500] and many houses barely maintained the conventual minimum of thirteen for long periods in their history'.

3 At Oxford in 1377 there were 90 Preachers, 84 Minors, 45 Carmelites and 15 Austin Friars (Russell, 'Clerical Population', 207).

4 At Cambridge there were *c.* 75 Preachers and Minors in 1289 (*VCH, Cambs*, II, 270, 277); there were 55 Preachers in 1305 and 70 Minors. (A. G. Little, *Franciscan Papers*, 138.)

the Preachers Kings Langley, the common noviciate house, was in a place by itself with a maximum of 60 shortly after its foundation by Edward II.

With the pestilence the days of very large communities passed, never to return, save at Oxford and Cambridge;[1] London shrank to a mere 30 or so, yet many of the friaries in large towns were maintained at a strength of 20—a total which few had exceeded before 1348. The Carmelites and Austin friars followed a similar pattern on a reduced scale: thus the Carmelite communities at Oxford and Cambridge were between 40 and 50 strong, and few others exceeded 30; for the Austin friars the corresponding figures are 30 and 20. These two lesser orders, and in particular the Carmelites, recovered more fully than their greater rivals in the late fourteenth century, and *c.* 1400 the Carmelites are found maintaining 20 or more friars at a number of urban houses.

Although the numbers of women leading the religious life under fully claustral conditions in England were far less than those of the monks, canons and friars, historians who have noted this fact with some surprise and have contrasted it with the preponderance of women in recent centuries seem often to have failed to note that throughout the Middle Ages there were generally small groups of women engaged in caring for the sick and aged at many of the numerous hospitals. These women were almost all under some form of religious discipline, and were in effect as fully devoted to their life of religious charity as their sisters in nursing communities at the present day, though their number cannot be estimated for the purpose of a statistical total. When all reservations are made, however, it remains true that the religious orders organized for external work such as nursing, teaching or missionary enterprise are creations of the modern world, and that the Englishwomen of the later Middle Ages never became acquainted with the new and fervent forms of convent life that came into being in the Rhineland and the Low Countries; their total was therefore relatively small.

Of the nunneries that existed the Benedictine houses were the largest; a few were indeed very large, especially in the thirteenth century, when conditions seem best to have favoured the choice and accomplishment of a religious vocation for women in England. Thus Shaftesbury abbey, with over 120 nuns in 1326, was probably the largest religious community of its day, and Romsey, Wherwell and Wilton had each some 80 or 90 inmates.[2] These abbeys, and indeed a majority of the larger houses for women save perhaps for the Gilbertine priories, were largely recruited from the upper ranks of society. Close upon the Benedictines in numbers came the nuns of Sempringham, who retained their popularity till 1348 at least.

1 Oxford had 70 Preachers and 103 Minors in 1377. As Russell suggests (*art. cit.* 208), these large figures may have been caused by a post-pestilence 'bulge' of young friars being put to their divinity.
2 For Shaftesbury, *v.* references in *VCH, Dorset,* II, 77

Sempringham itself in its thirteenth-century heyday is said to have had 200 nuns, and Chicksand and Watton some 50. Of the other orders the Dominicanesses of Dartford and the Minoresses of Denney and the Minories in London had communities of 40 before the Pestilence and 30 in later times. No house of Austin canonesses rivalled these, but in the last phase of the Middle Ages the Bridgettine house of Syon had 60 nuns throughout its century of existence.

A consideration of all the available statistics suggests certain general reflections.

The first is, that the black monks throughout the whole medieval period had the largest communities in the country. This was primarily due to their great resources, which were more varied in character and more readily exploitable than those of the Cistercians, and usually scattered more broadly than those of the canons. This great wealth gave them a flexibility which the other monastic and canonical orders did not enjoy; although they might have an ideal number for their communities, this was so large and their wealth on the whole appreciated so greatly that the larger houses in normal times were able to accept all who wished to come. For all the other orders the small or moderately sized community was the norm, and the canons almost invariably had a fixed 'establishment' which they could not easily exceed. Indeed, there is evidence that the houses of the black canons in the later Middle Ages came almost to regard themselves as a house of prebendaries, and the instructions given by bishops at a visitation suggest that vacancies could at need be announced and filled.

A consequence of this is that monastic historians of modern times have not been altogether in error when they have concentrated their attention primarily upon the great Benedictine houses. They alone were sufficiently and permanently large to allow a rich and varied community life and tradition to continue from age to age, and thus to present the true material for history. It is with monasteries as with schools or any other type of institution—only the largest can exhibit continuously sufficiently varied manifestations of life to give a significant picture to posterity; a history of St Swithun's Cathedral priory, and of St Mary's College, at Winchester can be written, whereas from Alcester Abbey and the now-defunct grammar school of Alcester only a few scattered facts and incidents remain recorded.

A second impression is perhaps one of surprise that the orders of all kinds succeeded in maintaining themselves at what was after all very great numerical strength until the end of the Middle Ages, long after the Black Death with all its consequences and through all the wars and disturbances of the fifteenth century. Not only did they maintain the level they had reached fifty years after the pestilences, but towards the end of the century they reached a figure higher than any since 1350. It would seem clear that, whatever may have been the ill fortune of certain houses, and even of one or two orders, the religious life as it was then lived was showing no signs of extinction through lack of recruits in the first decades of Tudor rule. Certain orders, no doubt, had fared better than others. The friars, particularly the Franciscans and the Carmelites, had shown a remarkable buoyancy after the pestilences, and the circumstance may have given contemporaries the impression that they were considerably more numerous than was actually the case.[1] The greater black monk houses also had risen again, where they had suffered severely, to respectable totals, while the Carthusians continued to feel a certain pressure upon their very limited accommodation, as is shown by the additional cells constructed at Mount Grace early in the fifteenth century, and in the London house a hundred years later. The Cistercians, on the other hand, and the Austin canons had remained in general relatively few in number. A consideration of all the houses, other than the friaries, suggests that a monastery could usually, by dint of positive effort, make up its numbers to the strength permitted by its funds; the purely economic factor, so alien to present-day religious sentiment, was powerful in the later Middle Ages. Nevertheless, this motive told both ways; if a well-to-do house could maintain a fair rate of recruitment, its inmates were not all so sure of their vocation that they would stand by a sinking ship.

1 *V. supra*, pp. 103, 113, for the exaggerations of the satirists and the fantasies of Wyclif and the Lollards.

CHAPTER XXI

LITERARY WORK

I. HISTORIES, CHRONICLES, ANNALS AND LIVES

The extraordinary fertility of historical talent and industry among the monks and canons of the twelfth century, to which we owe so much of our knowledge both of the period and of themselves, had ceased before the reign of Henry III, and we have noted elsewhere that although the day was yet to come of one of the most remarkable historians of all the monastic centuries, Matthew Paris of St Albans, yet the thirteenth century saw the dwindling and extinction, one by one, of the greater number of the monastic and other religious chronicles that had hitherto served as precious sources for history of every kind.[1]

The extinction was never, indeed, complete before the very last years of the fifteenth century. Besides three or four great monastic houses, to be mentioned shortly, where the traditions of the past lingered on to inspire either a continuous or an interrupted succession of writers, individuals appeared here and there to revive literary forms that had disappeared outside the cloister, or to keep the record of national events. Of the latter class several, in addition to those shortly to be mentioned, deserve remembrance: Henry Knighton, a canon of Leicester Abbey, compiled a history of England from earlier sources, adding numerous local and national items from his own knowledge in the later books. He died in 1366, and his work was carried on by another hand to 1395.[2] Ralph Higden, Knighton's contemporary, a monk of Chester, compiled a valuable chronicle from early times to 1352, which was continued in turn by a monk of Malvern and one of Westminster. More important still is the fifteenth-century continuation of the Croyland chronicle which, beginning with the exuberance of pseudo-Ingulph, became for a century or more a sober domestic chronicle, and in its last phase appeared as 'by far the most important source of English origin' for the country's history. The last continuation, however, is probably not monastic for its whole length. While the earlier part, to 1470, is an undistinguished narrative by a monk, the final section, 1484–6, which was written by a public servant who was in the King's Council, and is of the greatest value, must probably be reckoned as non-monastic.[3]

The purely domestic chronicles, though more numerous, are of little importance after the end of the fourteenth century. The chronicle of

---

1 *RO*, I, 291 *seqq.*
2 For Knighton, *v. DNB* and A. H. Thompson, *Leicester Abbey.*
3 For the Croyland continuators, *v.* C. L. Kingsford, *English Historical Literature in the Fifteenth Century*, 179 *seqq.*

Peterborough continued after a fashion till 1400; that of Gloucester till 1412; that of the Cistercian Louth Park till 1413; that of Evesham till 1418; and the annals of Bermondsey till 1432. In every case, however, it is a flickering light that ultimately vanishes into the dark. Elsewhere, as for example from St Benet's of Holme, Waltham, Ely and Sherborne, fragments only survive.[1] More notable are the very full and valuable *Chronicle* of the Cistercian abbey of Meaux in the East Riding, which received its final shape from Thomas of Burton, who carried the story down to 1396 when he was elected abbot,[2] and the final continuation of the Glastonbury chronicle of John of Glastonbury which does not end till 1493.[3] It is perhaps worth noting that the minor annals of the fifteenth century (of which the Waltham annals are an example) while extremely jejune, nevertheless record natural phenomena in extravagant terms, thus unconsciously reverting to the practice of their more primitive predecessors of the centuries before the great age of monastic historians.

In the midst of this scanty and stunted literary herbage three or four clusters of more luxurious vegetation appear, and among them one stands notably out from the rest. The celebrated abbey of St Albans, ever since the days when Lanfranc's nephew, Abbot Paul, breathed new life into it, had been distinguished as a home of art and letters second to none throughout the centuries, and remarkable above all others for a constant tradition of historical writing, both domestic and national in scope, which reached the point of highest achievement in the days of Matthew Paris. This tradition never failed till the very end of the Middle Ages: there was a vigour in the air breathed in that great abbey that stimulated one or more of its sons in almost every generation to record and to assess the deeds and characters of its own great men, and also the actions of others on the wider stage of their country's history. The work of these historians, though often encouraged, inspired and assisted by an abbot, was essentially something spontaneous and unorganized; a precentor wrote himself, and gathered scribes and pupils round him; the impulse endured for twenty or thirty years and then died away, to be reborn after an interval of silence.

Roger of Wendover and Matthew Paris, the two earliest historians of the series, left behind them a tradition of historical writing which lasted for almost two centuries.[4] Paris had taken his *Chronica majora* down to 1259. It was continued almost immediately by an unknown writer whose work runs from 1259 to 1265 in the *Flores historiarum*. Then historical composition ceased for some forty years, to be resumed, at the instigation of Abbot John de Maryns, in 1307–8, with the *Opus chronicorum* which

1 Kingsford, *op. cit.* 158–61; the Sherborne fragment is printed pp. 347–9.
2 *Chronicon monasterii de Melsa*, ed. E. A. Bond.
3 *Johannis Glastoniensis historia de rebus Glastoniensibus*, ed. T. Hearne, 17–26.
4 The historiography of St Albans has found a masterly and sympathetic expositor in V. H. Galbraith, *The St Albans Chronicle*, 1406–20. The text above relies upon his valuable account of the succession of writers, which is contained in a long introduction to the book.

carried the story from 1259 to 1297. This in turn is continued by a small treatise of William of Rishanger, who related the events of the years 1297–1307; there is indeed good reason to believe that he was the author of the *Opus chronicorum*. He joined the monastery in 1270, when the memory of Paris must still have been fresh, and though he published nothing (so to say) for some thirty years, his preparations must have been made much earlier, leaving, in fact, only a short gap between Paris and himself. Rishanger was an industrious writer, and it has been suggested that the so-called *Annals of John Trokelowe*, covering the years 1307–23, are substantially his. Trokelowe's *Annals* were continued for 1323–4 by the short chronicle of Henry Blaneforde, and shortly afterwards another anonymous hand went over the same ground in the so-called *Chronicle of William Rishanger*, which in fact consists of excerpts from Rishanger and Nicholas Trivet, and runs from 1259 to 1307.

Save for this anonymous compiler, who worked *c.* 1350, there was no historian writing at St Albans in the early and mid-fourteenth century, though records of domestic events were kept and were later used, as will be seen, for the lives of the abbots. About the year 1376, however, there began to write another monk who, in the range of his interests and his industry, is not unworthy of comparison with Matthew Paris himself. This was Thomas Walsingham, who is found as precentor with some seniority in 1380, and who remained in that office till he was appointed prior of Wymondham in 1394–6. This last event fell within the last decade of the long abbacy of Thomas de la Mare, who at some time in his reign had constructed a large new scriptorium, and it is natural to connect this event and the interest in letters which it implies, with the rebirth of literary and artistic activity under Walsingham. He remained only for a short time at Wymondham. There is some evidence that he was not a successful administrator, and events were to show that Wymondham was not a peaceful house, but it does not seem that he was again precentor.

Walsingham's chief works in the field of general history were: a continuation of the *Chronica majora* of Matthew Paris (1272–1392); a condensed version of this (1327–92) compiled while he was at Wymondham; a history of his own times (1376–1420), now scattered over four separate manuscript volumes; a short history of the period 1327–1422; and the *Ypodigma Neustriae*, an epitome of English history from 911 to 1419, which has won very high praise from a distinguished historian of our own time.[1] Alongside of these works of national scope, the writers of St Albans had accomplished equally valuable work in domestic history. Matthew Paris's *Gesta abbatum*, being the lives of the abbots from earliest times to 1255, is a work that displays all his various characteristics to perfection— his industry in assembling material, his skill in constructing a narrative,

---

1 Galbraith, *op. cit.* introd. lx: 'It is a most skilful compilation, marked by a power of selection which makes it perhaps the best short history of England produced in the Middle Ages.'

his patriotic love of his home and (not least in evidence) that dislike of authority and those oblique references to the failings of those in power that enliven his wider histories and have coloured so many accounts of monastic life that derive from him. The series was continued by Rishanger (1255–1308) and then again by Walsingham, whose account of the great Abbot Thomas de la Mare and his two predecessors equals in fulness and vivacity the work of any contemporary medieval biographer.

As has been justly said, 'no such series of histories was produced in any other house at so late a date'.[1] The scriptorium of St Albans, indeed, in the last years of Walsingham's precentorship (1390–4), reached a height of productivity and technical achievement worthy of the days of Paris. Besides the works of history, domestic and national, Walsingham's elaborate *Liber benefactorum* and other similar books, together with a great series of administrative records, survive, all written in a hand, regular and legible, which, since it is used by a number of scribes, is clearly a 'St Albans' hand.[2] The impulse, and the output of well-written books, continued for a decade or two after Walsingham's departure for Wymondham. Nevertheless, he was in fact the last great historian at St Albans. The early part of the fifteenth century was a time of decline from the summertime of Thomas de la Mare, and neither the histories of England nor the lives of the abbots were continued in their original form. Interest in domestic history continued; some at least of the monks had the sense, almost peculiar to St Albans at this time, that their abbey was their world, and that its politics and personalities were as interesting and as important as the pacts and sects of the greater world without. The registers of the abbots of the century, especially, in their different ways, those of Whethamstede's two terms of office and of Wallingford show this—the former probably written, or at least controlled, by the abbot himself, the latter by no friend of the abbot. Both represent a decline from the *Gesta abbatum*; the former by its wordy preciosity and the latter by its narrow range of interests and its degeneration into a series of connecting links between documents; but taken together they still represent an attempt at connected history, sometimes touching the history of the country, such as is found in no other monastery, and which, alike in its ambitions and in its critical reflections on the abbots concerned, faintly echoes the celebrated master who had given lustre to its scriptorium two hundred years before.[3]

Walsingham had another side to his learning. He was a classical adept of the medieval model, and encouraged by his prior, Simon Sutherey, he devoted his energies after his return from Wymondham principally to

---

1 Galbraith, *ibid*. xl.

2 *Ibid*. lxi: 'The merit of the distinctive hand in which they are written is, above all, its legibility. The letter-forms of this script are those of the ordinary cursive writing of the time, the Court Letter; but so boldly and clearly is the writing done as almost to raise it to the status of a book hand.'

3 *Annales Johannis de Amundesham*; *Reg. quorundam abbatum*. Both are edited by H. T. Riley.

works illustrating classical subjects taken from mythology and history. The *Archana Deorum* is a commentary on the *Metamorphoses* of Ovid, giving an account of the origins of the gods; *Dictys Cretensis* is an enlargement of a post-classical history of Alexander the Great. Walsingham's Latin style is correct, but flowery, and it has been suggested[1] with great probability that his writings and example did much to influence the last notable figure in the literary history of St Albans, Abbot John Whethamstede.

John Whethamstede has been variously judged by historians and critics in the past eighty years.[2] The editor of his register in the Rolls Series and other writers of the last century, approaching the subject either with an exaggerated notion of monastic rusticity, or seeking in vain in his verses for the precise and polished Ovidian felicities of Calverley or the *Sabrina corolla*, see in him a precursor of the English Renaissance or dismiss him as a tasteless and pedantic monk. Perhaps, if his work is viewed as a whole, both in itself and in the wider Europe of his day, we shall feel that when compared from a purely humanistic point of view with the great Italians— with Petrarch or Poggio or Aeneas Sylvius—Whethamstede cuts a very poor figure, lacking both measure and style and thought. Nevertheless, he appears as a noteworthy harbinger of the English humanists, in his imitation of Boccaccio and others, in his use of classical writers in preference to medieval authorities for all kinds of topics, and in his endeavour to imitate classical flowers of speech in his own compositions.

Whethamstede's voluminous works, at present scattered and dismembered, are worthy of note, if not for their intrinsic value, at least for the indication they give of the tastes of the age. The following are known to be extant:[3] the *Granarium* (in part), the *Pabularium poetarum* and the *Palearium poetarum*; two others, entitled *Propinarium* and *Manipularium*, have hitherto escaped discovery, if indeed they exist. The *Granarium* was the abbot's most considerable work, and regarded as such by Duke Humphrey, who presented a copy to the university of Oxford in 1444. It is an encyclopedia of the medieval pattern, and the first part, containing more than a hundred long articles, deals with historical events, personages and writers, and particularly with contemporary happenings such as the Councils and the trials of Hus, Wyclif and Jerome of Prague; Whethamstede uses classical and medieval authorities, including Adam Easton, in

---

1 Galbraith, *op. cit.* introd. xlv.

2 L. F. R. Williams, *History of the Abbey of St Albans,* 204, considers his style 'florid, obscure and incomprehensible'. H. T. Riley, *Amundesham,* II, lvi–lvii, remarks that 'the demerits of these effusions [i.e. Whethamstede's verses] may be summed up in a few words; they are written without regard to the laws of either grammar, metre or sense, being a mass of mere gibberish, to a great extent, and in the eyes of an ordinary scholar, alike beneath criticism and contempt', while his prose is 'often in bad taste, inflated, involved and verbose'. For a balanced judgement on the Latinity of the early English humanists, *v.* E. F. Jacob, 'Florida Verborum Venustas', in *BJRL,* XVII (1933), 264–90.

3 What follows owes much to Chapter V of an unpublished Ph.D. thesis of Manchester University by Miss C. E. Hodge, 'The Abbey of St Albans under John of Whethamstede' (1933).

the article on the cardinalate. The second part, mostly on ethical topics, uses the classics almost exclusively.

The *Palearium* [chaff-bin] *poetarum*, a work of some seven hundred articles on classical mythology, is taken for the most part directly from Boccaccio's *De genealogiis deorum*, and has been described as the first truly humanistic book written by an Englishman. Whethamstede lacked the genius and the personality of Petrarch and Boccaccio; he also lacked their sense of form and style. What is interesting in his work is his recourse to the pagan classical authors exclusively for teaching on such subjects as the nature of the soul. The *Pabularium* [food-store] *poetarum* is no more than a collection of quotations from the poets, medieval and classical alike. Ovid and Virgil are the favourites.

Two groups of articles in the *Granarium* deserve further notice. The one is of monastic subjects, and here Whethamstede uses almost exclusively the tract on monastic origins which, as will be seen, was current in England from the middle of the fourteenth century. The other is of Councils and Church government, a topic on which the writer must have heard and read a great deal. Here he uses a wide selection of recent writers: Alexander of Hales, Pierre de la Palu, James of Viterbo, Aquinas, Dante and Marsiglio. While he nowhere elaborates his own views, he seems to favour the claim of a Council to be, when in existence, able to judge and act independently of an erring pope. Thoughout these articles he uses contemporary sources and documents such as the *Acta* of the Council of Basel.[1] Indeed, it may well be that anxiety to see in Whethamstede an early English humanist has obscured his greater claim to be regarded as a serious historian. His wide reading in contemporary and recent authors, and his use of them and of documents to illustrate the history of his own times, together with his interest in current theories of ecclesiastical government, raise him above the level of the monastic chroniclers, even of a Walsingham, and place him on the margin of the territory of the political thinker and critical historian.

Second only to St Albans in its tradition of historical writing was the great northern cathedral priory (often, indeed, even by contemporaries styled 'abbey') of Durham. Here the tradition was even older than the Conquest, looking back to Bede and his pupils and resuming soon after the refoundation with Simeon and his successors. It continued in writings of varied length and value till the end. Geoffrey of Coldingham (1152–1214) wrote a chronicle that was continued by Robert of Greystanes (1214–1336), and this in turn by William de Chambre whose narrative, based on earlier records, continued beyond the Dissolution to 1571.[2]

---

1 Miss Hodge suggests that Whethamstede borrowed the *Acta* of Constance from Humphrey of Gloucester, whose copy is now B.M. Cott. Nero, E V, and those of Basel from Norwich (now MS. 142 of Emmanuel College, Cambridge); it is of course possible that St Albans had both.

2 *Hist. Dunelmensis scriptores tres*, ed. J. Raine.

Alongside of these there are, besides the incomparable treasures of the archives, valuable accounts of fifteenth-century elections, while the aspect of the monastery and something of its spirit is preserved in the idealized account of the old conservative written in the reign of Elizabeth I.[1] Durham, in addition, might well have had a still fuller history of its medieval life, for John Wessyngton, probably before his election as prior in 1416, spent a great deal of time and labour in collecting and arranging charters and documents, after the manner of Thomas Elmham of Canterbury, and in building up a history from earlier chronicles. The result, covering the history of the community and bishopric from the foundation of Lindisfarne in 635 to the death of Hugh du Puiset in 1195, is extant, and has recently been identified, but unfortunately Wessyngton did not continue his narrative down to the fourteenth century, when it would have been of the greatest interest.[2]

A third centre where chroniclers continued to work was Canterbury. Here in the twelfth and early thirteenth centuries the cathedral monastery of Christ Church had been the home of Eadmer, historian of his times and biographer of St Anselm, of several of the biographers of St Thomas, and of Gervase and his continuator. Then the stream dried up, though here and there a fragment survives, such as the fifteenth-century chronicle of John Stone (1415–71) and still less ambitious annals.[3] In the fourteenth century, however, the neighbouring abbey of St Augustine's housed the most industrious chronicler of his day, William Thorne (fl. 1380–1400) who, working over an elusive predecessor, Sprot, produced what is perhaps the most bulky continuous monastic chronicle of the age, *Chronicon de rebus gestis abbatum S. Augustini Cantuariae*. Thorne used and reproduced a vast quantity of charters and papal documents, some of them spurious; his interests lay in administration and litigation rather than in the personalities and activities of abbots and monks, but here and there, and particularly when he reached his own times and when he describes his adventures as proctor of his abbey at Rome 1387–90, he has many vivid touches. Shortly after Thorne had ceased writing in 1397, another monk of the house, Thomas Elmham, began an even more exhaustive overhaul of the documents with a view to producing what may be called a full documentary history of the abbey. Before he had completed his task, however, he departed in 1414 to be prior of Lenton, then much decayed; before settling down he was perhaps caught up into great affairs as chaplain to Henry V, whom he would thus have accompanied on the

1 *Rites of Durham*, ed. (1) J. Raine; ed. (2) J. T. Fowler. The date of composition is perhaps 1593.
2 For Wessyngton's work *v*. H. H. E. (later Sir Edmund) Craster, 'The Red Book of Durham'.
3 *V. Chronicle of John Stone*, ed. W. G. Searle; 'Chronicle of William Glastynbury, monk of Christ Church Priory, 1418–48', ed. C. E. Woodruff, and 'Monastic Chronicle of Christ Church, 1331–1415' (anonymous), ed. C. E. Woodruff.

campaign of Agincourt and later celebrated both in verse and prose, the prose life being the *Gesta Henrici Quinti*, a vivid eye-witness's account, and the other the *Liber metricus*, partly based on the *Gesta*. The *Liber metricus* is certainly his, but his identity with the chaplain must be considered doubtful in the extreme.[1]

II. MONASTIC HISTORY AND THEORY

In addition to the writings which can be grouped conveniently under the name of an individual or of a monastery there are one or two examples of a literary topic which, in true medieval fashion, went the rounds, so to say, of the monastic world, being copied, improved, defined, abbreviated or amplified as the case might be. Its career, therefore, is in a sense analogous to the fate of some of the great enterprises of Maurist scholarship which, begun as individual undertakings, were taken up as a corporate work by the monks and then, after a long lapse, were again revived in a more ambitious and critical form by one of the national academies. One such topic, which has been investigated in some detail, was exploited in a series of treatises and disquisitions on the origins of the monastic life, and as such floated about for more than a century.[2] The subject probably had its beginnings in the controversies which had long been smouldering and which broke into new flame in the fourteenth century, between the Austin canons and the black monks, as to the relative antiquity of their respective institutes, and between the old property-holding orders and the mendicant friars on the subject of evangelical poverty, the latter controversy being amalgamated with the former by the claim of the Carmelites and Austin friars to an antiquity superior to that of the black monks and canons. The purely controversial aspect of the matter was partly lost sight of behind a more loosely apologetic trend, which stressed the excellence of early monasticism and the examples of monastic sanctity, while the whole subject received additional elaboration from the 'genuine historical and antiquarian enthusiasm' present in the scriptoria of several of the larger abbeys.

The work seems to have originated at Bury St Edmunds between *c.* 1300 and *c.* 1350, for a manuscript attributing it to this source was written at Tournus in Burgundy *c.* 1365. It had four themes: monastic origins; monastic saints; the history of other, non-monastic orders; and a defence

---

1 Thorne's chronicle was printed by R. Twysden in *Scriptores X* (1652); cf. also *William Thorn's Chronicle of St Augustine's, Canterbury*, trans. A. H. Davis (1934, introduction). For Elmham, *v.* C. L. Kingsford, *English Historical Literature*, 45 *seqq.*; the *Gesta Henrici Quinti*, commonly attributed to him, was ed. by B. Williams for the Church Hist. Soc. 1850; his *Liber metricus* was ed. by C. A. Cole for *Memorials of Henry V* (RS), 1858. Professor V. H. Galbraith, *The St Albans Chronicle*, introd. xxiii, has contested Elmham's authorship of the *Gesta*, and certainly the tone and style of the work are foreign to Elmham's capacity, as seen in his other writings. The *Vita et gesta Henrici Quinti*, ed. by T. Hearne under Elmham's name in 1727, has no connexion whatever with him.

2 W. A. Pantin, 'Some Medieval English Treatises on the Origins of Monasticism'.

of the 'possessioners' against the mendicants. Ten years later, the first section only was worked up at Bury into an instruction for novices, with an emphasis on the primitive purity of the monastic life, and a little later was excerpted by a monk of Durham, Richard of Segbroke, a devotional writer. At about the same time, that is, c. 1390, the whole was worked over and amplified by Thomas of Walsingham at St Albans, and appears in a work of two volumes, immediately following the *Gesta abbatum*. This version was given actuality by its adaptation to the needs of time and place. The black monks were being attacked by Wyclif and his followers and defended by Sutherey and Binham, doctors of theology of St Albans; proposals for confiscation were in the air, and Lollardy was active in the parishes of the abbey. A second St Albans book, compiled ten or twenty years later, contains part of Walsingham's treatise, while Abbot Whethamstede's *Granarium* of about the same date uses it for the articles on monastic life.[1] Meanwhile it had penetrated to Glastonbury c. 1420 in a revised version, compiled at Bury St Edmunds possibly by no less a person than John Boston the bibliographer; and c. 1440 this emended version had reached Durham where, either at the date at which the manuscript was written or earlier in the time of Segbroke, it was augmented by some parts of an independent treatise on monastic history which was the work of Uthred of Boldon. Yet a third version of part of the same work comes from Durham at almost the same time, when the great Prior Wessyngton excerpted or revised the original, adding lists of monastic saints and a defence of the antiquity of the monastic order as against the regular canons. This does not exhaust the developments of the story. Extracts dating from the fifteenth and early sixteenth centuries can be assigned to Mount Grace and Colchester as places of origin, while in the fourteenth century its influence can be traced in a letter from Walter Hilton, a canon of Thurgarton, written to Adam Horsley, afterwards a Carthusian; in a sermon preached at a provincial chapter of unknown date;[2] and even in the discourse of Henry V to the delegates summoned to meet him at Westminster in May 1421.[3] Finally, and again from Durham, comes a compilation from Wessyngton's work, made by William Todd, a monk of Durham who survived the Dissolution as a prebendary and was still alive in 1567.

Altogether, this long series of copies and alterations is an excellent example of the slow and conservative motion of monastic thought and composition in the last centuries of the medieval world. We see a work, which in an ealier century might have come out as a finished treatise by Malmesbury or Ailred, and which at a later time would have crystallized rapidly in print, now passing from house to house and from hand to hand in the process of adaptation to more than one purpose or need. We see also how four of the most distinguished monks of the period—Uthred,

1 *V. supra*, p. 268.   2 Printed by W. A. Pantin in *DR*, LI, 295 *seqq.*
3 *V. MC*, II, 99.

Walsingham, Whethamstede, Wessyngton—and perhaps John Boston also, have a part, in this manner or in that, in its growth. Though destined ultimately to remain buried in its manuscript forms it is nevertheless, as has been well pointed out, a true ancestor of the antiquarian and biblio-graphical collections of Bale and Leland, and of other antiquaries of the Continent. It is in a sense the English pendant of Trithemius.

Born of the same circumstances, and perhaps related in some fashion to these apologetic treatises on monastic origins, are two compositions on the value of the monastic life by Uthred of Boldon.[1] These in their turn may depend upon lost predecessors; one of them certainly has a link with a commentary on the Rule of St Benedict written by another monk of Durham and prior of Durham College, John of Beverley, *c.* 1340. Of Uthred's two treatises the one sets out to prove how the monastic life began and whether it is a lawful form of life, while the other is concerned with the relative worth of the monastic and secular lives. Although in the former the writer is clearly concerned to discomfit his two opponents, the mendicants and Wyclif, yet his tone is calm and moderate, and he cuts the ground from beneath Wyclif by arguing that the monastic ideal is as old as the human race, and corresponds to a profound need in human nature. In the second, he avoids making any claim that monastic observances have any magical or purely mechanical efficacy apart from the good will and the love of God of the individual, which may be found equally in any walk of life, and he takes up the position, classical among theologians since Aquinas, that the 'mixed' life, made up of active and contemplative elements, is the best. A very sensitive critic has seen in these treatises an unexpected 'Aristotelianism' of outlook: while the monastic life is in a sense natural and reasonable, spiritual men, being by definition more virtuous and reasonable than others, are, like the Aristotelian well-balanced citizen, best qualified to govern others. Such a view which, as has been suggested, may have been in part a rationalization of Uthred's own long contentment with the dignified, ordered, courteous and intellectual family life at Durham, is in a number of ways a more attractive one than the obscurantist and formalist picture given by Erasmus, or even of the fierce and almost inhuman zeal of some of the writers of earlier centuries. It lacks, however, the living power of the words that nerve men to keep difficult ways, and it wants the theological strength of Aquinas, who teaches that while the moral virtues, as Aristotle held, are a mean between extremes, the Christian and supernatural virtues tend always to the limit of their powers: 'Be ye perfect, as your heavenly father is perfect.' In the lack of this impulse in Uthred's work it may be allowable to see the reason for the lack of strength in the English monastic world in any hour of crisis.

1 W. A. Pantin, 'Two treatises of Uthred of Boldon on the Monastic Life'.

III. POETS AND HAGIOGRAPHERS

The fifteenth century in England has often been characterized as a literary desert, belying the promise of the age of Rolle, of Langland, and of Chaucer, and though the labours of a series of distinguished scholars have shown that the output in verse and prose, and the popularity of much that was written, were both very considerable, even the most recent and learned of those who have given general surveys of the age, and who have endeavoured to rebut the charges of sterility and incompetence in its writers, are forced to cast their net very wide, and to include private letters and anonymous lyrics, in order to make any show with their spoils.[1] From what has been said of the libraries and studies of the monks and, *mutatis mutandis*, of the friars also, no great share in the groundwork of English literature will be expected of those whose reading and writing was still predominantly in Latin.

There is, however, a notable and unexpected figure in the early fifteenth century who has always been given a prominent place in the history of English poetry. John Lydgate (?1370–?1451), a monk of Bury St Edmunds from his fifteenth year, is one of the trio of contemporary poets who knew Chaucer well.[2] Lydgate, like Hoccleve, regarded that great poet as his master whom he desired to imitate; what jewels there may be among the dross of his verses (he tells us with obvious sincerity) are the reflections of Chaucer's phrases. Of Lydgate's movements and employments, apart from his literary work and its rewards, very little is known, and his biographers and critics have been forced to make what they can out of his writings. In consequence, two very different pictures have been drawn of him. The eminent scholar[3] who contributed a very full account to the *Dictionary of National Biography* more than fifty years ago assumed that Lydgate spent much of his mature life in attendance on his patrons at the English Court and in France; a more recent critic, assuming that the poet spent almost his whole working life within the cloister uses this

---

1 Cf. C. L. Kingsford, *Prejudice and Promise in the Fifteenth Century* (1925); chapters by G. Saintsbury in *Cambridge History of English Literature*, II (1908); H. S. Bennett, 'Chaucer and the Fifteenth Century' (*Oxford History of English Literature*, II (1947)), and the relevant sections in the *Cambridge Bibliography of English Literature*, I. For a few doubtful or probable ascriptions of Miracles and Moralities to monastic authors *v*. E. K. Chambers, *Oxford History of English Literature*, III, Ch. I.

2 The bibliography of Lydgate is extensive; part of it may be found in *CBEL*, I. Since the text of this chapter was written a full-length study of Lydgate has appeared in W. F. Schirmer's *John Lydgate, Ein Kulturbild aus den 15 Jahrhundert*. This is an extremely learned and thorough study of Lydgate's individual works, broken up by sections of political and social history. It is a mine of references to philological literature, but there are few literary or personal judgements, and despite its detail it is extremely difficult to discover the writer's answer to several large questions, e.g. how long was Lydgate actually resident at Bury, or at the Court? A critical list of the poet's authentic works is to be found in *The Minor Poems of John Lydgate*, ed. H. N. MacCracken, Part I, introd., 'The Lydgate Canon', v–lviii; this is reproduced, with minor alterations and criticisms, by W. F. Schirmer, *op. cit.* 228–43; he has also a valuable Excursus (223–8) on Lydgate's posthumous fame with a full bibliography.

3 Sir Sidney Lee.

circumstance to give substance and point to his judgement on his poetic work.[1] Absolute certainty is unattainable, but the internal evidence of Lydgate's poetry, added to the fairly numerous references to his financial position and to what we know of the conditions of society, monastic and aristocratic, of his day, would seem to show that the former of these two views is substantially correct:[2] Lydgate would thus be seen as passing much of his life outside the cloister and on the fringes of court life, a prominent example of a tendency, visible in so many directions at the time, towards relaxation of the bonds of community life, while at the same time his close links with his patrons are another aspect of that phase of social life immediately preceding the Wars of the Roses, seen also in the domestic history of St Albans, in which the families both of national and regional importance engaged themselves in patronal relationships of every kind, with monks and men of letters as well as with retainers.

Lydgate's works, as was his life, were long. He is in some ways a magnified version, an extension, of the monk of Chaucer as seen in his tale, medieval in his formlessness and his pillaging of classical stories and his easy passage through every field—devotional, scientific, philosophical, legendary, historical and purely personal—and akin in so many ways to the contemporary encyclopaedic and classical spirit of Whethamstede. Certainly it is not easy to understand how a cloistered monk, even of such a great house as Bury, could have obtained the patronage, known the circumstances, and met the demands of so many distinguished patrons, and the indications that he was often in London between 1399 and 1413, and that he was in Paris, at least in 1426, are strong. His visit to Paris, indeed, probably in the train of the Earl of Warwick, was a tribute to his position as poet laureate, an ambassador of English letters. He wrote on a great variety of subjects: London life, autobiography, translations of psalms and hymns, devotional expositions of the liturgy, translations of long poems, and a number of shorter verses, some satirical on the foibles of women,

---

1 Bennett, *op. cit.* 110–11; 138–46. Mr Bennett assumes (p. 138) that from Lydgate's fifteenth year 'the rest of his life was spent mainly in the cloister at Bury, or nearby at Hatfield Broadoak. Life passed him by while he spent endless hours in the scriptorium turning out verses', and he concludes (p. 110) that Lydgate 'may well serve as a horrid example of the worst that this system could evolve'. Without denying the uninspired verbosity of much of Lydgate's verse (which nevertheless had considerable influence in moulding the English literary vocabulary), it might be argued that dulness and prolixity are not confined to monastic poets, and that some of Lydgate's work does in fact show considerable sympathy with various aspects of extra-claustral life. Indeed, a case might be made against him as a monk on this very score. And after all, does a poet (as opposed to a dramatist or a novelist) live by contact with the world? Did Lydgate lack all 'precious experience of life' (p. 110) and live 'above the battle' (p. 138) any more than the distributor of stamps for the county of Westmorland who regarded poetry as 'emotion recollected in tranquillity'?

2 According to Sir Sidney Lee, Lydgate was born *c.* 1370, professed at Bury in 1386, and spent much time in London at Court 1399–1413. He was in Paris in 1426, and from 1423 to 1434 nominally prior of Hatfield Broadoak, though often in London and Windsor at Court. From 1434 till his death he was at Bury. It does not seem that Schirmer greatly alters this picture; he adds interesting details (from EETS, LXVI (o.s.), p. xxiii) of Lydgate's pension (*op. cit.* 214–15, n. 427).

some written in the person of a lover to his absent mistress, together with 'mummings' for the young King Henry VI and an official ode for his coronation. His fame was wide, and we find Abbot Whethamstede commissioning a poem on St Alban.[1] Though he complains of poverty (another indication that he was not living in his monastic home) he received fair rewards for his poems, and in the last twenty-odd years of his life enjoyed a royal pension.

As a poet Lydgate has been the object of the most diverse judgements. In his lifetime and for fifty years or more after his death he was consistently ranked along with Gower and Chaucer as one of the three ornaments of English poetry. Although a monk and a medieval man in every line, he was in high favour with the Elizabethans, and in later centuries Thomas Gray, Coleridge and Churton Collins have been his warm advocates. Recently, though his works have been assiduously edited and studied by scholars of Middle English and though his importance as a master of prosody and coiner of words has been amply proved, literary opinion has been harsh even to cruelty. Lydgate's fecundity is certainly formidable; his total output of verse has been assessed at 140,000 lines; and if only those who have read him in totality are competent to judge him, few would dare to praise. If, on the other hand, it counts for anything that several of his autobiographical and occasional, as well as some of his religious poems can be read with interest and even with pleasure, then Lydgate may be placed, if not among the great, yet among those who deserve recognition. Regarded not as a poet but as a type, Lydgate is a true child of his age. His outlook and his limitations are largely those of a Whethamstede. He has the same learning, the same acquaintance with the great Italians of the thirteenth century, and fails equally to appreciate and imitate what to us is most admirable in them. Like Whethamstede, also, he lacks a sense of form and proportion. It may be added in his favour that even if his life was spent largely outside the cloister, there was nothing either in it or in his writings to give scandal, and his religious poems have a note of genuine piety and sincerity, though they lack depth and any trace of spiritual vision.

The only other notable name in poetry connected with a religious house is that of John Audelay, now principally remembered for a quatrain of haunting pathos which probably appeals rather through the modern 'romantic' associations of its language than by intrinsic poetic qualities.[2]

---

1 *Reg. J. Whethamstede*, ed. H. T. Riley, I, 462; *Amundesham*, I, 256. The poet received £3. 6s. 8d.

2 For all that is known of Audelay *v. The Poems of John Audelay*, ed. E. K. Whiting. For his disabilities, cf. his own words, *ibid.* 224: 'John, the blynde Awdelay...deef, sick, blynd as he lay.' The quatrain occurs *ibid.* 148:

> 'As I lay seke in my langure
> In an abbey here be west,
> This boke I made with gret dolour
> When I might not slep ne haue no rest.'

Audelay, who, as he himself tells us, composed much of his poetry when blind and deaf, was probably not a religious, but a secular chaplain who ended his days as a corrodian in the infirmary, but his memory clings to the quiet ruins of Haughmond, his 'abbey here be west', just as his perhaps unthinking association of heart-sickness with the setting sun recalls the 'western brookland' of another poet, only a few miles to the south beyond the Wrekin.

Biography, which had been a literary genre of such importance in the eleventh and twelfth centuries, languished with the decline of a humanistic education before 1200, and did not fully revive until the new humanism of the early sixteenth century inspired Cavendish and Roper. Hagiography, however, understood not as the direct record of a disciple or a contemporary, but as the production in bulk of saints' lives from existing material, was in favour in the late fourteenth and early fifteenth centuries, and we have already seen how a succession of monastic writers compiled lists and notes on the lives of sainted monks of the past.[1] Much of the work was done in response to individual requests. Thus Lydgate produced for his patrons and confrères lives of St Margaret, St Edmund and St Fremund, and the Austin friar Osbern Bokenham of Stoke-by-Clare (?1392–?1447) translated into verse lives of holy women for friends and patronesses.[2] The most industrious worker in this field was, however, the Austin friar of Lynn, later provincial of his order, John Capgrave (1393–1464), who besides his *Chronicle of England* compiled in Latin a great collection of saints' lives known as the *Nova Legenda Angliae*, and wrote in English the lives of St Gilbert of Sempringham and St Katherine. Capgrave also extended his biographical activities into contemporary history, and in his *Liber de illustribus Henricis* dealt with Henry IV and Henry V, while in his vanished life of Humphrey Duke of Gloucester he celebrated the patron whom he shared with the leading literary men of his age.[3] Capgrave's work on Henry V may serve to introduce a little group of royal biographies of the early fifteenth century: a history of the life of Richard II by a monk of Evesham; two lives of Henry V attributed to Elmham, one in verse, and the other, of greater value as embodying many details of personal observation, in prose. A little later John Blakman, Fellow of Merton and Eton, and later a Carthusian, wrote on the life and miracles of Henry VI.[4] Yet another piece of biography is the history of the death of Archbishop Scrope by Clement Maidstone, originally a Trinitarian of Hounslow, later a priest of Syon.[5]

1 For saints' lives, v. CBEL; CHEL, II, ch. viii and Bennett, *op. cit.* 151–2.
2 Bennett, *op. cit.* 112. Cf. also the introduction to EETS, CCVI (o.s.), 1938.
3 For Capgrave, v. CBEL and Bennett, *op. cit.* 267. For an account of his life and works see also the foreword by F. J. Furnivall to Capgrave's *Life of St Katherine of Alexandria*, ed. C. Horstman.
4 For these v. C. L. Kingsford, *English Historical Literature in the Fifteenth Century.*
5 H. Wharton, *Anglia sacra*, II, 369–72.

A figure of a different type, round whom another group of treatises crystallized, was that of the Swedish noblewoman, St Birgitta or Bridget (1303–73; canonized 1391). Two circumstances combined to commend this saint to English writers. The less important was the presence in Rome, during the process of canonization, of Adam Easton, monk of Norwich and cardinal, who wrote a tract in defence of her actions and revelations, and may also have encouraged Abbot Geoffrey of Byland, and Richard Lavenham, a Carmelite confessor of Richard II, who did likewise. The other and more influential circumstance was the foundation by Henry V of the Bridgettine house of Syon and the close connexion with Sweden brought about by the Swedish marriage of the Princess Philippa. This led a number of writers to engage upon the task of presenting St Bridget to their countrymen; one of the first was John Audelay, the poet of Haughmond.[1]

The field of late Middle English literature has been so assiduously cultivated in recent years by English and American scholars that any attempt at a full treatment of religious writers would be out of place here. Enough has perhaps been said to show that while the monks and religious in general made no such decisive mark in vernacular literature in the later centuries of the Middle Ages as they had in the Latin literature of the twelfth century, yet a considerable fraction of the total output of writings of all kinds, English and Latin, was still coming from them, and in particular they were taking their full share of the fruits of patronage in an age when much of the literature of the times owed its existence to the requests or favour of individuals.

IV. ILLUMINATION

On an earlier occasion we noted the gradual shifting of the art of illustrating and decorating manuscripts from the cloister to the commercial *atelier*, followed after a brief interval by the gradual decline of this particular branch of art in England shortly before the middle of the fourteenth century. Though there was a notable revival during the reign of Richard II which resulted in the production of works of high excellence in this country, often by artists of foreign provenance, the monasteries had no share in this and never recaptured their early pre-eminence. The art continued to be practised in the cloister by individuals, as surviving examples show, but it was usually on a modest scale, in service books of secondary importance and in chronicles and lists of benefactors. Only one artist of eminence from among the religious deserves particular notice, together with another attribution, less certain and in any case nameless.

The first to be mentioned, a Friar Preacher, is the only medieval artist of note in the English province of his order of whom any record survives.

[1] The topic has been investigated in an unpublished Manchester M.A. thesis (no date) by F. R. Johnston, 'The Cult of St Bridget of Sweden in fifteenth-century England'. For Adam Easton *v. supra* pp. 57–8.

His name was John Siferwas, and research and his own love of blazonry have supplied a few facts about his origin and religious life.[1] The scion of a landed family of Berkshire, he appears in 1380 as a friar of Guildford receiving the first of the minor orders; he has besides left us several portraits of himself (and portraiture was a forte with him) including a large painting of himself and Lord Lovel of Tichmersh.[2] Two important works of his survive: the so-called Sherborne Missal, executed between 1396 and 1407 for the abbot of Sherborne and the bishop of Salisbury,[3] and a gospel-lectionary commissioned by Lord Lovel for Salisbury Cathedral.[4] Siferwas, the exponent of a style wholly different from that of East Anglia and possibly deriving from Flanders, was an artist of genius. His strength does not lie precisely either in minute design or harmonious and grand composition but in the richness of his work, in his portraits and liturgical groups and above all in his skill as a painter of birds.[5] In the last-named genre, indeed, he reaches the highest level, anticipating by five centuries the art of Bewick and the illustrators of Gilbert White; his minutely accurate and extremely beautiful portrayal of the different species, male and female, could have resulted only from long and loving observation; each bird or animal is a sensitive and finished picture; there is no question of mere line-drawing or semi-humorous treatment, as in the East Anglian psalters; his birds are studies from nature.[6] Whether such illustrations, half aesthetic, half scientific in their appeal, not forming an integral part of a great design, but rather distracting the mind from the purpose of the book, are any more suitable to the margin of a missal than are the humorous and grotesque sketches of the East Anglian psalters, must be left to the judgement of those who can assess without prejudice the claims of human nature and of spiritual edification.

Competent criticism has seen in the Sherborne Missal the work of several inferior hands, those of pupils of Siferwas, but all indications are that his school was a personal one and in no sense a tradition of his order or of a particular house. Moreover, the missal came to him as a written work; the script was finished at Sherborne by a monk, John Whas;[7]

---

1 For Siferwas *v.* introduction to the Roxburghe Club's publication of *The Sherborne Missal* (1920), by J. A. Herbert, and M. Rickert, *Painting in Britain: the Middle Ages*, 178–80.

2 This, a page from the lectionary, is reproduced in colour as the frontispiece of Dr Millar's second volume of *English Manuscript Illumination*.

3 The missal is now in the library of the Duke of Northumberland at Alnwick Castle.

4 This is now B.M. MS. Harl. 7026.

5 Many of the birds have the name of their species and sex written against them. Siferwas, like some of his successors, has a liking for finches and waterbirds, and it is worth remarking that while some of his subjects (e.g. the cock and hen chaffinch) resemble exactly in plumage their descendants of to-day, others (e.g. the moorhen and kingfisher) are so different as to be scarcely recognizable.

6 A selection of these bird-studies, reproduced in colour, forms the frontispiece to the Roxburghe Club's volume. Sketch-books of birds were in circulation at this time.

7 It was perhaps this fact that caused the slip of memory by which Miss Saunders (*English Art*, 156 and fig. 46) assigned to the illuminator of the Sherborne Missal and Lovel Lectionary a Sherborne origin. The resemblance between the names is curious.

whether the finished quires were painted by Siferwas at the abbey, or were sent to a neighbouring friary such as Wilton or Salisbury cannot be decided, but the share taken by pupils, and the existence of another great work by Siferwas destined for Salisbury Cathedral suggest the second of the two alternatives. In any case, the art of Siferwas was personal; though not contrary to his vocation as a friar—for in a few years' time a still greater artist among the Preachers was to be at work in San Marco—it was in no sense the outcome of a tradition.

Siferwas is the last known instance of an eminent artist among the monks and friars, but it has been suggested that one, at least, of the hands at work on a contemporary masterpiece, the missal painted for the Carmelites of London, may have been that of a friar of the house.[1] If so, he was one of the last of his kind. Save for a few manuscripts of outstanding excellence, most of which show direct foreign influence, surviving examples from the fifteenth century are commonplace or inferior, and are the work of a commercialized art, as are the contemporary alabaster and other small carvings. There is indeed direct evidence of an even earlier date that not only painting, but the routine copying of books other than the common liturgical texts went out of the monastic *scriptoria* and became almost exclusively the employment of professionals. This evidence, as regards writing at least, must not be pressed beyond due measure; it is probable that at many of the larger houses a certain quantity of passably good work was still forthcoming to meet the normal demand for decorated service books; there were, however, no more series of artists, and any illumination done within the cloister was the outcome of private enterprise and talent. The schools of the early Renaissance, which in Italy continued to produce painted work of good quality for almost a century after the invention of printing, had no counterpart in the monasteries of this country.

1 Only the miniatures and capitals remain from this missal. They have been assembled from various sources (which include an early Victorian child's scrap-book) and put together with infinite patience and critical acumen by Margaret Rickert (*The reconstructed Carmelite Missal*, London, 1952), who considers (p. 91) that the book 'may have been made at White-friars Convent in London by craftsmen and artists introduced there for the purpose.... The frequent occurrence of Carmelites in the Style C miniatures strongly suggests...that one or two of the six artists may have been Carmelites.' The work was done *c.* 1382–1400 (p. 98).

CHAPTER XXII

THE MONASTERIES AND SOCIETY

I. THE INFLUENCE OF THE MONKS

The position of an abbot and his monastery in contemporary society had altered considerably between the twelfth century and the age of the Lancastrian kings. In some ways it was less important. In earlier times, when the great monastery was the only organized community and almost the only institution in the land, as well as being the most powerful religious and intellectual centre, the abbot had been an important tenant-in-chief, an equal among the great barons and their superior in education and prestige, a member of the Great Council, often in attendance on the king at home and abroad, or acting for him in the public life of the country, and in every way the social equal of the bishops. Now, both abbot and monastery had passed into the background of public life. The intellectual leadership had passed to the universities and the spiritual leadership, so far as it existed at all, was shared by all the religious and bishops in so far as any of them by personal character were able to assert it. Abbots, as figures in the national life, had fallen far behind the bishops and were rarely employed on public business; though a number of the heads of important houses received regular summons to parliament they were rarely members of the King's Council, now chiefly composed of ambitious magnates and high officials.

For a century after the Conquest the principal abbeys held a position among the landholders, lay and ecclesiastical, and in both public life and the counsels of the king, which was of the very first importance. In wealth, birth and ability the abbots formed a college which was often more distinguished than that of the bishops, and their numbers, at least in the first fifty years after the Conquest, gave them great weight in Council. Already by the reign of Henry II this influence was lessening, owing to the great multiplication of monasteries and orders, which acted as a diluting rather than as a strengthening agent. In the thirteenth century still further changes came about. Though still summoned in fairly large numbers to the Council and to the assembly of lords which developed from it, the abbots were now, as a large heterogeneous class, less distinguished, less influential and less concerned with public affairs than the episcopate of the time. Many of them were great administrators of their estates but few were public figures, and the direction of politics and administration passed away from them as it was long after to pass from the Church altogether. Though they still remained among the greatest landowners, the sum of the country's wealth and the number of wealthy men was larger, and the intelligence of the country centred itself more and more at the universities and about the courts of law and in the administrative departments of the government. The heads of houses were too numerous and their interests too varied and too detailed for them to form a class, and the relatively few who were summoned to parliament were in no sense representatives of their order. Individual abbots might be used by the king, but the number of such names in the national history during the fourteenth and fifteenth centuries is small, even if it was still possible for an abbot such as Thomas de la Mare, who combined social position with eminent personal qualities, to become a figure of national significance.

They still, however, were a power to be reckoned with in local or regional society, in proportion to the wealth of their house and its peculiar circumstances. In this respect a place apart was held by the abbots of such houses as St Albans, Bury St Edmunds, Evesham and Glastonbury who, besides wide estates, controlled extensive franchises and exercised spiritual jurisdiction over enclaves in the diocese that contained them. At St Albans the ecclesiastical liberty was almost conterminous with the civil one, comprising twenty-four parishes in Hertfordshire and Buckinghamshire. Within this area the abbot exercised all the powers of an ordinary save those dependent upon the episcopal character: Abbot Wallingford, indeed, even petitioned the Holy See for powers of ordination, though without success, thus anticipating in design what has in modern times become common canonical practice for abbacies *nullius diocesis*.[1] The normal administration of the exempt parishes was carried out by a monk-archdeacon, but certain acts were reserved to the abbot, who often took cases into his own hands. From his decision, or that of his archdeacon, there was no appeal to the metropolitan; Rome was the only refuge, and there the abbot was likely to have agents capable of safeguarding his interests. The abbot or his archdeacon held synods, issued statutes, collated and instituted to benefices, dealt with misdemeanours of the clergy and laity, settled matrimonial cases and gave probate of wills. St Albans controlled a more extensive territory than any other house, but Evesham Abbey and Glastonbury had a number of parishes and Bury, Westminster and a few other houses had one or more parishes in the town or city where they lay. To the inhabitants of these the abbot was spiritual father, and it is at least possible that in the later Middle Ages he or his archdeacon was more efficient and accessible than the bishop and his officials in such a vast diocese as Lincoln.

Alongside of this spiritual jurisdiction went the civil control of the liberty. Thus in addition to the manorial courts held by the various officials there was the abbot's court 'under the ash tree' at St Albans, and in 1440 the abbot secured the privilege of return of writs, thus excluding the king's justices from his territory.[2] Civil immunity, in one form or

<hr>

1 *Reg. J. Whethamstede*, ed. H. T. Riley, II, 287–9.
2 Miss C. E. Hodges, in her thesis on Whethamstede, gives a very full account of the exempt territory of St Albans and its organization (chap. IV). Cf. also the article by Miss M. Reddan in *VCH, Herts*, IV, 398, 401.

another, was more common than ecclesiastical exemption, and was enjoyed by some of the priors of cathedral monasteries, such as Canterbury and (though under peculiar circumstances) Durham.

In addition to his extraordinary position as holder of civil or ecclesiastical immunities the abbot had a public position in society at large. Though rarely a figure in governmental circles he was the representative of a great establishment, the dispenser of patronage and hospitality on a grand scale. The patronage was both spiritual and temporal: the bestowal of benefices or vicarages and the appointment to numerous offices, both in his own household and in the name of the whole community as well as the presentation to the more honourable, and often lucrative posts, of steward and seneschal. The hospitality was lavish, though varying greatly in volume from house to house; at some of the greater abbeys, such as St Albans, Bury, Westminster and Gloucester the king frequently stayed and even held parliaments; at the lesser houses the local magnates were the most distinguished guests. Situation on a highroad, control of a shrine or proximity to the border regions of Wales or Scotland might entail sudden and extraordinary visits from the king or the commander of an army, which impoverished the house for years, as at Lanercost in 1306–7.[1]

Perhaps the most vivid impression of a great abbey's social liabilities is given by John Amundesham's chronicle of St Albans in the seven years 1424–30, a time when, during the young king's minority, the magnates with their clients and retainers took such a large part in the political life of the country. St Albans, lying on the main road to the north within easy reach of London, was a stage on many journeys besides those of pilgrimage, and was an ideal hostelry for a great man who wished to combine his Christmas or Easter devotions with comfort and intelligent converse. Thus during the Christmas season of 1423–4 Duke Humphrey with his wife and three hundred attendants kept the festival in and about the abbey; in 1426 convocation assembled there for ten days, with nine bishops to provide for at the altar and at table; only a few weeks after they had gone Duke Humphrey was there again with his household, and a little later in the year the Duke and Duchess of Bedford with three hundred attendants. In 1427–8 Humphrey again kept Christmas in the abbey, and in the Easter week following the young king with the queen mother stayed for nine days; later in the spring the Earl of Warwick chose to be ill for a month in the precinct, though he paid for what he consumed and arranged for his own catering. So the story goes on, and the chronicler makes no mention of the multitude of lesser men and women who must have filled the guest halls.[2]

A microcosm of all the relationships of an abbey is seen in its book of confraternity, and here again that of St Albans is peculiarly revealing.

1 Cf. J. R. H. Moorman, 'Edward I at Lanercost Priory, 1306–7' in *EHR*, LXVII (April, 1952), 161–74.
2 *Amundesham*, I, 4–64.

In the decades between the death of Henry V and the outbreak of the Wars of the Roses the entries show how closely a great abbey was still bound to the fabric of society. Henry VI, a client at so many shrines, was of course a confrater here, though not till 1459, as was his uncle the Duke of Bedford (1417), while his other uncle, Humphrey, apparently joined the list twice, once with his first wife Jacqueline (1424) and again with his second wife in 1431; the Earl of Warwick was admitted in 1428, and the Countess of Westmorland and the Duchess of Clarence in 1429. At all such notable ceremonies the brethren turned out in processional copes, and there was a special choral service followed by a feast.

Then, on a somewhat less magnificent level, were the lawyers and royal officials, who had done, or might be expected to do, some service to the abbot or convent, for example, Sir William Babington, Chief Justice of the Common Pleas (1428), Sir John Juyn, chief baron of the Exchequer (1433), and in the same year John Hotost, Treasurer of the Royal Household. Aristocracy of birth or talent was, however, by no means an essential. In 1421 John Shaw, a vintner of London, John Chitterne, a canon of St Paul's, and Dame Katherine, ancress in the local anchor-hold of St Martin, were admitted, and in the following year William the schoolmaster, the prioress of St Margaret's, and a number of townspeople. It is pleasant to note that even old servants of the abbey, porters and waiters in the infirmary, were rewarded with the fraternity when they retired after long service. Finally, when one of the great received the honour, he carried with him onto the roll a host of retainers. Thus twenty-two *generosi* accompanied Richard, Earl of Warwick, and Henry Beauchamp his son in 1428, while fifty followers were received along with the Duchess of Clarence in 1429 and two hundred with Henry VI in 1459.[1]

II. THE CLAIMS OF PATRONS

Between the reign of Richard II and that of Henry VIII there was a slow but continuous shift in the centre of gravity of the more substantial social groups, and this ultimately left the monasteries, taken as a body, far less influential than before. The shift was in origin due to the growth of the total wealth of the country, through foreign trade and through the more efficient realization of existing resources, and it became apparent when the class of prosperous and even wealthy gentry and yeomen, some of them drawn from merchant families who had invested in land, came to form an influential class all over the country between the great titled landowners and the small leaseholders and peasants. The movement was no new one;

[1] For the *Liber Benefactorum of St Albans* (B.M. MS. Nero D vii), *v.* V. H. Galbraith in *EHR*, XLVII (January 1932), 13–15; a shorter version is printed from Corp. Christi Coll. Cambridge MS. vii in Trokelowe, *Chronic. et annales*, ed. H. T. Riley, 427–64. For the Durham *Liber Vitae* see the edition by J. Stevenson, and for that of New Minster the edition by W. de Gray Birch.

it had been in progress since the end of the twelfth century, and its consequences were delayed rather than accelerated by the political and other changes of the early fifteenth century. Nevertheless, it had resulted, long before the end of that century, in a very notable lowering of the relative importance of the monasteries and their heads as compared with other groups and individuals of weight, especially as it was accompanied by the almost total disappearance of the abbots from the service and councils of the king.

While the heads of houses and their communities thus sank gradually into the landscape the laymen connected with their establishments rose more into view. In early days the English abbeys had been a strong contrast to the French and German houses in their independence of the aristocracy. Few of the greater houses were *Eigenklöstern*, and the lay patron or advocate, the *avoué* or *vocht* of the Continent, figured little in English monastic history. The oldest and greatest abbeys were either nominally royal foundations, or else, like Burton and Coventry, the foundations of Saxon or Danish earls and thanes whose claims disappeared from view at the Conquest. The Cistercians and Premonstratensians had by their original statutes kept free from lay influence. The Normans, however, had done something to introduce the Continental practice, especially in the dependent priories of the black monks and Cluniacs which they founded. Here the founder from the beginning had claimed certain rights of election and supervision as against the monastic mother-house, and these had often been the subject of concordats and charters.[1] The same state of things prevailed at some of the smaller houses of black canons. As the centuries passed, and the bond between the smaller priories, especially those of foreign or Cluniac allegiance, and the mother-house became looser, the lay founder or patron, often one of the greater magnates of the district, if not of the country, gained in importance. It is symptomatic of the shift in the relative positions of abbey and patron that already in the fourteenth century the king and other magnates step in as founders to regulate the affairs of disordered houses, while groups of local gentry are found interesting themselves in visitations and elections in a way that would not have been thinkable two centuries before.[2]

In other ways, too, the powerful lay element was finding its way into the monastic economy. We have already seen how in the early thirteenth century the abbot's council had grown to a considerable stature.[3] This was in origin a group of those most closely associated with the prelate in administration and litigation, and included the steward or seneschal of the estates, the bursar and, when one existed, the archdeacon, and two or three lawyers, often eminent men of national celebrity. Gradually it

---

1 *V. MO*, 156–7.

2 Examples of royal interference by virtue of patronage have been studied by Miss K. Wood-Legh, *Studies in Church Life under Edward III*, ch. 1. For the visitations of Thomas de la Mare, generally supported if not solicited by the king, *v. supra*, pp. 204–5.

3 *RO*, 1, 271–2.

became customary to retain civilians, canonists, advocates and perhaps also clerks from the royal service as advisers and assistants. The office carried a pension and robes and sometimes a chamber in the precinct, while ecclesiastical members were retained or rewarded by presentation to the richest livings in the gift of the house. Gradually, what may be called the influential element encroached upon the professional; magnates of the neighbourhood or (as for example at Durham) wealthy merchants from the nearest town sat beside the lawyers, thus broadening the social relations of the abbot and giving a wider circle of neighbours an insight into the resources of the house of whose private affairs they were professionally cognizant.

At the same time certain of the administrative offices were rising very considerably in dignity. The steward (*senescallus*), the receiver (*receptor*) and the professional auditor, who between them held the courts, collected the rents and checked the accounts, had originally been clerks in the employ of the house, or at most (in the case of the steward) one of the knights or small landowners of the locality, in the days before the emergence of these worthies into the social class of lower gentry. Originally essential posts in the administration, connected with the supervision of the estates, they tended, as the monasteries abandoned direct exploitation, to become honourable and lucrative sinecures enjoyed by powerful landowners who could help the house by their patronage at court and elsewhere, such parts of the practical work as remained being accomplished by smaller-salaried officials. As with the office of chancellor of a university or of a great complex such as the Duchy of Lancaster or of Cornwall, the greater the dignity of the holder, the less grew the burden of the office. The salary was retained and even increased, while the functions were transferred to a deputy, who himself was often of considerable social influence. When the households of the magnates grew in number and magnificence from the early fourteenth century onwards, the larger monasteries followed the fashion, and the staff of high officials, counsel, attendant gentlemen, pages and squires grew. In the age of disturbance that followed the reign of Edward III it became more and more of advantage to retain as the abbey's advocate one of the greatest of the realm who had ready access to the king's ear; consequently, the leading figures on both sides of the Wars of the Roses are found as stewards of the greater monasteries, and these, for their part, did not hesitate to make changes when their advocate ceased to command attention at court. The nobility and gentry, very naturally, had no objection to drawing large salaries for little or no routine work, while they enjoyed the hospitality and social amenities afforded by a rich abbey. Many of them were pluralists, acting as steward for several houses.

Although England had never known the Continental 'advocate', certain rights of the founder or patron of a monastery, as also of the patron of a church, were recognized in English law.[1] Thus the Second Statute of Westminster (1285) allowed patrons to have an opportunity of recovering lands alienated by their monasteries;[2] they could sue a writ *Praecipe tali abbati*. Similarly they could have recourse to a writ *Cessavit* for the recovery of lands given for a special spiritual service if that service had ceased to be rendered.[3] Behind this special legislation, also, lay the principle of canon law that a destitute founder (or his descendants) had a right to assistance from a religious house. Though rarely used, these legal sanctions represented a deep and continuous sentiment, quite alien to modern habits of thought, which saw in the deathless community and the founder's descendants a body and persons with an undying relationship and obligations to one another. The cry that was raised in the days of Wyclif, and by the landowners who supported Lollardy, that the king and other founders had a right to resume ownership of property that was no longer used in the service of God for which it had been given, though often crudely expressed and insincerely exploited, was nevertheless an echo of an old and respectable tradition, which was to continue to reverberate as long as there were lands and houses that a founder's descendant could consider desirable.

Less drastic, and more often successfully made, were the various claims of a founder to certain material advantages and amenities. Thus he could claim and, in the case of many small houses, did repeatedly enjoy, hospitality from his foundation not only for himself but for his servants, horses and hounds. The last-named, indeed, might be kennelled on the monastery for an indefinite period, prowling about the church and cloister, consuming the provisions of the house and making life unendurable with their baying. A corollary of the right to hospitality and prayers was the right to a permanent resting-place in the choir or nave or chantry chapel after death; Bardney, Haughmond, Christchurch (Hants), and Tewkesbury are names taken at random of religious houses which still show traces of the numerous tombs that once were, or that still are, a prominent feature in their aisles or on their pavement. Between hospitality and burial stood a series of other rights. Constant prayers were taken for granted; they were the service which originally took the place of other services in return for gifts in frankalmoin. An extension was the privilege of fraternity, rarely denied to a founder or patron. In early centuries this was often bestowed in the form of an actual clothing with the habit during the last illness, followed by reception into the monastic infirmary. This practice was rare after the

---

1 In this section use has been made of an Oxford University D.Phil. dissertation by Miss Susan Chenevix-Trench (Mrs S. Wood), since published with the title 'English Monasteries and their Patrons in the Thirteenth Century'. My thanks are due to Mrs Wood for the loan of a copy, with permission to use its valuable data.

2 Stat. West. II, c. 41 in *Statutes of the Realm*, I, 91–2.

3 Stat. Glouc. c. 4; Stat. West. II, c. 21, in *Statutes of the Realm*, I, 48; I, 82–3. Cf. Pollock and Maitland, *History of English Law*, I, 353, and T. F. Plucknett, *The legislation of Edward I*, 92–4.

beginning of the thirteenth century, but the multiplication of Offices and Masses and anniversaries for the dead continued to the end of the Middle Ages, though founders came to prefer the chantry to the monastery, as less costly to endow and more explicitly devoted to intercessory prayer for the dead.

Other rights besides these existed. In theory the founder often had the right of nomination to one or more places in the house. This was rarely exercised in the case of monks and canons, but the placing of a girl or young woman in a nunnery had often an economic or social motive as strong or stronger than the purely religious, and convents, especially those of which a bishop was patron, had regularly to receive novices of this kind. Less of an intrusion, but often more of an incubus, was the corrodian, one or several, whom the patron could by right appoint to his house. This, in the case of royal foundations, allowed the king to make considerable economies in his pension list, and many an abbey was saddled with aged and infirm huntsmen, grooms and cooks, sent down from Westminster or Windsor with a royal letter, and resolved to set up their rest in the abbey precinct. In another sphere, the patron was usually one of the most importunate of the suitors for the monastery's clerical patronage on behalf of his relatives or agents, and he might even demand a loan from the house, which he also treated as a bank and safe-deposit for charters, testaments and valuables of every kind. All these and similar contacts, which tended to become less spiritual and more social and economic as the years passed, wove the monasteries, and especially perhaps the lesser monasteries, more and more into the social fabric and rural pattern of the countryside.

CHAPTER XXIII

VICARAGES, THE CURE OF SOULS AND SCHOOLS

The relationship of the religious houses to the parochial organization of the country is a complicated topic which has too often been treated in a hasty or superficial manner, and by those who have failed to distinguish between century and century, or who have seen the problems from the point of view of a zealous churchman or nonconformist of the present day. Two weighty circumstances, both independently and in conjunction, have profoundly altered the framework of the Church and the outlook of its members since the end of the Middle Ages. In the first place, the Reformation with its rivalries and counter-reforms, followed by the ages of enlightenment and liberalism, have brought it about that Christians of every confession now regard pastoral and apostolic work as the imperative common task of all ministers of religion. Not only in the Churches separated from Rome, in which the pastoral work is the universal task of the clergy, but even in the Catholic Church itself pastoral work of a parochial kind—the work of the secular clergy *par excellence*—has been undertaken by monastic orders and regular canons as well as by friars and regular clerks such as the Jesuits. Abstention from such work on the part of any community of clergy has therefore something in it of the unfamiliar. In the second place the conception of the ecclesiastical benefice as primarily a pecuniary asset, a piece of real property, susceptible of most of the transactions associated with other forms of property and legally recognized as having this quality, has now practically vanished from the world: in Continental Europe through successive waves of confiscation and secularization, and in England, its last stronghold, through the efforts of reformers and the multiple economic changes of the past eighty years. In the Middle Ages, on the other hand, it was taken for granted by all parties at all times that a parochial cure of souls was a benefice, a piece of property, and by most parties that the sole normal holder of such a benefice was a secular, and not a regular, clerk.

At the time of the Conquest the churches of England, to which a cure of souls of the laity was attached,[1] were, almost without exception, served by secular priests. The great reform, however, which was already well under way on the Continent, was directed by monks, and the monastic ideals of chastity, poverty, the common life and the discipline of obedience were the means which they applied to every department of their great task.

[1] The parochial cure was not the only 'cure of souls' known to canon law; the head of a religious community and of a chapter were in the same category, a circumstance of significance in regard to papal legislation on pluralism; benefices with a cure were distinguished from 'sinecures' in the reckoning (*v*. A. H. Thompson, 'Pluralism in the Medieval Church').

The Western Church was, as a result, to a certain extent 'monachized' during the eleventh and twelfth centuries. A part of this process was an attempt to use the regular clergy as instruments in the reform of clerical life. In the case of the monks the result was negligible, save in so far as they directed the work on the high level of the episcopacy; a few only of the small priories founded soon after the Conquest were in churches used by the laity, and only in the rarest cases were other churches served by monks.[1] With the regular canons it was otherwise. The Augustinian canons were in origin servants of a large church, and though the first effect of the reforming movement was to give them a semi-monastic life, a second result was their use as a leavening element in the clerical life of the country. A number of their early foundations in England, especially those made in rural districts by a few canons only, were designed for this purpose and occupied a church in public use.[2] With the later white canons the apostolic purpose was still more marked, and from the beginning they were regarded as canonically capable of occupying parish churches and serving them. In the event, however, the tide of apostolic purpose receded, partly from a genuine desire on the part of many Austin canons and Premonstratensians for a strict and remote monastic life, partly from a wish to be free of ties and obligations, and in course of time the parochial duties in the churches of the canons were often carried out by stipendiary vicars. By the beginning of the thirteenth century it was again normal for all churches with a cure of souls to be administered by secular priests.

The coming of the friars made no change in the general outlook. Both by the principles of their institute and by later canon law the friars were the auxiliaries of the parish clergy, and were neither substitutes nor alternatives to them. Though they preached and absolved in their own churches, these were never parochial. Thus it may be said that in the thirteenth century the only members of the regular clergy who undertook the duties of a beneficed parochial cure were the rare Premonstratensian canons.

Meanwhile, however, the whole economic balance of the Church in England was being shaken by the introduction and rapid increase of the vicarage system, by which a large part of the revenues of a church were 'appropriated' to a purpose other than the maintenance of the incumbent and the needs of charity and hospitality; the 'vicar' who served the church as representative of the 'rector' received only a part, usually only in the region of a third part, of the total fruit of the benefice.

The details of this system and a judgement upon the use made of the revenues by the appropriators, together with a verdict upon the long-term effects upon the Church in England, are no part of the present outline. Though the subject has attracted considerable attention, it still offers

1 Cf. *MO*, 595, n. 2.
2 For this, *v.* J. C. Dickinson, *The Origins of the Austin Canons*, 224–33.

scope for a definitive study.[1] It will not, however, be out of place to give some indication of the stages of the growth of the practice.

At first, during the earlier half of the twelfth century, it was probably not uncommon for a baron or even a bishop to give churches to a monastery with the understanding that the monks would enjoy the greater part of the fruits: the regime of the proprietary church was passing, and conscientious lords welcomed the opportunity of disembarrassing themselves of tithe and other spiritual incomes, and of securing better service for the church from vicars chosen and supervised by the monks. Very soon, however, the normal process of appropriation began at the demand of the monastery; the monks wished to transform one of the churches of which they held the advowson from a rectory to a vicarage. It was the task, and in great part the achievement, of a generation of great diocesan bishops in the thirteenth century to regularize this procedure and to change the precarious tenure of a poorly paid priest who could be dismissed at will into a life-tenancy supported by an adequate, if moderate, income drawn from specified sources. It may seem strange that zealous bishops, with no prepossessions towards the monks and canons, did not set their faces firmly against any further appropriation. Sometimes, indeed, at least from the beginning of the fourteenth century onwards, they had no choice: a papal mandate had been obtained or, as they knew well, would be solicited if they refused, and from the time of the Great Schism onwards this was the normal way of initiating the process. But in earlier times numerous appropriations were in fact allowed with goodwill, and instances are not unknown of the gift of a church by the bishop himself to a cause deemed good. This perhaps should warn us that the disadvantages of a vicarage from the spiritual point of view were not always apparent, and that the attitude of a bishop towards his diocesan clergy was not the same then as now; and that, in the last resort, no medieval administrator could forget that a church was primarily a bundle of economic assets.

During the first half of the thirteenth century a remarkable work of stabilization was thus achieved in the ordination of vicarages. Speaking very generally, the impropriator secured two-thirds of the revenue and the incumbent one-third, composed of house and garden (but not glebe), small tithes and all regular offerings (altarage); the burdens, such as synodal dues, maintenance of assistants, and entertainment of the arch-deacon, were sometimes divided, sometimes borne by the vicar, and more rarely by the impropriator, while the latter as rector usually bore the

---

1 The monograph of the late R. A. R. Hartridge, *A History of Vicarages in the Middle Ages*, though valuable, cannot be pronounced definitive. It contains a great deal of detailed information, for the writer studied under G. G. Coulton and used his unrivalled collection of notes. On the other hand, the sketch of the origins and early history of the system is inadequate, and appropriation by those other than religious receives less than due attention. Moreover, Hartridge viewed the subject with the 'slant' characteristic of Coulton, and shared his mentor's readiness to pass abruptly from country to country and from century to century in quest of instances.

obligation of keeping the chancel in repair and furnished with books and the rest. The very greatest variety of allotment, however, prevailed and in a great number of cases the vicar received a fixed pension charged on the net profits of the church.[1] During the same period appropriations continued to multiply; the reasons given by religious houses were of all kinds: the demands of hospitality, loss of revenues from other sources, calamities of all sorts. When the records of the taxation of Pope Nicholas IV were compiled in 1291–2 there were some 1500 vicarages out of a total of 8100 churches;[2] by far the greater number (though certainly not all) were in the churches of monks and canons. The practice continued in the fourteenth century, when Scottish wars, pestilences, and changes in the social and economic conditions of the country were added to the existing reasons alleged in support of appropriation. From the last decades of the fourteenth century, however, the increase diminished; partly, no doubt, because the number of churches still not 'appropriated', and desirable for this reason or that, had decreased, but partly also because the value of those that remained was no longer solely of a pecuniary nature: the monasteries had lawyers to reward, suitors great and small to satisfy, and magnates to placate by the bestowal of patronage at their disposal, even if they did not on occasion gain a material advantage as well as an access of goodwill from the transference of rectors from one church to another. Nevertheless, the number of appropriated churches held by the English religious increased appreciably between 1380 and 1450 owing to the transference to a relatively small group of houses, among which the Carthusians and Bridgettines were pre-eminent, of the already appropriated churches belonging to foreign abbeys and suppressed alien priories.[3] Direct appropriations did not cease, indeed, but in the fifteenth century the beneficiary was more often a college, a chantry or a hospital than a religious house. At the end, when the existing state of things was about to be frozen by the Dissolution, the *Valor Ecclesiasticus* of 1535 shows that out of 8838 rectories 3307 had been appropriated with vicarages; that is, about 37 per cent of the total.[4]

In the last century of the Middle Ages, however, yet another refinement had been introduced. One of the reasons for the decrease of fresh requests for appropriation had been the difficulty of realizing the assets in churches with peculiar local conditions, or at a great distance from the monastery. To remedy this the practice came in of farming the rector's portion of the

1 Hartridge, *op. cit.* ch. viii, 'The division of duties and burdens'; cf. also A. H. Thompson, *The English Clergy and their organization in the later Middle Ages*, 116–19.

2 Hartridge, *op. cit.* 79, reproducing with slight modification the table given by E. L. Cutts, in *Parish Priests and their People in the Middle Ages*, 385, gives 1514 vicarages out of a total of 8085 churches. The *Taxatio*, however, cannot be taken as an entirely accurate or complete survey; cf. R. Graham, 'The Taxation of Pope Nicholas IV'.

3 Kirkstall Abbey (Yorks) was one of the few older religious houses to secure as many as seven ex-alien churches; cf. Thompson, *op. cit.* 117, n. 1; and *Bolton Priory*, 100.

4 The figures are taken from the table given by Hartridge, *op. cit.* 204, from Cutts, *op. cit.* 394.

church, sometimes to the vicar, but more often to a layman. Indulgences for this were frequently given by popes of the Great Schism; thus between 1397 and 1403 a number of houses great and small were given permission to put their churches to farm without permission of the ordinary.[1] Thirty years later the Carthusians and others were obtaining similar privileges.[2] Thus by the end of the fifteenth century a large number of religious houses had farmed (i.e. leased) their spiritual property; it was one more instance of that movement from direct exploitation to an economy of fixed income from rents which made so much of monastic ownership in the Tudor age an affair of parchment only, and so greatly facilitated the great transference when it came, as it also helped to perpetuate the economic arrangements of the *ancien régime*.[3]

Hitherto we have been considering the religious merely as owners of spiritual property. A word remains to be said about their share in spiritual ministration.

Here we must once more distinguish between the orders. The Premonstratensians, as has been seen, recognized the cure of souls as a part of their vocation. Their historian and copious documentary evidence alike make it clear that throughout their existence in England they served directly some of the churches they owned; these were sometimes near, but more often at some distance from the abbey.[4] The number of canons so engaged can never have been large, for the rule that the canon-vicar must have a canon-*socius* was long honoured, and houses of a dozen or less could ill afford to allow more than four at the most to be absent in quasi-perpetuity from the abbey. Probably for the whole order in England in the fifteenth century a maximum of forty canons, with or without *socii*, engaged in parochial duties was rarely attained—a negligible fraction of the nine thousand benefices of England.[5]

The Austin canons who, though a less austere order than their white brethren, were in a more equivocal position in the matter of the cure of souls, did in fact receive the same papal indulgences as the Premonstratensians, and when, from the mid-fourteenth century onwards, privileges of appropriation were sued out by them direct from the Curia, the formula employed usually allowed them to fill the vicarage either from among their own number or with secular vicars removable at will. Only long and detailed research could establish the approximate number of Austin canons

---

1 E.g. York, Eynsham (1397); Welbeck (1400); Kyme, Spalding, Carmarthen, Thurgarton, Peterborough, Lewes (1402); Lenton (1403), in *CPL*, v (1396–1404); *v*. index *s.vv.*

2 The privileges of the Carthusians, Daventry and Winchcomb are in *CPL*, VIII (1427–47).

3 A. R. Savin, *The English Monasteries on the Eve of the Dissolution*, 112–13, shows that many monasteries had farmed out all, or nearly all, their churches, sometimes to the number of a dozen or more, before 1535.

4 *V. supra*, pp. 139–40 with references to H. M. Colvin, *The White Canons in England*.

5 Hartridge, *op. cit.* 173, lists all cases found in the records stretching over the forty years of Bishop Redman's visitations.

serving churches at any given date, but to judge from occasional notices in bishops' registers and visitation documents the total at any moment was not large.[1] The presence of a *socius* was a canonical requirement for the black canons as for the white, but there is evidence that they honoured the rule less faithfully. In any case, the small numbers in so many houses of Austin canons must have rendered nugatory the privileges they possessed.

For the monks, both black and white, the cure of souls was no part of their vocation; popes, councils and monastic writers alike had prohibited them from the holding of benefices. Consequently, it is only in the rarest cases and most exceptional circumstances that the practice was allowed so long as strict discipline was maintained.[2] Towards the end of the fourteenth century, however, when, as has been seen in another connexion, privileges of a novel kind and most ample scope were bestowed without wisdom, it became common form in the Curia, even when monks were the petitioners for appropriation, to insert the clause allowing of the service of the church either by vicars or by members of their own community. The clause was probably common form and no more, and though it has been calculated that some fifty churches were liable to receive monastic vicars,[3] there is little evidence that the power was ever used.

Besides the development just mentioned, which may be considered as a normal part of ecclesiastical administration, monks were occasionally empowered to hold the cure of souls in exceptional circumstances or by personal privilege. Thus the abbey of Hailes was allowed to hold and serve the church of Pinnock as being a poor church to which no parson would go, and Pipewell was empowered to appoint monks to two neighbouring chapels.[4] Of far more significance than these isolated cases, however, which may or may not have been bona fide attempts to remedy distress, was the spate of privileges issued from *c.* 1390 onwards to members of all orders, friars included and Carthusians not excepted, to hold benefices.[5] How often these privileges were taken up by the grantees, and how often, even when used, the monk or canon or friar was an absentee rector making a career at the Curia, or following the fortunes of a patron, cannot be said; it is only rarely that we find a bishop instituting a monk,[6] and even so there is rarely record of residence. As regards the numbers of religious so empowered, they were indeed large if regarded as breaches of regular discipline, but considered as a factor in the parochial life of England over a century and a half, they were negligible.

---

1 Hartridge, *op. cit.* 178–9, gives some instances; Thompson, *The English Clergy*, gives others. Bolton and Nostell are examples; *v.* Thompson, *Bolton Priory*, 100.

2 Hartridge, who doubtless had Coulton's files at his disposal, remarks (p. 185) that save for one exceptional and temporary case, he has 'had no success in his search for churches served by monks in England during the thirteenth century'.

3 Hartridge, *op. cit.* 185.   4 *CPL*, VI (1404–15), 388 (Hailes), 393 (Pipewell).

5 For a fuller treatment, *v. supra*, pp. 171–3.

6 E.g. *Reg. T. Bekynton*, ed. H. C. Maxwell-Lyte and M. C. B. Dawes, has (no. 760) D. John Cadbury, monk of Glastonbury, as rector of Weston Bampfylde, and (no. 1329) a monk of Montacute as incumbent of another parish.

In conclusion, then, we may say that, save for a small number of churches served by the canons, and in particular by the Premonstratensians, the religious orders took no part in the cure of souls, though it will not be forgotten that the friars, working extra-parochially, performed, especially in the towns, many of the functions both then and now associated with the conception of pastoral work.

In the sphere of ownership, on the other hand, the share of the religious was great, and it was they who were primarily responsible for the significant change in the funds and status of one-third of the parishes of England, for the other classes of appropriators would probably not have existed had the monks not shown the way. Much has been written of the unfortunate consequences of the vicarage system, both in the Middle Ages and since, to the Church in England; it is an irony of history that it should have survived the monasteries, not only in its original form as a variety of organization, but with the added anomaly of the lay rector and owner of tithe.

Throughout the fourteenth and fifteenth centuries three types of school were in existence in the monastic world, which for the purposes of this section includes the Austin canons, but not the Cistercians. These were the internal school for the young monks and canons, the almonry school, and the song school. In addition, the abbot or prior occasionally kept as boarders some of the nobility and gentry, who learnt in his company the manners and some of the accomplishments of their class.

The three types of school were all in different ways the outcome of the disappearance of child oblation in the monasteries. Until the middle of the twelfth century each monastery had had its complement of children and boys who were given such teaching as the monastic life demanded until their profession as monks at the age of seventeen or eighteen. Some of these, at least, were the objects of monastic charity, and as such were a complete charge on the establishment; in return they supplied the monks with a personnel of ministers for all Masses and services, and with treble and alto voices for the choir. When child oblation ceased,[1] and at almost the same time education increased in popularity and complexity, the monasteries gradually adjusted themselves to the change, and of the three schools that evolved one was a prolongation of, and the other two substitutes for, the functions of the earlier cloister school: the school 'of primitive sciences'[2] within the monastery took the young monks a stage further than before; the almonry school supplied the claims of charity and provided clerks for the Masses; while the song school filled, at some distance of time, the void left by the disappearance of children from the monastic choir.

1 *MO*, 418–22. It would seem to have ceased in England earlier and more completely than abroad. The mendicants continued to accept young aspirants.

2 This was the official phrase used, for example, by Benedict XII in his Constitutions. Grammar, logic and philosophy were understood by it; cf. *MC*, II, 84.

The internal school for the young monks was the only one of the three to be, in theory at least, ubiquitous at all times in the larger houses. Originally catering for all the young population of the monastery, conducted by one or more of the senior monks, and providing a basis of grammar, letters and other elementary learning that might fit the boy, when he became a monk, to take his place in the community, it now took an advanced and secondary form. When, a little later, the monks began to frequent the university, a course in arts was needed to fit them for the studies in divinity which they insisted, like the friars, on beginning without the previous university course and degree in arts. The formal establishment of this school was decreed for monks and canons by the Constitutions of Benedict XII, which laid down that a master should teach the primitive sciences, that is, grammar, logic and philosophy, to the young monks of the cloister.[1] Later, however, it became customary to provide an arts course for young monks at the monastic colleges, and though some of the larger houses refused to accept a postulant till he had made at least some progress in grammar,[2] the claustral school tended again to become a higher grammar school or, at the smaller houses, a mere grounding in grammar. The chapter of 1444 reflected contemporary conditions when it decreed that a master with professional training, either a monk or a secular, should teach the primitive sciences, or at least grammar, in a room appointed for the purpose near the cloister.[3] Thenceforward till the Dissolution the provision of such a school with its master is a constantly recurring theme at visitations. At larger monasteries the master was no doubt often a religious, as this was the simplest and cheapest expedient, but at St Albans in the days of Whethamstede it was noted that there had been no grammar master for some years, and one was retained for the school (*domus eruditionis*) at a mark *per annum* to be paid by the treasurers.[4] At Durham, on the other hand, shortly before the end, 'one of the oldest Mounckes that was lernede was appoynted to be ther tuter'.[5]

The almonry school was a somewhat later institution, often of the early fourteenth century, but it was common, if not ubiquitous, among the black monks. At St Albans accommodation for the boys and their masters was provided by abbot Richard of Wallingford *c.* 1330, but the school may have existed previously.[6] There was one at Ely at least as early as 1314, when it was decreed that boys should stay for four years only.[7] The Durham conservative gives a succinct description of the school there as he knew it: 'Ther weare certaine poor children..which weare called the

1 Wilkins, *Concilia*, II, 588 *seqq.* cap. 7, 'De studiis'.
2 A candidate was rejected at Christ Church, Canterbury, in 1324 till he should have learnt grammar, reading and singing (*Lit. Cant.* I, 126–7).
3 *MC*, II, 205. 'Habeatur unus ydoneus et scientificus, sive secularis, sive religiosus, qui monachis in claustris ipsorum sciencias primitivas horis debitis legat et doceat, grammaticam videlicet ad minus.' The last clause is very significant.
4 *Reg. J. Whethamstede*, ed. H. T. Riley, 25; *Amundesham*, 109–10.
5 *Rites of Durham*, ed. (1) J. Raine, 81; ed. (2) J. T. Fowler, 96.
6 *GASA*, II, 282.   7 *Ely Chapter Ordinances*, ed. S. J. A. Evans, 38, n. 12.

children of the Aumery going daily to the Fermery schole.'[1] It was indeed
the poverty and often, no doubt, the orphanhood of these children that
differentiated them from the ordinary children of the neighbourhood at
the grammar school; their numbers were necessarily limited by the available
funds and accommodation, but a fairly large group was needed to fulfil
the function of ministration at the private Masses of the monks. Norwich
had a complement of fourteen at the end of the fifteenth century; the
Augustinian Thornton had the same number in 1422–3; Leicester had only
six in 1440; the Augustinian Newnham in 1422 only four, who shared a
master with the young canons; this master was paid out of the common
wages-fund (*peculium*).[2] Their presence was so essential that at Whitby in
1366 it was asserted that the number of private Masses had been reduced
to three or four through lack of boys to serve.[3] These clerks probably
themselves became monks far more often than the records suggest.[4]

The song school was a still later introduction than the almonry school.
Its purpose was to provide boys' voices for certain daily chant, in particular for the Lady Mass and the evening Salve. It was far less ubiquitous
than the almonry school, and probably only existed at the greater black
monk houses. The clearest account of it comes from Durham, where a
series of documents give the conditions imposed on choirmasters when
engaged.[5] There were singing boys at Westminster,[6] and the boys who
accompanied a deputation sent by Christ Church, Canterbury, to assist the
archbishop to bless a great ship, *La Trinité*, were no doubt choir boys.[7]
At Hyde at the end of the fifteenth century the recent disappearance of the
fourteen boys who sang the Mass of Our Lady is noted, but the number
suggests that these may have been almonry children.[8] Elsewhere, the
singing children were an appreciable help to the monks in choir in the
days of reduced numbers.[9] Normally these boys would have been younger
than those of the almonry school, and some of them may have been
sufficiently occupied in reading their psalter and learning to read and
write and cipher and sing, but at Hyde they seem to have attended a
grammar school.

1 *Rites of Durham*, (1) 77; (2) 91.
2 *Visitations of the Diocese of Norwich*, ed. A. Jessopp, II, 192; *LV*, I, 89, 121; II, 214.
3 *MC*, III, 281: 'Pauperes scolares minime sustentantur, qua de causa in dicto monasterio
pre defectu hujusmodi administrancium...nisi tres vel quatuor misse in die in ecclesia
communiter celebrantur.'
4 According to the Canterbury (Christ Church) chronicler John Stone (*Chronicle of John
Stone*, ed. W. G. Searle, p. 106), four boys from the almonry became monks in 1468. Cf.
E. H. Pearce, *Monks of Westminster*, introd. p. 37.
5 *Hist. Dunelmensis scriptores tres*, ed. J. Raine, Appendix, nos. ccxcv, ccc, cccx, cccxxiii,
and *Rites of Durham*, (1) 54; (2) 62. The master had to teach 'pleynsange, priknot, faburden,
dischaunte et countre' and to play the organ at High Mass and Vespers on great feasts.
6 Pearce, *op. cit.* introd. p. 37.
7 *Chronicle of John Stone*, 110.
8 C. Jenkins, 'Cardinal Morton's Register', 54.
9 *MC*, III, 84. At a visitation of St Mary's, York, *c.* 1384–93, complaint is made: 'quod
solebant esse clerici cantantes organum et adjuvantes monachos in cantu qui dicitur trebill,
et jam non sunt, in magnum nocumentum et tedium fratrum cantancium in choro'.

Finally, there are references in the fifteenth century to the sons of the gentry, especially in the houses of canons. In previous centuries, and perhaps until the Dissolution, some abbots and cathedral priors boarded young noblemen as pages in their households; these seldom appear in monastic documents any more than do the abbot's yeomen or gentlemen. As the 'gentlemen's sons' of the fifteenth century are usually closely associated with the superior of the house, they are probably to be regarded as enjoying a more modest form of courtly training, verging on a school. Thus at Bicester in 1445 they are both boarded and educated,[1] and at Westacre in 1493 they are so numerous that the prior does not see how he can feed them.[2] At Torre in 1478 they are 'assigned to the abbot's house'.[3]

It is no part of our task to discuss the vexed and often curiously obscure question of the monastic origin of well-known schools such as Westminster or Sherborne.[4] While in general an urban grammar school, where one existed, should probably be regarded as the parent rather than the almonry school, it is not impossible that at some abbeys, such as Westminster, the connexion may have come down from the latter.

1 *LV*, II, 35: 'Filii duorum generosorum...aluntur et informantur in domo.'
2 *Visitations of the Diocese of Norwich*, 50: 'Multi sunt pueri generosi in domo de quibus non percipit prior quomodo pro eorum mensa solvitur.'
3 *Collectanea Anglo-Premonstratensia*, ed. F. A. Gasquet, III, 143.
4 For Sherborne, *v.* J. Fowler, *Medieval Sherborne*, 353.

CHAPTER XXIV

PUBLIC OBLIGATIONS OF HEADS OF HOUSES

I. MILITARY SERVICE

In an earlier volume some account was given of the imposition of military service upon a certain number of religious houses.[1] This, as has been shown by Round and others, was accomplished once and for all within a few years of the Conquest, probably in 1070, and was entirely arbitrary in its incidence, bearing relation neither to the wealth nor to the importance of the house concerned, but solely to the actual state, troubled or otherwise, of the locality. In the centuries that came after, the religious houses holding by military service followed in general the current practices of other military tenants: they succeeded, for example, by the end of the reign of Henry III, in establishing the principle of tendering for military purposes less than one-sixth of their original *servicium debitum*, and of acquitting themselves of their remaining responsibility, in default of corporal service, either by the money payment of scutage or by a pecuniary fine.[2] Corporal service, which had early tended to fall into desuetude, can be shown to have been revived, even in the case of religious fees, in the reign of Henry III, thus giving an interesting parallel to the roughly contemporary revival of labour service, and, with the latter, indicating clearly that in feudal incidents as in other matters the medieval centuries do not provide a clear picture of a continuous change from a fully feudal to a fully pecuniary or other economy. Nevertheless, by the reign of Edward I the conditions of military service had come to be, in the main, stereotyped in the form described, though perhaps also antedated, by Maitland;[3] the tenant-in-chief either gave corporal service or fined (in each case for the accepted fraction of his original obligation), while scutage had now come to be a tax levied in the royal interest upon the under-tenants. The feudal muster became less frequent after the reign of Edward II but Richard II summoned the feudal host to Newcastle as late as 1385; after the summons of that year no other is recorded.[4]

While the course of the development of military service and its alternatives is clear, its incidence is at first sight more confused. There is no doubt which houses were originally liable. They were twenty-four in number, and appear again, neither more nor fewer, in the *cartae* of 1166.

1 *MO*, 607–12, and Appendix xv.
2 The whole subject has been fully treated by Miss H. M. Chew, *The English Ecclesiastical Tenants-in-Chief and Knight Service*. The only noteworthy lacuna in this book is a failure to note the analogous but dissimilar service attached to some estates in Yorkshire, Durham and Northumberland.
3 Pollock and Maitland, *History of English Law*, I, 269 *seqq.*
4 Chew, *op. cit.* 59, 76.

But when, towards the end of the reign of Henry III, the record of military summonses becomes available, many houses other than the nuclear twenty-four appear as receiving writs. In all, twenty-six additions, first and last, appear, including several houses of Austin canons and three abbeys of Benedictine nuns.[1] Nevertheless, it has been shown conclusively from the abundant records surviving, such as scutage rolls, marshal's rolls and fine rolls, which enable us to determine the composition of the feudal host as actually mobilized, that the writs to these additional houses, however frequently issued, were never obeyed and ultimately successfully challenged.[2] What prompted such numerous and arbitrary summonses, and why they were repeated in spite of the Exchequer's experience of their futility, cannot be precisely said, but it is noteworthy that exactly the same process is discernible during the same period in the issue of parliamentary writs; there, however, where the immediate consequences of acceptance were less acutely formidable, the summonses were not always resisted and a permanent obligation was in some cases incurred, even though the house forensically and successfully resisted concurrent writs of summons to fulfil military obligations.

II. ATTENDANCE AT PARLIAMENT

Few topics of English medieval history have been debated in recent years more fully than the origins and early characteristics of the institution which became, towards the end of the fourteenth century, recognizable as the Parliament of two Houses which has continued ever since, with only temporary interruptions, to be an essential feature of English political life. With these technical discussions we are concerned no further than to note a general agreement that parliament developed from, or was grafted upon, the Great Council of Norman and Angevin days which, though itself essentially feudal in nature, occupied the place and inherited many of the functions of the Anglo-Saxon Witenagemot. To the last-named gathering came, besides the bishops and lay magnates, the abbots of England, and when the Great Council of William the Conqueror took shape, the abbots were found there also.

This Great Council, which met at least three times a year, at the crown-wearings of Christmas, Easter and Whitsuntide, had from the beginning a feudal character as an assemblage of the great vassals, the tenants-in-chief of the Crown. As all the black monk abbeys in existence in 1086, the date of Domesday, were tenants-in-chief, their duty to be present was clear, and during the first century after the Conquest chroniclers and the signatures

---

1 *Ibid.* 11.

2 *Ibid.* 12: 'In spite of the evidence of writs of summons, there is nothing in the records of feudal service to indicate that any addition was made in the thirteenth century to the ranks of the clerical tenants of the Crown by knight service...only those ecclesiastics responded in money or men who had recognized military liabilities under Henry II or William I.'

of charters show that their attendance was constant. So matters continued for almost another century, the only change being that a few of the heads of remote and less important houses attended but infrequently, while a few newcomers, such as the royal foundations of Reading and Faversham among the monks, and of Waltham and Cirencester among the canons, joined the original members. The new orders, such as the Cistercians and Premonstratensians, founded in frankalmoin and keeping aloof of set purpose, did not as a rule attend, though towards the end of the twelfth century they were sometimes summoned to a gathering when it was a question of mulcting them of some of their wool for the benefit of the king.

Towards the middle of the thirteenth century a development took place: the Great Council, afforced to a varying degree and from time to time by new classes and groups, began to be called, as a body, a parliament, and to acquire a formality, and soon to transact business, unknown to the earlier Council; at the same time the royal summonses to this and similar assemblies, enrolled on a Close Roll, were preserved and have come down to us in what is from the reign of Edward I onwards something approaching to a complete series. It is therefore possible to know with some accuracy the composition of these assemblies and even, in the case of lay peers and others, the names of those summoned. The series of parliaments recognizable as such is often held to begin with the meeting at Oxford in 1258.[1] Thenceforward until the Dissolution of the monasteries certain abbots and other religious prelates were summoned, together with the bishops, and ultimately formed with them a part, and often a majority, of the House of Lords. It is the aim of the present section to note the change in composition of this group from the earliest records until, towards the end of the fourteenth century, a stereotyped list was formed of those who alone had the right and duty to receive and obey the royal summons to parliament.

The lists, taken from the Close Rolls and printed more than a century ago,[2] contain summonses to three types of gathering: the feudal muster, ordinary meetings of the Great Council, and parliament. Something has already been said about the summons to discharge the obligations of military service. The second and third kinds differ little, if at all, so far as the abbatial contingent is concerned, but as the Great Council ultimately

---

1 This is the date chosen by the editors of the *Handbook of British Chronology* (Royal Historical Society, 1939) as the *terminus a quo* of their list of parliaments, citing previous literature (pp. 339–50). This list has been taken as a convenient basis of reference for what follows.

2 They form part of Appendix no. 1 to the *Report on the Dignity of a Peer of the Realm, &c., &c.* Originally published in 1819–20, this was reprinted with a different division of volumes in 1826 and again in 1829, but the pagination remained the same; references are here given to the last reprint, where the Summonses occur in vols. III (part i) and IV (part ii). Lists are also printed in C. H. Parry, *Parliaments and Councils of England . . . from the reign of William I.* For the history of peers in parliament, *v.* also L. O. Pike, *Constitutional History of the House of Lords*, which uses many record sources, and is generally reliable, save in the author's views as to what constituted peerage.

ceased to exist as an independent institution, and as we are interested here solely in the body that became parliament, we can confine our attention to the lists, where they exist, of those assemblies which are commonly regarded as parliaments. Of these we have lists for perhaps four-fifths of the meetings known to have been held before the reign of Richard II; thenceforward the record is still more complete, though for the present purpose it is of slighter interest, as the personnel has become unchanging. The facts given by the lists shall be presented first; the interpretation will follow.

The most remarkable feature of the early lists is their great variety. Not only does the total number of religious called to parliament vary from less than twenty to near one hundred, but the individual houses represented vary greatly from one parliament to another. Still more remarkable, in view of the conservatism of medieval administrative methods, is the variation in the order of names from one list to the next. It might have been expected that the royal clerks would work from a basic list, with additions and subtractions, but in fact the order changes almost from one summons to the next, and in many cases the various religious families are completely intermingled. Even the nucleus of old black monk houses which is found in almost all the lists can only be extracted by the patient noting of every name as it occurs, and the first member of the group, who receives mention before and apart from the rest, varies five or six times in the course of the series, the relatively unimportant abbey of Peterborough ultimately holding the position for more than a century, having ousted both St Albans and St Augustine's, Canterbury, the two houses which for different reasons claimed a primacy among their peers.[1] The fact that in almost all the lists one or two sequences of two or more names resemble those of the previous summons only complicates the problem of discovering what principle guided the clerks in compiling the roll of summons. It need scarcely be said that the variation is not due to any personal qualities in those summoned. There is no indication whatsoever that an abbot was ever summoned because the king valued his counsel as an individual. He was summoned simply as the *persona* of his house. This perpetual variation, however, makes any examination of the lists extremely tedious, for it is only when all the lists over the whole period have been analysed that a pattern begins to emerge.

Of the lists of those summoned to parliament, as opposed to the feudal muster, only one has survived in full from the reign of Henry III: this is

---

1 The following is a representative summons (*Report*, III, i, 287 (Michaelmas, 1318)): 'Rex dilecto sibi in Christo abbati sancti Augustini Cantuariae salutem. Quia super diversis et arduis negociis, &c., vobis mandamus in fide et dilectione quibus nobis tenemini firmiter injungentes quod dictis die et loco omnibus aliis praetermissis personaliter intersitis ibidem nobiscum et cum ceteris prelatis magnatibus et proceribus supradictis super dictis negociis tractaturi vestrumque consilium impensuri. Et hoc nullatenus omittatis. Teste ut supra [the king himself has attested]. Eodem modo mandatum est subscriptis, videlicet Abbati de Rameseye, &c.'

the meeting summoned to London for 21 January 1265, and subsequently postponed to 8 March.[1] This was an altogether unusual occasion. The civil war was still continuing, the Lord Edward was a hostage, and the parliament called was composed of the partisans of Simon de Montfort. The intended gathering, to which writs of summons went out to eighty-seven abbots and priors of all orders, including such insignificant personages as the Augustinian priors of Studley and Fineshead, was in size and composition quite unique. Unfortunately the lists for the early years of the reign of Edward I have vanished, but in the year 1295 a regular series begins. Thenceforward till 1334, when the pattern of the summonses had become in essentials fixed, lists of the writs to forty-four out of the fifty-seven generally accepted parliaments are extant.

The first list, that of the Parliament of Westminster summoned for 1 August 1295, may have had precedents, but is unlike any that followed. It is made up of some forty-six black monk prelates, including eight of the priors of the cathedral monasteries, and seven Austin canons.[2] The next list, of the same year, called a parliament to meet the French threat to Gascony on 27 November. This list also has a pattern of its own. As the assembly was to be in the fullest degree representative—it is the so-called 'Model Parliament' with its resounding prologue in which occurs the celebrated phrase *quod omnes tangit ab omnibus approbetur*—the clergy, great and small, were summoned by the bishops, who would thus have been responsible for the ordinary, non-exempt, houses of black monks and black canons. It was left for the king to call five exempt abbots, nineteen Premonstratensians, forty-three Cistercians, the master of the Temple, the prior of the Hospitallers at Clerkenwell, and the master of Sempringham.[3] Another assembly of almost identical composition took place in the following autumn.[4]

Of an entirely different type was the gathering of Michaelmas 1297, to which were summoned nineteen black monks, two canons, the prior of the Hospitallers and the master of Sempringham. This, indeed, an assembly called on an ordinary occasion when there were no great schemes of war or taxation to announce, was in essentials, though not in details, the kind of list that was to become common form twenty-five years later. Two similar lists follow, and then, in 1301, an almost exact replica of that of the great assemblies of 1295 and 1296. In the next year, however, a new series begins.[5] It was an era of heavy new taxation, of which the brunt fell upon wool, and it was therefore natural that the white monks and white canons, the growers of the finest wool, should be present in strength. Between 1300 and 1322 summonses of this type to some twenty parliaments exist. Though varying considerably in detail and number, the general pattern is the same: twenty to thirty black monks, three or four black canons, five to fifteen white canons and fifteen to forty white monks.

1 *Report*, III, i, 33–4.   2 *Ibid.* 64–5.   3 *Ibid.* 66–8.
4 *Ibid.* 70–1.   5 *Ibid.* 87.

In general, the numbers of the two first orders remain constant, while those of the two last decline steadily over the series, the Premonstratensians falling from fourteen to three, and the Cistercians from forty-four to fourteen. As there are considerable changes in the lists, apart from variations of number, and as even the largest is far from containing all the houses of the two orders, it would appear that selection depended entirely on the royal initiative, translated into the practical decision of the curial clerks, though bargaining may have taken place behind the scenes. The Welsh houses are not summoned, save for the wealthy Strata Florida, rich in flocks, on some three occasions, and the two Marcher houses of Basingwerk and Buildwas. Among other houses such notable ones as Revesby in Lincolnshire, Warden in Huntingdonshire, Coggeshall in Essex and Bordesley in Worcestershire do not appear to have been called.[1]

The run of large contingents ceases with the Easter gathering of 1322, and with the parliament of 23 February 1324, a type begins which continues with only slight rearrangements until the end.[2] The list consists of twenty-two black monk abbots, two black monk priors (Spalding and Lewes), six Austin canons, one Cistercian (Beaulieu), and the prior of St John of Jerusalem at Clerkenwell. The Templars had by now ceased to be. Henceforward it is necessary only to note successive approximations to the list that finally became standard. With the Winchester Parliament of 1330 a number (twenty-nine) was reached which remained fixed for a considerable time: twenty-three black monks, five canons, one Cistercian and the Hospitaller.[3] As the decades passed there was a slight sifting. Of the Austin canons Thornton (after 1338), Oseney (1346) and Leicester (1352) dropped finally out, leaving only Waltham and Cirencester. Beaulieu, whose position had long been anomalous, disappeared in 1341–2,[4] as did the master of Sempringham. Lewes, another anomalous member with a long record of attendance, went after 1363–4. The black monk list had all but settled down in 1340, but there were a few changes afterwards. Spalding vanished after 1341–2, and Battle, which had rarely appeared in early days, and had recently been in and out by turns, finally established its place in the reign of Richard II. Winchcombe, an ancient member, hovered round the door for long, but ultimately stayed in; Eynsham, another venerable member, now much decayed, likewise lingered at the door but finally passed out. Accidental variations occurred

1 *Ibid.* 143–319. It may be noted, however, that in the midst of this long series of large parliaments occur four, dating from 1308 and 1309, containing only between eleven and nineteen black monks, one Austin canon, and no other religious (*Report*, III, i, 178–90).

2 *Ibid.* 346. 3 *Report*, IV, ii, 392.

4 In the list of summonses for 11 September 1346, the abbot of Oseney is cancelled with the note: 'vacet quia idem abbas habet cartam Regis quod quietus sit de summonitione parliamenti et ideo cancellatur'. In the summonses for 25 January 1352, the abbot of Leicester is cancelled with the note: 'abbas de Leycestria cancellatur quia habet cartam Regis quod non compellatur venire ad parliamentum'. Similarly Beaulieu is cancelled in the Easter writs of 1342 with the note: 'memorandum quod habetur carta Regis irrotulata in rotulo patenti de hoc abbate quod de cetero non summoneatur ad parliamentum'.

from year to year, but at the Westminster Parliament of 1364–5 there appeared for the first time the exact list that was to be the stereotype.[1] Henceforth there were no further accessions (save for the altogether eccentric appearance of Christ Church, Canterbury, at Coventry on 6 October 1406),[2] and the occasional absences must have been due to purely accidental circumstances. The final list, which remained standard for the last 140 years of existence of the abbeys concerned, contained twenty-three black monk abbots, the prior of Coventry, and two abbots of the Austin canons; in addition the prior of St John of Jerusalem held his place, and was reckoned as the premier peer of the House of Lords.[3] The houses represented were as follows, in the order followed in the issue of writs: Peterborough, Colchester, Bury, Abingdon, Shrewsbury, Gloucester, Westminster, St Albans, Bardney, Selby, St Benet's of Holme, Thorney, Evesham, Ramsey, Hyde, Glastonbury, Malmesbury, Croyland, Battle, Winchcomb, Reading, St Augustine's Canterbury, St Mary's, York, Coventry, Waltham and Cirencester. To these were added, by royal act of power early in the reign of Henry VIII, Tavistock, Tewkesbury and Burton.

If we now consider the development of ideas and purposes that lies behind these facts and figures we shall find that the history of the religious in parliament follows very closely that of the lay lords. In their case, as is generally agreed, the Great Council had as its potential members all the tenants-in-chief of the Crown. Originally these may have had a right as well as a duty of attendance, but as attendance was a burden, particularly when it implied granting aids to the king, the obligation was emphasized rather than the privilege, and in the form of liability to suit of court it was given formal expression in the eleventh section of the Constitutions of Clarendon (1165).[4] The obligation, however, was to come when summoned, and the royal summons became the constitutive agency for coun-

1 *Report*, IV (ii), 704. 2 *Ibid.* 791.

3 J. R. Tanner, *Tudor Constitutional Documents*, 514, states that to the parliaments of Henry VII 'there were summoned...28 mitred abbots'. This statement has been widely repeated in short histories and text-books. It is incorrect, and seems to be derived either from a loose statement of Pike, *Constitutional History of the House of Lords*, 349, that 'the number of Abbots and Priors who had seats was about the same (i.e. 29)', or from a misreading of a note added to a list of summons in the reign of Edward III giving a list of twenty-eight abbots and priors whom it had not been usual to call (Pike, 347). Stubbs, *more suo*, has the correct figure (*Constitutional History* (5th ed. 1896), 460) and he also explodes the theory (which goes back to Browne Willis, if not further) that 'mitred abbot' and 'parliamentary abbot' were convertible terms. This misconception can be killed even more decisively than in Stubbs; the mitre, like other pontifical insignia, was a papal gift, which was obtained with growing frequency throughout the thirteenth, fourteenth and fifteenth centuries. In 1350 several parliamentary abbots were without the mitre; by 1500 not only all those in parliament, but many outside, had the privilege, which soon after became inseparable from the abbatial dignity in the Catholic Church.

4 Stubbs, *Select Charters* (9th ed. 1921), 166: 'Archiepiscopi, episcopi, et universae personae regni, qui de rege tenent in capite, et habent possessiones suas de domino rege sicut baroniam...debent interesse judiciis curiae domini regis cum baronibus.'

cils and later for parliaments. As has been seen, the free choice of the king was very real in the latter half of the thirteenth century, and though there seems to have been a 'short list' of prelates based on feudal relationships, which was used on occasion throughout the period, there were also many assemblies of larger, and some of much larger, proportions. There was in fact a broadening of the base, a 'defeudalization' of the summons to the religious, similar to the contemporary broadening of the basis of lay liability to include representatives of the shires and boroughs, and for similar reasons: originally, to get the largest measure of agreement and support in the disturbances of Henry III's reign, and later to get the widest possible representation of taxable communities. There can be no doubt that the large gatherings of Cistercian and Premonstratensian abbots were directly connected with the endeavours of Edward I to realize for his own purposes some of the country's wealth in wool; when, on the one hand, taxation became more stereotyped and, on the other, the merchants rather than the growers became the immediate victims, the need to summon the wool-growing abbots passed, and the parliamentary tide receded, leaving the feudal nucleus once more exposed.

At almost the same time, when the strong hand of Edward I was removed, the first instances occur of attempts on the part of certain prelates to relieve themselves of a duty which had become in every way irksome. As they based these efforts on evidence that they were not liable to summons, they raised for the royal justices and for historians the whole question of the law or convention behind the writ of summons. There is a general agreement among both classes that liability to summons rested in some way on tenure by barony. This indeed had been commonly agreed long before the reign of Edward II, but what exactly was understood by tenure by barony is still a matter of controversy.[1] It seems probable that it was originally a name given somewhat loosely to the tenure of a fairly considerable group of knights' fees; in other words, a baron was an important tenant-in-chief holding by military service. This conception was later modified by the omission of any emphasis on military service: a barony was a sizeable group of estates held and organized as a unit, and a baron was a considerable tenant-in-chief. Even a complex of estates held of the king in frankalmoin came to be reckoned as a barony. This, perhaps, may have been the legal and conventional doctrine, but as kings and lawyers had consistently held that suit of court was a unilateral obligation, and as only a small number of religious had regularly received writs of summons, the existence or absence of regular summonses came to be an alternative criterion of the duty of attendance at parliaments. In the event, tradition of summons by writ came, with the religious as with the lay lords, to be the decisive title to presence in parliament, though a few prelates were successful in breaking a tradition by proving the absence of baronial tenure. The drift away from parliament began, as has been noted,

1 Chew, *op. cit.* 159–88.

after the death of Edward I, when the white monks and canons, summoned by individual writs, dwindled almost to vanishing point, the royal foundation of Beaulieu alone remaining. The disappearance of these houses encouraged some other marginal prelates to defect, and in 1319 and 1331 the Augustinian abbot of St James at Northampton and the prior of Bridlington successfully claimed that they were exempt as not being tenants-in-chief or barons. They thus used the clause of the Constitutions of Clarendon as a liberating agency: those who did not hold in barony were not bound to attend.[1] A further incentive to defection was provided by the royal decision, ending a controversy, in 1341, by which the clergy as a body contributed to subsidies one-tenth of their produce, while tenants-in-chief summoned to parliament contributed the lay one-ninth. Eleven heads of houses consequently sought to prove a right to exemption, followed by two others a little later. Eight were successful, though their evidence did violence to history; five failed, though historically their claims were equally strong. In all these cases the Crown relied principally on the argument from precedent: they had or had not in the past regularly received and obeyed writs of summons.[2]

The group of houses that remained is by no means a complete list of the greater monasteries of abbatial rank. There were at least a dozen or so from the black monks alone that in wealth and general importance could have challenged several of the parliamentary houses. Nor does any other criterion serve to account for this precise selection. Admittedly the abbots in parliament derived in unbroken succession from those attending the Great Council. But this test would argue for the inclusion of many not admitted to the final list. Nor is mere antiquity a criterion, for though most of those remaining were pre-Conquest houses, Colchester, Bardney, Selby, Battle and Reading were not, whereas Chertsey, Burton and Pershore, ultimately excluded, were pre-Conquest houses of some standing. Tenure by military service is no criterion, for though fourteen of the group held by knight-service, nine did not, whereas eight of those owing service had fallen out. It has often been peremptorily stated that real or reputed foundation by a monarch was the criterion,[3] yet this certainly gave no right, as the case of Faversham shows, and though a royal founder, real or legendary, was a common boast, several of the abbeys remaining in parliament had at one time or another successfully established their tenure in frankalmoin, as Croyland, or had never at any time claimed, or been claimed by, a royal founder. Such, for instance, was the

1 Chew, *op. cit.* 172 *seqq.*, with references to record sources.
2 *Ibid.* 174.
3 Even Stubbs takes this view (*Constitutional History*, III, 460) where he states that the religious in parliament were made up of 'twenty-three Benedictine abbeys of royal or reputed royal foundation'. Royal foundation is nowhere urged by the Crown or disclaimed by the religious in their suits to secure exemption from attendance at parliament, and several of the abbeys had no royal founder, real or reputed.

position of Bardney. In short, the reasons for the inclusion of some of those that remained cannot now be discovered; no obvious claim kept Selby so consistently in its place, and Bardney, never important and often materially and spiritually insolvent, would seem to have had no clear title. In the last resort, we have to acknowledge, here as with so many other medieval institutions, that the ultimate and decisive factor was either accident or free choice—in this case the royal choice expressed by the regular issue of a writ of summons—for which no precise reason can now be ascertained.[1]

The burden of attendance at councils and parliaments was a very considerable one for the prelates concerned. In the latter part of the thirteenth century, when the records of summonses become available, it is clear that attendance at councils or parliaments was required as a rule at least thrice a year, and when parliaments finally superseded the Great Council early in the fourteenth century its meetings were both more regular and more prolonged than before. Though statistics taken from the duration of parliaments do not truly give us the total time consumed in the public service, they are at least something of a guide. We know that parliaments occupied about 700 days in the seventeen years of Edward II's reign, and some 2300 days in the period 1440–1504, thus giving an average of six and five weeks per annum respectively.[2] Actually, the irregular incidence and sometimes the prolonged attendance, together with the time spent on travel and wasted between sessions, would be a greater burden than six or eight weeks regular annual employment. The attendance of abbots in the thirteenth and fourteenth centuries was certainly as regular as that of lay lords, though of their activities in parliament itself little is known; some of their number were regularly appointed triers of English and Gascon petitions, though their quota was smaller than that of lay peers in relation to their numbers.[3] Attendance at parliament necessitated the upkeep of a household of some size in London or Westminster, and the constant entanglement with secular business and intrigues must have been a permanent influence sapping whatever was left of the spiritual conception of an abbot's office.

Abbots and priors who were not summoned by writ to parliament did not wholly escape disturbance. They were summoned to Church Councils, either legatine (of which no instance occurred between 1268 and 1519,

1 The claim of Archbishop Courtenay in the parliament of 1388 (*Rot. Parl.* iii, 236–7), that 'of right and custom of the realm of England...it belongeth to the...abbots and other prelates whatsoever, holding of the lord the king by barony, to be present in person and in all the king's parliaments whatsoever as peers of the realm', was equally contrary to history and contemporary practice.

2 Parry, in *Parliaments and Councils of England*, gives notes of the duration of parliaments, and for the period 1439–1509 full and accurate dates and details of members present are to be found in the Register of the Ministers and of the Members of both Houses in Lord Wedgwood's *History of Parliament* (London, 1938).

3 So *History of Parliament*, ii, Introd. lvi.

save in 1332) or provincial. The latter became, at least from the early fourteenth century onwards, indistinguishable from convocations, which about the same time came to be summoned simultaneously with each parliament, though their duration was far less. In the period of the fifteenth century noted above, some forty-four convocations, either national or of the province of Canterbury, took place, as compared with fifty-seven parliaments.[1]

1 *V. Handbook of British Chronology*, 347–9, 366–70.

CHAPTER XXV

THE MONASTIC ECONOMY,
1320–1480

In considering the exploitation of estates and the administering of funds
attention will be confined to the monastic and canonical orders which
came into being before 1200. These were all, to a greater or less degree,
possessed of land and other sources of wealth and thus, in the term current
in the controversies of the fourteenth century, were the 'possessioners',
as opposed to the various orders of friars who were, in principle and to a
large degree in fact also, possessionless and mendicant. Within the class of
the possessioners a further division may be made between the old orders—
the black monks and canons—and the new—the white monks and canons,
together with the Gilbertines, the Grandmontines and the Carthusians.
The old orders will be treated here, and attention will be given principally
to the black monks, if only because their estates were in so many cases
large, wealthy and widely scattered, whereas the canons' houses, with a
few notable exceptions, had estates of moderate size which, in the vast
majority of cases, lay around or near the abbey or priory. It may be added
that through accident of survival the original documents are most plentiful
for a small group of large black monk houses, and that through accident
of accessibility, the printing and interpreting of these documents has
hitherto been all but confined to the small but important class of cathedral
priories.

In all these houses the administration was carried on within the framework of what has been called the 'obedientiary system'. The origins and
normal features of the organization of this system have been recounted
elsewhere;[1] here, it is sufficient to recall that the original scheme of St
Benedict's Rule, in which all the temporal affairs of the monastery were
conducted, under the abbot, by a single cellarer,[2] had been almost universally supplanted by one resulting from a wholesale decentralization of
domestic management and finance, as a result of which half a dozen or
more departmental officials had direct control both of the funds with
which to run their departments and of the lands, tenements, mills, churches,
courts and the rest from which these funds were derived. An account has
also been given of the resolute attempt made in the late thirteenth century
by authority at every level—abbatial, capitular, episcopal and papal—to
secure a strict and regular system of account and audit and, as a general
rule, to centralize at least the greater part of the receipt of revenues by the

---

1 MO, 433–9.
2 Regula S. Benedicti, c. xxxi: '[Cellararius] curam gerat de omnibus: sine iussione
abbatis nihil faciat.' Cf. Constitutiones Cong. Ang. O.S.B. (1931), ad cap. xxxi Regulae,
declaratio 47: 'Cellararius omnia monasterii temporalia administret sub abbatis moderamine.'

establishment of a single chest or treasury.[1] The last two centuries of the Middle Ages saw repeated attempts to make this system a working reality. As regards accounting, these attempts were as successful as could be expected in an age and country where administrative uniformity and efficiency were only partially and sporadically achieved. At the greater houses, at least, the accounts were regularly presented for audit each year with a technique that grew in accuracy during the fourteenth century. The voluminous material still extant in such repositories as the chapter libraries at Canterbury, Durham, Worcester, Ely and Winchester, and which consists largely of the annual accounts of receipt and expenditure presented by the obedientiaries, remains as a silent witness to the financial competence of the monks. Lesser houses, in some such way as the small family business of a century ago, or the petty village shop of yesterday, were less regular.

Centralization or rationalization of management was a more difficult affair. Here, speaking very generally, two movements may be discerned, the one later in time than the other. The first was a general attempt at all the greater houses during the period of 'high farming' to secure a greater efficiency, economy and uniformity of policy and management than was possible under the obedientiary system. This attempt, as might be expected, took a number of different forms, some of which will be noted later. The second movement developed later, in the latter part of the fifteenth century, when on the one hand the religious had become *rentiers* rather than exploiters, and on the other new and more efficient methods of central control were being employed in governmental and mercantile affairs throughout Europe. This tendency took the form, in the religious houses, of the combination of several or all offices in a few hands or even in a single hand, and particularly in the hand of the abbot or prior.

No complete account of late medieval monastic administration will be possible until further research has been made by individual workers among the archives of the great monasteries. Recently, however, half a dozen competent scholars and students have examined the documents of as many representative houses, and a synthesis of their findings will probably indicate with some accuracy not only the general movements and methods and influences common to all, but also some divergences of procedure and organization which further investigation will emphasize.[2]

---

1 *RO*, I, 55–63.

2 The principal groups of monastic accounts hitherto published are: ABINGDON: *Accounts of the Obedientiars of Abingdon Abbey*, ed. R. E. G. Kirk. DURHAM: *The Priory of Finchale, Historia Dunelmensis scriptores tres, The Accounts of the Bursar of the Monastery of Durham from 1530 to 1534, Inventories of the Benedictine Houses of Jarrow and Monk Wearmouth*, all ed. J. Raine; *Feodarium prioratus Dunelmensis*, ed. W. Greenwell; *Extracts from the Account Rolls of the Abbey of Durham*, ed. J. T. Fowler, henceforward abbreviated as *DAR*. NORWICH: H. W. Saunders, *Introduction to the Obedientiary and Manor Rolls of Norwich Cathedral Priory*. WINCHESTER: *Obedientiary Rolls of St Swithun's, Winchester*, ed. G. W. Kitchin. WORCESTER: *Accounts of the Priory of Worcester*, ed. J. M. Wilson; *Early Compotus Rolls of the Priory of Worcester*, ed. J. M. Wilson and Cosmo Gordon; *Compotus Rolls of*

In what follows attention will be paid principally to four or five of the great cathedral priories, such as Canterbury, Winchester, Durham, Norwich and Ely. Their buildings and the documents within them have in large part survived, and have remained the property of the capitular body which followed the monks, and it is natural that students should have selected these treasures first for examination. This is in one respect fortunate, for the cathedral priories, with their wide estates unbroken by the internal dichotomy between abbot and convent, and their more democratic and flexible government, were freer to adopt new methods and policies than was an abbey, where there was always potential tension between abbot and convent. They therefore show a variety of methods within a similar framework. It is probable that the abbeys, a far more numerous class, would show a greater family likeness; if so, while less interesting, perhaps, to the investigator they might supply firmer ground for general judgements.

The monastic economy may be considered in three of its activities: the exploitation of the land; the realization and distribution of the funds; and the collection, disposal and internal distribution of the produce of the land and of the goods purchased with the funds accruing from the estates.

The exploitation of the land may itself be considered on two levels: the immediate control of the labour force and its assignment to this or that agricultural or pastoral task; and the higher direction of policy, including improvement in methods of cultivation, changes in cropping or marketing policy, and the grouping or centralization of this or that activity.

The immediate direction of the labourers, whether villeins or free, was never in the hands of the religious, save perhaps in the earlier occasional practice when a manor was controlled by a resident monk, or in the later use of the same practice by the Augustinian canons.[1] Normally it was carried out either by the reeve (*praepositus*) of the manor, or by a sergeant (*serviens*) employed by the convent to oversee one or more manors. It was

the *Priory of Worcester of the Fourteenth and Fifteenth Centuries*, ed. S. G. Hamilton. To these may be added the accounts of the Augustinian houses of BRISTOL: *Two Compotus Rolls of St Augustine's Abbey*, ed. G. Beachcroft and A. Sabin, and BICESTER: J. C. Blomfield, *History of the deanery of Bicester*.

For a general aid to the understanding of medieval systems of accounting *v*. R. H. Hilton, *The Economic Development of some Leicestershire Estates*; E. Levett, *Studies in Manorial History*; N. Denholm-Young, *Seignorial Administration*; R. A. L. Smith, *Canterbury Cathedral Priory* and *Collected Papers*. In the treatment of Durham that follows a first draft had already been written when Miss E. M. Halcrow kindly allowed me to read and make use of the very valuable results of her researches among the Durham archives; the wide range of her findings was of the greatest assistance, and it is to be hoped that some of her work may see the light in due course.

Since the above was printed a valuable study of medieval agrarian development, by R. H. Hilton, has appeared in *VCH Leics.* II, 145–198.

1 Cf. the practice at Oseney, in *Cartulary of Oseney Abbey*, ed. H. E. Salter, vi, 184, and at Owston. Of the latter Hilton, *op. cit.*, 139, writes: 'It would appear that in the middle of the fourteenth century the Owston Abbey manors were supervised not by bailiffs but by canons of the abbey who resided on the manor and performed the functions of manorial bailiffs, accounting to the receiver as a bailiff would account.'

these officials who directed the labour force, collected and forwarded the surplus produce to headquarters or to the market, and who answered to the agent of the convent, the monastic or secular auditor or official, for moneys received and spent.

As regards the higher control practice varied. At some houses it was the task of monks or canons appointed for that purpose alone, as were the monk-wardens of the groups or 'custodies' of manors at Christ Church, Canterbury, or the canons in charge of the bailiwicks of Oseney Abbey.[1] At all other houses some or all of the manors were directly controlled by individual obedientiaries; the almoner in particular, whose funds, being charitable bequests, were never merged, and the sacrist almost always retained control of their lands to the end, and there may have been houses where all the manors were throughout administered by the obedientiaries to whom they had originally been allotted. Elsewhere, however, other methods were employed in the interests of efficiency, and a pair of officials, or a single monk, received charge of all or most of the property. Thus at Durham the bursar, with his *alter ego* the terrar, at Norwich the master of the cellar, at Winchester the prior's receiver, at Ely the monk-seneschal (or steward), and at Westminster the monk-bailiff and the warden of Queen Eleanor's manors had charge of a large proportion, if not all, of the house's property. Elsewhere, again, and more generally as the fifteenth century wore on, the monk overseer was replaced by a lay functionary, often the seneschal or steward who had previously been his official assistant; this was the case in later days at Croyland, and throughout the fifteenth century at Pershore.[2]

Originally, the manor had been treated for the purpose of financial and economic administration as a unit. The accounting official, whether reeve, sergeant or monk-warden, had received and accounted for all revenues in money and kind, and when compotus rolls give their earliest information receipts of all kinds are entered against the sums received from the convent for running expenses. This continued to be the normal practice, but in some houses, notably Durham, the sergeant was responsible and accounted for only what we should now call the farming or producing activities— the yield of grain, hay and vegetables. Rents for land and houses, dues and fees of all kinds were here collected by a separate official, and paid directly to the bursar. In consequence, it is extremely difficult and often impossible to arrive at a profit and loss balance, the more so, as all flocks, herds and dairy-work were managed on an intermanorial basis and accounted for by an official other than the sergeant of the manor.

For the collection and disposal of the produce, likewise, more than one system obtained. Originally, many or most of the demesne lands had contributed the bulk of their yield to the monastic landlord, either for the

1 Smith, *Canterbury Cathedral Priory*, 100–12.
2 For Croyland *v*. F. M. Page, *The Estates of Crowland Abbey*; for Pershore, *v*. the un-published London University M.A. thesis by R. A. L. Smith, 198–9.

routine provisioning of the convent, its guests, servants and dependants, or for the use of the abbot and officials during their visits to their manors. If a small surplus remained, after seed had been kept for the next year, it was sold locally. Gradually, as the monasteries developed the technique of agriculture and brought more land under plough, much of the yield, and sometimes the whole of the produce of certain demesnes, was sent to market. Finally, when business methods were still further developed, the grain and legumes of distant estates were sold in their totality, and the convent obtained its own supplies by local purchases where the monks could control the market or where prices were in their favour.

Greater definition may perhaps be given to a composite picture if a more detailed view is taken of the administration of a single house. For this purpose, and during the period under review, the great cathedral priory of Durham is perhaps the most attractive choice. The wealth of material still extant in the library and archives of the Dean and Chapter equals, if it does not surpass, the riches of Canterbury, Winchester and Norwich, and of this abundance much has already appeared in print, while of recent years additional work of high excellence has been done upon the original documents. With these materials it is possible to give a general view of the Durham economy that may show the organs and machinery of the whole establishment at work, together with their adaptation to the changing conditions of the last two medieval centuries, thus providing matter for comparison with the sketch of the Canterbury administration already given.[1]

The original system at Durham from at least the middle of the twelfth century onwards would appear to have conformed to the normal pattern. The lands of the bishop were separated from those of the monks, but within the estates of the convent there was no division between community and prior. The obedientiary system was in existence, controlled somewhat more tightly by the prior than it would have been by an abbot. The prior himself had no special sources of income allotted to him, but received contributions from various obedientiaries. Among these officials were the normal sacrist, almoner, chamberlain, cellarer, granator and the rest, and, in addition, one with the uncommon title of terrar who, it may be suggested, was the external counterpart of the cellarer.

Durham, in common with most black monk houses, moved towards financial centralization in the late thirteenth century, but instead of the treasurers or receivers instituted elsewhere a bursar appears as receiving officer for all revenues save the relatively small amounts accruing to a few other obedientiaries. Thus the bursar, throughout the last three centuries of the monastery's existence, came very near to being the universal receiver and provider of the house. The author of the *Rites of Durham*, indeed, speaks of him in general terms which at a first reading suggest that all

1 *RO*, I, 49–54.

revenues were collected, and all expenses met, by the bursar alone, as by the monastic procurator of to-day.[1] This, as will be seen, was not the case, but it is unquestionable that the bursar's office outweighed those of all the other obedientiaries taken collectively. Into his hands came directly some four-fifths of the gross income, and he controlled directly at least half of the spending.

It is natural to ask whether this important office was a direct legacy, with slight modifications, from early days when a single official handled all the business of finance and purveying, or whether, at some time in the thirteenth century, the control of separate incomes was removed in large part from the various officials and lodged in the hands of a central functionary. The documents hitherto printed or examined give no certain information on the point. It might have been alleged in favour of the first alternative that a monastic community was intensely conservative, in the twelfth as in the thirteenth century, and that the central treasury when newly established in other monasteries had a function purely financial or at most directive, whereas the Durham bursar appears in his earliest accounts as personally engaged in all the transactions of getting and spending, purveying and planning, building and furnishing, that pass through his books.[2] For the other alternative an argument may be found in the office of terrar. This official, as his name implies, must in origin have been in charge of the estates of the house, but at his first appearance in the rolls he is a simulacrum only, with a small income derived from unimportant dues, which he spends on a variety of minute affairs, often to the advantage of other officials.[3] At the same time he was engaged, outside the financial sphere, in constant managerial collaboration with the bursar in visiting manors and dealing with sales of wool and stock. When demesne farming was abandoned, the office was all but otiose, and before the Dissolution the terrar had vanished in all but name, being then in function as guest-master. It is natural, therefore, to suppose that at some early period the financial responsibilities of the office were removed from the terrar's hands and lodged in those of the bursar. There seems, indeed, to be no reasonable doubt that the bursary was a new creation of Prior Hugh de Darlington (1258–73), who in many ways showed himself a gifted and original administrator. There is no mention of the office in constitutions

---

1 *Rites of Durham*, ed. (1) J. Raine, 83; ed. (2) J. T. Fowler, 99: 'Hiss office was to Receave all the Rentes that was pertaining to the house, and all other officers of the house mayde there accomptes to him, and he discharged all the servants wages, and paide all the expences that the house was charged withall.'

2 *V. Scriptores tres*, p. xlix, and *DAR*, II, 484.

3 In the terrar's rolls between 1414 and 1509 the receipts are very constant, amounting always to between £31 and £39; they come chiefly from numerous small customary payments (cornage, elsilver, brasinage, etc.). The expenses, besides servants' wages and office and stable costs, are for purchases of grain, presents and allotments at the command of the prior. The author of the *Rites* says merely (1) 83; (2) 99: 'His office was to see that all the gests chambers to be [*sic*] cleanly kept, etc.' Yet the hostillar, who is not mentioned in the *Rites*, was giving full accounts for about £200 as late as 1529 (*DAR*, I, 162 *seqq.*).

drawn up prior to that date, whereas a bursar is referred to in a constitution of Prior Hugh's in 1265, and the first surviving bursar's roll is of 1278.

Only a careful examination of the very rich collection of account rolls still unprinted would establish the precise limits of the bursar's activity.[1] Certain broad outlines, however, are clear. On the side of revenue he received all income from lands, churches, pensions, sales, dues and payments in kind from all the lands of the convent save for the relatively small sources of income in each of these categories attached to the office of other obedientiaries. On the side of expense, he paid the regular salaries and wages to the majority of servants and dependants, met the prior's needs for cash for journeys, presents and alms, and paid his other bills; he also, for part of the period, found most of the money needed by Durham College and its students, and in general issued cash for all journeys, suits, gifts and taxes, besides advancing money for much of the regular almsgiving of the convent.[2] In addition, he bought at least some of the regular supplies of the house, including the bulk of the wine. Finally, he appears from the first as paying over annually, by tally or indenture, the large lump sum needed by the cellarer, master of the granaries and marshal in the course of their annual administration.[3] It is, however, quite impossible to draw a perfectly distinct and logical line, for while several other obedientiaries with their own sources of income joined in making contributions to the support of the prior, the upkeep of Durham College, and other funds,[4] the bursar for his part regularly augmented what would have seemed to be the peculiarly independent resources of the almoner, while many of his purchases might have been taken to fall within the province of the cellarer or sacrist.[5]

1 The main printed source is the selection of account rolls edited by Canon J. T. Fowler for the Surtees Society (noted above, p. 310, n. 2). As it would clearly have been impossible to publish the complete series without monopolizing the funds of the Society for an indefinite period, Canon Fowler, whose industry is beyond praise, decided to print a few representative rolls in full and extract salient items from the rest. Unfortunately for the social and economic historian, his interests were primarily antiquarian; he selected the unusual or picturesque items and gave no summary of the rest, not even giving the annual financial balance. Consequently, the volumes are of little use for economic or statistical purposes; it is, for example, impossible to draw a graph of the revenue and expenses of the obedientiaries, or to check the sales of grain, stock, etc., over a period of years. As it is most unlikely that the imperfect and remaining rolls will be printed, there is a wide and promising field in the Durham archives for a succession of students.

2 The bursar was apparently responsible for the doles made on behalf of the community on anniversaries of priors, bishops, etc. The almoner was principally concerned with the three hospitals: at Witton, St Mary Magdalen's, and that within the priory precinct. The income for these, it is to be supposed, was drawn from sources assigned to this end by benefactors, and such sources, like those assigned to the church for special purposes, usually escaped when a general pooling was in progress.

3 Cf. *DAR*, II, 493 (1292); 509 (1310–1).

4 Cf. *DAR*, II, 381 (sacrist, 1350–1): 'clericis Oxon. studentibus, 20 s.' *Ibid.* 383, the same and 'in pitanciis et exhenniis missis d'no Priori, etc.'

5 E.g. *DAR*, II, 518 (1330): 'in 2 paribus Tualium pro altar. & 2 Manutergiis . . . 2 vestimentis integris cum tunicis et dalmaticis.' Cf. *Ibid.* 519, for 35 quarters of salt purchased.

The functions of the bursar underwent no essential change between 1300 and 1530, though his activities were considerably changed in scope by the abandonment of demesne farming. There were, however, a few notable modifications during the period. Thus the cellarer, financially the official next in importance, originally received nearly all his income direct from the bursar by tally or indenture. This arrangement was still in force in the middle of the fourteenth century, but when, after an interval, a new series of long cellarer's rolls begins in 1438–9, the cellarer is found directly receiving and accounting for a long list of rents and dues, and as administering the property concerned, in complete independence of the bursar.[1] He lost this independence again, however, before the end,[2] and it would seem to be established that the temporary system was introduced by Prior Wessyngton (1416–46) to remedy the damage caused by an inefficient bursar.[3] As if to balance this devolution, a contrary development took place, apparently later than c. 1450, in the office of master of the granaries. Previously, this official had received, like the cellarer, an annual lump sum from the bursar; henceforth, the bursar takes over the purchase of grain and pulse, and the master of the garner is concerned solely with receiving, storing and distributing the materials. A similar change had occurred still earlier in the marshal's department; he was originally responsible for the farrier's work and stable care of the horses; now, the small sum originally issued no longer appears, and instead purchases or the materials required are made by the bursar.[4]

The offices other than the bursar's may be divided into two financial groups. Of major importance were the cellarer (£424), hostillar (£220), chamberlain (£190), sacrist (£102) and almoner (£74); all these had considerable receipts;[5] together with corresponding duties of land and property management. The infirmarian, commoner, terrar (on the financial side) and keeper of the shrine were of less significance. Their

1 In the earliest bursar's roll of 1292 (*DAR*, II, 493), £492. 18s. 2d. are given by tally to the cellarer. In the cellarer's roll of 1438–9 (*DAR*, I, 62 *seqq.*) there is the first extant (printed) list of properties with their income accounted for. In 1460 he is noted as paying £351 to kitchen expenses (*Feodarium Dunelm.* 211).

2 In the bursar's roll of 1536–7 (*DAR*, III, 707) there is a note of £531 paid by tally and indenture to the cellarer *pro expensis coquine*. It is impossible, owing to the editor's method of printing excerpts, to find when this practice recommenced; Miss E. M. Halcrow believes it to have been shortly after Wessyngton's death.

3 So Miss Halcrow, confirming a conclusion arrived at previously by the present writer; *v. infra*, n. 5.

4 The marshal received £12. 19s. 1d. in 1292 (*DAR*, II, 493), but in 1299 and subsequently the bursar is found buying horse-shoes, harness, etc. (e.g. *DAR*, II, 496), and the marshalry accounts printed by Fowler are for quite a different department, viz. fines for petty market faults, etc.

5 These figures are taken from different years which seemed normal, as the editor of *DAR* never gives a complete statement of all the officials for any one single year. The list in the appendices of *Scriptores tres*, p. ccli (1436) seems too symmetrical to be trustworthy; it is worth noting that the cellarer does not appear therein, i.e. he was presumably still paid by tally by the bursar. If this was really the case the change must certainly have been made in 1437 by Prior Wessyngton.

incomes, save for that of the last-named, which was in a class by itself and not administered by the official, were small and their expenses petty.

There is no trace in the Durham records as hitherto printed of a finance committee of seniors comparable to that constituted by the small group meeting at the exchequer at Christ Church, Canterbury, though it is probable that a few of the more experienced monks took part in the counsels of the prior, bursar and terrar. Nor, though the author of the *Rites* states that all the officials accounted to the bursar, is there a written trace of this audit. In an important respect, however, the bursar discharged the functions of a central treasury: throughout the centuries under review, and especially in the period of the greatest financial returns in the fourteenth century, the revenues of his office exceeded the visible expenses by a margin not wholly due to good management, and the surplus, carried forward from year to year, formed a mass of floating capital which was presumably used for extraordinary expenses and building operations, though these transactions cannot be traced in the fragmentary samples of the rolls as printed.

It would seem that the income reached a peak at the end of the thirteenth century. In 1292 the bursar's receipts were £3741,[1] and in 1308 £4526. These huge totals included the revenues of both cellarer and master of the garner, which may have amounted together to some £600, but it is probable that the residue accruing to the bursar in his own right was never greatly surpassed. Scottish wars, the permanent loss of 'spiritual' income north of the Border, inability on the part of tenants to repair damages and reclaim waste caused by Border raids, added to the pestilences of the time and the rising costs of labour, all combined to lower the income from Durham property. Receipts fell sharply to £1752 in 1335; in 1373 the net receipts were £2114, but were considerably increased by arrears.[2] By the middle of the fifteenth century the net total was £1144;[3] from this receipts rose to some £1400 at the end of the century, and on the eve of the Dissolution, in 1536–7, they stood at £1462.[4] As regards the churches of the priory, there are lists giving the income for seven annual periods between 1293 and 1436; they are as follows: (1293) £1466; (1348, two years after the battle of Neville's Cross) £616; (1350, the year after the Black Death) £410; (1392) £452; (1420, after more Border trouble and much conversion of arable to pasture) £396; (1430) £432; (1436, after the loss of Norham and the Holy Isle) £353.

1 *DAR*, II, 492. The floating capital of the year was apparently £1587 (*ibid.* 493).
2 They stood at £1931 in 1340–1 (*DAR*, II, 538), falling to £1212 in 1348–9 (*ibid.* 549) and rising again to £1732 in 1390–1 (*ibid.* III, 597). The first of these totals includes a few miscellaneous loans; in the other two, these have been subtracted by the accounting official.
3 This is the net total arrived at in 1446 by the public notary who audited the accounts and viewed the property. His full and most interesting report is printed in *Scriptores tres*, pp. cclxxxv–cccviii. In 1446 the gross income was £1227, but there was a loss of £246 on the year's working.
4 The totals for the two financial years 1499–1501 are £1399 and £1397 (*DAR*, III, 656); for that of 1536–7, v. *ibid.* 690. It was £1462.

The considerable estates of Durham priory were scattered over the north-eastern counties from Lincolnshire to Northumberland, but from the early thirteenth century onwards, and probably from the first years of the priory, no attempt was made at the direct exploitation of all. Those retained in hand by the bursar at the end of the thirteenth century formed compact groups round Durham itself and elsewhere in the county; to these must be added the three manors of Elvet, Sacristonhaugh and Witton, which throughout the period to the Dissolution were controlled and exploited by the hostillar, sacrist and almoner respectively.[1]

Besides being controlled by a single master, the manors of the bursar were centralized in several other respects. Not only were pasture and dairy farming intermanorial, as at most houses, with cattle concentration at Muggleswick in the Derwent valley, Witton in Weardale, Pittington and Le Holme, in addition to a stud of mares at Beaurepaire, but the direct organization of manorial business was centralized to an unusual degree. While originally the manor, when held in hand, had been treated as a single unit of account, all rents, fees, dues and fines being reckoned along with the sales and renders of produce in the total income of the manor, to be answered for by the sergeant or reeve, and balanced in the rolls and budget against the running expenses and capital outlay, at Durham in the period under review a financial line was drawn between agricultural activity and all other sources of income. The former was the concern of the sergeant or reeve in account with the bursar and under the oversight of the bursar and terrar; the latter were the concern of rent-collectors, sent down from Durham by the bursar, and were in no way part of the responsibility of the sergeant.[2]

There were no monk-wardens at Durham. Where they existed, as at Canterbury, they were almost invariably the regularization of an existing abuse, and it is possible that at Durham the abuse of monks farming manors for the convent had never existed. Instead of monk-wardens, the manors were controlled by paid sergeants or (less often) reeves. The bursar and terrar visited each manor at least once in the early part of the year, for a view of the stock and resources, and for planning the summer's crop; this was round Eastertide. A schedule of this visit, containing an inventory of the manor, was kept on the spot. Other and less formal visits

---

1 To be exact, the cellarer had Aldinridge in 1438–9 (*DAR*, 1, 66), though in 1446 it appears in the bursar's hand (*Scriptores tres*, ccci); the almoner had Witton well stocked and sown in 1338 (*DAR*, 1, 199–200), besides land round the hospital of St Mary Magdalen (*ibid.*); the chamberlain had the church and manor of Dalton, *c.* 1340–6 (*DAR*, 1, 171, 176); the hostillar had Elvet, *c.* 1300–5 (*DAR*, 1, 113, 114, 121), and still held it in 1528–9 (*ibid.* 162); the sacrist's activities at Sacristonhaugh (in its various spellings) can be traced *passim* in the accounts.

2 Miss Halcrow notes that on the contiguous estates of the bishop of Durham and of the Percys the contrary (i.e. the normal) practice was in vogue: all rents were paid to the manorial bailiffs or sergeants; *v.* Bishop Hatfield's survey (SS, 32; roll in appendix) and Percy Bailiff rolls (SS, 117).

by the two officials were frequent.[1] The prior, also, who spent about a third of the year in residence on the estates, sometimes made a set progress round the manors, usually in September or October.[2] At Michaelmas the audit took place. This, in Durham practice, was always carried through on the manor, either by the bursar or terrar (or the other obedientiaries concerned), or by a professional auditor employed by them. The sergeant's account roll was examined, criticized and annotated, and a new roll drawn up embodying the corrections; this roll was destined for preservation in the archives at Durham, and was often accompanied thither by the sergeant's roll. This procedure differed notably from that of Christ Church Canterbury, St Swithun's Winchester, and other houses, where the effective accounting was done at the monastery itself.[3]

Thus procedure followed in accounting and the technique of the accounts varied considerably from period to period, as it did also from house to house, and this variety and constant change affords one more example of the fallacy of regarding any medieval institution as either static or uniform. When once the principle of annual audit had been admitted, the normal practice would seem to have been for the sergeants to come up to the monastery and remain till they had been submitted to examination and a final balance had been struck. This was the practice at Christ Church, Canterbury, at the beginning of the fourteenth century, and it apparently continued to be the Winchester practice for at least a hundred years after.[4] This made of the chapter, or rather of a financial committee of the chapter sitting at the exchequer, the sole auditing body, and made a long business of the audit itself. Gradually it became customary for professional auditors to audit the sergeants' accounts on the manor. The members of the chapter or seniors now had little more to do than to receive the audited account, which they could then use as material for a full survey of the finances of the house, and as a basis for discussions of administrative and economic policy. At Durham the first stage, if it ever existed, has left no clear trace in the records, and throughout the fourteenth and fifteenth centuries the auditing was done on the manors.

It is possible to see in the compotus rolls that have been printed or analysed a development in the technique of accounting and in the methods and aims of the auditors. Two great differences between medieval and

1 Expenses connected with these visits are frequently noted on the (unpublished) manorial rolls; they do not appear in the published bursarial rolls where, however, the visits of the bursar and terrar to fairs and markets are recorded.

2 E.g. in bursar's roll of 1340–1: 'In expensis d'ni Prioris circumeundo maneria Prioratus per 7em dies post fest. S. Mich. Archang., 73s 2d'. (*DAR*, II, 539).

3 For the usual auditing procedure *v.* Denholm-Young, *Seignorial Admin stration*, 132. Miss Halcrow draws attention to occasional instances of a similar practice at Durham, e.g. for the chamberlain (*DAR*, I, 197): '[receptori] pro exp. suis versus Dunelm. pro compoto suo audiendo et determinando'.

4 Smith, *Collected Papers*, 56, 60–5; J. S. Drew, 'Manorial Accounts of St Swithun's Priory, Winchester'.

modern practice at once strike the reader of early fourteenth-century accounts. The first is the absence of any attempt to express a balance between expenditure and total receipts—in other words, to show a profit or loss; this, as we shall see, was remedied as the century wore on.[1] A corollary of this was that no effective reserve fund existed. The centralized treasury did not imply the existence of such a fund, and even when the common chest was instituted, as it was at many houses in the fifteenth century, it normally enjoyed only a small and fixed annual income. Monastic accounts therefore did not normally allow for the carrying of profits to reserve or to a capital account. A partial exception must, however, be made for the cathedral priory of St Swithun at Winchester, a house that had always been in the forefront of financial advance since the days of that great financier, Henry of Blois. Here the treasury from its first institution seems to have had a wide competence. It received all unappropriated revenues, and regularly paid extraordinary expenses. Moreover, it received any surplus that might remain after the audit of the accounts of obedientiaries.

The other difference between medieval and modern accounts is still more fundamental. It is the failure to differentiate between capital and regular income, with the consequence in accounting that no valuation of stock or property is included in the year's accounts, and that sales of land and timber and the like are counted among income just as are sales of grain and milk. The manorial and obediential accounts of c. 1300 are in fact mere lists of day-to-day expenses and receipts.

As regards the running of a manor, the function of the audit at the opening of the fourteenth century was chiefly to check the statements of the bailiff or reeve against the tallies, receipts or stores, and to examine the plausibility of his expenses for particular purposes. During the thirteenth and fourteenth centuries there was a fairly general development of technique in the direction of a statement of profit and loss,[2] and from the beginning of the fourteenth century or earlier, the 'profit of the manor' is in fact an important item on manorial accounts, though it is not always carried over into the copy enrolled for the archives. The *proficuum manerii*, indeed, is not always the net profit on the year's working as understood in modern practice, all expenses having been taken into account; it is more often at first the gross yield of demesne[3] less the running expenses, other income (such as profits of the manorial court) and overheads having been neglected.[4] The parallel *proficuum wainagii* of the fourteenth century was,

1 As, for example, at St Swithun's, Winchester, always an advanced house in financial matters, *v.* references in last note; for what follows I am in part indebted to Professor Postan for suggestions.

2 Miss Halcrow has demonstrated this very clearly from Durham sources.

3 Formulas such as 'respondet semen ad iii granum', and more complicated ones such as 'plus semen iiiito per viii quarteria' (i.e. a fourfold yield, plus 8 quarters of grain per acre) are common. For Norwich, *v.* Saunders, *Norwich Rolls*, 29–31 *et al.*; for Winchester, *v.* Drew, *art. cit.*

4 N. Denholm-Young, *op. cit.* 126–30; Saunders, *op. cit.* 11–14.

it would seem, a more accurate statement, giving an exact balance between the internal income and expenses of the demesne, to be used against a valuation of the land to show the prospective advantage or disadvantage of leasing as opposed to direct exploitation by the lord.

The advance in the technique of accountancy was accompanied by a development of equal significance in the procedure of auditing. If the decades shortly before the year 1300 were a 'boom' period in grain farming for the market, they were immediately followed by what may be called the golden age of keen, if not always as profitable, administration of estates. There is evidence that at the cathedral priories, at least, the auditing committee, which at Christ Church, Canterbury, Winchester, and doubtless elsewhere was composed of a few experienced senior monks, took an active and enlightened part not only in scrutinizing accounts and directing economic policy but in using the annual audit as an instrument of great efficiency in securing the best returns from the manors. Here again there was a divergence of method. At Christ Church the seniors, after receiving the annual statements and the reports of the wardens, budgeted for the coming year by demanding that such and such an acreage should be devoted to various crops as against such and such an allowance for upkeep.[1] At St Swithun's, Winchester, the practice was to set what would now be called a 'target' in each department of farming: grain sown was to produce such and such an increase, the wool crop was to be of a certain weight, lactage per animal was to result in this or that weight of cheese, stock was to multiply in this or that ratio per head. If the sergeant or reeve failed to achieve the desired result he was mulcted for the deficit, save in rare cases when mercy was shown; a surplus was to the good for the convent.[2]

This period of intensive and detailed direction from above came to an end, as had the 'boom' in grain and wool sales, even before the transfer of the convent's economy from sales to rents had been completed. At Canterbury the disappearance of the monk-wardens from effective control when Prior Chillenden went over to rents in 1391–6 marked the end of an epoch; personal vigilance and forecasting were no longer needed.[3] At Winchester there is evidence that the quantities demanded from the reeves of the various manors, which hitherto had reflected the circumstances of the year, were 'pegged' at a conventional figure by the middle of the fourteenth century. They thus became in effect fixed produce-rents rather than indices or stimulants of production, and it is to be presumed that enterprising reeves, having achieved the modest target, sold for their own profit such surplus as they could produce.

From the time of the earliest surviving account-roll and probably for a long period previously the production and marketing of wool and the

1 Cf. Smith, *Canterbury Cathedral Priory*, especially Appendix 1, 'Chapter and Exchequer ordinances'.   2 *V*. Drew, *art. cit.* 27–8.   3 Smith, *op. cit.* 191.

rearing of stock, both cattle and horses, together with the whole business of dairy farming, were conducted at Durham and elsewhere on an inter-manorial basis. The bursar and the terrar, with their subalterns the stock-keeper and the overseer of the stud, had charge, and the local sergeants had no responsibility whatsoever; payments and receipts appear on the books of the two departmental officials. The centre of the Durham sheep-farming was Le Holme,[1] but sheep in large numbers were kept also on manors devoted primarily to cattle. Muggleswick on the Derwent was the principal stock-farm; others were at Witton in Weardale and around the prior's country-house of Beaurepaire (Bearpark), where there was also a stud. In 1341 the bursar had 1082 sheep and 720 lambs of the year at Holm, and 204 *hogastri* or sheep of the second year at Bellasis, besides numbers of sheep and cattle at Muggleswick, Beaurepaire, Fery and Wystow. A century later, in 1447, there were at Holm 405 wethers, 699 ewes and 99 young sheep, together with 304 lambs, a total of 1507 in all. In the same year there were at Muggleswick 433 head of cattle of various descriptions and ages, in addition to 340 sheep, while at Beaure-paire there was an extensive concentration of all kinds of stock, including a stud of forty mares and colts, with fifty more from elsewhere on agist-ment.[2] In addition to these undertakings of the bursar, the obedientiaries had some sheep and cattle on their manors; the cellarer in particular, on his manor of Rilley, besides a flock of some three hundred sheep, had a large dairy farm which provided some, at least, of the milk and cheese needed for the establishment.[3] The bursar's stock, as has been said, was managed by the stock-keeper and by the overseer of the stud; the former accounted for all sales and losses of sheep and cattle, and arranged for the transfer of beasts from one folding place or steading to another, according to their class and age, while the latter, besides supervising the breeding, purchase and sales of the horses, arranged for the agistment of animals from elsewhere. These two officials, who had no revenues or estates appropriated to their office, worked under the bursar; they did not, there-fore, control the stock on the manors of the obedientiaries, and the almoner, who had at one time sixty head of cattle and 180 sheep in Wear-dale,[4] the cellarer, with his animals at Rilley and Aldingridge, and the hostillar, with his cattle at Elvet, made their own arrangements and profits.

The Durham agrarian economy underwent a steady process of change during the fourteenth century. At the opening of the period every manor

---

1 Le Holme is a portion of Coupon (Cowpen) in Billinghamshire, north-east of Stockton-on-Tees.

2 For the above figures *v.* the rolls of the instaurarius (*DAR*, ii, 308–22) and supervisor equicii (*DAR*, ii, 323–5).

3 See the cellarer's roll of 1438–9 (*DAR*, i, 67): 'nil de firma de Rylley cellararii, quia assignatur eidem pro butiro et caseo'. There does not seem to be any clear trace in the printed accounts of an organized food-farm, though several places contributed eggs and poultry at set times.   4 *DAR*, i, 200–1.

of the groups held in hand by the bursar sent up to the priory stocks of provisions—grain, milk, cheese, eggs, vegetables—and sold only the surplus that remained after seed had been kept back for the next year. Gradually it became common for this produce, in the case of manors at any distance, to be sold for cash on the spot or in the nearest profitable market; the money was forwarded to Durham and used to buy the necessary stores locally:[1] the normal source of these was the group of manors near Durham, where the convent could use their powers as landlords, through the agency of the terrar, to restrict the tenants' access to market, thus preventing competition and high prices for the grain available, which was needed at Durham itself.[2] This change of policy, which had come about earlier at many monasteries in the Midlands, meant the virtual extinction of demesne on their more distant property, and the parts of the demesne formerly cultivated for the bursar were let to tenants at an annual lease. As elsewhere in the country, the peak period of demesne high farming was shortly before 1300; grain production was decreasing by 1325, and the era in which commercial grain-growing was practised on a large scale by Durham was passing by 1370.

The gradual change from the economy of exploitation to one of rents took place at Durham, as elsewhere, during the fourteenth century. Even during the period of high farming, and concurrently with an intensive use of demesne, land had been purchased for leasing at Canterbury,[3] and at Durham and other houses some demesne was leased from time to time in the early decades of the century. At that time, and until *c.* 1350, the value of land was rising, and rents could be steadily raised; demesne land, in particular, could often command a rent appreciably higher than that obtainable for tenants' holdings. At the same time, rising land and rent values will not account for the movement away from farming on the part of the monks, for it grew in scale towards the end of the century, when land and rent values were falling. Probably a whole series of causes was at work: a steep fall in the population contracted markets and made labour dear; there was probably also a notable decrease in the number of skilled and honest sergeants and reeves available; while the universal fall in the monastic population after 1350 no doubt caused a corresponding decrease in the number of monks able and willing to devote themselves to estate management. All these causes, which at Durham were greatly intensified by the permanent damage done to land by Border warfare and the abandonment of cultivation, may have contributed to render the monks ready to exchange the strain and technical difficulties of estate management for the less exacting, and often more secure, business of rent-collecting.

But indeed the abandonment of farming for a rent economy is universal

---

1 For similar trends elsewhere *v.* Smith, *op. cit.* 131, and Saunders, *op. cit.* 25; also F. M. Page, *Wellingborough Manorial Accounts* (Northamptonshire Record Society, VIII, 1936).
2 *Durham Halmote Rolls*, 33, 90–3, 127. I owe these references to Miss Halcrow.
3 Smith, *op. cit.* 116–18.

among lay lords as well as among religious of all orders. At Leicester abbey, a large house of Austin canons, the process is perceptible before 1341; at Owston, a small house of canons in Leicestershire, before 1350; at Norwich before 1358; at St Albans throughout the second half of the century; at Christ Church, Canterbury, where it had occurred between 1300–40, it became a fixed and logically developed policy under Prior Chillenden in the short period 1391–6.[1] Similar changes could probably be found at almost all the religious houses of the country. At first the common practice was to lease the demesne only, or portions of it, annually to tenants at agreed rents which varied greatly from manor to manor and district to district. Later, whole manors were farmed out, at first for an annual lease, then for leases of nine, fifteen, twenty-one or more years. In the fifteenth century it became common to charge an entry fine in addition to the quit-rent, and this gave ample opportunities for unscrupulous or harassed abbots and priors to get large sums of ready money at the expense of their successors by increasing the fine and lowering the rent. A few manors, however, were always kept in hand. By the middle of the fifteenth century the number of manors directly exploited by the bursar of Durham had fallen to six, and of these it is expressly stated that one is kept for pasture while two others are held in hand owing to lack of tenants.[2] Seventeen years later four of the remaining manors are leased, and only the stock farms are in hand.[3] By the time of the Dissolution the land directly farmed had decreased still further; indeed, the only complete manor exploited for mixed crops by the bursar was that containing the prior's principal country house of Beaurepaire. The other obedientiaries, however, were still apparently working their single estates to the end.

The prior of the cathedral monastery or, as it was often called in medieval times, the 'abbey' of Durham was, after the archbishop of York and the bishop of the diocese, unquestionably the most considerable ecclesiastic north of the Humber, and probably also the landlord and administrator with the greatest influence. The estates and the prestige of his house were as great as those of the greatest abbeys, and the direct and unfettered control he could exercise over every detail of the life and policy of his house in day-to-day activities more than compensated for the lack of the abbatial

1 Details may be found in the works of R. H. Hilton, H. W. Saunders, E. Levett and R. A. L. Smith referred to above. An interesting parallel from a lay estate is seen in the practice of the Berkeleys from 1300 to 1400; cf. John Smyth's *Lives of the Berkeleys*, ed. Sir John Maclean (Bristol and Gloucester Archaeological Soc., 1883). Contrast II, 5–6, with I, 301–2. On p. 301 note the 'itinerating' esp. II, 5–6 around the manors.

2 Pittington and Beaurepaire are in hand, and Muggleswick is given over to stock; at Beaulieu and Fery the prior holds the manor *propter defectum tenentium*; at Dalton the tenants have left through fear of Sir W. Bowes (cf. list in *Scriptores tres*, ccxc *seqq.*). Of the other manors previously kept in hand Westow, Merrington and Hoghall are let complete with stock.

3 Cf. inventory of 1464 (*Feodarium Dunelm.* 98 *seqq.*). Dalton is now let to the vicar, Pettington has been let for four years, and Beaulieu and Fery are leased.

style and consecration. The monks of Durham were no less jealous of their rights and given to litigation than their brethren of Bury or Westminster, but between themselves and their prior there was almost always a solidarity of interest and feeling which was far from being permanent between monks and their abbot.

Title and consecration were in fact all that was wanting, for from 1379 onwards the prior enjoyed the right of using the pontifical insignia;[1] in other respects also his state was fully equal to that of an abbot. Like an abbot, he had a monk-chaplain as agent and factotum who handled all his funds, made all purchases and was in his turn assisted by another monk, the seneschal of the hospice, and by a chamberlain. Below these administrative officials was a whole company of servants, high and low, from butler and cup-bearer down to grooms, valets, washerwoman, fool, gardener, caterer, pages and boys.[2] There was a carter with a long cart to take the prior's baggage and chapel-furnishings round the manors, and a clerk to write letters and keep records. The whole troop of servants was dressed in a livery of light green and blue.[3]

Like an abbot, the prior spent much of his time in peregrinating the manors; he could thus get a view of the whole economy and its problems, and could make appointments to meet the bursar or terrar far from Durham. The length of these absences varied from year to year, but in the fourteenth century it was very considerable: it has been calculated for the year 1298–9 as 119 days, and for the year 1310–11 as 249.[4] Much of the time, however, was spent within easy reach of Durham at his country house of Beaurepaire, where there was a large manor-house, with a park and stud farm, and where there were opportunities for hunting of all kinds. There he entertained magnates and the bishop of Durham; thither also, three times a year, came parties of monks for recreation or *ludi*.[5] At the end of the fifteenth century, it may be noted, Prior Castell is found as the Master of Game to the bishop. At Durham itself, in the prior's hospice, hospitality was given as frequently and as lavishly as on the manors.

The prior, like a black monk abbot, had little direct control over the daily life and discipline of the house, which was the province of the sub-

---

1 *Scriptores tres*, appendix, nos. cxxx, cxxxi.

2 There is an interesting but incomplete list of servants in *DAR*, III, 702–4. The most distinguished of the priors' fools would seem to have been *Thomas fatuus* (*fl.* 1330; *ob.* 1356–7), whose career may be traced in various entries (*v.* index to *DAR*, *s.v. fatuus*).

3 *DAR*, III, 617 (1420): 'In 3 pannis et di. de grene Ray [= a striped textile] pro vestura capellanorum, clericorum et generosorum; 7 pannis...de lyghtgrene et 7 pannis...de Violet Ray...pro vestura valect...8 uln. de blewmedled pro duobus garniamentis duorum clericorum.'

4 The amounts paid at each manor (*expensa prioris per maneria*) are entered in early bursar's rolls. Details for 1310–11 are given in *DAR*, II, 507; those for 1298–9 (unprinted) are supplied by Miss Halcrow.

5 Cf. almoner's roll 1402–3 (*DAR*, I, 220): 'Item in tribus exenniis pro tribus ludis dni Prioris 30s.': 'Et pro vino dato in eisdem ludis 10s 6d.' Another year's *ludi* absorbed 24 sheep and 30 lambs; *v.* stock-keeper's roll, 1447 (*DAR*, II, 319). For many other references *v.* index of *DAR*, *s.v. ludi*.

prior. He was, however, in complete control of administration and enjoyed the initiative in every direction. He clothed novices and received professions; appointed obedientiaries and issued constitutions in chapter.[1] Moreover, as Durham had a family of satellite priories, these also were under the control of the prior, who appointed the priors and obedientiaries, and sent out or recalled monks. One of these priories was Durham College at Oxford, and here the prior, besides appointing the superior, was the ultimate judge in the selection of students and thus controlled the first step in the career of those who in a few years' time would enter the *cursus honorum* of office and fill the highest posts in the next generation.

Outside the monastic family the prior commanded a very wide range of appointments. He presented to the lay scholarships at Durham College, and to the numerous benefices in the gift of the priory. On a higher level he filled the places on his council from the ranks of leading canonists, civilians and exchequer clerks, and later from among the great merchants of Newcastle. Three times a year, either in person or through the bursar, he held the prior's court or halmote.

All these varied contacts gave the priors of Durham, especially in the fourteenth and early fifteenth centuries, a high social position and wide influence. They met on equal terms not only the bishop but the great northern families such as the Nevilles and Percys, whose children they received from the font and later brought up in their household. Their standards were those of the peerage rather than those of the country squire. They entertained king and queen, great nobles and ecclesiastics, and interchanged servants and minstrels, as well as horses, hounds and presents of game, with them. Nevilles and Percys borrowed their chariots and hunted their deer. They were bidden to all the social events of the north, to weddings, christenings and funerals. Their treasury at the priory was a repository for valuables and wills for the palatinate; one family at least, that of Scrope, stored all its muniments there; they dispensed corrodies to modest folk and confraternity to the more distinguished; the royal family, nobles and bishops besieged them with requests for places and benefices in their gift for clerks and old retainers and poor relations.

The prior disposed also of much valuable patronage. Besides the numerous churches in his gift, he controlled prebends at Howden and Hemingborough and was the recipient of a constant flow of requests from kings, queens, bishops and magnates on behalf of their clients for actual or prospective vacancies. On a lower level there were suitors for corrodies and letters of confraternity, and requests for such offices as that of porter or for places for poor scholars at Durham College. County families, Newcastle merchants and landed members of parliament were eager to hold the stewardship of the priory; Thomas Surtees (1368–78),

---

1 The prior of Durham had thus somewhat more power than the prior of Canterbury. The arrangements for profession were a compromise; after reading his vows before the prior, the novice repeated them before the bishop.

William Bulmer (1496–1531) and Thomas Neville (1531–9) bear well-known names. In the king's service the prior was a suitable diplomatic agent to be used in missions to the Scots, while the bishop could depend upon him for a loan of cash or as a liaison when litigants wished to arrive at a composition.[1]

In spite of these social and secular activities the priors of Durham found time to direct the affairs of their house. They were, it must be remembered, almost without exception men of intellectual abilities above the average, who had been chosen on account of their gifts to study at Oxford, and who, having achieved academic distinction and a training in theology or canon law, had then passed from one office to another, first at Durham College, then at Jarrow or Finchale, or as precentor or subprior of the mother-house.[2] They were thus, as a line, of a distinctly more intellectual and scholarly type than the contemporary sequence of abbots at all save perhaps one or two of the abbeys would have been, and they brought a trained and precise mind, fortified and rendered supple by years of experience in dealing with men and affairs, to the direction of a great and dignified institution. They were able administrators, always prepared to scrutinize methods of account-keeping and to review financial machinery, notable as builders of munificence, ultimately responsible for the outward form of a fabric which still, five centuries after they ceased to rule, remains one of the most imposing in Europe, nor were they wholly contemptible as scholars who enlarged the library both in space and content, and who themselves searched into monastic antiquities. Priors John Fossor, John Wessyngton, John Hemingborough and Richard Bell may take rank with the most distinguished abbots and prelates of their age, and the traditions which they embodied and perpetuated gave Durham a place apart and a recognizable individuality among the monasteries of the later Middle Ages, adding to the opulence and splendour which distinguished all the greater abbeys a northern virility which appears in intellectual shape in the divines and canonists who handled multifarious tasks with quiet success, and in spiritual form in the solitaries who, almost to the end, went from Durham to the windswept islands of the unharvested sea. There was a *genius loci* at Durham, as at St Albans; it vanished in the sixteenth century, and though Durham has had its tale of celebrated names since Tunstall—a Cosin, a Van Mildert, a Lightfoot and a Westcott—it is not of them that the great tower, the long dormitory and the store of rolls and volumes speak.

The financial and administrative activities of the religious houses were influenced between *c.* 1350 and the Dissolution by two innovations, the

1 I am indebted to Miss E. M. Halcrow for the loan of a valuable paper dealing with this subject and based on unpublished Durham muniments.

2 Two separate *cursus honorum* can be distinguished at Durham. Those with intellectual gifts followed the sequence given above; those with practical abilities rose from posts such as prior's chaplain, stock-keeper or overseer of the horses to the offices of cellarer, terrar and bursar.

one entirely financial, the other principally administrative. The first was the establishment, at a number of houses, of a chest which received stated funds and was to be used as a reserve fund. As has already been noted the financial system of the medieval monasteries did not normally allow of surplus revenue or profits being carried into a reserve fund or merged in a capital account;[1] they were carried forward by the obedientiary or the treasurer concerned as a cash balance or floating capital to be used in day-to-day administration and merged with the current account. Nor was the common chest, when instituted, in any sense a bank for the profits on the year's working; it received annually a fixed and relatively small sum from fixed sources or officials. Thus at Durham eighty marks and the profits of the common seal not already appropriated to the *librarius* went in; it was established under Prior John Fossor *c.* 1370.[2] At St Albans the chest was instituted by Abbot Whethamstede *c.* 1439–34, and received a tenth of all gifts to the community, all moneys left by deceased monks, and £3. 6s. 8d. per annum from the manor of Gorham. At Ely the small reserve fund, under the charge of the subprior, makes its appearance *c.* 1416–20, and there was something of the kind at Norwich at the end of the century. Pershore had receivers of unassigned revenue in 1471 and the existence of a common chest at the small Austin priory of Bicester as early as 1420 shows that the institution was widespread, if not almost universal.[3]

The other innovation was as widespread and far more important for the domestic life of the house; it was nothing less than a partial, and in some instances an almost complete, supersession of the monastic officials by the abbot or prior. The fully articulated obedientiary system had been seriously breached in the thirteenth century by the widespread introduction of a central treasury or receiving office which inevitably and indeed of set purpose took from the obedientiaries some of their sense of independence in both realizing and spending their revenues. They were still left, however, with the external administration of their property and with the domestic functions of their office. As the practice of leasing demesne and whole manors increased, the transference to a rent-economy became more and more complete, and the external activities of the obedientiaries diminished in proportion. Revenues could now be gathered in and a general oversight given by rent-collectors and agents, and the duties of an obedientiary became notably less onerous and less vital. In consequence, the amalgamation of offices became more practicable and did in fact occur very frequently. It is found most often in conjunction with another tendency, by which an able or domineering superior took upon himself one or more of the important offices of the house. Such an assumption had been

---

1 St Swithun's, Winchester, has been noted as a partial exception, and there may have been others.

2 The constitution establishing the chest is in the Durham archives, Misc. Ch. 421, fo. 6b

3 For St Albans, *Reg. J. Whethamstede*, I, 275–9; for Ely, Smith, *Collected Papers*, 62–3; for Pershore, the same writer's unpublished thesis (*v. supra*, p. 312, n. 2), 64; for Norwich, H. W. Saunders, *op. cit.*; for Bicester, J. C. Blomfield, *Deanery of Bicester*, II 136–205.

known in the twelfth century, when the obedientiary system was in process of crystallization; in that age an abbot would undertake the duties and financial responsibilities of an incompetent or unworthy obedientiary as a temporary measure, much as a Prime Minister has been known to do in a time of crisis by acting as his own Foreign Secretary or Minister for War.[1] In the fifteenth century the case was different; he now assumed the financial and administrative direction of the house in quasi-permanence, thus superseding one or more of the important obedientiaries altogether.

The course no doubt had its attractions for an energetic superior whose house was in financial difficulties, or who wished to inaugurate an ambitious building programme, and in some cases the results were certainly beneficial, at least to external appearance. It was, however, a fundamentally undesirable procedure, both as depriving energetic monks of a sense of responsibility and of a stake in the fortunes of their house, and still more as making the superior virtually irresponsible, with full powers of acquiring and spending funds. These dangers did not pass unnoticed, and attempts were made in the last decades of the old order to limit the practice; it is noteworthy that the point was taken up by the royal visitors in 1535.[2]

Certainly it had become a widespread practice before 1500, and would necessarily have formed an important item in any thorough scheme of reform, though it did but reflect in the monastic world a tendency seen throughout Europe, in secular as well as ecclesiastical administration, to concentrate power in a pair of capable hands by means of an amalgamation of offices. Wolsey, quite apart from his pluralism, is an example, and Thomas Cromwell another, as, in other countries, are Cardinals Ximenes de Cisneros and Georges d'Amboise. A striking early example among the English monks of such a step towards autocracy can be seen at Christ Church, Canterbury, in 1391, when Prior Chillenden not only constituted himself the unique treasurer, but made of the treasury a central fund whence he paid allowances of his own assessment to the obedientiaries, and was able to amass and dispose of funds for his magnificent and unceasing building operations. The practice was continued by his successor, John Woodnesburgh. In effect, it defeated the whole purpose for which the central treasury had been instituted, and, at a great institution such as Christ Church, demanded ability and steadfastness of purpose quite out of the ordinary in any prior who was to retain efficient control. In the event, it broke down within a few years, and the obedientiaries evaded control by reverting to the pre-treasury practice of receiving direct revenues and making cross-payments to each other.[3]

Canterbury did not stand alone. At the neighbouring cathedral priory

1 *MO*, 439.
2 Wilkins, *Concilia*, III, 787: 'Whether any religious person of this house do bear, occupy or exercise more offices than one.'
3 Smith, *Canterbury Cathedral Priory*, 190–7; idem, *Collected Papers*, 51–3.

of Rochester the prior is found acting as treasurer and paying his obedientiaries *c.* 1380. Rochester, indeed, a century later abandoned as completely as could be wished both treasury and obediences, and in 1511 the then prior is found combining, and accounting for, the offices of treasurer, cellarer, chamberlain, almoner, precentor and infirmarer. Long before that date such engrossing is frequent, if not normal.[1] Thus at Abingdon the abbot is one of the treasurers from 1441, at Pershore he is receiver in 1479, at Bristol the energetic Abbot Newland is treasurer and cellarer in 1491 and master of the new works in 1511.[2] Sometimes the abbot was alone, sometimes he was one of two treasurers, but in such circumstances the colleague can have had little more real power than had Bibulus in yoke with Caesar.

Not all monasteries had effectively centralized their finances under treasurers or receivers; some remained throughout with the full obedientiary system under abbot or prior, with a bursar or cellarer as principal spending and executive officer. In such houses, when an abbot desired and was able to capture complete control he did so by assuming the executive post. Thus at Tewkesbury and Winchcomb the abbot held the cellarer's office in 1536.[3] One of the most striking instances of successful monopolization is that of the great Abbot Islip of Westminster (1500–32), who carried through his building schemes while holding the offices of sacrist and master of the new works.[4]

Hitherto the examples given have all been of superiors assuming and combining inferior offices. It would indeed be scarcely possible for one who was not a superior to engross offices to the detriment of the abbot's authority and the interests of his confrères. At least one example may be given, however, of the powerful favourite of a weak abbot obtaining almost complete control of a great abbey's administration. The enigmatic William Wallingford is found as early as *c.* 1445 holding, under Abbot Stoke of St Albans, the offices of archdeacon, cellarer, bursar, forester and subcellarer, and was called by the chronicler, perhaps ironically but certainly not inappropriately, the 'general official'.[5] Even under severe attack from his enemies, and deprived of all save one of his offices, he was able to recover some of his power and under Abbot Albon, in 1465, was prior and kitchener in addition to retaining his post as archdeacon.[6]

---

1 *Ibid.* 52–3.
2 Cf. *Abingdon Account Rolls* under date 1440–1; for Pershore, Smith, *Collected Papers*, 52, n. 4; for Bristol, *Two Compotus Rolls*, 10–13.
3 *VCH, Glos.* II, 64.
4 *V.* E. H. Pearce, *Monks of Westminster*, 167–8.
5 *Reg. J. Whethamstede*, H. T. Riley, ed, II, 5, 102.
6 *Ibid.* II, 50.

CHAPTER XXVI

MONASTIC LIBRARIES

The libraries of the religious houses, and in particular those of the great and ancient houses of the black monks, were throughout the Middle Ages by far the most considerable repositories of books in the country. Only two other classes of library existed: those attached to a cathedral, and those belonging to an academic college or to the university itself. Neither of these could rival the great monastic libraries of England. No English cathedral at any time, with the possible exception of Canterbury, could show a collection of ancient books at all comparable with those of the cathedrals of northern Italy or southern Germany which could trace an unbroken existence back to Lombardic or Merovingian times. Moreover, during the centuries from the Conquest onwards ten of the seventeen English cathedrals, including several of the most important, had regular chapters; their libraries therefore were monastic. Of the rest, only Exeter could boast a respectable nucleus of ancient books coming down from before the Conquest, and all secular cathedrals lacked the corporate wealth and jealous care of an undying community. As for the academic libraries, they were of late origin and less catholic in their choice of books, and though by the end of the fifteenth century the aggregate wealth of books at Oxford and Cambridge was great, and in late scholastic and early humanistic literature surpassed any single monastic library, the greater abbeys and cathedral priories possessed to the end the largest collections of books of all dates and classes. Something has already been written of their state in the twelfth century in a previous volume, but it will be well to glance here over the whole epoch.[1]

Speaking broadly it may be said that the collections continued to grow from the foundation of the house till the Dissolution. No universal catastrophe occurred between the age of Dunstan and that of Thomas Cromwell, and no wholesale change of culture or literary technique took place such as had led in earlier centuries to the neglect or destruction of ancient literature or was in the fifteenth and sixteenth centuries to lead to the neglect of the manuscript book, when ousted by printing. Although within the period there were notable changes in taste and methods of

1 A few general surveys of the early period were noted in *MO*, 522-3. Since that book was written (1937) two comprehensive works of importance have appeared: *The Medieval Library*, (ed. J. W. Thompson), and N. R. Ker, *Medieval Libraries of Great Britain*. The latter is a record of almost all books, with present location, from the libraries of cathedrals, monasteries, colleges and hospitals, known to be still in existence. Like all such lists, it is capable of gradual extension and correction, but in itself it is a masterpiece of research and scholarship, executed by a genius in the field, in close collaboration with another scholar, C. R. Cheney, whose name does not appear. Besides medieval books, Ker gives under each house references to printed and unprinted catalogues and lists, where such exist, and notes of the press marks.

education, the rise of commercial writing and copying made it possible
even for monasteries distant from the universities and law schools to keep
abreast of the new literature of the age.

Nevertheless, there were inevitably serious casualties between 1066 and
1540. Accidents of fire and flood, damage by damp and insects, loss by
sale, theft and borrowing, and, finally, deterioration by legitimate wear and
tear and the obliteration of a supposedly useless book to provide wrappers
and fly-leaves for fresh writing, led to the loss of many ancient volumes,
and where catalogues of different dates exist for one and the same library
there are invariably volumes present in the earlier lists which are absent
from the later. During the last two centuries before the Dissolution, however, such losses of ancient books probably decreased, owing to a general
lack of interest in the types of literature or learning they represented; they
were preserved through neglect rather than through esteem.

The growth of a monastic collection of books in the Middle Ages was
almost always haphazard. There was rarely any attempt to 'create' or to
'develop' or to 'bring up to date' a library, save in the fifty years after the
Conquest, when the abbot of a newly founded or reorganized house
might collect books and make arrangements for their multiplication, as was
done by a succession of abbots at St Albans. After the twelfth century
the growth of a library depended almost wholly upon chance: the tastes
or needs of an abbot or an individual monk; the demands of teachers or
scholars when the monks began to frequent the universities; bequests of
all kinds; the changing devotional practices of the community. Extant
catalogues suggest that by far the most valuable accessions came at the
death of a superior or of a monk of distinction or at least of individuality
who had supplemented the general store with a small collection of
specialized books, as it might be theology or canon law, Latin classical
authors, medical books, French poetry, alchemy and astrology, English
devotional literature. Consequently, the monastic library, even the
greatest, had something of the appearance of a heap even though the
nucleus was an ordered whole; at the best, it was the sum of many
collections, great and small, rather than a planned, articulated unit.

In this unceasing growth and change it is perhaps possible to distinguish
four phases, though it must not be thought that any clear boundary
existed between one and another.

The first was the great age of amassing and copying, which continued
in Europe from the reign of Charlemagne to the end of the twelfth century; it was during this time that all great libraries came to acquire a
greater or less portion of the common stock of writings, theological,
Biblical, grammatical, literary, medical and astronomical, that the Middle
Ages inherited from the classical and patristic past. In England this age
had dawned for the monasteries in the days of Dunstan, but it reached full
day only after the Norman Conquest. Thence onwards until the end of

the following century the legacy of the past continued to be imported and multiplied. The libraries that were to be among the richest of all—those of Christ Church, Canterbury, and Durham—as seen in their twelfth-century catalogues are almost entirely made up of works which, in one field or another, were *auctoritates* or as we should say, using the term loosely, 'classics'.[1]

From the middle of the twelfth century onwards, however, the libraries began to reflect the creative achievement of the age. Not only new *auctoritates*, such as Anselm, Bernard and the Victorines, but also a whole new flood of technical literature, that of the schools, of the universities, of the canonists, began to pour in. From the days of Gratian to those of Ockham the most numerous accessions were of this class. Some were brought to the monastery by recruits from the schools, as Warin of St Albans from Salerno and Thomas of Marlberge at Evesham from Oxford, others were acquired by abbots either for study, as Abbot John of Taunton at Glastonbury, or to assist administration, as Henry of Eastry at Canterbury; others still, from the end of the thirteenth century onwards, were purchased by or for the monk-students. In the case of the friars, the nucleus of their collections was almost entirely academic or pastoral in scope.

The third period may be taken as running from *c.* 1350 to *c.* 1470. In this there was still a gradual increase of theological and canon law books, but the relative decline in creative thought in the schools made this accumulation less significant, and for historians and antiquaries of to-day the chief interest of this period lies in the appearance of certain other types of book such as English mystical and hagiographical writing, French poetry and chronicles and the science and lore of the Arabs.

Finally, in the sixty-odd years preceding the Dissolution there was an infiltration of books characteristic of the Italian and German Renaissance: a few humanistic texts and newly discovered classics, and a selection of the learned and devotional works now beginning to pour from the printing presses. In the last group of wares the monks were conservative customers; it is chiefly the early editions of the fathers, schoolmen and canonists that appear among their incunabula. Only at an isolated house such as Christ Church, Canterbury, would any interest have been taken in the *editiones principes* of an Aldus Manutius, and even Caxton would have found few purchasers. Almost the only printed books that do not merely duplicate manuscripts already in the library are volumes of the statutes of England, which in Tudor days were becoming as necessary a part of an abbot's reference collection as had been the canonists of an earlier day.

A library is to our thinking a large and comprehensive collection of books, gathered together according to a carefully prepared scheme to

---

1 For a conspectus of the 'authorities' recognized by medieval scholars down to the twelfth century, *v.* M. Manitius, *Handschriften antiker Autoren in mittelalterlichen Bibliothekskatologen.* (*v.* Bibliography.)

serve determined purposes, and housed from the beginning in a building
designed to accommodate both the books and those who wish to consult
or to study them. Such had been, at least to a certain degree, the libraries
of the ancient world in the Hellenistic East and in the more cultured parts
of the Roman Empire; such were, during the early medieval period, the
libraries both of Constantinople and other cities of the Greek Empire and
of Cordova and the cities of Islam. Such, from the fifteenth century
onwards, have been the libraries of western Europe, including not a few
libraries of monks and other religious. The English monastic library, at
least for the three centuries following the Conquest, was something quite
different. In the f ·st place, it was not a library at all, if by a library is understood a building housing a collection of books. Rather, it was a gathering
of books, originally made with a few restricted ends in view, and only
gradually becoming large and fairly comprehensive.

The nucleus of the collection consisted of service books. These had
formed a principal part of the church furniture imported by Augustine and
his companions and successors; they again were among the more precious
of the objects collected by Benedict Biscop; they remain as principal
evidence of the genius of monastic artists between the days of Dunstan and
those of Lanfranc, and from the time of the Conquest onwards down to
the reign of Henry VIII they were multiplied in every decade. The psalters
and missals of the thirteenth century and the Westminster missal of the
fourteenth carry on the tradition of which the missal of Robert of
Jumièges is an earlier link, and on the eve of the Reformation Prior More
of Worcester is seen furnishing the chapels of his manor-houses with carefully written books. Throughout the medieval period references can be
found to the elaborate writing and illumination of service books, and they
were still being multiplied when the printing press was already active.
It was because service books were an indispensable instrument of the
monastic life, and the earliest literary object of care and embellishment,
that the monastic library began with a cupboard in the neighbourhood of
the church and under the care of the precentor, and even a large monastic
library might find almost a quarter of its space filled by these books, though
in the later centuries they ceased to be counted along with the others.
Of equal importance with the service books, and indeed partly indistinguishable from them, were the books of Scripture. In theory at least,
the reading of the whole of the Old and New Testaments (exclusive of the
gospels) formed part of the Divine Office. Later, the task was divided
between choir and refectory, but this increased rather than decreased the
need for copies. In the early Middle Ages the Bible as a single book, or
even as two books, was very rare. In general it was divided into some
nine parts,[1] and it is only in the twelfth century that great Bibles, elaborately

---

[1] For the customary partition of the Bible, *v.* A. Mundó, '"Bibliotheca"', in *RB*, LX
(1950), 78–83. The nine sections were: Octateuch, Kings, Prophets, Psalms, Sapiential
Books, Histories, Gospels, Epistles, Acts and Apocalypse.

written and decorated for liturgical purposes, became common. In addition to its use for public reading in choir and refectory, the text of the Bible always formed the principal basis both of the private devotional reading of the monks and of all theological study.[1] Bibles, therefore, or the parts of Scripture, together with commentaries upon them, were the second great nuclear element of the monastic library and were, like the first, closely connected with the Church.

The third essential component was that described by St Benedict in the last chapter of his Rule: the devotional reading that was to supply matter for the monk's claustral meditation. The saint describes this succinctly as the teaching of the elders, the pages of Scripture and the writings of the Fathers of the Church.[2] In practice the teaching of the elders came to be restricted to a few books, such as the Lives of the Fathers of the Desert, the Conferences and Institutions of Cassian and commentaries on the Rule.[3] The writings of the Fathers, on the other hand, were multiplied and came to include all that had been written, or had survived, of theology in the works of bishops and doctors in the ages before the complete collapse of the Empire—all, that is, written in Latin, for the great Greek fathers, with the partial exceptions of Origen and St John Chrysostom, had been scarcely at all transmitted to the West, and throughout the Middle Ages the works of even the greatest, such as Basil and the two Gregories, were rare in monastic libraries. The core (or perhaps we should rather say the bulk) of the early library was made up of the four great Latin doctors, Jerome, Augustine, Ambrose and Gregory, and of these Augustine by reason of his fame and his fecundity, and Gregory by reason of his monastic reputation and recent date, surpassed the other two. Alongside the four greatest, others of secondary rank appeared, among whom Isidore of Seville and Bede the Venerable were pre-eminent. Cyprian and Leo the Great were rare; Tertullian almost unknown.

These three categories, liturgy, Scripture and devotional reading, made up the original, essential and (in numbers that varied from house to house) ubiquitous basis of the monastic library. They and they alone are implied as part of the furniture of the abbey of the Rule. But from the first another class of book must have been present, and in fact is found in all later libraries; it is that included in many later catalogues under the heading of 'Grammar'. Books of grammar, during the long centuries when the great majority of recruits came into the monastery in childhood, were indis-

1 J. de Ghellinck, *L'Essor de la Littérature latine*, I, 93 *seqq.*
2 *Regula S. Benedicti*, c. 73.
3 In *MO*, 12, n. 1 it was suggested that Cassian and the teaching of the desert was neglected in England in post-Conquest times, and that the texts themselves were rare in this country. N. R. Ker pointed out at once—what further research has amply confirmed—that manuscripts of Cassian were fairly common in England, and that at more than one house (e.g. Durham, *v. Catalogi veteres Dunelmensis*, 10) the book was definitely allotted for public reading at 'collation'. Despite this undoubted fact, it still appears to the present writer that there is very little to be seen in the monasteries of the ascetical and mystical influence of Cassian.

pensable for the teaching of letters. Here, as in so many other ways, the Middle Ages preserved at least the skeleton of the rhetorical education of the Empire, and the text-books were Donatus, Priscian and the other grammarians and commentators of the Roman schools, together with the *disjecta membra* of the liberal arts: Boethius, Macrobius, Marcianus Capella and the rest.[1]

It was no doubt possible, especially in the early centuries of monasticism, to use the text-books of grammar and rhetoric simply as an aid to mastery of the Latin language, and thenceforth to read Scripture and the Fathers only, but from the earliest times here and there, and from the Carolingian age universally, the study and exploitation and imitation of the ancient heritage of literature and knowledge became the practice in monasteries, and from the age of Alcuin onwards the amassing and multiplication of texts of all kinds became an important part of a great monastery's activity. Of such texts the Latin writers first and *par excellence* called classical formed a notable part, and by reason of their importance to the modern world deserve a fuller mention.[2]

The Latin classics, the writings, that is, in pure literature of the poets, orators, historians and critics of ancient Rome, from the time of Plautus to that of the younger Pliny, form a relatively small body of writings, far smaller than the extant Greek literature of equivalent excellence. Their transmission to the centres of Carolingian literary activity in Gaul, Germany and Italy is a story with which we are not concerned. Through earlier neglect, for which the monks were not responsible, some works, such as the poems of Ennius, the satires of Naevius and the speeches of Hortensius never reached the Middle Ages at all. Others, also by accident, survived hidden, as did the poems of Catullus. A few more, such as Tacitus and the *Silvae* of Statius, actually fell into monastic hands but by chance or neglect were never copied or diffused. The remainder became the common stock from which all monasteries between the death of Charlemagne and the thirteenth century drew in varying proportions.

The interest of the subject both in the general history of literature and as a measure of the culture of a religious house or an epoch of history, has led to the production of a number of specialist studies, and it is at least roughly possible to obtain a view of the distribution of the principal Latin classics in the monasteries of medieval England. The works can be grouped quite arbitrarily in three classes: those used as normal educational text-

---

1 For this see J. de Ghellinck (*supra*, p. 335, n. 1), and G. Paré, P. Tremblay and A. Brunet, *La renaissance du xiie siècle*.

2 The indispensable guide here is M. Manitius, *op. cit.*, who lists all occurrences of Latin authors down to Bede who occur in medieval libraries of the West, with dates and references. It should be noted, however, that, excellent as the work is, it is by no means (at least so far as England is concerned) immune from errors and there are very many omissions. R. A. B. Mynors, as the result of work as yet unpublished, has been able to make additions amounting in number to something approaching one-sixth of Manitius's total to the instances of classical authors in English libraries.

books; those generally known to exist and read by the more gifted whenever available; and those which were so rare as to escape notice altogether or to be known only to the rare investigator. While the first class was made up chiefly of books familiar to the schools of western Europe throughout our era, the other two result far more from the chances of transmission, and all include works of admitted excellence and undoubted mediocrity.

In the first class, that of the school text-book, may be reckoned either the whole or parts of Terence, Sallust, Cicero, Virgil, Horace, Ovid, Lucan, Persius, Statius, Juvenal and Seneca. In equally common use were some writers of the post-classical period such as Prudentius, Claudian, Prosper, Apollinaris Sidonius, Dares Phrygius and Sedulius. If any of the dozen or so medieval catalogues of large libraries are examined, they will be found to contain works of all, or of most, of the above. These writers, however, are seldom present in their entirety as known to modern scholarship. Thus the *Catiline* of Sallust is more frequently met with than his *Jugurtha*. In Cicero several groups may be distinguished.[1] The *Rhetorics* are ubiquitous; the *de Senectute* and *de Amicitia* common; the other philosophical works and the Catilinarian and Philippic orations less so; other orations, including several of those, such as the *pro Cluentio*, which are now most familiar, are rare; the *Epistles* are found nowhere in England. Of Virgil the *Aeneid*, *Georgics* and *Eclogues* are ubiquitous, and there is a fair scattering of the *Opuscula*, both genuine and spurious. Horace also is ubiquitous, though the *Odes* and *Epodes* are less common than the *Satires* and *Epistles*. Lucan is complete and frequent, but Statius, though common, is represented only by the *Thebaid* and *Achilleid*. Juvenal and Persius are substantially complete and very common. As all these authors were school text-books it is natural that there should have been several copies at the larger houses. Thus, to give but two examples, Christ Church, Canterbury, at the middle of the twelfth century possessed eight copies of Sallust, eight of Virgil, eight of Horace, nine of Persius, six of Statius and five each of Lucan, Terence and the *Rhetoric* of Cicero: Durham, in the catalogue of 1391, which probably includes fewer copies than were available two centuries earlier, has six *Rhetorics*, four Lucans, three Virgils, three Horaces and two copies of Persius.

In the next class, that of books that were neither text-books nor rarities come parts of Cicero and Seneca, the elder Pliny, Quintilian, Suetonius, the so-called Latin Homer and the Latin version of Plato's *Timaeus*. Among rarities must be counted Plautus, found only at Bury St Edmunds; Livy, only at Glastonbury and Canterbury; and Valerius Maximus, found only at six houses.[2] Caesar's *Commentaries* occur only at Bury and among the books of the Austin friar John Erghome *c.* 1375. Lucretius, Manilius and Catullus are non-existent.

1 The following distinction is based on the notes of Mynors.
2 The Bury St Edmunds references (from John Boston of Bury) and two of those to Valerius Maximus are due to Mynors.

As regards England, the golden age of the multiplication and diffusion of the Latin literary classics was the century between the Conquest and the death of Henry II. During the greater part of this time the vast majority of the black monks and black canons were broken to letters by a lengthy course of grammar and the Latin classics, and, if they had a literary or reflective bent, it was in the idiom of the Latin classics, and particularly of the more rhetorical and satirical of the classics, that their thoughts and emotions found expression. There is, therefore, no reason to wonder at the suppleness of their language and the sophistication of their thought, which in such men as William of Malmesbury and John of Salisbury attain a maturity not found again for four centuries in the genres of history and political thought. They reproduced, indeed, in a fair measure almost all the excellences of Latin classical prose save a control of the period and the compression of a subject into an ordered framework.

The number and range of classical authors existing in England between 1150 and 1200 was probably never surpassed, and certainly their works were never again so widely and intelligently used. They ceased in great part to be daily handled in the cloister when recruitment from children and boys largely ceased; the youths or young men who succeeded them in the thirteenth and later centuries had already learnt their grammar, and had sometimes passed through an arts course, outside. Copies of the classics were worn out and not replaced. Certainly the later catalogues, not to speak of the later monastic writings, create the impression that the classics were far less familiar and numerous in the fourteenth and early fifteenth century than they had been in the twelfth, and when Boston of Bury compiled his list of classical authors in monastic libraries he makes mistakes of title and ascription that would scarcely have been committed by William of Malmesbury, to say nothing of John of Salisbury.[1]

Hitherto we have considered only the purely literary works of the ancient Latin authors, as if they alone made up the collection of Latin classics. Poetry and studied prose, however, did not come down to the medieval monasteries, as they come down to the classical sixth form of a public school, in isolation. They were merely a part of the heritage of the past, and it would give a totally false picture of the classical nucleus of the monastic library if we considered them to the exclusion of what invariably accompanied them on the shelves. Max Manitius, in his great catalogue of classical authors in medieval libraries, lists an equal or greater number of what we may be allowed to call scientific and technical authors of all kinds, whose works found their way into even the remotest monastic book-cupboard.[2] Vitruvius on architecture, Frontinus and Vegetius on the art of war, Euclid on geometry, Palladius on agriculture, Solinus on geography, Hyginus on astrology, Oribasius and Diaskorides on herbs,

---

1 R. A. B. Mynors, 'Classical writers in Boston of Bury'.
2 Of the three hundred and fifty-odd authors catalogued by Manitius less than fifty bear names familiar to the normal classical scholar.

Soranus, 'Cleopatra' and the Medicina Plinii on medicine, grammarians, metrists and writers on harmonics are all found along with the poets and formed a part of the mental furniture not only of the technical practitioners, but of the more curious and bookish of the monks. Here again there was a shift from the beginning of the twelfth century onwards. Greek scientific books gradually filtered even into monastic libraries, and Greco-Arabian medicine and astronomy replaced the Græco-Roman tradition of the past. But by this time expertise in medicine and science had left the cloister for the university, and the monastic physician and astrologer was replaced by the lay professional or amateur.

During the eleventh and twelfth centuries the monastic libraries increased rapidly by the acquisition of books from elsewhere and still more by the copying of loaned volumes and the multiplication of existing ones. Though all three processes continued sporadically throughout the medieval centuries they were not, after c. 1200, the chief means of increasing the size of the libraries or of bringing more recent literature to their shelves. Taking the monasteries as a whole, there seems to have been comparatively little provision made for the regular purchase of new books for the community. The collection, like those of some of the Oxford and Cambridge colleges at certain periods of their history, seems to have been regarded rather as a static asset than as an ever-growing organism.

The accessions, and especially those which altered the character of a library and put it into touch with contemporary thought, came largely through the gifts of individuals. This is in some ways surprising. One of the basic principles of the monastic life is that, while the community can acquire and possess property, the individual cannot, and in modern times if the common library is found wanting in a particular field which a member of the house is cultivating, the deficiency is made good through the librarian, so far as funds allow. In the later centuries of the Middle Ages, on the other hand, it was the individual who acquired and held his stock of specialized books, which fell into the common store only at his death. That this should have been the case with abbots and monastic bishops is perhaps to be expected, and in fact they are among the principal donors of books from the earliest times, but individual monks and canons, and in time friars also, appear as givers of volumes, and it is from these that the libraries in later centuries received their most numerous, as also their most interesting and valuable, additions.

One of the earliest of which we have detailed information is the collection given by William of St Carilef to Durham at the end of the eleventh century;[1] another is the group of books, notable for its classical and canonical items, left to Christ Church, Canterbury, by Archbishop Thomas;[2] a third, only a few years later than this, is that left by Benedict,

---

[1] *Catalogi veteres Dunelmensis*, 117–18.
[2] M. R. James, *The Ancient Libraries of Canterbury and Dover*, 82–5.

sometime prior of the same monastery, to Peterborough where he had been abbot from 1177 to 1194.[1] This last, besides containing the anonymous contemporary chronicle which takes its current title from its owner, is interesting evidence of the rapidity with which books and ideas penetrated the monasteries, for among Benedict's books are the *Historia scholastica* of Peter Comestor, two copies of the Lombard's *Sentences*, two of Gratian's *Decretum*, three volumes of Decretals, two complete copies of the *Corpus Juris* of Justinian, and two canonistic *Summae*, those of Rufinus and Faguntinus.[2]

Of all extant catalogues that of Christ Church, Canterbury is, as might be expected, the richest in celebrities among its donors. Besides St Thomas, Archbishops Lanfranc, Hubert Walter, Stephen Langton and Robert Winchelsey figure in its pages, the last named bequeathing a peculiarly large and revealing collection of Thomist and other theological works. A long series of priors also left books, among them Prior Thomas (1279–85) who gave a considerable medical library, Henry of Eastry, who left eighty volumes chiefly of legal collections useful in administration, and, in later times, Chillenden and William Selling, whose unique collection of Greek and other Renaissance texts was never incorporated with the main collection of the monastery, perhaps from want of space, and thus perished by fire in the prior's lodging only a few years before the Dissolution.[3] Among unexpected donors may be noted Antony Bek, the combative bishop of Durham, and Roger Norris, the unsavoury abbot of the Evesham case, who presented an unexceptionable collection of current theological literature.[4] More interesting still, as revealing the interests and personalities of the monks, as also the potentialities of private specialization, are the legacies of individual members in private station in the priory. Thus Michael of Berham was interested in canon law, Robert of Cornwall in medicine, and William of Ledbury in theology, with a strong section of Aquinas's works. Altogether about 200 donors appear in the catalogue of 1331, subscribing over 300 books, or a sixth of the total.[5]

The neighbouring abbey of St Augustine shows exactly the same process. There also more than 200 donors furnish some 400 books, the abbots cutting the best figure, with Abbot Thomas Findon (1283–1309) contributing some 120 items.[6] An interesting study might be made of the monks' gifts; here can only be noticed Thomas Arnold, with his collection of

---

1 M. R. James, 'Lists of MSS. formerly in Peterborough Abbey Library', 20–1.
2 *Ibid.*
3 James, *Canterbury and Dover*, 122 (Prior Thomas), 143–5 (Prior Eastry), 150–1 (Prior Chillenden), Introd. l–li (Prior Selling).
4 *Ibid.* 139, no. 1730 (Bek); 102, nos. 1100–10 (Roger Norris).
5 *Ibid.* 138 (Michael of Berham and Robert of Cornwall); 140 (William of Ledbury). The figure 300 is that of James (introd. xxxix), but it is not clear from the printed text how he has arrived at it. A considerably higher figure would seem to be obtainable from his data.
6 For Findon and others see James, *Canterbury and Dover*, introd. lxxii–lxxvii; for the books see index. It is possible that some of the books attributed by James to Abbot Findon were contributed by other abbots named Thomas.

French romances and poems, John of London, with his texts of Roger Bacon and mathematical books, and Michael of Northgate, author of the *Ayenbite of Inwyt*, who, besides leaving his own book, gave a substantial collection in two separate fields, that of devotional literature, and that of alchemy.

That all libraries, and not the great ones only, owed much of their increase and variety to individual members of the community is shown by the catalogue of Dover Priory, a relatively small dependency of Christ Church, where no less than fifty donors appear. Undoubtedly the practice was universal, even where the catalogue does not mention any names or where, as at Peterborough and Glastonbury, we hear only of the gifts of the abbots. The libraries of the friars were to owe as much or more to individuals than did those of monks and canons, as can be seen from the palmary instance of the magnificent legacy of John Erghome to the Austin friars of York.

Hitherto we have considered only the houses of the black monks and, for the most part, the greater and wealthier houses. In the matter of libraries, however, as in so much else, it will be found that the other groups of monks and canons, and even the orders of friars, had a basic similarity and, as the years went on, tended to approach, rather than to depart from, a greater resemblance.

As for the old Augustinian houses, they resembled the black monks in almost every respect. The early catalogue of Waltham Abbey, equally with the late fifteenth-century one of Leicester Abbey, might be that of any black monk house, as might also the library, unusually rich for a mediocre house, of Lanthony by Gloucester.

The Cistercians, in their origin and during their first fifty years of primitive observance, had libraries of the same species as the black monks but reduced, so to say, to their lowest terms and without any of the accretions of the centuries. Like the black monks, they needed service books, Bibles, and the monastic and patristic classics, but in all these categories they aimed at simplicity both in quantity and quality. Since in every department economy was practised tropers, processionals and elaborate antiphoners were dispensed with, and the great illuminated Bibles of the twelfth century were never introduced. As there was no claustral school, grammar- and text-books were not needed and no attempt was made to collect books for the sake of collecting. The early catalogue of Rievaulx (*c.* 1200) resembles a contemporary black monk catalogue shorn of almost all its profane numbers and with only a few of the less common patristic works. Cicero's *Rhetorics* and the letters of Seneca are almost the only classical Latin authors, but it is noteworthy that even thus early Rievaulx had both *Codex* and *Decretum*, together with a collection of canons and several theological and canonical commentaries. The catalogue of the small abbey of Flaxley, a decade or so later, has no classics and few

Fathers, and contains chiefly Biblical texts and commentaries and a few devotional works.

At the same time, strong influences were making for a wider scope. The example and influence of Bernard, and of the many men of education, such as Ailred, Baldwin of Ford and later Stephen of Lexington tended to create a demand for books, and the Cistercian library soon grew. When the monks began to frequent the universities theology of all kinds came in, though since the study of law was prohibited the abundant thirteenth-century literature on that subject did not enter. As might be expected, Cistercian libraries welcomed the writings of confrères. Bernard belonged to the universal Church, and the collections of the black monks were fairly complete, but for complete sets of Ailred and for the writings of Baldwin of Ford and Gilbert of Hoiland Cistercian libraries were the place to search. Ailred's works in particular are found far afield in the Cistercian abbeys of Essex and others visited by Leland. Like the black monks, the Cistercians preserved psalters of distinguished brethren, but the extant catalogues do not provide much evidence of acquisitions by gift. Later, at the end of the thirteenth century, the medium-sized Yorkshire abbey of Meaux shows a considerable increase over Rievaulx in ancient literature and scientific works.

The Premonstratensians may be supposed at first to have followed Cistercian simplicity. In later centuries, for reasons that have not yet been discovered, but which do not seem to have issued from any particular austerity of principles, they were less affected by the university movement, and less productive of writers and ecclesiastical administrators than any other order. Nevertheless, the few extant Premonstratensian catalogues show adequate and conventional collections of books, and one, that of the unimportant house of Titchfield in Hampshire, is one of the most individual of the admittedly few libraries of which we have detailed knowledge. Dating precisely from 1400, it is remarkable as containing no scholastic writings on theology, though it has many canonistic and a few civil law books. It is particularly strong in three sections: a medical collection of some twenty books almost all of them dating from before 1250; a good selection of French poems and romances twenty strong, and a still more remarkable group of books covering the law and institutions of England, including Magna Carta, a charter of the liberties of the forest, the tract *De modo habendi parliamentum*, and collections of statutes. One or all of these groups may well have come by legacy or donation, but this does not make their assemblage in this small abbey less noteworthy.

The friars' libraries might be expected to have two characteristics: modesty of size and a preponderance of scholastic theology. Of the first there is little definite evidence save some general observations of chroniclers in early days; of the latter there is considerable record, and it is certain that the larger houses of friars, and especially those at Oxford and Cambridge, ultimately contained larger and more comprehensive collections of scholastic writings than any other libraries. They were perhaps also stronger in contemporary literature of all kinds, not of set policy but by the accidents of individual legacies. The popular preacher and limiter may well have often combined with a gift of music a taste for current light literature and curious knowledge. Certainly we have one notable example of this in the late fourteenth-century catalogue of the house of Austin friars at York. Though no doubt a centre of the order's northern activity it was not of great size, and certainly not comparable either to the university friaries or a fair-sized abbey. Yet the library was large and well stocked, and contained, besides the normal Biblical commentaries and *summae* an exceptionally large store of English theological writings of the fourteenth century, particularly Franciscan and northern authors. What renders the collection unique, however, is the large library of Friar John Erghome, consisting of more than 200 volumes which reflect the wide and very individual interests of its original owner—Latin classical texts in plenty including the very rare *Commentaries* of Caesar and a wide selection of Ovid; English legal tracts and English chronicles, Goliardic poetry, medical books, astrological treatises, packets of sermons and a group of magical treatises. As a contrast to all this at York we happen to possess the inventory (1365) and catalogue (1443) of the remote and primitive Carmelite house of Hulne in Northumberland. Here was a library of a more normal, semi-monastic type, well found in patristic, canonical and hagiographical literature, strong in Aquinas, and with none of the Latin poets or English chronicles.

Two orders remain with characteristics of their own. No Carthusian catalogue is known to be extant, but a number of short lists of books and survivors exist. These bear out what would otherwise have been a natural assumption, that the Carthusians were more conservative and austere than any other order in their choice of books, and that they confined themselves to the Bible, a few ancient and medieval devotional classics, and a few of the Fathers. The lists, however, give us a little more positive information than this, and show the Carthusians to have collected more readily than others the mystical and pietistic works of the later Middle Ages, especially the group of the so-called English mystics. Richard Rolle, Walter Hilton, *The Cloud of Unknowing* and Margery Kempe, as well as the French *Mirror of Simple Souls* and several works on the Passion of Christ in English and Latin are found at one or more of the four or five Charterhouses of which we have any information.

The other order, that of the Bridgettines, had only one house, but that was both large, rich and enlightened, and in fact the abbey of Syon had a library which must have ranked among the larger ones and which had a character that set it apart, so far as can be seen, from any other. No other had such an array of printed books from all over Europe, and no other was so rich in recent literature or contemporary devotional works. There were many reasons for this: Syon was a recent foundation, and therefore had none of the inheritance of the twelfth century or the accumulations from the schools; it was wealthy, and also attracted wealthy benefactors; above all, it was fervent and yet not eremitical, and in the last fifty years of its existence counted among its recruits several university men of the modern school, among them two or three fellows of colleges. These combined piety with the new scholarship and a knowledge of Greek and of the Italian Renaissance, and the result was a collection which in all save profane literature is in many respects what one coming for the first time to the period might have expected many of the monastic libraries to be: a reflection of what was best in the religious and learned world of the day.

The historian may approach the study of medieval monastic libraries with one or both of two possible ends in view. He may wish to know exactly what books a number of libraries contained, so as to be able to gauge the precise resources at the command of a given group of monks, and to be able to compare one such library both with several others, and with itself at different periods, and thus to form a general idea of the intellectual climate of monastic life at various moments of the Middle Ages; or he may wish to acquire a knowledge of the medieval books in themselves, their size, contents, marginalia, binding, calligraphy, illumination, accommodation, migrations, donors and so forth, so as to have in his mind a picture of the actual instruments and surroundings of the monks' work. Both ends would of course be obtained if only a single great medieval library had remained in existence and virtually intact to the present day. This, unfortunately, is not the case with any monastic library. By far the largest number of medieval manuscripts remaining from a single house are those that once belonged to the cathedral priory of Durham. These number 500, and the majority are still preserved at Durham itself and within the conventual buildings, though not within the medieval library; but we know from catalogues, in which also Durham is well-found, that the library contained in all some 3000 volumes.

Failing, therefore, one or more complete libraries, only a number of catalogues can afford sufficient material for a general judgement, for even if three-quarters of a library were preserved there could be no certainty about the missing volumes, which might or might not have included books either unique, rare or ubiquitous. To the historian, therefore, a complete catalogue of an ascertainable date is in many ways more revealing than even the richest collection of medieval books, though clearly a long and familiar acquaintance with such a collection as that of Durham or Worcester will give to all his judgements an actuality, a reality and a sense of detail that no catalogue can furnish, and will add in a thousand different ways to his knowledge of the material and intellectual atmosphere of a monastic library. Yet it must always be remembered that in many cases survival is due to the intrinsic interest or rarity of a book; it therefore often happens that such classes of book as, for example, illuminated texts,

English chronicles, or early and Middle English writings have survived on the shelves, but have not been listed in any extant catalogue.

In point of fact, the study and publication of catalogues and of lists of surviving medieval books have proceeded *pari passu* during the past sixty years, and the most eminent pioneer scholar in the field, M. R. James, did equally extensive and original work in printing and commenting upon catalogues, and in identifying and describing existing medieval volumes.[1] Fortunately, medieval catalogues have come down to us in sufficient number to allow of several general judgements being made, and before going further it may be well to give a short survey of the material. While it is certain that some fragmentary catalogues still exist unpublished, and no limits can be set to contents of unexplored libraries and archives, it was the opinion of James himself, when publishing the catalogue of Leicester Abbey shortly before his death, that this was the only major catalogue known to exist unpublished.

A beginning may be made with the ancient Benedictine abbeys, which in fact possessed a large proportion of the richest and most comprehensive collections of books. The two great Canterbury houses are well covered.[2] From Christ Church there is an imperfect but valuable catalogue of *c.* 1150, and a complete one of 1331, together with several later lists of donations by individuals. St Augustine's provides what is perhaps the largest single catalogue from *c.* 1497, showing the great library in its final stage of development. From Durham comes a mass of very varied information:[3] a catalogue of *c.* 1150 and a fragmentary one of a little later date; two incomplete catalogues of the fourteenth century; an almost complete one of 1391, giving the allocation of the books to various repositories throughout the house, and a fairly full inventory of 1395, together with a list of a somewhat earlier date used in 1416 as a control when books were moved to the new library. Peterborough furnishes a full catalogue of the late fourteenth century, with other lists,[4] and Bury

1 M. R. James has inspired or guided many followers; the names of several of these will appear in the notes to this and subsequent pages. Among his successors the chief place (in view of his printed work) is taken by N. R. Ker (*Medieval Libraries of Great Britain*). Mr Ker has continued to make additions to his lists of medieval catalogues and guide to press-marks, aided by colleagues, and these, pending a new edition of his book, are available for consultation at the Bodleian Library.

2 M. R. James, *The Ancient Libraries of Canterbury and Dover*. This is probably the most important single publication of its author and it remains, in its combination of texts, analyses and comments, the best introduction the reader can have to the subject of medieval libraries. The long introduction is full of matter: for all that the author says, it would be rendered far more accessible for reference by an index. For other lists of Canterbury books, *v.* Ker, *op. cit.* 18, and *Archaeologia Cantiana*, XLIII (1931), 105.

3 *Catalogi veteres librorum ecclesiae cathedralis Dunelmensis*, ed. J. Raine. This is one of the most remarkable works of that great antiquary, James Raine the elder, and both in conception and execution anticipates the work of James by half a century. Other Durham lists not in *Catalogi veteres Dunelmensis* are printed in C. H. Turner's, 'The earliest list of Durham MSS.' and R. A. B. Mynors, *Durham Cathedral MSS. to the end of the twelfth century. V.* also M. D. Hughes, *History of Durham Cathedral Library*, and Ker, *op. cit.*

4 M. R. James, 'MSS. formerly in Peterborough Abbey library'.

St Edmunds parts of three catalogues of *c.* 1200.[1] Glastonbury has a partial catalogue of 1247 and some later lists of donations,[2] and Rochester an imperfect list of *c.* 1150.[3] These are the principal catalogues from the greater houses, though fragmentary lists are extant from many others such as Reading[4] and Worcester.[5] As a sample, though perhaps scarcely a typical one, of the class of lesser and dependent monasteries there is the full catalogue of Dover Priory,[6] rendered somewhat atypical by its close connexion with the exceptionally well-stocked Christ Church. Finally, from the various surviving lists and inventories we can form some idea of the resources of an academic monastic house from the remains of Canterbury College, Oxford.[7] No complete Cluniac catalogue survives, but there is a partial one of the twelfth century from Reading,[8] then still under Cluniac influence.

From Cistercian abbeys come the catalogue of Rievaulx of *c.* 1200,[9] the early fifteenth-century one of Meaux,[10] and the early thirteenth-century list from Flaxley.[11]

From the older Augustinian houses there are the imperfect early thirteenth-century list of Waltham,[12] the fourteenth-century catalogue of Lanthony[13] and the very elaborate and full catalogue of Leicester Abbey *c.* 1500;[14] for the Premonstratensians we may consult the late thirteenth-century list from St Radegund's[15] and the somewhat unusual catalogue of Titchfield dated 1400.[16] No Carthusian or Gilbertine catalogue is known

---

1 M. R. James, *On the Abbey of S. Edmund at Bury: (i) the library; (ii) the church.* This is James's first major essay in the field and difficult to come by; it contains a great deal of information, to which James added in an article, 'Bury St Edmunds manuscripts'.

2 The 1247 catalogue was edited excellently by T. Hearne, *J. Glaston. chronica,* 423–44, and reprinted in *Somerset medieval libraries* 55–78, by T. W. Williams. For other lists, see Ker, *op. cit.* 49.

3 Printed from *Textus Roffensis* in *Archaeologia Cantiana,* VI, 120 *seqq.*

4 *V. EHR,* III (1888), 117–25, and J. R. Liddell in *Bodleian Quarterly Record,* VIII (1935), 47–54.

5 There is an early list, very probably from Worcester, in *EHR,* XXXII (1917), 388–9. It is worth noting that M. Manitius, *op. cit. supra,* p. 333, n. 1, consistently refers to this as a Keynsham list, led astray by the title of the article in which it occurs. Cf. also *Catalogue of MSS. of Worcester Cathedral* by J. K. Floyer and S. G. Hamilton; C. H. Turner, *Early Worcester MSS;* and J. M. Wilson, 'The library of printed books in Worcester Cathedral'.

6 Printed with introduction and comment by James, *Canterbury and Dover.*

7 For lists and catalogues *v.* James, *op. cit.* 165–9, and W. A. Pantin, *Canterbury College.*

8 *V. supra,* n. 4.

9 Printed several times, the latest and most accurate version being that of M. R. James in *Catalogue of MSS. of Jesus College, Cambridge,* 44–52.

10 In *Chronica monasterii de Melsa,* ed. E. A. Bond, III, lxxxiii–c.

11 Printed several times, most recently by T. W. Williams in *Trans. Brist. and Glos. Arch. Soc.* XXXI (1908), 113–5.

12 M. R. James, 'MSS from Essex monastic libraries'; N. Ker, 'More manuscripts from Essex monastic libraries'.

13 Printed by T. W. Williams, *Trans. Brist. and Glos. Arch. Soc.* XXXI (1908), 141 *seqq.*

14 M. R. James, 'Catalogue of the Library of Leicester Abbey', with corrections by A. Hamilton Thompson.

15 Printed by A. H. Sweet in *EHR,* LIII (1938), 88–93.

16 R. M. Wilson, 'The Medieval Library of Titchfield Abbey'.

to exist;[1] the Bridgettines supply the great early sixteenth-century catalogue of the library of the brethren at Syon.[2]

As for the friars, a complete list from a Dominican or Franciscan house has yet to be found; for the Carmelites we have an inventory of 1365 and an imperfect catalogue of 1443 from Hulne;[3] for the Austin friars the magnificent catalogue of 1372 from York.[4]

The library of one religious house in the century before the Dissolution stands so far apart from all others as to deserve particular mention. We are fortunate in having a careful and complete catalogue of Syon Abbey library, and a number of surviving volumes from both library and church.[5] The origin and history of Syon have been glanced at elsewhere; here we need only recall that the house was founded in 1415 and was both wealthy and fervent to the end. As the Bridgettine monasteries contained two communities there were also two collections of books, but although the nuns were far more numerous than the brethren their library was apparently small and probably contained only devotional books. The catalogue and volumes that survive belonged to the library of the thirteen priests and four deacons who, with their guests and those who were allowed to borrow books, had sole enjoyment of the very considerable collection. Syon, throughout its existence and not least in its closing decades, provided what is nowadays called a 'late vocation' to mature and in many cases learned secular priests, and a glance at the names of donors and contents of the catalogue shows clearly that this library, even more than that of the typical monastery, owed its riches largely to its inmates. Thus five members, Bracebridge soon after the foundation and Fewterer, Reynolds, Steyke and Westhawe in the subsequent period contributed no less than 400 volumes, and six others between twenty and thirty apiece. The five just mentioned, some of whom were still alive when the catalogue was drawn up, had contributed more than a quarter of the whole library, including the majority of its most interesting numbers. It is clear that new arrivals who had been collectors of books put all, and not merely new accessions, into the library, and this shooting of volumes into the common store resulted in a great number of duplications. This is particularly noticeable in the devotional section: half a dozen brothers contributed the works of Rolle and Hilton or both, and there are several copies of *Ludolph of Saxony* and the *Imitation of Christ*. Clearly the library of Syon owed its strength not so much to policy or wealth as to the resources and tastes of its recruits. In particular, the numerous printed books from Italy,

1 E. M. Thompson in *The Carthusian Order in England* has collected all the known lists of books. See under the individual houses in Ker, *op. cit.*

2 *Catalogue of the library of Syon Monastery, Isleworth*, ed. M. Bateson.

3 In *Catalogi veteres Dunelmensis*, 128, 131.

4 M. R. James, 'The Catalogue of the Library of the Augustinian Friars at York' in *Fasciculus J. W. Clark dicatus*, 2–96. See also Fr A. Gwynn, S.J., *The English Austin Friars*, 130–4.

5 *Supra*, pp. 343–4.

including translations of Plato, Aristotle, Plotinus and the Greek Fathers and some of the works of Platina, Poggio, Politian, Pico della Mirandola and Savonarola, as well as the productions of Reuchlin, Erasmus and Beatus Rhenanus are due to the ex-fellows of Cambridge colleges, especially Fewterer, Reynolds and Westhawe.

If we now turn to consider the numbers of surviving books from various houses a very great inequality is observable.[1] Durham is easily first with some 560 survivors, of which about 350 are still in the Chapter Library. Next comes Worcester, which owes its strength to the same circumstance as Durham, a great part of its library, some 275 volumes, having remained *in situ* at the Dissolution, while 115 others are extant elsewhere, mainly in the British Museum and at Oxford. After these comes Christ Church, Canterbury, with 370 books, of which only thirty are still in the Chapter Library, the remainder being for the most part at Cambridge, particularly in the libraries of Trinity and Corpus Christi Colleges. Bury St Edmunds and St Augustine's, Canterbury, have each some 260 books surviving: a large fraction of the Bury books is at Pembroke College, Cambridge, while those of St Augustine's are divided fairly equally between the British Museum, Oxford and Cambridge, with a strong contingent at Corpus Christi (Cambridge). Norwich, Rochester, Reading, St Albans have each over a hundred survivors: the Norwich books are almost all in Cambridge, mainly in the University Library, only two remaining at Norwich; the Rochester books are chiefly in the British Museum; the Reading books are distributed between Oxford (with the largest share), Cambridge and London; the St Albans books are similarly dispersed, with the largest portion in the British Museum. Finally, quite *sui generis*, and particularly interesting as showing the accidents of survival, is the mediocre priory of Lanthony by Gloucester, from whose library of five hundred volumes some 180 survive, the great majority being at Lambeth Palace.[2] Of the rest Syon has left over eighty and a number of others fifty or so. It has been computed that somewhat less than 5000 library and service books survive from the Middle Ages; the monastic contribution to this is somewhat over 4000, or a little more than the combined libraries of the two Canterbury houses at the time of the Dissolution.

With the aid of catalogues and lists of surviving books some idea may be gained both of the contents of a large medieval monastic library and of the aspect and quality of its books. The scene can be viewed from a

1 The following statistics are taken chiefly from Ker (*op. cit.*), and are therefore conservative, as a number of books have since been identified. There is a slight inconsistency in his introduction, p. xi, where the books *in situ* are included in the Durham total, but not in that of Worcester (cf. *ibid.* n. 1). Worcester has in fact the second highest total.

2 The Lanthony books, by reason of their compact survival in strength, have attracted an attention which is perhaps disproportionate. The collection itself is not distinguished either by the rarity or by the beauty of the books, though James is perhaps unduly harsh when he remarks ('The MSS. in the Library at Lambeth Palace', 4): 'Whether considered in the light of its catalogue or in that of extant volumes, the collection as a whole does not rise above mediocrity.'

slightly different angle by glancing at the attempts which have been made to describe the libraries of a region, as in the full and careful survey of Gloucestershire, or in the less rewarding views of Somerset and Essex.[1] Yet another impression can be obtained by a reading of Leland's *Collectanea*, where the antiquary notes the handful of books at each religious house he visited that appeared to him to be of particular interest, either a Latin classic or a rare ancient text or a source for English history. Occasionally, as at Glastonbury, he lets fall a word of admiration at the wealth and antiquity of the books he saw, but perhaps the most impressive evidence of the riches and variety of the libraries of even small and upland houses is the record of his selections from the small Gilbertine and other houses in the fens and wolds of Lincolnshire.[2]

Leland, unfortunately for posterity, was guided by no fixed principles of critical or scientific bibliography in his jottings, but a few entries gleaned from his notes may serve to show that any monastic library might contain rare books, particularly if the writer had been a son of the house or of the order. Thus at Bath Leland found, not perhaps with surprise, some rare medical books, along with the extremely rare *Commentaries* of Caesar;[3] Battle had glosses on the Psalter and the first book of Kings by Abbot Odo (1175–1200);[4] the Cistercian Beaulieu had Abbot John of Ford on the Canticle,[5] and Bridlington the works, fourteen in all, of Robert 'the scribe', their fourth prior.[6] At Buckfast Leland found *Quaestiones* by William Slade, abbot of the house (*fl.* 1380) on the Sentences, on the soul and on moral topics; doubtless Slade was also responsible for the collection there of some unusual scholastic treatises mainly of the Dominican school.[7] Byland, true in early days to its newly won Cistercian status, had works by Gilbert of Hoiland and Baldwin of Ford;[8] at Cambridge the Minors had 127 letters of Grosseteste and one of William of Nottingham, the hero of Eccleston the chronicler, on obedience;[9] at Cirencester the canons not unnaturally had works of Alexander Nequam and Robert of Cricklade.[10] At Coggeshall, besides an unusually good collection of classical poetry, there was some Ailred;[11] Faversham had William of Malmesbury, and Ford works by their abbot, John;[12] Hyde, besides Malmesbury's *Gesta regum*, had an otherwise unknown encomium of Walter Espec by Ailred.[13] Keynsham had Malmesbury and lives of St Alphege (by Osbern of Canterbury) and St Aldhelm.[14] The London friaries yielded a rich harvest of scholastics, including a great deal of Ockham and some Wyclif;[15] Norwich and Oxford also had scholastics,[16] and Oseney

1 T. W. Williams, 'Gloucestershire Medieval Libraries'; *idem.* 'Somerset Medieval Libraries'; M. R. James, 'MSS. from Essex monastic libraries', supplemented by N. R. Ker.
2 J. R. Liddell, 'Leland's lists of manuscripts in Lincolnshire monasteries'.
3 Leland, *Collectanea*, IV, 156.   4 *Ibid.* 68.
5 *Ibid.* 149.   6 *Ibid.* 35.   7 *Ibid.* 152.
8 *Ibid.* 38.   9 *Ibid.* 16.   10 *Ibid.* 158.
11 *Ibid.* 162: 'Omnes fere latinae poetae.'   12 *Ibid.* 6.
13 *Ibid.* 148. This may, of course, be simply the tract on the Battle of the Standard.
14 *Ibid.* 68.   15 *Ibid.* 49–54.   16 *Ibid.* 28, 59.

lives of Anglo-Saxon saints;[1] Pershore had Aelfric's Latin grammar,[2] and Rievaulx a truly magnificent collection of the writings (nine volumes in each case) of Walter Daniel and Ailred, including the letters of the saint since lost.[3] Sherborne had poems by its monk Adam of Barking on sacred subjects,[4] and Stratford Langthorne an almost complete set of Stephen Langton's works.[5] Waltham had Langton, Robert Pullen and William the Little,[6] and Winchcombe several works by Ailred.[7]

Too little is known of the great majority of the monastic libraries to allow of any statistics of total numbers. The libraries of which complete catalogues exist seem to show that the largest collections at what may be assumed to have been the maximum of expansion c. 1500 numbered about 2000 books. Thus James on the basis of catalogues and press marks suggests that Christ Church, Canterbury, held 2100 books, Bury St Edmunds probably 2000, St Augustine's, Canterbury, 1900, and Syon Abbey, 1450. At a somewhat lower level Leicester had upwards of 900, Lanthony 500, Peterborough, c. 1400, perhaps 350, Titchfield, c. 1400, 224, and Flaxley, c. 1200, some eighty volumes.[8] It is generally assumed that all these figures should be multiplied between four and fivefold, as most volumes contain a large number of items, ranging from two to as many as ten or more, which in a modern library would almost all be bound in separate covers. Even thus multiplied the largest libraries appear relatively small by modern standards, while that of Syon Abbey, collected in a century for the use of less than twenty men, is astonishingly large in comparison with even the greatest. The principal reason for the increase in the size of libraries since the sixteenth century is, of course, the diffusion of the printing press, with the consequent multiplication of and incentive to book-production. Another reason may be found in the essential character of a medieval monastic collection. It was from the beginning, and remained in part till the end, the sacred and profane legacy of the ancient world, multiplied and broadcast under the peculiarly favourable conditions of the eleventh and twelfth centuries, and with the original comments and additions made during that century. All that came after that was in a sense accidental, the infiltration of other disciplines, theological and legal, that were not monastic. Of creative monastic writing between 1250 and 1540 there was relatively very little, and no monastic library ever seriously attempted to collect all the Latin Continental books of the later Middle Ages, still less the vernacular literatures of the new Europe. Of the twenty or so books that spring first to the mind of a reader of to-day when he thinks of the Middle Ages—*Beowulf*, the *Chanson de Roland*, the *Romaunt de la Rose*, the *Monarchia* and the *Divina Commedia*, the *Decameron*, the *Defensor Pacis*, *Piers Plowman* and the *Canterbury Tales*,

---

1 *Ibid.* 57.   2 *Ibid.* 160.   3 ? *Ibid.* 38.   4 *Ibid.* 150.
5 *Ibid.* 161.   6 *Ibid.*   7 *Ibid.*
8 These numbers are conservative, as several houses have numerous survivors not listed in their extant catalogues.

the *Morte d'Arthur*, the *Chronicles* of Froissart and de Commines, the autobiography of Suso, the writings of Ruysbroeck, the *Imitation of Christ*—
a few indeed were in a monastic library here and there, but they were there
by chance and uncared for.

The foregoing pages will have shown that the collections of books in
the English monasteries, at least from the end of the twelfth century, were
often large, and almost always respectable in size. The volumes were also
carefully and elaborately written and bound, and often also very beauti-
fully illustrated and ornamented. The composition, copying, binding and
reading of books formed, indeed, the basic employment of the major part
of the community, at least until the end of the thirteenth century. It comes,
therefore, as something of a surprise to find that a library or book-room
is no part of a monastic plan for more than three centuries after the
Conquest, and that only in the early fifteenth century is any architectural
provision made for the storing and reading of books. This surprise is not
lessened by the reflection that in the Carolingian age a large book-room,
closely connected with the *scriptorium*, was a feature of the complete
monastery as shown in the exemplary plan known as the plan of St Gall
of *c.* 820,[1] and such accommodation must undoubtedly have existed in
some form or other in the great abbeys of Gaul and Germany.

In the monasteries built within fifty years or so of the Conquest the
books were stored in two places:[2] the service books in a cupboard in the
church in the neighbourhood of the choir; the books for claustral reading
in a cupboard in the thickness of the western (exterior) wall of the transept
opening upon the east walk of the cloister between the chapter-house and
the door into the church, conveniently near the walk of the cloister
contiguous to the nave of the church (north or south as the case might be)
in which the monks sat and worked.[3] An alternative position for this
book-cupboard seems to have been in the wall common to the aisle of the
church and the cloister, near the door from the cloister that gave access
to the choir.

When the Cistercians arrived they took over this element in their
planning from the existing monasticism. The original Cistercian book-
cupboard (*armarium*) was in the wall of the eastern walk of the cloister,
between the chapter-house and the door to the church. Later, as the
numbers of books increased, the usual practice of the white monks was to
secure more space by reducing by half the area of the narrow sacristy

1 *Der Karolingische Klosterplan von St Gallen* (Historical Society of St Gall, 1952), with
monograph by H. Reinhardt and others. On the plan itself a large area to the north of the
choir of the church bears the legend: '*Infra* [i.e. on the ground floor] sedes scribentium,
supra [i.e. on first floor] bibliotheca.'

2 J. W. Clark, *The Care of Books* (2nd ed. Cambridge, 1908) is still indispensable as an
account of the medieval library; reference is given to the sources and there are numerous
plans.

3 A description of this cupboard and its uses, a *locus communis* of Augustinian customaries,
may be found in J. W. Clark, *The Observances...of Barnwell*, 15.

between the end of the transept and the chapter-house, and devoting the half nearest to the cloister to the storage of books. Yet another expedient, when the architectural features allowed, was to use as stores two out of the three bays of the ante-room that sometimes lay between cloister and chapter-house.[1]

As for the black monks, the next stage, when the books grew in number, was to erect a series of wooden presses along the wall of the cloister next the church. These have without exception disappeared, but their position can sometimes be recognized owing to the mutilation of the stone seats and mouldings in order to place them against, or at least very near, the wall; this is also a clear indication that they were an afterthought, not reckoned for by the original builders.[2] These presses were extended from east to west as need demanded, and a separate cupboard was often provided in the western alley of the cloister to serve the novices' needs, while others were put near the door of the refectory, to store the books usually read in that room, and near the infirmary, for the use of its inmates. As late as 1391, the books at Durham Cathedral Priory were divided in almost equal proportions between presses in the cloister and shelves in the outer part of the room used as the treasury in the ground-floor of the western range.[3] In addition, some of the more valuable books were kept behind bars in the inner part of the treasury. At some houses (Westminster is an example) part of the walk of the cloister near the church was in effect converted into a book-room by partitions enclosing the area of the cloister in which the book-presses stood.

Finally, in the early part of the fifteenth century the great age of library-building began. The movement was not peculiar to the monasteries; the friaries, as also the cathedrals and the colleges of Oxford and Cambridge constructed and furnished at this time separate buildings for the housing and use of books.[4] For the last-named institutes the architectural problem was relatively simple, but in the monasteries the buildings round the cloister had long been complete, and no site generally available could be found in the existing complex. For convenience' sake a position near church and cloister was demanded, and there would seem to be no extant example in England of a monastic library standing free outside the claustral buildings. A favourite position, adopted at Durham, Gloucester

1 For this v. Clark, *Care of Books*. The arrangement may clearly be seen in many Cistercian ruins at the present day. For similar arrangements in France v. M. Aubert, *Architecture Cistercienne en France*, II, 39–47.

2 Clark, *op. cit.*; J. T. Micklethwaite, 'Notes on the Abbey Buildings of Westminster', in *Archaeological Journal*, XXXIII, 15–49.

3 Clark, *op. cit.* 97. The data are in *Catologi veteres Dunelmensis*. The numbers of volumes were: cloister, 386; spendiment: outer, 408, inner, 87; novices, 23; infirmary, 17. Other lists show that yet another small collection stood by the door of the refectory.

4 Duke Humphrey's library at Oxford is perhaps the best known of these works. Of the cathedral libraries Lincoln dates from *ante* 1419; Wells, *ante* 1424; Salisbury, 1444–5; St Paul's, 1449. Christ Church, Canterbury, *ante* 1443; Bury, *ante* 1445; Durham, *ante* 1446, St Albans, 1452. The library of the London Greyfriars is of *c.* 1420.

and Winchester, was over the sacristy, when this lay between the transept of the church and the chapter-house: this was in effect the Cistercian library raised to first-floor level and enlarged. At Christ Church, Canterbury, Archbishop Chichele built a room over the prior's chapel; at Worcester the library, here somewhat older, extended over the south aisle of the nave; at Much Wenlock it lay at first-floor level in a space which accident had rendered available between the west wall of the south transept and the cloister. With the friars it was usual to build over a walk of the cloister, which with these orders normally lay within the ranges of domestic buildings.

Within these fifteenth-century libraries the presses stood at right angles to the longer walls; between the presses were desks at which readers could stand before the open book. The medieval library was rarely a workroom; writing or painting was during this period accomplished in the carrells of the cloister or in a special *scriptorium*.

CHAPTER XXVII

IN RETROSPECT

Having passed in review so many of the activities of the religious, and the phases of their common experience, it becomes possible, and it is the historian's duty, to draw together the various strands and to consider the pattern of the fabric that the years have woven.[1]

The period opened with what was destined to be the last attempt on the part of a medieval pope to issue reforming decrees affecting the monks and canons of western Europe. True, they were of limited scope, and aimed at doing little more than to sanction and delimit existing practice. They were, nevertheless, the act of authority, and were accepted as such. The constitutional provision, which united the black monks of both provinces in a single chapter, had a permanent effect; it created an English congregation, which survived the revolutions of the sixteenth century in a single life, and endures to-day. The practical effect on the life of the monks was, however, small. The movement towards centralization and control from above by the abbots president had exhausted itself before the two chapters were united, and in the two hundred years that remained the monks did not once use the machinery of chapter to devise and implement a common design. Even Thomas de la Mare, the most eminent and active of the presidents, never attempted to direct the policy or promote the unity of the whole body; he contented himself with disciplinary visitations, and his one attempt to force a recalcitrant house into line was not successful. Paradoxically enough, the chief dissolvent of the loosely cemented union was precisely that movement which Benedict XII had hoped to foster by united effort, the frequentation of the universities. Despite papal decree and the machinery of chapter both Canterbury and Durham insisted on establishing colleges of their own at Oxford and received therein monks from other houses. From 1380 onwards, indeed, though the chapter met with regularity and with lengthy solemnity, its functions were in fact restricted to appointing visitors and hearing their reports, and to administering the affairs of the common houses of study at Oxford and Cambridge.

Yet although the papal hopes of united action were not realized, the Benedictine constitutions did much to protect the higher studies of the monks. It is true that the golden age of Oxford was drawing to a close when the monks arrived there, and the silver age of the logicians and mathematicians developed without the aid of the religious, but in the age of lesser men that began when Bradwardine and the greatest of his 'Pelagians' died in 1349, the monks played a not inglorious part. Uthred

[1] Several of the paragraphs that follow bear resemblance to an article 'The English Monasteries in the Later Middle Ages' which appeared in *History*, xxxix 135, (1954). Thanks are due to the editor (Professor R. F. Treharne) for his permission to take this liberty.

of Boldon, Simon Sutherey, Adam of Easton, William Worstede and John Wells could make a fair show both in teaching and in controversy. The Cistercians, for whatever reason, were less remarkable. Henry Crump, the most distinguished or notorious of the white monks at Oxford, was an Irishman; his contemporary, William of Rymington, later prior of Sawley, was perhaps the only Cistercian to be chancellor of Oxford. Nevertheless, even had there been no celebrated masters, the university training of the later Middle Ages, like that of the Oxford school of *literae humaniores* in the nineteenth century, might well have left a most valuable monument in the work of men outside the academic profession. For some two centuries, from the day of Richard of Wallingford to that of Richard Whiting, the monastic colleges of Oxford and Cambridge gave a series of distinguished monks to rule the dozen or so houses that were most assiduous in their academic service, Durham, Canterbury, St Albans, Norwich, Westminster and Worcester above all. Yet from the private monk's point of view a university education had the drawback that it failed to train him for any kind of claustral work. Unless the university monk remained at Oxford to teach, he could do little with his learning. When the controversies of the fourteenth century had died away, he became silent and has remained unknown.

The Benedictine constitutions had been effective for only a few years when Europe was ravaged by the Great Pestilence. We have seen that the religious orders suffered heavily with the rest of the nation, and that their numbers never again reached the level at which they had stood in the early years of the century. Yet the monks themselves never regarded the Black Death as the end of an epoch, or even of a chapter, and the historian cannot in fact bring forward evidence to show that one did in fact then end for the monasteries. The pestilence was the direct occasion for the advance to power of two young monks who were to prove respectively the greatest and the highest in place of the monks of the century. Thomas de la Mare, abbot of St Albans, following upon two predecessors of distinction, guided his abbey into another period of prosperity and was directly responsible for a rebirth of letters; while in office he became a figure of national importance, the father and patriarch of monks, summoned again and again to deal with houses in difficulty or distress. Over and above this, he gave an example of a life not only austere and edifying of itself, but showing also those qualities of love and fatherly care for his monks that must always be the hall-mark of an abbot faithful to the counsels of the Rule. Simon Langham of Westminster was of smaller spiritual stature, but as abbot, as king's servant, as archbishop and as cardinal he was an able and commanding figure, and his legacy to his abbey had a large share in creating much of the fabric as later ages have known it. Yet another sign that the pestilences were not the end of an epoch may be found in the two new monastic colleges of Canterbury and Durham, which were founded in the decades that immediately followed.

Meanwhile, a series of disputes, as so often happens, had called forth the talents of a number of divines, from Uthred of Boldon to Thomas Netter the Carmelite. The latter was perhaps the ablest defender of the traditional faith between the age of the great schoolmen and that of Luther.

Uthred was not indeed the only eminent theologian of his age, but he was perhaps the greatest of the 'university monks' and he rose, both as regent master and as wise monastic counsellor, to a position of esteem in his order and of celebrity in the schools such as was attained by no other. Adam Easton and Thomas Brunton, both of Norwich, might have rivalled him had not their fortune taken them to the Curia, where one was caught up into the rivalries of the Schism and the other was sent back to the see of Rochester and the service of the king.

The monks at the university between the middle and the end of the century were engaged in a number of controversies of some importance. Beginning in the realm of pure theory, the issue of Dominion and Grace developed first into a debate between the mendicants and the monastic 'possessioners', next into one between all the religious and their enemies intent on their destruction, and finally into a purely theological issue in which the religious and clergy together resisted heretical innovation. The two last phases coincided with an attack on the part of a small but powerful party upon the social and economic position of the monks, which broadened into an assault upon the first principles of the religious life. The attack developed very suddenly, fostered by the political malaise of a time of war, and at different moments was joined by forces of another order when, in 1381, the peasants and townspeople broke into the precincts and preserves of their landlords and when, a little later, the two great poets of their age pilloried the luxury of the monks and the intrigues of the friars. Though the words and acts of all these opponents were prophetic of many things that were to come in due time, the attack was strangely transient in its violence. The religious weathered the storm with little apparent loss, partly because their most convinced enemies became identified with social and doctrinal novelties which united all the forces of conservatism, and brought the monks nearer to the other clergy and the secular power than they had been for many decades. The tide of hostility, which had flowed so high in the petitions to Parliament for total secularization, ebbed back as rapidly out of sight, and when, early in the fifteenth century, an orthodox and devout monarch was active in the cause of religion, the turmoil of the recent past might well have seemed an evil dream.

The movement for confiscation coincided with the consummation of another process which has sometimes been confused with it, that of the elimination of the so-called alien priories, monasteries or cells owned by, or depending directly upon, mother-houses across the Channel. This process, which had been going on by fits and starts ever since war with France began under Edward I, was in part a manifestation of national prejudice and in part what would now be called a security measure. Time and again the foreign priories had been taken into hand by the king during a period of warfare, to be released again when peace returned, and there had been a steady drift on the part of these sorely vexed communities to end their troubles either by denization or by withdrawal and sale. Many, however, still remained in 1400, and it was left to Henry IV and his son to settle the matter for good. More denizations took place, and the remainder were suppressed by petition and statute. There was no anti-monastic animus displayed; almost all the sizeable houses remained as denizens, and the lands and buildings of the lesser were in almost every case bestowed upon other religious institutions. The process was no precedent for Cromwell, and if the disappearance of these minute houses was felt at all, it was as the removal of a withering bough.

If the monks and other religious showed no lack of mental vitality in the generations after the plague, a similar impression of continuity and life is given by the ambitious building schemes of the age. Foremost among these, at least in the eyes of posterity, are those of Ely and Gloucester. At Ely a great catastrophe had led to an undertaking which gave birth to more than one work of unusual beauty and originality; it was carried through by a man of genius, and the accompanying works, which had nothing to do with the fall of the central tower, show that both enterprise and artistic skill were present in full measure. At Gloucester a sudden influx of pilgrims and their gold prompted an extensive remodelling which soon took the form of a major revolution in architecture.

Meanwhile, in the economic order a slow change of some significance was taking place. Here again the Black Death, once invoked as the great stimulant of revolution, is now seen to be chiefly an accelerator of changes already under way. The fourteenth century, during almost its entire span, saw an important change of policy developing on the great estates, ecclesiastical and lay. From a regime of high farming and direct exploitation of demesne there was a gradual but unceasing shift towards an economy of rents and leases which ended by breaking down the old economic and tenurial structure of the manor, though it did not affect its administrative and judicial significance. The movement, whatever its cause, had begun before the Black Death. The pestilences, by rendering land masterless, by lessening the labour force, and by raising the wages of labour, were a major agency in shaking the balance of the manorial economy, and in hastening the change from direct exploitation to a regime of rents on the great estates. By 1400 many of the manors, and almost all the demesne, save for a few manors serving as home farms, had been leased out on most monastic estates. The process, still not fully explored, was common to all landowners, but it had results for the monks which others did not feel. For centuries out of mind the monks had been a class—and indeed a very great class—of landowners whose wide acres remained for century after century under the direction of a deathless master, suffering little from political disturbances, private ambitions, changes of inheritance, forfeitures or escheats, and gradually increasing and consolidating by gift, purchase and reclamation. The great fiefs changed, lords differed in character and policy, while some regions had experience only of small landholders, but the monks and canons were everywhere. Now, their economic and social power was being gradually and subtly undermined. During the late fourteenth and the fifteenth centuries the pattern of the countryside, with its farms and hamlets, was taking the shape it was to hold until the eighteenth century and beyond. The substantial men were establishing themselves, fellows of Chaucer's Reeve and Franklin, who were to found families and become in a generation or two the lesser gentry of early Tudor times. They were building their houses in their first shape of irregular stone or timber framework, as it might be an Ockwells or a Wanswell Court, that were to grow into the many-chimneyed moated hall, and to rise or fall in the social scale and to survive to our own day in the mellow beauty of Compton Wynyates or the decay of an old manor house, long ago broken into a nest of labourers' dwellings. For a time these new families lived on marginal lands on the fringe of a wood or marsh, or at the end of a high-banked lane; some were the creation of a successful villein or bailiff on the lands of the monastery; but gradually, as the monks ceased to exploit the demesne for themselves, the pattern altered. The yeoman, the small squire and the estate staff entered in, and as the years passed the manor and its lands seemed more and more their own. The monasteries had lost the initiative on their estates.

The speed and extent of this process must not be exaggerated. It had only begun by the reign of Henry IV—Shallow and Silence are Elizabethans, not Lancastrians—and it was far from complete at the Dissolution. It was, nevertheless, a real and most significant change, for it meant that the monasteries were no longer a necessity or even an integral factor in the country's economic stability. Few may have realized this, and still fewer expressed it in words. The priors and abbots who had given their names to Abbot's Morton and Cleeve Prior, the nuns and canons of White Ladies Aston and Whitchurch Canonicorum, were still casting their shadow over the land, but those whom they overshadowed were other than before.

For the Cistercians the change of economy, together with the effects, immediate and remote, of the plague, helped to complete the last stage in a great transformation. Their economy had originally depended entirely upon the lay brother and the grange. As social and religious conditions changed, lay brethren were harder to come by and less patient of control; in many abbeys they were a liability even in the thirteenth century. Here there is need for a more emphatic revision of past theory. It was not the Black Death and the social upheaval that extinguished the class of *conversi*; it is more true to say that the monks, going over to rents and leases, had of set purpose reduced their intake of lay brothers before 1348, and that the pestilence did no more than hasten the end of the process. In any case, the lay brothers had all but disappeared by 1360, and for the last two centuries of their existence the Cistercians were indistinguishable from the other monks in their estate management.

The four orders of friars followed a somewhat different rhythm of change. Economic and manorial movements had no significance for them, and they would seem to have been more numerically resilient than the 'possessioners' in the decades immediately following the plagues. The Austin friars and the Carmelites in particular entered upon new eras of prosperity, the former in the third, and the latter in the fourth quarter of the fourteenth century; they drew towards something of an equality in numbers and influence with the two larger orders, and each gave men of ability to the new controversies of the age. It is perhaps significant of the vitality of all the friars that, although statistics show clearly that their total numbers were considerably less than they had been in the pre-plague epoch, their contemporaries had a sense of their ubiquity which led to gross exaggeration whenever an estimate of their numbers was attempted. They presented a broad target to critics and satirists, and we must beware of allowing ourselves to trust exclusively to the fierce invective of Wyclif, the broad humour of Chaucer or the sharp thrusts of Langland. Whatever the faults of individuals, the services of friars to the Church were very real. Again and again representative groups were employed by Archbishop Langham and his successors to examine alleged false doctrine, whether of Wyclif or Uthred or the Lollards, and in every case the panels of distinguished friars forgot their rivalries to stand fast by the central tradition; to them, far more than to the bishops as a body, are owing the firm condemnations and the clear apologetics that threw off the attacks of the Lollards, and it is clear, both from the researches of Owst and from the narrative of Margery Kempe, that they were ubiquitous as effective preachers to the city folk and as advisers and directors of those who strove for a more perfect following of Christ.

We have seen that the legislation of Benedict XII gave the sanction of law to the drift of monks to the universities. That pope also sanctioned a practice of a different kind that had long been existing on sufferance, the eating of flesh meat on certain days, by half the community, and in a place apart from the regular refectory. Without canvassing the arguments of a spiritual kind for or against this relaxation of the Rule, we can at least point to two historical consequences: it permanently broke the unity of the common life in an important respect, and it sanctioned a frame of mind that looked upon the Rule as something that must be modified to suit modern times. It is one of the most telling and topical hits in Chaucer's account of the Monk that he should have wished to 'let olde thinges pace'.

The same spirit is seen in a number of subtle changes that became stereotyped in the fourteenth century, and that have been passed in review on an earlier page, as consequences of the universal prevalence of the 'wage-system'. Clothes-money was followed by spice-money, and that in turn by a string of payments for work done, for degrees and dignities attained, and even simply as dividends accruing yearly from a legacy. The last stage of the process was reached when the annual income was consolidated and spoken of as a monk's annual 'wages', and we have seen that this at the larger houses gave a considerable surplus, after the purchase of clothing and other necessities, for the purchase of books, vestments and even jewellery.

Concurrently with this there was a slow movement towards greater comfort and privacy. This had begun before our present period and was in part a movement sympathetic to the change of society at large towards something more civilized; it should not therefore be counted too readily against the monks unto condemnation. Nevertheless, it might be argued that the monks were in the van as regards domestic improvements, as they had long been as water engineers and plumbers. The move towards comfort developed during this period chiefly in the infirmary, which was very commonly rebuilt with rows of private rooms for the sick and the aged, and in the abbot's quarters. These last had expanded steadily from a modest cell to an elaborate lodging with a large hall, parlour, chapel and bedchamber, with wainscoted walls, glazed oriels, fireplaces and garderobes. The taste for private apartments spread downwards; the prior or second-in-command had a small suite of rooms, and the subprior and principal officials had checkers or offices, often with bedroom and solar attached, while at many monasteries a row of rooms existed either for doctors of theology or for any old monks who might have deserved so well of the republic as to have been rewarded with a chamber, an attendant, and a small pension. In addition, it was the universal custom to equip a set of rooms, not greatly inferior to those of the reigning abbot or prior, for any superior who might have resigned from old age or any honourable reason.

These developments were considerable in sum, and had a very real effect, not always salutary, on the community life, as was recognized by reformers and conscientious visitors. This effect, however, must not be exaggerated. Not every abbey had them all, and at no abbey did every monk enjoy all that were there. The official routine of the day's employment in choir and cloister had altered little, and the monks whom it affected in full, perhaps two-thirds of the able-bodied, were still living a life recognizably the same as that of earlier centuries. Nevertheless, when the attacks of the Lollards had subsided, a feeling of dissatisfaction continued in some quarters, and in 1421 Henry V summoned all the black monks to a conference at Westminster, and proposed some articles of reform. The impulse was bogged down, as so often before and after in the history of the black monks, by a deluge of protests and counter-proposals, and the sands of Henry's short life ran out before he could return to the charge. The reforms he had sponsored were not drastic, but he might well have renewed his attempt, and he was giving proof of his earnestness by his foundations of strict life at Sheen and Syon. It was the last time that a strong, conscientious and benevolent monarch offered himself to the monks to help them set their house in order. The offer was neglected;

what might have happened if a de la Mare or one holier still had been there to accept it, who can say?

After the alarms and excursions of the second half of the fourteenth century the first decades of the fifteenth were a time of peace for the religious. For a brief thirty or forty years before the outbreak of party strife in 1451 the aristocracy were of more significance in the social, political and cultural life of England than they had been fifty years before, or were again to be for more than a century. It was an age of patronage, and in it the monasteries, themselves at once both clients and patrons, enjoyed an Indian summer of some magnificence. The larger houses were more than ever hostels where the king, with his uncles and cousins, together with barons and knights of every degree, spent the great festivals and were received into fraternity, and where the treasure of vestments and plate accumulated every year. Yet it was an age singularly barren in great issues and in great men. Rarely, if ever, between the Conquest and the present day, has a space of seventy years passed over an England so devoid of men of distinction in any walk of life as the age between the death of Henry V and the adolescence of More and Wolsey. The autumnal sunshine vanished with the civil strife, and although the monasteries were affected very little in their domestic and economic life, they lost in the slaughter and proscriptions their somewhat artificial link with high and courtly life, and were left to meet the new era that followed more isolated than before from the centres of political power and intellectual life.

Perhaps the most noticeable change over the whole period is the gradual obliteration of the differences between the various orders that had been so marked in the twelfth and early thirteenth centuries. This gradual process had begun early, but now it was becoming wellnigh complete. Among the black monks the Cluniacs, together with a few minor groups such as the Grandimontines, by escaping from their dependence upon overseas superiors and by their ultimate denization, had become all but indistinguishable from the monks of the old English chapter-body. Still more remarkable was the assimilation of the Cistercians. When the choir monks had ceased to take part in field work, when the abbeys had ceased to recruit lay brothers and had passed over to a regime of hired labour or rents, and when by numerous small relaxations their domestic life had become less rigorous, while frequentation of the universities had opened the door to a life of study, the differences between them and the black monks had become accidental rather than essential. As for the Austin canons, their larger houses had from the first resembled very closely those of the black monks, while the austere, quasi-eremitical characteristics of the smaller and more remote priories had gone long since. Taken as a whole, they were by the fifteenth century the least fervent, the worst disciplined and the most decayed of all the religious houses, but where, in the north, they still flourished, as at Bridlington, Nostell, Guisborough and elsewhere, they differed little from the monks.

Even among the friars a similar process was at work. As was seen in an earlier volume, the original sharp distinction between Minors and Preachers had quickly been softened by mutual give and take, and they had drawn into their way of life the eremitical Carmelites and Austin Hermits. Nevertheless, their conflicts, rivalries and differences of doctrine had for long preserved the individuality of the four bodies. This undoubtedly became less marked in the late fourteenth century, as they drew together against their common enemies. Wyclif and the satirical poets make no distinction between them. 'Freres and feendes be but lyte asonder'; all the 'ordres foure' contribute to the naming of Caim's castles; the character in Chaucer's *Prologue* is a friar *tout court*. Between the monks and canons, however, on the one hand, and the orders of friars on the other, the gulf remained. The lack of real property, and the close contact with the society of town and village in preaching, visiting, directing and confessing, fixed an impassable barrier of sentiment between friars and monks, and although there was never in England, as in some continental countries, a prevailing difference in social standing between the recruits to the two bodies—for no English monastery ever established a heraldic test for postulants—yet the friar's career and vocation remained essentially different from the monk's.

Yet while the differences of spirit and doctrine, and the degrees of strict and less strict, had thus largely vanished in the great body of English religious, there had been no such levelling in the matter of wealth and influence and social prestige. Here the black monks, whatever they may have lost in more imponderable treasure, had more than held their own. In no respect is this more remarkable than in numerical strength. While, as we have seen, all orders had suffered a falling-off from their first days of expansion, and had received from the pestilences of the fourteenth century a blow from which they never fully recovered, the greater houses of the black monks, almost alone of the religious houses of the land, retained in the fifteenth century complements which in any age would rank as large. By the same token the Cistercians had lost ground. When the armies of lay brothers disappeared, and the monks no longer took part in agricultural and pastoral work, they ceased to occupy a privileged economic position and thus, all other considerations apart, could support no more monks than their funds allowed. Few white monk abbeys in the fifteenth century could have supported a community of fifty, with a household staff to match, even had recruits been plentiful. In fact, they were much smaller. Economic considerations weighed likewise with the canons, black and white. The normal endowment of a Premonstratensian abbey was for thirteen canons, and that of the Augustinians, though showing a wider range, was in many cases smaller still, and could support a mere half-dozen. When such small incomes were in question, a few years of bad management or natural shocks could bring a house to the brink of ruin.

Whatever the causes (and only a few have been suggested here) the fact is incontrovertible: the relative importance of the old black monk abbeys and cathedral monasteries grew as the Middle Ages drew to a close. It is a sign of their importance that the literary and administrative monuments they have left behind are far more numerous than those from other sources, and it is they who are to the fore in controversies and in relations with the great in Church and State. As the chapters in this book may have suggested, the history of the monks and canons in this age is largely drawn from some twenty black monk houses, together with less than half-a-dozen of other orders, and this must inevitably be so. Save on the rare occasions when the presence of a saint or a genius lends significance to the history of a Carmel at Lisieux or Dijon, or an Oratory at Edgbaston, the life of such communities, however useful or devout, passes in a narrow round of duties and relationships. A large abbey, on the other hand, such as Solesmes or Maredsous in the recent past, with wide commitments and associations, may easily originate movements of reform or produce works of art and literature, to say nothing of the rich variety of mind and character that may be developed. The point has been laboured, because it is natural, after studying the multifarious records of St Albans or Westminster, to desire some knowledge of the life and social relations of a smaller house. For such a smaller house—a Coldingham, a Blyth, a Stogursey—materials for an economic picture often exist, and a history of the dependencies of Durham or St Albans could be compiled without difficulty, but the inner life and personal activities of such places must almost always elude observation.

The monks were still a great social force. It would be difficult to express this in words, but no one who reads the records of the early fifteenth century can fail to realize the fact. Perhaps it was that no other class or institution had as yet arisen to take their place. They still retained that aura of sanctity, half local, half personal, that tradition of learning that had deservedly won them reverence long ago. The monks of Durham, like the monks in the cloister that Langland dreamed of, 'did study daily in their books'. What they studied, and what came of it all, who could say? But, in the fifteenth century at least, the new learning, with its different methods and its critical spirit, had not yet come to question and to ridicule. The monasteries were, besides, still the only vast complexes of building in the land, with their gatehouses and gables surrounding the towers and spires of the minster, with the comings and goings of a vast household and its guests, the outward image of wealth and power. The kings had as yet no palaces or courts or government buildings that could strike the imagination; their castles and those of the nobles were still for the most part strongholds with menace in them. The only rivals to the monasteries were the cathedrals with the bishop's palace and the lodgings of the canons, and of these many of the greatest were themselves monastic. It was this, no doubt, that lent a certain unreality to the attacks of the Lollards, and that permitted a wide licence to the poets. Langland was not self-contradictory, but expressing two aspects of experience, when he recognized that studious quiet and a recognition of beauty were to be found only in those cloisters, which yet would be shaken like Nineveh if their inmates did no penance.

The monasteries were not notably less observant or more decadent in the fifteenth century than before, but the age was undoubtedly marked by a lack of distinction, and by the lack of an absolute standard of excellence. The abbots and priors could show themselves as the practical and munificent builders of spacious cloisters and majestic towers and sumptuous chantries, but it is by its ideas and its aspirations that an age lives and is aroused to action, and these, in the realm of the mind and spirit, were either conventions or fantasies. The fifteenth century saw no great English churchman and no English saint. When all has been said that can be said of causes and influences, in things of the spirit it is, humanly speaking, the men that matter, and they were not forthcoming. Whatever there may have been of silent and hidden sanctity—and this, *ex hypothesi*, may equally well be assumed or neglected in any ge—no Englishman arose in the fifteenth century to show his countrymen the truth and the charity of Christ, which alone would have been able to make the dry bones live, or to see himself, and convey to others, the fullness of meaning of the First Commandment. An eminent religious of the early seventeenth century, the saintly Jesuit, Louis Lallemant,[1] writing in a very different world when the fervour of the Counter-Reformation was beginning to cool, gave to his novices his reflections on the signs of the times:

There are [he said] four kinds of religious: there are, first of all, the perfect; then there are those who are evil—proud, full of vanity, sensual, opposed to all regularity; a third class is of the lukewarm, slothful and careless; and lastly there are the virtuous who are on the road to perfection, although perhaps they may never attain to it. The holiest religious orders [he continued] may contain these four kinds among their members, as may also those orders that have fallen into laxity. There is, however, this difference: in an order that has fallen from its first fervour, the majority are lukewarm, and of the others some are positively evil, a few are striving after perfection, and a very few are truly perfect. Contrariwise, in an order where discipline is still strictly observed, the bulk of the community is composed of those who are striving after perfection, while of the others some are perfect, a few lukewarm, and a very few evil. A religious order [he added] is verging upon its final decline when the number of the lukewarm begins to equal that of the perfect.

These measured words, of which all who have experience of the religious life must acknowledge the truth, may be set before the reader who takes his backward glance upon the religious orders of England in the last centuries of peace, before the swelling of Jordan; the time of ease that was soon to be followed by the day when Jerusalem was searched with lighted candles, and visitation made upon men that were settled upon their lees.

1 The passage that follows is translated from Lallemant's *Doctrine spirituelle* (ed. 1927, Paris, Gabalda, p. 474). H. Bremond wrote of this book in his *Histoire littéraire du sentiment religieux en France*, v, 64: 'Inconnu des profanes, le modeste livre...n'en reste pas moins l'un des trois ou quatre livres essentiels de la littérature religieuse moderne.'

APPENDIX I

CHAUCER'S MONK

The account of the Monk in the *Prologue* to the Canterbury Tales is naturally of interest to the monastic historian, if only as being by far the most familiar (and therefore most influential) picture of a monk in the whole of English literature. Quite apart from this, however, the short description contains two points to intrigue the exegete and the historian.

1. It is assumed by everyone, the Ellesmere illustrator included, that Chaucer's monk is a black (or Benedictine) monk, not a Cistercian or (still more emphatically) an Austin canon. Why then the references to the rules of St Maurus and St Augustine?

Annotators point out very correctly that St Maurus, whose only authentic appearance is as a boy-monk at Subiaco in the *Dialogues* of St Gregory (II, cc. 3, 6, 7), has never been claimed as the author of a monastic rule, nor has any Chaucerian scholar or monastic historian, to my knowledge, discovered a clear parallel to Chaucer's phrase. It is also common knowledge that according to a venerable legend (which in Chaucer's day was universally accepted and was in fact not then susceptible of attack) Maurus had migrated to France on St Benedict's death, taking the Rule with him, and had established a 'Benedictine' monastery at Glanfeuil (the most readily accessible of the many critical treatments of the legend is perhaps that of Dom H. Leclercq in the *Dictionnaire d'Archéologie chrétienne, s.v.*). In consequence, St Maurus was always regarded as the patriarch and patron of French monachism, later giving his name to the celebrated reformed Congregation of the seventeenth century. It has therefore been suggested that Chaucer had met or heard of monks who treated the alleged customs of St Maurus as a kind of supplementary or alternative Rule; this may have been so, but these monks can scarcely have been native Englishmen, and until a clear documentary parallel is found the phrase must remain enigmatic. Equally strange at first sight is Chaucer's reference to the so-called Rule of St Augustine. Medieval monks were not bound by this and took no interest in it, and Chaucer could not well (and in fact shows elsewhere that he did not) confuse canons with monks. Here, however, there are many literary parallels which may well be also sources. The instructions on work given by St Augustine are frequently produced for the castigation of religious by moralists and satirists, and had recently so been used by Gower.[1] The medieval instinct to follow a model, even in another context, together with the unusual felicity of the lines, may have led Chaucer to introduce the passage *coûte que coûte*. Alternatively, he may, for reasons to be suggested later, have deliberately fused the picture of a canon with that of a monk.

2. The description of the monk is seemingly so sharply defined that many (including the present writer) have been led to spend time in attempts to identify the original, or at least to suggest his provenance. The temptation to do this has become the more powerful owing to the ingenuity of Professor Manly and his followers in producing without a doubt the historical exemplar of the Host, and in identifying with great probability the models of the Shipman, Reeve, Yeoman and Somnour.[2] Manly himself, while referring to the Monk as a problem, hinted that he could name his abbey with some probability. Looked at more closely, however, the only clear piece of evidence—that the monk was in charge of a cell with a chapel: that is, neither a grange nor a small priory—would, if pressed hard, go far to restricting his habitat

---

1 Gower, *Mirour de l'Omme*, ed. G. C. Macaulay, lines 20,845 *seqq.*, 20,995 *seqq.* 21,014 *seqq.* *Vox Clamantis*, IV, 281–2. There are many other passages of similar import.

2 J. M. Manly, *Some New Light on Chaucer* (New York, 1926).

to one of the small alien cells (loosely called priories) and would in effect make identification impossible, for the wardens of such places were never men of such importance as to get into the records. As for his characteristics—expensive dress, love of good cheer, rejection of austerity and appeals to the Rule, and above all a love of hunting—these, as generations of commentators have pointed out, are qualities found in monks by medieval satirists all over Europe and in every age, in various combinations. Indeed, they are faults all but endemic in the monastic body, and even in our own day there are those whose withers might well be wrung by Chaucer's lines. In particular, Wyclif, Gower and Langland (especially the two latter) have passages which resemble Chaucer's very closely and must, one would think, have been familiar to him.[1] All this doubtless accounts for the fact that until very recently no attempt had been made to identify the Monk with any known individual of the fourteenth century.

Some years ago, however, the present writer, reading Knighton's *Chronicle* for the first time, was immediately arrested by the description of William Clown, that great hunter whose activities were so nearly contemporary with Chaucer's, and in due course he wrote the passage in the text (*supra*, pp. 185–6). It was only very recently that his attention was called by Mr H. S. Bennett to a commentary[2] that cited a scholarly article by Ramona Bressie in *Modern Language Notes* (LIV, 7 (November 1939), 476–90) in which the identification of Clown with the Monk is urged with a wealth of learning and corroborative detail. The resemblance is indeed very striking, and there are numerous interesting points, such as the presence of the King of Cyprus, one of the examples of tragedy in the *Monk's Tale*, as a guest of Abbot Clown, and the existence at Inwardby, one of the properties of Leicester Abbey, of a large grange with a chapel. Moreover, if Clown was in Chaucer's mind the reference to the Rule of St Augustine becomes properly pointed.

Nevertheless, attractive as the identification is, the copious literary source-material must not be forgotten. If Chaucer drew his picture from the life, as seen in Abbot Clown, whence did Gower and Langland draw theirs? In short, we have to choose between regarding Clown as (in some respects, at least) an unwitting personification of the imaginary figure of the poets, or seeing him as the living person whose portrait Chaucer and possibly Langland also painted. If a choice of this kind must be made, the former alternative would seem that to be preferred. We may well feel, however, that whatever be the truth of the matter, it is next to unthinkable that Chaucer, with his connexions with the Court circle, should not have known of Abbot Clown and his hunting, while it is even more inconceivable that his courtly readers, when they heard the lines of the *Prologue*, should not have been reminded of the prowess of the late abbot of Leicester.

[1] For Gower, see *supra*, p. 365, n. 1; for the others, *v.* the sections in the text, pp. 108–14.

[2] Muriel Bowden, *A Commentary on the General Prologue to the Canterbury Tales* (New York, 1948).

APPENDIX II

HENRY V AND THE WESTMINSTER RECLUSE

The anonymous biographer of Henry V, edited by Thomas Hearne as *Thomae de E.mham vita et gesta Henrici Quinti* (Oxford, 1727), and now generally known as 'pseudo-Elmham', relates that on the evening following his father's funeral the new king 'quendam reclusum perfectae vitae virum apud Westmonasterium secreto adiit', made to him a general confession of his past life, and received penance and absolution. J. H. Wylie, in his *Henry V* (1, 199, n. 5) suggested with some hesitation that this was William of Alnwick; he promised to devote an appendix to the topic, but died without writing it. As the apparently simple issue is in fact somewhat complicated, a few paragraphs may be devoted to its presentation.

The difficulty is principally due to the existence of at least four contemporary Williams of Alnwick,[1] who have been conflated by historians in varying degrees of strength. They are:

(1) William of Alnwick, Premonstratensian canon of Alnwick, *c.* 1408; involved in the rebellion of 1407.

(2) William of Alnwick, bishop of Norwich (1426–36) and Lincoln (1436–49).

(3) William of Alnwick, monk of St Albans, prior of Wymondham 1420; archdeacon of St Albans, 1428–*c.* 1434; prior of Belvoir 1435.

(4) William of Alnwick, recluse of Westminster and first confessor-general of the Bridgettines of Twickenham from *c.* 1416/7 to *c.* 1418.

It is certainly a remarkable (and for historians a vexatious) coincidence that four clerics of the same name and provenance should have found a place in the records at almost the same moment, three of them in the south of England; but the conflation of two by the writer in the *VCH, Norfolk*, of three by E. Venables in the *DNB* and of all four by the still more learned Dr Wylie (*Henry IV*, III, 149, somewhat modified in *Henry V*, I, 199) seem to be unwarrantable simplifications of an undesirable complexity. The late A. H. Thompson took cognizance of the problem when compiling a biographical sketch of Bishop Alnwick in the introduction to his edition of *Lincoln Visitations* (II, xiv–xix), and brought to it his unique knowledge of ecclesiastical personalities and his habitual lucidity. He effectually distinguished the bishop from the canon, the monk and the recluse, but he would not commit himself finally to a distinction between the bishop and the confessor-general, even though he unwittingly opened the door to a fifth William by splitting the personality of the recluse. Here we are only concerned with the last-mentioned, the fourth on our list, William of Alnwick, recluse of Westminster. We may note:

1. The recluse is introduced to us in the following passage from John Amundesham's *Chronica rerum gestarum in monasterio S. Albani* (*Amundesham*, I, 27):

Dominus Thomas Fyschebourn, primo dapifer Domini Abbatis Willelmi, postea Romam adiens dispensationem Curiae ut sacerdotio fungeretur adeptus est, et vitam solitariam ducens apud Sanctum Germanum, sic familiariter Alienorae Hulle et Elizabeth Beauchamp et aliarum inhaerendo et obsequendo in magnam notitiam Regis profusus [? profectus] est; et post, Willelmus Alnwyk, reclusus monachus Westmonasterii, cum aliis monachis diversorum locorum, in custodiam foeminarum praefectus est: sed post anni circulum, taedio et senio confectus, ad cellam suam, unde egressus fuerat, reversus est. In

---

1 There is always a possibility that in the case of one or more of them 'Alnwick' was a corruption or assimilation of another word. In *The Book of Margery Kempe*, ed. Meech and Allen, Appendix III, iii, pp. 366–7, there occurs a certain Willelmus Ambewyk, Amwyke or Amwyk, *c.* 1400.

tempore vero Willelmi Alnwyk, prima Abbatissa monialis de Berkyng a dignitate sua per Regem exonerata est; cui successit in honorem et reclusionem monialis de Markyate.

This short passage has been misread in whole or in part by most of those who have made use of it. Wylie identified S. Germanus with S. Germain des Près near Paris, whereas in fact there was a chapel and hermitage with that dedication among the ruins of Verulamium; while Thompson, besides confusing the order of the succession of confessors at Twickenham, took the 'wardenship of women' to refer to those in the nunneries around St Albans. Actually Amundesham tells us:

(a) that Thomas Fishbourne, with St Albans connexions, came to be well known to the king;

(b) that subsequently William Alnwick, a recluse of Westminster, together with monks of other houses, was put in charge of (religious) women (i.e. the Bridgettines);

(c) that after a year he returned to his cell at Westminster;

(d) that while he was in charge at Twickenham the first abbess (from Barking) was allowed to resign;

(e) that she was succeeded in office by a nun of Markyate, near St Albans. This last circumstance, together with the connexion of Fishbourne and Alnwick with the abbey, helps to explain and to guarantee the information at the disposal of Amundesham.

2. The foundation charter of the Bridgettine abbey (*Monasticon*, vi, i, 542) tells us that the king appointed as first confessor-general 'fratrem Willelmum Alnewyk, in ordine sacerdotali constitutum, ordinis praedicti professum', i.e. the Bridgettine order, not as Thompson, *op. cit.* xviii, takes it, that of the Austin canons.

3. A letter from Richard Clifford, bishop of London (Ellis, *Original Letters*, 2nd ser., I. 90) informs the king that the bishop has confirmed the elections of the new abbess and of Fishbourne as confessor-general on 5 May 1421. Fishbourne died 14 September 1428.

From all this it seems clear that the first confessor-general of the Bridgettines was William Alnwick, late recluse of Westminster, who after a year at Twickenham retired to his old cell. The king must have known him well and trusted him, and the inference seems clear that he was the recluse to whom Henry had made his confession in March 1413. The identification of this William of Alnwick with his contemporary namesake, the archdeacon of St Albans, who occurs almost on the same page of Amundesham's chronicle, will not bear examination.

There is, however, a small difficulty still to be resolved. E. H. Pearce, in his annotated list of the monks of Westminster, notes a John of London, recluse of Westminster, as figuring in the documents between 1424/5 and 1428. Pearce was not interested in the problem of Henry's confessor, and apparently unaware of the recluse William of Alnwick, but this very fact shows that his name does not appear in the Westminster muniments either as a recluse or as a monk of the house. It is by no means impossible that there were two recluses exactly contemporary with each other; Pearce himself notes such an occurrence some twenty years later (*v. supra*, p. 221). It is also possible that William of Alnwick was directly supported by royal alms and therefore failed to appear in the monastic records. But it is certainly curious that a recluse, not a monk of the house yet enjoying the confidence of the king, should have come into residence at Westminster without leaving any trace of his name.

A further small complication is occasioned by Amundesham's notice (c. 1429) of the death of Dan John, hermit of Westminster for 40 years (*Amundesham*, I, 33). This monk appears as recluse in Pearce's lists, and according to the same authority was perhaps still on tour as late as 1401–2 in the active post of treasurer of Queen Eleanor's manors. Did the chronicler, who was primarily interested in Alnwick, confuse or conflate two obituary notices? This, however, scarcely affects the main issue, supported as it is by direct evidence. It must remain probable almost to certainty that Henry's confessor was the recluse William of Alnwick.

APPENDIX III

REGULARS AS BISHOPS

As in previous volumes (*MO*, Appendix XII, pp. 709–10; *RO*, I, Appendix I, pp. 321–2) an attempt has been made to catalogue the regulars in episcopal orders during the period. Besides those appointed to English and Welsh dioceses, note has been taken of insular and Irish sees, and those with foreign or *in partibus* titles who worked in England as suffragans, but the numbers in these latter classes cannot be regarded as complete. In general, the task of compilation is more difficult for these centuries owing to the absence of monastic chroniclers and annalists who faithfully recorded the advancement of monks and canons in earlier times. In compiling the list of Friars Preachers, I have been greatly helped by a paper kindly sent by the Rev. Fr T. W. Gumbley, O.P., which reproduced with a few additions that published by him in *Analecta Historica Ordinis Praedicatorum*, 1925–6. For the Minors I am equally indebted to the late A. G. Little, who sent me a list compiled by himself shortly before his death. No scholar has hitherto examined the Carmelites and Austin friars with equal care, and it is probable that additions could be made to their totals, especially for the Irish and titular sees. A few remarks suggest themselves:

1. The numbers of religious in English and Welsh sees continue to remain curiously constant, e.g. in 1325, 2 (Hamo de Hethe and John Eaglescliff); in 1365, 3; in 1395, 5; in 1425, 4; in 1455, 4; in 1475, 6. The black monks continue to be represented at short intervals throughout, but the other older orders of monks and canons virtually disappear from the lists.

2. While appointments in the thirteenth century were normally the outcome, directly or indirectly, of canonical elections, the fourteenth and fifteenth centuries saw the establishment of an equilibrium between the papal claim to provide directly and the royal endeavour to control appointments; in the event the pope generally accepted any moderately respectable royal nominee. There were, however, some canonical elections and numerous direct papal provisions and translations. As was to be expected, the regular cathedral chapters were the most persistent in maintaining canonical forms, and it is scarcely accidental that eight out of the thirteen appointments of regulars were to the sees of Canterbury, Carlisle, Ely and Rochester. It is equally comprehensible that the king should not have lavished the richest patronage on religious, and in fact, with the exception of Langham (an ex-official), almost all the appointments of religious were to three of the poorest sees: Hereford (6), Lichfield (3) and Chichester (2).

3. The practice of appointing friars to Welsh sees, begun in the thirteenth century, was continued throughout this period, and at Bangor and Llandaff in particular an almost unbroken succession was maintained. In all the Preachers had twelve, the Carmelites four, and the Minors three Welsh bishops. The Carmelites, here as elsewhere, were most in evidence between 1380 and 1450.

4. Papal provision of friars to Irish sees was also continued. Three ends were in view at various times—the provision of a diocesan bishop; the rewarding of a distinguished curialist; and the securing of a title for a friar destined to act as suffragan in England. The last of these preponderated, and as the dates of work in England often show, the bishop concerned can rarely, if ever, have crossed the Irish Channel.

5. Concurrently the practice continued of providing future suffragans to titular sees. This became frequent in the fifteenth century and continued till the Reformation.

6. In two centuries, marked throughout by the mediocrity of most of the bishops, it is noticeable that, apart again from Langham, the religious earned advancement

neither by proved ability as heads of houses nor by theological eminence. Most of them had either done public service or had been the advisers and confessors to the king. A Welsh diocese was the regular method of rewarding friars of these classes. Taking all classes of appointment together, the Preachers exceeded any other order, and it is worth remarking that the Minors alone of the four orders provided no occupant of an English see between 1320 and 1480.

I. ENGLISH SEES

BLACK MONKS

[Hamo of Hethe	pr. Rochester	ROCHESTER	1319–1352]
Simon Langham	abb. Westminster	ELY	1362–1366
		CANTERBURY	1366–1368
Thomas Brunton	m. Norwich	ROCHESTER	1373–1389
Thomas Merks	m. Westminster	CARLISLE	1397–1399
Alex. Tottington	m. Norwich	NORWICH	1407–1413
William Heywood	abb. St Albans	LICHFIELD	1420–1445
Thomas Spofford	abb. St Mary's, York	HEREFORD	1422–1445
John Langdon	m. Chr. Ch., Canterbury	ROCHESTER	1422–1434
William Wells	abb. St Mary's, York	ROCHESTER	1437–1444
Reynold Boulers	abb. Gloucester	HEREFORD	1451–1453
		LICHFIELD	1453–1459
Richard Bell	pr. Durham	CARLISLE	1473–1495
Thomas Milling	abb. Westminster	HEREFORD	1475–1492

AUSTIN CANONS

Philip Repyndon	abb. Leicester	LINCOLN	1405–1419

FRIARS PREACHERS

Thomas de Lisle		ELY	1345–1361
John Gilbert	[from Bangor]	HEREFORD	1375–1389
		[tr. St David's]	
William Bottisham	pr. prov. 1366–70 [from Llandaff]	ROCHESTER	1389–1400
Robert Reade	pr. prov. [from Waterford]	CARLISLE	1396 [tr. Chichester]
		CHICHESTER	1396–1415
John Burghill	[from Llandaff]	LICHFIELD	1398–1414

CARMELITES

Robert Mascall		HEREFORD	1404–1416
Thomas Peverell	[from Llandaff]	WORCESTER	1407–1419
Stephen Patrington	provincial [from St David's]	CHICHESTER	1417
John Stanbury	[from Bangor]	HEREFORD	1453–1474

AUSTIN FRIARS

Robert Waldeby	[from Dublin]	CHICHESTER	1395–1396
		YORK	1396–1398
John Lowe	[from St Asaph]	ROCHESTER	1444–1467

II. WELSH SEES

BANGOR

Thomas Rinstead	O.P.	1357–1366
Gervase de Castro	O.P.	1366–1370
John Gilbert	O.P.	1372–1375 [tr. Hereford]
John Swaffham	O.Carm. [from Cloyne]	1376–1398
Thomas Cheriton	O.P.	1436–1447
John Stanbury	O.Carm.	1448–1453 [tr. Hereford]
James Blakeden	O.P. [from Achonry]	1453–1464
Richard Ednam		1465–1494

LLANDAFF

Roger Cradock	O.M.	1361–1382
Thomas Rushook	O.P.	1383–1385 [tr. Chichester]
William Bottisham	O.P. [from Nantes]	1385–1389 [tr. Rochester]
John Burghill	O.P.	1396–1398 [tr. Lichfield]
Thomas Peverell	O.Carm. [from Leighlin]	1398–1407 [tr. Worcester]
John de la Zouche	O.M.	1408–1423
John Wells	O.M.	1425–1440
John Hunden	O.P.	1458–1476 [resigned]

ST ASAPH

Alexander Bache	O.P.	1390–1394
John Lowe	O.S.A.	1433–1444 [tr. Rochester]
Thomas Bird	O.P.	1451–? 1471
Richard Redman	O.Prem.	1471–1496 [tr. Exeter]

ST DAVID'S

John Gilbert	O.P. [from Hereford]	1389–1397
Stephen Patrington	O.Carm.	1415–1417 [tr. Chichester, but possibly died before moving]
Robert Tully	O.S.B.	1460–c. 1481

III. SCOTTISH SEES

John Framysden	O.M. ? Provided in error	Glasgow 1391, 1396 [suffragan Lond. 1393–1394, Sar. 1396]

IV. THE ISLES

William Northburg	O.P. FAROE ISLES	c. 1380 [suffr. Lichf. 1380–1387, Ebor. 1387–1408]
John Sproton	O.P. SODOR AND MAN	1392–1402
Richard Messing	O.P. SODOR AND MAN	1410–1421
John Seyre	O.P. SODOR AND MAN	1435–1441

For lists V and VI that follow I am indebted to Professor Aubrey Gwynn, who is engaged upon the preparation of Irish lists for a new edition of *A Handbook of British Chronology* for the Royal Historical Society. List V is of the resident occupants of sees under English control. List VI is of Englishmen appointed (usually by papal provision) to other Irish sees of whose residence there is no evidence, and who are known to have acted as suffragans for English diocesan bishops. One or two names are common to both lists; they are of bishops who at a given date are known to have ceased to reside in Ireland. These lists are the fruit of original research, and omit several names previously included in Irish lists, either because trustworthy evidence is lacking, or because they are disqualified for various reasons.

V. IRISH BISHOPS (RESIDENT)

FRIARS PREACHERS

William Charnels	FERNS	1350–1362
John Tattenhall	OSSORY	1361–1370
William Andrews	ACHONRY	1374–1380
	MEATH	1380–1386
Thomas Rushook	KILMORE	1389–1393 [? resident]
Robert Rede	LISMORE AND WATERFORD	1394–1396
Adam Lynns	ARDAGH	1400–1416
John Babingle	TUAM	1410–1420 [left diocese]
Geoffrey Herford	KILDARE	1449–1454 [left diocese]
John Payn	MEATH	1483–1507

FRIARS MINOR

Richard Leatherhead	OSSORY	1318–1360
Thomas Brakenberg	LEIGHLIN	1349–1360
Roger Cradock	WATERFORD	1350–1361 [tr. Llandaff]
Philip Torrington	CASHEL	1374–1380
James Vale (? Wall)	KILDARE	1475 [? resigned]
John Foxalis	ARMAGH	1471–4

CARMELITES

William Paul	MEATH	1327–1349
John Swaffham	CLOYNE	1363–1376 [tr. Bangor]
Richard Wye	CLOYNE	1376–1394 [deprived]
Richard Northalis	OSSORY	1386–1396
	DUBLIN	1396–1397
Thomas Peverell	OSSORY	1397–1398 [tr. Llandaff]
John Geese	LISMORE AND WATERFORD	1409–1425
Edmund Oldhall	MEATH	1450–1459

AUSTIN FRIARS

Geoffrey Cranfield	FERNS	1347–1348
Robert Waldby	DUBLIN	1391–1395 [tr. Chichester; York, 1396]
Gerald Canton	CLOYNE	1394–1412

BLACK MONKS

Roger Appleby (pr. Nuneaton)	OSSORY	1400–1402
	DROMORE	1402–1407
	WATERFORD	1407–1409
Thomas Knight	DOWN AND CONNOR	1453–1469 (?)

(Down had a Benedictine chapter; but few of the bishops seem to have been black monks; those that were came from the local community.)

CISTERCIANS

John Brid (? Bird)	CLOYNE	1335–1351
Robert Mulfield (m. Meaux)	KILLALOE	1411–1418 [left diocese]

AUSTIN CANONS

John Waltham	OSSORY	1398–1399
	DROMORE	1399–1402
	OSSORY	1402–1405
Ralph Alderle	DOWN	1445– ? [? resident]

CARTHUSIANS

Thomas Pollard (m. Hinton)	DOWN	1447–1450

VI. IRISH BISHOPS (NON-RESIDENT) AS ENGLISH SUFFRAGANS

FRIARS PREACHERS

Roland Jorz	ARMAGH, 1312–1322 [deprived]	Ebor. 1332
Henry Nony	ARDAGH, 1392–1400	Ex. 1396
John Babingle	TUAM, 1410– [left dioc.]	Sar. 1425
Richard Belmer (?)	INNISCATTERY, 1414–1417	Sar. 1414; Bath. 1414–18; Ex. to 1433
James Blackdon	ACHONRY, 1442–1453 [tr. to Bangor, 1453]	Bath. 1442–53; Sar. Wig.
Geoffrey Herford	KILDARE, 1449–1454	Her. 1449–1454
Richard Wolsey	DOWN, 1451–1479	Lich. 1452–65; Wig. 1465–78; Her. 1479
Thomas Knight	DOWN, 1454–1463	Lond. 1459–63
Simon Elvington	CONNOR, 1459–1481	Sar. 1459–81; Ex. 1463
John de Pygge	ARDFERT, 1463–1483	Lond. 1463–83

FRIARS MINOR

Robert Petit	CLONFERT, 1319–1326 [tr. Enachdun, 1326]	Wig. Ex. Sar.
Thomas Orwell	KILLALOE, 1389–1404	El. 1389–1404
Henry Thurlow	ENACHDUN, 1394–1402	Ex. 1395–8; Sar. 1397; Wint. 1399–1400
John Britt (? Brill)	ENACHDUN, 1402–1403	Wint. 1402–3

Robert Foston	ELPHIN, 1418–1426	Dun. 1426
Nicholas Wartre	DROMORE, 1419–1445	Ebor. 1420–45
Robert Wyndell	EMLY, 1422–1441	Nor. 1424; Wig. 1433–4; Sar. 1435–41
Robert Portland	EMLY, 1428–	Wint. 1456
John Heyne	CLONFERT, 1438–1459	Lond. 1443–59; Wig. 1443; Ex. 1447
Robert Wellys	ACHONRY, 1472–	??
James Vale (? Wall)	KILDARE, 1475– [? res.]	??

CARMELITES

Stephen Brown	ROSS, c. 1402–1420	St David's 1408; Bath 1410; Her. 1418; Wig. 1420
David Chirbury	DROMORE, 1431–1456	St David's 1437
Thomas Scrope	DROMORE, 1448–1489	Nor. 1450–77
Richard Messing	DROMORE, 1457–	Ebor. 1460

AUSTIN FRIARS

| Thomas Radcliff | DROMORE, 1429–1434 | Ebor. |
| William Egremond | DROMORE, 1463–1501 | Ebor. 1463–1501 |

BLACK MONKS

| John Stokes | KILMORE [before 1407] | Lich. 1407 |
| John Chourles | DROMORE, 1410–1433 | Cant. 1420–33 |

CISTERCIANS

| Robert Mulfield (m. Meaux) | KILLALOE, 1411– [left dioc. c. 1418] | Lich. 1418–c. 1440 |

AUSTIN CANONS

John Bonner	ENACHDUN, 1421–1433	Sar. 1421–33
Thomas Legger	LIMERICK, 1456–	??
Ralph Alderle	DOWN, 1445–	??

VII. RELIGIOUS IN FOREIGN SEES: IN SEES IN PARTIBUS: FOREIGN BISHOPS AS ENGLISH SUFFRAGANS

FRIARS PREACHERS

Richard	CHERSON	1333–?
Thomas Walleys	LYCOSTOMIUM	1353–?
William Bottisham	NANTES	1383–1385 [tr. Llandaff]
Maurice of Usk	AIRE (Gascony)	1390–? 1403
William Bellers	SOLTANIA	1403–*post* Linc.; Cant. 1437
Matthew Moore	HEBRON	*occurs* 1410 Her. 1410

FRIARS MINOR

Peter of Bologna	CORBAVA (Croatia)	1318–1332	Wint. 1321–3; Cant. 1326
Boniface of Pisa	CORBAVA	1332–?1340	Dun. 1338–41
Matthew	MANCHENSIS	occ. 1344	at Neville's Cross 1346
Richard	NAZARETH	1348–1366	Cant. 1349; Wig. 1350; Lond.; Roff. 1362
John de Langebrugge	BUDIA (Dalmatia)	1362–	Bath 1362–3; Linc. 1367
Thomas Ilsshawe	COUTANCES	1391–1401	
Thomas Butler	CHRYSOPOLIS	1395–1420	Wint. 1402; Bath; Sar. ? 1395
John son of Richard Blunt	ACRE	1400	
John Greenlaw	SOLDAYA (Crimea)	1400–1422	Bath. 1401–8; Sar. 1409; Ebor. 1421
John Cheveley	GALLIPOLI	1402–1408	Sar. 1407–8
Richard Multon	CAPITOLIAS (Palestine)	1403, 1414	
John Greyby	NORENTA (Dalmatia)	1403–?1443	Linc. 1423–31; El. 1424–43
William Yeurde	SOLUVRI (suffr. to Constantinople)	1404–1418	Ex. ? 1395–1419; Wint. 1407–1417; Sar. 1409–17
Robert Mabire	RAPHANENSIS (Syria)	1414	
Simon Brampton	TRIPOLI (Syria)	1414	
John Walkote	NISH (Bulgaria)	1414, 1419	Ebor. 1418–9
Robert Ryngman	GARDAR (Greenland)	1425, 1453	Nor. 1425–52
John Kegill	PHILIPPOLIS (Syria)	1421–1458	Ebor. 1442–58

CARMELITES

John Leicester	SMYRNA	1400–1424	Nor. 1400–24

CISTERCIANS

Thomas (m. Merevale)	MAGNATIENSIS	1353–1365	Lich. 1360; Lland. 1361; Her. 1361; Eb. 1365

GILBERTINES

John Crancroyt (can. Malton)	ANACORADENSIS	?	El. 1402; Linc. 1420–32; Cant. 1425

AUSTIN CANONS

William Westcarr	SINDON	c. 1450	Cant., etc. c. 1460

BIBLIOGRAPHY

The lists which follow are in no sense a complete bibliography of the subject. They are intended to include all, and only, those manuscripts, books, articles and theses that have been used or quoted in the text or notes of this book. The omission of any work, therefore, does not necessarily imply that it has not been consulted, or that it is of slight value, but simply that it has not been used by the writer in this particular connexion.

An asterisk (*) denotes that the book referred to is in another section of the bibliography.

I. CONTEMPORARY SOURCES

(a) MANUSCRIPTS

Cambridge

Pembroke College MS. 223 (Richard Methley's transcript of *The Mirror of Simple Souls*).

Trinity College MS. O. 2. 56 (Writings of Richard Methley).

Durham

Dean and Chapter Library MS. A III 57 ff. 26ᵛ–64ᵛ (*De naturali et necessaria connexione ac ordine sacerdotalis officii et regalis*); 69ʳ–99ᵛ (*De dotacione ecclesie sponse Christi*); 99ᵛ–110ʳ (*Contra garrulos fratrum dotacionem ecclesie impugnantes*); all works of Uthred of Boldon.

London

B.M. Add. MS. 6162 (*Vita compendiosa* of Uthred of Boldon).

B.M. Add. MS. 22,285 (Martiloge of Syon Abbey).

B.M. Cott. Vit. F 17 (Register of Leicester Abbey).

Harley 139 (Cheshire documents connected with John Whethamstede).

Royal D x (Uthred's tract *Contra querelas fratrum*).

Oxford

Laud Misc. MS. 296 (Homilies of John Waldeby).

Bodley MS. Wood Empt. 1 (*Secretum Domini* of Abbot Monington).

Bodley MS. Wood Rolls 1 (Access. 25277) (Uthred's defence of his articles).

Worcester

Cathedral MS. F 65 (Determination of Hatton against Uthred of Boldon).

(b) PRINTED SOURCES

Abingdon Abbey, Accounts of the Obedientiaries of, ed. R. E. G. Kirk (CS, n.s., LI, 1892).

Ailredi, Vita, ed. F. M. Powicke (Medieval Classics, Edinburgh, 1950).

Albani, Gesta Abbatum Sancti, ed. H. T. Riley (*MSAC,* IV, i–iii).

Amundesham, Annales Joannis de, ed. H. T. Riley (*MSAC,* V, i–ii).

Analecta Premonstratensia (Tongerloo, 1925–   ).

Analectes de l'Ordre de Prémontré (Brussels, 1905–14); revived as *Analecta Premonstratensia.*

Anglo-Premonstratensia, Collectanea, ed. F. A. Gasquet (CS, 3 ser., VI, X, XII; 1904, 1906).

Annales Monastici, ed. W. R. Luard (RS, 36, 5 vols., 1864–9).

Audelay, The Poems of John, ed. E. K. Whiting (EETS, o.s., CLXXXI, 1931).

Bekynton, T., *v.s.* Henry VI.

Benedicti, S., Regula Monasteriorum, ed. C. Butler (2 ed., Freiburg-im-Breisgau, 1927).

Berkeleys, Lives of the, ed. J. Maclean (*BGAS*, 1883).

Bicester, *v.s.* *Blomfield.

Bradwardine, T., *De causa Dei adversus Pelagianos*, ed. H. Savile (London, 1618).

Brinton, Bishop of Rochester (1373–1389), The Sermons of Thomas, ed. M. A. Devlin (CS, 3 ser., LXXXV–LXXXVI, 1954).

[*Bristol*], *Two Compotus Rolls of St Augustine's Abbey*, ed. G. Beachcroft and A. Sabin (Bristol Record Soc. IX, 1938).

Brut y Tywsogion, ed. J. Williams ap Ithel (EETS, o.s., CXXXVI, 1906–8).

Bullarium Franciscanum, ed. I. H. Sbaralea *et al.* (Rome and Quaracchi, 1759–1908).

Bullarium Romanum, ed. L. Cherubini, etc. (Luxembourg, 1727)

Calendar of Close Rolls (RP, London, 1892–).

Calendar of Fine Rolls (RP, London, 1911–).

Calendar of Letters and Papers, Foreign and Domestic, Henry VIII (RP, London, 1864–1(32)).

Calendar of Liberate Rolls (RP, London, 1917–).

Calendar of Papal Letters (RP, London, 1893–).

Calendar of Patent Rolls (RP, London, 1903–).

Calendar of Wills, Court of Hustings, 1258–1688 (ed. R. R. Sharpe, 2 vols., London, 1889–90).

Canterbury College, *v.s.* *Pantin, W.A.

Cantuarienses, Literae, ed. J. B. Sheppard (RS, 85, 3 vols., 1887–9).

Capgrave, J., *Life of St Katharine of Alexandria*, ed. C. Horstman (EETS, o.s., CVIII, 1893).

Carmelite Missal, *v.s.* *Rickert, M.

Chapters of the Augustinian Canons, ed. H. E. Salter (OHS, LXXIV, 1920; and C & YS, LXX, 1921–2).

Chapters of the Black Monks, ed. W. A. Pantin (CS, 3 ser., XLV, XLVIII, LIV, 1931–7).

Charter Rolls (RP, 1903–).

Chauncy, Dom Maurice, *Historia aliquot martyrum...Cartusianorum*, ed. V. M. Doreau (Montreuiel, 1888).

Chronicles of Edward I and Edward II, ed. W. Stubbs (RS, 76, 2 vols., 1882–3).

Chronicles of London, ed. C. L. Kingsford (Oxford, 1905).

Cisterciensis Ordinis Statuta, *v.s.* Statuta.

Clare, Letters of Osbert of, ed. F.W. Williamson (London, 1929).

Cloud of Unknowing, The, ed. (1) P. Hodgson (EETS, o.s., CCXVIII, 1944); (2) P. J. McCann (London, 1924, 1942).

Duckett, G. F., *Charters and Records of Cluni* (2 vols., Lewes, 1888).

Dunelmensia, Gesta, in *Camden Miscellany XIII* (CS, 3 ser., XXXIV, 1924).

Dunelmensis ecclesiae cathedralis, catalogi veteres librorum, ed. J. Raine (SS, VII, 1838).

Dunelmensis, Feodarium Prioratus, ed. W. Greenwell (SS, LVIII, 1872).

Dunelmensis, Halmota Prioratus, ed. J.B. (SS, LXXXII, 1889).

Dunelmensis, Liber Vitae ecclesiae, ed. (1) J. Stevenson (SS, XIII, 1841); ed. (2) A. H. Thompson (SS, CXXXVI, 1923).

Dunelmensis scriptores tres, Historiae, ed. J. Raine (SS, IX, 1839).

Durham, The Accounts of the Bursar of the Monastery of, ed. J. Raine (SS, XVIII, 1844).

Durham Account Rolls, *v.s.* *Blakiston, H.E.D.

Durham, Extracts from the Account Rolls of the Abbey of, ed. J. T. Fowler (SS, XCIX, C, CIII, 1898, 1900).

Durham Obituary Rolls, *v.s. Dunelmensis Liber Vitae.*

Durham, Rites of, ed. (1) J. Raine (SS, xv, 1842); ed. (2) J. T. Fowler (SS, CVII, 1903).

Eliensis, Historia [*Chronica abbatum et episcoporum Eliensium*], ed. H. Wharton in *Anglia Sacra*, vol. II (London, 1689).

Ellis, H., *Original Letters* (three series, 11 vols; London, 1824–46).

Elmham, T., *Historia Monasterii S. Augustini*, ed. C. Hardwick (RS, 8, 1858).

—— *Liber Metricus de Henrico Quinto*, ed. C. A. Cole, *v.s. Henry V.*

—— [spurious] *Vita et Gesta Henrici Quinti*, ed. T. Hearne (Oxford, 1727).

Ely Chapter Ordinances, ed. S. J. A. Evans, in Camden Miscellany XVII (CS, 3 ser., LXIV, 1940).

Ely, Sacrist Rolls of, ed. F. R. Chapman (2 vols. Cambridge, 1907).

English Chronicle of the reigns of Richard II, etc., An, ed. J. S. Davies (CS, o.s., LXIV, 1856).

Eulogium Historiarum, ed. F. S. Haydon (RS, 9, 3 vols. 1858–63).

Eynsham, Cartulary of, ed. H. E. Salter (OHS, XLIX, 1906–7).

Finchale, The Priory of, ed. J. Raine (SS, VI, 1857).

Fitzralph, Archbishop Richard, *De Pauperie Salvatoris* I–IV, ed. R. L. Poole with Wyclif's *De dominio divino*, *q.v.* Also *v.s.* *Hammerich, L. L.

Flete, John, *The History of Westminster Abbey*, ed. J. A. Robinson (Cambridge, 1909).

Fountains, Memorials of St Mary's Abbey of, ed. J. Walbran (SS, XLII, 1863).

Gale, T., *Historiae Britannicae et Anglicanae Scriptores XX* (2 vols. Oxford, 1691, 1687), a continuation of W. Fulman's *Rerum Anglicarum Scriptorum Veterum*, tom. I (Oxford, 1684).

Glastoniensis, Johannis, Historia de rebus Glastoniensibus, ed. T. Hearne (Oxford, 1726).

Gloucestriae, Historia et Cartularium monasterii S. Petri, ed. W. H. Hart (RS, 33, 3 vols. 1863–7).

Gower, John, *Complete Works*, ed. G. C. Macaulay, vol. I (Oxford, 1899).

Hatfield's Survey, Bishop, ed. W. Greenwell (SS, XXXII, 1856).

Henry V, Memorials of, ed. C. A. Cole (RS, 11, 1858).

Henry VI, Memorials of the Reign of [Official correspondence of Thomas Bekynton], ed. G. Williams (RS, 56, 2 vols. 1872).

Hilton, Walter, *The Scale of Perfection*, ed. E. Underhill (London, 1923).

Horstman, C., *Nova Legenda Anglie* (2 vols, Oxford, 1901).

Jarrow and Monk-Wearmouth, Inventories of..., ed. J. Raine (SS, XXIX, 1854).

John of the Cross, S., *Complete Works*, ed. E. Allison Peers (2 ed. London, 1952).

Kempe, The Book of Margery, (1) Selections in modern English, ed. W. Butler-Bowdon (London, 1936; Oxford, 1954); (2) ed. S. B. Meech and H. E. Allen (EETS, o.s., CCXII, 1940).

Kirkstall Chronicle, The, ed. M.V. Clarke and N. Denholm-Young in *BJRL*, XV (1931), 100–37.

Knighton, Chronicon Henrici, ed. J. R. Lumby (RS, 92, 2 vols. 1889–95).

Lanfranc, The Monastic Customs of, ed. M. D. Knowles (Edinburgh, 1951).

Letters and Papers of Henry VIII, *v.s.* Calendar of Letters. ...

Lincoln Visitations, ed. A. H. Thompson, *v.s. Visitations.*

Lydgate, The Minor Poems of John, ed. H. N. MacCracken (EETS, CVII, 1911).

Melsa, Chronicon monasterii de, ed. E. A. Bond (RS, 3 vols. 1866–8).

Miroir of the blessed lyf of Jesu Christ, by N. Love (Oxford, 1908).

Mirror of Simple Souls, The, ed. C. Kirchberger (London, 1928).

Monasticon Anglicanum, ed. W. Dugdale (re-ed. J. Caley, H. Ellis and B. Bandinel, 6 vols in 8, London 1817–30).

More, Journal of Prior William, ed. E. S. Fegan (WHS, 1914).

Netter of Wa den, Thomas, *Doctrinale de Sacramentis* (3 vols, Venice, 1571); *v.* also *Waldensis.*

New Minster, The Liber Vitae of, ed. W. de Gray Birch (Hants Record Society, 1892).

Northern Registers, Papers and Letters from the, ed. J. Raine (RS, 61, 1873).

Norwich Visitations, v.s. Visitations.

Oxoniensia, Munimenta Academica, ed. H. Anstey (RS, 50, 1868).

Parco Lude [*Louth Park*], *Chronicon abbatie de,* ed. E. Venables (Lincs. Record Society, 1891).

Parisiensis, Cartularium Universitatis, ed. H. Denifle and A. Chatelain (4 vols. Paris, 1888–7).

Parliamentary Writs and Writs of Military Summons (RP, 2 vols. 1827–34).

Paston Letters, The, ed. J. Gairdner (London, 1904).

Percy Cartulary, The [Bailiff Rolls], ed. M. T. Martin (SS, CXVII, 1909).

Piers Plowman, by W. Langland, ed. W. W. Skeat (2 vols. Oxford, 1886).

Premonstratensia, Collectanea Anglo-, v.s. Anglo-Premonstratensia.

Registers, Episcopal:
    Bath and Wells. *T. Bekynton,* ed. H. C. Maxwell-Lyte and M. C. B. Dawes (SRS, 2 vols. 1934).
    —— *J. Stafford,* ed. T. Scott Holmes (SRS, 2 vols. 1915–16).
    Canterbury. *S. Langham,* ed. A. C. Wood (C & YS, CXX, 1947–8).
    Exeter. *T. Brantyngham,* ed. F. C. Hingeston-Randolph (2 vols. Exeter, 1901, 6).
    —— *J. Grandisson,* ed. F. C. Hingeston-Randolph (3 vols. Exeter, 1894–9).
    Hereford. *T. Spofford,* ed. A. T. Bannister (C & YS and Cantilupe Soc. 1919).
    —— *R. Swinfield,* ed. W. W. Capes (C & YS, 1908–9).
    —— *J. Trefnant,* ed. W. W. Capes (C & YS and Cantilupe Soc. 1916).
    St David's. *The Episcopal Registers of the Diocese of St David's, 1397–1518. Vol.* I, *G. Mone, 1397–1407* (Hon. Soc. of Cymmrodorion, 1917).

Registra quorundam abbatum Monasterii S. Albani, ed. H. T. Riley = *MSAC,* IV, VI.

Reyner, C., *Apostolatus Benedictinorum in Anglia* (Douai, 1626),

Rolle, Richard, *Incendium Amoris,* ed. O. Deanesly (Manchester, 1915).

—— *Works,* ed. C. Horstman (2 vols. London, 1895–6).

Rotuli Parliamentorum: Edward I–Henry VII (RP, 6 vols. 1783).

Rymer, T., *Foedera, etc.* (London, 20 vols. 1704–35. Re-ed. RP, 4 vols. 1816–69).

Scholz, R., *Unbekannte kirchenpolitische Streitschriften* (containing Ockham's Tract for Edward III) (Rome, 1911–14).

Sherborne Missal, The, ed. J. A. Herbert (Roxburghe Club, 1920).

Snappe's Formulary, ed. H. E. Salter (OHS, LXXX, 1924).

State Papers during the reign of Henry VIII (RP, 11 vols. 1830–52).

Statuta Capitulorum Generalium Ordinis Cisterciensis, ed. J. M. Canivez (Louvain, 1933–41).

Statutes of the Realm (RP, 11 vols. 1810–28).

Stone, Chronicle of John, ed. W. G. Searle (Cambridge Antiquarian Soc. Publications, XXXIV, 1902).

Stubbs, W., *Select Charters* (9 ed. Oxford, 1921).

Subsidy Roll of 51 Edward III, ed. John Topham, in *Archaeologia,* VII (1785), 337–47.

Suecarum, Diplomatarium, ed. C. Silfverstolpe (Stockholm, 1885–1902).

Suecicarum medii aevi, Scriptores rerum, ed. E. M. Fant (Uppsala, 1818).

Suppression of the Monasteries, Letters relating to, ed. T. Wright (CS, o.s. XXVI, 1843).

Thorne, William, *v.s.* Twysden and *Davis, A. H.

Trokelowe, Chronica et Annales Johannis de, ed. H. T. Riley = *MSAC,* III.

Tryvytlam, De laude Universitatis Oxoniae, ed. H. Furneaux (OHS, Collectanea, III, 188–209) (Oxford, 1652).

Twysden, R., *Scriptores Decem* (Oxford, 1652).

Uthredi monachi Dunelmensis, Vita compendiosa, in *Bulletin of the Institute of Historical Research,* XIII 44.

Visitations in the diocese of Lincoln, 1517–31, ed. A. H. Thompson (Lincoln Record Soc. Pub. 33, 35, 37, 1940–7).

Visitations of religious houses in the diocese of Lincoln (1420–49), ed. A. H. Thompson (Lincoln Record Soc. Pub. 7, 14, 21, 1914–29).

Visitations of the diocese of Norwich, ed. A. Jessopp (CS, n.s., XLIII, 1888).

Visitations of Somerset Religious Houses, ed. H. C. Maxwell-Lyte (SRS, XXXIX, 1924).

Waldensis, Epistolae, ed. B. Zimmerman, in *Monumenta Historica Carmelitana*, I, 444–82 (Lérins, 1907).

Walsingham, Thomas of, *Historia Anglicana*, ed. H. T. Riley = *MSAC* I, i–ii.

Wazstense, Diarium [Vadstena chronicle], ed. Bengelius (Upsala, 1721); *v.* also *Suecicarum*.

Wellingborough Manorial Accounts, ed. F. M. Page (Northants. Rec. Soc. VIII, 1936).

Westminster, Customary of, ed. E. M. Thompson (HBS, 2 vols. XXIII, 1902).

Westminster, v.s. Flete.

Wharton, H., *Anglia Sacra* (2 parts, London, 1691).

Whethamstede, Registrum J., ed. H. T. Riley = *MSAC*, VI, i.

Whiteby, Chartularium abbathiae de, ed. J. C. Atkinson (SS, LXIX, LXXII, 1879, 1881).

Wilkins, D., *Concilia Magnae Britanniae et Hiberniae* (4 vols. London, 1737).

Winchester, Obedientiary Rolls of St Swithun's, ed. G. W. Kitchin (Hants. Rec. Soc. 1892).

Woodruff, C. E., Chronicle of William Glastynbury, monk of Christ Church Priory, 1418–48, in *ACant.* XXXVII (1925).

—— Monastic Chronicle of Christ Church, 1331–1415 (anonymous), in *ACant.* XXIX (1911).

Worcester, Accounts of the Priory of, ed. J. M. Wilson (WHS, 1907).

Worcester, Early Compotus Rolls of the Priory of, ed. J. M. Wilson and C. Gordon (WHS, 1908).

Worcester of the fourteenth and fifteenth centuries, Compotus Rolls of the Priory of, ed. S. G. Hamilton (WHS, 1910).

Worcester Cathedral, Catalogue of manuscripts preserved in the Chapter Library of, ed. J. K. Floyer and S. G. Hamilton (WHS, 1906).

Wright, T. (ed.), *Political Poems and Songs* (RS 14, 2 vols., 1859–61).

The following works of Wyclif are cited in the present book. There is a full list of Wyclif's writings in *CMH* VII, 900–4.

Wyclif, J., *The Church and her Members* (Select English Works, III).

—— *De apostasia*, ed. M. H. Dziewicki (WS, 1889).

—— *De civili dominio*, I, ed. R. L. Poole; II, III, ed. J. Loserth (WS, 1885, 1900, 1903–4).

—— *De detectione perfidiarum Antichristi* (Polemical Works, I, xi).

—— *De dominio divino*, ed. R. L. Poole (WS, 1890).

—— *De ecclesia*, ed. J. Loserth (WS, 1886).

—— *De eucharistia*, ed. J. Loserth (WS, 1892).

—— *De fratribus ad scholares* (Opera Minora, I (i)).

—— *De fundatione sectarum* (Polemical Works, I, i).

—— *De nova praevaricatione mandatorum* (Polemical Works, I, iii).

—— *De oratione* (Polemical Works, I, ix).

—— *De potestate papae*, ed. J. Loserth (WS, 1907).

—— *De quattuor sectis novellis* (Polemical Works, I, vi).

—— *De septem peccatis* (Select English Works, III, ix).

—— *De solutione Satanae* (Polemical Works, II, xii).

—— *Determinacio ad argumenta magistri Outredi* (Opera Minora, 18).

—— *De triplici vinculo amoris* (Polemical Works, I, iv).

—— The English Works of Wyclif hitherto unprinted, ed. F. D. Mathew (EETS, o.s., LXXIV, 1880).

—— Latin Works, ed. J. Loserth (*v.* list in *CMH*).

—— *Opera Minora*, ed. J. Loserth (WS, 1913).

—— Polemical Works, ed. R. Buddensieg (WS, 1883).

—— *Responsiones ad xliv conclusiones monachales* (Opera Minora, 17).

Wyclif, J., Select English Works, ed. T. A. Arnold (3 vols. Oxford, 1869–71).
—— Sermones, ed. J. Loserth (4 vols. WS, 1887–90).
Zizaniorum, Fasciculi, ed. W. W. Shirley (RS, 5, 1858).

II. MODERN WORKS

(a) PRINTED WORKS

Allen, H. E., *Writings ascribed to Richard Rolle* (*PMLA*, New York and Oxford, 1927).

Archer, M., Philip Repingdon, Bishop of Lincoln, and his cathedral chapter, in *University of Birmingham Historical Journal*, IV ii (1954), 81–97.

Atkinson, T. D., *An Architectural History of the Benedictine Monastery of St Etheldreda at Ely* (2 vols. Cambridge, 1937).

—— Article on Ely Cathedral in *VCH Cambs.* IV (1953).

Aubert, M., *Architecture cistercienne en France* (2 vols. Paris, 1947).

Aungier, G. J., *History and Antiquities of Syon Monastery* (London, 1840).

Bale, J., *Illustrium maioris Britanniae Scriptorum Catalogus* (Basel, 1557, 9).

Bateson, M., Archbishop Warham's Visitations, in *EHR*, VI (1891), 28–30.

—— *Catalogue of the library of Syon Monastery, Isleworth* (Cambridge, 1898).

Batsford, H., and Fry, C., *The Cathedrals of England* (London, 1934).

Baudry, L., *Guillaume d'Occam,* vol. 1 (Paris, 1949).

Beeching, H. C. and James, M. R., The Library of the cathedral church of Norwich and priory MSS. now in English libraries, in *Norfolk Archaeology*, XIX (1917), 67 seqq., 174 seqq.

Bennett, H. S., Chaucer and the Fifteenth Century, in *Oxford History of English Literature*, II, i (Oxford, 1947).

Blakiston, H. E. D., Durham Account Rolls, in *Collectanea*, III (OHS, XXXII, 1–76).

Blomefield, F., *An Essay towards a topographical history of the county of Norfolk* (London, 11 vols. 1805–10).

Blomfield, J. C., *History of the deanery of Bicester* (8 parts, London, etc., 1882–94).

Bloomfield, M. W., The present state of *Piers Plowman* studies, in *Speculum*, XIV (1939), 215–32.

Blore, W. P., Recent Discoveries in the Archives of Canterbury Cathedral, in *ACant.* LVIII (1945).

Bond, F., *The Cathedrals of England and Wales* (London, 1912).

—— *Gothic Architecture in England* (London, 1905).

Bowden, M., *A Commentary on the General Prologue to the Canterbury Tales* (New York, 1948).

Bressie, R., 'A Governour wily and wys', in *Modern Language Notes*, LIV, 7 (Nov. 1939), 477–90.

Britton, J., *History and Antiquities of Bath Abbey Church* (Bath, 1887).

Brown, W. and Hope, W. H. St J., The Charterhouse of Mount Grace, in *YAJ*, XVIII (1905), 252–309.

Bruel, A., Les Chapîtres Généraux de l'Ordre de Cluny, in *Bibliothèque de l'école des Chartes*, XXXIV (1873), 542–79.

Butler-Bowdon, W., *The Book of Margery Kempe* (London, 1936). Also, *v.s.* *Kempe.

Cambridge Bibliography of English Literature, I (Cambridge, 1940).

Cambridge Economic History, The, vol. 2, ed. M. M. Postan and E. E. Rich (Cambridge, 1952).

Cambridge History of English Literature, The (Cambridge, 1907–16).

Campbell, A. M., *The Black Death and Men of Learning* (New York, 1931).

Cargill, O., The Langland myth, in *PMLA*, L, 35–56.

Chambers, E. K., English Literature at the close of the Middle Ages, in *Oxford History of English Literature* vol. II, ii (Oxford, 1945).

Chambers, R. W., On the continuity of English prose from Alfred to More and his school (EETS, O.S., CLXXXVI, 1932 and, apart, London, 1932).

Chaucer, Geoffrey, *Complete Works*, ed. W. W. Skeat (Oxford, 7 vols. 1894–7).

Chew, H. M., *The English ecclesiastical Tenants-in-chief and Knight Service* (Oxford, 1934).

Chronology, Handbook of British, ed. F. M. Powicke (Royal Historical Society, 1939).

Clark dicatus, Fasciculus J. W. (Cambridge, 1909).

Clark, J. W., *The care of books* (Cambridge, 2 ed. 1908).

—— *The Observances in use at the Augustinian Priory of Barnwell* (Cambridge, 1897).

Clarke, M. V., *Medieval Representation and Consent* (London, 1936).

Clay, R. M., *The Hermits and Anchorites of England* (London, 1914).

Coghill, N., Two notes on Piers Plowman: the Abbot of Abingdon, in *Medium Aevum*, 4 (1935), 83 *seqq.*

Colvin, H. M., *The White Canons in England* (Oxford, 1951).

Coulton, G. G., *The Black Death* (London, 1929).

Craster, H. H. E., The Red Book of Durham, in *EHR*, XL (1925), 504–32.

Cutts, E. L., *Parish Priests and their People in the Middle Ages* (London, 1914).

Daniel, C. H., *Worcester College* (London, 1900).

Davis, A. H., *William Thorn's Chronicle of St Augustine's Canterbury* (London, 1934).

Denholm-Young, N., *Seignorial administration in England* (Oxford, 1947).

Denzinger-Bannwart, *Enchiridion symbolorum* (28 ed. 1952).

Devlin, M. A., Bishop Thomas Brunton and his Sermons, in *Speculum*, XIV (1939), 324–44.

Dickinson, J. C., *The Origins of the Austin Canons* (London, 1950).

Donnelly, J. S., *The decline of the Cistercian Laybrotherhood* (Fordham University Studies: History series No. 3; New York, 1949).

Drew, J. S., Manorial Accounts of St Swithun's Priory, Winchester, in *EHR*, LXII (1947), 20 *seqq.*

Ducarel, A. C., *Some account of the alien priories, etc.* (London, 1779).

Ehrle, F., *Der Sentenzenkommentar Peters von Candia* (München, 1925).

—— Die Spiritualen, ihr Verhaltniss zum Franziskanerorden und zu den Fraticellen, in *Archiv für Litteratur- und Kirchengeschichte*, II, 103–64; III, 553–623; IV, 1–190.

Esmein, A., L'unanimité et la majorité dans les élections canoniques, in *Mélanges Fitting* (Montpellier, 1907), 355–82.

Evans, E., St Mary's College in Oxford for Austin Canons, in *Oxfordshire Archaeological Society Reports*, nos. 74–8 (1929–32), 367–91.

Fawtier, R., *Ste Cathérine de Sienne* (Paris, 2 vols. 1921).

Fletcher, F., Recent excavations at Hinton Priory, in *Proceedings of the Somerset Archaeological Society*, XCVI, 160–5.

Floyer, J. K., *v.s.* *Worcester Cathedral.*

Fowler, J., *Medieval Sherborne* (Dorchester, 1951).

Fry, C., *v.s.* Batsford, H.

Gairdner, J., *Lollardy and the Reformation in England* (London, 4 vols. 1908).

Galbraith, V. H., Articles laid before the Parliament of 1371, in *EHR*, XXXIV (1914), 579–82.

—— *The St Albans Chronicle* (Oxford, 1937).

—— Thomas Walsingham and the St Albans Chronicle, 1272–1422, in *EHR*, XLVII (1932), 12–30.

Gasquet, F. A., *The Black Death* (London, 2 ed. 1908).

—— A forgotten English preacher, in *The Old English Bible and other Essays* (London, 1897).

—— *A history of the Venerable English College in Rome* (London, 1920).

Also *v.s.* *Anglo-premonstratensia.*

Geyer, B., *v.s.* Ueberweg, F.

Ghellinck, J. de, *L'Essor de la littérature latine* (Brussels, 2 vols. 1946).

Gierke, O., Über die Geschichte des Majoritatsprinzip, in *Essays in Legal History*, ed. P. Vinogradoff (Oxford, 1913), 312–27.

Graham, R., The History of the Alien Priory of Wenlock, in *JBAA*, 3 ser., IV (1939), 117–40.

—— *English Ecclesiastical Studies* (London, 1929).

—— Four Alien Priories in Monmouthshire, in *JBAA*, 2 ser., XXXV (1929), 102–21.

—— The Great Schism and the English Monasteries of the Cistercian Order, in *EHR* XLIV (1929), 373–87 (reprinted *Eng. Eccl. St.*).

—— The Order of Grandmont and its Houses in England, in *Archaeologia*, LXXV (1926), 159–210 (reprinted *Eng. Eccl. St.*).

—— The Papal Schism of 1378 and the English Province of the Order of Cluny, in *EHR* XXXVIII (1925), 481–95 (reprinted *Eng. Eccl. St.*).

—— Roland Gosenell, Prior of Wenlock, 1521–6, in *Transactions of the Shropshire Archaeological Society*, XLII (1923), 151–68 (reprinted *Eng. Eccl. St.*).

—— The Taxation of Pope Nicholas IV, in *EHR* XXIII (1908), 434–54 (reprinted *Eng. Eccl. St.*).

Graham, Medieval Essays presented to Rose (Oxford, 1950).

Grimké-Drayton, T. D., The East Window of Gloucester Cathedral, in *BGAS*, XXXVIII (1915), 69–97.

Grosjean, P., De S. Joanni Bridlingtoniensi Collectanea, in *Analecta Bollandiana*, LIII (1935), 101–29.

Gwynn, A., *The English Austin Friars* (Oxford, 1940).

—— Archbishop Fitzralph and the Friars, in *Studies* (March, 1937), 50–67.

—— The Sermon-Diary of Richard Fitzralph, Archbishop of Armagh, in *Proceedings of the Royal Irish Academy* (1937), 1–57.

Hadcock, R. N., *v.s.* Knowles, M. D.

Hamilton, S. G., *v.s.* *Worcester Cathedral.

Hammerich, L. L., *The Beginning of the Strife between Richard Fitzralph and the Mendicants* (Copenhagen, 1938).

Hartridge, R. A. R., *A History of Vicarages in the Middle Ages* (Cambridge, 1930).

Harvey, J. H., Henry Yevele, Architect, and his work in Kent, in *ACant.* LVI (1943), 48–53.

Hepple, R. B., Uthred of Boldon, in *Archaeologia Aeliana*, 3 ser. XVII (1920), 153–68.

Hilton, R. H., *The Economic Development of some Leicestershire Estates* (Oxford, 1947).

—— 'Medieval Agrarian History, in *VCH Leics.* (1954), 145–98.

Höjer, T., *Studier i Vadstena Klosters och Birgittinordens Historia ontill mitten af 1400-talet* (Upsala, 1905).

Hope, W. H. St J., *The London Charterhouse* (London, 1925). Also *v.s.* Brown, W.

Hughes, M. D., *History of Durham Cathedral Library* (Durham, 1925).

Hughes, P., *The Reformation in England*, I (London, 1950).

Hutton, E., *Highways and Byways in Gloucestershire* (London, 1932).

Jacob, E. F., 'Florida verborum venustas', in *BJRL*, XVII, 9 (1933), 264–90.

James, M. R., On the Abbey of St Edmund at Bury; 1, the library; 2, the church, in *Cambridge Antiquarian Society*, 8vo publications, no. 28 (1895).

—— *The Ancient Libraries of Canterbury and Dover* (Cambridge, 1903).

—— Bury St Edmund's manuscripts, in *EHR*, XLI (1926), 251–60.

—— The Catalogue of the Library of the Augustinian Friars at York, in *Fasciculus J. W. Clark dicatus, q.v.*

—— Catalogue of the Library of Leicester Abbey, in *Transactions of the Leics. Archaeological Society*, XIX (1936–7), 111–62, 378–440; XXI (1940–1), 1–88.

—— *Catalogue of the MSS. of Jesus College, Cambridge* (Cambridge, 1895).

—— *Catalogue of the MSS. of Pembroke College, Cambridge* (Cambridge, 1905).

—— *Catalogue of the MSS. of Trinity College, Cambridge* (Cambridge, 1900).

James, M. R., Lists of MSS. formerly in Peterborough Abbey Library, in *Biblio-graphical Society Transactions*, Suppl. V (1926).

—— MSS. from Essex monastic libraries, in *Transactions of the Essex Archaeological Society*, n.s. XXI (1933), 34–46.

—— The MSS. in the Library at Lambeth Palace, in *Cambridge Archaeological Society Publications*, XXXIII (1900).

—— *The MSS. in the Library at Lambeth Palace* (Cambridge, 1900).

James, M. R. and Robinson, J. A., *The MSS. of Westminster Abbey* (Cambridge, 1908).

Jenkins, C., Cardinal Morton's Register, in *Tudor Studies presented to A. F. Pollard*, ed. R. W. Seton-Watson (London, 1924).

Jones, A. H. M., Worcester College Buildings, in *VCH Oxon*, III (1954), 301–9.

Kellogg, E., Bishop Brunton and the Rat Parliament, in *PMLA* (1935), 57–68.

Ker, N. R., More Manuscripts from Essex monastic libraries, in *Transactions of the Essex Archaeological Society*, XXIII, part 2.

—— *The Medieval Libraries of Great Britain* (Royal Historical Society, 1941).

Kingsford, C. L., *English Historical Literature in the Fifteenth Century* (Oxford, 1913).

—— *Prejudice and Promise in the Fifteenth Century* (Oxford, 1925).

Knowles, M. D., Abbot Butler: a Memoir, in *DR*, XXXIII (1934).

—— The Censured Opinions of Uthred of Boldon, in *Proceedings of the British Academy*, XXXVII (1952), 305–42.

—— The English monasteries in the later Middle Ages, in *History*, XXXIX, 135 (1954).

—— The excellence of *The Cloud*, in *DR*, LII, 149 (1934), 71–92.

Knowles, M. D. and Grimes, W. F., *Charterhouse* (London, 1954).

Knowles, M. D. and Hadcock, R. N., *Medieval Religious Houses* (London, 1953).

Knowles, M. D. and St Joseph, J. K., *Monastic Sites from the Air* (Cambridge, 1952).

Lagarde, G. de, *La naissance de l'esprit laïque* (Paris, 6 vols. 1934–46).

Langland, William, *v.s.* *Piers Plowman.

Leland, J., *Collectanea de rebus Britannicis*, ed. T. Hearne (London, 1770).

—— *Itinerary*, ed. L. Toulmin Smith (London, 1907).

Levett, A. E., The Black Death on the estates of the see of Winchester, in *Oxford Studies in Social and Legal History*, ed. P. Vinogradoff, vol. V (Oxford, 1916).

—— *Studies in Manorial History* (Oxford, 1938).

Liddell, J. R., Leland's lists of manuscripts in Lincolnshire monasteries, in *EHR*, LIV (1939), 88–95.

—— Some notes on the library of Reading Abbey, in *Bodleian Quarterly Record*, VIII (1935), 47–54.

Little, A. G., The Dominicans versus the University of Cambridge, in *EHR*, L (1935), 686–96.

—— *Franciscan Papers, Lists and Documents* (Manchester, 1943).

—— *The Grey Friars in Oxford* (OHS, XX, 1892).

Lodge, E. C. and Thornton, G. A., *English Constitutional Documents, 1307–1485* (Cambridge, 1935).

McFarlane, K. B., *John Wyclif* (London, 1952).

—— An English Account of the Election of Urban VI, 1378, in *Bulletin of the Institute of Historical Research*, XXVI, 75–85.

Mahn, J. B., Le Pape Benoît XII et les Cisterciens, in *Bibliothèque de l'École des Hautes Études* (Paris, 1944).

Maitland, F. W., *v.s.* Pollock, F.

Manitius, M., *Handschriften antiker Autoren in mittelalterlichen Bibliothekskatalogen* (Leipsig, 1935).

Manly, J. M., *Some new light on Chaucer* (New York, 1926).

Marcett, M. E., *Uhtred de Boldon, Friar William Jordan, and Piers Plowman* (New York, privately printed, 1938).

Martin, A. R., *Franciscan Architecture in England* (British Society of Franciscan Studies, no. 18. Manchester, 1937).

Michalski, K., *Le problème de la volonté à Oxford et à Paris au xive siècle* (Lemberg, 1937).

Micklethwaite, J. T., Notes on the Abbey buildings of Westminster, in *AJ*, XXXIII, 15–49.

Millar, E. G., *English Manuscript Illumination of the XIVth and XVth centuries* (Paris, Brussels, 1928).

Mode, P. G., *The Influence of the Black Death on the English Monasteries* (Chicago, 1916).

Moorman, J. R. H., Edward I at Lanercost Priory, 1306–7, in *EHR*, LXVII (1952), 161–74.

—— *The Grey Friars in Cambridge* (Cambridge, 1952).

Morgan, M. M. (Mrs Chibnall), The Abbey of Bec-Hellouin and its English Priories, in *JBAA*, 3, s. v (1940), 33–61.

—— The Suppression of the Alien Priories, in *History*, XXVI, 103 (1941), 204–12.

Mundó, A., 'Bibliotheca', in *RB*, LX (1950), 78–83.

Mynors, R. A. B., Classical writers in Boston of Bury, in memorial volume to F. Saxl (still unpublished).

—— *Durham Cathedral MSS. to the end of the twelfth century* (Durham, 1939).

New, C. H., *History of the Alien Priories to the Confiscation of Henry V* (Chicago, privately distributed, 1914).

Oliger, L., Regulae tres reclusorum et eremitarum Angliae saec. xiii–xiv, in *Antonianum* (Rome), III (1928), 151–90, 299–320, and *ibid.* IX (1934), 37–84, 243–65.

—— Speculum Inclusarum, in *Lateranum*, n.s., ann. IV, no. 1 (Rome, 1938).

Owst, G. R., The *Angel* and the *Goliardeys* of Langland's Prologue, in *Modern Language Review*, XX (1925), 270–9.

—— *Literature and Pulpit in Medieval England* (Cambridge, 1933).

—— *Preaching in Medieval England* (Cambridge, 1926).

Oxford History of English Literature, II (1945).

Page, F. M., *The Estates of Crowland Abbey* (Cambridge, 1934).

Pantin, W. A., *Canterbury College* (OHS, n.s. 6–8, 1947–50).

—— The *Defensorium* of Adam Easton, in *EHR*, LI (1936), 675–80.

—— *The English Church in the Fourteenth Century* (Cambridge, 1955).

—— Gloucester College, in *Oxoniensia*, XI–XII (1945–7), 65–74.

—— The Monk-Solitary of Farne: a Fourteenth-Century English Mystic, in *EHR*, LIX (1944), 162–86.

—— A Sermon for Provincial Chapter, in *DR*, LI (1933), 291 *seqq.*

—— Some Medieval English Treatises on the Origins of Monasticism, in *Medieval Studies presented to Rose Graham* (Oxford, 1950), 189–215.

—— Two treatises by Uthred of Boldon on the Monastic Life, in *Studies in Medieval History presented to F. M. Powicke* (Oxford, 1948), 363–85.

Parry, C. H., *Parliaments and Councils of England* (London, 1839).

Pearce, E. H., *The Monks of Westminster* (Cambridge, 1916).

Peers, C. and Tanner, L. E., On some recent discoveries in Westminster Abbey, in *Archaeologia*, XCIII (1949), 151–64.

Pelzer, A., Les 51 articles de Guillaume Occam censurés en Avignon en 1326, in *Revue d'Histoire ecclésiastique*, XVIII (1922), 250–1.

Perroy, É., *L'Angleterre et le Grand Schisme d'Occident* (Paris, 1933).

Perry, G. G., Visitation of the monastery of Thame, in *EHR*, III (1888), 704 *seqq.*

Pike, L. O., *Constitutional History of the House of Lords* (London, 1894).

Plucknett, T. F., *Legislation of Edward I* (Oxford, 1949).

Pollock, F. and Maitland, F. W., *History of English Law* (Cambridge, 2 vols. 1923).

Postan, M. M., Some economic evidence of falling population in the later Middle Ages, in *EcHR*, 2 ser. no. 3 (1950), 221–46. Also *v.s. Cambridge Economic History*.

Powicke, F. M., *v.s. Chronology*, and Rashdall, H.

Prior, E. S., *The Cathedral Builders of England* (London, 1905).
Purvis, J. S., *St John of Bridlington* (Bridlington, 1924).
Rashdall, H. [*Medieval Universities.*] *The Universities of Europe in the Middle Ages*
    (ed. F. M. Powicke and A. B. Emden, Oxford, 3 vols. 1936).
—— The Friars Preachers versus the University, in OHS, *Collectanea*, II (1890),
    193–273.
Reinhardt, H., *Der Karolingische Klosterplan von St Gallen* (St Gall, 1952).
Report on the Dignity of a Peer of the Realm, etc., etc. (RP, 1829, etc.)
Repyngdon, Cardinal, and the followers of Wycliffe (anonymous), in *Church Quarterly
    Review*, XIX (1884), 39–82.
Rickert, E., John But, Messenger and Maker, in *Modern Philology*, XI, 107–16.
Rickert, M., *The reconstructed Carmelite Missal* (London, 1952).
—— The reconstruction of an English Carmelite Missal, in *Speculum*, XVI (1), 1941,
    92–102.
—— *Painting in Britain: the Middle Ages* (Pelican History of Art, London,
    1954).
Robinson, J. A., Simon Langham, Abbot of Westminster, in *Church Quarterly Review*,
    LXVI (1908), 339–66.
Roth, F., Cardinal Richard Annibaldi, First Protector of the Augustinian Order, in
    Augustiniana, II, 1–60; 108–49; 230–47; III, 21–34.
Rushforth, G. McN., The East Window of Gloucester Cathedral, in *TBGAS*, XLIV
    (1922), 293–304.
Russell, J. C., *British Medieval Population* (Albuquerque, 1948).
—— The Clerical Population of Medieval England, in *Traditio*, II (1944), 177–
    212.
Salter, H. E. *v.s.* Stevenson, W. H.
Salzman, L. F., [*Medieval Building*] *Building in England down to 1540* (Oxford, 1952).
Saunders, H. W., *An introduction to the obedientiary and manor rolls of Norwich Cathedral
    Priory* (Norwich, 1930).
Saunders, O. E., *A history of English art in the Middle Ages* (Oxford, 1932).
Savin, A., The English Monasteries on the Eve of the Dissolution, in *Oxford Studies
    in Social and Legal History*, I, ed. P. Vinogradoff (Oxford, 1909).
Schirmer, W. F., *Der englische Frühhumanismus* (Leipzig, 1931).
—— *John Lydgate, ein Kulturbild aus dem 15 Jahrhundert* (Tübingen, 1952).
Sikes, J. G., John de Pouilli and Peter de la Palu, in *EHR*, XLIX (1934), 219–40.
Smalley, B., Thomas Waleys, O.P., in *Archivum Fratrum Praedicatorum*, XXIV (1954),
    50–107.
Smith, R. A. L., *Canterbury Cathedral Priory* (Cambridge, 1943).
—— *Collected Papers* (London, 1947).
Snape, R. H., *English Monastic Finances in the later Middle Ages* (Cambridge, 1926).
Stevenson, W. H. and Salter, H. E., *The Early History of St John's College, Oxford*
    (OHS, n.s. 1, 1939).
Stow, J., *Chronicle of England* (London, ed. 1631).
Syon Abbey, *v.s.* Bateson, M.
Stubbs, W., *Constitutional History of England* (Oxford, 5 ed. 1896).
Sweet, A. H., The Apostolic See and the Heads of English Religious Houses, in
    Speculum, XXVIII (1953), 468–84.
—— The library of St Radegund's, in *EHR*, LIII (1938), 88–93.
Tanner, J. R., *Tudor Constitutional Documents* (Cambridge, reprinted 1940).
Tanner, L. E., *v.s.* Peers, C.
Thompson, A. H., *The Abbey of St Mary of the Meadows, Leicester* [*Leicester Abbey*]
    (Leicester, 1949).
—— *The English Clergy and their organization in the later Middle Ages* (Oxford,
    1947).

Thompson, A. H., *History of the Priory of St Mary, Bolton in Wharfedale* [*Bolton Priory*] (Leeds, 1928).

—— Pluralism in the Medieval Church, in *Associated Architectural Societies' Reports and Papers*, XXXIII (1915), 35–73.

Thompson, E. M., *The Carthusian Order in England* (London, 1930).

—— *A History of the Somerset Carthusians* (London, 1895).

Thompson, J. W., ed., *The Medieval Library* (Chicago, 1938).

Turner, C. H., The earliest list of Durham MSS., in *JTS*, XIX (1918), 121–32.

Twemlow, J. O., The Liturgical Credentials of a forgotten English saint, in *Mélanges Bémont* (Paris, 1913), 365–71.

Ueberweg, F. and Geyer, B., *Grundrisse der Geschichte des Philosophie*, vol. II (photo-electric reproduction of 11th (1928) ed., Berlin, 1951).

Valois, N., *La France et le Grand Schisme d'Occident* (Paris, 1896).

Victoria History of the Counties of England, The (London and Oxford, 1900–).

Vignaux, J., *Justification et Prédestination au XIVe siècle* (Bibliothèque de l'Ecole des Hautes Etudes: sciences religieuses, vol. 48, Paris, 1934).

Waugh, W. T., Sir John Oldcastle, in *EHR*, XX (1905), 434–56, 637–58. Also *v.s.* Wylie, J. H.

Wedgwood, Lord, *History of Parliament* (London, 2 vols. 1938).

Weiss, R., *Humanism in England during the Fifteenth Century* (Oxford, 1941).

Westlake, H. F., *History of Westminster Abbey* (London, 2 vols. 1923).

Wey, J., The *Sermo Finalis* of Robert Holcot, in *Medieval Studies*, XI (1949), 219–23.

Williams, L. F. R., *History of the Abbey of St Albans* (London, 1917).

Williams, T. W., Gloucestershire Medieval Libraries, in *TBGAS*, XXXI (1908), 78–195.

—— *Somerset Medieval Libraries* (Bistol, 1897).

Wilson, J. M., The library of printed books in Worcester Cathedral, in *The Library*, 3 ser. II (1911), 1–33. Also *v.s.* **Worcester.*

Wilson, R. M., The Medieval Library of Titchfield Abbey, in *Proceedings of the Leeds Philosophical and Literary Society*; Literary and historical section, V, iii (1940), 150 *seqq.*, 252 *seqq.*

Wood, S., *English Monasteries and their Patrons in the XIIIth Century* (Oxford, 1955).

Wood-Legh, K. L., *Studies in Church Life in England under Edward III* (Cambridge, 1934).

Woodruff, C. E., Note on the inner life and domestic economy of the priory of Christ Church in the fifteenth century, in *ACant.* LIII (1940), 1–16.

Workman, H. B., *John Wyclif* (2 vols. Oxford, 1926).

Wulf, M. de, *Histoire de philosophie médiévale*, III (6 ed., Louvain and Paris, 1947).

Wylie, J. H., *History of England under Henry IV* (London, 4 vols. 1884–98).

—— *The reign of Henry V* (Cambridge, 3 vols. 1914–29). Vol. III was completed by A. T. Waugh.

(*b*) UNPUBLISHED THESES, DISSERTATIONS, ETC.

Forte, S. L., *A study of some Oxford scholars of the middle of the fourteenth century* (B.Litt., Oxford, 1947).

Gumbley, W., List of Friars Preachers in episcopal orders in England.

Halcrow, E. M., *The administration and agrarian policy of the manors of Durham cathedral priory* (B.Litt., Oxford, 1949).

—— Several papers on the economy of Durham priory.

Hodge, C. E., *The abbey of St Albans under John of Whethamstede* (Ph.D., Manchester, 1933).

Johnston, F. R., *The cult of St Bridget of Sweden in fifteenth-century England* (M.A., Manchester, 1947).

Leff, G., *A study of Thomas Bradwardine's* De causa Dei *and its relations to contemporary Oxford thought* (Ph.D., Cambridge, 1954).

Rogers, L. E., edition of *Advice to recluses* from B.M. MS. Harl. 2372 (B.Litt., Oxford, 1933).

Smith, R. A., *The organization and financing of monastic building* (M.A., London, 1951).

Smith, R. A. L., *The estates of Pershore Abbey* (M.A., London, 1939).

Thompson, G. H., *Uhtred of Boldon* (Ph.D., Manchester, 1936).

Trench, S. Chenevix-, *The relations between English monasteries and their patrons in the thirteenth century.* See under *Wood.

Turner, M. E., *Some aspects of the English Carmelites in the first half of the fifteenth century* (M.A., Manchester, 1933).

INDEX

As the custom of using surnames was almost universal in the later Middle Ages, persons are so entered in this index; a very few exceptions have been made for names of an earlier age and for saints (e.g. Bonaventura) and others who are currently known by their Christian name alone. Reference to modern scholars whose works are mentioned in the footnotes is only given when an appraisal or discussion of particular points occurs.

The following abbreviations are used: A = Augustinian; abb. = abbey, abbot; archb. = archbishop; b. = bishop; B. = black monk (Benedictine); c. = canon; Carm. = Carmelite; Carth. = Carthusian; cath. = cathedral; Chr. Ch. = Christ Church; Cist. = Cistercian; Cl. = Cluniac; Gilb. = Gilbertine; Grand. = Grandmontine; m. = monk; Min. = Minoresses; n. = nun, nunnery; OM = Franciscan; OP = Dominican; OSA = Augustinian (Austin); Pr. = Premonstratensian; pr. = prior, priory; St Aug.'s = St Augustine's; Tir. = Tironian.